SOCIAL EXCHANGE
IN
DEVELOPING
RELATIONSHIPS

SOCIAL EXCHANGE IN DEVELOPING RELATIONSHIPS

Edited by

Robert L. Burgess
Ted L. Huston

College of Human Development
The Pennsylvania State University
University Park, Pennsylvania

Foreword by George C. Homans

ACADEMIC PRESS   New York   San Francisco   London
A Subsidiary of Harcourt Brace Jovanovich, Publishers

ACADEMIC PRESS, INC.
111 Fifth Avenue, New York, New York 10003

United Kingdom Edition published by
ACADEMIC PRESS, INC. (LONDON) LTD.
24/28 Oval Road, London NW1 7DX

Library of Congress Cataloging in Publication Data

Main entry under title:

Social exchange in developing relationships.

    Includes bibliographies.
    1. Interpersonal relations—Addresses, essays,
lectures. 2. Social exchange—Addresses, essays,
lectures. I. Burgess, Robert Lee. II. Huston, Ted L.
HM132.S568   301.11   79—6934
ISBN 0–12–143550–4

PRINTED IN THE UNITED STATES OF AMERICA

79 80 81 82   9 8 7 6 5 4 3 2 1

TO JUDY AND CHRIS

Contents

List of Contributors	xiii
Foreword	xv
Preface	xxi

Part I Introduction

1 Social Exchange in Developing Relationships: An Overview   3

TED L. HUSTON AND ROBERT L. BURGESS

I.	Introduction	3
II.	The Nature of Close Relationships	6
III.	The Development of Closeness in Relationships	8
IV.	Social Exchange in Developing Relationships	10
V.	The Social Context of Relationships	21
VI.	Conclusion	24
	References	25

Part II The Development Course
of Close Relationships

2 *The Initiation of Social Relationships and
Interpersonal Attraction*   *31*

    ELLEN BERSCHEID AND WILLIAM GRAZIANO

  I. The Importance of Understanding the Antecedents of the
    Initiation of Social Relationships   31
  II. A Perceptual Approach to the Problem of
    Relationship Initiation   34
  III. Outcome Dependency: A Framework for Viewing
    Relationship Initiation   41
  IV. · Identification of the Social Environment   47
  V. Some Comments on the Relationship between Attention
    and Attraction   54
  VI. Conclusions   57
    References   58

3 *Social Exchange and Behavioral Interdependence*   61

    JOHN SCANZONI

  I. Introduction   61
  II. Stage I: Exploration   65
  III. Stage II: Expansion of Interlocking Interest-Spheres   79
  IV. Stage III: Commitment   86
  V. Summary   94
    References   96

4 *Equity Theory and Intimate Relationships*   99

    ELAINE HATFIELD, MARY K. UTNE, AND
    JANE TRAUPMANN

  I. Introduction   99
  II. The Equity Formulation   100
  III. The Theorists' Debate: Is Equity Theory Applicable to
    Intimate Relationships?   104
  IV. The Accumulating Evidence   111
  V. Summary   131
    References   131

5 *Conflict in the Development of Close Relationships*   135

    HARRIET B. BRAIKER AND HAROLD H. KELLEY

  I. The Structure of Close Relationships   136
  II. The Development of Close Relationships   142

III. The Role of Conflict in the Development of Close Relationships   157
References   167

6 *A Social Exchange View on the Dissolution of Pair Relationships*   169

GEORGE LEVINGER

I. Introduction   169
II. An Exchange Perspective on Relationships   170
III. Determinants of Pair Dissolution   181
IV. Conclusion   189
References   191

Part III *Beyond the Dyad: Approaches to Explaining Exchange in Developing Relationships*

7 *Natural Selection and Social Exchange*   197

RICHARD D. ALEXANDER

I. Introduction   197
II. The Sexual Organism as Nepotist   202
III. Historical Relationships between Nepotism and Reciprocity   208
IV. Analyses of Human Nepotism and Reciprocity   211
V. The Evolution of Nepotism and Recipocity in Humans   215
VI. Ontogeny and Social Exchange   216
VII. Conclusions   219
References   220

8 *Social Network Influence on the Dyadic Relationship*   223

CARL A. RIDLEY AND ARTHUR W. AVERY

I. Introduction   223
II. Social Networks   224
III. Interactional Criteria   226
IV. Structural Criteria   227
V. Network Influences   228
VI. Social Exchange within Dyads   232
VII. Social-Exchange Theory Assumptions   233
VIII. Types of Dyadic Exchange Patterns   233
IX. Sequencing of Exchange Patterns within Dyadic Relationships   238
X. Social Network Influence on Dyadic Relationships   239
XI. Summary and Conclusions   244
References   245

9 *Personality and Exchange in Developing Relationships*   247

ROBERT C. CARSON

    I. Introduction   247
   II. The Nature of Personality   248
  III. Personality and Commodities of Exchange   251
  IV. Complementary Needs and Resource Exchange   256
    V. Reciprocal Patterns of Activity   258
  VI. Foresight of Future Satisfaction, or Rebuff   260
 VII. Construal Style Revisited   264
VIII. Conclusion   265
     References   266

10 *A Dynamic Interactional Concept of Individual and Social Relationship Development*   271

RICHARD M. LERNER

    I. Introduction   271
  II. Mechanistic and Organismic Models of Human Development   273
  III. Components of Development   276
  IV. Relationship Development   286
    V. Implications for Social Exchange   293
  VI. The Nature of Reward in Social Exchanges   298
 VII. Conclusions   301
     References   303

11 *Sexual Involvement and Relationship Development: A Cognitive Developmental Approach*   307

JUDITH FRANKEL D'AUGELLI AND
ANTHONY R. D'AUGELLI

    I. Introduction   307
  II. Person Variables Influencing Sexual Involvement   309
  III. Relationship Variables: Sex and Social Exchange   315
  IV. Sexual Decision Making and Moral Reasoning   320
    V. Relationship Reasoning   332
  VI. A Model for Sexual Involvement in Relationships   341
 VII. Summary   345
     References   347

12 *Relationship Initiation and Development: A Life-Span Developmental Approach*   351

DOUGLAS C. KIMMEL

    I. Introduction   351
  II. Critique and Recasting of Social Exchange Theory   352

III. Social Interactions and the Personality System 355
IV. Symbolic–Interactionist Approach to Social Relationships 359
V. Developmental Themes and Relationships 361
VI. Social Factors and Relationships 373
VII. Research Possibilities in Life-Span Social Interaction 375
References 376

Part IV   Epilogue

13 *Dynamic Theories of Social Relationships and Resulting Research Strategies* *381*

JAMES A. WIGGINS

I. A Theoretical Introduction 381
II. A Methodological Introduction 384
III. Concept Validity 385
IV. Propositional (Internal) Validity 393
V. Generalization (External) Validity 402
VI. A Final Note 405
References 406

Author Index 409
Subject Index 419

List of Contributors

Numbers in parentheses indicate the pages on which the authors' contributions begin.

RICHARD D. ALEXANDER (197), Museum of Zoology, Department of Zoology, University of Michigan, Ann Arbor, Michigan 48104

ARTHUR W. AVERY (223), Division of Child Development and Family Relations, University of Arizona, Tucson, Arizona 85721

ELLEN BERSCHEID (31), Department of Psychology, University of Minnesota, Minneapolis, Minnesota 55455

HARRIET B. BRAIKER (135), The Rand Corporation, Santa Monica, California 90406

ROBERT L. BURGESS (3), College of Human Development, The Pennsylvania State University, University Park, Pennsylvania 16802

ROBERT C. CARSON (247), Department of Psychology, Duke University, Durham, North Carolina 27706

ANTHONY R. D'AUGELLI (307), College of Human Development, Pennsylvania State University, University Park, Pennsylvania 16802

JUDITH FRANKEL D'AUGELLI (307), State College, Pennsylvania 16801

WILLIAM GRAZIANO (31), Department of Psychology, University of Georgia, Athens, Georgia 30602

ELAINE HATFIELD (99), Department of Sociology, University of Wisconsin—Madison, Madison, Wisconsin 53706

TED L. HUSTON (3), College of Human Development, The Pennsylvania State University, University Park, Pennsylvania 16802

HAROLD H. KELLEY (135), Department of Psychology, University of California, Los Angeles, Los Angeles, California 90024

DOUGLAS C. KIMMEL (351), Department of Psychology, City College, City University of New York, New York, New York 10031

RICHARD M. LERNER (271), College of Human Development, The Pennsylvania State University, University Park, Pennsylvania 16802

GEORGE LEVINGER (169), Department of Psychology, University of Massachusetts, Amherst, Amherst, Massachusetts 01002

CARL A. RIDLEY (223), Division of Child Development and Family Relations, University of Arizona, Tucson, Arizona 85721

JOHN SCANZONI* (61), Department of Sociology, Indiana University, Bloomington, Indiana 47401

JANE TRAUPMANN (99), Fane McBeath Institute on Aging and Adult Life, University of Wisconsin–Madison, Madison, Wisconsin 53706

MARY K. UTNE (99), Police Foundation, Newark, New Jersey 07102

JAMES A. WIGGINS (381), Department of Sociology, University of North Carolina, Chapel Hill, North Carolina 27514

* Present Address: Sociology and Child and Family Relations, University of North Carolina, Greensboro, North Carolina 27412

Foreword

In the chapters of this book certain words recur, such as *behavioral, exchange, relationship,* and *development.* I would like to open the book by commenting on these words, without trying to impose my own views on anyone else.

Speaking, then, for myself, I do not like to use *behavioral science,* as it is so often used now, to refer to all studies that purport to be concerned with human behavior. For me, behavioral science means something more specific than that. It constitutes a particular way of studying human behavior. It starts from the assumption that the object of study should be the actions of persons—and their actions include their words—insofar as their actions have consequences for their future behavior. This assumption implies that behavioral science is much less interested in actions, such as the answers people give to questionnaires, that may make little difference to their future behavior.

Behavioral science further assumes—but this I think is more than an assumption—that people's actions are functions of the consequences of those actions. Behaviorally, a person is a feedback mechanism, in the sense that, if he or she performs an action that has favorable consequences, the probability that the person will repeat that action increases. If the action has unfavorable consequences, the probability of repeating it decreases. Behavioral science further assumes that the circumstances accompanying an action and its consequences also affect the probability that the action will be repeated: If one or more of the circumstances accompanying a successful action recur, then the action is more likely to be repeated than if none of the circumstances recur. Finally behavioral science assumes, even more clearly now that Herrnstein has formulated the "matching law,"[1] that a person is seldom in such straits as to have only one course of action. Instead, alternatives are weighed in such a way that, other circumstances remaining unchanged, a person tends over time to choose alternatives that will maximize probable payoffs.

These assumptions have further implications. First, since all the so-called social sciences—history, government, economics, sociology, anthropology—have to do with human behavior, they must all, in fundamentals, be one science. Indeed, I think it can be shown that they all share the same assumptions about human behavior, though it is often impossible to get their practitioners to admit it. Second, since the general assumptions made about human behavior also apply to the behavior of other higher animals, there is a continuity between the behavior of these animals and man. This statement does not imply that behavior of animals is, in detail, identical with that of man, nor that the behaviors of different animal species are identical. Third, since behavioral science implies that a person's past experiences determine in part present behavior, behavioral science is inherently historical (evolutionary, developmental—call it what you will) not only for individuals but for the groups they belong to. This does not mean that the history need always be salient in explaining particular findings. For example, if we want to explain what a seaman does when handling a vessel under sail, the laws of physics are more relevant than individual past history. The seaman doubtless learned how to sail according to behavioral principles, but if the learned actions were not compatible with the laws of physics the seaman would not be sailing now.

In trying to explain human behavior, we behaviorists begin and end with the directly observable environment of the actor—with the stimulus features of the environment and with the environmental conditions that allow or prevent the rewarding of actions. But I always thought it unfair that we should be accused of treating what happens in between, interior to the acting person, as a "black box," as if we were wholly ignorant of, or uninterested in, what happens inside the box. Like everyone else, we are ignorant to a great degree, but we are certainly interested in what happens there, if only to understand what allows the behavioral connections we observe between the initial and final environmental conditions to have the features they do. What, for instance, are the characteristics of the human

---

[1] See, for instance, R. J. Herrnstein, "Quantitative Hedonism," *Journal of Psychiatric Research*, Vol. 8 (1971), pp. 399–412.

nervous system that allow the recurrence of the stimuli under which an action was rewarded in the distant past to resume their control over much later behavior?

Let me mention one other feature of the internal constitution of an actor that has recently received increasing attention. The genetic differences between individuals and between species may include, for instance, differences in their capacity to be rewarded by certain kinds of actions of others, that is, to be rewarded by social behavior. Such genetic variations may not affect behavior directly, which was believed to be true of what used to be called instincts, but only indirectly, by changing the contingencies that affect the learning process. Thus a person or a species with a low capacity for being rewarded socially might, when faced with the same kinds of social conditions as others differently constituted were faced with, learn and maintain rather different kinds of overt behavior. The effort to understand genetic and other biological differences will start some of us studying behavioral evolution, and, accordingly, I am glad that Richard Alexander has a chapter in this volume entitled "Natural Selection and Social Exchange."

Another feature I deplore in the current intellectual climate of psychology is the habit of drawing a sharp line between "behavioral" and "cognitive" psychology, as if they were contrasting or even competing psychologies. My difficulty here is that I cannot help viewing cognition itself as an active process—a type of action, if you will, which seems to exemplify some of the same kinds of laws as other actions do. Thus, if seeing a configuration of objects in a certain way allows a person to take successful action on the environment, that way of seeing it will be learned and will tend to persist. Even when the configuration has changed in some respect, cognition will still try to make sense of it in terms of the old learning. This phenomenon can be observed when we look at an aerial photograph of a terrain instead of the terrain itself, and turn the photograph at an inappropriate angle with respect to the direction from which the original terrain was lighted. Thus when we look from an inappropriate angle at photographs of the surface of the moon, we see what are actually craters as mounds.

And now a word about *exchange*. I confess that I do not much like phrases such as exchange theory, equity theory, balance theory, and so forth as they are currently used, more often by psychologists than by sociologists. I do not much like these phrases, even though I am given credit for being a founder of both exchange theory and equity theory. (The founder of equity theory was in fact Aristotle.[2]) I do not like these phrases because they give the impression that the theories are somehow self-contained, without relation to one another or to a more general theory of

---

[2] See especially *Nicomachean Ethics*, Book V.

human behavior. Indeed, some of the investigators in these fields try to treat them as if they were in fact self-contained. I believe, and have tried to show, that the propositions of these theories all follow, under special given conditions, from the propositions of a more general theory of human behavior.[3]

Yet whatever one may think of the phrase "exchange theory," exchange itself is a reality, and a vital one, for exchange is what makes human behavior specifically social. When I speak of exchange I mean a situation in which the actions of one person provide the rewards or punishments for the actions of another person and vice versa. Though many features of behavior emerge from exchange that would not have appeared without it, one of the tenets of what it is now fashionable to call my metatheoretical position is that no new general propositions are needed to explain the emergent features. The propositions that hold when a person's actions are rewarded by the nonhuman environment are the same propositions that hold when the actions are rewarded by the actions of another person. What has changed is the situation, not the propositions. This position appears to be unacceptable to some sociologists, though they have been unable to put forward any further propositions that, in their view, might be needed to explain the allegedly unique features of social behavior. That is, there are social scientists who insist on a solution of continuity between individual and social behavior, just as there are those who insist on a solution of continuity between the behavior of men and that of other animals.

Next, the term *relationship*. Exchanges may take place and behavior thus be social without the emergence of anything that I would be prepared to call a relationship between persons. An example is the classical market in economics. In such a market, a buyer is presumed to be able to enter into exchange with one seller on one occasion, with another on another occasion, and so forth, depending on which one demands the lowest price on each occasion. There is no presumption that a buyer will enter into repeated exchanges with a particular seller, although some buyers probably do so. Not until a person enters into repeated exchanges with the same other person may we even begin to speak of a relationship existing between them. Or, to move to a more complex level of social organization, only then can we begin to speak of a relationship between the occupant of a particular office in a formal organization and the occupant of another such office.

Again, no new general propositions are needed to explain these differences between exchange without the development of a relationship and exchange with such a development. The situations to which the

---

[3] G. C. Homans, *Social Behavior: Its Elementary Forms*, revised ed., New York: Harcourt Brace Jovanovich, 1974.

general laws apply change, but not the laws themselves. Still, the different situations help us to distinguish between classical economics and some of the other social sciences. Economics is much less interested in relationships than the others are. Indeed the others are profoundly interested, for relationships—repeated exchanges between particular persons, offices, or groups—are the very stuff of social structures, and the characteristics of enduring social structures are what sociologists, for instance, are most interested in. I have said for years that my chief intellectual aim has been to explain, using propositions about individual behavior, how the interactions (exchanges) between individuals could give rise to such structures.

And, finally, the *development* of a relationship. When we consider this kind of social elaboration, we should keep our eyes on two different kinds of processes. First, as the relationship between two persons develops, the partners almost inevitably add new kinds of exchanges to the one that brought the relationship into being in the first place; and these new exchanges may further cement the original one or undermine it through conflict. The interaction effects between the different exchanges are what so-called balance theory tries to explain. Again, I think it a mistake to treat balance theory as a distinct theory. The fundamental propositions about human behavior do not change in balance theory, but the given conditions to which they apply do.

Second, a relationship between two persons seldom develops in isolation from the relationships between each of them and other persons; and these latter relationships may interact with the changes that might otherwise have been expected to occur within the original one. Sometimes the new relationships cut down the variety of exchanges that might otherwise have proliferated between the original partners, in such a way that each now seeks one type of reward from the original partner and other types from the other persons. An example is the tendency for so-called instrumental exchanges to occur between persons unequal in status and more purely "social" exchanges, such as going to parties together, to occur between equals.[4]

Especially interesting, at least for me, is what occurs when a number of small groups, such as families, are placed in very similar conditions, so that similar patterns of relationships tend to develop among the members of every group. Then the recurrence of the pattern tends to make it highly visible. And since a relationship that is seen to exist in fact always tends to become one that people believe ought to exist, they begin to say, for instance, that a boy ought to treat his mother's brother in a particular way. And since in turn norms imply sanctions for their nonfulfillment, the norms tend further to stabilize the pattern. But let us not overdo the

[4] *Ibid.*, pp. 229–318.

stability. If the conditions that produced the original similarity of pattern disappear, the norms will sooner or later disappear, too. No regularity of behavior was ever maintained by norms alone. In any event, no student of developing relationships need be ashamed of an interest in complicated kinship systems—and many not so complicated.

What I have done is to start with some of the most general assumptions of a behavioral psychology, and then to suggest how we might apply these assumptions to increasingly specific and increasingly complex situations, first to exchange, or social behavior, then to repeated exchanges between two persons, which we may call a relationship between them, then to the elaboration of that relationship and finally to the development of patterns of relationships among several persons. I hope that this brief effort to lay out the general field will allow one to appreciate better the particular contributions made by each of the contributors to this volume.

Let me add an epilogue about our own behavior as social scientists. The behavioral psychology, including the social psychology, of mankind is an experimental science, but it certainly cannot be just an experimental science. For one thing, we cannot experimentally manipulate the behavior of human beings by using really powerful means of influencing their motivations. We are not, for instance, allowed to keep them half-starved as we keep experimental pigeons, and we usually cannot afford to offer them big monetary rewards. One result, I suspect, is that there is a large unexplained random element in our findings. The correlations we discover are relatively weak. This does not mean that our results are worthless, but only that we must always remember that their truth may be limited to particular circumstances, and we must beware of extrapolating them without circumspection to large areas of what is called "real life." In real life, the motivations of people are often far stronger than they can be in our experiments. To encourage a certain circumspection, an experimental social psychologist might well spend a part of the time carrying out field research with natural groups, even if the findings cannot be under experimental control. How much has field research on animal behavior told us that we should never have been in a position to discover by experiment! And why should recent field research on lions and baboons have to remind us of the virtues of our own older tradition of field research on human groups? Above all, field research can suggest to us ideas that might be tested experimentally. And if we cannot do fieldwork, let us at least read widely in good novels, memoirs, and history. Finally let us examine critically our own personal experience of social behavior, which is the richest source of data that we, as individuals, possess.

GEORGE C. HOMANS
Harvard University

Preface

We trust the reader will agree with us that people need to learn more about close, interpersonal relations, yet our emphasis on exchange processes may seem puzzling. The reasons we have decided to concentrate on exchange are several. First, as Homans notes in his Foreword, it is exchange which makes human behavior social. An exchange perspective accepts as fundamental the reciprocal impacts that partners have on one another. Second, by explicitly looking at exchange processes, the stage is set for taking the relationship itself as a unit of analysis in its own right. Third, the exchange process can be examined in terms of (a) the individual biological and psychological characteristics of the actors; (b) the history of their interactions with one another; (c) the nature of the social network each actor maintains; and (d) the larger cultural context within which the relationship is embedded. Indeed, given the focus on reciprocal effects, how those effects take place, and the level of generality of exchange principles, it is possible to bring some order to the jumble of theoretically colliding approaches that have been applied to the analysis of relationships.

Our intent in preparing this book was to encourage the systematic study of the development of relationships. Throughout, several theoretical perspectives are presented, including evolutionary theory, cognitive developmental theory, personality theory, role theory, equity theory, and attribution theory. In each case, however, the authors address the issue of exchange in developing relations. Their views of the exchange process differ as a function of their own theoretical perspectives. Such is the state of the art.

In Part I, we have provided a conceptual home base of what follows. We deliberately have tried not to produce premature closure by writing a summary chapter. Instead, we have simply discussed some of the major topics that are examined in varying ways throughout the book. In doing this, we may have placed undue emphasis on romantic relationships and we may not have discussed sufficiently a number of important topics such as conflict or the metatheoretical underpinnings of an exchange approach. On the other hand, at least two chapters in Part II deal with the former, and Homans in the Foreword, Wiggins in the Epilogue, and the various chapters in Part III deal with the latter.

Many of the chapters in this book have grown out of a conference sponsored by the Division of Individual and Family Studies in the College of Human Development at The Pennsylvania State University. We wish to express our gratitude to the many people who supported the conference and participated in it. This book has been much longer in the making than we had planned. The major reason for this is that we have worked very hard in trying to ensure that the individual chapters separately and collectively make the strongest case possible. We, thus, would like publicly to thank the authors for their patience but, especially, for their outstanding contributions. We, the editors, are excited about this book. We invite you, the reader, to join us in our attempt to chart and understand the developmental course of human social relationships.

SOCIAL EXCHANGE
IN
DEVELOPING
RELATIONSHIPS

PART I

Introduction

1

Social Exchange in Developing Relationships: An Overview

TED L. HUSTON
ROBERT L. BURGESS

I. Introduction

The motives behind the establishment of social relationships have intrigued social philosophers and social scientists for a long time. During the eighteenth century, men such as Jean Jacques Rousseau, Thomas Hobbes, John Locke, and Adam Smith wrestled with the problem. Rousseau suggested that people's needs and desires usually outstrip their capacity to satisfy them individually. Hobbes argued that individual passions are the ultimate determinants of behavior and that there always are irreconcilable conflicts between the interests of one person and another. According to him, in the absence of some form of imposed order, each individual's unregulated attempts to gain his or her own ends would inevitably result in open conflict and hostility.

John Locke and Adam Smith, on the other hand, emphasized the beneficial consequences of social relationships beyond their role in preventing unrestrained war and chaos. Smith, in particular, stressed mutual self-interest as the basis of social relationships:

> In civilized society [man] stands at all times in need of the co-operation and assistance of great multitudes. . . . He will be more likely to prevail if he can interest their self-love in his favour, and show them that it is for their own advan-

3

tage to do for him what he requires of them. Whoever offers to another a bargain of any kind, proposes to do this: Give me that which I want, and you shall have this which you want, is the meaning of every such offer; and it is in this manner that we obtain from one another the far greater part of those good offices which we stand in need of. It is not from the benevolence of the butcher, the brewer or the baker that we expect our dinner, but from their regard to their own interest. We address ourselves, not to their humanity, but to their self-love, and never talk to them of our own necessities but of their advantages [Smith, 1850, p. 7].

This theme was later developed by such social philosophers as Jeremy Bentham, John Stuart Mill, and Karl Marx, all of whom believed that there is no inherent incompatibility between individual and social interest. Indeed, whereas an individual's weakness may lie in an excess of wants over an ability to satisfy them, together individuals can simultaneously gratify their own desires as well as those of others. Thus, networks of relationships, both within the family and outside it, lead to individual survival and success.

That people join together only insofar as they believe and subsequently find it in their mutual interest to do so is the central theme of this book. The premise behind the theme is that through interaction, people learn about one another, and that over time they try as best they can to balance their social involvements so as to satisfy as fully as possible their private interests. Relationships, we assume, grow, develop, deteriorate, and dissolve as a consequence of an unfolding social-exchange process, which may be conceived as a bartering of rewards and costs both between the partners and between members of the partnership and others. In beginning with such a premise, we do not mean to imply that all aspects of social activity can be explained in such terms, or that persons succeed equally well in structuring their relationships so as to maximize benefit to themselves. Those enjoying good fortune may, sometimes, anonymously give to others with no hope or expectation of being repaid in kind, either in this world or the next. And some, moreover, may learn or decide not to depend on others, even when doing so would enhance both their own and the other's well-being.

There are, nonetheless, a number of reasons why we focus on articulating an approach to relationships based on the notion of exchange. First, an explicit look at exchange processes sets the stage for considering the relationship itself—rather than the individuals or the larger social system as a unit of analysis. Though relationships are influenced by the personality makeup of the partners as well as by the social system in which they are embedded, the developmental course of particular relationships cannot be fully understood by recourse either to individual psychology or to the social system. The interpersonal structures of relationships are worked out, at least partly, through actual social transactions. Exchange analyses of social life accept as fundamental the reciprocal effects partners have on one another and scrutinize the development of relationships over time. Another analytical advantage of a focus on exchange processes is that other approaches can be readily synthesized with an exchange interpretation (Emerson, 1976). Thus, the exchange process can be examined in terms of the biological (Alexander, Chapter 7) and psychological (Carson, Chapter 9; Lerner, Chapter 10; D'Augelli & D'Augelli, Chapter 11; Kimmel, Chapter 12) characteristics of the partners, the nature of the partners' social network (Ridley & Avery, Chapter 8), the larger cultural context within which the relationship is embedded, and the history of the partners' interactions with one another. Given the widespread utility of exchange theory, it is not surprising to find students of it working within several disciplines, among them anthropology, biology, economics, psychology, and sociology.

Figure 1.1 portrays our conceptual schema. Person (P) and other (O) are shown to proceed through three levels of involvement (see Levinger & Snoek, 1972; Levinger, 1974):

1. *Awareness,* in which one knows of the other—or where both P and O know of one another—but they have not interacted.
2. *Surface contact,* characterized by formal, or superficial, contact.
3. *Mutuality,* in which the relationship is personal, intense, and intimate.

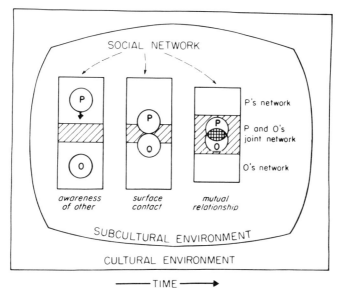

Figure 1.1 A person–other relationship in its social context. [From Huston and Levinger (1974). Reproduced, with permission from the *Annual Review of Psychology,* Volume 29. © 1978 by Annual Reviews Inc.]

Relationships proceed to or stop short of mutuality depending on the reward-cost history of the exchange between P and O. Similarly, from an exchange perspective, relationships move back from one level to an earlier one if the reward-cost ratio declines to the detriment of one or both partners. The next section reviews material concerning the nature of mutual (i.e., close) relationships. The third section (page 8) discusses the ways relationships change as they move from surface contact to mutuality. The section beginning on page 10 applies social-exchange theory to the analysis of the evolution of relationships from first impressions to surface contact through mutuality to termination.

Partners in a relationship simultaneously maintain ties to one another and to others. This is illustrated in Figure 1.1, where it is shown that as P and O move ever closer together their social network decreases in size and becomes more integrated (i.e., jointly shared). Thus, the partnership of a couple involves a marriage of sorts of each with the other's family, friends, and associates. Social networks structure relationships by providing normative standards and by approving some activities and prohibiting others; relationships, in turn, incline people to restructure their networks. The fifth section (beginning on page 21) considers the reciprocal effects of networks and relationships within various sociohistorical contexts, and ties our analysis to the sociohistorical boundaries illustrated in Figure 1.1.

II. The Nature of Close Relationships

According to exchange theory, close relationships are characterized by high interdependency, or mutual dependency. There exists no comprehensive taxonomy of relationships; nor has a systematic attempt been made to classify relationships according to closeness. Levinger, Rands, and Talaber (1977) found that persons tend to differentiate relationships according to the following five considerations: (a) kin or nonkin, the latter divisible into socially oriented or task-oriented relationships; (b) sex composition; (c) age composition; (d) degree of affective involvement; and (e) content of interaction. The first three considerations locate relationships within a structural space, whereas the latter two index the quality of the partners' involvement with one another.

Several researchers (e.g., Marwell & Hage, 1970; Triandis, Vassiliou, & Nassiakou, 1968; Wish, Deutsch, & Kaplan, 1976) have asked persons to make judgments concerning the interpersonal characteristics of various role relationships. Wish and his colleagues (Wish et al., 1976), for instance, using multidimensional scaling techniques, uncovered four fundamental dimensions of relatedness: (a) cooperative–friendly, as opposed to competitive–hostile; (b) equal, as opposed to unequal; (c) intense, as opposed to superficial; and (d) socioemotional–informal, as opposed to task-oriented–formal. The first pole of each dimension implies closeness or intimacy, whereas the second indicates distance or surface involvement.

Participants in the Wish *et al.* (1976) study rated their own relationships, both those of their childhood (e.g., with their mothers, fathers, close friends, and disliked acquaintances) and those of their adulthood at present (e.g., with their spouses, mothers, fathers, coworkers). The participants also rated 44 "typical relations." Included among these were most of the types of relationships they had rated for themselves, as well as relations such as those of salesman and regular customer, business rivals, and second cousins. Each of the relationships was located in terms of each of the four dimensions. Thus a profile of how relationships are seen in comparison with one another emerged.

Data gathered by Marwell and Hage (1970) and Triandis *et al.* (1968) differ in details, but the general pattern of results is the same. Taken as a whole, the empirical work provides guidelines to characterize what is meant when a relationship is described as "close." The studies suggest that kin relationships are generally closer than those between nonkin, but that close relationships cut across kinship, sex, and age boundaries.

While perceptual approaches to identifying and characterizing close relationships are useful, the data gathered should be interpreted cautiously. For one thing, relationships not ordinarily seen as intimate sometimes are, and relationships that are typically viewed as intimate sometimes are not. Wish *et al.* (1976), in fact, found, when their respondents described their own relationships, that relationships stereotyped as close were actually quite varied in regard to closeness. Marriages, in general, were perceived as intimate in terms of each pole of the Wish *et al.* (1976) dimensions; but some participants did not describe their own marriages as intimate.

Accordingly, several observers (e.g., Burgess & Wallin, 1953; Bernard, 1964; Cuber & Harroff, 1965) have attempted to capture some of the variability in the character of specific relationships by classifying marriages as, for instance, primarily "companionate" or primarily "instrumental" in character. Recent divorce statistics (see Norton & Glick, 1976) may be taken to suggest that conflict and hostility may characterize many marriages as much as cooperation and friendship. And even within generally harmonious families, conflict, hostility, and attempts at coercion occur at times (Birchler, Weiss, & Vincent, 1975; Burgess, 1979; Patterson & Reig, 1970; Vincent, Weiss, & Birchler, 1974). It appears safe to assume that, given the degree of interdependence involved, almost all, or at least many, intense relationships have more conflict than perceptual models are likely to attribute to them.

III. The Development of Closeness
in Relationships

Studies concerned with perceptions of the interpersonal properties of role relationships provide guidance for identifying where within a culture close relationships are most likely to be found. They also indicate fundamental properties of relationships; such properties can be used to describe how relationships move from distance, or surface contact, to closeness.

Since the extent and nature of interdependency cannot be directly measured, several exchange theorists (Altman & Taylor, 1973; Hatfield, Utne & Traupmann, Chapter 4 of this volume; Hinde, 1976; Levinger, 1974; Levinger & Snoek, 1972; Scanzoni, Chapter 3 of this volume) have attempted to describe intimate relationships and to differentiate them from superficial ones. A composite of their descriptions, as well as some we have added ourselves, suggests that as partners grow increasingly closer, the following changes take place in their relationship.

1. They interact more often, for longer periods of time, and in a widening array of settings.
2. They attempt to restore proximity when separated, and feel comforted when proximity is regained.
3. They "open up" to each other, in the sense that they disclose secrets and share physical intimacies.
4. They become less inhibited, more willing to share positive and negative feelings, and to praise and criticize each other.
5. They develop their own communication system, and become ever more efficient in using it.
6. They increase their ability to map and anticipate each other's views of social reality.
7. They begin to synchronize their goals and behavior, and develop stable interaction patterns.
8. They increase their investment in the relationship, thus enhancing its importance in their life space.
9. They begin increasingly to feel that their separate interests are inextricably tied to the well-being of their relationship.
10. They increase their liking, trust, and love for each other.
11. They see the relationship as irreplaceable, or at least as unique.
12. They more and more relate to others as a couple rather than as individuals.

This list of changes is by no means exhaustive; nor do all relationships change in the same ways as the partners grow closer. Intimate relationships have personalities, just as people do, and the ways couples shape their relationships allow them to express their own versions of intimacy. No one knows for sure which of the elements, if any, are essential ingredients of interdependency (used here as a synonym for closeness) in the sense that they necessarily ebb and flow as the relationship alters.

There is little systematic behavioral science work describing changes in relationships. Research concerned with premarital couples has usually focused on determinants of "courtship progress," measured by changes in commitment to marriage (e.g., Kerckhoff & Davis, 1962; Levinger, Senn, & Jorgensen, 1970). Work on marriage has rarely been longitudinal; most studies have taken cross-sectional samples of partners who have been married for varying lengths of time, or who are in different stages of the family life cycle, and compared them in regard to marital adjustment (e.g., Burr, 1970; Spanier, Lewis, & Cole, 1975). Longitudinal studies of friendship have focused more on the determinants of friendship than on its description (e.g., Duck, 1977a; Newcomb, 1961).

Each type of relationship has spawned its own form of behavioral-science literature. Not only has each literature developed independently, but the study of change has tended to examine only one aspect of involvement at a time. Attempts to map the evolution of relationships within a multidimensional space are rare.

Braiker and Kelley (Chapter 5), using retrospective longitudinal data, show how such work might proceed. Their goal was to reconstruct the movement of premarital relationships from their beginnings up to and into marrriage. They first postulated basic dimensions of involvement and then developed scales to measure these. They generated a pool of items on the basis of descriptive data provided by newly married couples. Responses to the pool of items were factor analyzed, and the following dimensions identified: (a) love; (b) conflict and negativity; (c) ambivalence; and (d) maintenance (including self-disclosure, problem-solving behavior, and attempts of persons to change themselves or their partners). Relationships changed in terms of each dimension as the partners moved from casual dating to engagement. The dimensions also tied together differently at various stages of involvement. Early in the cycle, love was associated with maintenance activities; later, love had little to do with maintenance. Instead, maintenance activities were associated with conflict. Ambivalence was tied to conflict early in the relationship; later on, ambivalence had more to do with concerns about love than the experience of conflict. At all stages, the degree of love and the amount of conflict were uncorrelated. Some couples reported conflict throughout their relationship; others said that they experienced little at any stage.

Within the next decade, further research will undoubtedly build on this pioneering work of Braiker and Kelley (Chapter 5)—as it should on the work of Wohlwill (1973), who has organized a framework for investigating developmental phenomena within the individual that could provide a model for research on change in relationships. The framework sets forth a five-step process for studying developmental change: (a) the discovery of meaningful change dimensions; (b) the quantitative and qualitative description of change; (c) the correlational analysis of the patterning of change along the stipulated dimensions; (d) the investigation of the determinants of developmental change; and (e) the study of variations in patterns of development.

Braiker and Kelley's (Chapter 5) study offers a descriptive focus on the first three steps. The last two steps deal with issues of explanation. The Braiker and Kelley (Chapter 5) work contrasts with most research on relationships, which has not been adequately descriptive, and has dealt with explanations of poorly explicated phenomena. Consider, for instance, the previously mentioned work on courtship progress. Usually, the assessment of courtship progress is based on a single question: "Are you closer to marriage, further apart, or about the same (as you were 6–8 months ago)?" Some couples were casually committed at the beginning; others said that they were seriously committed—even engaged. Such data are difficult to interpret unless it is assumed that "closer to marriage" means the same to all respondents, regardless of their degree of involvement, and unless one believes that the determinants of change in commitment are the same regardless of whether the partners are committing themselves to dating, living with, or marrying one another.

IV. Social Exchange in Developing Relationships

A. Equity, Equality, and Intimate Relationships

The recent application by social scientists of exchange principles to intimate relationships (Altman & Taylor, 1973; Huesmann & Levinger, 1976; Leik & Leik, 1976; Levinger & Snoek, 1972) is interesting in part because the basic tenets of exchange theory seem contrary to Western views about the nature of love and intimacy. Love is supposed to involve caring, altruism, communion, and selflessness; certainly persons "in love" often feel and act in ways that reveal such virtues. The view that love is tied to the exchange of rewards seems crass. Even those who believe exchange principles can be usefully applied to a wide variety of situations and relationships sometimes shy away from applying them to close relationships (e.g., Deutsch, 1975; Lerner, 1975; Rubin, 1973; Sampson, 1975). Rubin (1973), for instance, takes an uncertain stance regarding the ability of exchange principles to account for intimate relationships:

As an interpersonal bond becomes more firmly established . . . it begins to go beyond exchange. In close relationships one becomes decreasingly concerned with what he gets *from* the other person and increasingly concerned with what he can do *for* the other. But even in the closest of relationships, the principles of the interpersonal marketplace are never entirely repealed . . . even in the case of love the dual themes of what we can get and what we give remain closely intertwined [pp. 86–87].

Rubin (1973) and other scholars (e.g., Deutsch, 1975; Sampson, 1975) object in particular to the *equity* interpretation of exchange (see Hatfield, Utne, & Traupmann, Chapter 4). According to equity theory, people become more committed to relationships when they perceive that the value of each participant's outcomes are proportional to the relative value of each individual's investments. Such a frame of reference, according to both Deutsch (1975) and Sampson (1975), encourages status differentiation and discourages cooperation. Allocation according to the principle of equity, Deutsch (1975) believes,

tends to be disruptive of social relations because it undermines the bases for mutual respect and self-respect. . . . It does this by signifying that the different participants in the relationship do not have the same value. A relatively low evaluation may lead to envy, self-devaluation, or conflict over the valuations—all of which may destroy the enjoyability of the relationship. . . . Moreover, respect and esteem are more valuable if they are received from those whom one respects; equal status relations represent the optimum distribution of status for the mutual support of self-esteem [p. 146].

We agree with Deutsch's assessment; but we also agree with Hatfield and her colleagues (Chapter 4) that partners are more likely to be satisfied with relationships in which equity prevails. This contrariety disappears when one grants that equity and equality can exist side by side.[1] If both partners contribute and gain equally, their equality of benefits (rewards) and responsibilities (or other costs) amounts to equity: equal returns have derived from equal investments. Judgments partners make regarding the equity or equality of their relationship are apt to be rooted in their overall satisfaction with the relationship which, in turn, is tied to its reward-cost history and to the partners' respective alternatives outside the relationship. If the partners are getting a great deal from the relationship, compared with their available alternatives, they are likely to be unconcerned with whether the distribution is equitable, equal, neither equitable nor

[1] Persons seeking intimacy are likely to try to attach themselves to someone with whom equal sharing is equitable; to the extent that they succeed (at least in their own eyes) in making such a match, they are likely to try to share equally. The difficulty of achieving and maintaining equity and equality simultaneously in a relationship over long periods of time, coupled with the tendency to become impatient with even short periods of either inequity or inequality, probably explains, at least partly, the fragility of intimacy.

equal, or both (Burgess & Nielsen, 1974). It is when a relationship is of arguable value that partners are apt to show great concern with calibrating the rewards and costs according to rules of equity. Similarly, it is only after the partners conclude that they are of equal merit that they ought to show regular concern with whether the benefits and responsibilities are allocated equally. This suggests, then, that when persons are dissatisfied with their relationship they are apt to view it as inequitable; and that when they are satisfied, they are likely to see it as both equitable and equal. This interpretation is not inconsistent with the data gathered by Hatfield *et al.* (Chapter 4), but whereas Hatfield *et al.* view equity as producing satisfaction, we suspect that both satisfaction and judgments of equity–inequity are tied to the reward–cost history of the relationship.

B. *Application of Exchange Principles to Intimate Relationships*

How does exchange theory interpret the manner in which relationships might evolve from superficial liaisons—in which the partners are likely to recognize the exchange basis of their involvement—to close, intimate bonds (wherein the partners may seem almost selfless in their devotion to each other) to breakups (with their attendant alienation and hostility). The interpretation uses basic reinforcement and exchange principles as set down by Blau (1964), Homans (1961, 1974), and Thibaut and Kelley (1959).[2] Our analysis focuses on romantic relationships, not because the reasoning developed is not applicable to other relationships, but because such relationships have been most thoroughly studied (see Huston & Levinger, 1978).

Exchange theorists view "love" as the product of a long history of interaction. Affection, caring, trust, and dependency, all of which are generally thought to be components of love, are assumed to be part of the couple's involvement with each other. Love, if it is to be conceived in

---

[2] The reader is referred to Chadwick-Jones (1976) for a summary comparisons of various versions of exchange theory. Our analysis explicates what Ekeh (1974) has referred to as the *individualistic* approach to social exchange, as set forth by Homans (1961, 1974), Thibaut and Kelley (1959), and Blau (1964), and as further explicated by Burgess and Bushell (1969), among others. In focusing our discussion on an individualistic approach to exchange, however, we do not wish to imply that society at large does not have a stake in how relationships are structured, or that people do not consider both societal and personal interests in working out their relationships. In this chapter, we maintain that social partnerships are apt to be strengthened when the partners find that their personal interests are best furthered by working toward their collective interests. The same type of reasoning can be applied to the linkages of relationships to one another within a culture (see Sampson, 1977), and it is likely that persons are aware of these linkages and take them into consideration as they make their way through their interpersonal world (see Scanzoni, Chapter 3).

terms of exchange theory, must be interpersonally based. Such a view of love differs from that in which it is portrayed as infused with irrationality, romance, and fantasy (see Berscheid & Walster, 1974, for an elucidation of this view), and from the belief that love (at least in its so-called pure form) requires absolute selflessness (Fromm, 1956).

Close romantic relationships generally evolve from a first meeting to acquaintanceship to casual dating to serious dating and finally to some kind of formal commitment between the partners (Braiker & Kelley, Chapter 5). First meetings, acquaintanceships, and casual dating can generally be described as "surface" relationships. As relationships evolve toward greater commitment, however, the partners develop private norms for regulating their relationship, increase their investment in it, share intimate information about themselves, and increasingly take responsibility for furthering the pleasures and benefits ("returns") their partners reap.

Why do some relationships remain superficial and others evolve to a deeper, committed involvement? The key element from an exchange-theory perspective is growth in the extent and nature of "interdependency" (see Huesmann & Levinger, 1976; Levinger & Huesmann, in press; Scanzoni, Chapter 3 of this volume). Partners are interdependent to the extent to which each one's outcomes ("returns") depend on the outcomes received by the partner, and to the degree to which each one's profits exceed customary profits or those likely in another relationship (Thibaut & Kelley, 1959). As persons interact, they begin to discover the extent to which shared activities are mutually rewarding. They also discover the degree to which the relationship is beneficial to them independent of direct interaction with one another. One partner's managerial capabilities, for instance, may heighten the other's satisfaction. In addition, as the relationship becomes public, parents, peers, and others react to it, thus strengthening or disrupting the partners' commitment to each other (Driscoll, Davis, & Lipetz, 1972; Ridley & Avery, Chapter 8).

1. SOCIAL EXCHANGE AND THE INITIATION OF RELATIONSHIPS

Many first encounters are structured by social circumstance which leave the interactants with little choice concerning with whom or how they interact. Encounters such as those between customers and merchants or first meetings between businessmen operate under such constraints. Other circumstances are less constrained and allow greater latitude and choice. Since exchange theorists assume social interest is anchored in self-interest, according to the theory persons in open-ended situations ought to seek out partners with whom they anticipate interaction will prove rewarding. Another assumpton of exchange theory is that one must be able to provide rewards in order to get them. An actor, therefore, must

consider two things before making an overture to another. He must calculate the degree to which he finds the attributes of potential partners
attractive, and hence their approval rewarding; and he must consider the
degree to which they would find him attractive and, as a consequence,
respond favorably to him.

The operation of "marketplace" considerations in evaluations of potential partners is illustrated by the following thoughts on the beginnings
of "love." They are those of Ezekiel Farragut, the protagonist of John
Cheever's (1977) novel, *Falconer*:

> I am today and will be forever astonished at the perspicacity with which a man can,
> in a glimpse, judge the scope and beauty of a woman's memory, her tastes in color,
> food, climate and language, the precise clinical dimensions of her visceral, cranial
> and reproductive tracts, the conditions of her teeth, hair, skin, toenails, eyesight
> and bronchial tree, that he can, in a second, exalted by the diagnostics of love, seize
> on the fact that she is meant for him or that they are meant for one another [pp.
> 76–77].

And he then notes, "I am speaking of a glimpse and the image seems to be
transitory, although this not so much romantic as it is practical since I am
thinking of a stranger, seen by a stranger [p. 77]."

The nature of the rewards sought and offered—and, thus, the determinants of reciprocal attraction—are of less central interest to exchange
theory than the reciprocity itself, except insofar as it is necessary to
identify them in order to test the central propositions.[3] Rather than try to
ascertain what people seek, and therefore what features of others they
attend to, and what they offer in initial encounters, exchange theorists
have attempted to design their research so that they know in advance
which people actors will find attractive, and which people the actors
believe will find them attractive. The prediction is then made that actors
will seek out (or find desirable) only those partners who are *both* attractive
to them and who seem likely to reciprocate their attraction.

Confirmation of the importance of the dual role of attraction and
concern for reciprocity is provided by several studies of the processes
involved in choosing dating partners (Berscheid, Dion, Walster, & Walster, 1971; Huston, 1973; Kiesler & Baral, 1970; Shanteau & Nagy, 1976;
Stroebe, Insko, Layton, & Thompson, 1971). Shanteau and Nagy (1976),
for instance, conducted a series of studies demonstrating how attraction
and expectations of reciprocity combine to determine the desirability of

---

[3] Generally, when persons associate they seek acceptance or approval. The value of the
approval, according to attraction researchers, is dependent on, among other things, such
factors as the status of the other, the other's physical beauty, and the similarity of the other's
attitudes, personality, and social characteristics to one's own. Recent reviews of the literature on attraction can be found in Berscheid and Walster (1977), Clore (1975), Duck (1977b),
Huston (1974), and Huston and Levinger (1978).

persons as dates. In one study, participants were shown a set of pictures of persons of the opposite sex paired together in all possible combinations; for each pair in the series, the participants were asked to pick the person they most desired to date. At another time, the participants rated each photo for physical beauty and also indicated the likelihood that each of the photographed persons would accept them as a date. The relative desirability of the pictured persons was better predicted by taking into account both the attractiveness ratings and the probability-of-acceptance ratings than by either set of ratings taken alone.

In a second study (Shanteau & Nagy, 1976), participants rated the desirability of several persons after examining their pictures and bogus information concerning the likelihood that each would date them. When the participants were led to believe that there was no chance of acceptance by any of the persons, the relative desirability of the persons was indistinguishable and low. When chances of acceptance were represented as good, however, the highly attractive persons were rated as increasingly desirable compared with those who were less attractive.

It is easy, perhaps, to read into the above analysis the idea that the decision to begin interaction is discrete, and based on a more or less objective appraisal of the degree of balance between what one person has to offer and what others have to offer in return. Most freely initiated encounters, however, are probably low-key, with neither party investing much nor expecting much in return. In some situations, though, a person is immediately attracted to another, and at the same time finds it difficult to estimate how the other will react. In such circumstances, the person may intensify his or her attention, or gather information over an extended period of time in order to make the assessments necessary to determine the most beneficial course of action (see Berscheid & Graziano, Chapter 2, for a discussion of the impact of dependency on attention).

Those seeking someone to love may base their decision to initiate interaction not only on immediate rewards and costs but also on anticipated future returns (see Altman & Taylor, 1973; Huesmann & Levinger, 1976). Shanteau and Nagy (1976), in one of their studies, found that the desirability of persons as dates was not only predicated on their attractiveness and receptivity to an offer but also on the degree to which they were seen as likely to be compatible.

2. FROM ENCOUNTER TO RELATIONSHIP

Regardless of what precedes the start of an encounter, the behavioral data the partners gather about each other begin to replace preliminary assessments as a basis for further interaction. A rebuke, for instance, may dash what were high hopes for a rewarding experience; or the discovery of common interests may transform what was anticipated to be an unpromising relationship into one of considerable satisfaction. Such sudden developments, however, do not occur every day; indeed, social life is culturally designed so that much of the give and take is controlled by convention. Yet encounters are apt to move people emotionally when seemingly routine relationships or interactions produce surprises in the form of unexpected rewards or costs (Tedeschi, 1974).

According to exchange theory, most relationships remain superficial for two reasons:

1. The types of rewards exchanged (e.g., approval for information) are readily available from a number of sources.
2. The interaction has not been sufficiently profitable to motivate the partners to intensify their involvement (Altman & Taylor, 1973; Huesmann & Levinger, 1976).

When partners find superficial interaction unusually rewarding, or when they begin to feel each has the potential to reward the other in ways few people do and that others who can offer such rare rewards are unavailable, they begin to deepen and develop their relationship. As they do, both gather new information about their own investments, as well their partner's, and revise their forecasts of future rewards (see Altman & Taylor, 1973; Huesmann & Levinger, 1976; Levinger & Huesmann, in press; Scanzoni, Chapter 3). Forecasts, according to exchange theory, are rooted not only in the absolute amount of profit (i.e., rewards minus costs) derived from the partners' previous exchanges, but also in the perceived pattern of profit over time, and, especially, the degree to which the relationship compares favorably with others.

How can we predict before interaction whether two persons are apt to become highly involved with each other? Patterson and Reid (1970) believe the answer lies in a comparison of the similarity between persons in their repertoire of social behaviors. These authors suggest we view persons as having stable repertoires of social behaviors, and that these behaviors can be rank-ordered according to their frequency of occurrence. A rough correspondence is assumed between the frequency of a social behavior and its reinforcing value to the actor. According to Patterson and Reid (1970), the fact that two persons were raised

in the same culture would lead to the prediction that there would be *some* overlap in their repertoires of social behaviors. For short periods of time almost any combination of two persons is likely to provide mutual reinforcement for each other's behavior. This may relate to the fact . . . that "proximity" is one of the primary determinants of friendship selections. . . . However, extended interactions, or friendship pairings, are most likely to occur as a function of overlapping hierarchies for behaviors which are major sources of reinforcement for both persons involved. This would suggest, of course, that friendship pairings are partially made on the basis of similarities of interests, work, and hobbies. Interacting with another person with similar interests would not only increase the probability that you will attend to his behavior and thereby reinforce him, but it also increases the probability that he will reinforce you [pp. 141–142].

Patterson and Reid (1970) further note that because partners—whether friends or spouses—reinforce the behavior of one another that is similar to their own, they are likely to become more similar over time.

In the early stages of relationships, it is likely that attraction is based on the degree to which the partners find rewards in shared behavior. As relationships evolve, however, other reward–cost considerations take on increasing importance. Levinger and Huesmann (in press) have stressed the "slope of rewards" (and costs) over time as a factor influencing attraction. Thus, a person may be attracted to a particular person not so much because previous interaction has been notably profitable, but because the profits have been steadily increasing. The partners may also be apt to find that an increasing amount of the rewards are mediated not through direct interaction but indirectly through the partners' transactions with the surrounding physical and social world. Thus, individuals may take pleasure in the material goods that their joining together has allowed them to acquire, or they may enjoy the status that they have achieved in their community by virtue of their union.

Several recent studies (Berscheid & Fei, 1977; Dion & Dion, 1976; Rubin, 1974; Braiker & Kelley, Chapter 5) chart the growth of relationships in terms of interdependency and affection. In the early stages, partners appear to experience the beginnings of dependency, accompanied by a sense of vulnerability, insecurity, and ambivalence (Berscheid & Fei, 1977; Braiker & Kelley, Chapter 5). Much of the early absorption lovers show may be directed toward transforming the ambivalence of dependency into the security of interdependency. Data from several studies (Berscheid & Fei, 1977; Dion & Dion, 1976; Driscoll, Davis, & Lipetz, 1972; Braiker & Kelley, Chapter 5), taken as a whole, show that as partners grow emotionally close, they feel more dependent, yet less ambivalent and insecure in their relationship. They increasingly begin to recognize their mutual dependency, and to have reason to trust that their partner needs them just as much as they need their partner. Some research (Driscoll, Davis, & Lipetz, 1973) seems to suggest that as relationships evolve, love and trust become increasingly intertwined, and recent attempts (Rubin, 1970; Braiker & Kelley, Chapter 5) to measure love as it develops in heterosexual relationships suggest that when persons say they are "in love," much of what they mean is contained in the concept of interdependency.[4]

---

[4] We have erected our analysis on a foundation of data provided by couples involved in heterosexual romantic relationships. By extension, however, we are addressing the role of

Persons deeply in love, in the way just indicated, sense that their own well-being and that of their partner are intimately tied together. It is possible, in theory at least, that partners can be so perfectly meshed that what is rewarding to one is rewarding to the other. In such a circumstance, it becomes difficult if not impossible to differentiate self-interest from altruistic interest; moreover, since such a differentiation entails no practical consequences, the partners are apt to conceive of their relationship more as a communion than as an exchange.

Such may have been the nature of the relationship of Frieda and D. H. Lawrence, whose enduring romance severed her from a previous marriage and lasted until his death. She recalls this early period of their life together:

> I didn't want people, I didn't want anything. I only wanted to revel in this new world Lawrence had given me. I had found what I needed, I could now flourish like a trout in a stream or a daisy in the sun. His generosity in giving himself: "Take all you want of me, everything, I am yours"; and I took and gave equally, without thought.
>
> When I asked him: "What do I give you, that you didn't get from others?" he answered: "You make me sure of myself, whole."
>
> And he would say: "You are so young, so young!" When I remonstrated: "But I am older than you."—"Ah, it isn't years, it's something else. You don't understand."
>
> Anyhow I knew he loved the essence of me. . . . Whatever faults I had. It was life to me.
>
> "You have a genius for living," he told me.
>
> "Maybe, but you brought it out in me." [Frieda Lawrence Ravagli (in Nehls, 1957, p. 167).]

Most stable close relationships, of course, will have periods of communal feeling rather than an all-pervasive sense of communality. The extent to which the partners' individual concerns and their joint interests converge may be viewed as a continuum, with couples evidencing varying degrees of convergence. The greater the convergence, the more likely the rewards flowing from the interaction will exceed their expectations—or, in Thibaut and Kelley's (1959) terms, their "comparison level." Moreover, the greater the convergence, the more likely the rewards will exceed what the two believe they could receive in other relationships they might establish—that is, their "comparison level for alternatives" (Thibaut & Kelley, 1959).[5]

---

social exchange in fostering cooperation in general. Pruitt and Kimmel (1977), in a recent critique of research on experimental gaming, suggest a set of conditions similar to those we have identified as facilitating cooperation between game partners. In short, the development of a cooperative relationship involves the discovery within a wide range of settings of the mutual benefits of cooperation over noncooperation.

[5] People's expectations of what they ought to get and what they could get elsewhere are rooted not only in their direct experience but in the ethos of their culture. People become

As relationships take on a "public" character, further reward–cost considerations come into play. Persons involved with either partner or with the couple react to the relationship either by supporting it (and therefore rewarding the partners for maintaining the relationship) or by attempting to thwart it (see Ridley and Avery, Chapter 8). Sir Kenneth Clark (1974), the art historian, provides an illustration of how parental response bears upon relationships:

> My parents took the news of my attachment (we were never officially "engaged") very well. They were completely unworldly and it never struck them that I should "make a good match." They had, indeed, received some advance warning of the situation, as my father, to relieve his boredom, used to open and read all my letters. Usually they were from Charlie Bell, and his boredom was increased. A few were from Jane and on one of them he wrote "Don't let the girl catch you." As soon as they met they adored each other. [My mother] too behaved to Jane with the utmost sweetness and consideration. I think they were genuinely glad to see me so happy; perhaps they were also relieved to have me out of the way [p. 122].

Clark's parents provided support for a decision that he and his fiancée had reached. What if his parents had opposed the marriage? The only data bearing on the issue of parental opposition seem to suggest that, if anything, it intensifies the commitment of premarital partners to each other (Driscoll *et al.*, 1972). These data should be interpreted cautiously, however, because the effect of parental attitudes on relationships is apt to be qualified by a host of variables, including the strength of the bond between parent and offspring, the extent to which the parent controls needed resources, and the way in which the parent makes his or her feelings known.

3. DETERIORATION AND DISSOLUTION
OF RELATIONSHIPS

According to exchange notions, commitment is strengthened to the extent that both partners discover they have uncommon abilities to reward each other. One criterion of commitment, in the view of Leik and Leik (1976), is the cessation of comparisons between one's present relationship and others one has had or might have.

Why do couples either fail to seek or fail to achieve such a commitment, or if they have become intensely committed, what leads them to break off the relationship? There are at least two approaches to examining

---

interdependent—in the sense that the word is used in exchange theory—through a history of mutually profitable exchanges; how profitable is profitable enough, however, is a subjective judgment much influenced by the values dominant in the larger cultural milieu. The steady rise in the divorce rate (Norton & Glick, 1976) may be due, in part, to rising expectations for marriage and, upon the failure of a marriage, for remarriage.

why relationships deteriorate and dissolve from the perspective of exchange theory. The relationship may be viewed in terms of the transactions that occur between the partners, or examined in terms of the relationships that each partner maintains with others.

Within relationships, some ties are never consolidated, either because the partners find the interaction insufficiently rewarding to sustain affection or because a one-sided sense of dependency develops. Data gathered by Hill, Rubin, and Peplau (1976) on breakups of premarital involvements bear on this proposition, at least insofar as love reflects feelings of dependency, and that symmetry of commitment implies equality in dependency. In their study of 231 dating couples, Hill et al. (1976) found that those who had stayed together over a 2-year period were more "in love" and more equally committed to each other than those who had broken up.

The fact that partners have a weak bond does not mean they will necessarily break up. Hill et al. (1976) found that couples tended to terminate their relationships before or after periods of separation. Gustave Flaubert, in *Madame Bovary*, has portrayed the agonized weariness of remaining too long in a lifeless relationship:

> He was bored now when Emma suddenly began to sob on his breast, and his heart, like the people who can only stand a certain amount of music, dozed to the sound of a love whose delicacies he no longer noted.
>
> They knew one another too well for any of those surprises of possession that increase its joy a hundred-fold. She was as sick of him as he was weary of her. Emma found again in adultery all the platitudes of marriage.
>
> But how to get rid of him? She accused Leon of her baffled hopes, as if he had betrayed her, and she even longed for some catastrophe that would bring about their separation, since she had not the courage to make up her mind to effect it herself.
>
> She none the less went on writing him love letters, in virtue of the notion that a woman must write to her lover [1950 (orig., 1857), p. 332].

Why might people remain in a relationship which is no longer satisfying? One reason is that people sometimes feel that the failure of a close relationship represents a personal failure. They may also stay in a relationship because breaking it would require them to restructure their life—to develop new habits of living, to refashion old friendships, and to find new ones. Earlier, we suggested that as partners begin to see each other as unique sources of reward, they begin to build barriers around their relationship. These barriers can be moral, as when partners expressly affirm their love for each other and vow to establish a lifelong bond. Or they can be erected in collaboration with a network of kin and friends. In the latter case the partners may receive subtle (and sometimes not so subtle) indications of how relatives and friends feel about one of them, as well as indications of whether a committed, long-term relationship is believed to be propitious. Levinger (Chapter 6 of this volume) suggests ways in which forces—both within the dyad and outside it—combine to build relationships and tear them down.

V. The Social Context of Relationships

Up to this point, we have stressed factors internal to relationships—the charges transmitted between the partners—with little emphasis given to the larger social context and how it conditions relationships. In a thoughtful essay on the history of intimacy in the United States, Gadlin (1977) traces the evolution of close relationships from the colonial period, when they were primarily a community matter, to the present, when relationships are often subordinated to the separate needs and goals of each partner. By extending his analysis to include the effect of kin relationships, it is possible to compare the development of close relationship in two different social circumstances: in a close-knit community, where the larger group and the kinship group play a particularly dominant role, and in a metropolis, where the importance of the larger community tends to be slight, because of anonymity, pluralism, and the isolation of romance from other relationships.

The two contrasting social contexts—the small community and the metropolis—are compared in terms of social networks in Table 1.1. The close-knit community, as described by Boissevain (1974), is small and dense. Relationships are diversified and fields of activity overlap. Persons play multiple roles with each other, and exchange a variety of things—information, services, and affection—with the same people over extended periods of time. Moreover, a large proportion of people are linked with their neighbors—a fact that, according to Alexander's (Chapter 7) analysis, may be expected to influence the community ethos.

Small, close-knit communities tend to have a high degree of consensus regarding norms and values (Boissevain, 1974). People learn their place in the community, usually early in life, because, as a collectivity of like-minded individuals, the community withholds or confers benefits and punishments, depending on conformity with local standards. People learn to anticipate consequences, and most generally develop desires and dispositions congruent with prevailing social norms. Failures of acculturation are punished, thereby affirming social norms and providing an example to potential norm violators (Durkheim, 1895/1950).

Within such communities, considerable social control is likely to be exercised on close relationships. Partners are apt to have known each other—or known about each other—for a long time before their close relationship began. As they confirm their commitment, they become further enmeshed within the larger community. As the partners join

TABLE 1.1

Social Networks and Community Context

Network Characteristics[a]	Close-knit community	Metropolis
A. *Structural Aspects*		
1. Size	Small	Large
2. Density (*degree to which network is interconnected, independent of a particular dyad*)	High; many persons are related through kinship	Low; few are tied by kinship
3. Connectedness (*proportion of persons with whom the average individual has a relationship*)	High; large proportion are with kin	Low; considerable variation exists with regard to the proportion of people with kin
4. Values, attitudes, and rules of conduct	Considerable community consensus	Pluralism within community
B. *Interactional Criteria*		
1. Diversity of linkage (*refers to the number of roles that connect persons to one another*)	Nearly all relationships are diversified (multiplex)	Large proportion of relationships are narrowly circumscribed (uniplex)
2. Exchange content[b] (*information, services, goods, money, status, love*)	Most relationships involve variety of content	Most relationships involve restricted content
3. Directional flow (*refers to the direction elements move—are exchanged—in transactions*)	Bidirectional, but dyads are dependent on network resources	Bidirectional, but dyads search the larger network for persons who are able and ready to supply needed resources
4. Frequency and duration of interaction	Interaction is frequent, and relationships of long duration	Interaction is infrequent, and network system is continually changing in composition

[a] See Boissevain (1974) and Ridley and Avery (Chapter 8 of this volume) for further elaboration of characteristics of networks

[b] These areas of exchange content have been identified by Foa and Foa (1974)

together, their social network becomes increasingly intertwined. It seems likely that in small communities relationships are encouraged and held together or discouraged or broken apart as much by community reaction as by the interpersonal transactions that occur within the dyad.[6] Erikson

[6] Data reviewed by Bott (1971) suggests that the greater the density of a community, the less intimate the marital bonds. Thus, it is important to keep in mind that heterosexual relationships spawned in different community contexts may differ in interpersonal and psychological content.

(1976) provides a description of the profound influence networks exert on the course and stability of intimate relationships within close-knit communities:

> No act in life seems more private, more intimate, than the decision by two people to get married, particularly in this age when we celebrate the distance we have come since the times of arranged marriages. It is true, of course, that people "select" their mates now, whatever that may mean. But there are other ways to arrange marriages than becoming a formal party to the contract—spoken and unspoken encouragements that pass among families and friends beforehand, as well as a million other hints and suggestions that become a part of the marriage scene afterward. While we do not know much about those subtle chemistries, it is clear enough that marriage, too, is something of a community affair. It is validated by the community, commemorated by the community, and every married couple in the world knows something about the pressures exerted on that union by interests outside of it. In one sense, then, a marriage between two persons lies in a kind of gravitational field. The human particles who form the union are held together by all the other magnetic forces passing through the larger field; and when the outer currents lose their force, the particles find the inner charge, the interpersonal bond begins to fade as well [p. 218].

In large urban contexts, the partners in a relationship are less influenced by community reaction. They generally know each other for only a short period of time before pairing up; what is more, they are likely to have few friends in common and, of those they have, even fewer are likely to be linked by common knowledge, affection, or geographical residence. Thus, partners have much more control over who is in their network of relationships. Moreover, given the pluralism in values characteristic of the metropolis, they are likely to be in a position to fashion a network to support their relationship rather than vice versa.[7]

More so than in a small-community setting, relationships in an urban context are developed and maintained, or dissolved, because what happens inside the relationship is or is not mutually rewarding. The dyad withdraws from the urban community as the partners become more involved with each other (see Slater, 1963). This withdrawal is illustrated in Figure 1.1 (p. 5), which shows the overall size of the partners' social network shrinking as the partners move from surface contact to mutuality. If the interior of a close relationship breaks down, the partners are more apt than in a small community to break up both their relationship and their joint social network, move on, and reestablish themselves with a

---

[7] Such restructuring is not always possible, or as easy as our analysis may seem to imply. If a person (or cluster of individuals) controls resources scarce and valuable to the partners, the person(s) may have considerable influence on the relationship (see Ridley & Avery, Chapter 8), depending on how the attempt at influence is manifested. Overt and direct attempts to control relationships may produce psychological resistance (see Brehm, 1966) and boomerang. The tie of external constraint to internal cohesion (or commitment) within long-term relationships is complex. Recent observers (e.g., Fischer, 1977; Levinger, 1977; Rosenblatt, 1977), however, agree that high external constraint, if anything, reduces internal resolve.

new group of friends, often geographically removed from the now dis-
carded relationship and network.

Undoubtedly, the foregoing describes relationships within contexts
at the two ends of a continuum. Even in large urban settings, kinship ties
and other primary relationships play an important role in the establishment of relatively enduring social relationships. Indeed, a recent study of
urban residents by Shulman (1975) found that over 40% of social networks are kin-related.

VI. Conclusion

This chapter has offered an introduction to the application of social-
exchange concepts to the analysis of the evolution of relationships from
first acquaintance to close, intimate commitment. In setting forth such an
analysis, we did not wish to imply that all features of relationships are
readily interpretable by exchange theory, or that close relationships in
contemporary society are necessarily sustained by the kind of affection
based on exchange. As Erikson (1976) has noted with regard to families in
Appalachia:

> The bonds of the family were close. . . . But those bonds were of a rather
> special cast. The family did not operate like an assembly of separate individuals,
> each of whom was expected to develop a personal bond of intimacy with each of the
> others. It was a generalized entity, a living tissue, from which every member drew
> some measure of warmth and to which every member offered some measure of
> allegiance. . . . Visitors to the areas have expressed surprise at the degree to which
> individuals will cherish, protect, nurture, and make particular allowances for their
> mates without appearing to know them very well as distinct personalities. Part of
> this is the celebrated individualism of the mountains: people will not presume to
> speak for anyone else, not even a husband or wife. But part of it stems from a real
> indifference to the interior furnishings of another's mind, as if one's tastes and
> attitudes belong to the sphere of privacy to which no one else has access [p. 59].

This description of the nature of bondedness in Appalachian families
can be interpreted so as to fit exchange principles, but much would be lost
by such an interpretation. As it stands, Erikson's (1976) vignette is of
interest because it focuses attention on the nature of familial interconnec-
tedness, and illustrates the distinctive way such connectedness is manifested as a function of the subcultural milieu. It is difficult, however,
without recourse to exchange principles, to understand how relationship
patterns emerge, are maintained, or are changed in various social milieus,
or to conceive how relationships within a particular subculture develop
(see Homans, 1975).

The strength of social-exchange theory, in contrast with either purely individualistic or socio-cultural examinations of social relations, inheres in its focus on the interpersonal transactions which occur between and among people (see Gergen, 1976). It is through such transactions that relationships are built or torn asunder. It is also through social intercourse that people develop and change and institutions and organizations evolve. The following chapters provide background data for further investigations of social relationships and provide empirical foundations, speculative ideas, and ideological fuel for further inquiry. The effort to understand social interaction is just beginning. We will be pleased if this volume moves that struggle a bit further along toward understanding the interpersonal underpinnings of social life.

References

Altman, I., & Taylor, D. *Social penetration: The development of interpersonal relationships.* New York: Holt, 1973.

Bernard, J. The adjustment of married mates. In H. C. Christensen (Ed.), *Handbook of marriage and the family.* Chicago, Illinois: Rand McNally, 1964.

Berscheid, E., Dion, K., Walster, E., & Walster, G. W. Physical attractiveness and dating choice: A test of the matching hypothesis. *Journal of Experimental Social Psychology,* 1971, *7*, 173–189.

Berscheid, E., & Fei, J. Romantic love and sexual jealousy. In G. Clanton & L. G. Smith (Eds.), *Jealousy.* Englewood Cliffs, New Jersey: Prentice-Hall, 1977.

Berscheid, E., & Walster, E. A little bit about love. In T. L. Huston (Ed.), *Foundations of interpersonal attraction.* New York: Academic Press, 1974.

Berscheid, E., & Walster, E. *Interpersonal attraction,* 2nd ed. Reading, Massachusetts: Addison-Wesley, 1977.

Birchler, G. R., Weiss, R. L., & Vincent, J. P. Multimethod analysis of social reinforcement exchange in maritally distressed and nondistressed spouse and stranger dyads. *Journal of Personality and Social Psychology,* 1975, *31*, 349–360.

Blau, P. *Exchange and power in social life.* New York: Wiley, 1964.

Boissevain, J. P. *Friends of friends.* Oxford: Blackwell, 1974.

Bott, E. *Family and social networks* (2nd ed.). London: Tavistock, 1971.

Brehm, J. *Theory of psychological reactance.* New York: Academic Press, 1966.

Burgess, E., & Wallin, P. W. *Engagement and marriage.* Philadelphia: Lippincott, 1953.

Burgess, R. L. Child abuse: A social interactional analysis. In B. B. Lahey & A. G. Kazdin (Eds.), *Advances in clinical child psychology,* vol. 2, New York: Plenum Publishing Company, 1979.

Burgess, R. L., & Bushnell, D. *Behavioral sociology: Experimental analysis of social process.* New York: Columbia Univ. Press, 1969.

Burgess, R. L., & Nielsen, J. An experimental analysis of some structural determinants of equitable and inequitable exchange relations. *American Sociological Review,* 1974, *39*, 427–443.

Burr, W. R. Satisfaction with various aspects of marriage over the life cycle: A random middle class sample. *Journal of Marriage and the Family,* 1970, *32*, 29–37.

Chadwick-Jones, J. K. *Social exchange theory: Its structure and influence on social psychology.* London: Academic Press, 1976.

Cheever, J. *Falconer.* New York: Knopf, 1977.

Clark, K. *Another part of the wood: A self-portrait.* New York: Harper & Row, 1974.

Clore, G. *Interpersonal attraction.* Morristown, New Jersey: General Learning Press, 1975.

Cuber, J., & Harroff, P. *The significant Americans.* New York: Appleton-Century-Crofts, 1965.

Deutsch, M. Equity, equality, and need: What determines which will be used as the basis of distributive justice? *Journal of Social Issues,* 1975, *31,* 137–149.

Dion, K., & Dion, K. Love, liking, and trust in heterosexual relationships. *Personality and Social Psychology Bulletin,* 1976, *2,* 187–190.

Driscoll, R., Davis, K. E., & Lipetz, M. E. Parental interference and romantic love: The Romeo and Juliet effect. *Journal of Personality and Social Psychology,* 1972, *24,* 1–10.

Duck, S. W. *The study of acquaintance.* Westmead, England: Saxon House, 1977 (a).

Duck, S. W. (Ed.), *Theory and practice in interpersonal attraction.* New York: Academic Press, 1977 (b).

Durkheim, E. [*The rules of sociological method*] S. A. Solovay & J. H. Mueller, (trs.). New York: Free Press, 1938. (Originally published, 1895.)

Ekeh, P. P. *Social exchange theory: The two traditions.* Cambridge, Massachusetts: Harvard Univ. Press, 1974.

Emerson, R. M. Social exchange theory. In A. Inkeles, J. Coleman, & N. Smelser (Eds.) *Annual Review of Sociology* (Vol. 2). Palo Alto: Annual Reviews, 1976.

Erikson, K. T. *Everything in its path: Destruction of community in the Buffalo Creek flood.* New York: Simon & Schuster, 1976.

Fischer, C. S. *Networks and places: Social relations in the urban setting.* New York: Free Press, 1977.

Flaubert, G. *Madame Bovary* (Francis Steegmuller trans.) New York: Modern Library, 1950. (Originally published, 1857.)

Foa, U. G., & Foa, E. B. *Societal structures of the mind.* Springfield, Illinois: Thomas, 1974.

Fromm, E. *The art of loving.* New York: Harper, 1956.

Gadlin, H. Private lives and public order: A critical view of the history of intimate relations in the U.S. In G. Levinger & H. Raush (Eds.), *Close relationships: Perspectives on the meaning of intimacy.* Amherst, Massachusetts: Univ. of Mass. Press, 1977.

Gergen, K. J. Social exchange in a world of transient fact. In R. Hamblin & R. J. Runkel (Eds.), *Behavioral theory in sociology.* New Brunswick, New Jersey: Transaction, 1976.

Hill, C. T., Rubin, Z., & Peplau, L. A. Breakups before marriage: The end of 103 affairs. *Journal of Social Issues,* 1976, *32,* 147–168.

Hinde, R. A. On describing relationships. *Journal of Child Psychology and Psychiatry,* 1976, *17,* 1–19.

Homans, G. C. *Social behavior: Its elementary forms.* New York: Harcourt, 1961.

Homans, G. C. *Social behavior: Its elementary forms* (Rev. Ed.). New York: Harcourt, 1974.

Homans, G. C. What do we mean by social "structure"? In P. Blau (Ed.), *Approaches to the study of social structure.* New York: Free Press, 1975.

Huesmann, L. R., & Levinger, G. Incremental exchange theory: A formal model for progression in dyadic social interaction. In L. Berkowitz & E. Walster (Eds.), *Advances in experimental social psychology* (Vol. 9). New York: Academic Press, 1976.

Huston, T. Ambiguity of acceptance, social desirability, and dating choice. *Journal of Experimental Social Psychology,* 1973, *9,* 32–42.

Huston, T. (Ed.), *Foundations of interpersonal attraction.* New York: Academic Press, 1974.

Huston, T. & Levinger, G. Interpersonal attraction and relationships. In M. R. Rosenzweig & L. Porter (Eds.), *Annual Review of Psychology* (Vol. 29). Palo Alto, Calif.: Annual Reviews, 1978.

Kerckhoff, A. C., & Davis, K. Value consensus and need complementarity in mate selection. *American Sociological Review,* 1962, *27,* 295–303.

Kiesler, S., & Baral, R. The search for a romantic partner: The effects of self-esteem and physical attractiveness on romantic behavior. In K. J. Gergen & D. Marlowe (Eds.), *Personality and social behavior*. Reading, Massachusetts: Addison-Wesley, 1970.

Leik, R. K., & Leik, S. K. Transition to interpersonal commitment. In R. L. & J. H. Kunkel (Eds.), *Behavioral theory in sociology*. New Brunswick, New Jersey: Transaction, 1976.

Lerner, M. J. The justice motive in social behavior: Introduction. *Journal of Social Issues,* 1975, *31,* 1–19.

Levinger, G. A three-level approach to attraction: Toward an understanding of pair related-ness. In T. Huston (Ed.), *Foundations of interpersonal attraction*. New York: Academic Press, 1974.

Levinger, G. The embrace of lives: Changing and unchanging. In G. Levinger & H. Raush (Eds.), *Close relationships: Perspectives on the meaning of intimacy*. Amherst, Massa-chusetts: Univ. of Massachusetts Press, 1977.

Levinger, G., & Huesmann, L. R. An incremental exchange perspective on the pair relation-ship: Interpersonal reward and level of involvement. In K. J. Gergen, M. S. Greenberg, & R. H. Willis (Eds.), *Social exchange: Advances in theory and research*. New York: Wiley, in press.

Levinger, G., Rands, M., & Talaber, R. *The assessment of rewardingness in close and casual pair relationships*. Technical Report submitted to the National Science Foundation, June, 1977.

Levinger, G., Senn, D. J., & Jorgensen, B. Progress toward permanence in courtship: A test of the Kerckhoff-Davis hypothesis. *Sociometry,* 1970, *33,* 427–433.

Levinger, G., & Snoek, J. D. *Attraction in relationship: A new look at interpersonal attrac-tion*. New York: General Learning Press, 1972.

Marwell, G., & Hage, J. The organization of role relationships: A systematic description. *American Sociological Review,* 1970, *35,* 884–900.

Nehls, E. (Ed.), *D. H. Lawrence: A composite biography* (Vol. 1). Madison, Wisconsin: Univ. of Wisconsin Press, 1957.

Newcomb, T. *The acquaintance process*. New York: Holt, 1961.

Norton, A. J., & Glick, P. C. Marital instability: Past, present, and future. *Journal of Social Issues,* 1976, *32,* 5–20.

Patterson, G. R., & Reid, J. B. Reciprocity and coercion: Two facets of social systems. In C. Neuringer & J. Michael (Eds.), *The experimental analysis of social behavior*. New York: Appleton-Century-Crofts, 1970.

Pruitt, D. G., & Kimmel, M. J. Twenty years of experimental gaming: Critique, synthesis, and suggestions for the future. In M. R. Rosenzweig & L. Porter (Eds.), *Annual Review of Psychology* (Vol. 28). Palo Alto, Calif.: Annual Reviews, 1977.

Rosenblatt, P. C. Needed research on commitment in marriage. In G. Levinger & H. Raush (Eds.), *Close relationships: Perspectives on the meaning of intimacy*. Amherst, Massa-chusetts: Univ. of Massachusetts Press, 1977.

Rubin, Z. Measurement of romantic love. *Journal of Personality and Social Psychology,* 1970, *16,* 265–273.

Rubin, Z. *Liking and loving*. New York: Holt, 1973.

Rubin, Z. From liking to loving: Patterns of attraction in dating relationships. In T. L. Huston (Ed.), *Foundations of interpersonal attraction*. New York: Academic Press, 1974.

Sampson, E. E. On justice as equality. *Journal of Social Issues,* 1975, *31,* 45–64.

Sampson, E. E. Psychology and the American ideal. *Journal of Personality and Social Psychology,* 1977, *35,* 767–782.

Shanteau, J., & Nagy, G. Decisions made about other people: A human judgment analysis of dating choice. In J. Carroll & J. Payne (Eds.), *Cognition and social judgment*. Hillsdale, New Jersey: Erlbaum, 1976.

Shulman, N. Life cycle variation in patterns of close relationships. *Journal of Marriage and the Family,* 1975, *37,* 813–821.

Slater, P. E. On social regression. *American Sociological Review*, 1963, *28*, 339–358.

Smith, A. *An Inquiry into the Nature and Causes of the Wealth of Nations*. Edinburgh: Black, 1850.

Spanier, G., Lewis, R., & Cole, C. L. Marital adjustment over the family life cycle: The issue of curvilinearity. *Journal of Marriage and the Family*, 1975, *37*, 263–275.

Stroebe, W., Insko, C. A., Thompson, V. D., & Layton, B. D. Effects of physical attractiveness, attitude similarity, and sex on various aspects of interpersonal attraction. *Journal of Personality and Social Psychology*, 1971, *18*, 79–91.

Tedeschi, J. T. Attributions, liking, and power. In T. L. Huston (Ed.), *Foundations of interpersonal attraction*. New York: Academic Press, 1974.

Thibaut, J. W., & Kelley, H. H. *The social psychology of groups*. New York: Wiley, 1959.

Triandis, H. C., Vassiliou, V. & Nassiakou, M. Three cross-cultural studies of subjective culture. *Journal of Personality and Social Psychology Monograph Supplement*, 1968, *8*, (No. 4), 1–42.

Vincent, J. P., Weiss, R. L., & Birchler, G. R. A behavioral analysis of problem solving in distressed and nondistressed married and stranger dyads. *Behavior Therapy*, 1975, *6*, 475–487.

Wish, M., Deutsch, M., & Kaplan, S. J. Perceived dimensions of interpersonal relations. *Journal of Personality and Social Psychology*, 1976, *33*, 409–420.

Wohlwill, J. *The study of behavioral development*. New York: Academic Press, 1973.

PART II

The Developmental Course of Close Relationships

2

The Initiation of Social Relationships and Interpersonal Attraction[1]

ELLEN BERSCHEID
WILLIAM GRAZIANO

I. The Importance of Understanding the Antecedents of the Initiation of Social Relationships

Famous for her acid social commentary, one of Alice Roosevelt Longworth's frequently quoted observations concerns the genesis of the high number of marital mismatches in her social milieu. "Washington, D.C., is full of fascinating men . . . and the women they married when they were very young," she quipped. There may be wisdom as well as wit in Ms. Longworth's remark (quite apart from the general status of women that it reflects). It directs those of us who marvel at some of the odder odd couples of our acquaintance, and who seek to understand these and other social pairings, to pause and consider the circumstances under which those relationships were initiated.

Ms. Longworth's assumption is that if we are to understand social relationships, it is necessary for us to do more than look exclusively for contemporaneous reasons why, or contemporaneous explanations of how,

[1] Preparation of this paper and the research described was facilitated by National Science Foundation Grant GS 35157X to the senior author.

a social relationship is maintained. If this assumption is correct, then the importance of identifying the causal antecedents of one person's attempt to initiate a relationship with another may extend far beyond our ability to predict such social outcomes as who will ultimately pair up with whom. The prediction of who will ultimately choose whom as a roommate, as a colleague, or as a spouse (and of whose choices are likely to be reciprocated by whom) is, of course, of interest. But an understanding of the factors that determine whether a social relationship will be initiated assumes even greater importance if these initiating factors cast their influence beyond the point of initiation and affect the relationship itself, both its nature and its course.

It is this possibility we will consider here. We will maintain the thesis that the *raison d'être* of any social relationship, as well as the relationship's complexity of character at any stage of its growth or deterioration, cannot be fully understood unless one also understands the conditions under which it was initiated. But we will contend that to analyze the contemporaneous characteristics of a relationship that has evolved over time in order to discern the circumstances under which it was initiated is much like trying to examine the various characteristics of a raging forest fire in order to discover if the precipitating cause of the holocaust was a fragment of glass lying on a bed of pine needles in the noonday sun three days earlier. The task might not be impossible, but it would be extremely difficult; history is easier to record than to reconstruct, and causal chains are easier to identify if one can begin at the beginning rather than at the end.

Accordingly, we disagree with those who have faulted social psychologists for focusing so intensely upon nascent social relationships and, within attraction research, upon attraction as it may occur and develop in the immediate postnatal stage of a relationship—often between persons who, only moments before they came within the researcher's purview, were strangers to each other. We believe that those of us interested in understanding interpersonal attraction, as well as other characteristics of social relationships, generally have not begun our study of these phenomena early enough in the development of the relationship. For example, those of us interested in heterosexual attraction and courtship typically pick up the tale of Jane and Joe *after* their eyes have met across a crowded room on some enchanted evening—after, that is, they have already become a "couple," or at least some time (and often a relatively long time) after the birth of their relationship.

Experimental social psychologists working in the laboratory also do not usually begin their study of social relationships at the beginning, even though the experimenter is, typically, not only present at the birth of the relationship but also has often served as the midwife who brought it into existence. The relationship between Jane and Joe in the laboratory is usually picked up for examination after Jane, at the experimenter's instruction and to earn two points or $2, has scrutinized Joe's responses to an attitude questionnaire, looked at Joe's picture, or read a list of the traits Joe presumably possesses.

This traditional laboratory procedure used to investigate interpersonal attraction and other dyadic phenomena bears an unsettling similarity to the procedure traditionally followed in perception experiments before the revolutionary work of J. J. Gibson (1966). Just as the person's freedom of choice and movement is greatly restricted in the typical attraction laboratory experiment, in which he is placed before a video screen or at a table, so in the traditional perception experiment the person–perceiver was physically restrained, his head clasped in a rigid position by various mechanical devices. And just as in the attraction experiment, in which the passive person's attention is directed toward certain social stimuli, so in the traditional perception experiment, the perceiver's attention was directed toward certain stimuli that were to be evaluated in various ways.

Gibson argued that the conclusions about perceptual processes that were drawn from data obtained under these restrained conditions had little to do with how the world is normally perceived. The perception experimenters had systematically eliminated all opportunity for, and thus all processes related to, the perceiver's spontaneous initiation of interaction with his physical environment—processes which are critical for an understanding of perception. So, too, our experimental practice of systematically eliminating opportunities for people to actively and spontaneously explore their social environments may produce similarly misleading results (see Harré & Secord, 1973, for a general discussion of this point). At the least, this practice would seem to be intimately associated with the desultory interest in determining the antecedents of relationship initiation that social psychologists historically have shown.

Fortunately, however, the situation seems to be changing, at least within the interpersonal attraction framework. Such recent theoretical efforts as Murstein's (1970) "stimulus–value–role" theory and Levinger and Snoek's (1972) schema are addressed, at least in part, to the problem of predicting when social relationships will be initiated. Furthermore, certain recent and major theoretical developments within the mainstream of experimental social psychology may encourage the study of relationship initiation. The considerable theoretical and empirical effort currently devoted to an understanding of social perception, particularly within the attribution theory framework, would seem to signal that the study of the antecedents of relationship initiation, and of their influence upon such relationship characteristics as attraction, may now be in an especially favorable position for progress. While attribution researchers do not always begin the study of relationships at their beginning, their efforts to explicate how it is that we come to know the persons who constitute our social environment has obvious relevance to the problem of sketching the principle ways in which the determinants of relationship initiation carry over to influence the nature of the relationship.

II. A Perceptual Approach to the Problem of Relationship Initiation

Much of the evidence relevant to our thesis has been gathered in a social perception theoretical framework, rather than in the more restricted attraction framework or even in a strictly reinforcement or social exchange framework (although, as will become clear, we believe reinforcement-related considerations are central to perceptual processes in general and social relationship initiation processes in particular). This framework, which we will sketch below, is regrettably loose. There are several reasons for this, and two of the most prominent might be explicitly noted here by way of an apologia.

First, the traditional physical perception literature contains, we believe, exceptionally valuable information for the prediction of relationship initiation. Unfortunately, not only has this literature not been integrated with the social perception literature, but the two bodies of knowledge rarely even occupy the same bookcase. Second, we believe that the solution of the mysteries of relationship initiation depends critically upon the development of adequate motivational constructs and theory. We mean *motivational* in the sense that "motivation is the process (a) of arousing or initiating behavior, (b) of sustaining an activity in progress, and (c) of channeling activity into a given course [Young, 1961, in Madsen, 1968]." Building a theory of relationship initiation on a motivation foundation is, these days, not unlike building a house on a foundation of sand. The psychology of motivation is in disarray. Or perhaps it would be more accurate to say that it has simply vanished as a cohesive body of knowledge. A portion of concern with motivation appears to have moved into the psychology of learning under the influence of Bolles (1967), but it has been incorporated in such a way that the perceiver (or the "learner") is viewed as relatively passive and passionless; the motivational action has been transferred from the perceiver to a stimulus that may or may not possess "incentive value." Another portion of motivational concern appears to have moved to more friendly social-psychological terrain, but not, sad to say for present purposes, to the social perception area that still retains the amotivational imprint of its Gestaltist heritage.

A. The Beginning of a Relationship: Attention

If we are to look for the antecedents of the initiation of a social relationship, what is our dependent variable? Where is the beginning of a relationship? The answer may be: at the point where one person attends to another.

Many theorists have argued that attention must occupy a central place not only in perceptual theory but also in psychological theory in general. Titchener (1908), for example, went so far as to declare that "The doctrine of attention is the nerve of the whole psychological system. . . . As men judge of it, so shall they be judged before the general tribunal of psychology [p. 173]." Whatever its relevance for psychological theory in general, attention may be an especially important variable for theories of social relationship. In particular, attention may be an especially promising variable for the study of relationship initiation, as Levinger and Snoek (1972) suggest: "The beginnings of a relationship appear when one person becomes aware of another. In defining this level, it is unimportant whether or not O in turn notices P. The only pertinent event is that P has information that forms a basis for his unilateral evaluation of O [p. 6]."

We agree that our primary problem, at least at this point in the study of relationship initiation, should be to identify the antecedents of whether a person notices another, rather than to attempt the more complex task of identifying the factors that are associated with reciprocity of notice. Throughout this paper, then, we will approach the problem of relationship initiation from the point of view of the "initiator"; we will relatively ignore the problem of the reactions of the initiatee, although we acknowledge its vital importance along many dimensions, not the least of which is the question of the continuation of the relationship.

Perhaps more importantly, we also agree with Levinger and Snoek that the point of a person's awareness of another may be a useful conceptualization of the beginning point of a relationship. We believe it desirable, however, to refine the phrase "becomes aware of another." In our own research, in reframing the problem of relationship initiation as a problem in social perception, we have found it useful to posit the beginning of a relationship as somewhere around the point at which one person, the initiator, perceptually *attends* to a particular other—observes the other person and the other's behavior (or attends to such artifacts of the other as the responses the other has made to a questionnaire, the other's picture, an account by a third person of the other's behavior or characteristics, and so on).

The way in which we mean the term *attention* is very much as Berlyne (1960, 1974) has described; that is, to refer to processes or conditions within the organism that determine how effective a particular stimulus will be. But by *attention* we do not mean an orienting response, such as may occur in reaction to stimuli of high intensity—for example, a person who has emitted a very loud noise or one whose sartorial splendor at a dimly lit cocktail party includes a brightly blinking battery-operated necktie. Rather, by the term we mean something more sustained than the involuntary kind of noticing reaction that stimuli of very high intensities often provoke.

Furthermore, the aspect of attention that most interests us in the relationship initiation context is its selective and directive aspects. As Berlyne (1974) puts it, "Many stimulus elements, present simultaneously, generally compete for control over behavior or, in other words, for occupation of the nervous system's limited information-transmitting capacity. Events inside the organism may grant predominant influence to one property of a stimulus object, causing other properties of the same object to be ignored [p. 124]." Similarly, at a more molar level and in a field of social stimuli, "events inside the organism" may lead an initiator to attend to one person in his social environment (or to certain properties of that person) causing other persons in the initiator's social environment to be relatively or wholly ignored. Thus, the person who has won the competition "for control over behavior" occupies the initiator's "nervous system's limited information-transmitting capacity"—and it is for that person that the initiator, in an effort to learn more about the stimulus person, is likely to activate such perceptual–cognitive machinery as attribution processes.

B. A Prototypical Problem for the Study of Relationship Initiation

If initial attention to another is designated as the beginning of a relationship, then the problem of identifying the factors which determine relationship initiation may be formulated within a social perception framework as follows: Given a potential initiator, in a social environment consisting of relatively unfamiliar others A, B, C, . . . N, to whom, if to any of these, will P spontaneously attend?

Framing the relationship initiation problem as a problem in selective attention has certain virtues, one of which is that the competitive nature of the relationship initiation process is emphasized. Thus, in congruence with virtually all exchange theories that assume that one of the costs of interacting with any one person is the foregoing of interaction with others, one of the potential costs of relationship initiation with any one person is recognized (e.g., Homans, 1961; Thibaut & Kelley, 1959).

Readers who are familiar with Murstein's "stimulus–value–role" theory of marital choice will recognize that this problem prototype for the study of relationship initiation—predicting to whom of the various persons in the initiator's social environment he awards his attention—is an open, as opposed to a closed, field situation for the initiator. According to Murstein, an open field encounter, between a man and a woman, for example,

> refers to a situation in which the man and woman do not as yet know each other or have only a nodding acquaintance. Examples of such "open field" situations are "mixers," presence in a large school class at the beginning of a semester, and brief contacts in the office. The fact that the field is "open" indicates that either the man or the woman is free to start the relationship or to abstain from initiating it, as they wish [1970, p. 466].

Another common denominator in these examples of open field situations seems to be the element of competing social stimuli. At the mixer, in the large school class, and in the office, there are a number of relationship alternatives open to the potential initiator. Thus the open field situation generally may be one in which the initiator's social environment consists of more than one stimulus person. The potential initiator may spontaneously pay attention to any one of the competing social stimuli, but not to all simultaneously—a situation analogous to our prototypical relationship initiation problem as well as to that of a person who has just entered a cocktail party.

Murstein goes on to elaborate his concept of an open field by stating that:

> The contrary concept is the "closed field" situation in which both the man and the woman are forced to interact by reason of the environmental setting in which they find themselves. Examples of such situations might be that of students in a small seminar in a college, members in a law firm, and workers in complementary professions such as doctor–nurse and "boss"–secretary [p. 466].

Perhaps an even better example of a closed field situation is the typical laboratory situation in which the stimulus person in the potential initiator's social environment has no social competition (and very little competition from physical stimuli, as well). Thus, the probability that the potential initiator will attend to the stimulus person in the closed field situation of the laboratory is extremely high—just as the experimenter intended.

C. Motivational Factors in Selective Attention

If one accepts the prototypical problem in relationship initiation to be analogous to that of predicting to whom a person standing at the threshold of a cocktail party will award his or her attention, then theories of selective attention, and related data, become directly relevant (although these theories, as well as virtually all attention research, focus almost exclusively upon the perception of physical rather than social stimuli).

The factors that perception theorists and researchers have identified as governing attentional processes may be subsumed under the two general principles *novelty* and *importance* (cf. Berlyne, 1960, 1974). Novel stimuli—which disconfirm the perceiver's predictions and are incongruent with his expectations, or stimuli which are so unfamiliar that no predictions readily can be made about them—have been demonstrated to capture the perceiver's attention in competition with less novel stimuli. In formulating our prototypical initiation problem, we have been careful to pose the question as one of predicting to whom of several social stimuli, all relatively unfamiliar (and equally so), the potential initiator will award his attention. We have done this in order to simplify the problem; we wish to focus temporarily on the role of the other principle of selective attention in relationship initiation. The principle of novelty does have direct relevance, however, to the prediction of attention when the initiator's social perceptual field contains persons of varying degrees of familiarity, and we shall return to this point and some of its implications later.

The second principle that appears to govern attentional processes concerns the fact that, as Berlyne (1960) puts it, some stimuli are more "important" than others. Unfortunately, however, perception researchers have not strictly specified the determinants of importance (e.g., Lanzetta, 1968). It is at this point that we must face squarely that what is perceptually important to any given perceiver is a motivational problem, and, thus, that the problem of selective attention to social stimuli in an open field is a motivational one.

Regrettably, most social perception theorists and researchers, following the lead of their brethren in learning theory, exhibit an amotivational bias. Within attribution theory frameworks, for example, the person who is attempting to acquaint himself with his social environment is often seen as a bloodless causal schemata-constructor who goes about his business dispassionately and "objectively," much as a scientist collecting and analyzing data. Thus, although attribution researchers have gone to great length to describe the complex blueprint of the processes by which we come to know others, we cannot identify the factors—the *motivators*, if you will—that are likely to initiate these complex perceptual–cognitive processes within the perceiver. The position in which we find ourselves is similar to that of a child who discovers a mechanical wooden horse at a supermarket, but can find no slot for a coin; the child is well aware of the structure and function of the horse, yet he doesn't know how this interesting piece of machinery is activated.

We said earlier that we were optimistic that a focus on basic perceptual variables in the social perception process would be helpful in the study of relationship initiation, since it would allow us to capitalize on the theoretical and empirical advances made recently in the attribution framework (e.g., Jones, Kanouse, Kelley, Nisbett, Valins, & Weiner, 1972). We also believe that research effort on the problem of relationship initiation may, reciprocally, help enrich the social perception literature in general, and the attribution literature in particular, by returning the prodigal son of motivation to the place in attribution that Heider envisioned—as the spark that ignites the attribution process.

1. RENDERING THE SOCIAL ENVIRONMENT PREDICTABLE

Heider (1958), the grandfather of attribution theories, did, in fact, lay a motivational foundation for his model of social perception. Within his structuralist approach to perceptual processes, Heider incorporated the Brunswickian notion that the function of person-perception is to make the social environment stable and predictable. Perceivers are assumed to activate their perceptual–cognitive machinery in order to get to know certain objects and persons in order to discover how these persons will act in future encounters. When the social environment is rendered predictable, the perceiver is able to guide his own behaviors in such a way as to maximize his chances of obtaining rewards and avoiding punishments; whereas in an unpredictable social environment, where rewards and punishments are delivered randomly, the perceiver is unable to act in his best interests.

Although those who have followed in Heider's footsteps endorse the Brunswickian–Heiderian belief that perceptual acts function to stabilize and make predictable the phenomenal world, this view has not played an important role in attribution theory and research. Kelley (1972a), for example, found it desirable to explicitly remind attribution researchers that "the attributor is not simply an attributor, a seeker of knowledge. His latent goal in gaining knowledge is that of effective management of himself and his environment [p. 22]." Kelley comments further, "The attributional process can be well understood only in the context of a comprehensive analysis of the exercise of control."

It seems reasonable that the relationship initiation process, which necessarily precedes the attributional process, also can be well understood only in the context of control. For example, Kelley's comment suggests that among those people that constitute our social environment, those persons who represent potential problems of control to us are likely targets for an attributional analysis. If so, they are also likely targets for attention in the service of such an analysis. Such a conclusion makes sense if, as Heider believed, perceptual acts are motivated by the perceiver's desire to predict the contingencies of his social environment in order to control it.

Who is likely to represent a potential problem of control? Not all of the people who constitute our social environment are equally potent sources of reward and punishment. First, some people have more power than others to meet our needs and affect our outcomes, while others have little or no power to influence the comfort of our daily lives. Thus, whether another represents a problem of control to us should be a function of our perception of whether that person can (has the power to) satisfy or frustrate our needs.

Second, even given another's power to affect our outcomes, not all persons in our social environment are equally likely to use it. It seems reasonable that through past experience we have learned to anticipate that some persons are more likely to satisfy, or to frustrate, our needs than others. Thus the anticipation that the other may, given the proper contingencies, exert power to deliver need-gratification (or frustration) should also play a role in determining whether that person represents a problem of control to us. If we perceive that another has enormous power to influence our well-being, but is highly unlikely to use that power for either our good or our ill, then it seems doubtful that we will expend our limited perceptual–cognitive time and energy to know the person better and to learn of the contingencies governing that person's behavior. But by becoming acquainted with a person who not only has control over our outcomes but may use it, the perceiver may acquire counter–control: He learns of the possible contingencies for acquiring the things he needs and avoiding the events which may frustrate his aims.

Within the framework of Thibaut and Kelley's (1959) social exchange theory, we would say that for relationship initiation to occur, the perceiver must be "outcome-dependent" on the other. These theorists may be interpreted to posit that a person (P) is dependent on another (O) to the extent that: (a) P has some need; (b) P perceives that O possesses the resources that P needs; (c) there is some likelihood less than certainty that O may deliver, or withhold, those resources. (With respect to this last point, we note that conditions of outcome dependency are likely to be conditions of considerable uncertainty. If O consistently and regularly delivers needed resources to P, it is unlikely that P will even perceive himself to be dependent on O. We might also note that Lanzetta (1968; 1971) and others have hypothesized that uncertainty is an important determiner of perceptual search and receptivity to information. The more uncertain the outcome, the stronger the preference for information relevant to it. Attention is just such a perceptual search.) In the Thibaut and Kelley framework, then, O is said to have "outcome control" over P to the extent that P expects that O can and may reward (or punish) P; P is then outcome dependent on O.

The prediction that those who are associated with the delivery of rewards and punishments are likely to win the competition for the perceiver's selective attention, and are likely targets of such perceptual–cognitive processes as attributional analyses, has some slight research support. There is evidence that both inanimate objects (Nunnally, Duchnowski, & Parker, 1965) are persons (Yussen, 1974) who are associated with the delivery of rewards are likely to be awarded the perceiver's attention. These findings are consistent with the view that both selective attention and attributional analysis are perceptual acts that function for a similar purpose: to render the environment predictable so that the perceiver may maximize his rewards and minimize his discomfort.

Although we are here primarily interested in the problem of relationship initiation, we might note here that the preceding analysis represents a foundation for the prediction of attraction in the relationship that is consistent with the theoretical views of many attraction theorists (e.g., Blau, 1967; Byrne, 1971; Maslow, 1954; Reik, 1944, 1957, 1963). For example, we have proposed that persons who possess no power to affect our welfare and persons who do possess such power but are unlikely to use it are unlikely targets for our attention and for relationship initiation. These are also the people for whom, according to attraction theorists who take a social-exchange approach, we are unlikely to develop affection or dislike, for they are irrelevant to us and indifference is our probable response to them. This view also places the primary source of attraction in the state of the perceiver, where it belongs. If a person feels no need that can be satisfied or frustrated, he is unlikely to develop any attraction or disaffection for another. Further, the greater the perceiver's needs, the greater the perceptual–cognitive effort he is likely to be willing to expend on getting acquainted with social targets associated with anticipated need satisfaction (or frustration) and the greater the attraction (or dislike) he is likely to exhibit toward them.

There is, then, a clear correspondence between the principles we believe underlie relationship initiation—at least as we have conceived it, as a problem in selective attention—and the principles most social exchange theorists believe underlie interpersonal attraction. Nevertheless, the relationship between attention and attraction is neither as direct nor as simple as one could wish. We shall return to this point after further developing our view of relationship initiation.

III. Outcome Dependency: A Framework for Viewing Relationship Initiation

We have conceptualized both attentional and attributional processes as a manifestation of a perceiver's motivation to predict the behavioral contingencies of those persons in his social environment who represent problems of control to him. Thus we have hypothesized that persons on whom the perceiver is outcome dependent are likely targets of his attention and, subsequently, of his attempts to learn the contingencies associated with their behavior.

A. Hypotheses: How Outcome Dependency May Influence the Initiation and Development of a Relationship

Returning to the prototypical relationship initiation problem, it will be recalled that we asked: Given a potential initiator in a social environment consisting of relatively unfamiliar others A, B, C, . . . N, to whom, if to any of these, will the initiator attend? We said that if a major human motive is to make stable and predictable the social environment in order to exercise control over it, then a person should be especially eager to learn the behavioral contingencies of another person who has outcome control over him. This motive to predict should be reflected in the perceiver's efforts to collect data (attention) about the other to render the other predictable (trait attributions). Thus, we can hypothesize that, other things being equal (especially the degree of unfamiliarity of those who compose his social environment), the initiator is likely to attend to those others who have outcome control over him. Further, we can predict that as the initiator's outcome dependency on a particular person in his social environment increases, selective attention to that person is also likely to increase.

Attention, of course, is only part of the story. It is the central thesis of this chapter that the same factors that initiate attentional processes are also likely to steer such cognitive processes as memory and causal attributional analyses, and influence affective processes as well. If we view all of these cognitive–perceptual acts as manifestations of an underlying motive to exercise control over our social environment in order to maximize need satisfaction, we can now also predict the direction in which the perceiver's cognitions will be steered when the relationship-initiating variable is outcome dependency.

First, as his outcome dependency on a particular person in his social environment increases, so should the perceiver's preference that the causal analysis he performs conclude in a dispositional rather than a situational attribution. Intuitively, knowledge of another's dispositions to behave in certain ways would seem to be a more useful bit of information to the perceiver who hopes to exercise control over that part of his social environment than an attribution of the other's behavior to nonpersonal situational factors (see Shaver, 1975). Thus, we may predict that the factor triggering the causal analysis may influence the ultimate *form* of the causal attribution.

Second, when the triggering factor is outcome dependency, the social perception literature allows us to predict that it will influence the *substance* of the dispositional attribution as well. The results of several studies investigating the influence of perceiver need states on social perception may be interpreted to support the thesis that persons who are outcome dependent on another tend to arrive at wish-fulfilling conclusions about the other's dispositional traits (e.g., Berscheid, Boye, & Darley, 1968; Darley & Berscheid, 1967; Levine, Chein, & Murphy, 1942; Pepitone, 1950; Stephan, Berscheid, & Walster, 1971). Thus, as the perceiver's outcome dependency on another increases, the dispositional attributions made about the other should be in the direction of wish-fulfillment. This should be true despite the fact that dependency should lead the perceiver to pay close attention to the other's behavior and the context in which it occurred, a factor which is commonly thought to be associated with lack of distortion of the nature of another's predispositions.

B. A Test of Outcome Dependency Hypotheses

1. PROCEDURE.

In order to investigate these hypotheses, Berscheid, Graziano, Monson, and Dermer (1976) tried to devise a situation, analogous to the prototypical relationship initiation situation, in which (a) the degree to which persons in the perceiver's social–perceptual field represented potential problems of control to him could be manipulated; specifically, the perceiver's outcome dependency on each person could be varied while the novelty or unfamiliarity of each person could be held constant; (b) the degree of attention the perceiver subsequently awarded to each of these others; (c) the extent to which the perceiver arrived at dispositional inferences about each could also be ascertained; and (d) the degree to which these dispositional attributions reflected wish-fulfilling distortions about the other could be specified a priori, and the degree of attraction to the other measured.

Our requirements were satisfied by a situation in which young men and women volunteered to participate in a study of heterosexual dating relationships. These individuals had contacted the Laboratory for Research in Social Relations in response to an advertisement and had indicated that they were not currently romantically involved with any one person (i.e., married, engaged, going steady, etc.), and were seriously interested in meeting persons of the other sex. Since all but three were willing to commit themselves formally and in writing to the dating terms outlined to them, there were 27 men and 27 women who participated in the study.

All of these volunteers agreed to turn over complete control of their heterosexual dating lives to us for 5 weeks. Each agreed to date only that person or those individuals assigned to them and no one else for the 5-week period. It was explained that they might date one person for the entire period or several different people. It was also explained that all dating assignments would be determined by random lottery.

Each man and woman who participated in the study was randomly assigned to one of three outcome dependency conditions. To meet our theoretical and logistical requirements, "outcome dependency" was operationalized in terms of three levels of exclusiveness of the dating relationship: high-, low-, and zero-exclusiveness.

In the *high exclusiveness* condition, the participant was given the prospective date's name and phone number, and was informed that he or she would be dating that person exclusively for the entire 5-week period. Thus each was highly dependent on that person for his or her dating outcomes for the next 5 weeks.

In the *low exclusiveness* condition the procedure was the same, except that the participant was informed that he or she would be dating a particular person only once, and that a different person would be dated for each of the remaining 4 weeks. To the extent that participants antici- pated dating someone only once, they were less dependent on him or her for their dating outcomes.

The procedure for the zero *exclusiveness* condition was identical to that of the low exclusiveness condition, except that the person named as the prospective date was not among those the participant would shortly see in a videotape. This condition was not included as part of the factorial design, but rather was included to provide base-rate levels of response on the principal dependent measures (cf. Himmelfarb, 1975).

In addition to our situational manipulation of outcome dependency, we examined each person's status on an individual-difference variable we predicted to be related to the perception of outcome dependency. Snyder (1974) has hypothesized that persons scoring high in "self-monitoring" on his scale are particularly concerned with the appropriateness of their own behavior and, for this reason, are especially attentive to the behaviors of others. Thus the behaviors believed to characterize perceivers scoring high on this individual-difference measure resemble the behaviors we hypothesize to characterize perceivers who find themselves in a situation in which their outcomes are highly dependent on another (and who, therefore, would be especially concerned with determining the appro- priateness of their behavior vis-à-vis the person on whom they are dependent). For this reason, we hypothesized that high self-monitors should exhibit, other things being equal, a pattern of behaviors similar to that hypothesized to characterize persons in the high situational outcome dependency condition.

After each participant received his or her date's name and phone number, the experimenter asked him or her to view a videotape of other-sex participants in the study for the ostensible purpose of gaining perspective on the dating problems of the other sex. Male participants were shown a videotape of three women (confederates) who were engaged in an apparently spontaneous 15-minute conversation of dating problems. Female participants viewed a similar tape of three men (also confederates).

The confederates were selected, and the tapes edited, on the basis of extensive pretesting, such that (a) all three stimulus persons within each tape appeared to be distinctively dressed, but equal to one another in degree of physical attractiveness (slightly above average); (b) each person spoke for about the same length of time; (c) each mentioned a distinctive set of interests, hobbies, academic major, etc., during the conversation; and (d) in general, each appeared to be about equal to the others in dating desirability.

For the first 7.5 minutes of conversation, the confederates did not mention their names. Then, exactly halfway through the tape, they introduced themselves using their names. Among the three names spoken were the names the high- and low-exclusiveness participants had been given as their anticipated dates.

Each participant was asked to view the discussion by means of a specially designed system that consisted in part of a television monitor and a switch box on which three toggle switches were mounted. The experimenter explained that due to the limitations of the video equipment, it would be possible to view only one of the three people on the videotape at a time. He indicated that when a switch was depressed only the person corresponding to it would appear on the monitor (e.g., if the left switch was depressed only the participant who had been sitting in that location of the discussion room would appear). If no switch was depressed there was neither video nor audio. If more than one switch was depressed, the video was scrambled. For a switch to be operative, it had to be held down; release resulted in loss of both video and audio. Connected to each switch was a remote cumulative timer that measured the time a participant attended to each of the discussants. The experimenter was not present while the participant viewed the videotape.

After the participant had viewed the tape, the experimenter returned and asked the participant to complete an "impression questionnaire." The first items on the questionnaire were memory (both recall and recognition) items for each of the three stimulus persons. The memory items required the participant to answer questions pertaining to specific things said or articles of clothing worn by each of the stimulus persons.

Next, participants were asked to complete 15 bipolar trait scales (e.g., warm–cold, strong–weak) for each of the three stimulus persons. Immediately beneath each trait scale was a bipolar "confidence" scale. Thus, after each trait rating was made, participants rated their confidence in the rating they had made. Both trait scales *and* confidence scales were used, because Jones and Davis (1965) have suggested that trait ratings alone do not tell us whether dispositional attributions have been made to another; attributions of dispositions to a stimulus person are evidenced by perceiver ratings of the stimulus person that are extreme on trait dimensions, and ratings in which the perceiver indicates confidence. If a perceiver rates another in the middle of every bipolar trait scale, the perceiver has probably made few dispositional attributions to the other. Further evidence that no dispositional attributions have been made would be provided if the respondent indicated that his trait ratings were made with little confidence. Finally, participants were asked to rate their attraction to each stimulus person on a bipolar scale.

2. RESULTS

We hypothesized, it will be recalled, that the same factors that prompt the spontaneous initiation of the attribution process may guide, in predictable ways, the manner in which the process unfolds, influencing both the form and the substance of its conclusion. We reasoned that outcome dependency upon another, under conditions of high novelty, may be one such initiating factor.

With outcome dependency viewed either from the perspective of differences created between our situational experimental conditions or from the perspective of individual differences measured by the self-monitoring scale, and with divergences only in some particulars, our results generally supported the specific hypotheses deduced from the preceding reasoning. For example, with increases in a person's dependency upon another (for his or her dating outcomes, in this case), he or she tended to award more attention to the other. The amount of attention awarded to a stimulus person in his or her competition for the perceiver's attention was a monotonically increasing function of the degree to which the perceiver was outcome dependent on the person—from zero-date to one-date to five-dates.

Moreover, as the person's outcome dependency on another increased, the person tended to remember more about the other, both in terms of recall and recognition. This did not appear to be due solely to the fact that perceivers paid more attention to, and thus should have had more information about, the other on whom they anticipated dependence. Several lines of evidence within the experiment argued against a purely informational interpretation of the memory results (e.g., there were few significant correlations between attention time and the other dependent variables, including memory).

Finally, as outcome dependency upon another increased, so did the tendency to evaluate the other more confidently and with more extreme ratings on a variety of traits, and to be more attracted to the other as indicated both by the positivity of trait ratings of the other and by self-report of attraction to the other.

These results support the thesis that all of the data-processing operations of the social perceiver—the collection of data (attention), the selective storage and retrieval of data (memory), the inferential extrapolation on the basis of the data collected about persons in the perceiver's social environment (attribution)—are part of a unified whole and may be viewed as manifestations of an underlying motivation to predict and control the social environment to promote one's own welfare.

IV. Identification of the Social Environment

If the degree of a person's outcome dependency upon others in his social environment is an important factor to consider when predicting whether the person will attempt to initiate a relationship with a particular other, then it becomes important to be able to predict (a) what persons are likely to constitute the social environment of the initiator, and (b) among these persons, whom the initiator is likely to perceive as having outcome control over him or her.

A. Size, Homogeneity, and Similarity to Initiator of Social Environments

With respect to the first question, it seems reasonable that some general principles will be found to underlie the patterns of social environments within which people live. One important dimension which may prove interesting to investigate is simply the number of (easily) available people with whom a person may initiate a relationship and interact. Apart from its other implications, it is likely that this factor will be related to the difficulty of specifying the social environment of various types of individuals. For example, the social environment of the forest ranger who lives atop a tower and goes into a little town once a week to pick up his mail will be easier to specify than that of the airline stewardess.

Another dimension on which social environments may differ impor-, tantly for relationship-initiation predictions is the degree of similarity between a person and others in his environment. There is little doubt (given such bodies of evidence as the assortative mating literature, the attraction literature, and the conformity and deviance literatures) that, in general, a person's social environment is generally made up of people very much like himself—in education, in socioeconomic status, in religion, in ethnic background, in age, and so on. Nevertheless, there is undoubtedly some variance along this dimension that might be predictable. Such variation has consequences for relationship initiation, particularly if one assumes that dissimilarity is associated with high novelty–unfamiliarity–incongruence. For example, a highly dissimilar person in a highly homogeneous social environment that is otherwise similar to the initiator ought to be, other things being equal, the recipient of more initiation attempts than the same person in a social environment that is highly heterogeneous with respect to the initiator.

On the other hand, if we are to use the known principles of selective attention, the other thing that must be equal for predictive purposes is the relative importance of persons in the perceiver's social environment. If those who are similar to him are typically perceived to possess more power to provide need-gratification, and are more likely to do so, simply by virtue of their similarity, then this factor must be taken into account. It seems likely, however, that the type of similarity would be extremely important in making relationship-initiation predictions (e.g., similarity in poverty or other states associated with need-deprivation versus similarity of interests and values that may signal potential need-gratification in interaction with that person).

With respect to determining who has outcome control, and to what degree, over the potential initiator, a number of other considerations seem important. It could be argued, for example, that as the sheer number of people in the initiator's social environment increases, the likelihood that any one person will have high outcome control over the initiator should decrease; or, to put this speculation in another of Thibaut and Kelley's terms, the CL_{alt} of the potential initiator is likely to increase, and the relative importance of any single person is likely to decrease, as the size of his or her social environment increases.

B. Outcome Dependency and Expectation of Stability of the Social Environment

Another factor associated with outcome dependency is the prospect of future interaction, or the expectation of stability of various portions of the social environment. In the Berscheid *et al.* (1976) experiment discussed earlier, the person's degree of outcome dependency upon others was varied by manipulating the duration of future interaction he or she anticipated with each of the others. As a determinant of outcome dependency, this factor, anticipation of future interaction, probably has some ecological validity. In naturalistic situations, we are told that (for example) we will have a visiting professor for one quarter, a year, or (if a tenured appointment is made) perhaps indefinitely. Roommates, office coworkers, and car-pool mates are often assigned by external sources for specified and varying lengths of time. It might be possible, then, to place those in our social environment on a continuum of permanence and to make some predictions about relationship-initiation and relationship-deepening activities (taking into account again, of course, variations in familiarity among the social stimuli). At the least, the results of the Berscheid et al. (1976) experiment suggest that as the duration of the future interaction anticipated with another increases, so, too, should efforts to exert control over this portion of the social environment.

C. The Importance of Social Stereotypes in Predicting Relationship Initiation

Since the prediction of the importance (or incentive value, if you will) of social stimuli is essential to the prediction of relationship initiation, the content of social stereotypes, as they may exist and vary for different groups of people, is important to consider. Social stereotypes are simply predictive networks, composed of trait statements about a given group, that allow us to rapidly project the likely outcomes of interaction with its members. Stereotypes are usually triggered by easily discerned, often highly visible, characteristics of a stimulus person—race, age, sex, appearance, and role, for example—that can be quickly ascertained in the first moments of interaction. Thus the usefulness of social stereotypes is maximum in a situation in which one has no other information about the other.

In an open field situation, then, the extent to which the stereotypical information evoked by the other suggests that high rewards may be forthcoming in future interaction with him or her ought to be a determinant of relationship initiation (see Friedman, 1976). In closed field situations, however, we might expect a somewhat different pattern. If the perceiver is concerned with effective control of the social environment in a situation in which interactions are inevitable, he cannot afford the luxury of ignoring persons with powers of punishment. In these closed field situations, we might predict that a person would initiate a relationship with a noxious, punishing other if there is some prospect of eventual countercontrol. If there is no such prospect, we might predict that the negative stimuli will be "tuned out" attentionally (cf. Jones & Gerard's [1967] discussion of the perception of negatively valued stimuli). Such cognitive–attentional strategy in a closed field situation parallels active avoidance of a negative other in an open field situation.

We should explicitly note the underlying social exchange process at work even in relationship initiation attempts (or nonattempts) based on stereotypical information about the other. Several studies (cf. Berscheid & Walster, 1974) have suggested that those persons who possess similar social-incentive values tend to pair off socially. These studies make it clear that, other things being equal, attempts at relationship initiation are associated with higher incentive values of the other. But within this overall tendency, the initiator's expectation that the initiatee will rebuff his attempts to initiate or deepen the relationship appears to dampen the "upward drive" of social choice and hence reduce initiation attempts with all except those of matching or lesser incentive-value levels. Within the framework we have outlined, it seems clear that as the incentive value of another becomes higher and more discrepant with one's own, one's anticipation that the other will deliver the resources he possesses, and the perceiver needs, diminishes; the power the perceiver must have for countercontrol, even if he learns the proper contingencies governing the behavior of the other, is lacking.

Our central thesis, it will be recalled, is that the same factors that are associated with relationship initiation exert their influence over the whole of the relationship. We have presented some evidence that supports this proposition in the case in which the initiating factor is outcome dependency as manipulated by variations in the prospect of future interaction. The prospect-of-future-interaction variable presumably affects the incentive value of social stimuli, but it is extrinsic to them. Stereotypes largely confer information about the intrinsic value of a person. We should now like to present some additional evidence that is relevant to our thesis and that engages a stereotype that affects the incentive value of a social stimulus.

1. THE PHYSICAL ATTRACTIVENESS STEREOTYPE AS SELF-FULFILLING PROPHECY

That there exists a stereotype imparting high positive incentive value to those who are physically attractive has been extensively documented; the physically attractive are generally assumed to possess more socially desirable personality traits and are expected to lead more rewarding personal, social, and occupational lives than the unattractive. And, as we might expect, there is also much evidence that documents that the highly physically attractive are the recipients of significantly more relationship initiation attempts, at least from the opposite sex, than the physically unattractive are (cf. Berscheid & Walster [1974] for a review).

Mark Snyder and his associates at the University of Minnesota have been interested in tracing how a relationship initiated on the basis of the other's physical attractiveness may influence various characteristics of the relationship itself. Within his general theoretical framework of how we perceptually and behaviorally construct our individual social realities, Snyder (1975) has hypothesized that the earliest information we have about another (information that often derives from a social stereotype and leads to a relationship initiation attempt) plays a particularly important role in the development of the relationship, primarily because the initiator's subsequent information-gathering-and-processing activities may be conducted in ways that serve to bolster and strengthen his or her initial impressions of the other.

There is, indeed, some evidence for such a "cognitive bolstering" process, the end result of which is that the evidence upon which the initial impression was formed is no longer needed to sustain belief in it (Chapman & Chapman, 1967, 1969; McArthur, 1972; Regan, Straus, & Fazio, 1974; Rosenhan, 1975). The initial impression of the other gains a form of functional autonomy and may persevere even in the face of evidence which disconfirms the initial impression (e.g., Ross, Lepper, & Hubbard, 1975; Valins, 1974; Walster, Berscheid, Abrahams, & Aronson, 1967).

A study conducted by Zadney and Gerard (1974) provides a particularly good example of the cognitive bolstering process. Each participant in Zadney and Gerard's experiment saw a live skit in which a male college student attempted to enroll in classes. Before the skit began, the experimenters led some perceivers to expect that the actor they were about to see was a chemistry major, while others expected a music major, and still others expected a psychology major.

As the student–actor attempted to enroll, he stumbled and dropped the books and other items he was carrying. In all, he dropped nine items upon entering the stage. Three of the items were related to chemistry (e.g., a slide rule), three to music (e.g., Beethoven sheet music), and three to psychology (e.g., a copy of *Psychology Today*). After picking up the items, he proceeded to try to enroll in the various classes. His questions and the registrar's replies were planned so that six different classes in each of the three areas of specialization were eventually mentioned.

Immediately after the skit, each observer was asked to list from memory all of the objects dropped as well as all of the classes mentioned. Zadney and Gerard found that perceivers recalled a higher percentage of items and classes appropriate to their initial expectation (e.g., the music major was perceived to engage in more music related behaviors). And, in a subsequent comparable experiment, Zadney and Gerard demonstrated that the perceivers failed to report items incongruent with their expectations not because their memories failed them, but because they simply hadn't seen the objects incongruent with their expectations in the first place. Thus information processing tendencies on the part of the initiator lead him to direct his relationship with the initiatee along the lines in which he originally perceived the initiatee, lines which are often dictated by stereotypical information.

But quite apart from these tendencies, Snyder hypothesizes that the initiatee himself may do his part to assure that the initiator's initial information has special influence upon the relationship. Conceptually we might say that the initiator shapes behavior, the other's behavior, much as the behavior of a rat in a Skinner box is shaped.

To shed some light on the way such shaping might occur in social interaction, Snyder, Tanke, and Berscheid (1977) conducted an experiment to demonstrate the behavioral confirmation of the physical attractiveness stereotype in dyadic interaction. They also wished to trace how the other may participate in fulfilling the prophecy the initiator originally made about him or her.

In this laboratory experiment, ostensibly designed to investigate the way in which people become acquainted, a man and a woman interacted in a situation so constructed as to allow control of the information the man received regarding the woman's physical attractiveness. Some men believed that the woman they were to chat with over the telephone was highly attractive; others believed she was unattractive. Thus, it was possible to separate out the effect of the woman's *actual* physical attractiveness from the effect of her physical attractiveness as it was *perceived* by the man on her display of conversation behaviors associated with the physical attractiveness stereotype.

It was found that the men who believed they would be interacting with a physically attractive woman were more likely (than the men who believed they would be interacting with a physically unattractive woman) to indicate, on a first impression—pre-interaction questionnaire, that the woman they were going to talk to possessed many socially desirable traits. The men who believed that they would converse with an unattractive woman anticipated, however, that their partner would possess only the socially desirable traits of "modesty" and "altruism."

The telephone conversation of each pair (both naive participants) was recorded. Each participant's voice was recorded on a separate channel so that separate tapes could be made of the woman's contributions to the conversation, the man's contributions, and the contributions of both.

Observer—judges listened to two 4-minute segments (one from the beginning and one from the end) of the tape of the woman's contribution to the conversation. (The observer—judges were unaware of the experimental hypothesis and knew nothing of the actual or perceived physical attractiveness of the individuals whom they heard over the tapes.) After listening to each woman, the judges then indicated on a questionnaire their first impressions of her. Multivariate analyses indicated that, as predicted, the men must have reacted differently to the women they believed to be attractive from the way they reacted to the women they believed unattractive, for they elicited from their partners a differential display of behaviors associated with the physical attractiveness stereotype. Not only did the observer–judges tend to rate the women differentially (and in ways predicted by the physical attractiveness stereotype) on personality trait scales, but they tended to perceive the women whose male partners believed them to be physically attractive as being more confident of themselves, as being more animated, as enjoying the conversation more, and as liking their partners more than those women who interacted with men who perceived them as physically unattractive. Consistent with the stereotype of unattractive women, however, from the conversation of the women whose partners believed them to be unattractive, the observer–judges got the impression that they were more "sensitive," "altruistic," "kind," "genuine," and "modest" than the women whose partners believed them to be attractive.

The observer–judges also listened to the men's contributions to the conversation and evaluated them. It was found that men who interacted with women whom they believed to be physically attractive appeared to the observer–judges to be more sociable, sexually warm, interesting, independent, sexually permissive, bold, outgoing, humorous, and socially adept than their counterparts who believed they were talking to an unattractive woman. Moreover, these same men were seen by the judges to be more attractive, more confident, and more animated in their conversation than their counterparts. They were also considered to be more comfortable in the conversation, to enjoy themselves more, to like their partners more, to take the initiative more often, to use their voices more effectively, to be more inclined to see their partners as attractive, and to be more likely to be seen as attractive by their partners than men who believed they were talking to an unattractive woman.

This experiment, then, provides yet more evidence that factors leading to a relationship initiation attempt, such as physical attractiveness, may have special influence upon the relationship itself—molding it to the initiator's first expectations, not only through the initiator's perceptual processes but also through the self-fulfilling prophetic behaviors the initiator may elicit from the other. It also underscores the fact that a person who initiates a relationship with another because he or she believes need-gratification may ensue will try to behave in such a way as to encourage the other to provide the sought-for rewards. Thus, attention to others in the environment helps the individual decide not only with whom to interact but also how to structure his behavior toward the other. (See Figley & Huston, 1976, for further discussion of this point.)

V. Some Comments on the Relationship between Attention and Attraction

So far, we have drawn a close correspondence between the degree to which a person attends to another, or is likely to initiate a relationship with another, and that other's importance or incentive value to the person, a factor generally believed to be the major determinant of interpersonal attraction. The notion that attention and attraction are directly related has much precedent in folklore. People in their everyday language link visual regard to attraction. Expressions such as "love at first sight" and "girl watching" attest to the attraction associated with watching and attention. Even in the archetypal closed field situation—marriage—husbands and wives seem to use attention as an index of the other's attraction to them. Such complaints as "You never pay any attention to me; [therefore] you don't love me anymore!" are not unusual. Further, some marriage counselors would agree that a lack of attention to one's spouse signals a lack of interest in them and a lack of attraction to them.

One might be inclined to discount folklore, but popular notions of the attention–attraction link are buttressed by the way in which the phenomenon of attention has been treated in various areas of psychology, within the psychoanalytic framework, for example. As Berlyne (1974) notes, Freud's works contain numerous, if brief, references to attention. Freud believed that attention was a form of cathexis, or investment of energy, that could be directed either to mental content or to external stimuli associated with gratification. Since we know that the latter are usually stimuli toward which we are attracted, it does not require a great deal of extrapolation to arrive at the hypothesis that attention may be a good index of attraction.

Further, some attention researchers have suggested a direct hedonistic principle underlying attention. For example, Faw and Nunnally (1967) found that male college students spent more time looking at attractive females than at plain-looking females.

Moreover, the hypothesis that attention and attraction are directly related is not without some support from the empirical attraction literature. Exline (1971), in his paper for the Nebraska Symposium on Motivation, concludes that "The studies mentioned to date provide rather good evidence that persons are more prone to engage in mutual glances when they find the relationship with another attractive rather than aversive [p. 181]." Other researchers in the nonverbal communication area (e.g., Mehrabian, 1971; Rubin, 1974) also assert that the more a person likes or loves another, the more the person looks at the other. (We should note here, however, that, with the exception of Faw and Nunnally the researchers mentioned above are talking about a relatively unmonitored, bilateral, *mutual* attention. It seems to us, with the wisdom of hindsight provided by an experiment we shall shortly describe, that this type of visual interaction probably represents a relatively small share of the varieties of social attention.)

The often presumed attention–attraction link is, in fact, primarily responsible for our initial interest in attention as a dependent variable. We had the optimistic idea that the extent to which a person attends to another might be an excellent unobtrusive measure of attraction. Such a measure, we believed, would prove to be particularly useful in field situations. (We had visions of being able to walk into a living room and converse with a husband and wife and unobtrusively determine, if not the absolute level of attraction that existed between them, then at least the relative degree of attraction they felt for one another by measuring the relative amount of attention they awarded each other.) Having quickly surmounted the problem of measuring attraction in field situations, we were then going to proceed to test some interesting predictions about symmetrical and asymmetrical attraction relationships in marital dyads.

The first thing we overlooked was, of course, the factor of novelty (unfamiliarity– uncertainty– incongruence) as a determinant of attention. This factor would be especially important for the situation in which we hoped to use our unobtrusive measure of attraction, since most husbands and wives have known each other for quite some time and, particularly in the case of those who have been married for many years, the degree of uncertainty associated with one's spouse is (ordinarily) quite small. For example, when a husband begins, "Those people in Washington . . .", his wife often knows that what is to follow is Lecture Number 23, "The Need for Tax Reform." Thus, though attention and attraction may be related in some situations, novelty is the wild card that can quickly undo one's predictions.

The independence of attention and attraction—even in situations in which the others in the initiator's social environment are relatively unfamiliar to him or her—was brought home to us in the first experiment we conducted, in which both attention and attraction were used as dependent measures. This experiment, conducted to investigate what has been termed the "law of marital infidelity" (Berscheid, Brothen, & Graziano, 1976), illustrates how both principles of attention must be used to predict attention and how attraction appears to correspond to only one of these principles, that of importance or incentive value.

The "infidelity law," which has been derived from Aronson's Gain–
Loss Theory of Interpersonal Attraction, has been illustrated with the
following episode:

> Mr. and Mrs. Doting, who have been married for ten years, are preparing to leave
> their house for a cocktail party. He compliments her—"Gee, honey, you look great!"
> She yawns. She already knows that her husband thinks she is attractive.
>
> Mr. and Mrs. Doting arrive at the cocktail party. A male stranger begins to talk to
> Mrs. Doting, and after a while he says, with great sincerity, that he finds her very
> attractive. She does not yawn. The compliment increases her liking of the stranger
> [Aronson, 1970, p. 48].

In the situation described, Aronson and others suggest that Mrs. Doting
may abandon her faithful but tedious husband for the sincere stranger—
especially if her new admirer continues to ply her with "gains" in esteem
(cf. Aronson, 1969).

We reasoned, however, that the experimental situations that have
provided support for the gain principle of attraction are structurally
different from the naturalistic situations to which the principle is often
applied. In experiments conducted to test the gain hypothesis, the person
whose affective responses are measured typically receives evaluations
only from a single evaluator; this evaluator either delivers consistently
positive evaluations to the person or delivers initially negative but then
increasingly positive evaluations. The situation addressed by the infidelity law, however, is much like our prototypical relationship initiation
situation: the person whose affective responses are of concern is faced
with an array of social stimuli (at least two)—the admiring stranger and
the doting spouse. Thus, the person receives two sets of evaluations
simultaneously, or almost simultaneously.

We predicted that a Mr. Doting may fare better than the law of
infidelity would lead one to expect in such a competitive situation, for at
least one important reason: A steady stream of compliments might not
seem so boring to the recipient when viewed against the backdrop of the
initially hostile comments of the gain evaluator. In fact, in this open field
situation in which the recipient of the two sets of evaluations could
attentionally tune out one evaluator and direct his or her attention to the
more positive evaluator, we predicted that by the time the gain evaluator
got around to making his positive comments, the evaluatee simply
wouldn't be listening—rather, he or she would be attending to the pleas-
antries of the consistently laudatory Mr. Doting.

We tested this hypothesis in a situation in which a person—again,
sitting before a video monitor—could, by depressing one button or
another, watch either one of two evaluators, in two different rooms, who
were simultaneously giving their personal evaluations of him or her. We
predicted that the gain evaluator, who began with negative evaluations,

would be quickly tuned out in favor of the consistently positive evaluator; as a consequence, we predicted, the "gain" effect of attraction would not have a chance to occur and the consistently positive evaluator would be better liked.

We found, however, that the initially negative but then positive (gain) evaluator was not *not* tuned out. On the contrary, the evaluator who expressed affectively varied evaluations (whether his evaluations changed for the better or for the worse) *always* won more attention than the consistent evaluator (whether his consistent evaluations were affectively positive, affectively negative, or affectively neutral). Thus, our attention data supported, in a relatively complex social situation, the general finding of basic perceptual research; namely, that novel (or incongruous and changing) stimuli are awarded more attention than consistent stimuli.

What happened to attraction? Disconcertingly (considering the presumed attention–attraction link, our attention findings, and the gain principle), we were right when we predicted that the continuously positive evaluator would be better liked in this competitive situation. Although the consistently positive evaluator lost out in competition with the gain evaluator for attention, the consistently positive evaluator was liked significantly more than the gain evaluator.

These results indicate that the relationship between attention to others and attraction for others is considerably more complex than we and others suspected. The ultimate answer to the question Who likes whom and why? may not bear close correspondence to the answer to the question Who pays attention to whom and why? The positivity of social stimuli, or their positive incentive value, is an important consideration in attraction (as we know from voluminous research). It is also an important factor in attention. The critical element that may not always be equal, however, and that is of importance in determining attention is the extent to which the other is a novel, unfamiliar, or incongruous stimulus. Novel stimuli generally present special problems in control to the perceiver. While they invite attention, they are not necessarily attractive. This conclusion may be of some solace to doting husbands and wives who have lost out in the competition for attention to more novel social stimuli. If they themselves have become familiar and predictable, if they no longer constitute a control problem to their spouse, the spouse's attention may be safely directed toward other portions of the social environment.

VI. Conclusions

Our thesis has been that the factors that cause a relationship to be initiated are also likely to steer intermediate cognitive processes and, thus, ultimately influence the nature of the relationship. We have therefore argued that an understanding of the factors that cause a social relationship to be initiated are vital to an understanding of the relationship itself.

In developing this thesis, we have taken a perceptual–cognitive approach to the problem of relationship initiation. We, much like the attribution theorists, have viewed the relationship initiator as a scientist who, in his attempts to acquaint himself with the persons who constitute his social environment, collects and analyzes data relevant to them. Unlike many attribution theorists and researchers, however, we do not view the initiator as a pure scientist, a passionless seeker of information; rather, we view him as an applied scientist, one who is devoted to engineering his or her life toward the greatest possible comfort and reward.

The title of this paper associates the question of predicting relationship initiation with the question of predicting to whom a person will be attracted. We have tried to illustrate how the perceptual–cognitive acts of the social engineer are integrally related to his affective acts; that attention, attribution of characteristics to the other, and attraction—as well as, ultimately, the initiatee's reactions to the initiator—are all part of one continuous stream. While we typically break up portions of the stream into separate conceptual entities, particularly for laboratory study, perhaps we should be more aware than we usually are that the behavior we are interested in predicting and understanding resembles a fluid and continuous chain more than an aggregate of discrete categories that can be studied in isolation from the other categories, particularly those that comprise preceding events.

We have designated attention to an unfamiliar other as the point at which an individual may be said to have initiated a relationship with that other. We then attempted to show through our research findings and those of others how this event is of paramount importance in understanding the development of the relationship, since this event precedes all others in it. We took the position that attention is thus an extraordinarily important variable in the study of the evaluation of social relationships in general, and of social perception, in particular, even though attention has been almost wholly neglected.

References

Aronson, E. Some antecedents of interpersonal attraction. In W. J. Arnold & D. Levine (Eds.), *Nebraska Symposium on Motivation* (Vol. 17). Lincoln: Univ. of Nebraska Press, 1969.

Aronson, E. Who likes whom—and why. *Psychology Today*, August 1970, 74, pp. 48–50.

Berlyne, D. *Conflict, arousal and curiosity.* New York: Academic Press, 1960.

Berlyne, D. Attention. In E. Carterette & M. Friedman (Eds.), *Handbook of perception* (Vol. 1). New York: Academic Press, 1974.

Berscheid, E., Boye, D., & Darley, J. Effect of forced association upon voluntary choice of associate. *Journal of Personality and Social Psychology*, 1968, *8*, 13–19.

Berscheid, E., Brothen, T., & Graziano, W. Gain–loss theory and the "law of infidelity": Mr. Doting vs. the admiring stranger. *Journal of Personality and Social Psychology*, 1976, *33*, 709–718.

Berscheid, E., Graziano, W., Monson, T., & Dermer, M. Outcome dependency: Attention, attribution and attraction. *Journal of Personality and Social Psychology*, 1976, *34*, 978–989.

Berscheid, E., & Walster, E. Physical attractiveness. In L. Berkowitz (Ed.), *Advances in experimental social psychology* (Vol. 7). New York: Academic Press, 1974.

Blau, P. M. *Exchange and power in social life.* New York: Wiley, 1967.

Bolles, R. C. *Theory of motivation.* New York: Harper & Row, 1967.

Byrne, D. *The attraction paradigm: An annotated bibliography.* New York: Academic Press, 1971.

Chapman, L., & Chapman, J. The genesis of popular but erroneous psychodiagnostic observations. *Journal of Abnormal Psychology*, 1967, *72*, 193–204.

Chapman, L., & Chapman, J. Illusory correlations as an obstacle to the use of valid psychodiagnostic signs. *Journal of Abnormal Psychology*, 1969, *74*, 271–280.

Darley, J., & Berscheid, E. Increased liking as a result of the anticipation of personal contact. *Human Relations*, 1967, *20*, 29–40.

Exline, R. Visual interaction: The glances of power and preference. In J. Cole (Ed.), *Nebraska symposium on motivation* (Vol. 19). Lincoln: Univ. of Nebraska Press, 1971.

Faw, T., & Nunnally, J. The effects on eye movements of complexity, novelty and affective tone. *Perception and Psychophysics*, 1967, *2*, 263–267.

Figley, C., & Huston, T. L. *Attraction, ambiguity of acceptance, and self-preservation in a dating context.* Unpublished manuscript, 1976.

Flavell, J. Concept development. In P. Mussen (Ed.), *Carmichael's manual of child psychology* (Vol. 2). New York: Wiley, 1970. Friedman, H. F. Effects of self-esteem and expected duration of interaction on liking for a highly rewarding partner. *Journal of Personality and Social Psychology*, 1976, *33*, 686–690.

Gibson, J. J. *The senses considered as perceptual systems.* Boston: Houghton Mifflin, 1966.

Harré, R., & Secord, P. *The explanation of social behavior.* Totowa, New Jersey: Littlefield, Adams, 1973.

Heider, F. *The psychology of interpersonal relations.* New York: Wiley, 1958.

Himmelfarb, S. What do you do when the control group doesn't fit into the factorial design? *Psychological Bulletin*, 1975, *82*, 363–368.

Homans, G. *Social behavior: Its elementary forms.* New York: Harcourt, 1961.

Jones, E., & Davis, K. From acts to dispositions: The attribution process in person perception. In L. Berkowitz (Ed.), *Advances in experimental social psychology* (Vol. 2). New York: Academic Press, 1965.

Jones, E., & Gerard, H. *Foundations of social psychology.* New York: Wiley, 1967.

Jones, E., Kanouse, D., Kelley, H., Nisbett, R., Valins, S., & Weiner, B. *Attribution: Perceiving the causes of behavior.* Morristown, New Jersey: General Learning Press, 1972.

Kelley, H. Attribution in social interaction. In E. Jones, D. Kanouse, H. Kelley, R. Nisbett, S. Valins, & B. Weiner (eds.), *Attribution: Perceiving the causes of behavior.* Morristown, New Jersey: General Learning Press, 1972a.

Lanzetta, J. T., & Driscoll, J. M. Effects of uncertainty and importance on information search in decision making. *Journal of Personality and Social Psychology*, 1968, *10*, 479–486.

Lanzetta, J. T. The motivational properties of uncertainty. In H. I. Day, D. E. Berlyne, & D. E. Hunt (Eds.), *Intrinsic motivation: A new direction in education.* Montreal, Canada: Holt, 1971.

Levine, R., Chein, I., & Murphy, G. The relation of the intensity of a need to the amount of perceptual distortion: A preliminary report. *Journal of Psychology*, 1942, *13*, 283–293.

Levinger, G., & Snoek, J. *Attraction in relationships: A new look at interpersonal attraction.* Morristown, New Jersey: General Learning Press, 1972.

Madsen, K. B. *Theories of motivation.* Kent, Ohio: Kent State Univ. Press, 1968.

McArthur, L. Z. The how and what of why: Some determinants and consequences of causal attributions. *Journal of Personality and Social Psychology,* 1972, *22,* 171–193.

Maslow, A. H. *Motivation and personality.* New York: Harper & Row, 1954.

Mehrabian, A. *Silent messages.* Belmont, California: Wadsworth, 1971.

Murstein, B. Stimulus–value–role: A theory of marital choice. *Journal of Marriage and the Family,* 1970, *32,* 465–481.

Nunnally, J., Duchnowski, A., & Parker, R. Association of neutral objects with reward: Effects on verbal evaluation, reward expectancy and selective attention. *Journal of Personality and Social Psychology,* 1965, *1,* 270–274.

Pepitone, A. Motivational effects in social perception. *Human Relations,* 1950, *3,* 57–76.

Regan, D., Strauss, E., & Fazio, R. Liking and the attribution process. *Journal of Experimental Social Psychology,* 1974, *10,* 385–397.

Reik, T. *A psychologist looks at love.* New York: Farrar & Rinehart, Inc., 1944.

Reik, T. *Of love and lust.* New York: Farrar, Straus, & Cudahy, 1957.

Reik, T. *Need to be loved.* New York: Farrar, Straus & Co., 1963.

Rosenhan, D. L. The contextual nature of psychiatric diagnosis. *Journal of Abnormal Psychology,* 1975, *84,* 462–474.

Ross, L., Lepper, M., & Hubbard, M. Perseverance in self-perception and social perception: Biased attributional processes in the debriefing paradigm. *Journal of Personality and Social Psychology,* 1975, *32,* 880–892.

Rubin, Z. From liking to loving: Patterns of attraction in dating relationships. In T. Huston (Ed.), *Foundations of interpersonal attraction.* New York: Academic Press, 1974.

Shaver, K. G. *An introduction to attribution processes.* Cambridge, Mass.: Winthrop, 1975.

Snyder, M. The self-monitoring of expressive behavior. *Journal of Personality and Social Psychology,* 1974, *30,* 526–537.

Snyder, M. *Cognition and behavior. When belief creates reality.* National Science Foundation Grant manuscript, July, 1975.

Snyder, M., Tanke, E., & Berscheid, E. Social perception and interpersonal behavior: On the self-fulfilling nature of social stereotypes. *Journal of Personality and Social Psychology,* 1977, *35,* 656–666.

Stephan, W., Berscheid, E., & Walster, E. Sexual arousal and heterosexual perception. *Journal of Personality and Social Psychology,* 1971, *20,* 93–101.

Thibaut, J., & Kelley, H. *The social psychology of groups.* New York: Wiley, 1959.

Titchener, E. B. *Lectures on the elementary psychology of feeling and attention.* New York: Macmillan, 1908.

Valins, S. Persistent effects of information about internal reactions: Ineffectiveness of debriefing. In H. London & R. Nisbett (Eds.), *Thought and feeling: Cognitive modification of emotions and motives.* Chicago: Aldine, 1974.

Walster, E., Berscheid, E., Abrahams, D., & Aronson, V. Effectiveness of debriefing following deception experiments. *Journal of Personality and Social Psychology,* 1967, *6,* 371–380.

Young, P. T. *Motivation and emotion.* New York: Wiley, 1961.

Yussen, S. Determinants of visual attention and recall in observational learning by preschoolers and second graders. *Developmental Psychology,* 1974, *10,* 93–100.

Zadney, J., & Gerard, H. Attributed intentions and informational selectivity. *Journal of Experimental Social Psychology,* 1974, *10,* 34–52.

3

Social Exchange and Behavioral Interdependence

JOHN SCANZONI

I. Introduction

What follows is an examination of the stages of behavioral inter-dependence between exchange partners—an attempt to develop notions that are general enough to comprehend at least four different sets of partners: *peers* (same or cross sex), *lovers, husbands–wives, parents–children*. Interdependence is defined as the reliance of actors (or larger units) within any social system on other actors (units) within that system for valued rewards, benefits, gratifications. We assume that the evolution or progression of interdependence passes through at least three stages (and around them this chapter is organized): exploration, expansion, commitment. Exploration means relatively low interdependence, expansion a greater degree of interdependence, and commitment the highest level of interdependence. Interdependence is one way to approach the issue of "ongoingness," or the maintenance of a social system, irrespective of whether that system be dyadic or more than dyadic.

Ellis (1971) indicates that there are at least two ways to approach the problem of interdependence—the functionalist, or normative, solution, and what he calls the utilitarian solution. While the approach followed in this chapter is basically the utilitarian approach to interdependence, the importance of normative elements cannot be overlooked—they are, indeed, essential to any utilitarian perspective (Dahrendorf, 1959, 161–162). As far back as 1960, Gouldner was wrestling with the question of conjoining the two approaches. He concluded that the functionalist approach to the question of interdependence is that of learned moral norms. With regard to marriage, for example, men and women are said to learn norms that promote interdependence, and thus order (Pitts, 1964). Males learn task-oriented norms, women person-oriented norms. Gouldner (1960) argues that in the functionalist view it is the *complementarity* of these sets of norm (or role) behaviors that promotes interdependence and thus solidarity (p. 168). Complementarity implies that through socialization Actors learn the rights and duties of their own roles and also the expectations attached to the rights and duties of Others' roles (pp. 168, 172). As applied to the issue before us—interdependency among certain categories of partners—the functionalist might argue that such involvement is based on the *internalization* of norms pertaining to rights and obligations among Actors and Others. "The concept of complementarity takes mutually comparable expectations as given [Gouldner, 1960, p. 173]."

Therefore, the functionalist insight is that interdependence springs from learning—from socialization, though that process itself is not adequately distinguished from the vague notion of internalization. But "even if socialization were to work perfectly and so internalize such rights and obligations, there still remains the question as to what mechanism can sustain and reinforce [them]. Complementarity does not and cannot explain how [rights and duties] are maintained once established [Gouldner, 1960, p. 173]." The importance of these observations is that they underscore the fact that to resort to utilitarian perspectives to explain interdependence is not an arbitrary decision. Interdependence is both process and structure—or structure in process. Functionalism with its emphasis on *static* structure is unable to capture the actual empirical events of the *dynamics* of interdependence. For that reason we are forced to explore theoretical perspectives that deal more adequately with the questions Gouldner raises about reinforcement, maintenance, and solidarity. These are questions of process that functionalism is ill-equipped to handle because, as Gouldner argues, the functionalists fail to deal unambiguously with a notion that is central to exchange processes: *reciprocity*. This is defined as the performance of role rights and duties so that "What one party recieves from the other requires some return, so that giving and receiving are mutually contingent [Gouldner, 1960, p. 169]."

For Gouldner, reciprocity is the underlying energy that maintains ongoing social systems and relationships, that influences satisfactions with and thus commitments to them, and that also ultimately helps to account for their dissolution. He argues that reciprocity does not stem solely from the "sheer gratification" that A and B derive from each other, because of an exchange of rewards. Rather, to gratitude rectitude must also be added: A and B feel morally obliged "to give benefits to those from whom [each] has received them [Gouldner, 1960, p. 174]." (To be sure, as Ellis, 1971, indicates, Gouldner's notions are inadequate to account for conflict or coercive situations. That issue is dealt with later.)

Ekeh (1974) labels reciprocity based merely on gratitude as part of the "individualistic" or utilitarian tradition in sociology. He maintains that in that tradition stress is laid on "the centrality and autonomy of individual self-interests, wishes, and desires." Concern with rectitude and moral obligation moves closer to what he labels the "collectivist" tradition, which "postulates that social processes gain relevance according to the degree to which they contribute to a definition of the corporate existence of society or of particular groups [p. 13]." He contends that Homans is the "chief apostle" of the former tradition. The latter tradition is currently represented most strongly, he says, by Levi-Strauss (pp. 37ff). Obviously, Ekeh's dichotomy is somewhat rigid, because "there is little justification for making a sharp distinction between prudential [individualistic] and moral [collectivistic, or some principle beyond self-interest] obligation. To the extent that prudential obligation is derived from long-run self-interest and so far as long-run self-interest does in fact conflict with short-run interests, prudential obligation is moral obligation [Ellis, 1971, p. 696]."

Nevertheless, if we conceive of individualistic and group interests as opposite poles of a continuum, then the conception becomes germane to a discussion of interdependency among persons in a social system. To what degree and under what conditions does behavior tend towards one end of the continuum, that of *individualistic* interests? What are the conditions that shift behavior towards the opposite end, that of *collectivist* interests, or commitment to the group or system? Since we are interested in progressive involvement, we may ask whether part of the evolution of relationships is from the individualistic to the collectivist.

Continuing to interpret Levi-Strauss, Ekeh notes that reciprocity between *two* persons is, of necessity, *mutual*. But *univocal* reciprocity involves C (a third person), as well as A and B (two persons), and "demands that A gives to C in response to what A receives from B [p. 48]." (Examples of these several Levi-Strauss–Ekeh notions are provided below.) Mutual reciprocity is the basis for what Levi-Strauss calls *restricted exchange*; univocal reciprocity is the basis for what Levi-Strauss calls *generalized exchange*. Gouldner (1960) sees reciprocity (whether mutual or univocal) as contributing to maintenance and stability of relationships because it engenders enduring obligations among Actors. Persons can never be certain they have fully repaid enough of what they might owe. Thus, over an extended period of time they seek to keep repaying and in turn are themselves continually repaid (pp. 174–175). Ekeh's (1974) approach is basically the same as Gouldner's in that both analysts argue that obligations emerging from social exchange processes contribute to solidarity or commitment. In short, relationships are maintained when actors perform valued services for others, and vice versa; and also when these performances continue to generate ongoing feelings of moral obligations to reciprocate benefits received.

A. Purposive Action

These two general conclusions serve as the basis for the more detailed discussion to follow. Fundamental to the discussion will be a careful examination of processes that amplify exchange and reciprocity. These include processes such as power and conflict, apart from which exchange and reciprocity cannot be adequately understood. Our basic objective is to specify conditions that account for progressive interdependence and solidarity between exchange partners.

It will be helpful if we subsume processes such as attraction, exchange, power, and conflict under a general construct, such as *purposive action* (Coleman, 1975). Progressive interdependence may, after all, be conceived of as a series of decisions in which actors continually choose to decrease or else increase their involvement. In that sense, a process such as attraction may be considered the first of a whole series of purposive-action processes. Actor has chosen to engage in some association with Other, and that decision may have been motivated by varying degrees both of reward-seeking and obligation. (Heath's [1976] construct, *rational-choice theory*, is a similar attempt to subsume exchange and conflict theories under some general heading that tries to make explicit the assumption of goal-seeking or utilitarianism). Therefore, in the pages that follow, we may conceive of progressive interdependence as the unfolding of a series of purposive-action processes, some related more closely to the exchange tradition, others to the conflict tradition. As Ellis (1971) implies, distinctions between exchange and conflict theories are primarily artificial since both rely on utilitarian as against functionalist assumptions to explain social organization. For that reason Coleman's shorthand label of purposive or goal-directed behavior becomes extremely useful in subsuming the less abstract processes analyzed below.

The discussion will be divided into three parts. Each corresponds to stages of development or of progressive involvement among which various social processes may operate differently or not at all. These stages are labeled *exploration*, *consolidation*, and *commitment*. They are not discrete categories. Instead, very often relationships may be located on the border between, and indeed may overlap with, at least two stages. The assumption that relationships are seldom pure types—that is, seldom found totally in one stage or another—is underscored by Lerner's analogy of the concept of development as an *organismic* process (Chapter 10 of this volume). The organismic analogy emphasizes the wholeness, or unitary ongoingness, of social relationships. It is this ongoingness of relationships that we propose to explore, beginning with a relationship of merely slight interdependence and moving progressively to relationships of much interdependence.

Another point of considerable importance made by Lerner is that the development of relationships does not occur in a vacuum (Chapter 10 of this volume). The larger social environment, or social system, in which the association occurs is both cause and consequence of processes within the association. This systemic assumption is fundamental to virtually all of the analyses that follow.

The literature that accepts this assumption contains several descriptions and analyses of models of relationship change, or developmental progression. From among this literature the work of Leik and Leik (1977) is closest to the model developed here. However, there are some critical differences between their three stages of development and ours, and these will be identified at the appropriate time.

II. Stage I: Exploration

As "Exploration" suggests, this first stage covers the first meetings between Persons and their subsequent efforts to discover relevant information about Others. It might also be labeled *tentative, initial,* or *introductory.* The exploratory relationship or system may be thought of as fragile in the sense that unlike later stages it can be easily, quickly, and simply terminated. Relative ease of termination is owing, of course, to minimal investment and minimal interdependence. The major objective of Actors during this first stage is to discover whether or not it is worthwhile, profitable, or in their best interests to maintain or develop the relationship by further investments.

Of the four types of social relationships mentioned earlier two can reasonably be placed in this initial or exploratory stage, and two cannot. The dependent child has neither legal discretion nor resources to sever relationships with his parents. Moreover, the child has never had the opportunity to explore and test the desirability of movement toward an expanded, or committed, situation. As Blau (1964, pp. 20, 34) points out, the child was simply "set down," with no opportunity to weigh the costs and rewards of entrance, into a legally sanctioned exchange and power situation controlled by the parents. And, likewise, husbands and wives are beyond this first stage (unless their marriage was arranged). Their initial explorations have led them to conclude that it would indeed be worthwhile to try to establish a more or less permanent set of ongoing exchanges. Thus our major focus in this first stage will be on relationships between peers and lovers.

Leik and Leik label the first stage of their developmental model "strict exchange" (1977). Strict exchange is concerned "with immediate payoff, such that apparently preferable alternatives will be immediately sought, . . . [and with] what factors induce *strangers* to choose each other for various interaction purposes, whether friendship or coalition formation or cooperation on some simple task [italics added]." Our Stage 1 also includes concern with immediate payoff but extends considerably beyond it, as shall be seen later.

A. Attraction

The initial process that leads to and that exists at the outset of this first stage has been called attraction. Blau (1964), defines this as "the proclivity to associate with others. . . . He expects associations with them to be rewarding, specifically, to be more rewarding than alternatives [currently] open to him . . . [p. 34]." Two types of attractions are distinguished—intrinsic and extrinsic (p. 35). The former refers to intangible, the latter to tangible gratifications. As might be expected these two dimensions exist at polar ends of a continuum. Blau's overall approach to attraction and exchange leads Ekeh (1974) to charge that Blau, along with Homans, takes an individualistic and utilitarian, rather than collectivistic stance (p. 166ff). For example, by way of illustration of what has earlier been labeled as univocal reciprocity, it is not difficult to think of concrete instances where peer associations were formed primarily on the basis of obligation rather than attraction. Student B perceives that student C, who answers the instructor's questions abysmally, needs private tutoring. B received that kind of help from Student A a few weeks earlier. B, out of a sense of the need to repay the moral debt to A, then goes to C to offer assistance. Now C is in B's debt and must repay. And if C asks B why B gave unrequested assistance, and B tells C that B gave it because of a sense of obligation to A, then C becomes indirectly indebted to A and may feel obligated to repay in some fashion. Thus a rather complex social network can emerge from obligation, quite apart from attraction.

Nevertheless, as was discussed earlier in connection with Ellis' (1971) observation that prudential and moral obligations are equivalent, we may assume that obligation and attraction often operate simultaneously. B may genuinely have felt obligated to assist C while simultaneously perceiving certain intrinsic gratifications that C could provide. And whether or not B was concerned for rewards at the outset, C does in fact begin to provide gratifications to B whether out of gratitude, recitude, or both. If C refuses to repay in some fashion we may assume that B would eventually cease the inputs. Therefore rather than being polemic about the primacy of utilitarian (prudential) over obligatory (moral) concerns, the most fruitful way to proceed, both theoretically and empirically, would be to recognize that both mechanisms may govern associations. The research task is to discover the conditions under which one is or is not more significant than the other (Scanzoni, 1978). Likewise, if one element predominates at time 1, does the other emerge as more significant at time 2, and if so, why? Moreover, irrespective of initial circumstances, as the exploratory relationship continues, it seems clear that both reward-seeking and obligation would become significant for its maintenance, whether in lover or peer relations. Decisions regarding whether or not to continue the relationship may sometimes be made on purely utilitarian or individualistic grounds, but more often it is likely that group or collectivist considerations are weighed as well.

In discussing rewards as the basis for attraction, Lott and Lott (1974) make the point that it is hazardous to assume beforehand what is actually rewarding to Person A or to Person B: " 'one man's (or woman's!) nectar is another's poison' [p. 173]." If we consider Lerner's point (Chapter 10) that associations must be examined in their systemic context (see also Kerckhoff, 1974), it would seem to be naive to assert uniformity of rewards sought, for example, by lovers. To the degree that renascent feminism is influencing younger women, the kinds of rewards they seek from lovers may be in considerable flux compared with the much greater homogeneity of, say, 10 or 15 years ago.

Lott and Lott (1974) also describe varieties in the types and sources of rewards that may lead to attraction. These include rewards directly provided by Other; characteristics of Other as source of reward; Other's attitude similarity as a reinforcement of Actor's own competence; and receiving rewards from Other in the presence of some third party. These kinds of issues—relevant or irrelevant rewards, types and sources of rewards—are just two among many that are basic to a complete understanding of this crucial process ubiquitous to all social relationships. (The interested reader is referred to Huston, 1974, for a full discussion of the attraction process.) For our purposes in tracing here the development of associations, we assert that attraction is the foundational element, and that foundation consists of an intermixture of utilitarian and collectivist considerations.

B. Exchange and Exchange Rules

There are no neat, clear-cut, mutually exclusive boundaries between these several purposive-action processes. For instance, as attraction occurs and the association is being formed exchange processes are occurring simultaneously. Moreover Ekeh (1974), interpreting Levi-Strauss, argues that there are rules that govern exchange—"normative regulations" that existed "prior to, and brought into" this particular association (p. 45). Ekeh (p. 45) criticizes Homans because Homans ignores normative elements, a charge that cannot be brought against the structurally oriented Blau. The presence of these norms provides some guidelines for the initial probes that potential exchange partners may make towards each other. At the very least, these norms prescribe what elements may or may not be exchanged, how much, and what the larger reference group considers a fair exchange. Blau (1964) characterizes the reference group effect in terms of prevailing social norms [p. 22].

However, Blau also takes a position that seems to put him at odds with Ekeh's view of norms that exist prior to social interaction. He argues that when persons are "thrown together" and begin to exchange rewards, it is then that group norms emerge—norms that did not exist prior to the interaction (p. 92). Ellis (1971) would appear to reconcile the two views when he makes a crucial *temporal* distinction. In newly emerging situations where no norms exist, or where the actors or groups know of no appropriate or efficient norms, interaction does indeed shape the formation of emergent norms (p. 694).

Nevertheless, "in time, a subset of these norms may themselves achieve the status of generalized moral norms, or they may be linked up with another set of norms which already have the status of moral norms [Ellis, 1971, p. 694]." It is this latter ongoing phenomenon to which Ekeh refers, and on which Blau himself builds many of his arguments. Heath (1976) takes a similar conciliatory approach, according to which partners, rather than bargain continually and repeatedly, agree to establish a norm or "rule which has the 'function' of introducing predictability and regularity into the relationship [p. 68]."

In his attempt to refine the concept of norm, Scott moves away from Ellis' reconciliation. Scott seems to argue that instead of defining norms as "expected patterns of behavior [Lipset, 1975, p. 173]" that then might precede and govern interaction, we ought instead to define a norm as "a pattern of sanctions [1971, p. 72]." In that sense norms would seem to exist only when rewards and punishments are being applied during interaction. The obvious merit of this approach is that it sensitizes us to the distinction between the expectation and the sanction, a point overlooked by the early functionalists (Blake and Davis, 1964). However, it has serious drawbacks, the foremost of which is that normative expectations are part of social structure (Colson, 1974; Ellis, 1971; Holter, 1970; Lipset, 1975) and that therefore far more theoretical leverage is lost than is gained by focusing solely on sanctions and not on the expectations as well. This is particularly true in the analysis of social change, for change is often understood in the context of the dynamic ongoing interplay (often lack of fit or slippage) between expectations (preferences) and sanctions.

For example, 100 years ago, when men and women from respectable homes were introduced, their initial exchanges were governed by what Brickman (1974, pp. 11–12) labels a "fully structured" relationship: "the behavior of each party is completely specified or prescribed by social norms . . . . The orientation of parties . . . is a moral orientation. . . . The reactions of the parties are often the result of their concerns to guide, respect, and obey the other party . . . ." Brickman contends that such a relationship is one in which there are few "resources, options, or alternatives available . . ." and there are considerable "constraints" placed on the use of those that exist (p. 7). In Ekeh's terms such associations were "collectivistic" in that group loyalties were considered to be more significant than individual utilities. Gradually, over time, for reasons discussed elsewhere (Scanzoni, 1972; Scanzoni & Scanzoni, 1976) women began to challenge the normative expectations that bound them in those collectivist associations. They have sought to introduce more individualistic norms into male–female relationships, both prior and subsequent to marriage. The understanding of these fundamental evolutionary changes is far more greatly enhanced by comparing shifts in both preferences and sanctions than it is by looking solely at sanctions. Indeed, the latter approach would be woefully incomplete.

As fully structured or collectivist arrangements have become less common, there has emerged what Brickman calls the partially structured relationship, in which "rules constrain certain behaviors but leave others to the free choice of the parties [p. 7]." Such relationships are "established bargaining relationships . . . because they regularly involve a contest between actors with a rational orientation towards maximizing their respective share of the common resources [pp. 8–9]." "Parties in partially structured relationships are likely to use inducements or reinforcements to influence one another. . . . Intentional or selfish aggression, activated by calculation that this aggression will be rewarded by more favorable outcomes, is an important part of partially structured [relationships] [p. 11]."[1] Unfortunately, by this description Brickman creates the impression that persons in contemporary or "partially structured" relationships are concerned only or chiefly with individualistic gratifications, and not at all with collectivist concerns. This was the same pitfall into which Ekeh stumbled and from which, as we've noted, Ellis (1971) extricates us. Later in the chapter, we discuss more fully how the two types of gratifications are not necessarily mutually exclusive, even as relationships develop into increasing degrees of interdependence.

Fox (1974) apprehends distinctions similar to Brickman's when he uses the term "spontaneous consensus model." By this he mans a situation in which "participants acquiesce in the current definition of roles,

---

[1] Brickman uses the term, *conflict* relationships, but that additional terminology is neither requisite nor useful to our purposes.

with their differing degrees of discretion [power], and make no attempt, covert or overt, individual or collective, to redefine those roles, either their own or those of other participants. . . . All members legitimize the existing distribution of discretion [power] in the sense of accepting it and being prepared to work with and through it [p. 85]." Persons "who share common goals are capable of allocating roles among themselves in the light of what they perceive as 'functional necessities' [p. 86]." Fox contends that within contemporary modern societies few instances remain of that "spontaneous consensus" model. Rather, there exists a much greater incidence of what he calls a "power model," by which he means essentially the same thing as Brickman's "partially structured" relationship.

Respectable nineteenth-century men and women were governed by long-standing rules of exchange for whatever inputs they might wish to give to and receive from each other—including, of course, sex (McCall, 1966). Just as those particular rules of exchange ("spontaneous consensus") were altered, so exchange rules may also be altered in contemporary settings, as we shall discuss later. For now, we observe that even Ekeh (1974), who argued so strongly for structural norms that exist prior to interaction, acknowledges that "Exchange behavior is behaviorally creative and dynamic . . . [p. 45]." Changes of the rules may emerge by feedback out of the very exchanges which the rules themselves govern.

Having asserted that axiom, it would nonetheless be misleading to assume that partially structured relationships among contemporary peers or (potential) lovers exist apart from pre-existing rules of exchange. Even yet among, for instance, working-class and some middle-class youth, the woman would rarely if ever ask for, arrange, and pay for going out with a man. Instead of a woman being assertive in those matters, the man remains so, and he may seek sexual favors in exchange. The woman seeks the gratifications of status and prestige from being chosen by a desirable man, and looks forward to the benefits (including economic provision and security) that accompany marriage (Luker, 1975). Yet it appears that some younger women (and men) are changing those rules (Bayer, 1975; Mason et al., 1976; Parelius, 1975; Scanzoni, 1976). They are seeking to redefine the meaning of *peer* or *friend* to include cross-sex as well as same-sex persons. Thus as friend to friend (irrespective of sex) Actor could take the initiative and arrange for any activity with Other (or set of Others) and bear whatever financial costs might be incurred. This, of course, generates obligations on the part of Other(s), but critical additional redefinitions enter the situation at this point. Since the male is no longer uniquely assertive nor the unique economic source, the woman is no longer uniquely passive regarding sex, nor is sex any longer an obligation on her part. Indeed, she is no longer obligated to provide it at all. She is now free to actively seek sexual rewards from the male or to choose not to have them enter the exchange at all, depending on the details of the bargain that she wishes to strike (Collins, 1971, 1975).

1. GENDER ROLE NORMS

It would appear that variations in these particular kinds of exchange rules are part of the larger issue of changes in gender or sex role norms. As Holter (1970) indicates, such norms or preferences may be taken to represent the interests, goals, or rewards that men and women seek from each other especially across, but also within, sex lines. Traditional gender-based rules of exchange prescribed the situation of male assertiveness, economic provision, and sexual expectations. Contemporary or modern rules prescribe the egalitarian situations (Scanzoni & Scanzoni, 1976, Chapters 2 and 3). The outcomes of traditional exchanges were sharp contrasts in gender differentiation in terms of status, prestige, power, and control of material resources within the context of the larger society. Contemporary exchanges will very likely contribute toward reduction of those types of gender differentiation.

C. Communication and Bargaining

We may now return to a consideration of Persons A and B. Our aim is to trace a progressive development or change in their association. The first phase of that development has occurred through processes of attraction and exchange. Let us assume that for the most part they are in what Leik and Leik (1977) call "strict exchange" or what we might call exploration based primarily on individualistic considerations. Although collectivist concerns are present, we may assume that for the time being these are less nearly central to the association. Indeed, to the degree that they emerge as more nearly central, their emergence in itself becomes an indicator of significant developmental change. A and B are tentatively beginning to exchange gratifications based on sets of rules of exchanges prescribed by a variety of sources: parents, peers, teachers, religious figures, additional significant others.

Next, in the development of their association, two additional processes must now be taken into account. One has been called communication; the other is bargaining or negotiation. Deutsch (1973) defines the former as the process whereby Actor *relays* to Other his or her interests, objectives, norms, and so forth. Perhaps the most critical element in communication is accuracy—Actor relaying as precisely as possible what he or she actually intends, and Other grasping this as accurately as possible (Brickman, 1974, p. 228). Thus two persons, one of whom is gay, may interact. If they are of different sexes, the straight Actor may unintentionally communicate the impression that he or she desires sexual gratifications. But when Other (who is gay) reads it, she or he may therefore fail to respond with any gratifications. Subsequently, the relationship is terminated owing primarily to the miscommunication.

A similar situation may prevail between heterosexual persons. The point is that during exploratory stages, associations are exceedingly fragile. Investments on both sides have been minimal; dissolution is fairly simple. Though there may have been some attractions, few obligations have been incurred. There is little if any behavioral interdependence (as defined earlier) binding them. The very early phases of exploratory associations tend to furnish prime examples of Ekeh's *individualistic* exchanges in the sense that utilitarianism seems to outweigh (not obliterate) collectivist or group interests. This is chiefly because little if any sense of group interests has yet been developed.

However, a process that assists in the formation of collectivist or joint interests is negotiation or bargaining. A significant indicator of development or progressive change in any association is found at that point where partners perceive that the potential rewards are great enough to take the trouble, go to the bother, and expend the psychic and physical energies necessary to negotiate. Willingness to do so implies not only that Other has rewards worthwhile to Actor, but even more importantly that Actor is prepared to strike a bargain to obtain them, that is, to make certain investments and incur costs that heretofore have not been part of the association.

Let us assume, for instance, that a male and female begin to interact (early Stage I) with no prior history of exchanges. The female may accurately communicate to the male that she prefers that modern or egalitarian, not traditional, rules of exchange govern their association. Upon accurately receiving her preference he, preferring traditional rules, may wish to terminate their relationship. Nonetheless, she begins to negotiate with him. (Bargaining or negotiations can be defined as the process whereby in the face of resistance or disagreement Actor and Other *rearrange* or change their mutual distributions of rewards and obligations. In this instance, the negotiation is over rules that govern their relationship, or "basic" rules, as Coser [1956] puts it.) Presumably, the woman seeks to communicate to the man that it would be in his best interests to establish egalitarian rules to govern a peer–peer association rather than to insist on the traditional "ascendant male"–"cooperating female" relationship. She must present or offer to him an array of rewards that outweigh rewards he perceives as flowing from *traditional* male–female situations. Along with such utilitarian elements, she may use the element of obligation based on generalized exchange to seek to convince him that he owes her autonomy. She may argue that he owes her this largely because of the autonomy he has received from existing social arrangements that favor males.

D. Power and Justice

In any case it is impossible to carry on negotiations apart from the processes of power and distributive justice, along with phenomena labeled resources (Heath, 1976). These processes are crucial ones in delineating where an association may be placed on the continuum linking exploratory and consolidated associations. As will be seen, both processes can quickly result in the termination of associations. Conversely, if they emerge and termination does not occur, then we may assume that behavioral involvement or interdependence has increased considerably over what it was prior to their emergence. If termination does not occur, we will have passed a significant milestone in the progressive development of associations. If partners can tolerate the exercise of power or injustice by one another, then we may say that the degree of their interdependence has substantially increased. In exploring the bases for that assumption, let us first of all acknowledge that the notion of power has been exceedingly difficult to apprehend both formally and operationally (Dahl, 1968). Space does not permit us to consider here its complexities in depth, but such attempts have been made elsewhere (Cromwell & Olson, 1975; Scanzoni, 1979). Drawing on several sources we define power as the capability to achieve intended effects or goals at minimal costs.

Homans (1974) has dealt at great length with the notion of distributive justice. For him the term refers to the assessment by Actor of outputs received relative to inputs made. That ratio may range from just to unjust. Incidentally, Homans' discussions of distributive justice take into account the impact of a third party on a dyadic relationship, and thus to some degree can be fitted under generalized exchange notions. If C perceives that he or she receives fewer outputs from A than B does for the same or even fewer inputs, then C is likely to consider those distributions unjust. (See also Heath, 1976; Walster et al., 1978).

Emerson (1976) defines resource as an "ability, possession, or other attribute to an actor giving him the capacity to reward (or punish) another specified actor [p. 347]." By that definition resource (whether tangible or intangible) is always a *potential* sanction. The critical distinction is Emerson's use of "capacity." Returning to our illustration of the woman seeking to negotiate with the man regarding exchange rules, he may identify in her certain gratifications that he seeks and that attract him to her. These then may be resources she can use in bargaining with him. Simultaneously, she may be quite deft in the skills of bargaining and this may be an important resource that she utilizes, but this capacity is not necessarily a gratification that he seeks. As Emerson (1976, pp. 347–348) demonstrates, Actor's resources are transformed into social rewards only when Others *value* those resources.

In order to adequately combine these three purposive-action notions, Heath's phrase *bargaining power* becomes exceedingly useful. Heath (1976) concludes that most studies assume "that individuals will take advantage of their bargaining power and thus obtain an improved bargain [p. 105]." Thus a process that we earlier (and necessarily) abstracted from the purposive-action sequence (negotiation) is in reality inseparable from these adjoining processes. Both Actor and Other hold power vis-à-vis each other based on the relative amounts of resources each possesses, and based on alternative resources, outside the relationship, to which each has access. The degree of symmetry or balance of their bargaining power is computed on the ratio of goals attained and costs incurred by A *relative* to goals attained and costs incurred by B (Kuhn, 1975:111–112). In terms of the illustration we are considering, let us assume the woman is offered a job in another city, and seeks to get her male friend to quit his job (her goal), follow her, and look for a new job. She promises to pay his moving expenses and support him totally until such time as he can secure a position. Those are her costs, which she is willing to incur because she values the socio-emotional rewards he provides. He may counter by refusing to quit and move with her—his bargaining power, resting on the expressive resources he controls. He feels it would be too costly to move. The expressive rewards she can provide him as well as the merely potential and uncertain material rewards are not great enough to counterbalance the costs of quitting his job. But similarly, she feels the costs of her staying where she is are not outweighed by the expressive benefits he provides. In the usual traditional gender role situation, the woman would not have the alternative resource of an attractive occupation, and thus would conform to the man's bargaining power: "Stay here and enjoy the expressive rewards I provide you." As Burgess and Nielsen (1974) put it, exchanges continue so long as "the exchange is more profitable than other sources of reinforcement [p. 441]." But in modern settings, the woman often possesses *both* instrumental and expressive resources, just as the man does. Thus, continuation of an association such as the one in view is so far relatively problematic.

The association could change from what Leik and Leik call *strict exchange* to one of what they call *confidence*, if the man would be willing "to put up with temporary lower returns compared to alternative exchanges [1977]." However, though he is not willing to do that, the woman comes up with a resource that gives her greater bargaining power than he has, and enables her to tip the power balance her way. She finds him a job in the new city that is more attractive than the one he has now. Therefore, given the range of expressive and instrumental benefits he could secure by staying, it becomes more profitable for him to move. To be sure, he has paid a price by quitting his job, but she has made it profitable for him to do so. Assuming it cost her nothing (except energy) to locate a job for him, her costs have been relatively low (she does not now even have to take on his support) and her goals accomplished have been relatively great— indicative of high power. By comparison, his overall costs were relatively great, and his goal of keeping her in the first city was not achieved. Both elements (high costs, lack of goal-attainment) indicate less relative power on his part.

Had he been able to persuade her to give up her goal of moving, apart from his providing some additional reward (which he did not possess anyway), or else apart from upping current rewards, it is likely that she would have soon considered this unfair, unjust, inequitable (Walster *et al.*, 1978). She would soon have compared what she could have been getting with what she is actually receiving, and she would consider herself in a situation of relative deprivation or injustice. Based on her *comparison level for alternatives* (Thibaut & Kelley, 1959) she would consider herself poorly off, indeed. But precisely the same conclusions could hold if the man had moved without having been provided a job, and then had not been able to find one after many months. Upon comparing his new with his former situation, he too would very likely develop a keen sense of an injustice done him.

The fact that she *did* take the trouble to locate a job for him tends to illustrate the point made earlier: Associations that pass through mutual exercise of bargaining power—with its potential for creation and alleviation of feelings of injustice—may be said to have increased or changed their progressive developmental interdependence. In the case before us the new exchange or outcome itself has obviously increased and strengthened the bonds of their interdependence. So have the negotiation processes leading to the outcome, because of the *trust* and *maximum joint profit* it generated. Likewise, the relationship has apparently passed from a situation where individualistic interests are of prime concern to one where collectivist interests are taking on importance. This is seen most dramatically in her efforts to locate a job for him, thus simultaneously promoting his welfare and her own, and thus the association's. Moreover, the bonds of associational interdependence have been strengthened because now, in a very real sense, she is in his debt. Should he one day receive an attractive job offer from city C, he would be able to exercise considerable bargaining power to try to get her to move with him. One of his arguments would be that she is now morally obligated to reciprocate in kind for what he had earlier done for her. What the ultimate outcome of those negotiations might be would, of course, rest on the same kinds of conceptual elements that had governed their earlier move. Incidentally, we should note in passing that to possess strong feelings of justice and equity does not always imply that the actual level of associational interdependence has necessarily moved beyond exploratory Stage I and into Stage II. Additional purposive-action concepts must be introduced before we can say that we have made that type of significant transition. This point is underscored when we recall the earlier implication that had either the man or the woman at any time ceased negotiating, the association could have been terminated fairly simply.

Related to the notion of injustice and termination is a concept that can be traced at least as far back as Max Weber. During the course of the negotiations, either Actor or Other may seek to exercise *nonlegitimate* power in achieving their intentions. Buckley defines that as "control or influence over the actions of others to promote one's goals without their consent, against their 'will,' or without their knowledge or understanding [1967, p. 186]." In contrast, the type of legitimate power exercised in our illustration, where both finally perceived distributive justice, is known as authority: "The direction or control of the behavior of others for the promotion of collective goals, based on some ascertainable form of their knowledgeable consent. Authority thus implies informed voluntary compliance . . . [Buckley, 1967, p. 186]."

In discussing nonlegitimate power, Blau (1964, p. 228) describes it as an attempt by A to dominate or coerce or force B into some behavior without providing sufficient rewards to lead B to perceive that conformity is worthwhile. It is therefore apparent that nonlegitimate power and distributive *injustice* are closely allied processes. If, in our illustration, either seeks to coerce the other into moving or staying without gratifications sufficient to make conformity worthwhile, then Other may see that as an unfair attempt to exercise nonlegitimate bargaining power (which is in itself a painful cost to bear) leading to feelings of distributive injustice. Being unwilling to bear that type of cost, with no other meaningful ties of interdependence to bind them, and with readily available alternative sources of reward, Other may simply elect to terminate the still new association. Not that nonlegitimate power always results in termination, but only that it is more likely to do so during early stages of minimal interdependence. The shock of it may often be too much for exploratory relationships to bear.

E. Maximum Joint Profit and Trust

Returning to the situation where each perceives distributive justice over the rules of exchange they have negotiated, we may therefore assume that they actually begin to exchange gratifications within those rules. If Gouldner and Ekeh are correct then, as a result, mutual feelings of gratitude as well as rectitude (obligation) tend to develop. Actual behavioral interdependencies are thus being reinforced by, and are feeding back on, definitions of the situation and vice versa. At this point we may introduce two additional processes, the actual chronology of which, relative to adjoining purposive-action processes, may vary. The first of these is called *maximum joint profit*, or *MJP*. Kelley and Schenitzki (1972), drawing on the earlier work of Siegel and Fouraker (1960), have sought to investigate the conditions under which persons will negotiate and bargain so as to promote mutual or group interests rather than merely individual advantage. Thus during negotiations if Actor tries to exercise nonlegitimate bargaining power, Other immediately defines Actor as interested not in MJP but only in personal advantage. On the other hand, an awareness by either partner that Other does or does not seek MJP may not emerge until after the negotiations are completed, and actual exchange behaviors may continue for a while. This would be especially relevant during the exploratory stage of an association because there would be no earlier basis on which to assess Other's orientations toward MJP.

Kelley and Schenitzki (1972, p. 335) point out that a critical research task is to explore the conditions under which the pursuit of individual rewards meshes with the pursuit of mutual benefit. This is precisely the same issue that Ekeh (1974) raised in contrasting individualistic with collectivistic approaches to social exchange. And it is the issue that Ellis (1971) addressed, arguing that both approaches often tend to be congruent. One thing appears certain: There can be no MJP apart from each partner's sensing distributive justice. The more that each person in a group feels that his or her own interests are being met fairly, the more that each is convinced that the partner seeks his or her best interests (Walster et al., 1978). This conviction may occur at the same time that Actor perceives that Other is being reasonable with regard to Other's own objectives. That is MJP. And the more that Actor perceives that Other is pursuing MJP, the more obligated Actor is to pursue it. Clearly, a high level of perceived MJP on the part of both partners is very likely to promote progressive interdependence. (Later, when we discuss such concepts as solidarity, cohesion, and commitment, we shall maintain that a major component of these notions is MJP.)

The second of the two processes to be introduced here is *trust*. It is closely related both to MJP and to increased interdependence. Trust is defined by Deutsch (1973) as confidence that one "will find what is desired" from Other "rather than what is feared [p. 148]." Mistrust, therefore, amounts to expectations of punishments from Other (including the absence of positive inputs) rather than rewards. (See also Blau, 1964, pp. 97–99, 107–108, 112–113). As with MJP, exploratory relationships are not likely to be characterized by much trust, simply because there has been little or no past experience from which either trust or mistrust could develop. (As we shall observe shortly, with time and the emergence of both MJP and trust, we are prepared to move from Stage I to Stage II of behavioral involvement.) Based on Zand's small-group research, Fox (1974) observes that "trust tends to evoke trust, distrust to evoke distrust [p. 67]." He also draws on Zand's definition of trust: "the conscious regulation of one's dependence on another . . . [p. 69]." Deutsch's and Zand's definitions can be readily combined if we conceive of trust as Actor's willingness to arrange and repose his or her actions on Other because of confidence that Other will provide expected gratifications.

If this reasoning is valid, it seems virtually impossible for MJP and trust not to co-vary. Nevertheless, they are distinct variables. Being convinced that Other is concerned to cooperate with Actor is MJP; being willing to strike bargains with Other in which some element of risk is involved is trust. The former is a perception or evaluation based on past dealings; the latter involves some future behavior or action. For instance, a young newly married couple (both high school graduates) may negotiate an arrangement in which Actor agrees to work full time for two years while Other goes to college full time. They agree beforehand that at the end of that interval they shall reverse behaviors. Presumably they both possess MJP that co-varies, and indeed may be a cause of, the trusting, risk-taking behavior on the part of the one who first works. He or she is willing to arrange current behavior in dependence on Other. The arrangement means that Actor is willing to forego immediate gratifications and accept certain costs so that Other can enjoy those particular gratifications. This behavior is based on the expectation that Actor can *depend* on Other to reciprocate in kind at the agreed-upon time. And both are convinced that this exchange is beneficial to their association, that is, they are being collectivistic as well as individualistic.

The application of trust to this particular illustration is virtually identical to what Leik and Leik (1977) mean by *confidence*: the willingness to forgo the immediate in lieu of long-term rewards. Thus, in a sense our exploratory Stage I tends to subsume both of their two initial stages—the other being strict exchange. The use of a married couple to illustrate trust may seem to shift us out of our Stage I, since marriage presumably involves processes additional to those described so far. Nevertheless trust can exist at exploratory Stage I quite apart from any relationship such as marriage, though obviously it can do so only in the later phases of the stage. Therefore, in seeking to identify progressive change or development within associations, it seems apparent that when MJP and trust do finally emerge, we have moved a significant step to the right on the continuum displayed in Figure 3.1. When those processes become part of an association, we may say that its level or degree of interdependence has become substantially increased. An association possessing them is very different from one lacking them, and this not so subtle shift is reflected in Figure 3.1. When these processes appear the transition from concentra-

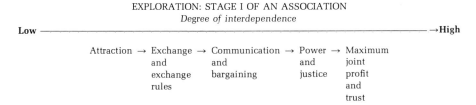

EXPLORATION: STAGE I OF AN ASSOCIATION
Degree of interdependence

Low ———————————————————————————————————— →**High**

Attraction → Exchange → Communication → Power → Maximum
and   and   and   joint
exchange   bargaining   justice   profit
rules   and
trust

Figure 3.1 Degree of progressive interdependence within the exploratory stage of an association as indicated by emergence of particular purposive-action processes.

tion on individualistic interests to concern with group interests is complete. However exclusive or limited individualistic seeking may have been in the past, now, by definition, that must be and is being balanced by seeking Other's interests, and thus collective interests as well.

III. Stage II: Expansion of Interlocking Interest-Spheres

The fundamental contrast between Stage I (exploration) and Stage II (expansion) is the enlargement or increase of intermeshing interest-spheres (or goals, ends, or objectives) that bind actors or groups. Throughout exploratory phases the range of goals sought by Actor from Other, and vice versa, tends to be limited—as does their interdependence. However, the emergence of MJP and especially of trust is a kind of catalyst or critical juncture in the association. Where trust is present, risk-taking, or bets on the future, are readily incurred. Almost inevitably, therefore, these risks are related to an increase of the range of gratifications that Actor seeks from Other, and vice versa. As this critical intersection is passed, and the range of goals sought from it are substantially widened, we may say that the association has developed or evolved significantly from one characterized by probing, testing, examination, and so on, to one characterized by continual enlargement of the kinds of rewards that partners supply one another, and thus of increased interdependence.

Take, for instance, the partners described earlier and the exchanges they were able to negotiate. Each person may be assumed to have interests or goals besides those discussed. These may include a variety of status, prestige, and consumption interests; academic or educational interests; peer interests; kin interests; other kinds of nonwork time objectives, and so forth. There are at least three ways by which the range of interests they exchange may gradually become expanded. The first way, of course, is the powerful and ubiquitous force of *attraction*. Either person can come to perceive that Other can provide an array of valued rewards. The woman, for instance, may perceive that the man can provide encouragement, advice, counsel or colleagueship in her career efforts within a traditionally male occupation (Blau, 1964; Fogarty, Rapoport, & Rapoport, 1971). Therefore her attraction to him expands to include these kinds of rewards. Or a more traditional woman, after fulfilling traditional exchange rules during the initial phases of Stage I, may perceive that her man can provide a good home and a secure future for her. Thus her attraction is expanded to include these interests.

The second way by which exchanges and the degree of interdependence may be expanded is *obligation* or a concern for collective well-being (as opposed to a concern for individualistic gratifications). For instance, let us assume that our partners are fulfilling their negotiated reciprocities. Perhaps the most distinguishing feature of social as distinct from economic exchange is the absence of strict accounting (Blau, 1964; Ekeh, 1974; Heath, 1976). Persons are never quite certain how much in debt they are to each other, and therefore strong feelings of moral obligation to repay are continually being generated and reinforced (Gouldner, 1960). Actor can fulfill this moral obligation in at least two ways. The first is by increasing the level of inputs already being provided; for example, a woman could go out with her friend five instead of four nights a week. But once the available resource is used to its capacity (seven nights), that way is no longer useful. In that situation, Homans (1961, p. 76) argues that persons may feel guilty because they are being out-given, are receiving more than they are giving, or perhaps are receiving more than they think they deserve. Therefore, a second way to demonstrate feelings of gratitude and rectitude is to identify an additional resource one has that would constitute a reward to Other. Actor's supplying this gratification expands the range of their exchanged resources. But not so obvious is the likelihood that Other will now feel more indebted than before the emergence of this most recent input. Therefore to discharge this felt obligation, Other will search for additional resources he has that will constitute a valued reward to Actor. As that occurs, *expansion*, and thus progressive interdependence, has enlarged by one more identifiable step. Though Ekeh (1974, p. 48) would label this type of reciprocity *mutual*, there is no reason that *univocal* reciprocities might not also contribute toward weaving an expanded network of overlapping interest-spheres among partners. Either person may have received considerable benefits from parents, peers, teachers, or clergy, and thus feel obligated to reciprocate to Other in terms of the latter's interests, beyond those already being met through mutual exchanges.

The third way, which does not necessarily exclude ways one and two, is that certain exchanges may impinge on or spill over onto other interests of either partner. An outcome may be negotiated or struck that ipso facto carries implications for intersecting interests, though neither partner originally intended that. For instance, when Actor (woman) negotiated Other (man) into the exchange previously described, two more sets of Other's interests (defined as spheres within which Actor or Other seek objectives or rewards that he or she defines as vital) may have been affected. Both peers and kin may have negatively sanctioned him through ridicule and criticism, and through reduction of whatever levels of prestige and authority he may have held with them. Thus, his negotiations with her may have been costly, and may have placed him in a less favorable bargaining position than he previously enjoyed in those two interest spheres. As he becomes aware of those costs his ongoing exchanges with her may begin to take account of intersects with those other spheres. Specifically, in attempting to renegotiate the earlier exchange, he may apprise her of the unforeseen costs he has now incurred. If he does, she may seek to compensate him through increased levels of current rewards, or she will expand the interdependence further by identifying an additional interest sphere of his. For example, he may have certain academic weaknesses in areas where she has strengths. Consequently, she may appeal to his interest in completing an educational program and utilize her resources to assist him to achieve that goal. Therefore the bargain they may now strike will be considerably more complex than the one before.

Expansion, therefore, is a kind of stochastic process in which attractions, obligations, negotiations continually lead to an ever widening network of intermeshed or interdependent interests. Behavior in one interest sphere affects behaviors in several others simultaneously. Processes executed in one sphere are inherently linked with processes in other spheres. Power, for instance, that is exercised nonlegitimately by Actor in sphere 1 may very well lead Other to respond in kind in sphere 2. Feelings of injustice in sphere 3 may cause Person to reduce inputs in sphere 2, thus disrupting the exchange to which they had previously agreed. These intimately linked processes connecting several interest spheres simultaneously are, of course, in constant motion, in the sense that they are the vehicles through which Actor and Other are making inputs to and receiving outputs from each other. At the same time the pair as a unit, as well as each partner separately, is involved in other exchange networks that increase or decrease inputs they can make to their association. Likewise these networks, by providing alternative resources, influence the bargaining power of Actor and Other with regard to the level of outputs they are able to gain from their association.

Moreover, as the expansion of overlapping interests proceeds, we may assume that MJP and trust both cause, and are also reinforced by, the increasing interdependence. As Actor learns that Other fulfills Other's obligations and indeed exceeds them, Actor defines Other as being concerned for MJP. As a consequence, Actor will become more willing to negotiate even more complex arrangements involving additional interest spheres and thus greater risk to Actor. This willingness is due to Actor's confidence (trust) that Other can be relied on in these new spheres as well. In turn, fulfillment by Other of these added obligations generates still greater perceived MJP and trust on Actor's part.

A. Sex and Expansion

Thus far, in examining expansion (and exploration) we have focused mostly, though not exclusively, on heterosexual pairs developing friendship associations. But the conceptual framework and expected relationships are general enough to apply to same-sex friendship relations. The same applies to associations in which the partners are lovers, whether hetero- or homosexual. Since sex is a resource that virtually all persons can supply and receive, it is not necessarily absent from friendship relations. But in terms of exchange rules agreed on by the pair, and often involving significant others with whom they maintain univocal exchanges, sexual gratifications (defined operationally by something like the continuum of the Reiss Scale [1967]) are not exchanged by the pair. But if, for whatever reasons, the rules are altered to incorporate those kinds of gratifications, then the pair may be said to have established a lover-type relationship. It is possible, of course, to have an exploratory association in which there is only one common interest, namely, sex. The incidence of such ongoing associations (in contrast to one-night stands) is open to empirical assessment, but they are not likely to be too frequent. More probably, sex is exchanged within an expanded association in which additional interests have either preceded or else followed the sexual interest sphere.

Conflict theoreticians, begining with Engels (1884) and including some recent feminists (Firestone, 1970; Mitchell, 1971) have argued that cross-gender sexual exchanges have in the past been exploitative. It is alleged that men, by virtue of their greater physical strength and social status, have gotten far more sexual gratification from women than they have given. And though many women may not define their situation as one in which they suffer injustice and endure nonlegitimate power, it is argued that historically such was and indeed often remains the case. In considering the issue of the sexual exploitation of women, it is not a simple matter to distinguish mere rhetoric from scientifically testable hypotheses about historic or present-day sexism. Gouldner (1960) has made an initial contribution to scientific-theory development regarding sexual exploitation, but the most thorough effort to date is the work of Collins (1971; 1975, p. 225ff.). He attempts to combine Freud (sex as a basic drive) with Marx (control of economic resources by men) to show that whereas men have had both sexual and economic resources with which to bargain, women have had only the former. Therefore they have tended to be in a subordinate position to men and have often been exploited both economically and sexually.

The question of how many women define their situations as exploitative as well as the strength of those definitions is not settled. Nevertheless, referring back to our earlier discussion of shifts in gender-role norms from traditional to modern, it may be argued that women who prefer the latter kinds of situations do sense more keenly the potential of exploitation (injustice) inherent in traditional gender arrangements. They may sense that traditional arrangements tend to deny women direct access to the achievement of tangible and intangible occupational gratifications, and that inequity in this interest sphere affects their bargaining position in other spheres, including the sexual. It was for these kinds of reasons that we earlier predicted that women who are more modern in their views of gender roles would seek to alter traditional exchange rules regarding sex (Walshok, 1973). We would also predict that modern gender norms and altered exchange rules will vary accoring to assertive female negotiating behaviors that are aimed at avoiding sexual exploitation (Scanzoni, 1978).

Regarding the general issue of progressive involvement, which this chapter addresses, we should observe that sex has the unique capability of suddenly engendering high degrees of extensive behavioral interdependence quite apart from the kinds of purposive-action processes that ordinarily contribute to group solidarity or commitment. Often, because of univocal or generalized exchanges and perceived obligations to kin, peers, or church, unintended pregnancy forces many lovers to marry legally, chiefly to avoid the costs of an illegitimate[2] child.[3] Such costs include not wanting to embarrass significant others (e.g., parents), because to do so would show ingratitude for inputs received. Significantly, Furstenburg (1976) reports that such rules of univocal exchange leading toward forced marriages tend to be much less pervasive among lower status blacks, chiefly because they have learned that young black men simply cannot supply the economic resources to make viable such forced interdependencies.

[2] See Scanzoni and Scanzoni, 1976, for data on relationships between premarital conceptions and marriages, and for a discussion of the possible obsolescence of the term *illegitimacy* in modern societies.

[3] Assuming, of course, that the couple cannot obtain or else will not tolerate the costs of an abortion, or giving up the infant for adoption. Refusal to abort may also be partially explained (as was avoidance of illegitimacy) by notions of *generalized exchange*. Certainly, many of the arguments of Right-to-Life and other anti-abortion groups are of that genre.

B. Negotiation and Contraception

It has been observed that between lovers who exchange sexual gratifications, there seems to be considerable ambivalence regarding negotiations over contraception (Kantner & Zelnick, 1972, 1973; Furstenburg,
1976). Apparently, there is some reticence on the part of such persons
even to communicate clearly and objectively whether to use contraceptives, and if so what types, much less to negotiate or bargain regarding
who is responsible for their use (Luker, 1975). If anything, there is a kind
of implied silence that the woman is ultimately responsible for contraception, and that she is to blame if a pregnancy occurs. It would appear that
this inability or unwillingness of lovers to communicate openly and to
negotiate firm bargains in regard to contraception is largely responsible
for many of the forced sudden interdependencies (legal marriages) just
described. There is evidence to suggest that married women—both black
and white—who are more gender-role modern tend to be more adept at
using contraceptives (Scanzoni, 1975). Likewise, among white undergraduate women those who are more strongly role modern intend to have
fewer children (Scanzoni, 1976). Earlier it was predicted that role moder-
nity would decrease the likelihood of a woman's being sexually exploited.
It is therefore axiomatic that such women are more likely to negotiate
openly and firmly regarding contraception, and also more likely to ensure
that they and their partners practice more effective contraceptive behavior.

C. Co-Residence

At this phase of our discussion of expansion, we must begin to raise
the issue of how we will be able to shift along a continuum from Stage II to
Stage III. How do relationships progress or develop to something beyond
Stage II or proliferation of interlocking interest spheres? When can we say
that interdependence is characterized by Stage III, or what is called
commitment? What phenomena must be brought into view in order to
help us grasp the evolution or development of behavioral interdependence? What is the relative function of collective versus individualistic
interests in a committed relationship? We have just suggested that the
extensive interdependencies of legal marriage sometimes emerge quite
apart from commitment, defined as feelings of solidarity and cohesion
with an association. But what are some ways we might identify evolutionary movement toward interdependence marked by commitment?

One first and partial indicator of that evolution is co-residence. When
friends or lovers choose to share the same household, we may assume that
their range of interest spheres has become highly interlocked by means of

the purposive-action processes described previously. In particular, together they have to a greater or lesser degree become economically interdependent. That kind of interest sphere is extremely significant for group maintenance for a host of reasons, of which we will enumerate two. Willingness to merge economic rights and duties within a household, as within a business, suggests that the partners have developed a relatively high degree of trust. Second, relative control over economic resources is, as Collins and others indicate, at the core of female–male subordination. Very likely it is also intrinsic to most other forms of differentiated bargaining power as well.

Nevertheless, in spite of its potential significance co-residence does not imply that commitment is *necessarily* present. Or if it does exist it may be no more than an initial untested commitment. The forced marriage is an example of co-residence and interdependence without the assurance of commitment. The same lack of assurance could apply to many voluntary marriages. Concomitantly, persons may maintain committed associations and not be in co-residence. But co-residence remains one salient indicator of extensive *interdependence*.

Moreover, variation in the rules that govern co-residence can shed some light on the degree of the extensiveness of that interdependence. For instance, Table 3.1 presents a set of categories describing varying types of co-residence by degree of interdependence. These categories were designed originally to apply to lovers (gay or straight), and would appear to have only limited relevance to friend–friend associations. They describe the nature of the expansion or proliferation of interests that lovers might experience. Living together covertly implies fewer areas of interest overlap than occur in an overt living arrangement. Insofar as the partners are concerned, the greater range of rewards in the latter situation outweighs

Table 3 .1
Types of Co-Residence Patterns and Degree of Behavioral Interdependence[a]

		Marriage			
		Sociological definition		Legal definition	
Premarriage					
The affair	Living together covertly	Living together overtly		Common law marriage	Legitimized union
(Regularized sexual liaisons)	Ad hoc arrangement	Trial marriage	Ongoing consensual union (not legally recognized)	(In states where legally recognized)	(Fulfilling state requirements for licensing and solemnization)

[a] From Scanzoni and Scanzoni (1976, p. 147).

any negative consequences they might encounter; however, in the former situation there may not be sufficient rewards to risk the costs of "going public." Subsequently, interest overlap and interdependence may be said to increase or expand as we move from ad hoc to legal union. We would hypothesize that accompanying such a transition the degree of commitment also increases, although there may be considerable variation as a function of processes now to be considered.

IV. Stage III: Commitment

Leik and Leik (1977) also label the third developmental stage of an association *commitment*, but they define it as a situation where "the members are no longer attending to alternatives. The feeling of each committed partner is that the current relationship is to be maintained and alternatives are simply irrelevant." Thus, in their view, commitment primarily involves collectivist or group goals or interests, whereas individualistic interests have become largely subordinated. Marriage, they suggest, is a prime example of a committed relationship but in contrast McCall (1966), drawing on Farber (1964), has argued that contemporary marriage is not marked by commitment, at least as it is defined by Leik and Leik. For McCall, marriage is characterized primarily by concern for individualistic interests.

> Every person with whom the individual comes in [to] contact is eligible as a possible mate, regardless of marital status. . . . Marriage may occur at any time in one's life, so one must make an effort to remain desirable and must polish up his skills in striking a good bargain. . . . Marriage [is a] restrictive trade agreement. The two individuals agree to exchange only with one another, at least until such time as the balance of trade becomes unfavorable in terms of broader market considerations [pp. 197–198].

Certainly, McCall's thesis as stated appears crass and lacks the refinements, subtleties, and sophistication that over a decade of work have contributed to the applications of social exchange theory to marriage (Chadwick-Jones, 1976). Nevertheless the intervening years have made the tenor of McCall's thesis more believable today than it was when first proposed. The major problem both with McCall and with Leik and Leik is that they have gotten into the same thicket as Ekeh by sharply contrasting collective and individualistic interests. There is no empirical or theoretical reason why a committed relationship could not be characterized by Ellis' (1971) notion that "prudential obligation *is* moral obligation [p. 696]." Indeed it can be argued quite strongly that in the evolutionary scale of associational interdependence, commitment stands high or is advanced precisely because the participants have been able to negotiate an optimum balance of long-range and short-term interests, beneficial both to participants and the association. That view of commitment excludes the Leik and Leik notion that alternatives ever become irrelevant. Should persons or groups become oblivious to the market they run the equally serious risks either of being exploited by or of exploiting their partners, either of which could undercut commitment and result in termination. This view of commitment also excludes McCall's implication of continuous shopping. Most persons or groups involved in committed associations have an awareness of the market without constant and frenetic testing. This view also calls into question the apparently common practice of attaching the idea of stability to committed relationships. Leik and Leik (1977) follow that practice, although they allow for what they call "continual interpersonal adjustment." Stability is a term more in keeping with a static functionalist image of reality than with a utilitarian view (Ellis, 1971). The latter view would lie closer to Gurvitch's notion that any association or structure (micro to macro) is a "permanent process [cited in Bottomore, 1975, p. 160]." By that reasoning, interdependence that has reached the commitment stage (while expected to be indefinitely ongoing) is not necessarily stable since the arrangement itself may be undergoing continual change, often in response to external forces (Lerner, Chapter 10 of this volume), some of which may indeed be alternative sets of gratifications. For these reasons, the notion of permanent process is theoretically much more meaningful than and thus preferable to stability.

Unfortunately, reviews of the literature treating the idea of commitment (Chadwick-Jones, 1976) force us to the conclusion that, like power, commitment is an extraordinarily slippery notion. What is available suggests that we conceive of commitment as a construct that may be defined as "the degree to which persons feel solidarity with or cohesion with an association." For instance, Blau's discussion (1964, pp. 76–85, 160–165) of commitment suggests at least two key dimensions which indicate solidarity within an association. One is the level of inputs which Actor provides; the second is the duration or period of time during which those inputs are made. If both level and duration are high, then we may say that solidarity is high—that commitment is great. But there is at least one additional dimension that implicitly runs throughout other discussions of commitment (Davis, 1973). We will label it the *consistency* or constancy with which these inputs are made. That is, within a given period of time input levels may be high at one point, but quite low at another, and Partner A may have some difficulty predicting when B's input levels will be the one or the other. Such fluctuations suggest *inconsistency*, which may be said to indicate B's relatively low commitment. Therefore, before we can say that Actor is committed to a relationship, at the very least all three (measurable) elements must be present: relatively high input levels, relatively lengthy duration, relatively great consis-tency.

A. Comparison Levels

Intrinsic to the notion of commitment as viewed here are *CL* (comparison level) and CL_{alt} (comparison levels for alternatives) (Thibaut & Kelley, 1959). Our earlier discussion of distributive justice was linked to a relatively narrow range of interest spheres. But Thibaut & Kelley (1959, p. 21) suggest that Actor's comparison level is tied to the *total* relationship: assessing overall costs and rewards in terms of what one deserves. *CL* is "influenced by *all* of these outcomes known to the member . . . [italics supplied]." By way of distinction, CL_{alt} is "the lowest level of outcomes a member will accept [from the total relationship] in the light of available alternative opportunities." Commitment is a construct applied to the *total* relationship, and where it is high, it is so because of *CL* and CL_{alt}. (See Heath, 1976, pp. 45–46.) The cumulative effect of negotiations, exchanges, legitimate power, MJP, trust, etc., over a series of expanding interest spheres produces an overall or global assessment of the relationship that may be conceptualized by Thibaut and Kelley's notions. With the growth of a positive or strong comparison level, there also develops solidarity and, hence, commitment as we have defined it. Very likely MJP and trust exert paths of influence both on *CL* and on commitment. Awareness that Other is concerned for group interests and also that Other can be counted on to provide gratifications is bound to increase *CL*. Alongside those influences, plus the effects of *CL* on commitment, we could also predict that MJP and trust would be having their own independent effects on commitment. Actor's willingness to raise input levels, extend their duration, and increase the consistency or constancy with which they are made should all be positively and highly related to MJP and trust.

In short, it is possible to argue that commitment emerges out of the types of purposive-action processes described so far that have accounted for expanding behavioral involvement. By definition, once commitment has been generated it feeds back on the interdependence, providing significant motivation to maintain it. These complex patterns would account for at least a certain level of commitment in a friend or peer association, in a lover relationship, or in an actual marriage whether legally sanctioned or not (see Figure 3.2). They would also account for a certain degree of commitment in a parent–child relationship, although there the situation cannot be analyzed apart from the age (dependency; lack of alternative resources) of the child. As noted earlier, when the child is young there is no exploratory stage. Within what might be termed the expansion stage, parents provide increasingly numerous inputs because of the immediate gratification they receive from the child, the long-term intrinsic and extrinsic benefits they expect, and the kinds of generalized obligations or exchanges (univocal reciprocities) to which Ekeh (1974) refers. Therefore, depending on the types of purposive-action processes that occur, and the degree of interdependence, as well as the range of interest spheres involved, any sampling of families is likely to reveal considerable variation in the level of commitment that exists on both the parents' side and the child's.

But since neither the dependent child nor the parent can voluntarily terminate the association except under the most unusual circumstances, the relevance of CL and CL_{alt} is questionable. However, as the child becomes an adolescent or a young adult, those global variables become extremely relevant, because both sides now gain the legal and social freedom to terminate their association. And when the child finally gains alternate resources sufficient to maintain economic independence, these resources can then be used by offspring to negotiate with parents for distributive justice over interest spheres that include objectives for both sides. At that point, their association may still maintain some rules of exchange that characterize a parent–child (superior–subordinate) relationship, but it is also very likely that the offspring has negotiated a change in some of the exchange rules so as to make it, in part at least, a peer or friend-type association. Such a change in norms would be analogous to our earlier discussion of the woman who negotiated a change from traditional (dependent) to modern (autonomous) male–female relations. The desire or capability of the offspring to negotiate change from child to peer status is contingent on a range of critical variables too numerous and complex to raise in this chapter (see Rollins & Thomas, 1975).

More pertinent to the central objective here is this issue: Whatever the relationship (peer, lover, marriage-partner, child), are there purposive-action processes beyond those already discussed that might contribute to still greater levels of commitment? If we had measures of the three concepts that underly commitment and if, via a regression model, we were to try to account for variations in them, what variables could we add to the equation besides those already discussed that might account for a significant increase in the amount of explained variance? Or to put it another way: Are there certain purposive-action processes that represent a critical test of commitment? Is it the case that unless these processes have occurred either the level of commitment is relatively low or at least it is potentially fragile because it is untested? The processes we have in mind are *conflict* and its resolution or regulation. Hostility and physical coercion can also be part of this range of variables.

Although exchange and conflict traditions have developed separately, there is in fact very little to distinguish them theoretically, since they are both premised on goal-seeking (Buckley, 1967; Heath, 1976; Ellis,

1971, pp. 182–184). For that reason conflict is included here as another of the series of purposive-action processes that explain behavioral inter-dependence.

B. Conflict

The discussion that follows is based in large part on data available in Scanzoni (1978, Chapters 4 and 5). In the real world conflict as a process is, like bargaining, inseparable from power. Therefore, it may emerge at any point in the exploratory stage of a relationship, as outlined in Figure 3.1, where power is being exercised. With a slight modification of Coser's (1956) definition, conflict may be defined as Actor's struggle against Other's resistance toward Actor's efforts to achieve intended effects. When we discussed power earlier, we assumed that both Actor and Other were exercising it in negotiations whose objective was to arrive at a settlement (new exchange, or changes of exchange rules, or changes in types or amounts of commodities exchanged) that both consider fair and just; that is where both were able to achieve reasonable intended effects. However, at any point during negotiations Other may resist Actor's efforts to achieve MJP by presenting inflexible, nonnegotiable demands. Or, sub-sequent to negotiations in which Actor and Other have agreed to exchange rights and duties, Other may violate their agreement and seek to exercise nonlegitimate power by behaving in a fashion that Actor considers unjust and for which Actor has not bargained.

If Actor accedes to Other in either instance, no struggle or actual conflict may be said to exist. Indeed, if Actor accedes we may say that Other has been able to bring about change in either the rules of exchange that govern their relationship or the items exchanged, or both. Actor may then harbor feelings of resentment and hostility towards Other, or else simply come to accept the legitimacy of Other's power to make those changes. If the latter, it is likely that feelings of trust and MJP have been restored. Since legitimate power rests on supplying rewards for de-manded conformity (Blau, 1964, p. 228) it is likely that Other has had to make considerable additional inputs in order to achieve either acquies-cence or change apart from negotiation. Our hypothesis is that this par-ticular chain of events, which clearly increases interdependence, is also likely to co-vary with increased commitment. Other, for instance, may be assumed to assess favorably his or her Cl given what has been accom-plished. And in terms of CL and CL_{alt}, Actor apparently feels that in spite of having had, at first, to endure nonlegitimate power, the ultimate outcomes have overall been quite beneficial relative to any alternative situation. Otherwise Actor would have become hostile, or resorted to conflict, or else possibly terminated the relationship.

If indeed Actor does resist or struggle, then we may say that conflict has been generated.[4] Struggle may take several forms, including refusal to submit or submission while constantly expressing dissatisfaction and continually seeking to renegotiate so as to remove the injustice. The longer the period of resistance continues, the more the conflict becomes institutionalized (Sprey, 1971); that is, becomes an integral component of the relationship. So long as the conflict continues we may say that the struggle is being regulated by one of the parties (Dahrendorf, 1959).

C. Conflict-Resolution

Conflict-resolution occurs when there is a renegotiation of obligations and gratifications—when Actor percieves that the injustice and nonlegitimate power have been removed and a new and fair exchange has been established. Resolution takes place when Actor is able and willing to exert enough power during renegotiating processes so as to end Other's resistance (change the conflict situation, or stalemate) and to achieve intended effects in this interest sphere. Yet Actor has done so in such a way that Other feels it is fair—a case of MJP.

Should conflict occur during the exploration stage of an association the probability is high that it would very often result in termination. The reasons for this eventuality are similar to those presented in connection with termination as a result of injustice. But the greater the degree of expansion (Stage II) of a relationship the greater the inevitability of conflict (Coser, 1956). If greater intermeshing of interests makes conflict more inevitable, it also makes termination potentially more costly. Therefore in Stage II or III Actor is more likely to acquiesce in nonlegitimate power, or to allow the conflict to become institutionalized, or else to resist it, than merely to terminate the association. Should conflict be resolved we may hypothesize that solidarity and thus commitment will be strengthened (Coser, 1956; Blau, 1964). One reason for this expectation is the increased interdependence that the resolution has presumably generated in the form of more complex sets of interlocking networks of rewards and costs than existed previously. But perhaps a more significant reason is the trust and MJP built up through the course of having to bargain, draw upon resources, utilize power, and eventually negotiate a fair exchange with which both can live. Our hypothesis is that a certain minimum level of interdependence and commitment has to precede these difficult processes. If none were present before conflict, the struggle would seem less worthwhile, and termination would be more likely. It is in that sense that conflict is a test of commitment.

Second, willingness to engage in conflict or struggle is a test of

---

[4] See Straus, 1976, for various assertions of when conflict may actually be said to exist.

commitment, inasmuch as conflict may be taken as an index of Actor's perception of Other's orientation to MJP. If, on the one hand, Actor is convinced that Other is strongly oriented towards the best interests of the association, then Actor is more willing to struggle with Other for justice in the confidence that Other will eventually be compelled by it. On the other hand, the perception that Other's MJP is low may lead to an unwillingness on Actor's part to struggle, because struggle, he would assume, would be futile; that is, bring about no significant change in Other's behavior.

Accordingly, the process of conflict resolution enchances the degree of commitment because it uniquely generates trust and MJP. Both Actor and Other learn that it is possible for them to initially withstand each other's intended effects, and yet eventually arrive at a satisfactory arrangement of costs and rewards involving, very likely, several of their interlocking interest spheres. Particularly significant for its effect on increasing and sustaining ongoing commitment, is the confidence that since conflict resolution has occurred in the present and past, there is no reason why it cannot be repeated in the future. And what is commitment if not a wager on the future?

For this reason it is probable that commitment is likely to be substantially greater here than where nonlegitimate power was exercised, acquiesced in, and accepted, but where Actor did not actively participate in and contribute to resolution of the struggle. Likewise, it hardly needs to be said that whereas resolution generates greater commitment regulation undermines it. Forced submission to nonlegitimate power is a severe punishment. Nevertheless, such a submission can also be a revealing test of commitment. If that cost is endured in a particular interest sphere and the entire relationship not terminated, then almost certainly other interests within the total relationship are relatively gratifying. Simultaneously, as discussed later, the range of costs is less than those perceived outside it. Therefore CL is at least adequate and CL_{alt} has not been reached.

D. Hostility and Violence

Two additional elements that need to be considered with regard to their effect on commitment are hostility and violence. As with conflict, we would not expect these phenomena to emerge during Stage I of an ongoing association, but only during the later stages of expansion, or during Stage III—commitment. Hostility can be defined as feelings of anger or resentment that are expressed to a greater or lesser degree and in varying ways (Homans, 1974, p. 257). Hostility and its expression can be incited in a variety of ways, such as by perceptions of distributive injustice as a result of inadequate rewards, nonlegitimate power, regulated conflict, mistrust, and so forth (Homans, 1974, pp. 257–261, 178–179). Two key features of hostility link it theoretically with conflict and commitment. One is variation in the degree to which it is actually expressed or suppressed. Based on Coser (1956) it is possible to argue that the more numerous the hostilities that are suppressed and the more strongly that they are, the more likely it is that an association will experience sudden upheaval, explosion, or termination.

As with conflict, it is likely that the suppression of hostility is in part related to perceived low MJP on the part of Other. Willingness to express hostility may sometimes indicate that Actor believes that Other genuinely wants MJP. That feature is related to a second key feature of hostility; namely, that expressed hostility can be "an instrumental act by which [Actor] tries to raise to a higher and more just level the amount of reward [Actor] gets [Homans, 1974, p. 257]." Though it is possible to have conflict apart from hostility, the two often co-vary together. When they do, hostile behaviors may indeed become one tactic or bargaining strategy used by Actor to help resolve the conflict (Scanzoni, 1978). Specifically, if Actor expresses anger or resentment towards Other, Other may believe that Actor is serious about removing the injustice, and thus the expression may provide support for Actor's efforts to negotiate and establish a new and fair exchange. Therefore, expressed hostility too can be construed as a sign of commitment; and insofar as it aids in conflict resolution it may also contribute indirectly to greater solidarity. On the other hand, where hostilities mushroom and are not expressed, they—in conjunction with nonlegitimate power, regulated conflict, and so forth—may contribute strongly to termination.

Violence has been described as the "ultimate resource" or strategy to achieve one's goals (Goode, 1971). Physical coercion is not the type of strategy we would expect to find in bargaining situations aimed at fair exchanges, as described for the exploration and expansion stages. Violence there is likely to result in rapid termination. Nevertheless, oddly enough, violence can sometimes be used as one way to gauge commitment (as defined above) if we think in terms of CL and CL_{alt}. For instance, the evidence is mounting that violence between husbands and wives is far more common than has been supposed (Steinmetz & Strauss, 1974). Violence is the polar extreme of domination, nonlegitimate power, and coercion. To the degree that those three are experienced and are already punishing to Actor, the addition of physical pain becomes an added cost. The family folk literature is replete with tales of longsuffering housewives whose drunken husbands beat them several nights a week, but who nonetheless persevere in their marriage.

Gelles' (1976) research suggests that the willingness by adults to endure great or consistent violence in a relationship is due to this: when all the elements in the relationship are weighed (CL), the association is seen to be more profitable than any alternative Actor might perceive (CL_{alt}). In the CL_{alt} sense, greater commitment is evidenced by persons who experience violence yet maintain system stability than by persons who experience similar violence but terminate. We would predict that adult friendships and nonlegal marriages (Table 3.1) are most likely to become terminated if violence persists. Among legal marriages, wives of lower-status husbands are most likely to tolerate violence, because among all wives they possess the fewest options in the form of viable, attractive, alternative associations (Scanzoni & Scanzoni, 1976). Moreover compared to higher-status wives, their commitment (in terms of the three dimensions that comprise it) is likely to be considerably less, and that is one reason they experience higher marital dissolution rates.

Children, of course, are routinely exposed to legally and socially approved violence. Only when the child is known to be abused do non-family members intervene on its behalf. The connections between parental coercion of dependent children (whether by nonphysical or physical means) and parent–child commitment are too vast and complicated to be dealt with adequately here. However, the key issue would seem to be perceived legitimacy of parental demands and coercions. Blau (1964, p. 228) contends that subordinates accord legitimacy to superiors' demands in ratio to the benefits accorded them. Thus, if parents coerce their children with respect to certain interest spheres, those "sticks" must presumably be balanced off by gratifications or "carrots" in the same or other interest spheres. Such balances would presumably enhance legitimacy of parental power and contribute to child–parent commitment. The need for such balances varies, of course, with the degree of actual or potential alternative resources perceived by the child. As the child becomes older and gains access to more alternate resources, commitment, we assume, would be enhanced the less that parental coercion (especially physical) is utilized and the more that the processes of bargaining, altered exchanges, and conflict resolution become part of the association. Precisely because the relationship is not voluntary, a dependent child's acceptance of parental violence cannot be considered a sign of commitment, as an adult's acceptance of violence might be. Indeed the expectation is that the older the child and the greater the violence to which he is subjected the less will be the child's commitment to the parents (Schulz, 1969).

V. Summary

Our intention in this chapter has been to examine the issue of progressive interdependence among persons, whether they be friends, lovers, spouses, or parents and children. We sought to distinguish interdependence from solidarity or commitment, yet at the same time to show how interdependence and commitment reinforce each other. First we began with an initial discussion of some of the implications of reciprocity and exchange. Next three stages of progressive involvement or solidarity were identified: (I) exploration, (II) expansion, (III) commitment. The construct that bridged all three stages was Coleman's (1975) one of purposive-action. That term was selected because it suggests the idea of some choice or volition on Actor's part to increase or terminate the level of behavioral interdependence by evolutionary participation in each of a number specific processes.

The broad and often amorphous notion of purposive-action includes concepts describing specific social processes that are discussed in most chapters in this book. Included within Stage I, for instance, were attraction, obligation, social exchange, communication, bargaining, power, distributive justice, maximum joint profit, and trust. Also included were three additional variables intrinsically linked with these processes— namely, rules of exchange, gender role norms, and resources. We suggested that Stage I (exploration) consists of all of these processes and variables with reference to a narrow set of interests common to Actor and Other.

Expansion, or Stage II, is an enlargement or branching out of these interest spheres. A variety of interconnected interests are brought into the relationship, and thus interdependence is increased or enlarged. The point was made that between heterosexual lovers unintended pregnancy can bring about substantial interdependence (legal marriage) without a corresponding increase in the levels of solidarity or commitment. At the same time it was noted that variation in the rules of co-residence may often be thought of as a reliable and valid indicator of associational commitment.

We suggested that commitment, like purposive-action, is a construct that requires measurement in terms of more specific concepts such as input levels made by Actor to the relationship, duration of those inputs, and the consistency with which they are made. Commitment evolves out of the types of purposive-action processes that simultaneously account for ever-increasing and extensive behavioral interdependence. In this regard Thibaut and Kelley's notions of *comparison level* and *comparison level for alternatives* become quite significant. Furthermore, commitment may be enhanced or else undercut by means of additional purposive-action processes, such as conflict, and conflict resolution. Indeed, conflict may often be thought of as a test of commitment. We also considered hostility and coercion (nonphysical and physical) and the ways in which they may be related either to varying levels of commitment or else to system termination.

We concluded that interdependence (the degree of reliance between partners for gratifications) may be said to increase with the transition from exploratory to expansion to commitment stages. That evolution is also marked by the relative primacy of individualistic versus collective interests. Although we assumed that both were always present to some degree in the kinds of relationships considered here, we acknowledge that during the early exploratory stage, individualistic concerns may predominate. However, as a relationship evolves into the commitment stage, the two sets of interests seem to become more balanced and, as some theorists claim, sometimes indistinguishable.

We noted that all three stages may characterize lover and peer relations. It would seem that only Stages II and III could be applied validly to husband–wife or to parent–child associations. A most significant factor in analyzing parent–child relations is the age of the child and the usually correlated economic independence. Commitment, as we described it, becomes a meaningful notion only in a context where termination is a viable option. Dependent children do not have that option. As the off-spring gain greater economic independence that option becomes ever more open to them. Concomitantly, with greater resources and bargaining power, the offspring gain the option to change the rules of exchange from parent–child to peer–peer.

Acknowledgements

Special thanks to Bob Burgess, Gary LaFree, Ted Huston, Gary Robinson, Bill Strahle, for numerous discussions and suggestions that have contributed significantly to the several versions of this chapter.

References

Bayer, A. E. Sexist students in American colleges: A descriptive note. *Journal of Marriage and Family*, 1975, *37*, 391–400.

Blake, J., Kingsley D., Norms, values, and sanctions. In R. E. L. Faris, (Ed.), *Handbook of modern sociology*. Chicago, Illinois; Rand McNally Co., 1964.

Blau, P. M. *Exchange and power in social life*. New York: Wiley, 1964.

Bottomore, T. Structure and history. In P. M. Blau, (Ed.) *Approaches to social structure*. New York: The Free Press, 1975.

Brickman, P. *Social conflict*. Lexington, Massachusets: Heath, 1974.

Buckley, W. *Sociology and modern systems theory*. Englewood Cliffs, New Jersey: Prentice-Hall, 1967.

Burgess, R. L., and Neilsen, J. M. An experimental analysis of some structural determinants of equitable and inequitable exchange relations. *American Sociological Review*. 1974 (June) *39*: 427–443.

Chadwick-Jones, J. K. *Social exchange theory: Its structure and influence in social psychology.* New York: Academic Press. 1976.

Coleman, J. S. Social structure and a theory of action. In P. M. Blau, (Ed.), *Approaches to the study of social structure.* New York: The Free Press, 1975.

Collins, A conflict theory of sexual stratification. *Social Problems,* 1971, *19,* 3–21.

Collins, *Conflict sociology.* New York: Academic Press, 1975.

Colson, E. *Tradition and contract.* Chicago: Aldine, 1974.

Coser, L. A. *The functions of social conflict.* New York: Free Press, 1956.

Cromwell, R. E., Olson, D. H. (Eds.). *Power in families.* New York: Wiley, 1975.

Dahl, R. A. Power, In D. L. Sills (Ed.), *International encyclopedia of the social sciences.* (Vol. 12.) New York: Macmillan, 1968.

Dahrendorf, *Class and class conflict in industrial society.* Stanford: Stanford Univ. Press, 1959.

Davis, M. S. *Intimate relations.* New York: The Free Press, 1973.

Deutsch, M. *The resolution of conflict.* New Haven: Yale Univ. Press, 1973.

Ekeh, P. P. *Social exchange: The two traditions.* Cambridge: Harvard Univ. Press, 1974.

Ellis, D. P. The Hobbesian problem of order. *American Sociological Review.* 36(August)pp. 692–703.

Emerson, R. M. Social exchange theory. In A. Inkeles, J. Coleman, & N. Smelser, (Eds.), *Annual Review of Sociology,* Palo Alto, California: Annual Reviews, Inc., 1976, pp. 335–362.

Engels, F. *The origin of the family, private property and the state.* (1902 ed.) Chicago: Kerr, 1884.

Firestone, S. *The dialectic of sex.* New York: Morrow, 1970.

Fogarty, M. P., Rapoport, R., & Rapoport, R. N. *Sex, career and family.* Beverly Hills: Sage, 1971.

Fox, A. *Beyond contract: Work power and trust relations.* London: Faber 3 Faber Ltd., 1974.

Furstenberg, F. F., Jr. *Unplanned parenthood: The social consequences of teenage childbearing.* New York: The Free Press, 1976.

Gelles, R. J. Abused wives: Why do they stay? *Journal of Marriage and Family,* 1976, *38*(November) pp. 659–668.

Goode, W. Force and violence in the family. *Journal of Marriage and the Family,* 1971, *33*(November), 624–636.

Gouldner, A. W. The norm of reciprocity: A preliminary statement. *American Sociological Review,* 1960, *25,* 161–178.

Heath, A., *Rational choice and social exchange.* New York: Cambridge Univ. Press, 1976.

Holter, H. *Sex roles and social structure.* Oslo: Universitetsforlaget, 1970.

Homans, G. C. *Social behavior: Its elementary forms.* New York: Harcourt, 1961 (rev., 1974).

Huston, T. L. A perspective on interpersonal attraction. In T. L. Huston, (Ed.), *Foundations of interpersonal attraction.* New York: Academic Press, 1974.

Kantner, J. F., & Zelnik, M. Sexual experience of young unmarried women in the U. S. *Family Planning Perspectives,* 1972, 4(October), 9–17.

Kantner, J. F., & Zelnik, M. Contraception and pregnancy: Experience of young unmarried women in the U.S. *Family Planning Perspectives,* 1973, 5(Winter), 21–35.

Kerckhoff, A. C. The social context of interpersonal attraction. In T. L. Huston, (Ed.), *Foundations of interpersonal attraction.* New York. Academic Press, 1974.

Kelley, H. H., & Schenitzki, D. F. Bargaining. In C. G. McClintock (Ed.), *Experimental social psychology.* New York: Holt, 1972.

Kuhn, A. *Unified social science: A system-based introduction.* Homewood, Illinois: Dorsey. 1975.

Lipset, S. M. Social structure and social change. In P. M. Blau, (Ed.), *Approaches to the study of social structure.* New York: The Free Press, 1975.

Leik, R., & Leik, S. A. Transition to interpersonal commitment. In R. L. Hamblin & J. H. Kunkel, (Eds.), *Behavioral Theory in Sociology*. New Brunswick, New Jersey: Transaction Books, 1977.

Lott, A. J., Lott, B. E. The role of reward in the formation of positive interpersonal attitudes. In T. L. Huston, (Ed.), *Foundations of interpersonal attraction*. New York: Academic Press, 1974.

Luker, K. *Taking chances: Abortion and the decision not to contracept*. Berkeley: Univ. of California Press, 1975.

Mason, K. O., Czajka, J., & Arber, S. *Change in U.S. women's sex-role attitudes, 1964–1975*. American Sociological Review, 1976, 41(August) 573–596.

McCall, M. Courtship as social exchange. In B. Farber (Ed.), *Kinship and family organization*. New York: Wiley. 1966.

Mitchell, J. *Woman's estate*. New York: Pantheon Books, 1971.

Parelius, A. P. Emerging sex role attitudes, expectations, and strains among college women. *Journal of Marriage and Family*, 1975, *37*, 146–154.

Pitts, J. R. The structural-functional approach. In H. T. Christensen (Ed.), *Handbook of marriage and the family*. Chicago: Rand McNally, 1964.

Reiss, I. L. *The social context of premarital sexual permissiveness*. New York: Holt 1967.

Rollins, B. C., Thomas, D. L. A theory of parental power and child compliance. In R. E. Cromwell D. H. Olson (Eds), *Power in Families*, New York: Wiley, 1975.

Scanzoni, J. *Sexual bargaining: Power politics in American marriage*. Englewood Cliffs, New Jersey: Prentice-Hall, 1972.

Scanzoni, J. *Sex roles, life-styles, and childbearing: Changing patterns in marriage and family*. New York: Free Press, 1975.

Scanzoni, J. Sex role change and influences in birth intentions. *Journal of Marriage and Family*, 1976, *38*(February), 43–60.

Scanzoni, J. Social processes and power in families. In W. R. Burr, R. Hill, F. I. Nye, & I. L. Reiss (Eds.), *Contemporary theories about families*. New York: Free Press, 1979.

Scanzoni, J. *Sex Roles, Women's Work and Marital Conflict: A Study of Family Change*. Lexington, Massachussets: Lexington Books/Heath, 1978.

Scanzoni, L., & Scanzoni, J. *Men, women, and change: A sociology of marriage and family*. New York: McGraw-Hill, 1976.

Schultz, D. A. *Coming up black*. Englewood Cliffs, New Jersey: Prentice-Hall, 1969.

Scott, J. F. *The internalization of norms: A theory of commitment*. Englewood Cliffs, New Jersey: Prentice-Hall, 1971.

Siegel, S., & Fouraker, L. *Bargaining and group decision making*. New York: McGraw-Hill, 1960.

Sprey, J. On the management of conflict in families. *Journal of Marriage and the Family*, 1971, *33*, 722–732.

Steinmetz, S., & Straus, M. (Eds.), *Violence in the family*. New York: Dodd, Mead, & Co., 1974.

Straus, M. *Measuring Intrafamily Conflict and Violence: The CRT Scales*. Unpublished paper. University of New Hampshire, Durham, 1976.

Thibaut, J. W., & Kelley, H. H. *The social psychology of groups*. New York: Wiley, 1959.

Walster, E., Walster, G. W., Berscheid, E. *Equity: Theory and research* Boston: Allyn-Bacon, 1978.

Walshok, M. L. *Sex Role Typing and Feminine Sexuality*. Paper read at Annual Meetings of American Sociological Association. New York, 1973.

4

Equity Theory and Intimate Relationships[1]

ELAINE HATFIELD
MARY K. UTNE
JANE TRAUPMANN

I. Introduction

Social psychologists have always been painfully aware that their field is in desperate need of a general theory of social behavior. Until recently, it was assumed that it was far too early to try to develop one. A number of optimistic, or foolhardy, social psychologists, however, have begun to challenge this assumption (see Moscovici, 1972). For example, equity theory (see Walster et al., 1978 and Walster, 1973) was developed in the hope of providing the glimmerings of the general theory that social psychologists so badly need. It attempts to integrate the insights of reinforcement theory, cognitive theory, psychoanalytic theory, and exchange theory.

Adams and Freedman (1976) argued that equity theory's integrative attempt has been strikingly successful. They observed,

> The theory in its present form (Walster et al., 1973) strikes us as having a well articulated structure, being parsimoniously elegant, and having an increased predictive range. These are characteristics that bode well for progress, for as Kuhn

[1] This research was supported in part by National Institutes of Mental Health Grant MH 26681.

99

Copyright © 1979 by Academic Press, Inc.
All rights of reproduction in any form reserved.
ISBN 0-12-143550-4

(1962) and Rosenberg (1972) have noted, the growth of a discipline, scientific or technological, is intimately tied to the existence and quality of theory [p. 44].

Equity theory has been applied to predict people's reactions in such diverse interactions as industrial relations, exploiter–victim relations, and philanthropist–recipient relations.[2] It has proved to be surprisingly successful in predicting people's reactions in such casual interactions. Would it be equally successful in predicting their reactions in deeply intimate interactions? Surprisingly, we do not know, for it has not been applied to the most profoundly important of human interactions: intimate relationships. No one has determined whether equity principles guide the interactions of lovers, married couples, or parents and children. In this chapter, we will explore the insights that formal equity theory gives us into intimate romantic and marital relationships. In Section II, we will briefly review equity theory. (Those who are already familiar with equity theory can skip ahead to Sections III and IV.) In Section III, we will review theorists' sharp disagreements as to whether or not equity considerations operate in romantic, mating, and marital relationships. In Section IV, we will review current research which may provide the glimmerings of a resolution to this controversy.

II. The Equity Formulation

Equity theory is a strikingly simple theory. It is composed of four interlocking propositions:

A. The Equity Propositions

PROPOSITION I: *Individuals will try to maximize their outcomes (where outcomes equal rewards minus punishments).*

PROPOSITION IIA: *Groups (or rather the individuals comprising these groups) can maximize collective reward by evolving accepted systems for equitably apportioning resources among members. Thus, groups will evolve such systems of equity, and will attempt to induce members to accept and adhere to these systems.*

PROPOSITION IIB: *Groups will generally reward members who treat others equitably, and generally punish members who treat others inequitably.*

[2] E. Walster, G. W. Walster, and E. Berscheid review this wide ranging and voluminous Equity research in *Equity: Theory and Research*, New York: Allyn & Bacon, 1978.

PROPOSITION III: When individuals find themselves participating in inequitable relationships, they will become distressed. The more inequitable the relationship, the more distress they will feel.

PROPOSITION IV: Individuals who discover they are in inequitable relationships will attempt to eliminate their distress by restoring equity. The greater the inequity that exists, the more distress they will feel, and the harder they will try to restore equity.

B. Definitional Formula[3]

Equity theorists define an equitable relationship to exist when the person scrutinizing the relationship—who could be Participant A, Participant B, or an outside observer—concludes that all participants are receiving equal relative gains from the relationship; that is, when

$$\frac{(O_A - I_A)}{(|I_A|)^{k_A}} = \frac{(O_B - I_B)}{(|I_B|)^{k_B}},$$

where I_A and I_B designate a scrutineer's perception of Person A's and Person B's inputs, O_A and O_B designate his perception of Person A's and Person B's outcomes, and $|I_A|$ and $|I_B|$ designate the *absolute value* of their inputs (i.e., the perceived value of their inputs, disregarding sign).[4]

C. Definition of Terms

Inputs (I_A or I_B) are defined as "the scrutineer's perception of the participant's contributions to the exchange, which are seen as entitling the participant to reward or punishment." The inputs that a participant contributes to a relationship can be either assets (entitling him to rewards) or liabilities (entitling him to punishment).

In different settings people consider different inputs to be relevant. For example, in industrial settings businessmen assume that such hard assets as capital or manual labor entitle one to rewards. Such liabilities as incompetence or disloyalty entitle one to punishment. In social settings, friends may assume that such social assets as beauty or kindness entitle one to reward, whereas such liabilities as drunkenness or cruelty entitle one to punishment.

In addition to assessing what participants have put into their rela-

---

[3] For a detailed explanation of the logic underlying this definition of Equity, see Walster et al., 1978.

[4] There is one restriction on inputs: The smallest absolute input must be ≥ 1, that is, $|I_A|$ and $|I_B|$ must both be ≥ 1.

tionship, the scrutineer must also assess whether or not participants are getting the outcomes they deserve from the relationship.

Outcomes $(O_A$ or $O_B)$ are defined as "the scrutineer's perception of the rewards and punishments that participants have received in the course of their relationship with one another." The participants' total outcomes, then, are equal to the rewards they obtain from the relationship minus the punishments that they incur.

The exponents k_A and k_B take on the value of $+1$ or -1 depending on the sign of A and B's inputs and the sign of A and B's gains (outputs — inputs). $[k_A = \text{sign } (I_A) \times \text{sign } (O_A - I_A)$ and $k_B = \text{sign } (I_B) \times \text{sign } (O_B - I_B)]$[5]

D. Who Decides Whether a Relationship Is Equitable?

According to equity theory, equity is in the eye of the beholder. An observer's perception of how equitable a relationship is will depend on his assessment of the value and relevance of the participants' inputs and outcomes. If different observers assess participants' inputs and outcomes differently—and it is likely that they will—it is inevitable that they will show disagreements as to whether or not a given relationship is equitable. For example, a wife, focusing on the fact that she works long hours, is trapped with no one over 5 to talk to all day, and is constantly engulfed by noise, mess, and confusion, may feel that her relative gains are extremely low. Her husband, focusing on the fact that she gets up in the morning whenever she pleases, and can see whom she wants when she wants may disagree. Moreover, an "objective" observer may calculate the participants' relative gains still differently.

E. The Psychological Consequences of Inequity

According to Proposition III, when individuals find themselves participating in inequitable relationships, they feel distress regardless of whether they are the beneficiaries or the victims of the inequity. The overbenefited may label their distress *guilt, dissonance, empathy, fear of retaliation,* or *conditioned anxiety.* The underbenefiteds' feelings can be labeled *anger* or *resentment.* Essentially, however, both the overbenefited

---

[5] The exponent's effect is simply to change the way relative outcomes are computed: If $k = +1$, then we have $\dfrac{O - I}{|I|}$ but if $k = -1$ then we have $(|I|) \cdot (O - I)$. Without the exponent k, the formula would yield meaningless results when $I < 0$ and $O - I > 0$, or $I > 0$ and $O - I < 0$.

and the underbenefited share certain feelings—they both experience subjective distress accompanied by physiological arousal (see Austin & Walster [1974]).

F. Techniques by Which Individuals Reduce Their Distress

Proposition IV states that individuals who are distressed by their inequitable relations will try to eliminate their distress by restoring equity to their relationship. There are only two ways by which participants can restore equity to a relationship: They can either restore *actual* equity or restore *psychological* equity to it. A participant can restore actual equity by altering his own or his partner's relative gains. For example, imagine that an unskilled laborer discovers that the contractor has been paying him less than the minimum wage. He can reestablish actual equity in four different ways: He can neglect his work (thus lowering his inputs), start to steal equipment from the company (thus raising his own outcomes), make mistakes so that the contractor will have to work far into the night undoing what he has done (thus raising his employer's inputs), or damage company equipment (thus lowering the contractor's outcomes). The ingenious ways people contrive to bring equity to inequitable relationships are documented by Adams (1963).

A participant can restore *psychological equity* to a relationship by changing his perceptions of the situation. He can try to convince himself that the inequitable relationship is, in fact, equitable. For example, suppose that the exploitative contractor starts to feel guilty about underpaying his unskilled laborers. He can try to convince himself that his relationship with his underpaid and overworked employees is equitable in four ways: He can restore psychological equity by minimizing their inputs ("You wouldn't believe how useless they are"), by exaggerating his own inputs ("Without my creative genius the company would fall apart"), by exaggerating their outcomes ("They really work for the variety it provides"), or by minimizing his outcomes ("The tension on this job is giving me an ulcer").

G. Actual versus Psychological Equity Restoration

At this point, equity theorists confront a crucial question: Can we specify when a person will try to restore actual equity to his relationship, *versus* when he will settle for restoring psychological equity? From equity theory's Propositions I and IV, we can make a straightforward derivation:

A person may be expected to follow a cost–benefit strategy in deciding how he will respond to perceived inequity. Whether an individual responds to injustice by attempting to restore actual equity, by distorting reality, or by doing a little of both has been found to depend on the costs and benefits a participant thinks will derive from each strategy. (See, for example, Berscheid & Walster, 1967; Berscheid et al., 1969; and Weick & Nesset, 1968.)

H. Summary

Equity theorists agree that people try to maximize their outcomes (Proposition I). A group of individuals can maximize its collective outcomes by devising an equitable system for sharing resources. Thus, groups try to induce members to behave equitably: That is, they try to ensure that all participants receive equal relative outcomes:

$$\frac{(O_A - I_A)}{(|I_A|)^{k_A}} = \frac{(O_B - I_B)}{(|I_B|)^{k_B}}$$

They can do this in only one way: by making it more profitable to be good than to be greedy. They reward members who behave equitably and punish members who behave inequitably (Proposition II). When socialized persons find themselves enmeshed in inequitable relationships, they experience distress and are moved to reduce such distress either by restoring actual equity or by restoring psychological equity to their relationship (Proposition IV).

III. The Theorists' Debate: Is Equity Theory Applicable to Intimate Relationships?

A. The Theorists' Debate

When equity theorists point out that equity considerations have a profound impact on a wide variety of casual encounters (i.e., business relationships, philanthropist–recipient relationships, and exploiter–victim relationships), few demur. However, when equity theorists proceed a step further, and begin to suggest that equity considerations shape romantic and marital relationships as well, objections are quickly raised.

It is easy to see why people find the suggestion that in intimate relationships there is quid pro quo distinctly unsettling. On the one hand, we all long to believe that love relationships are special—that they transcend social exchange. The longing for unconditional love is an immemorial one. We would like to believe that even if we lost our looks, openly expressed our most unacceptable feelings, and could no longer work, our family and friends would continue to love us. On the other hand, we suspect that such love is not to be had. We suspect that if we become incapable (or unwilling) to give anyone anything, we would soon cease to receive much of anything in return.

This uncertainty over whether love transcends or embodies market principles is reflected in the conflicting pronouncements of psychologists. Fromm (1956) is probably the most well-known proponent of the notion that true love goes beyond exchange. In *The Art of Loving*, he grants that most flawed "human love relations follow the same pattern of exchange which governs the commodity and labor market [p. 3]." But, he contends, unconditional love—love given without expectation or desire for anything in return—is the truest, strongest, and best type of love.[6]

Rubin (1973), too, argues that romantic relations are special relations:

> The principles of the interpersonal marketplace are most likely to prevail in encounters between strangers and casual acquaintances and in the early stages of the development of relationships. As an interpersonal bond becomes more firmly established, however, it begins to go beyond exchange. In close relationships one becomes decreasingly concerned with what he can get *from* the other person and increasingly concerned with what he can do *for* the other [pp. 86–87].

A number of other theorists agree with the contention that love transcends equity. See, for example, Douvan (1977), May (1953), Mills (1975), and Murstein *et al.* (1977).

An equally prominent group of theorists insists that equity considerations *do* apply in intimate relationships.

> Marriage is an interlocking, self-contained system. The behavior and the attitudes of one partner *always* stimulate some sort of reaction from the other. . . . We call this system of behavioral responses the *quid pro quo* (or "something for something"). . . . The *quid pro quo* process is an unconscious effort of both partners to assure themselves that they are equals, that they are peers. It is a technique enabling each to preserve his dignity and self-esteem. Their equality may not be apparent to the world at large; it may be based upon values meaningless to anyone else, yet serve to maintain the relationship because the people involved perceive their behavioral balance as fair and mutually satisfying [Lederer & Jackson, 1968, pp. 177–179].

Patterson (1971) adds:

---

[6] Even this champion of unconditional love, however, inadvertently finds himself in the equity camp. Although Fromm claims that equity considerations demean love relations, he is moved to promise his readers that if they love truly they will reap a handsome return. "[In] truly giving, he cannot help receiving that which is given back to him. Giving implies to make the other a giver also . . . [p. 21]."

> There is an odd kind of equity which holds when people interact with each other. In effect, we get what we give, both in amount and in kind. Each of us seems to have his own bookkeeping system for love, and for pain. Over time, the books are balanced [p. 26].

Other theorists agree that in love relationships—as in all other relationships—considerations of equity and the marketplace prevail (see, for example, Bernard, 1964; Blau, 1964; McCall, 1966; Scanzoni, 1972; and Storer, 1966). Walster *et al.* (1978) argue that the equity principles which operate so relentlessly in casual relations operate in intimate relations as well. They agree that casual and intimate relationships differ in a number of ways.[7] At the very least, they differ in the intensity of liking (or loving); the depth and breadth of information exchange; the duration of the relationship; the value of the resources exchanged; the variety of the resources exchanged; the substitutability of resources; and the unit of analysis (from "you" and "me" to "we"). However, they insist that the fact that casual and intimate relations differ in so many important ways should simply affect (a) how easy or how difficult it is to calculate equity in a casual versus an intimate relationship and (b) how the participants in the respective relationships choose to restore equity. However, the same equity *processes*, they assert, operate in both kinds of relationships.

When faced with the compelling arguments on both sides on the issue of whether intimate relationships transcend or embody equity principals, there is only one thing to do: gather systematic research. Let us begin by defining what we mean by intimacy. What are the characteristic features of an intimate relationship? Why are these relationships so hotly defended as special? Why are they so difficult to systematically examine and understand? What implications should the differences between casual and intimate relationships have for perceptions of and reactions to equity or inequity?

B. Definition: What Do We Mean by "Intimate Relations"?

> Intimate / 'int-a-mat / adj. [alter. of obs. intimate, fr. L intimat] 1: a: intrinsic, ESSENTIAL b: belonging to or characterizing one's deepest nature 2: marked by a warm friendship developing through long association 3: a: marked by very close association contact, or familiarity b: suggesting informal warmth or privacy 4: of a very personal or private nature [*Webster's Seventh New Collegiate Dictionary*, p. 444].

Supreme Court Justice Stewart once said of pornography that he couldn't define it, "But I know it when I see it." Most of us would second

---

[7] We will provide a lengthy discussion of these differences in Section III B.

his statement with regard to intimate relationships. We begin with a provisional definition: Intimates are loving persons whose lives are deeply entwined. When we reflect upon such relationships—relationships between best friends, lovers, spouses, and parents and children—it appears that they are generally marked by a number of characteristics, among them the following:

1. INTENSITY OF LIKING (LOVING)

Intimate relationships are carried on by people who like or love each other. Of course, human relationships are complex. Sometimes intimates feel unadulterated liking or love for each other. More often, their affection is veined with occasional feelings of dislike or even hatred. However, if an intimate relationship is to remain intimate, participants must basically like or love each other (see Walster & Walster, 1978).

2. DEPTH AND BREADTH OF INFORMATION EXCHANGE

In casual relationships, individuals usually exchange only the sketchiest of information. Intimates generally share profound information about each other's personal histories, values, strengths and weaknesses, idiosyncrasies, hopes, fears, etc.

Altman and Taylor (1973) provide a painstaking analysis of the social-penetration process. Their comparison of the extremes of intimacy provides a vivid example of the difference between casual and intimate relationships in the amount and kind of information exchanged. Altman and Taylor (1973) conclude that, with few exceptions, as intimacy progresses "interpersonal exchange gradually progresses from superficial, nonintimate areas to more intimate, deeper layers of the selves of the social actors [p. 6]." The more intimate we are with someone, the more information we are willing to reveal to him, and the more we expect him to reveal to us (see Altman & Taylor, 1973; Huesmann & Levinger, 1976; Jourard, 1971; & Worthy, Gary, & Kahn, 1968).

3. LENGTH OF RELATIONSHIP

Casual relationships are usually short-term. Intimate relationships are expected to endure, and generally do endure, over a long period of time. For example, Toffler (1970) cites husband–wife relationships and parent–child relationships as the most enduring of all relationships. " 'Til death do us part" is still our cultural ideal for marriage. This fact has two important consequences for the way equity principles operate in intimate relationships.

Perception of Inequity.   It should be easier to calculate equity in casual relationships than in intimate ones, for over a short span it is easy to assess who owes whom what. Strangers in a bar, for example, need only remember who bought the last drink to determine who should pick up the tab for the next. In intimate relationships it is far more difficult to calculate equity: Should the drinks I served my husband when we were dating count when determining who should pay for the case of Scotch we bought today? How far back in a relationship is it fair to go in making such calculations? In the short-term relationships equity theorists have studied heretofore, participants could usually distinguish what was equitable from what was not with some ease. We suspect, however, that participants in intimate relationships may have a far harder time defining equity–inequity.

Tolerance of Perceived Inequity.   Participants in casual and intimate relationships are likely to differ in regard to when perceived inequities should be redressed. Those in casual relationships are more likely to feel that unless existing imbalances are redressed soon they will probably never be redressed at all. Intimates, committed to long-range interaction, are more likely to be tolerant of imbalances, since they know that they will have ample time to set things right.

4. VALUE OF RESOURCES EXCHANGED

A number of exchange theorists (Aronson, 1970; Huesmann & Levinger, 1976; and Levinger & Snolk, 1972) have observed that as a relationship grows in intimacy, the value of the rewards and punishments a pair can give one another increases.

a. Value of rewards.   Many theorists have observed that intimates' rewards are especially potent. For example, Huesmann and Levinger's (1976) elegant incremental exchange model of dyadic interaction has as its fundamental assumption: "that the expected value of a dyad's rewards increases as the depth of the relationship increases . . . [p. 196]." Levinger, Senn, and Jorgensen (1970) point out that a reward such as the compliment "I'm glad I met you" is far more potent when it comes from an intimate than when it comes from a casual acquaintance. Moreover, intimates possess a bigger storehouse of rewards than acquaintances do. People are usually willing to invest far more of their resources in an intimate relationship than in a casual one. Thus, intimates are able to provide their partners with more valuable rewards (time, effort, intimate information, money, etc.) than acquaintances are.

b. Value of punishments.   The punishments intimates can inflict on each other are as potent as the rewards they can exchange. For example, if a stranger at a party loudly announces that I am a selfish bore, I lose little; I can dismiss his words as those of a boor who doesn't really know what kind of a person I am. But if my best friend were to tell me the same thing, I would be crushed—she knows me, and thinks that of me! Aronson (1970) put it succinctly: "Familiarity may breed reward, but it also breeds the capacity to hurt."

5. VARIETY OF RESOURCES EXCHANGED

As a relationship grows in intensity, the variety of rewards and punishments a pair can exchange increases. Recent theoretical and empirical work by Uriel Foa and his associates provide a useful framework for discussing this point. Foa and others (see Donnenworth & Foa, 1974; Foa, 1971; Teichman, 1971; and Turner, Foa, & Foa, 1971) have argued that the resources of interpersonal exchange fall into six classes: (a) love, (b) status, (c) information, (d) money, (e) goods, and (f) services. We suspect that casual as compared with intimate relationships differ markedly in both the types and the variety of resources exchanged. In casual exchanges, participants exchange only a few types of resources. Furthermore, since casual relationships are such short-term relationships, participants probably feel lucky if they can manage to negotiate an exchange only of those resources whose value is commonly understood—such as money, goods, and services. They simply are not in business long enough to work out any very complicated exchanges. Thus, their exchanges may be expected to be focused primarily on money and goods.

We suspect that in intimate exchanges, however, participants exchange resources from all six of the aforementioned classes. Like participants in a casual relationship, intimates can exchange money, goods, and services. But they also negotiate exchanges involving love, status, and information—it may even be that they are primarily concerned with such exchanges.

The contrast between the two kinds of relationships in regard to exchange suggests a second reason why it is easier for acquaintances than for intimates to calculate equity. The former exchange resources of set value. The latter exchange set-value commodities *plus* commodities of indeterminate value. It is no wonder, then, that intimates may find the calculation of equity–inequity a mind-boggling task.

6. SUBSTITUTABILITY OF RESOURCES

Within a particular exchange, participants in a casual relationship, we would venture, tend to be limited to exchanging resources from the same class, whereas intimates have far more freedom to exchange resources from entirely different classes. Casual relationships usually exist in a single context where like is exchanged for like. Consider, for example, an academic context: If I lend my notes to the classmate I see three times a week, I expect to be repaid in kind the next time I miss a lecture. If I invite my neighbor to a dinner party, I expect to be invited to one. In contrast, intimate relationships exist in a variety of contexts. Participants have at their disposal the whole range of interpersonal resources, and freely exchange one type of resource for another. Thus, the wife who owes her husband money can pay him back in a number of ways: She can defer to his wish to go golfing on Sunday (status), or bake him a special dinner (services), or tell him how much she loves him and how grateful she is for his generosity (love). These responses may be less satisfactory to her husband than direct monetary repayment, but not necessarily so. Intimates spend much of their time negotiating the values and exchangeability of various behaviors—the terms, so to speak, of their relationship. This is what much of getting acquainted is all about (see Scanzoni, 1972).

Once again, our comparison of the variety of resources involved in casual and intimate relationships leads us to the conclusion that it is easier to calculate equity in casual relationships than in intimate ones.

7. THE UNIT OF ANALYSIS: FROM YOU AND ME TO WE

Intimates, through identification with and empathy for their partners, come to define themselves as a unit—as one couple. They see themselves not merely as individuals interacting with others but also as part of a partnership, interacting with other individuals, partnerships, and groups. This characteristic may have a dramatic impact on intimates' perceptions of what is and what is not equitable.

Just what do we mean when we say that intimates see themselves as a unit? Perhaps the simplest way of describing this wholeness is by saying the unit is a *we*. Manifestations of this we-ness are the joy and pride parents feel at the success and happiness of their child ("That's our boy!"); the distress a wife experiences when her husband has been denied a hoped-for opportunity; the intense pleasure a lover feels while striving to make his beloved happy (see Boulding, 1973). Now, of course, parents, the wife, and the lover are directly affected by what happens to their partners. The parents may be supported in their old age by a successful son; the wife's household allowance as well as the husband's suffers when the husband is denied his hoped-for promotion; the lover may receive affection for his labors. But intimates' identification with their partners may cause them to experience genuine, first-hand emotions aside from such returns. A number of theorists have noted that intimates' outcomes often become hopelessly intertwined. Blau (1964), for instance, speculates, "The repeated experience of being rewarded by the increased attachment of a loved one after having done a variety of things to please him may have the effect that giving pleasure to loved ones becomes intrinsically gratifying [p. 77]."

What implications does the we-ness phenomenon have for the application of equity theory to intimate relationships? There is one very important implication. Equity theorists have always known that to explain and predict the behavior of individuals in a relationship, one must first be able to define the relationship—one must know who is interacting or relating with whom. The student of intimate relationships must constantly ask what is happening in the intimate relationship at the moment of observation. Are the individuals relating to each other as individuals? Or are they relating as a couple to others? If the intimates are relating as a couple to others, then the individual members are no longer the appropriate unit of analysis. It is the couple's inputs and outcomes which are important, and which form the basis for a prediction of the behavior of the individual members as a twosome.

C. Summary

In this section, we have maintained that the same equity processes operate in both casual and intimate relationships. We have acknowledged that casual and intimate relationships differ in a number of ways: (a) in the intensity of liking (loving), (b) in the depth and breadth of information exchange, (c) in the time span of the relationship, (d) in the value of resources exchanged, (e) in the variety of resources exchanged, (f) in the substitutability of resources, (g) in the unit of analysis (from You and Me to We). The fact the casual and intimate relations differ in so many important ways should affect (a) how easy or how difficult it is to calculate equity in a relationship and (b) how casual acquaintances and how intimates choose to restore equity.

We can now return to our original question: Is there any evidence that equity considerations shape not only casual interactions but intimate ones as well? There is some. In Section IV we will describe the NIMH project which pinpoints the equity hypotheses that need to be tested, and review the sparse experimental evidence that has already been collected in an effort to determine whether or not equity theory does provide some fresh insights into intimate relations.

IV. The Accumulating Evidence

Recently, we began a project designed to address the question of whether equity applies to intimate relationships.

A. Developing Scales to Measure the Equity–Inequity of a Relationship

Surprisingly, in spite of all the speculation about whether equity is, or is not, important in a relationship, theorists had never taken the trouble to develop any measures to assess how equitable relationships are. Thus, our first step was to develop such scales.

Marriage and family researchers[8]—as well as such social psychologists as Levinger, Murstein, Olson, Rubin, and Susman—have accumulated an abundance of scattered information about what couples think they ought to contribute to their relationships and what they think they have a right to expect from them. Equity researchers have now taken the next step and have developed scales that measure what couples believe they are both contributing to their relationships, what rewards and frustrations they are reaping from them, and, thus, how equitable their relationships are. These scales are the following:

1. THE HATFIELD (1978) GLOBAL MEASURE OF EQUITY–INEQUITY

This measure asks men and women's general impressions about the fairness of their relationship.

> *Considering what you put into your relationship, compared to what you get out of it . . . and what your partner puts in, compared to what s(he) gets out of it, how would you say your relationship "stacks up"?*

+3   I am getting a much better deal than my partner.
+2   I am getting a somewhat better deal.
+1   I am getting a slightly better deal.
0   We are both getting an equally good . . . or bad . . . deal.
−1   My partner is getting a slightly better deal.
−2   My partner is getting a somewhat better deal.
−3   My partner is getting a much better deal than I am.

2. THE TRAUPMANN, UTNE, HATFIELD (1978) SCALES: PARTICIPANTS' PERCEPTIONS OF EQUITY–INEQUITY[9]

This measure is designed to give us a fine-grained analysis of the romantic give and take.

---

[8] See Blood and Wolfe (1960), Burgess and Wallin (1953, Goode (1956), Hops, Wills, Weiss, and Patterson (1972), Hudson and Henzi (1969), Komarovsky (1971), Locke (1951), and Waller (1938).

[9] For detailed description of the administration procedure for these scales, a complete

Couples are asked to assess the fairness of their relationship in four different areas:

1. Personal concerns.
2. Emotional concerns.
3. Day-to-day concerns.
4. Opportunities gained and lost.

The *personal* area includes such characteristics as how attractive spouses are, how sociable, how intelligent. The *emotional* area touches such matters as how much spouses like each other, how much they love each other, their understanding of each others needs, their sexual relationship, and their commitment to the total relationship. *Day-to-day exchange* is concerned with the money they both bring in, the day-to-day maintenance of the house, being easy to live with, fitting in with each other's friends and relatives, and the like.

Another area assessed, *opportunities gained or lost*, includes such things as the opportunity to be married, the opportunity to have children, and such losses as the chance to have married someone else.

As in the *Hatfield (1978) Global Measures*, respondents are asked how their relationship "stacks up" in each of these areas. A total Equity score is calculated by simply summing up a person's responses to each of the 25 items that constitute the index.

Now that equity theorists are able to measure couples' inputs and outcomes and the equity–inequity of their relationships, we are able to move on to some fundamental questions.

B. Determining Whether or Not Equity Theory Provides Some Fresh Insights into Intimate Relations

According to equity theorists, participants in equitable as opposed to inequitable relationships should react in markedly different ways:

1. Men and women in equitable relationships should be fairly content. Men and women who feel they've received either far more, or far less, than they deserve, should be uncomfortable. The more inequitable their relationship, the more distressed they should be.

2. Since inequities are disturbing, couples may be expected to keep chipping away at them over the course of their marriages. Underbenefited men and women, who feel they are contributing far more than their fair share to the relationship, should be motivated to demand more from their partners. Their guilty partners may well agree to cede such rewards. Thus

---

description of the scales themselves, and reliability and validity information, see Traupmann (1978) or contact the authors.

(all things being equal) relationships should become more and more equitable over time.

3. In all marriages, there are certain crises periods, for example, when the dating couple marries, moves in together, and begins to discover what marriage is really like; when the first child arrives; when the children leave home; when the husband loses his job or retires. At such times of precipitous change, a couple may find that their once-equitable relationship is now woefully unbalanced. We would expect that if we contacted couples before such crises, in the midst of such crises, and then again after they had endured them for some time, we would find that the couples had conceived of effective ways to reestablish the equitableness of their relationship, or that their relationship had floundered.

4. When people find themselves enmeshed in markedly inequitable relationships, they may be expected either to work to change them, or to abandon the relationship for a more satisfying one. Thus, we would expect that if we examined equitable versus inequitable couples' marital satisfaction and happiness, their love versus hate, their perceptions of their marriages' permanence, and their divorce rates, we should find that equitable relationships are sturdy relationships, whereas inequitable relationships are fragile ones.

In our forthcoming research, we plan to test these Equity hypotheses.

Let us, then, review the evidence which does exist for each of these hypotheses:

HYPOTHESIS I: *The Impact of Equity on Contentment–Distress*

According to equity theory's Proposition III, couples in equitable relationships should be reasonably content; couples in inequitable relationships should be deeply distressed. Thus, we predict that *the more equitable a couple's relationship, the more satisfied they will be.*[10]

One additional question that anyone interested in the development of relationships would wish to ask is: What happens when inequity persists for a prolonged period—say, for example, when an individual knows full well that he or she is being shabbily treated, but is unable to do anything about it, and is unable to leave (perhaps because of religious sanctions or responsibility to children). Does he or she continue to experience underlying feelings of distress, as equity theory predicts he or she should? Or

---

[10] In pretesting, we found that *most* couples agree as to who is contributing more, and who is contributing less, to the relationship. Now and then, of course, there is disagreement. Both participants may insist *they* are the over-contributing partner—or the under-contributing one. When this happens, we would expect *both* participants to act as if they were the over-contributing (or under-contributing) partner—*both* insisting they are entitled to more (or less).

does injustice, somehow, become something he or she is emotionally resigned to? It is hoped that our data will help us to answer this question.

Previous researchers provide *some* support for Hypothesis I. Some examples: Berscheid *et al.* (1973) posed an intriguing question which is related to our analysis. What happens to a couple that is markedly mismatched—when one partner is clearly superior to the other? The authors predicted that both partners in an inappropriate match would be unhappy. It is obvious why the underbenefited partner should be dissatisfied. Every time he looks around, he realizes that he is sacrificing rewards to which he believes he is entitled. But, they argued, the lucky mate is not really so lucky, after all. The overbenefited mate is confronted with a wrenching dilemma. On the one hand, he is eager to keep his prestigious prize; he is well aware that he has little chance of again attracting so desirable a partner. On the other hand, he is also painfully aware that his partner has little reason to stay with him. For these reasons, Berscheid *et al.* predicted that both partners in an inequitable relationship would feel uneasy about their relationship; they would both suspect that their alliance might be an unstable one (see also Blau, 1964; Waller, 1937).

Berscheid *et al.* (1973) tested Hypothesis I in the following way: The authors requested *Psychology Today* readers to fill out a questionnaire concerning their current dating, mating, or marital relations. They measured readers' perceptions of the equitableness–inequitableness by means of a single question.[11]

Describe your partner's desirability:
 —Much more desirable than I.
 —Slightly more desirable than I.
 —As desirable as I.
 —Slightly less desirable than I.
 —Much less desirable than I.

Then, they asked readers how satisfied they were with their marital relationships. As predicted, readers who were matched with "appropriate" partners were more satisfied with their relationships than were individuals whose partners were far more, or far less desirable, than themselves.

Walster, Walster, and Traupmann (1978) interviewed 500 University of Wisconsin men and women, who were dating casually or steadily. First, they asked students to consider all the things a man or woman could put into and get out of a relationship, and then to estimate how their relationship "stacked up": Did they feel overbenefited?, Equitably treated?, Underbenefited?

---

[11] When Berscheid *et al.* (1973) did their early research, appropriate measures of Equity–Inequity did not yet exist.

Then they asked the men and women:

When you think about your relationship—what you put into it, and what you get out of it—how does that make you feel? How **content** *do you feel? How* **happy** *do you feel? How* **angry** *do you feel? How* **guilty** *do you feel?*

They found that the more equitable a couple's relationship, the more content and the happier they were.

As Table 4.1 indicates, those men and women who feel they are getting far more than they really deserve from their partners feel uncomfortable. They are less content, less happy, and a lot more guilty than their peers. Of course, those men and women who feel they deserve a lot more than they are getting are understandably upset too. They are a lot less content, less happy, and a lot angrier than their peers.

Recently, Jane Traupman (1978) and Mary Utne (1978) asked a random sample of newlyweds—couples who had been married between 3 and 8 months—to participate in an interview study of marriage. They asked couples how fair and equitable they considered their marriages to be. They measured Equity by two different scales[12]: (a) *The Hatfield (1978) Global Measures of Equity–Inequity,* and (b) *The Traupmann, Utne, Walster (1977) Scales: Participants' Perceptions of Equity–Inequity.*

From these estimates, the authors were able to calculate whether men and women considered themselves to be overbenefited, equitably treated, or underbenefited. Couples also completed a series of questionnaires that assessed their level of contentment or distress:

1. Austin's (1974) *Contentment–Distress Measure.*
2. The Locke–Wallace (1959) *Marital Adjustment Test* (modified version).
3. Hatfield's Measures of Passionate and Companionate Love.

Traupmann and Utne proposed that spouses who feel equitably treated will feel happier, more content, less angry, and less guilty than will spouses who feel underbenefited or overbenefited.

As Figure 4.1 illustrates, their hypothesis was confirmed with qualifications. Women in equitable marriages were more content than women who felt overbenefited or underbenefited. [$T-U-W: F_{4227}$(quadratic) $= 3.89$, $p < .5$.] They were also less happy. (But in this case, the F (quadratic) was not significant.) The men's results were similar, except that this time the "content" variable was not quite significant, whereas the "happy" variable was. Equitably treated men were significantly more happy than were their inequitably treated counterparts [F_{4227}(quadratic) $= 5.79$, $p < .01$.] Turning to negative affect, they found a significant curvilinear trend for

---

[12] These scales are available in Walster, Walster and Berscheid (1978).

TABLE 4.1
The Effect of Equity–Inequity on Contentment–Distress

How equitable– inequitable is the relationship?	How content[a]	How happy[a]	How angry[a]	How guilty[a]
Person is getting far more than he feels he deserves.	2.91	3.06	1.54	1.83
Person is getting somewhat more than he feels he deserves.	3.51	3.69	1.36	1.51
Person is getting just what he feels he deserves.	3.51	3.61	1.36	1.31
Person is getting somewhat less than he feels he deserves.	3.26	3.42	1.75	1.44
Person is getting far less than he feels he deserves.	2.70	2.98	1.98	1.39

[a] The higher the number, the more content, happy, angry, or guilty the person feels.

anger—both underbenefited *and* overbenefited women were more angry than the equitably treated women [T−U−W: F_{4227}(quadratic) = 7.08, $p <$ .01]. Overbenefited women were slightly, but not significantly, more guilty than the equitably treated and underbenefited women. The men were remarkably unmoved to guilt or anger. There were no significant differences between the three groups for either anger or guilt. The curve for guilt is virtually a straight line! The results for anger and guilt for women and men are illustrated in Figure 4.1.

Austin's (1978) *Total Mood Index* (reported in Walster, Walster, & Berscheid, 1978), an overall index of affect, was calculated by summing the respondents' "content" and "happy" scores and subtracting their "anger" and "guilt" scores: AFFECT = content + happy − guilty − angry. The higher the total score, the more content (and the less distressed) they are.

These results are also found in Figure 4.1. The curve for women is precisely what was predicted: Equitably treated women are significantly more content (and less distressed) than underbenefited and overbenefited women [T−U−W: F_{4227}(quadratic) = 9.38, $p <$ .01]. The results for men were not significant but did fall into the same pattern as that for women. The means were Underbenefited = 3.65; Equity = 4.53 and Overbenefited = 4.33.

In combination, then, the results for the four "affect" variables lend support to Hypothesis I. Equitably treated, as compared with inequitably

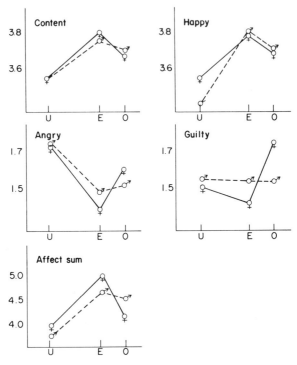

Figure 4.1   The affect variables of content, happy, angry, and guilty and the Austin Total Mood Measure as a function of the perceived equity–inequity in the marriage. ♂ = men; ♀ = women; U = Underbenefited; E = Equitably treated; O = Overbenefited.

treated women, show more positive and less negative affect. Equitably treated, as compared with inequitably treated, men report more positive affect. This pattern of results is especially convincing when one considers that the sample consists of newlyweds. According to cultural lore, for most couples the first year of marriage is blissfully happy—the disagreements are minor, the motivation to please is great. Nevertheless, in this fairly stringent test of the extent to which equity–inequity affects happiness, we see that perceptions that the marital exchange is unfair are related to discontent. We see that feeling underbenefited is damaging. We see that, to a lesser extent, feeling overbenefited is distressing. Equity is the most pleasant state for men and women.

The authors also expected equitably treated spouses to feel happier and more satisfied with their marriages than spouses who feel underbenefited or spouses who feel overbenefited.

The authors found strong confirmation for this hypothesis, for both men and women. Equitably treated men were significantly more happy with their marriages than overbenefited or underbenefited men [T–U–W: F_{4227}(quadratic) $= 14.08$, $p < .001$] and they were more satisfied with their marriages [T–U–W: F_{4227}(quadratic) $=$ 6.37, $p <$ .01]. Equitably treated women were also happier and more satisfied with their marriages than were their deprived or indulged counterparts. For the women, the (T–U–W) Fs were 7.31, $p <$ .01 for the "happy with marriage" responses and 4.78, $p <$ .05 for the "satisfied with marriage" responses. Figure 4.2 plots mean responses to the happiness and satisfaction questions for the underbenefited, equitably treated, and overbenefited men and women.

Hypotheses II–IV: The Restoration of Equity–Inequity

If we find that couples in equitable relationships are content, whereas those in equitable ones are deeply distressed, what then? According to equity theory's Proposition IV, when couples find themselves enmeshed in an inequitable relationship, they will be motivated to do one of three things to get things right: (a) They will work to make their relationship actually more equitable. Or (b) they will try to convince themselves (and their partner) that their relationship is really more equitable than it seems (they will try to restore psychological equity). Or (c) they will abandon their inequitable relationship.

1. RESTORATION OF ACTUAL EQUITY

One way participants in an inequitable relationship can restore equity is by inaugurating real changes in the relationship. Consider, for example, a marriage in which the husband is the overcontributing partner, the wife the undercontributing one. The overcontributing partner— who feels that he is contributing far more than his fair share to the relationship—will naturally be motivated to set things right by demanding better treatment from his partner. The undercontributing partner— who is contributing less than her share—may well reluctantly agree to grant such rewards:

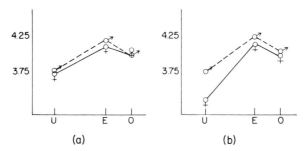

Figure 4.2 Satisfaction (a) and happiness (b) with marriage as a function of perceived equity–inequity in the marriage.

Physical attractiveness: The overcontributing partner can easily slip into becoming careless about the stylishness of his dress, his cleanliness, or his diet.

Conversation: The overcontributing partner might begin to feel that he's entitled to conversation or solitude, whichever is his inclination, and that he's entitled to be as grumpy as he pleases, and so on.

Finances: He might feel a little less pressure to work hard (or to save money) merely so that his partner's wants can be fulfilled.

Expressions of Love and Affection: He might become a little less careful about reassuring his partner of his love and admiration.

Self-sacrifice: He might become especially reluctant to make sacrifices for his partner's benefit. When an argument arises over who should take the car in for servicing, or over whose mother they should visit at Christmas, or over whether they should go to a play or go on a hunting trip, he might be inclined to take a strong stand.

Sex: The person who feels he is already putting too much into the marriage may well feel reluctant to sacrifice himself to make his partner's life fulfilling. He might feel that his partner should be as warm or as aloof as *he* prefers; that his partner should be willing to explore the sexual practices that *he* likes; that she should be tolerant of *his* extramarital affairs, but refrain from making him jealous and insecure.

Of course, the reactions of the undercontributing partner (assumed, in this case, to be the wife) would be quite different. She, believing she's already getting much more than she deserves, might be especially eager to set things right by agreeing to treat the partner better. There are a variety of ways, then, that a mismatched couple can restore actual equity to their relationship.

There are some anecdotal data showing that couples do try to "fine-tune" their relationships in such practical ways. See, for example, Jones (in Palmer [1974]), Komarovsky (1971), and Bakke (1940a,b).

2. RESTORATION OF PSYCHOLOGICAL EQUITY

Of course, sometimes people find it harder to change their behavior than to change their minds. Sometimes couples threatened by the discovery that their relationship is an unbalanced and unstable one prefer to close their eyes and to reassure themselves that, really, everything is in perfect order.

In intimate relationships, participants may find it fairly easy to restore psychological equity. Earlier, we attempted to enumerate characteristics of casual versus intimate relationships; we concluded that they differed in numerous ways, and that the long-term, complex nature of intimate relatiuonships means that, even in the best of circumstances, it is extremely difficult for partners to calculate their relationship's equitableness–inequitableness. If participants expand their horizons and try to calculate how equitable–inequitable a relationship will be over the course of a lifetime, such calculations become virtually impossible.

Probably many couples, then, when confronted with the fact that the balance of their marriage has changed, find it easiest to restore psychological equity to their relationship, and to convince themselves that these changes are not real changes, or that they are not really very important.

For example, the neglected wife might try to convince herself that her husband really loves her more than she thought he did, that working all the time is really evidence of his concern for her. Or she might convince herself that after he graduates, gets a job, gets promoted, or retires he will rectify what has been wrong or disappointing.

If equity theorists' speculations are correct, we would predict that couples, throughout their marriage, will try to improve the balance of their marriages. If couples are as concerned with equity as we think they are, we would expect to find two things occurring in the marriages we have chosen to investigate.

HYPOTHESIS II: *The longer a couple has been married, the more equitable everyone (i.e., both outside observers and the participants themselves) will perceive their relationship to be.*

HYPOTHESIS III: *Critical Periods in a Relationship*

Probably the strongest evidence that couples are profoundly concerned with the equitableness–inequitableness of their relationship might come from the observation of couples whose relationships are in the process of undergoing precipitous change. Marital shifts may be produced by a variety of factors:

a. Getting Acquainted. Regardless of how well engaged or newly married couples think they know each other, they are likely to make some marked discoveries about their own and their partner's characteristics once they began living together. Participants may come to realize that the relationship they thought would be so equitable is, in fact, grossly inequitable.

b. Having Children. When a couple has their first child, the balance of their relationship may shift remarkably.

c. Day-to-Day Changes. Over the years, people change. The shy young bride may become less shy and far more witty and compassionate after raising four or five impish children. Her devil-may-care bridegroom may settle down and become far more dependable, and more irritable, than the man she married. Such mundane changes as these may produce inequities.

d. Dramatic Changes.   Sometimes dramatic changes occur in partner's inputs. The ugly-duckling wife may join Weight Watchers and emerge a beautiful swan. Eventually, the impoverished medical student is transformed into an affluent doctor. The once good provider may be laid off. The handsome soldier may become a scarred paraplegic. Such changes may, of course, drastically alter a relationship's balance.

e. Retirement.   When a man or woman retires, the perceived equity of his or her relationships may shift markedly.

One exciting question that equity theorists have asked is: What effect do such changes in the equitableness–inequitableness of a relationship have on the dynamic equilibrium of a marriage? Equity theorists have maintained that the smallest of changes in a marriage's balance are likely to send reverberations throughout the entire system.

As an ancillary proposition of Hypothesis III, we maintain that: If we examine marriages at the time of crisis, we may well find them to be markedly inequitable. However, if we reexamine them many months later, we will find that, somehow, participants have found a way to begin to set things right. (See Figure 4.3 for a graphic depiction of this process.)

3. EQUITY THEORY VERSUS THE ALTERNATIVES

In this chapter, we have focused on the equity perspective so exclusively that it might seem as if the equity perspective were obviously the only valid one. We are fully aware, however, that Hypotheses I–III are controversial. Here are just two questions critics might pose:

a. Are happily married couples concerned with equity?   We should take a moment here to remind our readers that eminent marriage-and-the-family researchers and social psychologists have argued that (a) happily married couples should not be, and are not, concerned with equity, and (b) thus, there is no necessary connection between a relationship's duration and its equitableness, or, if there is, the relationship is the *opposite* of what we hypothesize. Moreover, Murstein et al. (1977) and Rubin (1973) argue that the time to calculate whether or not a relationship is equitable is *before* marriage. After that, it's too late. When one tries to keep tabs on a continuing relationship, the effort is destructive as well as futile. They maintain that equity considerations operate more strongly in dating relationships than in marital ones.

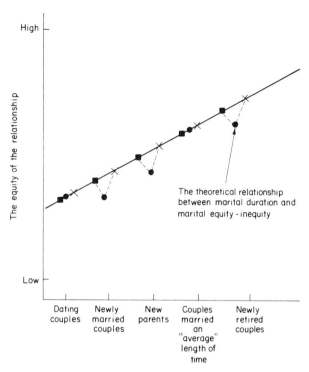

The theoretical relationship between marital duration and marital equity - inequity

Figure 4.3   The impact of an initial "crisis," followed by the passage of time on marital equity–inequity. ■—theoretical precrisis level of equity–inequity; ●—initial interview; X—second interview (1 year later).

An exchange-orientation . . . [was] . . . hypothesized to be quite appropriate for limited or beginning friendships, and exchange–exchange couples were predicted to develop greater friendship intensity than other combinations. . . . Perceived exchange equity is almost impossible to attain in marriage because of greater sensitivity to self than to others. It was hypothesized that exchange-orientation is inimical to marriage adjustment, with exchange–exchange couples being less happy than other possible exchange combinations (exchange–nonexchange, nonexchange–nonexchange) [p. 1].

Other social psychologists have admitted that there is good reason to argue both ways. They simply cannot predict whether equity considerations will be more important in dating or in marital relationships. On the one hand, one could argue that dating couples would be most prone to believe their relationship was equitable. Dating couples and newlyweds probably have only the sketchiest of ideas of what their partners are really like. Thus, they find it very easy to believe what they would like to believe. Long-married couples, on the other hand, have been forced to expose their illusions to reality. They are likely to have a painfully accurate idea of what their partners are really like. Thus, it may be that newlyweds find it far easier to believe that they are about to reap all the good things they so deserve than their more experienced counterparts do.

Yet, one might make the opposite prediction, maintaining that mar-. ried couples should be most prone to insist that their relationship is equitable. When one is trying to decide whether or not to marry, it is critically important to view reality with a clear eye. Once one has made the decision and is committed to it, however, it is less important to see things as they are; one is free to believe what one would like to believe. (There is evidence in support of this contention. For example, Festinger, 1964, found that before decision and commitment have occurred, individuals process data in an objective way. Brehm and Cohen, 1962, found that soon after a couple becomes engaged, they begin to convince themselves that engagement is a good idea.)

In any case, we hope that from our data, we will be able to determine whether it is in new or in well-established relationships that love is most equitable and/or "blind."

Critics might well raise a second set of objections with regard to the preceeding equity speculations.

b. Are couples concerned with equity or with quid-pro-quo or with power? Even theorists who are convinced that exchange principles apply in both casual and intimate relationships sometimes have radically different ideas of what exchange principles really count in relationships. They have proffered three radically different suggestions as to what factors count. Two groups of theorists—whose who support the equity formulation and those who support the quid-pro-quo formulation—insist that people are concerned about the fairness of their intimate relationships. The third group discounts fairness altogether.

1. Are couples concerned with equity? (The Equity Formulation) Equity theory insists that participants in both casual and intimate relationships consider both (a) what they and their partners are contributing to their relationship, and (b) what they are getting out of it, in calculating equity–inequity. According to equity theorists, couples *are* motivated to maintain a fair and equitable relationship.

$$\frac{(O_A - I_A)}{(\,|I_A|\,)^{k_A}} = \frac{(O_B - I_B)}{(\,|I_B|\,)^{k_B}}$$

2. Or are couples concerned with quid-pro-quo? (The Clinicians' Quid-Pro-Quo Formulation) Other theorists argue that casual relationships and intimate ones are different. In casual relationships, these theorists maintain, participants are well aware that contributions may be of far different value. An intimate relationship, however, is by definition a relationship between equals. Thus, clinicians insist, couples' day-to-day negotiations are far simpler than equity theorists think. A person, to calculate whether or not he is being fairly treated, need only make one simple determination: Am I getting as much as my partner is from this relationship?

$$\frac{(O_A - I_A)}{1} = \frac{(O_B - I_B)}{1}$$

3. Or are couples concerned with power? (The What-the-Market-Will-Bear Formulation)   Finally, another group of exchange theorists insist that fairness is irrelevant—all that counts in this world is power. Such theorists argue that what matters is not how a person is treated in his existing relationships (i.e., fairly or unfairly) but how well he could fare in an "open market." According to these theorists, the important thing to determine is who has the power in a given relationship. From this perspective, the important question is who—oneself or one's partner—would find it easier to secure a new partner as attractive as the present one if forced to seek a new one. One could tap power in questions such as the following:

> If **you** found yourself unattached again, for whatever reason, and wanted to find a new partner, how easy or difficult would that be? How do you think you would fare? That is, how would the new partner compare with your present partner?"

> If **your partner** were unattached again, and wanted to find a new partner, how easy or difficult would that be? How do you think your partner would fare in finding a new partner? That is, how would the new partner compare with you?"

In any case, from our data we will eventually be able to determine whether equity theory or its two popular competitors—the quid-pro-quo formulation or the what-the-market-will-bear formulation—is the best predictor of the mode of a couple's interaction.

Let us turn now to the equity theorists' final hypothesis:

HYPOTHESIS IV. *Equitable relationships will be stable relationships; inequitable relationships will be fragile ones.*

According to the equity theorists dating couples should be more likely to progress toward marriage if their relationship is equitable than if it is not; married couples should be more likely to stay married if their relationship is equitable than if it is not.

Exchange theorists (see Backman & Secord, 1966, and Blau, 1968) have long argued in favor of such a "matching hypothesis." They have proposed that the more equitable a romantic relationship, the more likely it is to progress to marriage. Equity theorists have also argued that the more equitable a marital relationship is, the more likely it is to endure.

Walster *et al.* (1973)—along with Adams and Freedman (1976), Bernard (1964), McCall (1966), Scanzoni (1972), and Thibaut and Fachaux (1965)—point out that if a couple's relationship becomes grossly inequitable, the couple should be tempted to sever it. Of course, it is far easier for dating couples than for married couples to part. The dating couples who break up suffer, but, as Bohannan (1971) documents, the married couples who divorce suffer even more: Their parents and friends express shock, one partner may lose rights to the children, and their close friends may drop them; it is, moreover, expensive to secure a divorce and to establish and maintain two households. Divorce, then, is costly in both emotional and financial terms. Yet equity theorists argue that if a marital relationship is unbalanced enough, and if couples can find no better way than divorce to set things right, participants may be expected to part. Udry (1971) calculates that from 20 to 25% of first marriages end in annulment, desertion, or divorce.

THE EXISTING EVIDENCE

Is there any evidence that equity considerations operate both in determining who gets together in the first place, and in determining who stays together? Is there any evidence that people end up with partners who are no better and no worse than they deserve? For years, marriage-and-the-family researchers have explored the process of homogamy (the tendency for similar individuals to be attracted to each other). This literature provides evidence that if a person possesses only one important asset in common with a prospective partner—say, physical attractiveness, or intelligence, or understanding and concern—he will be more successful than his peers who possess none in attracting and keeping that partner.

a. Beauty. A number of researchers have demonstrated that couples tend to date and marry those who are similar in physical attractiveness (see Berscheid & Walster, 1974; Huston, 1973; Murstein, 1972; Rubin (in press); Silverman, 1971; Stroebe *et al.*, 1971; Walster *et al.*, 1966).

b. Mental Health. Most clinicians agree that mentally healthy people, and emotionally disturbed people tend to pair up with their own kind. Perhaps Edmund Bergler (1948), a psychoanalyst, presents the case more strongly than anyone else:

> All stories about a normal woman who becomes the prey of a neurotic man, and vice versa, [sic] or a normal man who falls in love with a highly neurotic woman, are literary fairy tales. Real life is less romantic; two neurotics look for each other with uncanny regularity. Nothing is left to chance as far as emotional attachments are concerned [p. 11].

Equity theorists, of course, might interpret Bergler's data a little differently. It may be the case that both normal people and neurotics *desire* well-adjusted partners, but that only the former are able to attract and hold them. The neurotics must settle for partners whose adjustment is as poor as their own. In any case, there is some relatively hard evidence that people tend to date and marry those who are similar in level of adjustment (see, for example, Burgess & Wallin, 1953; Gottesman, 1965; Murstein, 1967a; and Murstein, 1967b).

c. *Physical Health.*   Eugenicists have observed that people are likely to marry partners who possess comparable physical disabilities. (See, for example, Spuhler, 1968.)

d. *Intelligence and Education.*   A great deal of attention has been given to the fact that people tend to pair up with partners who are similar in education and intelligence. (Evidence that men and women marry partners of comparable intelligence comes from Garrison, Anderson, & Reed, 1968; Jones, 1974; and Reed & Reed, 1965. Evidence that they marry partners of comparable educational attainment comes from Garrison, Anderson, & Reed, 1968; and Kiser, 1968.)

e. *Matching: More Complex Cases.*   Thus far, we have reviewed only the evidence that documents people's tendency to pair up with partners who possess traits identical with their own. Of course, previous theorists have noted that couples can be matched in a variety of ways. And we have contended that exchanges go on across as well as within resource types. For example, the handsome man (who is not especially dependable, warm, etc.) may use his assets to capture a beautiful partner, or he may decide to pursue a partner who is far plainer than himself, but far more dependable and warm. Murstein *et al.* (1977) provide a compelling description of the way such complex matching might operate:

> A handsome man is seen with a woman of mediocre attractiveness. "I wonder what he sees in her?" may be the quizzical question of a bystander. Quite possibly, she possesses compensating qualities such as greater intelligence, interpersonal competence, and wealth than he, of which the bystander knows nothing. . . .
>
> Another case of compensatory exchange might be indicated if an aged statesmen proposed marriage to a young beautiful woman. He would probably be trading his prestige and power for her physical attractiveness and youth [p. 3–4].

These is some evidence, sparse, in support of the contention that people do engage in such complicated balancing and counter-balancing when selecting mates (see, for example, Elder, 1969; Holmes & Hatch, 1938; and Berscheid *et al.*, 1973).

We have already described a study, based on interviews with 500 students, by Walster *et al.* (1978). Early in the questionnaire used, the students were asked to estimate how much they and their partners contributed to their relationship and how much they and their partners got out of it. From these estimates it was possible to determine how equitable or inequitable the students perceived their relationships to be. After asking the students a series of questions about their involvement, Walster *et al.* finished by asking them how long they thought their affair would last. They asked: "Are you still going with your partner?" "How certain are you that the two of you will be together one year from now?" "five years from now?" They found that men and women involved in equitable relationships were the most optimistic about the future of their relationships. (See Table 4.2). Men and women who felt their relationship was fair and equitable generally felt that it was currently a viable one, and were "somewhat certain" it would be that way a year or so from now. Men or women who knew that they were getting far more than they deserved from the relationship had every reason to hope it would last, but were not very optimistic that it would. (They were "somewhat" to "very" uncertain that their affair would last a year or more.) Men or women who felt they were getting far less from the relationship than they deserved were even more pessimistic about the future of their relationship.

TABLE 4.2
The Effect of Equity–Inequity on the Perceived Stability of a Relationship

Equity–inequity of Relationship	Are you currently going with partner?[a]	How certain are you that you will still be going together[b]	
		One year from now?	Five years from now?
Person is getting far more than he feels he deserves	1.44	1.68	1.37
Person is getting somewhat more than he feels he deserves.	1.73	2.10	1.56
Person is getting just what he feels he deserves.	1.75	2.60	2.11
Person is getting somewhat less than he feels he deserves.	1.69	2.23	1.73
Person is getting far less than he feels he deserves.	1.47	1.48	1.06

[a] A score of 1 = "No"; 2 "Yes"
[b] The higher the number, the more certain the man or woman is that the relationship will last.

Earlier we described a study in which Jane Traupmann and Mary Utne interviewed newlyweds about their marriages. In this study, the authors measured newlyweds' perceptions of how overbenefited, equitably treated, or underbenefited they were in their marriages as well as how stable they believed their marriages to be. The authors proposed that spouses who feel equitably treated will perceive their marriages to be more stable than will spouses who feel underbenefited or overbenefited. The authors measured perceived stability in marriage by asking their respondents how often they had considered moving out and how often they had considered divorce. To some extent these escape fantasies correlated with inequity.

Men who felt underbenefited were more likely to report that they had considered moving out than the equitably treated or overbenefited men [T−U−W: F_{4227} (linear) = 9.26, p < .01]. Underbenefited men were also more likely to have considered divorce [T−U−W: F_{4227}(linear) = 9.26, p < .01). (See Figure 4.4).

Though inequities don't seem to be related to ideas of moving out for women [(T−U−W) Fs were insignificant], there is a strong tendency for overbenefited women, compared with equitably treated and underbenefited women, to consider divorce [T−U−W: F_{4227}(quadratic) = 6.17, p < .01].

Despite the newness of these marriages, there are signs of instability in the inequitable relationships.

Walster, Traupmann, and Walster (1978) argued that inequitable relationships might be fragile relationships for still another reason. The man or woman who feels cheated in his or her marriage may be tempted to do some "cheating" of their own.

Walster, Traupmann, and Walster (1978) predicted that the more cheated a person feels in marriage the more likely the person will be to risk illicit, extramarital sex. To test this hypothesis, they retrieved the Berscheid et al. (1973) data and reanalyzed them. As before, they consid-

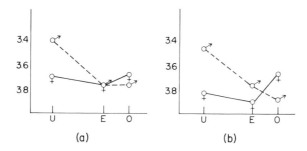

Figure 4.4 Reported functions of considerations of (a) moving out or (b) divorce as a function of the perceived equity–inequity in marriage.

ered overbenefited respondents to be those whose partners were much more or slightly more socially desirable than themselves. Equitably treated respondents were those whose partners were as socially desirable as themselves. *Deprived* respondents were those whose partners were slightly less or much less desirable than themselves.

Berscheid *et al.* assessed readers' willingness to engage in extramarital sex in two ways: (a) they asked how soon after they had begun living with or had got married to their partner they had first had sex with someone else. (b) they asked with how many people they had had extramarital affairs.

The results (see Figure 4.5) provide some support for the Walster *et al.* hypotheses: Overbenefited and equitably treated men and women were very reluctant to experiment with extramarital sex. On the average, overbenefited and equitably treated men and women waited from 12 to 15 years before getting involved with someone else. Deprived men and women began exploring extramarital sex far earlier—from 6 to 8 years after marriage. Similarly, the overbenefited had the fewest extramarital encounters (none or one). Equitably treated men and women had a few more. The deprived had the most (from one to three).

Once again, we see that, for a variety of reasons, equitable relations are likely to be more stable than inequitable ones.

Is equity theory useful for understanding intimate as well as nonintimate relationships? Can we use equity theory to make sense of the interplay between husband and wife? The preceeding evidence suggests that the answer is affirmative.

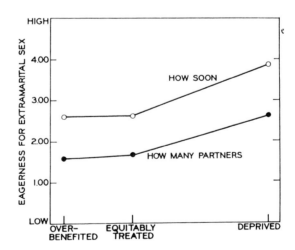

Figure 4.5 The impact of marital overbenefit or equity or deprivation on men and women's eagerness to engage in extramarital sex.

Summary

Equity theory does seem to provide a convenient method of examining romantic and marital relationships. And the data, however sparse, provide at least suggestive evidence that equity principles operate in determining whom one selects as a mate and how the partners will get along. Obviously, however, more research will have to be done before we can have greater confidence in these conclusions.

References

Adams, J. S. Toward an understanding of inequity. *Journal of Abnormal and Social Psychology*, 1963, 67, 422–436.

Adams, J. S., & Freedman, S. Equity theory revisited: Comments and annotated bibliography. In L. Berkowitz & E. Walster (Eds.), *Advances in experimental social psychology*. New York: Academic Press, 1976.

Altman, I., & Taylor, D. A. *Social penetration: The development of interpersonal relationships*. New York: Holt, Rinehart, Winston, 1973.

Aronson, E. Some antecedents of interpersonal attraction. In W. J. Arnold & D. Levine (Eds.), *Nebraska symposium on motivation*. Lincoln: Univ. of Nebraska Press, 1970.

Austin, W. G. *Studies in "Equity with the World:" A new application of Equity Theory*. Ph.D. Thesis, University of Wisconsin, 1974.

Austin, W., & Walster, W. Participants' reactions to "Equity with the World." *Journal of Experimental Social Psychology*, 1974, 10, 528–548.

Backman, C. W., & Secord, R. F. The compromise process and the affect structure of groups. In C. W. Backman & P. F. Secord (Eds.), *Problems in social psychology*. New York: McGraw-Hill, 1966.

Bakke, E. W. *The unemployed worker: A study of the task of making a living without a job*. New Haven: Yale Univ., 1940a.

Bakke, E. W. *Citizens without work*. New Haven: Yale Univ., 1940b.

Bergler, E. *Divorce Won't Help*. New York: Harper and Brothers, 1948.

Bernard, J. The adjustments of married mates. In H. T. Christensen (Ed.), *Handbook of marriage and the family*. Chicago: Rand McNally, 1964.

Berscheid, E., & Walster, E. When does a harm-doer compensate a victim? *Journal of Personality and Social Psychology*, 1967, 6, 435–441.

Berscheid, E., & Walster, E. A little bit about love. In T. L. Huston (Ed.), *Foundations of interpersonal attraction*. New York: Academic Press, 1974.

Berscheid, E., Walster, E., & Barclay, A. Effect of time on tendency to compensate a victim. *Psychological Reports*, 1969, 25, 431–436.

Berscheid, E., Walster, E., & Bohrnstedt, G. The body image report. *Psychology Today*, 1973, 7, 119–131.

Blau, P. M. *Exchange and power in social life*. New York: Wiley, 1964.

Bohannan, P. *Divorce and after*. Garden City, New York: Doubleday, 1971.

Boulding, E. *The economy of love and fear*. Belmont, California: Wadsworth, 1973.

Brehm, J. W., & Cohen, A. R. *Explorations in cognitive dissonance*. New York: Wiley, 1962.

Burgess, E. W., & Wallin, P. *Engagement and marriage*. Philadelphia: Lippincott, 1953.

Buss, A. *The psychology of aggression*. New York: Wiley, 1961.

Donnenwerth, G. V., & Foa, U. G. Effect of resource class on retaliation to injustice in interpersonal exchange. *Journal of Personality and Social Psychology,* 1974, *29,* 785–793.

Douvan, E. Interpersonal relationships: Some questions and observations. In G. Levinger & H. L. Raush. *Close relationships on the meaning of intimacy.* Amherst, Massachusetts: Univ. of Massachusetts Press, 1977.

Elder, G. H., Jr. Appearance and education in marriage mobility. *American Sociological Review,* 1969, *34,* 519–533.

Festinger, L. *Conflict, decision, and dissonance.* Stanford, California: Stanford Univ. Press, 1964.

Foa, U. G. Interpersonal and economic resources. *Science,* 1971, *171,* 345–351.

Fromm, E. *The art of loving.* New York: Harper, 1956.

Garrison, R. J., Anderson, V. E., & Reed, S. C. Assortive marriage. *Eugenics Quarterly,* 1968, *15,* 113–127.

Gottesman, I. I. Personality and natural selection. In S. G. Vandenberg (Ed.), *Methods and goals in human behavior genetics.* New York: Academic Press, 1965.

Holmes, S. J., & Hatch, C. D. Personal appearance as related to scholastic records and marriage selection in college women. *Human Biology,* 1938, *10,* 65–76.

Huston, T. L. Ambiguity of acceptance, social desirability, and dating choice. *Journal of Experimental Social Psychology,* 1973, *9,* 32–42.

Huesmann, L. R., & Levinger, G. Incremental exchange theory: A formal model for progression in dyadic social interaction. In L. Berkowitz & E. Walster (Eds.), *Advances in experimental social psychology* (Vol. 9), New York: Academic Press, 1976.

Jones, A. Reported in Marjorie Palmer, "Marriage and the formerly fat: The effect weight loss has on your life together." *Weight Watchers,* 1974, *7*(2), 23–50.

Jourard, S. M. *Self-disclosure.* New York: Wiley, 1971.

Kiser, C. V. Assortative mating by educational attainment in relation to fertility. *Eugenic Quarterly,* 1968, *15*(2), 98–112.

Komarovsky, M. *The unemployed man and his family.* New York: Octagon, 1971.

Lederer, W. J., & Jackson, D. D. *The mirages of marriage.* New York: Norton, 1968.

Levinger, G., Senn, D. J., & Jorgensen, P. W. Progress toward permanence in courtship: A test of Kerckhoff-Davis hypotheses. *Sociometry,* 1970, *33,* 427–443.

Levinger, G., & Snoek, J. D. *Attraction in relationship: A new look at interpersonal attraction.* Morristown, N.J.: General Learning Press, 1972.

May, R. *Man's search for himself.* New York: Norton, 1953.

McCall, M. M. Courtship as social exchange: Some historical comparisons. In B. Farber (Eds.), *Kinship and family organization.* New York: Wiley, 1966.

Mills, J. *Interpersonal attraction in exchange and communal relationships.* Unpublished manuscript, University of Maryland, 1975.

Moscovici, S. Society and theory in social psychology. In J. Israel & H. Tajfel (Eds.), *The context of social psychology: A critical assessment.* New York: Academic Press, 1972.

Murstein, B. I. The relationship of mental health to marital choice and courtship progress. *Journal of Marriage and the Family,* 1967a, *29,* 447–451.

Murstein, B. I. Empirical tests of role, complementary needs, and homogamy theories of marital choice. *Journal of Marriage and the Family,* 1967b, *29,* 689–696.

Murstein, B. I. Physical attractiveness and marital choice. *Journal of Personality and Social Psychology,* 1972, *22*(1), 8–12.

Murstein, B. I., Cerreto, M., & MacDonald, M. G. A theory and investigation of the effect of exchange orientation on marriage and friendship. *Journal of Marriage and the Family,* 1977, *39,* 543–548.

Patterson, G. R. *Families: Applications of social learning to family life.* Champaign, Ill.: Research Press, 1971.

Reed, E. W., & Reed, S. C. *Mental retardation: A family study.* Philadelphia: Saunders, 1965.

Rubin, Z. *Liking and loving: An invitation to social psychology.* New York: Holt, 1973.

Rubin, Z., Peplau, L. A., & Hill, C. T. *Becoming intimate: The development of male-female relationships.* (In press).

Scanzoni, J. *Sexual bargaining: Power politics in the American marriage.* Englewood Cliffs, New Jersey: Prentice-Hall, 1972.

Silverman, I. Physical attractiveness and courtship. *Sexual Behavior,* 1971, *3* (Sept.), 22–25.

Spuhler, J. N. Assortative mating with respect to physical characteristics. *Eugenics Quarterly,* 1968, *15,* 128–140.

Stroebe, W., Insko, C. A., Thompson, V. D., & Layton, B. D. Effects of physical attractiveness, attitude similarity, and sex on various aspects of interpersonal attraction. *Journal of Personality and Social Psychology,* 1971, *18,* 79–91.

Storer, N. W. *The social system of science.* New York: Holt, 1966.

Teichman, M. *Satisfaction from interpersonal relationship following resource exchange.* Unpublished doctoral dissertation, University of Missouri, at Columbia, 1971.

Thibaut, J., & Faucheux, C. The development of contractual norms in a bargaining situation under two types of stress. *Journal of Experimental Social Psychology,* 1965, *1,* 89–102.

Toffler, A. *Future shock.* New York: Bantam, 1970.

Traupmann, J. *Equity and intimate relations: An interview study of marriage.* Unpublished doctoral dissertation, University of Wisconsin, 1978.

Turner, J. L., Foa, E. B., & Foa, U. G. Interpersonal reinforcers: Classification in a relationship and some differential properties. *Journal of Personality and Social Psychology,* 1971, *19,* 168–180.

Udry, J. R. *The social context of marriage.* Philadelphia: Lippincott, 1971.

Waller, W. The rating and dating complex. *American Sociological Review,* 1937, *2,* 727–734.

Walster, E., Aronson, V., Abrahams, D., & Rottman, L. The importance of physical attractiveness in dating behavior. *Journal of Personality and Social Psychology,* 1966, *4,* 508–516.

Walster, E., Berscheid, E., & Walster, G. W. New directions in equity research. *Journal of Personality and Social Psychology,* 1973, *25,* 151–176.

Walster, E., Traupmann, J., & Walster, G. W. Equity and extramarital sex. *Archives of Sexual Behavior,* 1978, 121–141.

Walster, E., Walster, G. W., & Berscheid, E. *Equity: Theory and research.* Boston: Allyn and Bacon, 1978.

Walster, E., Walster, G. W., & Traupmann, J. Equity and premarital sex. *Journal of Personality and Social Psychology,* 1978, *36,* 82–92.

Walster, E., & Walster, G. W. *A new look at love.* Reading, Massachusetts: Addison-Wesley, 1978.

Walster, G. W. The Walster et al. (1973) equity formula: A correction. *Representative Research in Social Psychology,* 1975, *6,* 65–67.

Weick, K. E., & Nesset, B. Preferences among forms of equity. *Organizational Behavior and Human Performance,* 1968, *3,* 400–416.

Worthy, M., Gary, A. L., & Kahn, G. M. Self-disclosure as an exchange process. *Journal of Personality and Social Psychology,* 1969, *13,* 63–69.

5

Conflict in the Development of Close Relationships[1]

HARRIET B. BRAIKER
HAROLD H. KELLEY

This chapter will examine the phenomenon of conflict in close relationships and its role in their development. We begin by presenting our conceptual model of a close relationship, so that the ensuing analysis of developmental processes will be both logical and contextually explicit. Following our initial statements defining the nature and structure of close relationships, we shall present evidence about the developmental course of such relationships, with special attention to the occurrence and role of conflict. Finally, we shall speculate about the unique role that conflict plays in the developmental process and examine the relevant evidence.

Our considerations in this chapter will be limited to heterosexual dyadic relationships such as those involved in marriage and in pairings that sometimes lead to marriage. This focus is dictated by the fact that most of the existing evidence about close relationships comes from studies of heterosexual dyads. Moreover, there are certain potential advantages to this focus. It goes without saying that the course of premarital and marriage dyads is highly important in societies like ours, which rely on the family for such functions as moral training and the instilling of work motivation. On a theoretical level, heterosexual relations serve to

[1] The preparation of this paper and the original research reported in it were made possible by a grant from the National Science Foundation (GS-33069X) to Kelley.

135

keep our attention on certain asymmetries and possible differences that may exist within a close relationship as a consequence of the asymmetries and differences being sex linked. Furthermore, in this time of rapid changes in relations between the sexes, reliance on the heterosexual dyad as the target of analysis serves to make salient the possible culture- and history-bound nature of our generalizations.

Notwithstanding the potential advantages of this focus, it is important at the outset to specify the often unique properties of heterosexual dyads, especially of the courtship relationship, whose development is examined in detail in a subsequent section. Such properties, on the one hand, make the courtship process an excellent paradigm for studying the development of close relationships generally, and for illustrating the ideas about conflict and levels of interdependence we will propose in this chapter. On the other hand, the fact that the courtship relationship is unique in several respects, as compared with other types of close relationships, requires the exercise of caution in generalizing from the results of the studies to be described.

What are the special properties of the courtship relationship? First, the couple in courtship represents, by definition, a developing relationship. The language used in our culture to characterize the courtship process reveals its dynamic nature—couples "fall in love," "move toward marriage," "become involved," etc. Second, the courtship relationship is voluntary. Third, the courtship process and its culmination in marriage are highly valued by the culture. Thus, couples in courtship derive potential rewards both from the behavior-exchange process as well as from the intrinsic value of the relational state. Fourth, the courtship process has one of two culturally defined endpoints: either it culminates in a long-term commitment (marriage) or the relationship ultimately terminates or breaks off. For this reason, couples in courtship are continually confronted with a decision, either implicit or explicit, to proceed with the relationship and thereby move closer to commitment, or to terminate it. Finally, the courtship is a subset of the general category of heterosexual dyadic relationships and as such inevitably involves issues of sex role definitions and behaviors.

I. The Structure of Close Relationships

Having distinguished heterosexual courtships from other close relationships, the question arises: What is a *close* relationship? In this section, we will attempt to make explicit our view of the defining structure and dynamics of close relationships. As will be seen, this view is strongly influenced by social-exchange theory, particularly as conceptualized by

Thibaut and Kelley's (1959) model of dyadic interdependence. We have attempted here, however, to move beyond interdependence on a strictly behavioral level. Thus, our model of the close relationship involves, in addition to behavioral exchange, interdependence on the normative level, and on the level of personal characteristics and attitudes. We would suggest, in fact, that interdependence on this latter level might be the defining property of a close relationship. This is consistent with McCall's (1974) definition of a *personal* relationship as one in which the interaction "is constrained by what one person knows of the other and by what one thinks or hopes the other knows of him . . . [p. 218]."

In generating our model of a close relationship, we were not guided exclusively by prior theoretical views. Rather, many of our inferences about the properties of close relationships were based on some simple evidence of the kinds of conflict that occur in such relationships— evidence collected in an interview study that we conducted with John Cunningham in 1973. The details of that study, which essentially involved surveying young married or cohabiting couples about problems they were encountering in their relationships, are beyond the scope of this paper. We used that data on conflict—its substance, forms, and levels—as our "windows" on the inner structure and workings of close relationships.

The first and most obvious property of a dyadic close relationship is that the two persons are mutually dependent. In a sense, this interdependence is reflected in the mere fact of whatever conflict may exist between the two parties. A person who is not dependent upon another—that is, who has no special interest in what the other does—has no conflict with that other person. It is not, however, necessarily true that high interdependence must inevitably involve conflict, but the existence of interdependence, especially if it is extensive, as in the case of close relationships, does make the occurrence of conflict likely. The high probability of conflict being generated by the extensive interdependence in close relationships becomes more obvious when one views conflict in a broad context—that is, broad enough to cover both overt, interpersonal conflict, and conflict of interest resulting from noncorrespondence of outcomes in the domain of the partners' interaction (Thibaut & Kelley, 1959). Although the noncorrespondence of outcomes in heterosexual couples partly reflects sex-linked differences in needs and preferences, it probably also reflects simple differences between the two persons that are independent of gender.

A second property defining close relationships is that interdependence between the two persons exists on different levels. It follows then that persons in a close relationship gain rewards and incur costs (e.g., conflict) on each level of exchange. We have illustrated in Figure 5.1 what appear to be three levels of interdependence that characterize a close relationship, using the device of the payoff matrix from game theory and as employed by Thibaut and Kelley (1959).

The first level, interdependence of *specific behaviors*, has been the focus of Thibaut and Kelley's analysis. In Figure 5.1, the behavioral example shows the consequences for the two of each person's deciding to clean or not to clean their common quarters. Interdependence on the *normative* level has been the subject of sociological analyses of compatibility between persons in regard to the norms and role expectations they bring to the relationship. The example in Figure 5.1 shows the possible consequences of each person's holding one of two views about sex role obligations regarding household chores, the one being the norm of equality and the other being the traditional view of the female's greater responsibility regarding chores. Interdependence on the *personal* level has been described by Robert Carson in his book *The Interaction Basis of Personality* (1969). The example here follows his conclusions about the probable consequences of each person's being either a dominant or a submissive personality type.

We are not interested here in the details of these examples or payoff matrices. The purposes of Figure 5.1 are (*a*) to emphasize that interdepen-

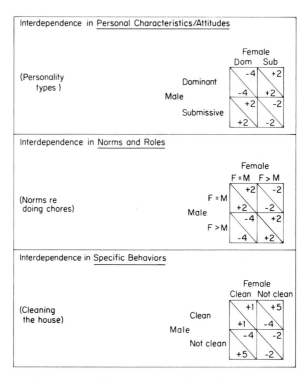

Figure 5.1   The structure of close relationships.

dence on these three levels has already, although on separate occasions and in different domains of social science, been the object of scientific analysis, and (b) to suggest that interdependence on the three levels can be analyzed in common terms (as, for example, with the payoff matrix).

Our multilevel model of interdependence in close relationships is supported by the data in the Kelley, Cunningham, and Braiker-Stambul (1973) study. The most striking findings of that study, in fact, were the diversity of the problems reported, and the different levels of generality on which the problems were defined. Thus, couples described concrete and focused conflicts over specific behaviors, more general conflicts about the unique norms and rules of their relationships, and highly generalized problems arising from attributions about the partner's characteristics, dispositions, and attitudes. Moreover, it is noteworthy that couples described a fourth type of conflict—one that cuts across, or may occur on all levels of interdependence. This fourth type is conflict over the conflict process itself. It seems that as couples attempt to resolve their differences on one or another level of interdependence, new sources of disagreement may arise from the actions involved in the conflict process. Some illustrative problems mentioned in the Kelley, Cunningham, and Braiker-Stambul couples include nagging, temper displays, and withdrawal or sulking.

The occurrence of conflict on different levels is indicated by research other than our own. Several other studies of the kinds of conflict issues reported in marriages also show that different levels are involved (De-Burger, 1967; Goode, 1956; Levinger, 1966). Similarly, investigations employing preset schedules of problems, constructed on the basis of, presumably, the investigator's general knowledge of interpersonal conflict, often entail a range of issues varying from the specific to the general (Bowerman, 1957; Brim, et al., 1961; Locke, 1951; Mathews & Milianovich, 1963; & Terman, 1938). In these various sets of results and lists, the behavioral level is most often represented by conflicts about recreation and about specific sexual behaviors; the normative level, by conflicts about household duties, economic-support responsibilities, and authority; and the personal level, by issues about life-values, selfishness and inconsiderateness, and affectional relations. Many items, such as drinking behavior and sexual relations, are ambiguous as to the level of conflict involved. The reason is that the same term (e.g., "excessive drinking") can specify a problem on any of the three levels. We find few indications in the literature that earlier investigators have been concerned about the level on which the persons conceptualize their problems.

The descriptions of conflicts also make it clear that interdependent persons place value not merely upon one another's behavior but also upon various combinations of behavior, or joint actions. Thus, in the terms proposed by Thibaut and Kelley (1959), the interdependence of persons in a close relationship is characterized not only by mutual fate control but also by mutual behavior control. The relationship therefore involves both problems of *exchange* and problems of *coordination*. As suggested by the matrices in Figure 5.1, this is probably true on all three levels of interdependence. Thus, the two persons must *coordinate* and *exchange* not only their specific behaviors but also the norms and roles, and personal characteristics and attitudes they display in the relationship.

As we have said, for two persons to be interdependent on the different levels, it is necessary that they incur costs and gain rewards on each level. Rewards and costs on the level of specific behavior are now well documented and taken for granted. Rewards and costs on the higher levels reflect the simple facts that each person tends to derive satisfaction from conforming to certain norms and from being a certain kind of person, and that each person also experiences discomfort and anxiety upon failing to meet such normative and personal standards. These evaluative criteria also exist for the partner and for the relationship itself. The person's "goals" include conceptions of the ideal partner, the ideal pattern of interaction, and the ideal interpersonal attitudes that underlie the relationship (e.g., romantic love). Accordingly, the person gains rewards or incurs costs from the partner's behavior as it relates to the higher-level concepts and from the joint pattern of behavior as it reveals the presence or the absence of the desired attitudes. This point has been well stated by Levinger and Huesmann (1978) in their concept of "relational rewards." They emphasize that the person gets rewards from various relational states, such as that of being loved or that of being seen in the company of an attractive partner.

The presence of rewards and costs at the higher levels is revealed by a particularly dramatic aspect of conflict in close relationships; namely, the tendency for issues to escalate to the higher levels of interdependence. This phenomenon reveals a *hierarchical ordering* of levels of conflict and, by extension, of levels of interdependence, as was shown in Figure 5.1. This particular ordering is indicated by two facts: (a) a set of issues at a lower level can give rise to a general issue at any higher level, and (b) resolution of an issue at a higher level reduces or eliminates conflict about a number of issues at any lower level. Thus, a normative conflict relating to obligations and privileges arises from numerous specific behavior conflicts, such as those concerning which person will do each of a number of cost-generating tasks, which person will be permitted to enjoy various rewarding activities, etc. Resolution of a normative conflict will (at least in principle) reduce or eliminate the numerous specific conflicts. For example, an explicit norm of turn-taking, such as among differently valued joint recreational activities, reduces the recurrent conflict over specific benefits and sacrifices.

Conflict about personal characteristics and attitudes has this *dual* relation to *both* the other levels of conflict, so it is located at the top of the hierarchy. Thus, on the one hand, charges of the partner's selfishness or thoughtlessness may reflect numerous instances either of his insistence on his own way at the behavioral level or of his pressing for superior prerogatives in norm-setting interactions, or both. On the other hand, an agreement at the level of personal characteristics or attitudes (e.g., that one person is far more intelligent than the other, or that they are deeply in love) has implications for the resolution of issues at both lower levels. Many specific interest conflicts can be settled by reference to this agreement, and norms (say, of authority or reciprocity) are implied and, in a sense, rendered superfluous.

Another way of describing this hierarchical order is in terms of two processes: (a) An upward, abstracting or generalizing process (in part, what has been called the "attribution" process, in social psychology), by which a number of specific issues at a lower level can be generalized or conceptualized in more abstract terms; and (b) a downward, specifying or particularizing process, where settlement of a single general issue has implications for numerous specific issues at a lower level.

It was our distinct impression from the Kelley, Cunningham, and Braiker-Stambul study that the tendency to raise conflict to higher levels of generality is a very powerful one. In that study, we did our best to elicit statements of problems exclusively at the level of specific behaviors. Despite our efforts, about one-third of the problems were given at the normative or personal level. It has since become clear that we are encountering a phenomenon that is the bane of behavior modification therapists working with marital conflict. The behavior modification approach requires a specific behavioral definition of the problem, but therapists using this approach are repeatedly frustrated in their efforts to elicit such a "pinpointing" definition from the marriage partners (Patterson & Hops, 1972).

Intuitively, it seems clear that this escalation phenomenon often reflects attempts to use higher-level incentives to control lower-level behavior. Thus, appeals are made to higher levels—the offending person is criticized and challenged at those levels—in order to attempt to control his choices at lower levels. This does not mean that the control aspect of escalation is always effective. When the unhappy person elevates the issue to the level where the offending partner can be hurt the most, the latter may become angry or avoidant. Aversive methods of behavior change work no better here than in other realms of life.

This control intention involved in escalation relates to our central assumption about the relation among the three levels of interdependence. *The higher levels serve to govern events at the lower levels.* Each person's normative preferences determine his decisions at the level of specific behaviors—how he weighs his own and his partner's interests, the value he attaches to equity, turn-taking, equal sharing in decisions, etc. His personal characteristics (neatness, sympathy) and attitudes toward the partner (love, superiority) place similar constraints upon both (a) numerous specific behavioral decisions and (b) his comfort with any particular set of norms and roles. This point was implicit in our earlier suggestion that resolution of conflict at a higher level has implications for numerous specific issues at lower levels.

Furthermore, we would argue that the factors underlying the interdependence at the higher levels evolve out of conflicts of interest at lower levels. Kelley and Thibaut (1978) present an analysis of the dilemmas and conflicts existing at the level of behavioral interdependence. From a systematic examination of patterns of interdependence, it is easy to show the potential functional value, both for the individual and for the pair, of various rules and choice criteria. These include such things as rules for turn-taking and exercising initiative, and the choice criteria for maximizing joint outcomes or minimizing differences in outcomes. Such rules and choice criteria correspond to items at the normative level. (They also correspond, in part, to the "social motives" investigated by Charles McClintock and his colleagues, 1972). Kelley and Thibaut argue that by virtue of their functional value, these rules and criteria are both represented in the moral teachings of the society and reinforced by the individual's experience in interdependent relationships. Thus, through their functional value and through the social incentives provided to encourage their acquisition, the rules and criteria come to be valued in themselves. Adherence to them and meeting the behavioral standards they define become rewarding to the individual; failure in these respects generates discomfort and anxiety. This is the basis for rewards and costs at the normative level. Undoubtedly, a similar analysis can be made for the personal level, inasmuch as there is a basis at the lower levels of interdependence for coming to value the display of certain personal characteristics and attitudes.

This conception of the close relationship gives conflict—now, in the sense of conflict of interest and decisional conflict—a central role in the development and continuation of the higher levels of interdependence. Conflicts of interest and decisional conflicts constitute the problems for which norms, traits, and attitudes provide the solutions. And because open interpersonal conflict stems from conflict of interest, it too may play some role in the development of the normative and personal standards that characterize a close relationship.

II. The Development of Close Relationships

In the present section, we will summarize an empirical investigation of the development of one type of close relationship: that of heterosexual couples in courtship. In examining the courtship process, we will focus on the phenomenon identified in the preceding sections. We will pay particular attention to the development of interdependence, both in degree and at different levels. The empirical data will be closely examined for what they suggest about the role of conflict in relationship development. Specifically, we will examine the forms of conflict, its meaning in the context of the dimensions of relationship growth, and how its occurrence changes as relationships develop toward increasing levels of commitment.

The empirical evidence on the development of close relationships presented here is based on data from samples of young married couples. In the studies described below, subjects provided retrospective accounts of their relationships during the period between their initial acquaintance with each other and the period of the first 6 months of their marriage.

Because of its special properties, described earlier, it seems likely that the "successful" courtship relationship has an inherent developmental course. Moreover, the kinds of conflicts that emerge and the role of conflict in the developmental process are probably strongly influenced and constrained by the special characteristics of courtship.

The explicit developmental character of the process and its seemingly inexorable culmination point are a potential source of both intrapersonal and interpersonal conflict concerning the relationship's continuation. Intrapersonally, an individual may experience conflict over the relative loss of independence, or over the psychological requirements of commitment. Asymmetries in willingness to increase the level of involvement may be sources of open interpersonal conflict. The occurrence of aversive conflict, in turn, may itself be a source of intrapersonal conflict (ambivalence) inasmuch as fighting and unhappiness are not congruent with the culturally prescribed couple-in-love expectations. The increasing interdependence of developing relationships raises the possibility of conflicts of interest, behavioral interference, and personality clashes between members of the pair. Finally, the occurrence of conflict, both intrapersonally and interpersonally, during the critical courtship phase provides information that may be used by individuals to assess whether, for example, the relationship is "good enough" (i.e., satisfying, strong, etc.) to continue, whether the partner is the kind of person "to spend a lifetime with," or what the partner's "true feelings" must be. A decision to proceed with the relationship raises the necessity of resolving meta-conflicts about how to deal with conflicts at lower levels—that is, the necessity of evolving norms and rules, idiosyncratic to the couple, to promote smooth relationship functioning in the future.

In the studies reported here, we present evidence that not only mirrors the special properties of the courtship process but also reflects a special outcome of that process. The data were collected from *married couples* and pertain to the developmental course of *their* relationship. Therefore, the results are subject to the critical qualification that they are derived from couples who withstood whatever conflicts occurred during their courtship. (The role of conflict in the deterioration and termination of relationships is the subject of Chapter 6 in this volume.)

A. The Development of Premarital Relationships

The central purpose of the studies to be described here was to generate a model of how heterosexual courtship relationships develop over time. The methodological approach used was retrospective and phenomenological, the intention being to conceptualize the process of relationship growth from acquaintance through marriage on the basis of how married couples reconstructed and reported the development of their relationships. This approach was chosen for two primary reasons. First, married couples were viewed as an identifiable population of ongoing relationships with the common past experience of a courtship that culminated in a formalized long-term commitment. Second, since the course of heterosexual relationship growth remains, for the most part, uncharted in the literature, couples' retrospective reports of their own experiences seemed an appropriate first step toward generating an empirical development model.

It should be noted, in this regard, that the studies to be described were conducted as part of the first-listed author's doctoral dissertation research in the winter and spring of 1975 (Stambul, 1975). The central purpose of that work, as has been stated, was to explore the developmental course of courtship relationships; the focus of the research as it was then formulated was not on the particular role of conflict in the developmental process or on the kinds of interdependence levels proposed in the present paper. For these reasons, the empirical evidence reported here on the role of conflict in the developmental course of courtship does not form an integrated picture. Rather, the evidence on conflict derived from this research is more like a set of snapshots taken when conflict appears during the course of relationship development. These snapshots, however, do fit into a larger view of how premarital relationships develop over time, and, from this view, the particular role of conflict in relationship development may be inferred.

A review of various theoretical models of relationship development (e.g., Altman & Taylor, 1973; Levinger & Snoek, 1972; & Ryder *et al.*, 1971) suggested three principal questions for the research: First, are there consensually recognized stages of courtship, as reported by married couples, from which a developmental model can be constructed? Second, which variables of heterosexual pair functioning are most useful for understanding the courtship process? And, third, how do such variables (including conflict) change as a function of progression toward commitment?

B. Study I: Stages in Relationship Development

A first step toward establishing a developmental model of heterosexual relationships consists of determining whether consensually perceived stages can be defined. If discrete developmental stages do exist, as is implied by the models of Levinger and Snoek (1972) and Ryder et al. (1971), then such stages should be recognized and reported by most couples and should therefore constitute a normative pattern. If, on the other hand, each couple's courtship is idiosyncratic, normative characterization would be precluded and the existence of a general developmental model would be cast in doubt.

A preliminary investigation of this question was conducted in a pilot study of 16 married couples. Husbands and wives were asked to provide independent retrospective views of the time period from their initial acquaintance to the date of their marriage. They were asked to divide that time period into what they considered to be "important stages, periods, or perhaps turning points" in the development of their relationships. They also provided brief written sketches describing each of the stages they delineated. These data were examined in order to detect possible developmental patterns common to most courtships. A consensus emerged from the stage descriptions indicating that a combination of some or all of eight stages could describe the developmental pattern of all the relationships. The eight stages, not necessarily in order, were labeled as follows:

1. Friends–Acquaintances (F)
2. Casual Dating (CD)
3. Serious Dating (SD)
4. Engaged—not living together (E)
5. Living together—not engaged (LT)
6. Living together and engaged (LT–E)
7. Break-Up (BU)
8. Physical separation not due to Break-up (PS)

The pilot study, then, suggested general common elements in the various couples' reports of their progress toward commitment. Study I was intended to provide a cross-validation of the eight stages as consensually recognized periods in courtship development. Beyond this basic purpose, the study sought to measure the frequency of occurrence of the various stages, and their sequence and length in the context of total courtship time, with the aim of establishing a normative pattern of relationship development.

Twenty married couples participated in the study. All the couples had been married less than 3 years. The mean length of marriage of 19.45 months. The couples were recruited from university populations through advertising in campus newspapers. The sample was further limited to individuals who were under 31 years of age, who were not foreign born, who had never been married before, who had no history of marriage counseling, and who had no children.

Data were collected through a self-administered form, completed by husbands and wives *independently* in a group session. The questionnaire, in part, presented the eight stages derived from the analysis of the pilot data and surveyed the respondents as to whether they had actually experienced such periods in their own courtship. Having indicated which of the eight stages (and any miscellaneous "Other" stages) had occurred in their own courtships, the respondents were then asked to arrange those stages in chronological order on a timeline bounded at the two ends by "Day we met," on the left, and "Day we married," on the right. They then provided open-ended written descriptions of each stage on their timeline, completed a set of structured sentence-completion items about each stage, and identified at which stage each of 13 important events (e.g., "When did you first feel you loved [your partner]") occurred.

Results of the stage survey indicated that a basic common pattern could be discerned across couples consisting of three major stages: casual dating, serious dating, and engagement. This is not to say that other stages did not enter into the developmental process; rather, the other five stages probably represented important, and perhaps idiosyncratic, variations on or additions to the basic pattern for some relationships, but they did not represent the experience of the majority of couples in the sample. Each of the three major stages was recognized by a majority of the respondents as comprising part of their own courtship experience. For the majority of the couples (65%), all three stages were reported, and in combination the three accounted for 83% of the total courtship period.

Although the qualitative nature of the data in this study permitted only subjective analyses, the respondents' "case history" reports did generate an overall picture of the courtship experience and a set of potentially useful dimensions for further research on relationship growth.

The open-ended descriptions of the stages of courtship were content analyzed to determine the prominent "themes" or content dimensions used by the subjects to describe the ways in which their relationships developed over the courtship period. The analysis yielded five content dimensions used most consistently by subjects in their stories of relationship growth. The five dimensions with examples of content scoring are listed in Table 5.1.

It may be noted that these content dimensions reflect both the nature of the interdependence and the kinds of conflicts occurring in the rela-

TABLE 5.1
Content Code for Themes of Relationship Development

I. *Love*
Score "1" if card contains reference to:
A. "Love," "in love," "falling in love"
B. Synonyms: strong affection, "deep" feelings, great caring, "real thing."
C. Description of closeness, need, belonging, attachment
D. Recognition of love: e.g., "the woman to spend my life with," "He (or she) was it," "I knew I felt the real thing," etc.

II. *Conflict–negative affect*
Score "1" if card contains reference to:
A. Fights, hassles, arguments, not getting along, hostility
B. Feeling badly because of relationship; e.g., frustrated, dissatisfied, jealous, unhappy
C. General mention of problems, "having problems"
[Note: excludes reference to loneliness or depression while physically separated.]

III. *Ambivalence*
Score "1" if card contains reference to:
A. Confusion about feelings toward partner or relationship
B. Unsure about future of relationship—whether or not to go ahead with it
C. Anxiety about commitment; concern over loss of independence
D. Feeling trapped or pressured—want to back out but feel constrained to proceed

IV. *Third party influence*
Score "1" if card contains any reference to either joining or separative influence of family or friends

V. *Unit relationship*
Score "1" if card contains reference to:
A. Feeling like a "couple"—being seen as a couple
B. Feeling like "husband–wife," "us," "together"
C. Exclusivity—i.e., mutual decision to see–date only one another
D. Doing "everything together," going "everywhere together"
E. Discussing future as a couple

tionship's course. The degree of interdependence of the pair is reflected in the *love* category by references to caring, needing, and attachment. The extent of interdependence is reflected in references to exclusivity ("doing mostly everything together"). The personal and attributional level of interdependence is indicated by attributions made about the self (being in love), the partner ("the person to spend my life with"), and the relationship (feeling like a couple). The *conflict–negative affect* category indicates conflict between the two persons (arguments, problems) and the *ambivalence* category reflects intrapersonal conflict of the type inherent to the courtship process (confusion about feelings toward the partner, anxiety about increasing the commitment and losing independence).

It is noteworthy that respondents often referred to feelings of love and belonging while simultaneously describing instances of conflict and ambivalence. This observation raises important theoretical questions (which we addressed in a second study, to be described later) about the relation between love and conflict, and the role of conflict in developing intimacy.

In order to analyze the relative importance of each content dimension as characterizing the three major developmental stages, the couples' stage descriptions were content scored, and analyzed for frequency-of-theme usage. The three stages were described differently, with respect to usage of all the content themes except ambivalence. References to love and third-party influence were most frequent for both the serious dating and engagement stages. For the conflict–negative affect and unit relationship themes, the serious dating descriptions contained the highest frequency of thematic reference. The sentence completion items and the important events scale were also analyzed for differences among the three major stages. Results of these analyses suggested that the three basic stages of courtship, as described by these couples, represent not only temporally distinct periods but also psychologically and socially different levels of interpersonal functioning arrayed on a continuum of increasing degrees of interdependence and intimacy.

The casual dating stage is described in these data as an initial, tentative, and largely superficial level of interaction. Generally, it is typified by feelings of attraction toward the partner (based on physical attributes and perceived personality traits), sexual exploration, and ambivalence about the continuance of the relationship. In comparison with the later stages, this stage is seldom characterized by reports of love, conflict, third party influence, or the sense of being a unit.

As couples' relationships move from the level of casual dating to that of serious dating, a number of important changes take place. The relationship during serious dating is characterized by increasing reports of love feelings, the sense of belonging with the partner, and public recognition of the pair as constituting a definite unit. Moreover, the transition to serious dating is marked by an increase in conflict and negativity between the partners. In this stage, couples also recognize the seriousness or depth of their feelings toward each other, are sexually intimate, discuss the possibility of marriage, and begin to plan their future together. The attraction to the partner now derives from need satisfactions as well as from the attractions of the previous stage.

The shift from serious dating to engagement is somewhat less pronounced than that from casual to serious dating. The most significant event in, and the clearest definition of, this stage is the couple's formalization of their commitment in a public decision to marry. The feelings reported to occur during engagement span the range from love, belonging, extreme happiness, and excitement to ambivalence, conflict, negativity, and anxiety, therefore suggesting that this stage of the courtship may be a rather turbulent and traumatic period.

Although the data in Study I do suggest that a basic common pattern of stages is experienced by most couples during their courtship, the data do not imply that the overall developmental patterns for these relationships are fully homogeneous. On the contrary, an examination of the complete "case histories" of courtships provided by the subjects (including all the stages described) reveals that different *styles of courtship* can be distinguished among them. In the context of the present chapter, these styles of courtship have implications for understanding the role of conflict in the developmental process. It is clear that open interpersonal conflict is a more salient characteristic of courtship for some couples than for others. What is more, the conflicts arising from the courtship process are not the same for all couples. For some couples the special intrapersonal and interpersonal conflicts that may arise from asymmetries of involvement at various stages in the developmental process are characteristic of their "style" of courtship; for others, asymmetries do not occur and do not, therefore, represent a potential source of conflict. Likewise, some relationships are characterized by transition points leading to levels of increased involvement that entail considerable decision conflict, whereas others are characterized by smooth transitions to a greater commitment that yet entails few or no explicit decision-making processes. And, finally, some courtships are characterized by conflict between the couple and third parties (e.g., parents), whereas such conflicts are nonexistent or inconsequential for other couples.

The data from Study I are obviously only qualitative in nature, and the subjective analyses they permit do not allow strong conclusions to be drawn. They do, however, provide some glimpses of the role of conflict in the development of courtships about which some tentative statements can be made. First, as relationships develop toward long-term commitment, members of the couple become increasingly interdependent. The interdependence grows not only in extent and degree but also on the level at which it exists. In moving toward love and in becoming a couple, the partners fulfill the general criteria they have for the close heterosexual relationship. With this increased interdependence come the circumstances for and the occurrence of conflict. Second, while a measure of conflict is common to virtually all courtship relationships, the types of developmental conflicts and the intensity of conflict in the developmental process are not the same for all couples. Third, it is clear that conflict is not *necessarily* destructive of or disruptive to relationship growth and continuation—all of these couples' courtships culminated in marriage. Furthermore, both interpersonal and intrapersonal conflict occur concurrently with feelings of love and belonging. These observations raise a number of conceptual questions that are addressed in Study II.

C. Study II: The Developmental Process: Relationship Change Over Time

The content analysis in Study I yielded a set of themes used by subjects to describe the development of their own relationships. In Study II, these themes were translated into quantifiable variables of relationship functioning. Developmental "stages" were used as sampling points in order to observe patterns of change in these variables over time.

The goals of Study II were twofold. First, the study sought to provide a systematic analysis of some of the major variables in courtship development by identifying the important dimensions of growth and describing their meaning and their relationship to one another. Explicitly addressed are the questions of how conflict and love are related to one another and how ambivalence fits into the developmental process.

The second goal of Study II was to examine systematically changes in relationship variables over time. At what stage, for example, does conflict begin to emerge? How do feelings of love develop? Are there very large increments in early stages followed by a leveling off, as a romantic view would suggest, or does love grow more gradually with time? The qualitative nature of the data in Study I permitted only a rough approximation of the way relationships dimensions varied across stages. Study II was designed to examine the developmental patterns of relationship variables across four stages: casual dating, serious dating, engagement, and the first 6 months of marriage.

Twenty-two married couples served as subjects in the study. They were recruited and screened according to the procedures described in Study I. As before, data was collected from husbands and wives through self-administered questionnaires. Before answering a series of questions about their relationships, the members of each pair worked together on defining the four stages in their relationship history. All the respondents then independently completed a questionnaire consisting of four sets—one for each of the four stages of their relationship or development—of 30 questions each. The sets of questions were identical; to control for possible biases introduced by the order of stages, the question sets for half the subjects were arranged in a sequence beginning with casual dating and ending with marriage, while for the other half the sequence was reversed. All of the questions were of the same basic form. They required the respondents to estimate the degree or extent of a particular attitude, feeling or behavior that they may have experienced during a particular stage in the relationship's history. The responses were presented on a nine-point scale. The questions were constructed so as to measure systematically the dimensions of relationship growth suggested by the content analysis of Study I.

A principal-components factor analysis with orthogonal rotations was performed separately on the questionnaire responses for each of the four stages. This statistical technique permitted us to identify the major dimensions or factors underlying the questionnaire items and to construct factor scales composed of items that remained highly intercorrelated across the four stages.

The analysis yielded two principal factors comprised of the questionnaire items listed in Table 5.2. Factor I is a general Love dimension defined most clearly by Items 1, 8, 19 and 28, which are questions that concern, respectively, belonging, love, closeness, and attachment. This factor reflects the degree to which the two persons make certain attributions to themselves of love and belonging, as well as the degree of interdependence (closeness, attachment). Factor II is a Conflict–Negativity dimension defined most clearly by overt behavioral conflict and communication of negative affect.

In addition to the two principal factors, two highly intercorrelated *clusters* of items were extracted to form scales. These clusters are presented in Table 5.3. The first cluster represents a dimension of Ambivalence defined most clearly by questions 7 and 16. The second cluster was termed Maintenance, and it includes primarily communication behaviors engaged in by members of the couple to reduce costs and maximize rewards from the relationship.

The Ambivalence and Maintenance clusters are not independent of the principal factors; however, the loadings of these clusters on the two principal factors present an intriguing pattern of change over the sequence of developmental stages. An examination of the rotated factor loadings indicates that the Love (Factor I) and Conflict–Negativity (Factor II) items demonstrate high stability and consistency in factor loadings across the four stages. In contrast, the Ambivalence items are highly loaded on Factor II in the casual dating and serious dating stages but become negatively

TABLE 5.2
Items Constituting Principal Factor Scales

Factor I. Love

1. To what extent did you have a sense of "belonging" with (____)?[a]
5. How much do you feel you gave to the relationship?
8. To what extent did you love (____) at this stage?
11. To what extent did you feel that the things that happened to (____) also affected or were important to you?
14. To what extent did you feel that your relationship was special compared with others you had been in?
17. How committed did you feel toward (____)?
19. How close did you feel to (____)?
22. How much did you need (____) at this stage?
26. How sexually intimate were you with (____)?
28. How attached did you feel to (____)?

Factor II: Conflict–negativity

4. How often did you and (____) argue with each other?
6. To what extent did you try to change things about (____) that bothered you (e.g., behaviors, attitudes, etc.)?
13. How often did you feel angry or resentful toward (____)?
29. When you and (____) argued, how serious were the problems or arguments?
30. To what extent did you communicate negative feelings toward (__)—e.g., anger, dissatisfaction, frustration, etc.?

---

[a] The symbol (____) is used throughout to represent the spouse's name.

loaded on Factor I in the post-marital stage. The Maintenance items are loaded on Factor I in the first two stages but, by the fourth stage (marriage), are more heavily loaded on Factor II. Figure 5.2 illustrates the movement across the principal factors of the Ambivalence and Maintenance loadings from Stage 2 (serious dating) to Stage 4 (marriage). While the pattern is not perfectly consistent for all items, the overall "factor flip" of the two clusters implies that the dimensions of Ambivalence and Maintenance change their meaning over time as reflected by their changing relationships to the main factors.

The central and conceptually most important result of the factor analyses is that the two principal factors, Love and Conflict–Negativity, are orthogonal dimensions of relationship growth. This result provides statistical support for the subjective impressions gained from the protocols of Study I: There appears to be no relation between the amount of interdependence and love in a relationship, on the one hand, and the amount of negative affect and open conflict, on the other hand.

A further, and unexpected, empirical finding of the factor analyses was the unusual phenomenon of "flipping" clusters—suggesting the probable complexity of ambivalence and maintenance behavior in relationship development. The possible causes or roots of ambivalence may

TABLE 5.3
Items Constituting Additional Cluster Scales

Cluster 1: Ambivalence

7. How confused were you about your feelings toward (___)?
10. How much did you think or worry about losing some of your independence by getting involved with (___)?
16. How ambivalent or unsure were you about continuing in the relationship with (___)?
20. To what extent did you feel that (___) demanded or required too much of your time and attention?
24. To what extent did you feel "trapped" or pressured to continue in the relationship?

Cluster 2: Maintenance

3. To what extend did you reveal or disclose very intimate things about yourself or personal feelings to (___)?
9. How much time did you and (___) spend discussing and trying to work out problems between you?
12. How much time did you and (___) talk about the quality of your relationship—for example, how good it was, how satisfying, how to improve it, etc.?
15. To what extent did you try to change your behavior to help solve certain problems between you and (___)?
27. How much did you tell (___) what you wanted or needed from the relationship?

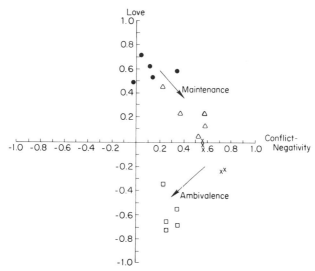

• Factor loadings of Maintenance items in Stage 2.
△ Factor loadings of Maintenance items in Stage 4.

x Factor loadings of Ambivalence items in Stage 2.
□ Factor loadings of Ambivalence items in Stage 4.

Figure 5.2   Movement across principal factors of maintenance and ambivalence clusters from Stage 2 to Stage 4.

be inferred from the pattern of factor loadings. In relatively early stages of relationship growth, ambivalence may arise in response to conflict and negativity in the relationship. Later, ambivalence appears to result from waning feelings of love. It should be noted, however, that the factor-analytic procedure does not provide a test of cause and effect relationships. It is therefore arguable whether ambivalence is a precursor or cause of increased conflict in early stages and of the reduction of love in later ones. Keeping in mind the limitation we ascribe to the factor analytic procedure, we suggest that the close communication described here as maintenance behavior serves to increase interdependence and love in the earlier stages of development and to resolve conflict in the later ones.

Having identified the major dimensions of development as measured in the questionnaire, the investigator's next task was to examine the nature of change in these dimensions of relationship growth over time. Using the factor loadings, four factor scales were constructed representing, respectively, love, conflict–negativity, ambivalence, and maintenance.

Figure 5.3 shows the mean score on the four scales plotted as a function of courtship stage. Analyses of variance (Sex of Respondent × Stage of Relationship) on each scale yielded significant main effects for stage. No significant main effects for sex or interactions with sex were

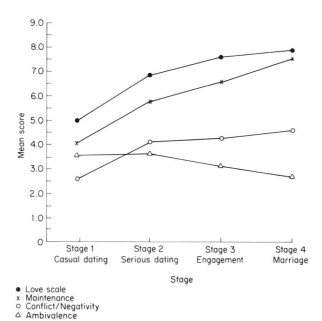

Figure 5.3 Mean scores on the four scales as a function of stage (sex and order factors collapsed).

found. Using the four designated relationship stages as time sampling points, it was found that the dimensions all exhibited linear developmental trends. The means on all four scales were found to change significantly over time, although the specific forms of the trends were different.

Behaviors and affect constituting the love dimension showed gradual incremental changes as the relationship progressed from casual dating to serious dating, and from serious dating to engagement and to marriage. A similar pattern was found for the maintenance items, although the slope of the trend from Stage 2 to Stage 4 was somewhat more gradual. The amount of conflict–negativity reported across all couples did not fully parallel increases in interdependence, at least as the latter is reflected in love-scale content. Instead, the overall degree of reported conflict–negativity substantially increased as the relationship progressed from the first stage to that of serious dating and greater interdependence. The conflict–negativity trend became asymptotic thereafter, showing no further significant increases or decreases as the relationship entered engagement and marriage.

The ambivalence trend across subjects followed a decreasing pattern from both dating stages to engagement and marriage. It is difficult, of course, to interpret the reasons for the observed changes. It may be that partial resolution or reduction in ambivalence about the relationship precedes and, in fact, precipitates the formalized commitment. Alternatively, a dissonance interpretation would hold that the decision to marry precedes and motivates the subsequent reduction in ambivalence.

D. Summary of the Studies

The two studies agree on the main outlines of the course of development of the close relationship. Not surprisingly, the most striking aspects of change are increases in the properties covered by the love scale. Prominent among these are feelings of dependence (need for, attachment to, and closeness to the partner). There is little doubt that the partner is seen as also being increasingly dependent upon the relationship, although measurements of this perception were not included in the research. The increasing interdependence is apparent not only on the specific behavioral level (e.g., sexual intimacy) but also on the normative level. This is reflected in Study I by an emerging norm of exclusivity, which is part of the unit-formation process at the serious dating stage. Paralleling this development is the finding in Study II (not reported earlier in this chapter) that jealousy sharply increases and is at its highest in the serious dating stage. It is not difficult to imagine that conflicts over the range of activities to be shared exclusively with each other are expressed in feelings of jealousy and are resolved through agreements about the extent of the interdependence. Along with the increase in behavioral and normative interdependence, there is also increasing interdependence on the level of personal characteristics and attitudes. Attributions are made about the self (being in love, affected by things that happen to the partner), the partner ("a person to spend a lifetme with"), and the relationship (special as compared with others, "a unit to which we belong"). The interdependence here constitutes the core meaning of the heterosexual relationship in its romantic version, where each person gains relationship rewards both from loving and from being loved, as well as from being in a relationship that is like none previously experienced. We believe that, as illustrated here, this level of interdependence must be regarded as being of particular importance to *close* relationships or even, as suggested earlier, as being a defining property of them. Of course, the specific rewards involved will vary, depending upon the particular kind of relationship (e.g., the close same-sex friendship versus the close heterosexual relationship).

The serious dating stage is serious not only in its sharp increment in interdependence but also in the sharp increase in conflict. The frequency of arguments and the seriousness of problems increase, as does the communication of negative feelings about each other. Consistent with our earlier assertion that conflict often involves the use of incentives to attempt to influence the partner, the reports of trying to change bothersome things about the partner are part of the conflict scale (i.e., these reports correlate with arguing and communicating angry feelings). The evidence on the increase in and the shifting meaning of maintenance activities (the close communication of feelings and needs, and discussions directed at improving the relationship) also suggests that conflict may motivate constructive work on the problems that the pair have encountered.

Although the typical couple reports an increase in conflict from the casual dating to the serious dating stage, not all couples experience conflicts (Study I). However, among these "successful" couples, who eventually get married, there is no correlation at any of the stages between the level of love–interdependence and the level of conflict. These appear to be two independent dimensions of close relationships. This finding is consistent with the results of an earlier study by Orden and Bradburn (1968), based on interviews with a large sample of married respondents from a nationwide set of metropolitan areas. They found that the reported frequency of recent pleasurable activities the couple had engaged in together did not correlate with the number of things that had recently caused differences of opinion or problems in their marriage. In short, conflict does not indicate lack of interdependence or love in these successful marital relationships.

The intrapersonal conflict tapped by the ambivalence measure shows that such conflict is most prevalent during the casual and serious dating stages and declines with *increased* commitment and movement toward marriage. During the early stages, ambivalence is associated with the occurrence of conflict, suggesting that open conflict raises doubts in the person's mind about the central issue in the courtship process; namely, whether to continue along the road toward long-term commitment. Of course, all the individuals in these studies finally resolved this issue in favor of continuance. However, in relationships that do not culminate in marriage, early conflict probably constitutes part of the information that leads to the decision to break off the courtship process.

III. The Role of Conflict in the Development of Close Relationships

We now turn to a *theoretical* analysis of the part that conflict plays in the development of close relationships. Our analysis will take account of the facts detailed in the preceding section about the typical course of development as well as of other relevant empirical evidence.

The reader will recall our earlier conceptualization of a close relationship as involving interdependence at three levels: the behavioral, the normative, and the personal. In the relationship-formation process, each person brings to the interaction preferences and propensities on each of these three levels. That is, he or she has a repertoire of *specific behaviors* appropriate to the relationship as well as desires and preferences about his other own behaviors, the partner's behaviors, and their joint outcomes. Similarly, each also has a set of propensities and preferences regarding *norms* and *roles* to guide the interaction, and each has *personal character- istics* and *attitudes* to be manifested in the relationship.

Given these preferences and propensities, the behavior, norms, and personal properties each person chooses to express may be mutually satisfying. Mutual satisfaction would mean that their pattern of inter- dependence at each level is characterized by high communicability be- tween their outcomes—they have little conflict of interest with respect to either specific behavior, rules and norms, or personal attitudes and char- acteristics. Each may find the interaction to be highly rewarding, and they may develop a high degree of interdependence. There would be little or no open conflict between them, and each person would feel little ambiva- lence about pursuing the relationship further.

More common, we suspect, than this scenario of conflict-free rela- tionship development is one in which conflict of interest figures promi- nently. The two persons enter the relationship with different ideas about the behavioral events they want to occur, or about the norms and roles they want for the relationship, or about the attitudes and personal properties they wish to see expressed there. Their awareness of these differences is not likely to be great during early interactions. As Altman and Taylor (1973) have shown, early interaction consists almost wholly of superficial information, with intimate information being revealed only later. Initial interaction, especially that in a relationship with a possible future, is constrained by norms of politeness and conflict avoidance as well as by the individuals' strategies of ingratiation (putting one's best foot forward).

These constraints are particularly significant in preventing the occurrence of open conflict. On the face of it, they seem to serve to give the relationship its "best chance," by permitting an exploration of areas of common interest and an avoidance of those of disagreement. In reality, however, the constraints keep the interaction on the level of the common and banal and away from areas of interchange that may potentially be most rewarding. By interfering with the flow of information, they encourage the development of separate conceptions of the relationship (rather than shared ones). These conceptions may be divergent or, as in the famous Waller and Hill example (1951, p. 186), convergent but not known to be such and, indeed, feared to be different.

As interaction proceeds, the pair is increasingly likely to encounter instances of objective difference and incompatibility on all three levels of interdependence. With increasing intimacy, there is decreasing presentation of a false self (Heiss, 1962). Conflicting interests are made plain as interaction moves beyond the superficial, stylized, culturally common domains (popular music, current arts and dance, and conversation topics and attitude domains common to the subculture) and becomes serious—that is, moves into the idiosyncratic domains of special attitudes and interests (unusual or special religious or political beliefs, attitudes toward friends and parents) and the intimate aspects of living together (personal habits, ideas about housekeeping, etc.). Undoubtedly, an important part of a relationship's becoming serious is the expression of the higher level preferences one has—in particular, those for the long-term heterosexual relationship.

With the uncovering and revelation of different preferences for the relationship, a variety of different and overlapping processes are set in motion. Insofar as the apparent differences are seen to portend the inability to gain high satisfaction and the likelihood of costly open conflict, one or both persons may become ambivalent about continuing the relationship. One or both may pull back from further expansion of the relationship, either breaking it off entirely or limiting it to certain domains of interaction where there are shared preferences. Tacit norms may be developed that promote an avoidance of conflict-inciting areas. Alternatively, more constructive norms may evolve, such as those of turn-taking and of openness to trying out new behaviors, which enable each person, at least occasionally, to enjoy the higher rewards available in the relationship. On the personal level, there may develop new attitudes (of loving and caring) and new goals that serve to reduce and resolve conflicts about norms and behavior.

In general, because of the information exchanged and the potential for change, the occasions on which the couple encounter conflicts of interest constitute some of the most significant events in the course of their relationship. On a theoretical level, the complex phenomena that can occur, which we have noted briefly, are represented in their extreme form by two opposing views of the formation process. The avoidance response to conflict, with total or partial discontinuance of further interaction, is consistent with the view that relationship development consists of a fitting together and an accommodation between relatively fixed entities (the two persons and their preferences and propensities). In the absence of conflict of interest, the relationship proceeds beautifully; given conflict of interest, the pair either works around it or breaks off interaction completely. This view is implicit in theories that relate pre-relationship indices of personal attitudes and characteristics to such relationship formation indices as progress in the relationship, becoming engaged or married, marital adjustment, and marriage continuation (versus separation or divorce). It is also implied by models of the developmental process (Altman & Taylor, 1973; Thibaut & Kelley, 1959) that emphasize exploring the reward–cost potentialities (presumed to be more or less fixed) and extrapolating from them unexperienced outcomes in order to predict how satisfying the relationship will be.

The constructive response to conflict, with the development of new norms, interpersonal attitudes, and personal goals, is consistent with the opposite view, namely that relationship formation consists of mutual influence between two relatively malleable entities and of the evolution of preferences and propensities unique to the relationship. This second view is characteristic of the interactionist analysis of relationships derived from George Herbert Mead and represented in the writings of Bolton (1961), Cottrell (1942), Foote (1957), McCall (1974), and Waller and Hill (1951). The interactionist view is well represented by Ingersoll's commentary on her observations of the development of authority patterns in the family (an example of interdependence at the normative level):

> the individual tends to express his introjected authority role . . . when he meets a situation (in this case, his own marriage) which he perceives as requiring a role similar to that learned under parental control in his childhood experience. However, if the expected response to his role is not forthcoming from his marriage partner, and the partner's expectations of . . . behavior with regard to authority in family living differ from his, then an interaction may take place which modifies the introjected authority roles of both partners, and a different pattern of control is evolved in the family relationship [1948, p. 269].

As this example illustrates, the interactionist view clearly implies that relationship development is not entirely predictable from the initial preferences and propensities with which the two persons enter their relationship. It also implies that the salient and crucial events in the developmental process will be instances of conflict. Accordingly, the development process will depend on the couple's competencies to deal with conflict and their flexibilities to give up old behavioral guidelines and adopt new ones.

A. Growth through Conflict

As the preceding discussion should have made clear, we do not agree with Altman and Taylor (1973, p. 166) that conflict is an essential part of the development of process. Close relationships can develop without it, though perhaps few do. Nor do we accept the view, implied by Waller and Hill (1951, p. 186–187), that relationship growth necessarily involves cycles of crisis and disruption. Braiker-Stambul's evidence suggests that such cycles are characteristic of some courtships but not of others. We do believe that conflict can play a positive role in relationship development and that the relationship that successfully moves through conflict episodes is thereby likely to be somewhat different from the one that grows without conflict. This belief is based on an analysis of the contribution of conflict (a) to thinking about and understanding the relationship and (b) to the evolution of new bases of interdependence, particularly on the higher levels.

A brief commentary on the fundamentals of conflict will serve to orient us to the relevant phenomena. *Intrapersonal* conflict occurs in a relationship when a person is uncertain about which of several courses of action to follow. For example, a person may experience a conflict between satisfying some long standing interest outside the relationship (e.g., the weekly bowling league) and fulfilling a valued role or personal ideal that is held within and for the relationship. As Braiker-Stambul's data on ambivalence show, an important kind of intrapersonal conflict during the courtship process has to do with maintaining and, possibly, increasing one's commitment to the relationship versus retaining one's independence or alternative commitments. *Structural interpersonal* conflict (conflict of interest) exists when the preferences of the two persons are different. For example, given discrepant goals for joint activities, the conflict of interest becomes apparent as the couple's actual activities fail to satisfy one or both persons. Structural interpersonal conflict gives rise to intrapersonal conflict, as when, having detected the differences, one is uncertain about whether to press for the fulfillment of one's own preferences, at the risk of open conflict, or to recognize and comply with the partner's preferences. Such intrapersonal conflict may also occasion open or *dynamic interpersonal* conflict. And as Braiker-Stambul's data suggest, open conflict may, in turn, give rise to still more intrapersonal conflict about the continuance of the interaction.

Conflict, whether intrapersonal or interpersonal (of the open, dynamic sort), produces aversive experiences and discomfort. During intrapersonal conflict, there are the tensions associated with counterpressures and decision under uncertainty. (These have been conceptualized as "emotional tension" by Lewin, 1951, and "frustration-produced drive" by Brown & Farber, 1951.) Interpersonal conflict involves the anxiety associated with the open expression of aggression and the possible loss of the benefits derived from the relationship, and the anger associated with the frustration of personal goals. In short, conflict is arousing and motivating.

If the conflict level is very high, the resultant emotional level is also high and the resolution of the conflict is likely to be simple, at least in the short term. Simple resolution takes the form either of *escape* (avoidance or denial of the problem in the intrapersonal case and withdrawal from interaction in the interpersonal case) or of *exaggerated action* (precipitous choice in the intrapersonal case and hasty surrender or aggressive attack in the interpersonal case).

With lower levels of conflict, more complex reactions are possible. At the intrapersonal level, the individual is motivated to think about the relationship and to assess it in relation to alternative activities. This process can be highly informative to him—for example, as he recognizes the benefits of the relationship that he has been taking for granted, or as he mentally tests his feelings about the partner and finds them to be somewhat different from what he had thought. At higher levels of conceptualization, intrapersonal conflict motivates thought about such questions as "What are my personal priorities in life?" and "How does what I'm doing compare with what I *want* to be doing?" Self-defining questions of this sort may be unlikely ever to be raised by the individual until he or she encounters choices and decisions such as those posed by the close relationship (e.g., the marriage commitment). Bolton (1961) describes very clearly how young people "use their love relations as vehicles for dealing with identity problems . . . [p. 240]."

As some of the preceding points have implied, interpersonal conflict may engender changes in feelings and attitudes. There may be a crystalization of sentiments about the relationship that supports a new self-attribution of "being in love." As the person resolves conflicts in favor of the partner's interests, there develops a basis for a self-attribution of "really caring" for the partner. Through cognitive restructuring, the person may reduce the perceived incompatibility between the relationship and other important life goals (e.g., career goals), and even perceive ways in which the relationship can promote those goals.

Similar informational and change effects may result from interpersonal conflict. Open conflict is often the occasion when persons first reveal to each other certain feelings, doubts, disappointments, expectations, ideals, and assessments they have about the relationship. For example, in the stress of open conflict, previously guarded feelings of love and dependence may be expressed. Differences in preferences also become explicitly revealed. Often, the new information exchanged may lead to a reinterpretation of the partner's past behavior, as, for example, altruistic when it may have been previously viewed as rational or self-interested. During the conflict, there may be opportunities for one person to show the empathy with the partner's anguish and the caring for the partner that bespeak love. Similarly, the joint compromises during conflict or the reconciliation following an open breach in the interaction provides each partner with evidence of the other's attachment to the relationship.

Change occurs as interpersonal conflict motivates and makes possible a joint conceptualization (or reconceptualization) of the relationship. Questions of the following sort are (implicitly or explicitly) raised and answered: What are we like as a pair? Where do we stand now and where are we headed? What kind of relationship should we have (or do we want to have)? To what do we, separately and together, attach greatest importance? How do my partner and I really feel about our relationship? In the course of conflict the two persons attempt to influence each other about these issues, and in so doing they may incorporate new norms for their relationship, new goals for each other, and a new definition of their relationship. These new conceptualizations are designed to eliminate further conflict and to serve control purposes—both in self-control, as the individual applies the rules and criteria to himself or herself, and in social control, as each person employs them as standards for the other.

From these properties of the conflict process, it can be seen that relationship development characterized by conflict will often exhibit sharp discontinuities. The discomfort generated by conflict that reaches some threshold point motivates the person and the pair to grasp for a rule or concept that will produce a reduction in conflict. Once the conflict is reduced, both reinforcement and attributional processes may operate to attach great emotional significance to the operative rule or concept. The particular formula of reconciliation, the terms of endearment used in the rapprochement, and even the time and place of the conflict resolution may take on special significance for the pair and be referred to later in order to enforce the new feelings of closeness and unity. Ambivalence and uncertainty may be transformed into a commitment that has few qualifications. Thus, the outcome of the conflict may become highly informative as to the future of the relationship, even though one might have had a difficult time predicting such a result. In this way, a strong conflict provides a point where the relationship may possibly take a sharp turn (subjectively, an unpredictable one.)

By making possible innovation, new levels of commitment, and discontinuities in the relationship, conflict also contributes to the pair's perceived sense of the uniqueness of their relationship. In the growth process, there is likely to be some movement of the couple away from rules and criteria shared with other, similar relationships and toward the development of unique standards. Even if the couple never invents anything novel, the experiences they share in thrashing out their differences are likely to lead them to feel that their arrangements are unique and that there is "something special" about their relationship.

In the foregoing, we have depicted the positive side of open interpersonal conflict. Our purpose has been to emphasize the constructive potentialities of conflict, which are too often overlooked. While not intending to detract from these positive potentialities, we must at least mention the more negative aspects. With respect to information transmission, the new information communicated during conflict will not always be accepted at face value. The two persons' assessments of prior events are likely to be different. Once in the open, the divergent views themselves may become a source of further conflict and conceptualization. For example, a husband's unacceptable attribution about his wife's behavior may encourage her to raise questions about his propensities as an attribution maker. Consequently, the use of the additional information provided during conflict may not always be the use intended by the person who provides the information.

The change or influence attempts that occur in conflict—and, indeed, in almost every aspect of conflict behavior—may themselves become objects of conflict. Things said in the heat of conflict are often interpreted as reflecting true feelings and attitudes, and there is often some justification for such an interpretation, insofar as the emotion incited by conflict weakens normative and self-presentation controls. The proliferation of issues caused by the trading of accusations, commonly observed in conflict, operates against keeping problems narrowly enough defined so that solutions can be easily invented. What is perhaps most serious, the escalation that is characteristic of open conflict often lays bare basic disagreements—differences at the higher levels of interdependence—that might have remained implicit had the interaction remained at the concrete level of specific behaviors. The two persons may realize that they have not only specific conflicts of interest but also basic and perhaps irreconcilable differences in moral principles and human values. Thus, conflict interactions may create barriers to good problem-solving, and they have the potentiality for bringing to the surface basic incompatibilities. Finally, the discontinuity in development, noted earlier, that is sometimes generated by conflict may now show up as a sharp turn from positive feelings to intense dislike: Kirkpatrick and Caplow (1945) found that following the breakup of love affairs, about 10% of a college-student sample reported feeling hostility toward the former partner. As Scanzoni (1970) observes, "Intimacy is no safeguard against hostility—indeed, it may be the breeding ground for its most severe forms [p. 136]."

B. Research Needs

The evidence on the role that conflict plays in the development of relationships is very sparse. It is fairly clear that most couples experience *conflict of interest* in their relationships. From their classic study of 1000 engaged couples, Burgess and Wallin (1953) conclude that "Evidently disagreements in one or more areas of the relationship are the rule and 'always' or 'almost always' agreeing the exception . . . [p. 247]." In their sample, the "rule" seems to apply to about 80% of the couples. Open conflict is probably also a part of the common experience. In Gurin, Veroff, and Feld's national-survey sample (1960), 45% of the married respondents admitted that they had had "problems getting along with each other." One suspects that an estimate of the proportion of marriages that include overt interpersonal conflict would be a conservative one if we assume that what was admitted in this sample corresponds to what is actual.

The net effect of conflict on courtship and marriage relations, whether positive or negative, is more difficult to assess. It is a well documented fact that reported conflict (problems, disagreement, un-realized expectations, behavior disliked by partner) is associated with marital unahppiness (e.g., Birchler, Weiss & Vincent, 1975; Gurin, Veroff, & Feld, 1960; Orden & Bradburn, 1968; and Ort, 1950) and with divorce (e.g., Locke, 1951). When interpreting this association, we must distinguish between conflict as an effect or a symptom and conflict as a cause. In part, open conflict undoubtedly reflects factors that make unlikely the development of a cohesive and satisfying relationship; for example, the inability of one person to provide appropriate rewards for the other; or one partner's propensities and preferences to act in ways that are aversive to the other. Moreover, the continued occurrence of unresolved conflict reflects a failure of one or both partners to change or modify maladaptive behavior. Thus, open conflict is partly a symptom of causal factors that prevent relationship happiness. However, open conflict also serves to contribute to unhappiness and instability. As the Kelley, Cunningham, and Braiker-Stambul study shows, conflict behavior itself becomes an object of conflict. The way two persons fight and the interpretations they place on each other's conflict actions often afford further reasons for unhappiness. Thus, as shown by Terman's (1938) early study, many of the grievances that most clearly differentiate between happy and unhappy couples have to do with conflict behavior: the partner is argumentative, critical, nagging, complaining, quick-tempered, oversensitive, etc.

While there is little doubting the often destructive nature of open conflict, a case can also be made that conflict does not necessarily threaten the close interpersonal relationship, a point on which, as Scanzoni asserts, "most sociologists have come to agree [1970, p. 147]." A first important fact is that a considerable number of happy couples have conflict. In Gurin, Veroff, and Feld's sample (1960), 32% of the persons describing their marriages in the most favorable terms ("very happy") reported that they had had problems getting along with each other. Locke's (1951) data on marital adjustment indicates that while over half of the divorced sample reported two or more disliked activities of the mate, about a fifth of the happily married sample also gave the same report. A similar view is provided by Birchler, Weiss, and Vincent (1975), based on diaries of conflicts and arguments. Couples "currently experiencing marital distress" reported an average of 3.4 conflicts over a 5-day period; happily married couples reported, on the average, one conflict over the same period.

More impressive than the incidence of conflict in happy couples is the fact that conflict can occur between partners who are also experiencing rewarding interaction. Both Braiker-Stambul's data, reported above, and those of Orden and Bradburn (1968) show that measures of positive aspects of the relationship (love and attachment, in the former study, frequency of pleasurable activities, in the latter) are not correlated with measures of conflict. Both sets of data are derived from partners in existing marriages, so they presumably reveal something about conflict in successful, happy, or at least continuing relationships.

At the very least, the lack of correlation means that in successful relationships, conflict can and does coexist with positive satisfactions. Beyond that, the result raises questions about the bases of conflict and the handling of conflict in such relationships. As was noted before, there are indications that happy relationships have fewer conflicts, whether conflicts of interest or open conflicts. Moreover, it is entirely possible that the conflicts that do occur are less severe in relatively happy as compared with relatively unhappy couples. As we observed earlier, a low degree of conflict may be stimulating for a relationship, whereas a high degree may be debilitating. Some successful relationships may experience an optimum level of conflict by virtue of encountering a small number of nonserious bases of disagreement. A different hypothesis is that successful couples have different kinds of problems from those that unsuccessful ones have. Mathews and Mihanovich (1963) set out to test the opposite hypothesis, but conclude, "Unhappy marriages have many more and different problems [p. 304]." Although their results are very clear on the more point, they are not at all convincing with regard to the *different* point. A close examination of the data leaves one with the impression that when the overall differential rates of problems are set aside, the remaining differences reflect the simple fact that in unhappy couples there is more often a schism between the two persons: feelings of neglect, lack of love, and lack of communication. In other words, the differences in problems may merely reflect the unhappy pairs' progress along the road to disruption and may tell us little about the basic problems in their relationships. Once again we encounter the problem of distinguishing between problems as causes and problems as effects.

The belief that successful couples have many of the same problems as unhappy ones is accompanied by the assumption that the good fortune of the former reflects their superior ability to deal with conflict when it arises. Terman's (1938) marital happiness scale included an item about the usual result of disagreements and the response "agreement by mutual give and take" was scored as indicating happiness. When allowance is made for the partial correlation thus generated, Terman's results show clearly that couples with higher happiness scores more often settle disagreements in this manner. This result is confirmed by Ort's (1950) study of marital happiness and Locke's (1951) comparison of happy and divorced couples. Both of these studies suggest that successful couples not only are more prone to settle conflict by discussion but are less likely to react by avoidance. It is tempting to conclude that a successful marriage may be partially dependent on the couple's possession of good conflict resolution skills, but once more, we must remember that conflict can be either cause or effect, or both. Discussion and give and take may not be very feasible for the unhappy couples in view of the frequency and intensity of problems they confront.

Unfortunately, we are not able to find any systematic evidence relating to the positive role of conflict. There has been a growing recognition in social science that conflict may be "productive" or "constructive" in its effects (see Altman & Taylor, 1973, for a brief summary of these views). However, as yet there is no documentation of these possibilities. We have summarized here a number of theoretical considerations to suggest that, under special conditions, conflict will contribute to the development of the close relationship and, particularly, to the properties that the couple feels characterizes their uniqueness. By their nature, the processes we have described may be very difficult to identify. All the evidence we have suggests that positive outcomes may not be the most common. Indeed, they may be rather rare, occurring only under optimal conditions of (a) frequency and intensity of conflict, (b) background of positive interchange, and (c) conflict-coping capabilities of the couple.

More generally, we would emphasize the double importance of studying conflict in close relationships. In its own right, such studying forms a basis for reducing the expensive negative consequences of marital conflict. Our analysis raises particular questions about the role of conflict in generating further conflict. Investigators in the field of predicting marital adjustment would be well advised, in our view, to give consideration to the hypothesis that an important basis for adjustment is found in a consensus within the couple about how to deal with conflict. Besides its direct importance, we believe that the investigation of conflict holds great promise for the understanding of basic aspects of close interpersonal relationships. The issues and processes of conflict reveal a great deal about the underlying structure and dynamics of the close relationship.

For either of the above purposes, conflict can be investigated meaningfully only by studies that are longitudinal and focus on the interaction process. This particular methodology affords the only definitive approach to disentangling the difficult issue of conflict as an effect versus conflict as a cause. It is distressing to note that even the best of the existing studies fall far short of satisfying these essential methodological requirements.

References

Altman, I. & Taylor, D. A. *Social penetration.* New York: Holt, 1973.

Birchler, G. R., Weiss, R. L., & Vincent, J. P. Multimethod analysis of social reinforcement exchange between maritally distressed and nondistressed spouse and stranger dyads. *Journal of Personality and Social Psychology,* 1975, *31,* 349–360.

Bolton, C. D. Mate selection as the development of a relationship. *Journal of Marriage and Family Living,* 1961, *23,* 234–240.

Bowerman, C. E. Adjustment in marriage: Over-all and in specific areas. *Sociology and Social Research,* 1957, *41,* 257–263.

Braiker-Stambul, H. B. *Stages of courtships: The development of premarital relationships.* Doctoral Dissertation, University of California, Los Angeles, 1975.

Brim, O. G., Jr., Fairchild, R. W., & Borgatta, E. F. Relations between family problems. *Marriage and Family Living,* 1961, *23,* 219–226.

Brown, J. S. & Farber, I. E. Emotions conceptualized as intervening variables with suggestions toward a theory of frustration. *Psychological Bulletin,* 1951, *48,* 465–495.

Burgess, E. W. & Wallin, P. *Engagement and marriage.* Philadelphia: Lippincott, 1953.

Cottrell, L. S., Jr. The analysis of situational fields in social psychology. *American Sociological Review,* 1942, *7,* 370–382.

DeBurger, J. E. Marital problems, help-seeking, and emotional orientation as revealed in help-request letters. *Journal of Marriage and the Family,* 1967, *29,* 712–721.

Foote, N. N. Concept and method in the study of human development. In M. Sherif & M. O. Wilson (Eds.), *Emerging problems in social psychology.* Normal, Oklahoma: University Book Exchange, 957.

Goode, W. J. *After divorce.* Glencoe, Illinois: Free Press, 1956.

Gurin, G., Veroff, J. & Feld, S. *Americans view their mental health.* New York: Basic Books, 1960.

Heiss, J. S. Degree of intimacy and male-female interaction. *Sociometry,* 1962, *25,* 197–208.

Ingersoll, H. L. A study of the transmission of authority patterns in the family. *Genetic Psychology Monographs,* 1948, *38,* 225–302.

Kelley, H. H. & Thibaut, J. W. *Interpersonal relations: A theory of interdependence*. New York: Wiley-Interscience, 1978.

Kirkpatrick, C. & Caplow, T. Emotional trends in the courtship experience of college students as expressed by graphs with some observations on methodological implications. *American Sociological Review*, 1945, *10*, 619–626.

Levinger, G. Sources of marital dissatisfaction among applicants for divorce. *American Journal of Orthopsychiatry*, 1966, *36*, 803–807.

Levinger, G. & Huesmann, L. R. An "incremental exchange" perspective on the pair relationship: Interpersonal reward and level of involvement. In K. J. Gergen, M. S. Greenberg, & R. H. Willis, (Eds.), *Social exchange: Advances in theory and research*. New York: Wiley, 1978.

Levinger, G. & Snoek, J. D. *Attraction in relationship: A new look at interpersonal attraction*. New York: General Learning Press, 1972.

Lewin, K. *Field theory in social sciences*. New York: Harper, 1951.

Locke, H. J. *Predicting adjustment in marriage*. New York: Holt, 1951.

Mathews, V. D. & Mihanovich, C. S. New orientations on marital adjustment. *Marriage and Family Living*, 1963, *25*, 300–304.

McCall, G. J. A symbolic interactionist approach to attraction. In T. L. Huston (Ed.), *Foundations of interpersonal attraction*. New York: Academic Press, 1974.

McClintock, C. G. Social motivation—a set of propositions. *Behavioral Science*, 1972, *17*, 438–454.

Orden, S. R. & Bradburn, N. M. Dimensions of marriage happiness. *American Journal of Sociology*, 1968, *73*, 715–731.

Ort, R. S. A study of role-conflicts as related to happiness in marriage. *Journal of Abnormal and Social Psychology*, 1950, *45*, 691–699.

Patterson, G. R. & Hops, H. Coercion, a game for two: Intervention techniques for marital conflict. In R. E. Ulrich & P. Mountjoy (Eds.), *The experimental analysis of social behavior*. New York: Appleton-Century-Crofts, 1972.

Ryder, R., Kafka, J. S., & Olson, D. H. Separating and joining influences in courtship and early marriage. *American Journal of Orthopsychiatry*, 1971, *41*, 450–464.

Scanzoni, J. *Opportunity and the family*. New York. Free Press, 1970.

Terman, L. M. *Psychological factors in marital happiness*. New York: McGraw-Hill, 1938.

Thibaut, J. W. and Kelley, H. H. *The social psychology of groups*. New York: Wiley, 1959.

Waller, W., & Hill, R. *The family: A dynamic interpretation*. New York: Dryden, 1951.

6

A Social Exchange View on the Dissolution of Pair Relationships[1]

GEORGE LEVINGER

I. Introduction

Two of the persons quoted below are describing a friendship, two a marriage. Two are telling about a gratifying current relationship; the others are reporting on ones that have deteriorated. The informants differ in age, in sex, and in the nature of their relationships. Here are their brief descriptions.

> *Ben and I really have a lot in common. I like being with him. We may not talk much, but we like doing things together— fishing, camping, canoeing. I can always count on him* [Man, 25, describing his strong ongoing friendship].

> *We both lead busy lives, but our time together is really important. We just enjoy being near one another . . . . One of my real joys in life is lying in bed hugging and being hugged by Steve* [Woman, 67, telling about her 42-year marriage].

[1] Work on this chapter was supported in part by Grant BNS-02575 from the National Science Foundation. I am indebted to Ann Levinger and Marylyn Rands for their extremely helpful comments and discussions on early versions of the manuscript, and also to Ted Huston, Joseph Pleck, and Ivan Steiner for their reactions to the last draft.

169

> *Things haven't been so good lately. I sometimes wonder if
> it's worth trying to make a go of things between Mary and me.
> We're at each other all the time lately, arguing or bickering . . . .
> There's not much fun now, not like it used to be* [Man, 41,
> reporting on his 16-year marriage that has gone into a tailspin].

> *Sue and I used to be really close friends, but we haven't seen
> much of each other since she went back to school. She's always
> so busy now* [Woman, 29, telling about her former good
> friendship].

All of these rather different relationships can be considered from a
single theoretical viewpoint—that of social exchange theory. As noted
elsewhere in this volume, social-exchange theory views human interaction as the ongoing exchange of mutually rewarding activities. It assumes
that activities differ in their rewardingness and costliness for different
actors and at different occasions, and that members of a relationship seek
to maximize their rewards and minimize their costs. Presumably, a rewarding association will continue; a costly one will eventually be terminated.

Despite the modesty of these assumptions—or perhaps because of
it—the exchange view of close interpersonal relationships has its critics.
They have argued that the approach is materialistic, that love defies
computation, or that members of intimate, as contrasted with superficial
relationships, do not think about equity or tit-for-tat.

This chapter will argue that exchange theory is indeed useful for
understanding a variety of phenomena that occur in close relationships,
even though its concepts and interpretations do not necessarily correspond to the partners' phenomenal experience. The chapter will suggest
that partners' deliberate attention to and evaluation of their exchange
balance differ at different stages and depend on the meaning of the
relationship.

The chapter is divided into two parts. The first part analyzes the
exchange orientation to relationships. It begins by examining four illustrative cases, and then considers some limitations in and modifications of
the analysis. The second part looks at the determinants of pair dissolution
from a social-exchange perspective.

II. An Exchange Perspective on Relationships

The present approach is influenced by Thibaut and Kelley's (1959)
model of dyadic interdependence and a later modification of it in the
"incremental-exchange" model of Huesmann and Levinger (1976;

Levinger & Huesmann, in press). The former focused mainly on the pair *situation*; the latter enlarged the perspective to the pair *relationship*.

A pair *situation* consists of the matrix of all possible interactions formed by two actors' behavior repertoires (Thibaut & Kelley, 1959). Each possible interaction has an associated outcome value, or payoff. Figure 6.1a shows an example of such an outcome matrix. Thibaut and Kelley assumed that interactants evaluate the goodness of their outcomes against two standards: the *comparison level* (CL), which refers to the average value of all outcomes one has experienced in a comparable situation; and the *comparison level for alternatives* (CL$_{alt}$), which is the level of outcomes expected in one's best currently available alternative to the present relationship.

A pair relationship consists of a set of such pair situations, as shown in Figure 6.1b. The actors' past experience with a variety of such situations indicates the extent of their familiarity with each other. The degree of their outcome interdependence indexes the level of their mutual involvement, or the depth of their relationship (Huesmann & Levinger, 1976). In superficial relationships, the actors have jointly experienced few situations or interpersonal outcomes; in deep relationships, they usually have experienced a large number of outcomes in diverse pair situations.

A. Illustrative Analyses

Consider the examples of the satisfying friendship and the satisfying marriage described briefly at the start of this chapter. In what ways are those persons' satisfactions interpretable in exchange-theory terms? To

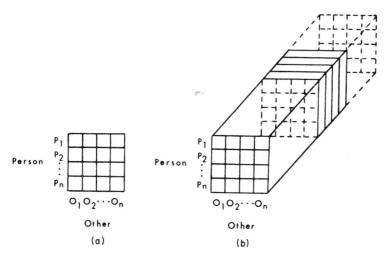

Figure 6.1 Two illustrations of dyadic outcome matrices: (a) the pair situation; (b) the pair relationship (from Levinger, 1974a).

begin with, note that both informants tell us that their time *together* with their partner is a particular source of enjoyment; their interaction generates pleasure for each other. This may partly derive from their good coordination or their special responsiveness to each other's needs. It partly stems from the similarity of their desires and from their compatible behavioral repertoires—whether outdoors in the woods (for the male friends) or indoors in bed (for the spouses).

By telling us that their relationships are good, both informants signify that their outcomes are generally above their personal comparison level or, CL (Thibaut & Kelley, 1959)—that is, each individual's subjective standard of satisfaction. (Other friends with higher CLs might find Ben's outdoors accomplishments below par; other women might be dissatisfied with Steve as a bedmate.) Their outcomes also appear to compare favorably with those expected from any alternative (CL_{alt}). Elsewhere in the interviews, neither respondent mentioned anyone whom he or she saw even nearly as attractive as the partner, implying that the outcomes far exceed CL_{alt}. In that sense, each informant is dependent on the relationship. A separate interview with the partner revealed that the dependence is mutual and is recognized as such by both members.

Now consider the unsatisfactory relationships described in the contrasting third and fourth excerpts. The marriage of Mary and her husband, Norm, has reached a point of malcoordination and miserable communication. Its outcomes have slid below Norm's CL; they compare unfavorably with those Norm remembers from the past, and he is clearly upset. Elsewhere in the interview he says that he is trying to find ways of improving things, to help put back a spark into the marriage, but at the moment he is in a quandary. Norm does not, at this time, admit to thinking about possible alternatives: The relationship remains above his CL_{alt}; he does not wish to break up the marriage; nor is he looking for more pleasurable female companions. Nonetheless, the pair's present relationship is unstable; if it does not soon begin to get better, it may well move toward dissolution. In a separate interview, Mary reported comparable unhappiness, and interests increasingly divergent from Norm's. Despite their unsatisfactory interaction, however, each spouse is still committed to the relationship, respects the other as a person, enjoys their home and mutual friends, and does not seriously contemplate the alternative of divorce. Although their dyadic outcomes have dropped below each spouse's CL, neither spouse currently finds them below CL_{alt}. Furthermore, their strong commitments to their children and mutual friends act as barriers against a breakup; in other words, even if they preferred an alternative status, they would be deterred by the high emotional cost of termination.

The fourth relationship—between Sue and Joyce, the interviewee—is rather different. Their friendship has not been formally broken, but the two women have drifted so far apart that Joyce no longer gets anything out of it. Joyce expresses regret tinged with bitterness, for she and Sue were once very close and she still feels a sense of loss. At one time the friendship's outcomes for Joyce were far above her CL. Although its loss has not been replaced by any other, her CL_{alt} is still below the outcomes she receives merely from remembering past pleasures. Sue's case, though, has been different; she has developed satisfying alternatives, which she finds more attractive than continuing her earlier friendship.

OUTCOME COMPARISON, ATTRACTION, AND STABILITY

Let us try to integrate the above analyses. In inventing the concepts CL and CL_{alt}, Thibaut and Kelley (1959) used them for defining *attraction* and *dependence*. One's *attraction* to a relationship is definable by whether or how far its outcomes are above one's comparison level. One's *dependence* on a relationship is an inverse function of one's CL_{alt}; the more attractive one's alternatives are, the less is one's dependence. If both partners are dependent on their dyadic relationship, its future appears to be stable.

Four major types of relatedness can thus be generated from this model of outcome comparison: (a) attractive stability, where each member's outcomes exceed both CL and CL_{alt}; (b) attractive instability, where either member's outcomes in the relationship are, or may be, below those obtainable elsewhere; (c) unattractive stability, where present outcomes are unsatisfying but still better than those one foresees anywhere else; and (d) unattractive instability, where one or both member's payoffs fall below *both* CL and CL_{alt} and the relationship either has been or soon will be terminated. Early formative relations are often instances of attractive instability; later long-term attachments frequently illustrate attractive stability; and declining relationships may first be marked by unattractive stability and subsequently by unattractive instability and breakup.

WHAT REWARDS ARE EXCHANGED?

Social-exchange theory assumes that social interaction consists of mutually rewarding exchanges. A difficulty, however, is that the theory itself provides no special basis for analyzing the value of the varying rewards that partners may gain from each other. My colleagues and I—aware that few empirical studies have inquired about the sorts of rewards people receive from each other—have recently begun to investigate this topic. In one study of steadily attached heterosexual couples, we found that partners reported the greatest rewards from joint activities, mutual help, supportive communication, and the display of physical affection (Levinger, Rands, & Talaber, 1977). In a study by Richard Mack (cited in Levinger, 1974a), close relationships were also marked by reports of shared ownership and exclusive commitment. And, in our recent research on mid- to upper-income married pairs who have remained satisfactorily together for many years, we find that members of such marriages report that they give much respect to each other and that they try hard to work together to solve common difficulties.

Most interpersonal rewards are interpretable according to a schema offered by Foa and Foa (1974), who propose that interpersonal rewards derive from six broad categories of resources, which they have labeled *money, goods, information, status, services,* and *love.* Their six categories arrange themselves into a two-dimensional circular order, reflecting the two dimensions of *particularism* and *concreteness.* For instance, love is the most particularistic resource, because its value depends most on the person from whom it is received. Money is the least particularistic, or most universal, resource, because its value is generally independent of its provider. Goods and services, which involve the exchange of tangible products or activities, are considered highest in concreteness. Giving or receiving status and information is considered lowest in concreteness and highest in symbolic content.

Interpersonal relations seem initially to develop on the basis of universalistic exchanges, whether concrete or symbolic. Thus at first goods, services, or information that are valued generally would be exchanged. Later, however, the most valued rewards are those that signify unique meaning to the partners. The value of various services or information depends greatly on who it is that offers them, and intimate feelings in relationships are maintained largely through the interchange of symbolic and affectional resources.

B. How Well Does the Exchange Concept Apply to the Close Relationship?

It is sometimes suggested that love relationships differ essentially from exchange relationships. For example, Boulding (1974) has argued that in love "the individual comes to identify his own desires with those of another [p. 160]," whereas exchange is marked by a belief that may be expressed thus: "I will do something good for you if you will do something good for me [p. 155]." In an analogous vein, Altman (1973) has suggested that intimates frequently deviate from the direct reciprocity that is observed in relations among strangers. Furthermore, in our own empirical study of rewards in relationships (Levinger, Rands, & Talaber, 1977), we found that members of stable intimate pairs often resisted thinking in terms of reward or cost, and that they felt uncomfortable about systematically analyzing the components of their interaction with their partner or alternative partners. None of these arguments or findings, however, are necessarily incompatible with the application of exchange theory.

To begin with, as a relationship becomes more intimate the partners' time perspectives become extended. A change occurs in the meaning of "I will do something good for you if you do something good for me." The *if* no longer applies, for each person can imagine countless instances where the other has already done good or is likely to do so again. Long-term friends are less concerned about immediate reciprocity than are short-term friends (this idea is further examined later).

Furthermore, increasing intimacy is marked by an increase in the number and the variety of particularistic exchanges (Foa & Foa, 1974), in which one does good for the other at little cost and much pleasure to the self. Sexual intercourse is one example, and there are many other complementary activities where two partners take mutually beneficial complementary roles. They continue to discover new areas of payoff correspondence: one person listening while the other is talking, one helping when the other desires help, one paddling astern while the other is at the bow.

Finally, it is possible to construct formal models of social exchange that incorporate the assumption that, as interpersonal involvement deepens, one's partner's satisfactions and dissatisfactions become more and more identified with one's own. Indeed, such a formal model, named RELATE, has been constructed so as to be suitable for computer simulation of relationship development (Huesmann & Levinger, 1976). RELATE employs a multiple, sequentially arranged set of outcome matrices such as those shown in Figure 6.1b. The interaction between Person and Other is postulated to move from one situation to another; situations differ in the nature of possible interactions and payoff consequences. In this incremental exchange model, situations of deeper involvement have potentially greater expected values for each partner. Furthermore, as relationships move toward greater depth, the partner's payoffs are increasingly weighted into one's own payoffs—an explicit acknowledgement of the notion that deepening intimacy implies increasing mutual identification.

An important aspect of the RELATE model is that one's past outcomes, whether positive or negative, are added into the cumulative payoff that one has experienced in the relationship. One of RELATE's rules is as follows: "An actor terminates a relationship if the expected payoff from a competing relationship minus the cost of terminating the current one exceeds the expected payoff from the current relationship by an amount sufficient to overcome the effect of past credits and debits [Huesmann & Levinger, 1976, p. 201]." In other words, even if current outcomes seem low, the model assumes that partners are encouraged to maintain their relationship by a high cumulative payoff or credit balance.

C. Awareness of the Exchange Balance at Different Stages of a Relationship

It is here proposed that the magnitude of one's perceived exchange balance (or cumulative payoff) in the relationship has an important bearing on one's attention to currently available rewards and costs. Imagine the analogy of a bank credit balance: If one's credit balance is high, one makes deposits and withdrawals without tension, and with less need for record keeping than if it is low. Similarly, in a relationship where the accumulated benefits are high and continuing, there is likely to be inattention to one's costs and little desire for a regular accounting. If, on the other hand, one's rewards have so far been slight—as in a casual acquaintanceship—or if one feels the other is overdrawing the account, one is prone to attend carefully to the rewardingness of current and anticipated outcomes.

It may be further hypothesized that pair members' awareness of the exchange aspects of their interaction differs at different stages of their relationship. Three such stages will be distinguished here: a formative stage, a stable middle or plateau stage, and a declining stage. This discussion will be limited to primarily voluntary social relations, rather than to kinship or business relations whose conduct is more strongly determined by the social environment.

TIME SPAN

Early in a relationship, interactions are usually seen in a limited time frame. Thus early acquaintances are likely to look for reciprocity of disclosure or to help each other on a near-term basis (Altman, 1973). As a relationship deepens and stabilizes, its time frame expands; current outcomes are evaluated with a regard to a longer past and a more foreseeable future. During the decline of a relationship, however, it is likely that both past pleasures and prospective gratifications will be discounted (Huesmann & Levinger, 1976); one's effective time span, therefore, has again become shorter and one's awareness of rewards and costs is more immediate.

THE FORMATIVE STAGE

During the formative stage, it may be difficult to distinguish between pair breakup and the failure of a pair to be formed. It is clear, though, that superficial interaction is marked by exploration and testing. Individuals are inclined to pursue those early contacts that appear likely to lead to later reward (Berscheid & Walster, 1969; Levinger & Snoek, 1972), and before forming commitments they are likely to consider alternative options. Thus early contacts are unstable. To the extent that one is concerned with the future of a relationship—and particularly in contemplating an exclusive long-term relationship—the magnitude of the exchange balance is likely to be salient in one's thoughts.

Experiences with new friends, then, would be analyzed more carefully than those with old friends. For example, if an evening with a new friend gives only small pleasure, it probably occasions more caution than would a similar evening with a steady friend. In heterosexual relations, men have been found to be more quickly romantic and women more cautiously pragmatic during early encounters (Rubin, 1975). This is easily understandable if it is assumed that women generally invest a greater portion of their lives in couple relationships; in marriage particularly, their status becomes more dependent on the male partner than vice versa. Writing about the process of mate selection, Hill, Rubin, and Peplau (1976) have interpreted these male–female differences as follows:

> In most marriages, the wife's status, income, and life chances are far more dependent on her husband's than vice versa. . . . In "free choice" systems of mate selection like our own, the woman must be especially discriminating. She cannot allow herself to fall in love too quickly, nor can she afford to stay in love too long with the wrong person. . . . The fact that a woman's years of marriageability tend to be more limited than a man's also contributes to her great need to be selective [p. 163].

THE PLATEAU STAGE

Let us now turn to pairs who have established an enduring relationship that both members value and desire to perpetuate—the case of attractive stability. In such a rich relationship, it does seem likely that the partners will deemphasize its exchange properties. I believe, however, that this is not because exchange principles cease to function, but because such a pair has an economy of surplus. People recognize that having a lot in common helps to make a partnership thrive. In exchange theory terms, common interests allow partners to engage in joint actions that enhance mutual pleasure at low cost, and thus promote a continuing high credit balance in their relationship.

To illustrate this, let us consider some activities associated with a traditional marriage: sexuality, earning a living, and recreation. If both partners get intense pleasure from their sexual interplay, every sexual contact will add to their common account. In contrast, if one partner sees his or her sexual activity as a sacrifice for the other's benefit, then it may be difficult to avoid a conscious or unconscious desire for compensation. Earning a living may provide one with great personal satisfaction or it may be perceived as distasteful, done only to support one's family; only in the latter case is one likely to mark it down on the debit side of the ledger. Recreational activities are frequently carried on jointly by married partners; spouses in satisfying marriages often report that they have adjusted their recreational preferences in order to spend much of their leisure time together (Rapoport, Rapoport, & Thiessen, 1974). If both get pleasure from an excursion, for example, then neither is likely to think in terms of social exchange. But if one spouse goes along grudgingly, just to comply with the other's wishes, then the other may well feel the need to make up in some way, so as to restore the balance.

From a theoretical standpoint, then, it should be possible to assess the working of an ongoing relationship by examining both partners' expressions of reward and sacrifice regarding each of the relationship's central activities. Either member's preoccupation with the reward–cost balance could be considered a signal of danger. In some marriages, such signals are attended to; they are a source of discussion, reevaluation, and possible redistribution. In many other marriages, though, such signals are ignored and the relationship is allowed to decline in attractiveness for one or both partners.

THE DECLINING STAGE

It is here hypothesized that, if a long-term relationship begins to turn sour, the partners will again pay close attention to its benefits and its costs, as well as to the benefits foregone by not exploring alternative possibilities. Whether one is mainly concerned with reestablishing the pair's former satisfactions (as is the case with the third pair, discussed before), with attempting to renegotiate the current arrangement, or with trying to withdraw entirely, one is likely to look carefully at the exchange balance.

One scenario played out frequently today is that in which a wife begins to feel that she has contributed far more than her share to her marriage, or that her accumulated returns do not match her investments. In the past, being single carried a stigma for a woman (her CL_{alt} was low). Through marriage, she could obtain status, income, and protection; in return, she expected to play a somewhat subservient role. Now, as a wife's opportunities for a rewarding life outside marriage increase (her CL_{alt} rises), she becomes less dependent on her marital existence. Concurrently, she raises her expectations of what she should be receiving from her marriage (her CL rises) and begins to find her current outcomes insufficient. She becomes dissatisfied with the role demand that she put her own needs behind those of her husband—that she continually nurture her husband more than he nurtures her. In other words, if wives develop satisfying lives outside the home, inequalities in their marital roles are more likely than before to be perceived and to become sources of friction (Scanzoni, 1979).

D. Attractions and Barriers

Until now, we have focused on exchanges within the dyad, with little attention to the external pressures that act either to hold together or to pull apart the union. Before we consider the determinants of pair dissolution, in the following section, it is necessary to examine the constellation of forces that operate on each member of the pair. It will be assumed that two sorts of psychological forces act to keep a person in a relationship—or act to tie him or her into an alternative relationship. Historically, these two types of pressures have been labelled *driving forces* and *restraining forces* (Lewin, 1951). In accordance with my more recent usage (Levinger, 1965, 1976), they are here called *attractions* and *barriers*.

Positive attractions refer to feelings of pleasure, comfort, or admiration of the partner; *negative attractions* (or *repulsions*) stem from the opposite of these feelings. Most of the time, one has both some positive and some negative feelings toward a partner (i.e., ambivalence), but in an intimate relationship positive feelings are expected to predominate. In the present context of social exchange, if, on the one hand, the partner's credit is perceived to be high, one tends to be highly attracted to him or her. On the other hand, if the partner is believed to have overdrawn the account, the belief entails a lowering of one's earlier attraction and a temptation to make comparisons with earlier times and with possible alternatives.

Barrier forces are orthogonal to attraction forces. Barriers derive from the social structure in which we live, or which we ourselves have created—such as the commitments or obligations we ourselves have entered into. They prevent us from acting solely according to our attractions and repulsions.

> Barriers—or psychological "restraining forces (Lewin, 1951)"—affect one's behavior only if one wishes to leave the relationship . . . . Barriers are important for keeping long-term relationships intact. An example is the partnership contract, legitimized by the norms of society. Barriers lessen the effect of temporary fluctuations in interpersonal attraction; even if attraction becomes negative, barriers act to continue the relationship [Levinger, 1976, pp. 24–26].

To explain the continuance of interpersonal relations, exchange theorists have concentrated on the comparative attractiveness of outcomes (Thibaut & Kelley, 1959) or of profits (Homans, 1961), but have neglected the importance of barriers to breakup. Although Thibaut and Kelley do mention that actors differ in dependence on a relationship (as an inverse function of the CL_{alt}), they do not consider that an actor may also be strongly influenced by the partner's own dependence on the relationship (i.e., by the other's low CL_{alt}). For instance, a husband's feelings of obligation to his wife may be raised by the extent of her dependence upon him, or lowered by her expression of independence. In previous exchange theorizing, barriers or termination costs have been merely an implicit component of CL_{alt}—that is, costs that would be deducted from the attractiveness of an alternative. In this analysis, they are an explicit new variable.

Barriers or commitments tend to be much stronger in marriages and other exclusive relationships than they are in friendships, which are usually perceived as non-exclusive (Shurkus, 1977). They become sources of oppression if a relationship's attractions disappear. To better understand the functioning of attractions and barriers, let us consider how they may operate differently during the formative, the stabilized, and the declining stage of a marriage relationship.

ATTRACTIONS AND BARRIERS AT DIFFERENT STAGES

During the formative stage, one seeks out a partner who appears attractive. One attends closely to the positive and negative aspects of the interaction, making explicit comparisons between one's feelings toward this acquaintance and one's feelings toward others. Early in a relationship, the attractiveness of one friend tends to be at most slightly greater than that of alternative friends. Activities rather than specific partners are the focus of one's interaction. If a relationship develops, though, one becomes increasingly concerned with the partner; the nature of one's attraction becomes more nearly unique. Barriers against termination, however, remain relatively low.

If the relationship continues to grow and to give pleasure to both its members, they may want to make a public declaration of their closeness and to ensure the perpetuation of their closeness. In doing so, partners are influenced by their kin, their friends, and the other members of their social network. Making such a declaration—that is, announcing their engagement—reinforces the commitment to each other that they have come to feel.

Subsequently, though, this public commitment takes on a force of its own: It becomes a new psychological and social barrier against dissolution. During a stable middle stage, one usually intends that both attractions and barriers shall continue to remain high. Indeed, if attractions remain high and salient, then it is unlikely that the partners will attend to the restraints against breaking the bond (Levinger, 1976). Nonetheless, marriages differ greatly in the constellation of the spouses' feelings. In some marriages, the spouses' attraction to each other continues to grow over time and few thoughts about the barriers against breakup are reported (Levinger, unpublished data). In other marriages, there is a drop in one or both partners' satisfaction, and they begin to seriously contemplate alternatives; if so, the existence of barriers becomes salient in their thinking.

If a marriage continues its decline, attractions are likely to drop still further, and each member will actively explore alternative possibilities in the interpersonal marketplace. Rather than concentrate on repairing the existing relationship, they may spend increasing time on establishing independence or on forming another pairing. In that eventuality, of course, it is unlikely that the first marriage will be improved; rather, its attractions and barriers erode further, and soon the partners take formal steps to end the legal contract.

III. Determinants of Pair Dissolution

Dissolution refers to "the undoing or breaking up of a tie, bond, or union; the act of resolving into parts or elements; death or decease [American College Dictionary, 1947]." Before something can be undone or broken apart, then, there must first exist an entity, a tie, or a union. When actual relationships split asunder, it may seem in retrospect that their ties of interchange had all along been weak. Note also that the dissolution of a union is assumed to require *acts*; such acts may be abrupt or gradual, open or disguised; but action is necessary. Finally, note that the decease of a pair relationship may occur in various ways: through the death or departure of either member, through the deterioration of their interconnections, or through the destruction of their external social support.

In this part of the chapter, the discussion will be limited to premarital or marital heterosexual relationships. Friendships, whether same-sex or cross-sex, will not be considered. Empirical research on the development or breakup of friendships is scarce in contrast to research on premarital or marital pairs (Huston & Levinger, 1978); the growth and the decline of friendships seem to be less noticeable than those of romantic relationships.

Pair termination will be considered at two different stages: (a) during the formation, and (b) after the formation of a relationship. During the early development of a pair and before there is a strong attachment, a breakup may be fairly abrupt. After the stabilizing of an affective attachment, termination is normally a gradual disengagement.

A. Termination during the Formative Period

By far, most terminations occur before any relationship has formed. Most interpersonal contacts end with one's first impression of someone, before there is any interaction. Another large portion consists of very shallow ones, which neither person has the intention to prolong. For example, a taxi driver picks up a rider only to drop him off a few miles later; a dancer at a contra dance pairs off with one partner, only to whirl away and join hands with another. In a tiny fraction of their relationships, however, people do develop lasting affection and interdependence.

Hinging on the extent of an interpersonal relation, different factors will influence its continuation or termination. Early contacts, for example, are affected by the operation of impersonal factors, such as the spatial and the social distance between two individuals; later contacts seem affected most by the quality of a pair's interaction (Levinger & Snoek, 1972, pp. 11–15). As either partner explores the outcomes that appear available from developing the interaction, he or she may soon find that the expected value is below CL or below CL_{alt} and will decide to discontinue it. The less involved an acquaintanceship, the more immediate are one's calculations about such a decision.

IMPERSONAL AND INDIVIDUAL DETERMINANTS

The continuation or discontinuation of superficial contacts is largely determined by the frequency of meetings imposed by factors outside the relationship. For example, neighbors or classmates continue to see one another regardless of their personal desires. A variety of studies on mate selection have shown that people who are near each other either physically or socially have a much higher probability of developing a relationship than those who are apart (Eckland, 1968). The converse of that finding—that those far apart have a higher probability of terminating their early contacts—is interpretable by exchange theorists as a result of the greater cost of forming or maintaining distant as opposed to nearby connections (Thibaut & Kelley, 1959).

Individual determinants of continuation derive from the characteristics of both the chooser and the chosen. For example, choosers are more likely to seek affiliation if they are high rather than low in affiliation need, or if they are relaxed rather than preoccupied (Levinger & Snoek, 1972). There are marked sex differences among choosers' desires in our culture. One analysis of choosers' pre-interactional expressions of wants and offers was recently derived from a large number of lonely-hearts advertisements in a nationally circulated tabloid. "Women were more likely than men to offer attractiveness, seek financial security, express concerns about the potential partner's motives, and seek someone who was older. In complementary fashion, men were more likely than women to seek attractiveness, offer financial security, profess an interest in marriage, and seek someone who was younger [Harrison & Saeed, 1977, p. 257]." These findings fit well into a social exchange interpretation of relationship formation.

A large variety of findings pertain to the rewardingness of the characteristics of the prospective choice. To begin with, the other's visible characteristics, such as physical attractiveness, height, and posture, play an important part in leading the perceiver to desire further contact (Huston & Levinger, 1978). In addition to such external qualities, signs of the other's inner resources—attitude similarity, or the approval likely to be accorded the chooser—also determine the probability of repeated contact. Presumably, each such perceived quality gives promise of reward; yet the overly high attractiveness of the other may deter one if one believes that pursuit will lead to rejection (Berscheid, Dion, Walster, & Walster, 1971).

INTERACTIONAL DETERMINANTS

Once two persons begin to interact with each other, they begin to respond to the satisfactoriness of their actual joint outcomes in the light of their earlier expectations. Outcomes will be sampled from a variety of their interaction matrices. Continuation or discontinuation of the interaction now depends on whether or not their sampling yields outcomes above CL and CL_{alt}. The higher the two actors' payoff correspondence in their salient outcome matrices, the more gratifying will be their interaction and the more it will promote their exchange balance; conversely, termination will occur if the two actors persist in giving each other unsatisfactory payoffs.

A "filter" model of relationship development (Kerckhoff & Davis, 1962) suggests that later in a relationship new factors are likely to become more important—e.g., another's external appearance will probably become less salient, whereas need compatibility will probably become more so. Recent studies, however, indicate that fixed-sequence filtering models do not adequately account for the multiple ways in which formative relationships break up (Hill, Rubin, & Peplau, 1976; Levinger, Senn, & Jorgensen, 1970). Levinger *et al.* (1970), for instance, found that the breakup of a serious heterosexual relationship depended more on the partners' previous lack of mutual investment than on any identifiable cluster of similar or complementary attitudes or of personal characteristics.

Hill *et al.* (1976) found that premarital pairs who had broken up reported significantly less closeness, love, or exclusiveness in the relationships they had had than pairs who still remained together reported. In contrast, there was no statistically significant difference between couples breaking up and couples remaining together in regard to any of fourteen background or attitudinal characteristics.[2] Retrospective reasons given for breaking up with the partner were most often expressed as follows: "be-

---

[2] A conservative test of statistical significance shows no reliable differences on those measures. Hill *et al.*'s findings parallel those of a previous study of dating pairs by Levinger, Senn, and Jorgensen (1970). In other words, similarity or dissimilarity on a priori background variables is less crucial for the progress of ongoing attachments than the partners' continuing investment in their relationship.

coming bored with the relationship," developing "differences in interests," or one or the other partner's "desire to be independent"—each of the three being reported by a majority of the respondents. In other words, these ex-partners' explanations focused on a decline in the relationship's current rewardingness or on the rise of alternative attractions.

NETWORK INFLUENCES

In the study by Hill *et al.* (1976), less than 15% of the respondents reported that parental pressures had any effect on their breakup; we are not told whether the parents favored or opposed the termination. Another research study has reported that, in fact, parental opposition tended to intensify their children's romantic involvements (Driscoll, Davis, & Lipetz, 1972). Neither of those studies, though, gives any information about the positivity or intensity of the parent–child attachment or the nature of the resources controlled by the kinship network. It would seem that the stronger the filial attachment and the more public the anticipated union, the more will parents exercise influence on their offspring.

Parents and relatives are, of course, only part of a couple's social network; friends and colleagues have often equal or greater influence. Elsewhere in this volume, Ridley and Avery (Chapter 8) propose that members of a social network will exert influence on the life of a relationship as a direct function of a number of variables—including the magnitude of their resources, the multiplexity of their relations to the pair members, and their unanimity regarding the issue. It seems indisputable, then, that significant third parties are important sources of rewards and costs, and of pressures either for or against the continuation of a couple's relationship.

B. The Dissolution of Married Attachments

In formative relations, partners do not usually commit themselves to remain together indefinitely. If they should decide to do so, however, their relationship enters a new phase, in which the barriers against its breakup have become explicit. Marriage is the major form of such a lasting commitment. Entrance into marriage has, at the least, a twofold implication: first, that both partners feel sufficiently attracted to each other to bind themselves formally in marriage; and, second, that once so bound together they will find it more costly than before to terminate their union.

Initially, engagement and marriage are likely to enhance the attraction that partners feel for each other; it is consonant with one's felt experience to believe that one's decision was correct and to suppress one's questions or uncertainties (Brehm & Cohen, 1962). Subsequently, many couples continue to find their marital commitment a source of security and growth, even if they encounter disappointments as well as delights in the course of their relationship. Now, an increasing percentage of spouses, however, are finding disenchantment in their marriage; they find themselves thinking about divorce and disengaging themselves from their relationship.

If disengagement does occur, how is it explainable by an exchange analysis? Here is one example of an exchange interpretation, offered by two economists: "Individuals implicitly weigh the social, economic, and personal benefits (or costs) of marriage. . . . They choose to divorce only when the future expected net benefits of a marriage compare unfavorably to its perceived alternatives [Ross & Sawhill, 1975, p. 38]." Within our present exchange framework, the events of marital dissolution would be interpreted in terms of one or more of the following sorts of changes: (a) a decrease in the net attraction of interacting with one's partner; perhaps the old touch has lost its magic, or once stable resources have deteriorated, or the spouses' interests have shifted so that once enjoyable activities no longer yield pleasure; (b) an increase in the attractiveness of alternative states; for example, a wife discovers her ability to benefit from experiences outside the confines of the home, or a husband gets to know a more pleasing sexual partner; (c) a decrease in the costs of getting gratification outside the relationship, or an erosion of the barriers against breakup. Each such change may stem from alterations in either partner's personal needs or from shifts in their social milieu, and such changes, be it noted, are rarely independent of one another.

DECLINING ATTRACTIONS

Most newlyweds probably expect to continue being in love, to remain sexually compatible, to enjoy a comfortable standard of living, to further develop similar interests and activities, and to resolve their conflicts through honest communication. Research on "happiness," however, indicates that the peak of happiness, the honeymoon, is followed by a slide toward a more prosaic routine that often fails to match earlier expectations (Blood & Wolfe, 1960; Campbell, Converse, & Rodgers, 1976). For instance, a couple's income, which (we'll assume) at the start is no problem, later fails to meet their financial needs, particularly if children are born (Furstenberg, 1976). Economic strain is frequently reflected in marital difficulties. Data from the U.S. Census and from national probability surveys show that a husband's low income and low-employment stability are strongly associated with marital instability (Cherlin, 1979; Cutright, 1971; Ross & Sawhill, 1975). In our society, economic poverty is associated with a complex of family problems that interfere with husbands' and wives' abilities to provide each other with ample interpersonal rewards, such as emotional supportiveness or warm togetherness (Rubin, 1976).

Other correlative elements of marital strain include the partners' lack of love, respect, or companionship, their lack of shared sexual enjoyment, and their feelings of neglect or abuse (Levinger, 1966, 1976). Dissatisfaction in one area of a marriage breeds difficulties in other areas (Goode, 1956), although one may not be able to specify the direction of causality. It does appear that the more serious or persistent complaints—such as employment instability, drunkenness, or brutality—are likely to lead to divorce. By contrast, less serious or more reversible complaints—such as the spouse's lack of love or mental cruelty—permit repair or reconciliation (Levinger, 1974b).

Despite a decline in their marital satisfaction, spouses do continue to stay married, often maintaining a placid relationship (Cuber & Harroff, 1965; Rubin, 1976). If their outcomes deteriorate, they may lower their expectations and deny to themselves that their life together is unsatisfactory. For instance, in national probability surveys (e.g., Campbell *et al.*, 1976), generally less than 5% of married respondents acknowledge dissatisfaction with their marriage; the vast majority report themselves satisfied or very satisfied. A growing fraction, though, may be contemplating alternative possibilities, and in one national survey (Campbell *et al.*, 1976), 16% of the sample had already been separated or divorced at least once.

RISING ALTERNATIVE ATTRACTIONS

Women initiate divorce proceedings about three-fourths of the time (Jacobson, 1959; U.S. Department of Health, Education, and Welfare, 1973). Although this proportion is influenced by legal custom and the technicalities of child support, at least two studies have found that wives wanted separation more than did their husbands (Brown, 1976; Goode, 1956); and in the Hill *et al.* (1976) study of premarital couples, more women than men initiated the breakup of their dating relationship.

A woman's opportunity for an independent life outside marriage, then, seems particularly important for her evaluation of alternative attractions. And indeed, recent studies show that at all economic levels a wife's actual or potential earnings are correlative with her propensity toward divorce (Cherlin, 1979; Ross & Sawhill, 1975).

Finding pleasure with alternative sexual partners is another form of increasing one's alternative attractions—and perhaps also of diminishing the positive outcomes inside one's marriage. There are few solid research findings on the causes and effects of extramarital affairs (Hunt, 1969). Following Hunt's (1969) intensive interview study of a sample of men and women who told him about their extramarital affairs, he wrote as follows:

"The desire for newness and variety is apparently deeply rooted in us all; fidelity to a single sexual partner is not an innate universal human need. . . . And this is why so many of the married—even the happily married—sometimes dream of other loves to refresh their dulled palates, to recall the taste and glow of new love, and to partially allay the harassing desire that comes over us with the years to know another and more exquisite love before it is too late [p. 37]." Nevertheless, most of Hunt's marital interviewees were propelled into their sexual search out of their disenchantment with their own spouse, and it seems very likely that alternative sexual liaisons contributed in turn toward further marital disengagement. A recent study found that even in the sexually liberal marriages of young couples living in communal households most of the breakups were preceded by "extra-couple sexual relationships [Jaffe & Kanter, 1976, p. 184]."

DECLINING BARRIERS

The third element that promotes separation is the erosion of the barriers that help contain the relationship. Normative expectations, both those held by persons outside the marriage and those constructed by the partners themselves influence the partners' continued commitment. When the norms upholding its permanence are put under question, the restraints against breakup tend to diminish.

In a culture that encourages alternative life styles, barriers to marital breakup may lose much of their force, although for highly satisfying relationships their erosion is unimportant. It becomes important only if either member begins to explore alternatives. In that event, the probability of breakup is affected by changes in both external and internal restraining forces: from the outside society or significant others, and from the obligations that partners feel. Let us consider each such source of barrier forces.

In regard to external restraining forces, it is obvious that divorce laws have become more permissive over the past half century and that Americans have become more accepting of the divorced and the remarried. American politicians are no longer disqualified by their divorce from being reelected. An increasing volume of literature (e.g., Longfellow, 1979; Nye, 1957) argues that divorce is less harmful to children than their continuing to live in a tense or conflict-torn home. Furthermore, the very increase in the number of divorced persons reduces the anticipation of deviancy of those who contemplate divorce today. Certainly, the societal context has reduced the social costs to be paid by those who consider marital breakup (Levinger, 1976).

Internal restraining forces reflect in one way or another, each of those outside changes. For example, if a substantial fraction of yesterday's marriages have ended in divorce, it becomes less meaningful today to vow solemnly to stay together "until death do us part"; instead of obligating themselves to continue a marriage "for better or worse," some of today's couples express the limited commitment of remaining together as long as the relationship is "growthful." The current mood appears to favor individual satisfaction at the expense of family or societal stability. Exchange benefits are viewed individualistically rather than collectively.

C. Some Thoughts about the Repair of Deteriorating Relationships

The decline of a relationship does not necessarily imply its continued descent, ending in breakup. If some declines are uncheckable, others are mere temporary "down" periods, to be soon followed by exhilarating "up" periods. Still other declines have a less certain status: They may go in either direction, being susceptible to reversal under the proper conditions. Various marital conflicts result from malcommunication or misunderstandings that are amenable to modification. Many couples can probably deal ably with such problems themselves, but many others need skilled outside intervention or counseling. This chapter cannot elaborate on marriage therapy or relationship enhancement, which have recently become an important topic for research (Gottman, Markman, & Notarius, 1977; Guerney, 1977; Thomas, 1977; Weiss, Hops, & Patterson, 1973), but it can take note of such strategies within the present framework.

A repair strategy, whether it comes from inside or outside the relationship, can focus on any combination of the attraction and barrier forces that affect the relationship. Traditional society's strategy for maintaining marriages was to keep rigid the barriers preventing formal exit and to remove all alternatives from realistic consideration. That strategy had its costs; it often bought public stability at the price of private tension or despair.

A more contemporary maintenance strategy is to revive or raise the couple's mutual feelings of attraction. This requires reducing the negative aspects of the marital interaction and augmenting the positive ones. This approach is consonant with recent advances in behavior modification and therapy. To illustrate this orientation, let us look at an excerpt from Thomas's (1977) suggestion of using explicit "exchange systems" for improving marital communication:

> A system of exchange as applied to marital behavior is a means by which given response consequences, such as reinforcement for engaging in desirable behavior, may be exchanged for particular verbal responses. The exchange is simply a means of achieving behavior-guiding response consequences. It can be mediated by tokens . . . or points . . . or contingency contracts [p. 99].

Thomas and various others (e.g., Weiss, Hops, & Patterson, 1973) report instances of the successful use of such exchange systems for altering distressful marital behavior.

This analysis suggests that attention be drawn to an issue that might be forgotten in attempts to implement purely behavioral solutions, namely, the notion that raising a couple's reward–cost ratio is only an intermediate step toward a more permanent peace.[3] A truly satisfying relationship, it has been argued, is one where both partners have stopped counting reinforcements, where both care for the other's pleasure as they do for their own, and where satisfaction is considered less in terms of "mine" than in terms of "ours." This cognitive–emotional view is not antithetical to behavioral approaches, but it warns of a potential pitfall: It would be ironic if, in their effort to remedy a couple's present ills, attempts at behavior modification were to extinguish the pair's future inclination to employ surprise or mystique. In other words, if our present hypothesis that precise reciprocity is more a sign of unstable than of stable relationships is correct, then efforts toward improving relationships should also develop ways of helping the clients move beyond the confines of literal exchange.

IV. Conclusion

This chapter has applied a social-exchange formulation to the development and dissolution of pair relationships. Concepts such as reward, cost, cumulative payoff, exchange balance, and outcome comparison were used in order to consider relationships differing in their attractiveness and their stability. To examine pair dissolution, those concepts were used in conjunction with the Lewinian constructs of attraction and barrier forces employed in this author's earlier discussions of divorce (Levinger, 1965, 1976). Exchange concepts were used despite the recognition that intimate partners themselves may find them inappropriate for contemplating their ongoing relationship. It was acknowledged that people appear far more ready to attend to the exchange implications of their interpersonal relations during a formative or a declining stage than when relating mutually during a stable middle stage.[4]

---

[3] This point was first suggested by Robert Burgess.

[4] In a manuscript I received while completing this one, Newman and Langer offer a parallel suggestion about intimate partners' cognitive arousal and attribution:

Relationship beginnings are characterized by high levels of stimulation and cognitive activity. . . . Relationship stabilization stages are characterized by a reduction in cognitive demands. Information processing proceeds in a more orderly

When persons first consider the development of a new acquaintanceship, it seems sensible to weigh both its potential benefits and its potential costs. Or, after a relationship has ended, it may be instructive to expose its transactions to ruthless retrospective analysis. Such analyses, of course, seem easier to make from the safe distance of separation than when one is intertwined with a partner in an ongoing relationship. Distance permits us to view others as objects and transactions as instrumentalities. Closeness blurs our focus; it clouds distinctions between self and other, between mine and thine.

A. *The Exchange Metaphor as a Source of Ambivalence*

In one sense, the concept of exchange or transaction is a step beyond the individualistic analyses that pervade Western social science and social psychology (see Sampson, 1977). Individual behavior is placed within an interactional perspective; one partner's outcomes are seen as interdependent with those of the other. By emphasizing the interpersonal, it permits us to accept the legitimacy of circular as against linear causality. It also encourages us to attribute interpersonal compatibility or incompatibility to relational coordination or malcoordination, rather than to see it as primarily the result of personal adequacy or inadequacy.

Nonetheless, the present analysis does not escape the intrusion of the individualistic perspective; it may even unintentionally foster it. Whether looking at one or the other partner, or at their mutual interaction, its concepts (e.g., outcome comparison or exchange balance) appear individually oriented. They reflect the free-enterprise marketplace economics that pervades our society (Deutsch, 1975). Though we can hardly escape its effect on our thinking—just as we cannot separate ourselves from the air that we breathe—we can foster an awareness of the normally unquestioned assumptions it presupposes.

One unsettled issue in social-exchange theory is the disjunction between individualistic and collectivistic orientations, as recently articulated by Ekeh (1974). What Ekeh calls the *individualistic orientation* considers exchange in terms of reciprocities that occur entirely within a dyad; he calls this a focus on "restricted exchange." In contrast, he argues that a *collectivistic orientation* looks at pair interaction as part of a larger structure of exchange processes in the wider social net, thus focusing on "generalized exchange." Collectivistic analyses draw attention to the

---

fashion and attributions are employed so as to support the level of positive interpersonal regard desired. . . . . Relationship endings are characterized by high levels of cognitive activity brought about by reevaluation and cognitive confusion [Newman & Langer, 1977, pp. 20–21].

influence of the community and social network, and to the fact that dyadic transfers are often a part of a larger system of transfers; such analyses have been applied most successfully to societies where communities and networks are fairly stable and interconnected. Ekeh (1974) notes that "radicalizing changes" in Western society—brought about by a series of "revolutions"—have led to "convulsive individualization, the abstraction of individual actors from their concrete traditional bases, and the generalization of the individual ties beyond the immediate context of family and community [p. 3]." Despite its importance, the collectivistic perspective is most applicable to relationships in stable societies, and less so to those in an impersonal social milieu.

While I am fascinated by the unexplored possibilities of the collective orientation, my own current compromise is to focus largely on the dyad. In doing so, I realize that I use many individualistic constructs, but I believe that it is possible to build connections between the differing levels of analysis. It is not only possible but necessary to move between (in Martin Buber's terms) the I–Thou (supra-individual) and the I–It (individual) level of analysis; Buber himself believed that I–Thou relations represent only a small fraction of the moments in even the most mature relationships. Although my human concern is that all of us enrich our interactive situations and relationships, my theoretical concern is that we build better bridges between the individual, pair, network, and even societal levels of analysis.

References

Altman, I. Reciprocity of interpersonal exchange. *Journal for the Theory of Social Behavior*, 1973, *3*, 249–261.

Berscheid, E., & Walster, E. *Interpersonal attraction.* Reading, Massachusetts: Addison-Wesley, 1969.

Berscheid, E., Dion, K. K., Walster, E., & Walster, G. W. Physical attractiveness and dating choice: A test of the matching hypothesis. *Journal of Experimental Social Psychology*, 1971, *7*, 173–189.

Blood, R. O., Jr., & Wolfe, D. M. *Husbands and wives.* Glencoe, Illinois: Free Press, 1960.

Boulding, K. E. The relations of economic, political, and social systems. in *Collected papers*, Vol. 4. Boulder: Univ. of Colorado Press, 1974.

Brehm, J. W., & Cohen, A. R. *Explorations in cognitive dissonance.* New York: Wiley, 1962.

Brown, P. *Psychological distress and personal growth among women coping with marital dissolution.* Unpublished doctoral dissertation, University of Michigan, 1976.

Campbell, A., Converse, P. E., & Rodgers, W. L. *The quality of American life.* New York: Russell Sage, 1976.

Cherlin, A. Work life and marital dissolution. In G. Levinger & O. C. Moles (Eds.), *Divorce and separation.* New York: Basic Books, 1979.

Cuber, J., & Harroff, P. B. *The significant Americans: A study of sexual behavior among the affluent.* New York: Appleton-Century-Crofts, 1965.

Cutright, P. Income and family events: Marital stability. *Journal of Marriage and the Family,* 1971, *33,* 291–306.

Deutsch, M. Equity, equality, and need: What determines which value will be used as the basis of distributive justice? *Journal of Social Issues,* 1975, *31,* 137–149.

Driscoll, R., Davis, K. E., & Lipetz, M. E. Parental interference and romantic love: The Romeo and Juliet effect. *Journal of Personality and Social Psychology,* 1972, *24,* 1–10.

Eckland, B. K. Theories of mate selection. *Eugenics Quarterly,* 1968, *15,* 71–84.

Ekeh, P. P. *Social exchange theory.* Cambridge, Massachusetts: Harvard Univ. Press, 1974.

Foa, U. G., & Foa, E. B. *Societal structures of the mind.* Springfield, Illinois: Thomas, 1974.

Furstenberg, F. F., Jr. Premarital preganancy and marital instability. *Journal of Social Issues,* 1976, *32* (1), 67–86.

Goode, W. J. *After divorce.* Glencoe, Illinois: Free Press, 1956.

Gottman, J., Markman, H., & Notarius, C. The topography of marital conflict: A sequential analysis of verbal and nonverbal behavior. *Journal of Marriage and the Family,* 1977, *39,* 461–477.

Guerney, B. G., Jr. *Relationship enhancement.* San Francisco: Jossey-Bass, 1977.

Harrison, A. A., & Saeed, L. Let's make a deal: An analysis of revelations and stipulations in lonely hearts advertisements. *Journal of Personality and Social Psychology,* 1977, *35,* 257–264.

Hill, C. T., Rubin, Z., & Peplau, L. A. Breakups before marriage: The end of 103 affairs. *Journal of Social Issues,* 1976, *32,* (1), 147–168.

Homans, G. C. *Social behavior: Its elementary forms.* New York: Harcourt, 1961.

Huesmann, L. R., & Levinger, G. Incremental exchange theory: A formal model for progression in dyadic social interaction. In L. Berkowitz & E. Walster (Eds.), *Advances in experimental social psychology* (Vol. 9). New York: Academic Press, 1976.

Hunt, M. M., *The affair.* New York: World, 1969.

Huston, T. L., & Levinger, G. Interpersonal attraction and relationships. In M. R. Rosenweig & L. W. Porter (Eds.), *Annual review of psychology* (Vol. 29). Palo Alto, California; Annual Reviews, 1978.

Jacobson, P. H. *American marriage and divorce.* New York; Rinehart, 1959.

Jaffe, D. T., & Kanter, R. M. Couple strains in communal households: A four-factor model of the separation process. *Journal of Social Issues,* 1976, *32* (1), 169–191.

Kerckhoff, A. C., & Davis, K. E. Value consensus and need complementarity in mate selection. *American Sociological Review,* 1962, *27,* 295–303.

Levinger, G. Marital cohesiveness and dissolution: An integrative review. *Journal of Marriage and the Family,* 1965, *27,* 19–28.

Levinger, G. Sources of marital dissatisfaction among applicants for divorce. *American Journal of Orthopsychiatry,* 1966, *36,* 803–807.

Levinger, G. A three-level approach to attraction: Toward an understanding of pair relatedness. In T. L. Huston (Ed.), *Foundations of interpersonal attraction.* New York. Academic Press, 1974 (a).

Levinger, G. *Expressed complaints of divorce applicants.* Unpublished manuscript, Univ. of Massachusetts, Amherst, 1974 (b).

Levinger, G. A social psychological perspective on marital dissolution. *Journal of Social Issues,* 1976, *32* (1), 21–47.

Levinger, G., & Huesmann, L. R. An "incremental exchange" perspective on the pair relationship: Interpersonal reward and level of involvement. In K. J. Gergen, M. S. Greenberg, & R. H. Willis (Eds.), *Social exchange: Advances in theory and research.* New York: V. H. Winston, in press.

Levinger, G., Rands, M., & Talaber, R. *The assessment of involvement and rewardingness in close and casual pair relationships.* Unpublished technical report, Univ. of Massachusetts, Amherst, 1977.

Levinger, G., Senn, D. J., & Jorgensen, B. W. Progress toward permanence in courtship: A test of the Kerckhoff-Davis hypotheses. *Sociometry,* 1970, *33,* 427–443.

Levinger, G., & Snoek, J. D. *Attraction in relationship; A new look at interpersonal attraction.* Morristown, New Jersey: General Learning Press, 1972.

Lewin, K. *Field theory in social science.* New York: Harper, 1951.

Longfellow, C. Divorce in context: Its impact on children. In G. Levinger & O. C. Moles (Eds.), *Divorce and separation.* New York: Basic Books, 1979.

Newman, H. M., & Langer, E. J. *A cognitive arousal model of intimate relationship formation, stabilization, and disintegration.* Unpublished manuscript, Graduate Center of City University of New York, 1977.

Nye, F. I. Child adjustment in broken and unhappy broken homes. *Marriage and Family Living.* 1957, *19,* 356–360.

Rapoport, R., Rapoport, R., & Thiessen, V. Couple symmetry and enjoyment. *Journal of Marriage and the Family,* 1974, *36,* 588–591.

Ross, H. L., & Sawhill, I. V. *Time of transition; The growth of families headed by women.* Washington, D.C.; Urban Institute, 1975.

Rubin, L. B. *Worlds of pain: Life in the working class family.* New York: Basic Books, 1976.

Rubin, Z. *Loving and leaving.* Unpublished paper, Harvard Univ., 1975.

Sampson, E. E. Psychology and the American ideal. *Journal of Personality and Social Psychology,* 1977, *35,* 767–782.

Scanzoni, J. A historical perspective on husband-wife bargaining power and marital dissolution. In G. Levinger & O. C. Moles (Eds.), *Divorce and separation.* New York: Basic Books, 1979.

Shurkus, J. P. *Perceived changes in friendly and romantic relationships.* Senior honors thesis, University of Massachusetts, Amherst, 1977.

Thibaut, J. W., & Kelley, H. H. *The social psychology of groups.* New York: Wiley, 1959.

Thomas, E. J. *Marital communication and decision making: Analysis, assessment, and change.* New York: Free Press, 1977.

U. S. Department of Health, Education, and Welfare. *One hundred years of marriage and divorce statistics: United States 1867–1967* (#74–1902, Series 21, Number 24). Washington, D.C.: U. S. Government Printing Office, 1973.

Weiss, R. L., Hops, H., & Patterson, G. R. A framework for conceptualizing marital conflict: A technology for altering it, some data for evaluating it. In L. A. Hammerlynck, L. C. Handy, & E. J. Mash (Eds.), *Behavior change: The Fourth Banff Conference on Behavior Modification.* Champaign, Illinois: Research Press, 1973.

PART III

Beyond the Dyad: Approaches to Explaining Exchange in Developing Relationships

7

Natural Selection and Social Exchange

RICHARD D. ALEXANDER

I. Introduction

The purpose of this chapter is to explain how exchange theory, as currently investigated, chiefly by psychologists and sociologists, would be modified if it were made consistent with evolutionary theory in biology, and if possible to point the way toward its constructive development as a result of such input.

Evolutionary approaches to the study of social behavior have been undergoing an extensive and dramatic refinement during the past decade. Unfortunately, narrow and sometimes thoroughly misleading caricatures of this revolution have appeared at intervals in the popular press. The new theories, however, are much broader and more solidly based than one can as yet infer by consulting popular or derived accounts. They actually affect our view of nearly every human attribute and enterprise, from senescence, sex ratios, and sexual dimorphisms to altruism, play, incest, and the rise of nations. I think it is important that social scientists absorb at least the generalities of this revolution, so that they will be able to accept or reject its various propositions from knowledge rather than from misinterpretations based on incomplete or prejudiced accounts. With this problem expressly in mind, I recently reviewed the history of the de-

SOCIAL EXCHANGE IN DEVELOPING RELATIONSHIPS

velopment of the major ideas used by current evolutionary social biologists and attempted to show how they can be applied in the analysis of human sociality (Alexander, 1977a). That review includes a fuller exposition of arguments mentioned and used in the pages that follow. The original sources for these arguments are represented by the following publications, or may be traced from them: Alexander (1971, 1974, 1975; 1977, a,b), Alexander *et al.* (1979), Alexander and Noonan (1979), Hamilton (1963, 1964, 1966, 1967, 1970, 1971, 1972), Lewontin (1970), Trivers (1971, 1972, 1974), West-Eberhard (1976), Williams (1957, 1966, 1975).

To understand an evolutionary biologist's view of social exchange it is necessary to begin with approaches and concepts normally unfamiliar to social scientists. Evolutionists differ from social scientists in at least two important regards. First, they are not primarily, and most often not at all, concerned with the human species. Second, they are, at least initially, concerned more with what are usually termed *ultimate* (historical, functional) causes than with *proximate* (ontogenetic, physiological) causes. That is to say, the primary motivation of the evolutionist is to understand the continuous history of differential reproduction, or natural selection, that biologists assume lies behind every trait of every organism. Even when an evolutionist studies ontogeny directly, he regards the organism's ability to respond to immediate sequences of stimuli and to change as a result of certain sequences of stimuli primarily as a product of the long history of natural selection working on the genetic systems of the organism's ancestors. In the evolutionist's terms, proximate rewards (such as pleasurable sensations) can be regarded as satisfactorily accounting for behavior only if we ignore the questions of why particular proximate rewards exist, and why there are variations in proximate rewards. It is one thing to understand why placing one's hand in a fire should hurt, or why eating when hungry should give pleasure; it is quite another to understand why one has a conscience that causes uneasiness when something is obtained for nothing, or why one sometimes experiences pleasure from giving costly aid to another person. From the social scientist's viewpoint, the relevant question may be whether or not enlightenment, from evolutionary approaches, in regard to such "why" questions can contribute to an understanding of the proximate mechanisms that interest them—for example, to an understanding of the ontogenetic backgrounds of tendencies to engage in certain kinds of social exchange. I hope that the arguments in this chapter demonstrate that the answer to this question is emphatically affirmative.

Two important consequences derive from the evolutionists' general inattention to the human species. One is that evolutionists' hypotheses may not seem quite in focus for questions of primary interest to social scientists. Another is that uniquely human attributes may be ignored completely (an example possibly relevant to this chapter is what I later discuss as "pure" reciprocity). Evolutionists, one must understand, seek their generalizations, not because they best describe or predict human behavior, but because they apply either to all organisms or to large numbers of species that share such attributes as particular kinds of breeding or communicative systems or particular patterns of group-living or parental care. An evolutionist may assume that if he locates principles that are broadly applicable they will have some significance for the study of humans; but he is unlikely to regard this as requisite, or even centrally important.

Moreover, evolutionists characteristically proceed by identifying phenotypic traits, including expressions of behavior, and then attempting to determine their adaptive (reproductive) significance, using field observations or experiments, preferably carried out under conditions resembling those to which the species has been subjected for a long time. This approach is one of the reasons that evolutionists are, at least initially, relatively unconcerned with the precise sequences of ontogenetic stimuli that lead to particular behaviors, and why they may defer ontogenetic studies, or leave them entirely to other kinds of investigators. Moreover, evolutionists obviously do not encounter the major stimulus to ontogenetic analyses characteristic of human-oriented studies; namely, the problem of how behavior can or should be modified in connection with social, educational, medical, or other such programs.

In the light of these differences it is not surprising that evolutionists' approaches to behavior should be regarded as alien by social scientists, who are interested in modifying behavior by altering its ontogenetic bases, and who deal with the one species whose behavior is, as a whole, ultimately modifiable, compared with that of other organisms. Also contributing to misunderstanding may be the fact that evolutionists, because of their kinds of questions, rely heavily upon comparative study and field observations, whereas social scientists, because of *their* kinds of questions, are often restricted to rigorously designed experiments and chiefly compare the different members of a single species.

In one sense the evolutionist's approach is incompatible with the peculiar nature of human behavior, except in a strictly historical context. How can one study the so-called "traits" of an organism when the results of the study are available to the organism as it progresses, and when the mere identification of a supposed trait sets in motion deliberate and not-so-deliberate cost–benefit analyses of the trait by the organism itself, newly aware of it, that may cause the trait to cease being one? Probably no other organism can accomplish this kind of alteration of its phenotype—at least not by deliberate reflection—and one can scarcely resist compounding the paradox by declaring this capability itself a human behavioral trait.

The ability of humans to change their behavior if, on reflection, they do not like what they see probably lies behind statements by self-declared antideterminists that there is no "human nature"—statements that raise another issue that distinguishes the approaches of biological and social scientists to the analysis of behavior. The evolutionists' tendency to assume that behavioral traits exist, and their associated neglect of ontogeny, have suggested to some an undue preoccupation with the genetic background of behavior—even an intolerable assumption of genetic determinism or behavioral rigidity. After all, natural selection can only work when there is heritability associated with the variations that are causing differential reproduction. Social scientists are keenly aware that all or nearly all of the behavioral variations they observe are learned, and from this knowledge they understandably acquire a certain skepticism about the significance of natural selection in shaping human behavior. It does not help that evolutionary biologists, who, as I have already said, tend to leave ontogenetic details to others, are relatively ignorant about both human behavior and its developmental background, and are thus prone to making naïve remarks on matters in this realm.

The common assumption that an evolutionary view of behavior requires a genetically deterministic or rigid behavioral ontogeny is, however, incorrect, even though no one can deny that evolutionists have sometimes promoted such an assumption by their attitudes. The very concept of *phenotype,* as opposed to *genotype* and as used by evolutionists, is antithetical to the notion of genetic determinism. The evolutionary *raison dêtre* for phenotypes, as products of genotypes, is that they represent flexibility in responding to variable environmental contingencies. Phenotypes are genotypes' ways of meeting unpredictable environmental outcomes in better (i.e., more reproductive) fashions. If genes were to determine phenotypes rigidly, regardless of environment, then there would be no reason for behavior as such to evolve or to be maintained; for behavior, from its evolutionary origins, has typified the ultimate in phenotypic flexibility. On the other hand, it does not follow that if environments determine phenotypes, at some given time or in some given population and regardless of genotype, then the nature of the phenotype is necessarily independent of evolutionary history (Alexander, 1977b).

The ability to learn, and directional tendencies in learning of whatever sort, are surely products of natural selection. Hence, learning must result from the action of genes that specify that the organism should develop in such a fashion as to be able to respond appropriately to any situation from some array of likely situations when the particular one that will eventuate cannot be identified ahead of time. In no way can evolution be a reasonable theory about life unless it has the power to explain learning and to encompass all theories of learning—indeed, unless it leads to more useful predictions about the nature of learning than any other theory does.

The ability of humans to learn different things is an evolved ability, and the evolutionary function or background of learning is such that we could predict on evolutionary grounds that most observable variations in behavior *in any species whatsoever* would be the result of learning. To refine and investigate this view of learning in regard to humans we need to know two kinds of things: (a) what is the *actual nature* of human learning (for example, its ease in different directions) and (b) in what kinds of situations has the human kind of learning ability been favored— hence, what has *actually been learned* during human history (and how has it helped the learners)?

I believe that these questions can be asked profitably about social exchange. How do we learn, for example, what constitutes an appropriate return on a social investment in different circumstances? What causes us to feel rewarded by, say, helping offspring who do not help us back, even by sacrificing our lives for them, yet consistently to begrudge lesser expenditures to most others, or to feel cheated if we are not compensated for such expenditures immediately?

Elsewhere I have argued (Alexander, 1977, a,b) that the differences between social and biological scientists that restrict the effectiveness of their cooperation are not likely to be resolved until both together have developed a mutually acceptable set of theories about the relationships between genes and human behavior, or genes and the structure of culture—in other words, a much better understanding of what learning is all about. I suggest that the search must be expressly for the ways in which genes and behavior *are related* (as they obviously must be, in some fashion), and not simply for evidence about the kinds of ways in which they are potentially independent.

Despite the various problems in attempting to understand our own behavior, I believe that the evolutionary approach of first locating and analyzing traits is easily justified. The initial interest of the evolutionist is in how a trait is expressed in the usual environment of a species, which is what determines its adaptiveness (again, its reproductive significance during the history of its expression). The evolutionist's approach thus parallels the way in which natural selection actually works. It does not matter, in selection, how a trait comes to be expressed—only that it is expressed in the optimal way and at the optimal time and place. Accordingly, ontogenies vary for different organisms and different behaviors simply because, first, different kinds of ontogenies deliver particular phenotypic responses more or less reliably, and, second, natural selection always begins with "last year's model" and the previous lines of specialization may have caused different routes of further specialization to be more or less likely. Thus, the best way for a young songbird to learn the appropriate song pattern may be by listening to its parent, but this is not possible for a cricket, because its parents die before it even hatches. Once an organism has evolved either of two such different systems of song acquisition as typify insects and birds, it is at least a little less likely to evolve the other. The same relationship may exist between different systems of behavior within a single species.

As applied to humans, the evolutionary approach of first locating and analyzing traits is valid if the analysis remains historical—that is to say, if we remind ourselves continually that in this approach we are justified only in examining the past and in analyzing what humans had done *before* the kinds of thinking we are undertaking here became a part of the causative or motivational background of the human behaviors we are attempting to investigate.

II. The Sexual Organism as Nepotist

Evolutionists develop their theories and investigations around the assumption that all of life has, since its origin, been subjected to a continual, unrelenting process of natural selection or differential reproduction. The overwhelming evidence for the correctness of this view causes evolutionists, since and including Darwin (1859), to assume that the traits of organisms, in their usual environments, tend to develop in the individual so as to maximize its reproductive success. Peculiar as it may seem to those unfamiliar with evolution, biologists assume that organisms are designed (by evolution) solely to reproduce. They tend to regard the abilities and tendencies of modern humans to behave otherwise, on occasion, as products of massive novelty in the human environment; and they tend to wonder whether humans are not behaving so as to maximize reproduction in many more circumstances than are usually suspected. That such a view does indeed seem bizarre or even ludicrous to most people is suggested by the fact that reproduction has not been mentioned in any of the publications on social exchange that I have encountered during the development of this chapter. Evolutionists, in the confidence of their perverseness, wonder why a reproductive interpretation of human behavior seems to lie so far outside the consciousness of most people, and why such a proposition so frequently evokes exaggerated humor or heated denials.

The evolutionary view of the organism as a reproductive system is crucial to an understanding of the evolutionary approach to social exchange. It assumes that organisms have evolved so as to pass through two phases during their lifetimes—a resource-garnering (or growing, developing, juvenile, or "somatic") phase and a resource-redistributing (or adult, parental, or "reproductive") phase (Figure 7.1). The first phase overlaps the second, except in species like salmon and soybeans, which reproduce once suddenly (hence, are called "semelparous"). In repeat breeders ("iteroparous" species), such as most mammals and birds, resource-garnering (e.g., eating) must go on after resource redistribution (e.g., production of offspring) has begun, at least to an extent sufficient to maintain the organism as long as it is able to reproduce.

Given the evolutionist's focus on reproduction, we can next turn to the point that most organisms reproduce sexually rather than by fissioning or budding. Associated with sexual reproduction, senescence has become prominent, evidently as a consequence of deleterious late-acting effects of genes that accumulate unavoidably because they are concomitants of beneficial early-acting effects that are reproductively more valuable because they affect (a) individuals with more of their reproduction left and also (b) a greater proportion of the population, because some individuals inevitably die as aging takes place (Hamilton, 1967; Williams, 1957). Reproduction in sexual organisms with finite lives because of the process of senescence necessarily occurs only through producing and assisting other genetically related individuals. The evolutionist thus sees sexual organisms like ourselves as having evolved to be wholly devoted to nepotism, which includes the production and care of offspring as well as assistance to other genetic relatives. In other words, if altruism is defined as passing benefits to others, humans along with all other social organisms are seen as having evolved to be altruists, but altruists of a very special sort, whose altruism has as its background the spreading of the genes each of us possesses in our individual genotypes. It is difficult to imagine a concept more crucial to the analysis of social exchange.

As a consequence of this approach, the evolutionist tends to divide instances of social exchange into two categories: those occurring between relatives (nepotism) and those occurring between nonrelatives (reciprocity). The difference is that, on the one hand, in the case of social benefits given to genetic relatives, including offspring, returns in kind are not necessarily expected; the "payoff," in historical terms, may be entirely genetic, through the reproduction of the assisted individual. In the case of nonrelatives, on the other hand, in historical terms the evolutionist would expect tendencies to give—or to be altruistic or to engage in social donorism—only when the likelihood is great that more than compensatory benefits will be returned by the recipient, either to the donor or to the donor's relatives. Every act of social donorism is seen as involving some cost, however slight, in calories, time, or risks.

With certain obvious exceptions, reciprocity and nepotism correspond roughly to what Blau (1964) distinguished as social exchange

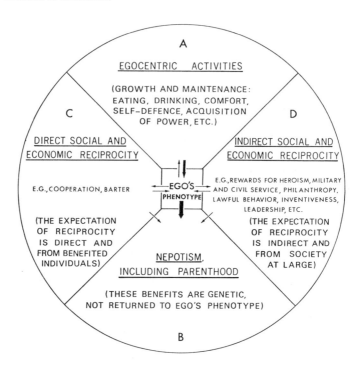

Figure 7.1   A diagram purporting to show all routes by which expenditures of calories and taking of risks by humans can lead, both directly and indirectly, to genetic reproduction. Reproduction will be maximized when the benefits from egocentric activities and reciprocal transactions (resource-garnering) maximally exceed their costs, and when their benefits are channeled to the closest relatives with the greatest ability to use the benefits to maximize the reproduction of their relatives in turn (resource redistribution). I suggest that as sociality increases in complexity during evolution from relatively nonsocial beginnings (A), following nepotism only to offspring (B) nepotism to nondescendant relatives becomes relatively more important, then (chiefly in humans) direct reciprocity (C), then (probably only in humans) indirect reciprocity (D). Expansion of nepotism to nondescendant relatives and increasing group size must, in human history, have set the stage for an increasing prominence of reciprocal transactions. In large and highly organized states or nations, as compared with simpler forms of social organization, indirect reciprocity must generally be more prominent—indeed, probably a criterion. Simple bands must have been predominantly systems of nepotism to descendant and nondescendant relatives with relatively little complexity in reciprocal transactions. Opportunities to engage advantageously in reciprocal transactions must begin to appear as systems of nepotism among nondescendant relatives become extensive and complex, a development that also increases the potential for cheating by potential recipients of nepotism. Selective pressures leading to larger groups thus represent pressure for increased engagement in reciprocal transactions, and increasingly elaborate cheating and the ability to detect and thwart cheating. Beyond some level of group size, only other competing groups of humans seem an appropriate source of such pressure for increasing group size and complexity (See also Alexander, 1977a).

based on, respectively, *extrinsic* and *intrinsic* personal attractiveness (note the relationship between (a) nepotism and (b) altruism to a mate, who represents the other parent to one's children) and what Hatfield *et al.* (Chapter 4 of this volume) have termed *casual* and *deeply intimate* social interactions. Using evolutionary theory, we would predict that in the Hatfield *et al.* proposed comparison of these two classes of interactions, profound differences will appear if the study is done in contexts appropriate to the history of human sociality. If the study is not done with careful reference to historical contexts, then analysis of the second class of interactions seems likely to give results that are complex and inconclusive compared with those of the first.

Even a casual examination of treatments of social exchange reveals that the aspects which evolutionists would label as nepotism have largely been ignored by social scientists investigating exchange systems. Homans (1974), for example, in his volume on elementary forms of social behavior, says, "Mother love and sexual love are surely elementary social behavior, yet I have nothing to say about them whatever [p. 15]." He also notes, of course, that he is forced to leave out much else. Sahlins (1965), discussing "the sociology of primitive exchange," proceeds from the household outward to the intertribal sector using the word reciprocity throughout and omitting all mention of nepotism or the possible significance of genetic kinship.

Why this consistent omission, downplaying, or confusion about a whole class of social interactions between individuals, and, no less, in books and articles devoted to this precise topic? Words like *nepotism*, *relatives, family, kinship,* and *marriage,* and terms of relationship such as those in the diagram in Figure 7.2, are entirely absent from the pages of most major works on social exchange.

To shed light on this question, let me return briefly to considering the significance of the relationship between proximate and ultimate mechanisms of behavior. Homans (1974) speaks of social exchange in the following words:

> Let not a reader reject our argument out of hand because he does not care for its horrid profit-seeking implications. Let him ask himself instead whether he and mankind have ever been able to advance any explanation why men change or fail to change their behavior other than that, in their circumstances, they would be better off doing something else, or that they are doing well enough already. On reflection he will find that neither he nor mankind has ever been able to offer another—the thing is a truism. It may ease his conscience to remember that if hedonists believe men take profits only in materialistic values, we are not hedonists here. So long as men's values are altruistic, they can take a profit in altruism too. Some of the greatest profiteers we know are altruists [p. 79]

Elsewhere Homans implies the significance and the difficulty of the question of ultimate causation, and then adroitly sidesteps it, with these

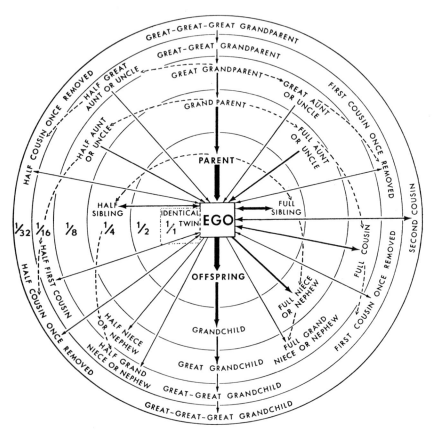

Figure 7.2 Genetic relatives potentially available to an individual, Ego, for reproductively self-serving nepotism. The arrows indicate the likely net flows of benefits. Half of the genes of parent and offspring are identical by immediate descent. Other relationships are averages. The dotted lines indicate closest relatives other than Ego, thus the most likely alternative sources of nepotistic benefits. The widths of the lines indicate the likely relative flows of benefits to or from Ego, based on the combination of genetic relatedness and the ability of recipients to use the benefits in reproduction. Extreme lateral relatives are less likely to be encountered or identified, because of social or geographic distance; extreme vertical relatives, because of temporal nonoverlap. The double-headed arrows indicate relatives whose statuses in regard to the need of benefits or the ability to use them to reproduce, and the ability to give benefits, are doubtful, owing to the uncertainty of the age relationships of the individuals involved. (Thus, one's second cousin may be much younger than, much older than, or of about the same age as one; one's sibling, on the other hand, is much more likely to be of comparable age). The relatives on the right side of the diagram are those resulting from monogamous marriages; polygyny results in the relatives indicated on the left.

words: "Sometimes it may be hard indeed to explain why [a man's] present values are what they are . . . . Nor, thank God, is it, as we shall see, the business of this book to explain [p. 45]."

But how can we deal with exchange theory in a truly general way until we know something about the circumstances in which altruism is its own reward, and the consequences of altruism in those circumstances? This is all the more true because what Homans has said about profit-seeking is indeed a truism. One gets the impression that altruism (in Homans' sense), "intrinsic attractiveness" (Blau's [1964] term), and "deeply intimate" interactions (Hatfield *et al.* Chapter 4 of this volume) have been avoided because sense has not yet been made of them in terms of social exchange. They are seen as different from exchanges in which goods or service is in evidence, but no one seems to know why, or even exactly how, they differ. They are described as having their own reward, but this does not explain why it should be so, given our obvious and heralded tendencies to adjust our situations constantly so as to profit or be better off in all other situations. The question is whether or not sense *can* be made of social exchange *without* considering these aspects. What is the real meaning of "profit" or "better off" in statements like Homans'? Do these terms refer to *personal* well-being? If we say, "Usually, but not always," then, when do they, and when not? The evolutionary answer is simple: whenever greater profit to one's genotype is possible by hurting one's self or helping someone else, or—as in our evolutionarily novel modern environment—whenever the historical equivalent of this situation occurs even though actual genetic relatives happen not to be involved. I do not believe that any human behaviors will be discovered that, when all the circumstances are known, and in the absence of obvious pathology, will gainsay this explanation.

Obviously, the evolutionary view of social exchange, as I have described it so far, is still oversimplified and unsophisticated, especially in respect to the very complex social organizations of modern humans in enormous technological nations; and it is almost certain to be regarded as bizarre by anyone encountering it here for the first time. Nevertheless, I see this view as an appropriate starting point for the study of human social interactions, and I am convinced that a history of differential reproduction will eventually be accepted as the basic principle upon which social exchange theory must be built. To put it another way, I believe that the general theory of social behavior that Hatfield *et al.* (Chapter 4 of this volume) mention but regard as not yet appropriately sought is already available and needs only refinement and development to be immediately and broadly applicable to our efforts to understand human sociality and its ontogeny. I think it is already obvious to anyone familiar with exchange theory in the social sciences that its findings have begun to converge dramatically with the predictions that derive from an evolutionary view of social exchange.

III. Historical Relationships Between Nepotism and Reciprocity

Although evolutionists tend to regard nepotism and reciprocity as entirely distinct, it is worthwhile to examine their probable historical and functional relationships to each other. Alexander and Borgia (1978) argue that nepotism to nondescendant and distant descendant relatives is an extension of (evolutionarily) earlier altruism extended solely as parental care. They cite the ubiquity of parental care in social organisms, the relative accuracy of assessment of parenthood as compared to other relationships, and the paucity of evidence for undirected altruism (i.e., equally toward all interactants) as opposed to individualized altruism toward relatives of different degree. I will argue here that reciprocity is in turn derived from nepotism.

Pure social reciprocity can be defined as interactions that normally occur between nonrelatives, the structure and circumstances of which indicate clearly that each party may be expected (by the observer) or expects (in the case of humans) to receive benefits greater than those given. This outcome is possible whenever there is a disparity between the needs of the participants and their abilities to give. For example, when anyone purchases an item in a shop, both proprietor and customer must feel that they will receive more value than they give, else the transaction will not occur. The exchange is agreed on because the customer has money and needs the product and the proprietor has the product and needs the money. Such exchange is the easiest to analyze without an evolutionary perspective, because the items of exchange and their values are apparent (see Homans, 1974, p. 62, for a nonevolutionary analysis using almost identical phrases).

As a case of pure reciprocity, we should expect that the above exchange, especially if it occurs between nonrelatives or strangers, is likely to involve an almost simultaneous transfer of money and goods; in this fashion each party's risks are minimized. This aspect of exchanges should be most evident in interactions likely to occur but once.

Aside from the interactions of unrelated mates in parental species, pure reciprocity must occur rarely in nonhuman species, and may actually be unusual in humans, outside modern nations. Although Trivers (1971) argued for the possibility of nonhuman cases of reciprocity—the two cases he cited involved cleaning and cleaned fish of different species and alarm calls in flocks of birds—his cases may be questionable. West-

Eberhard (1976) has explained the various ways in which the alarm calls can be viewed in strictly selfish or nepotistic terms, and there is no evidence that either species of fish in the cleaner–cleanee relationship ever actually behaves altruistically. The cleaner may be simply acquiring food in the best way available to it, and the cleaned fish may refrain from consuming its cleaner not because the cleaner will then be available for subsequent cleaning but, in evolutionary terms, because the cleaner is poisonous and ill-tasting.

The reason for suggesting the infrequency of pure reciprocity in humans outside modern nations is that nonrelatives probably interacted only rarely in the small, relatively sedentary bands in which humans are generally presumed to have lived throughout most of their evolutionary history. Wiessner (1977) has found that Kung Bushmen almost never engage in exchange (*xhora*) with individuals not known to be related to them. Among the Yanomamö Indians, neighboring tribes and even enemy groups are essentially always composed of known relatives (Chagnon, 1979, and personal communication).

The concept of pure reciprocity returns us to the question of the relationship of nepotism to reciprocity and the origins of pure reciprocity. Although either nepotism or reciprocity can exist in the absence of the other, most of the time the two probably occur together. Thus, every act of nepotism involves a certain risk. Even a mother nursing a baby and, for the purposes of this example, expecting no altruistic returns at all (hence, engaged in so-called "pure" nepotism) would be, like a bank loaning money (hence, engaged in so-called "pure" reciprocity), making an investment that carries with it a certain risk. The baby may be susceptible to an inevitable, and maybe inevitably fatal, childhood disease; it may be sterile; or for other reasons it may yield no genetic returns whatever to the mother. (Note: In an example like this I am suggesting nothing at all about the conscious motivations of the mother, or her attitude toward her motivations, although the enormous emotional concern and satisfaction of mothers in this kind of circumstance can scarcely be regarded as incidental to a history of differential reproduction.)

Pure nepotism, then, is represented by cases in which one who gives benefits to a genetic relative expects absolutely nothing in return except a further reproduction of the genes one shares with the recipient of one's altruism. Such cases must be more unusual than is commonly suspected, although much of parental care to very young and helpless juveniles would qualify, and certainly so in species in which the parent tends the offspring briefly, and then dies or leaves and never again interacts with them.

Nepotism in humans, however, seems usually to take a somewhat different form. Anyone who helps a cousin or other distant relative, though he may be satisfied even if no direct compensation ever occurs, is likely to expect that, should the situation later be reversed, the relative will return the favor. Even parents, among humans, commonly behave as though they expected their offspring to return certain kinds of favors or assistance to them because they have provided for the offspring. I suggest that this tendency is due, at least in part, to the long period of life during which humans are able to reproduce, or redistribute resources in their own interests—a period that commonly overlaps that of their offsprings' ability to redistribute resources, and during which the parents' interests will frequently differ from those of their offspring (Alexander, 1974; Trivers, 1974). That exchanges between relatives lead to special kinds of expectations is suggested by many aspects of everyday life, one being the commonly heard admonition to be cautious about doing business with a relative.

Reflecting upon cases in which nepotism and reciprocity are mixed, we perceive that their differences are not so profound as they might at first seem. Each involves investment, with some risk. From a reproductive, or evolutionary, viewpoint, if a social investment has some likelihood of not being returned, then it is better given to a close relative than to a distant one. Then, if reciprocity fails, there will at least be a chance of genetic return. We may expect that, during human history, frequent recurrence of disparities in ability to give and ability to use among social interactants—who in primitive societies would virtually always be relatives—would lead to social investments of a sort ordinarily calling for reciprocity but not necessarily requiring it for the interaction to have at least some reproductive benefit for the investor. Even in pure reciprocity the eventual fate of any resource garnered is—again, in historical terms—redistribution via nepotism in the interests of genetic reproduction. In the admonition about doing business with a relative the emphasis is on *business,* and it may be best interpreted as meaning that doing business with genetic relatives may severely prejudice the likelihood of overcompensating return—in other words, that relatives are more likely to feel free to renege on a debt, and to get away with it should they try. In-laws, who are commonly included among one's relatives (the explicit way in which this comes about, and the reasons for its acceptance, are themselves intersting to contemplate), are perhaps most notoriously regarded as poor risks in transactions. It is relevant to this chapter's concerns to reflect that we have no genetic interest whatever in our spouse's relatives (unless the spouse is a relative), and hence suffer no nepotistic loss if resources are not returned to "their side of the family." Thus, married adults (at least, those who have not considered the arguments presented here) might be expected to look favorably upon investments in the spouse's side of the family only if the spouse's family is wealthy or if there are other reasons to believe it likely that a debt will be more than repaid. I am not suggesting that it is impossible to teach someone to behave otherwise, or even to refrain from reproducing, for that matter; but only that such teaching has probably been quite rare during human history.

This comparison of nepotism and reciprocity exposes some problems in analyzing social interactions in terms of their backgrounds in differential reproduction. Perhaps the greatest difficulty evolutionists encounter in assessing the adaptive significance of traits is in identifying the environment in which the trait evolved and in which, therefore, it is adaptive. In an evolutionarily novel environment any trait may be expressed maladaptively, or its evolved function may be completely misinterpreted. It may not be widely appreciated that the resulting difficulties are problems not only for the evolutionists but also for other investigators. Every experiment carried out in an evolutionarily novel environment may mislead the experimenter in profound ways. Of this possibility it can be said that there may be no more general problem in behavioral science nor one that better reveals the reasonableness of attempting to understand the evolutionary approach to the study of life.

Probably no organism has ever modified its social environment as rapidly as have humans during recorded history. Within a few hundred generations we have gone from a simple, sedentary band structure in which nearly all social interactants were relatives of known (or assigned) degrees to enormous, mobile urban societies in which sometimes almost none of our lifelong associates are genetic relatives. In such novel situations, how can we understand social exchanges in evolutionary terms? On the other hand, how can we understand them otherwise?

The search for an answer, paradoxically, returns us to the question that I said earlier is deferred or ignored in most evolutionary studies: that of ontogeny. How do we, as individuals, acquire our social responses to others? How, in a clan of permanently interacting relatives of different degree, could patterns of nepotism and reciprocity appropriate to reproduction be generated and maintained? How would the mechanisms involved there translate into patterns of sociality in modern technological societies? What would the answers to these questions mean for tests of exchange and equity theory in experimental situations?

IV. Analyses of Human Nepotism and Reciprocity

I have made two attempts to test the model of human social altruism which divides altruism into nepotism and reciprocity (Alexander, 1974, 1975, 1977, a,b). The first effort (Alexander, 1975) centered on a lengthy review of the sociology of primitive exchange by a cultural anthropologist (Sahlins, 1965). Sahlins divided reciprocity into three classes, termed *generalized, balanced,* and *negative* reciprocity (Figure 7.3). He described *generalized* reciprocity as concentrated in the household and characterized by one-way flows of benefits, and he used the suckling of children as an example. The notion of balanced reciprocity he applied to (in his words) "transactions which stipulate returns of commensurate worth or utility." He described negative reciprocity as "the attempt to get something for nothing with impunity." Balanced reciprocity, he suggested, is concentrated within villages and lineages, among people who interact repeatedly, whereas negative reciprocity is centered outside tribal boundaries (see Alexander, 1975; and Sahlins, 1965, for more details).

I interpreted Sahlins' model to be "an uncanny match for that of the evolutionary biologist." Sahlins' generalized and balanced reciprocity I saw as "roughly the equivalent of what the biologists have called kin selection [i.e., nepotism] . . . and reciprocal altruism . . . respectively.

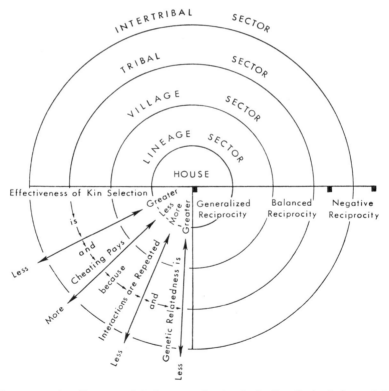

Figure 7.3 An effort to explain in terms of natural selection the basis for variations in the kinds of social interactions attributed to primitive societies by Sahlins (1965). The material in the lower left quadrant has been added to Sahlins' diagram. See text for further explanation.

Evolutionary theory not only recognizes the two categories almost precisely as Sahlins has distinguished them, with the exceptions noted, but it specifies the social levels at which generalized reciprocity gives way to balanced reciprocity . . . [Alexander, 1975, p. 92]." This match is especially significant because Sahlins then had no knowledge of the evolutionary viewpoint.

Sahlins (1976), in a book denouncing the use of evolutionary theory in the analysis of human sociality, has denied the match I suggested, in the following words:

> Sociobiologists, notably Alexander (1975), have taken the equally well-known tendency of economic reciprocity to vary in sociability with "kinship distance" as cultural evidence of biological "nepotism," hence as a proof of kin selection . . . . this conclusion is based on an elementary misunderstanding of the ethnography. The kinship sectors of "near" and "distant," such as "own lineage" vs. "other lineage," upon which reciprocity is predicated, do not correspond to coefficient of relationship, so the evidence cited in support of kin selection (e.g., Sahlins, 1965) in fact contradicts it . . . [p. 112].

Sahlins' denial seems to me preposterously careless and incomplete. He does not explain why his detailed descriptions of the three kinds of reciprocity are almost perfect reflections of evolutionary analyses of nepotism and reciprocity (Alexander, 1974; Trivers, 1971; others); or why, within the social system, they should center so precisely on what evolutionary theory predicts they will. His denial is focused on the nepotistic aspects of my analysis. But the example of suckling children was his own. Is he denying that people are altruistic toward their offspring, or that one-way flows of benefits typify such altruism? The word *lineage* was his own. Does he deny that persons in the same "lineage"— explicitly as anthropologists use the term—are more often genetically related, or more closely related, than persons in different lineages? He evidently refers at least in part to what anthropologists term the *classificatory* aspects of kinship systems. One aspect of classificatory kinship is that terms like *mother, father, brother, sister, aunt, uncle,* and *cousin* are frequently, and sometimes formally and consistently, applied to persons that do not have the genetic relationship to Ego of such relatives as are shown in Figure 7.2. Superficially, this might seem to prejudice the likelihood of a biological background for kinship systems; but the opposite argument can be made. Suppose that I as an individual, or the members of my society generally, should wish to adjust the apparent social distance, or the privileges and responsibilities, of some particular members or classes of members in the society. First, that such shifts are even possible indicates a certain regularity within society. And second, that terms commonly denoting classes of genetic relationship are employed to create the adjustments indicates that the regularity is based on genetic relationship. After all, if I should wish to draw inward, socially, a particular individual, what reason is there for me to use a kin term like *brother* except that *brother* ordinarily refers to someone with the close relationship that I wish to create?

A second classificatory aspect of kinship involves the fact that not every possible distinction among kin is made (see Figure 7.2). Maternal and paternal aunts and uncles may not be distinguished, or the various kinds of cousins. For example (as in Figure 7.2), mother's brother's daughter is not distinguished from mother's sister's daughter, father's sister's daughter, or father's brother's daughter. In many cases the sexes may not be distinguished. In other words, relatives derived through obviously different routes are classified together. On the other hand, Figure 7.2 indicates that, in this society at least, there are tendencies to lump together relatives of the same degree, the same dependency relationships, and the same sex, and to distinguish those that differ in these respects.

These two classificatory aspects of kinship systems, then, can be used to support rather than negate the notion that genetic relationships and nepotism represent the basic cement of human sociality (see Alexander, 1977, a,b, for a fuller discussion). Yet neither Sahlins' original analysis nor his denial includes any mention of the altruism of nepotism. Is he denying that nepotism exists? If not, then where does it fit into his scheme? Does he actually mean to deny that it contributes to the particular arrangement of sociality that he proposes? Obviously, this question is crucial to anyone examining the distribution and background of social exchange.

Sahlins indicates that the social relations of people involved in what he calls "primitive exchange" do not correspond to genetic relatedness. I am aware of no evidence to support this claim, and note that ethnographers commonly have not secured the necessary kind of information. Contrary evidence, however, is available. Wiessner (1977), in a 2-year study of reciprocity among Kung Bushmen, has discovered, first, that reciprocity (*xharo*) is almost always restricted to known relatives, and, second, that there is a direct correspondence between the percentage of each class of genetic relative with whom *xharo* is practiced and the actual degree of relatedness in genes identical by descent: A higher proportion of one's 50% relatives than of one's 25% relatives are objects of *xharo*, and an even higher proportion of them than of one's 12.5% relatives, etc. Sahlins' assertion is also countered by Chagnon's (1975) findings that among the Yanomamö Indians the genetic relatedness of the inhabitants is a better correlate than the size of the village of the likelihood of village fissioning: Villages composed of more closely related people are likely to grow to larger sizes before splitting.

In a footnote (Footnote 2 p. 109), Sahlins attempts to deny that humans tend to live in social groups composed of genetic relatives. He relies chiefly on the fact that marriages often occur between unrelated or distantly related groups. But he ignores two crucial facts: (a) that tending a spouse is essentially an act of nepotism toward one's offspring (as can be the social cultivation of the relatives of one's spouse and (b) that the common occurrence of marriages between nonrelatives or distant relatives (the human tendency to outbreed is shared widely throughout the animal and plant kingdoms) is surely the principal reason why marriage rules are one of the most prominent of all aspects of human culture—marriages literally determine patterns of inheritance.

Elsewhere (Alexander, 1977, a, b; 1974), I have deliberately considered other formal aspects of human kinship systems that do not seem to accord with nepotistic predictions, especially the phenomenon of a mother's brother acting as the chief or sole male parent and the asymmetrical treatment of cross- and parallel-cousins (i.e., offspring of different-sex and same-sex siblings, respectively). Those analyses have demonstrated that, although these phenomena have been used to deny a biological basis for patterns of kinship behavior, they actually support an evolutionary model rather strongly. The reasons are that in societies where a mother's brother is a prominent figure, this particular uncle because of low confidence of paternity is likely to be the closest identifiable adult male relative of at least some of his sister's offspring; and in polygynous societies, putative parallel cousins are on the average more closely related than cross-cousins, because they are often half-siblings.

V. The Evolution of Nepotism and Reciprocity in Humans

Nepotism and reciprocity are vastly more complex in humans than in any other organism. Some of the reasons, at least, are obvious (see Figures 7.1, 7.2). As Figure 7.2 suggests by the familiarity of its terms of relationship to all in this society, and as is known by all anthropologists, humans everywhere maintain a remarkably extensive and detailed knowledge of the identity of their genetic relatives. Indeed, there are no indications that in any other species has there developed such a complete and precise picture of what actually represents the potential avenues of genetic reproduction via nepotism. Noonan and I (1979) have argued that the expansion of the potential for reproduction via nepotism, both because of the expanding group of socially available relatives and because of increases in wealth and power differentials associated with the appearance of the cumulatively heritable accoutrements of culture, may have been largely responsible for the evolutionary divergence of humans from other primates, and even for the evolution of human cognitive capacity. We suggest that this situation was promoted by obligatory group-living, coupled with escape from the over-riding influences of large predators on the social structure (which we believe still largely structures the sociality of other group-living primates) into a condition in which bands of humans became one another's chief competitors and sources of mortal peril. A particularly important consequence, we suggest, was a dramatic increase in the value of paternal care, leading to an emphasis on the behaviors of females that increased their mates' confidence of paternity (e.g., the concealment of ovulation) and favoring males with high promise as capable and faithful fathers over males physically capable of acquiring and holding females during their display of oestrus (the latter kind of male predominates among most primates living in multi-male bands). All of these factors, we argue, combined to revolutionize the sociality of ancestral humans and to differentiate it from that of their primate relatives also living in polygynous, multimale bands. Whether or not this scenario is approximately correct, the complexity of human knowledge of genetic relatedness is a fact that bears directly upon efforts to develop satisfactory approaches to social exchange and its ontogenetic bases.

VI. Ontogeny and Social Exchange

Assuming that nepotism exists, and is at least sometimes correlated in its intensity with our obvious knowledge of the relatedness of different individuals in our network of kin, what causes this knowledge to develop in the individual, and how are systems of nepotism and reciprocity maintained from generation to generation? What kinds of gene action could account for individual humans behaving socially in such fashions as to maximize their reproduction via altruism to relatives?

Consider first the investments parents make in their offspring. Except for one of the two parents—usually but not always the mother—evidence of genetic relationship is always circumstantial. Some female mammals can observe their babies being born and keep them in direct contact until umistakable recognition has been established. Male seahorses, which take unfertilized eggs more or less directly from the female, place them in a brood pouch, and fertilize them there, are in a similar position. But all other assessments of genetic relationship, and thus all behavior appropriate to them, are necessarily based on circumstantial evidence. In other words, particular social interactions predict particular genealogical relationships. I may, with some accuracy, assume those individuals who are cared for by the same adult female and male as I to be my siblings; a caterpillar may assume its siblings to be whoever hatches next to it at about the same time. I assume my offspring to be those juveniles accepted as my offspring by the woman with whom I live. Error is obviously possible in all of these cases.

One might suppose that nepotism could be, or even has to be, based on the appearance of mutant genes that enable their bearers to recognize their own effects in other individuals. Such a gene would have to, first, have an effect on the phenotype; second, cause its bearer to be able to recognize the effect in others; and, third, also cause its bearer to take the appropriate social action (Hamilton, 1964). Not only are these requirements of gene action unreasonably complex, but any such mutant would act on the basis of its own presence in the genotype of the potential recipient of its bearer's altriusm, independent of the probability of the presence of other genes in its genotype that also contribute to its bearer's altruism, if only incidentally. Thus, the mutant would necessarily act against the interests of all other genes in its own genotype. The extraordinary organization of the genotype could not be sustained if such genes became prevalent. Any gene mutating so as to suppress such an "outlaw" effect would thereby help itself, and in any large genotype the mutational probabilities of suppression, as opposed to the probability of sustaining outlawry, would be enormously high (Alexander & Borgia, 1978).

If nepotism depends upon circumstantial evidence of relatedness, then social interactions must lead to an accurate assessment of genetic relationships. The interesting consequence is that the essential ontogenetic basis of appropriate patterns of nepotism in any species need be no more complex or deterministic than learning through ordinary positive and negative reinforcement schedules. In other words, whatever it is that enables us to construct a diagram of the sort seen in Figure 7.2, whatever it is that makes the labels there familiar to all of us, whatever enables us to put ourselves in the role of Ego and then fill in the diagram with actual names of actual people—whatever that learning process has been in each of us—it is entirely adequate to account for any ability by any of us to behave so as to maximize our genetic reproduction via nepotism. Indeed, it is the only proximate, genetic, ontogenetic, physiological series of events that is even an appropriate candidate. All that remains is to establish that the usual context of distinguishing relatives is favoritism, based on relatedness, needs, and available alternatives in dispensing altruism. If we do indeed treat our closer relatives better and help our dependent relatives more—that we do is, I believe, already an established fact (Alexander, 1974, 1975, 1977, a)—then an evolutionary model for the history of human sociality is appropriate. And nothing more deterministic is required than regular and predictable differences in our learning experiences with different relatives, which lead to regular and predictable differences in our treatment of them. What would have evolved would be our tendencies to behave exactly as learning psychologists already know we do under negative and positive reinforcement schedules—or, more precisely, our tendencies to react as we do to particular learning schedules that are then labelled as positive and negative *because* of our reactions to them.

The simplest relationship between gene effects and social behavior that might lead to the regularity of nepotism that this hypothesis requires is the accumulation of genes causing us to be positively reinforced according to the number and intensity of physiologically or socially "pleasant" interactions with any particular individuals. In small clans of genetic relatives that effect alone could cause us to favor closer relatives; and humans have almost certainly lived in such groups throughout nearly all of their history. The effects I am suggesting would have to be modified and qualified by many other kinds of learning in different circumstances to explain a great deal of sociality. For instance, an utterly and continuously dependent juvenile might gain by being positively reinforced by almost any kind of repeated interactions with an adult—even unpleasant, traumatic ones—and I believe there is good evidence that dependent juveniles are so reinforced. On the other hand, some degree of generality is implied. For example, parental teaching about who are relatives are becomes no more than a subset of this hypothesis.

When I initially had this rather simple idea about learning to be appropriately nepotistic, I immediately tried to think of exceptions: When do we treat with extreme altruism individuals with whom we have *not* had long histories of positive social interaction? It seemed to me that instances of such treatment should be unusually dramatic if genes with the effects I have just described have accumulated, for in such instances the postulated gene effects would in some sense have to be overridden. I thought of several cases, such as that of newborn babies, and that of strangers yoked together by disasters and wholly dependent upon one another for survival: Each of these deserves analysis. But the example that stuck in my mind is the event that we call "falling in love." Humans, apparently everywhere, tend to select as mates individuals with whom they have had relatively few social interactions, or, in some cases, who are even poorly known; and at least in our own society we draw them rapidly from strangeness to ultimate intimacy and make them long-term or lifetime partners, usually in what must be referred to as the dearest of all biological enterprises. There is much evidence in music, art, and literature that few events are more dramatic in human sociality than falling in love—*falling*, it seems to me, across the breach from social strangeness to social intimacy. I consider this phenomenon to be at least potentially supportive of the existence and importance of the kinds of gene effects I have here postulated (see also Alexander, 1977, b).

Now, perhaps, we can make certain rudimentary predictions about positive and negative reinforcements that should be associated with the altruism of social exchange. Thus (to speak of one extreme), we should be most positively reinforced by (i.e., experience the greatest pleasure from) altruism toward persons we have known intimately and for very long periods, because such individuals are overwhelmingly likely, in terms of the history of human sociality, to represent close genetic relatives such as parents, offspring, or siblings—that is, family, or members of the inner-most circle of the diagram in Figure 7.2. There are obvious exceptions—for example, when siblings are in intense competition for parental ben-efits that are all-important to each of them. In a modern urban environ-ment such persons as roommates, school friends, business associates, companions at work, or neighbors may assume roles causing us to treat them, in varying degrees, as if they were genetic relatives.

At the other extreme we should begrudge essentially all benefits given to virtual strangers whether or not, or maybe even especially when, they are able to translate the benefits into their own well-being or repro-duction. This will be most true, moreover, as the risk of not being repaid in kind increases, and certainly true in view of the fact that altruism to strangers is never likely to be rewarding unless there is a high likelihood that it will become public knowledge, or that some other circumstance will accrue that affords a likelihood of compensation in kind from others, or from society at large. One such circumstance is a probability of our being made a hero, or a public example of the fact that altruism is rewarded.

Between these two extremes will be a confusing mingling of the two tendencies they represent. Unfortunately for those interested in the de-velopment of exchange behavior in the social mixes of our modern envi-ronment, most of our responses to the possibilities of social exchange are likely to generate in this intermediate realm. Thus, the existence of a nepotistic human background can scarcely be ignored in efforts to under-stand what exchange theorists have termed *equity* and *social* and *dis-tributive justice* (Walster & Walster, 1975; Homans, 1974).

VII. Conclusions

A marriage of the approaches and theories of biological and social scientists, in the interests of solving problems about human behavior, is long overdue. It is time for biologists to realize that including humans in their theoretical considerations would be useful and broadening, espe-cially to their views of the mechanisms and evolution of ontogenies. It is time for social scientists to take more seriously the fact that evolution is the process behind all traits of all life, and that to consider behavior in terms of a history of natural selection does not require or even suggest an intolerably deterministic approach to ontogenies.

Evolutionists divide socially altruistic behavior into nepotism and reciprocity. The two usually occur together in humans. Predictions about these two kinds of altruism or social donorism differ. Nepotism is altruism directed at genetic relatives and does not necessarily call for returns in kind; reciprocity is altruism from which an overcompensating return is expected to the altruist or its genetic relatives. Analyses of several aspects of human social systems indicate that nepotism and reciprocity tend to be dispensed in genetically appropriate fashions. Both are necessarily based on learning, and raise fascinating questions about how their expressions maintain reproductively appropriate patterns, as they probably do most dramatically in societies least subjected to the extraordinary changes that have occurred in what are now large, mobile, urban societies.

From an evolutionary viewpoint, current exchange theory would likely be significantly more predictive if (a) genetic reproduction were seen as the historical force behind the functional aspects of social exchange, (b) serious efforts were made to incorporate analyses of nepotistic interactions, and their surrogates in modern society, and (c) the question of why particular proximate mechanisms have evolved in different circumstances were used to help distinguish the different categories of such mechanisms and to analyze their nature and effects.

References

Alexander, R. D. The search for an evolutionary philosophy of man. *Proceedings of the Royal Society of Victoria*, Melbourne, 1971, *84*, 99–120.

Alexander, R. D. The evolution of social behavior. *Annual Review of Ecology and Systematics*, 1974, *5*, 325–383.

Alexander, R. D. The search for a general theory of behavior. *Behavioral Science*, 1975, *20*, 72–100.

Alexander, R. D. Natural selection and the analysis of human sociality. In C. E. Goulden (Ed.), *Changing scenes in the natural sciences 1776–1976*. Bicentennial Symposium Monograph, Philadelphia Academy of Sciences, special publication 12, 1977a, 283–337.

Alexander, R. D. Evolution, human behavior, and determinism. *Proceedings, 1976 Biennial Meeting of the Philosophy of Science Association*, 1977b (Vol. 2), 3–21.

Alexander, R. D., & Borgia G., Group selection, altruism, and the levels of organization of life. *Annual Review of Ecology and Systematics*, 1978, *9*, 449–474.

Alexander, R. D., Noonan, K. M. In N. A. Chagnon & W. G. Irons (Eds.), *Evolutionary biology and human social behavior: An anthropological perspective*. North Scituate, Massachusetts: Duxbury Press, 1979, pp. 436–453.

Alexander, R. D., Hoogland, J. L., Howard, R. D., Noonan, K. M., & Sherman, P. W. Sexual dimorphism and breeding systems in pinnipeds, ungulates, primates, and humans. In N. A. Chagnon & W. G. Irons (Eds.), *Evolutionary biology and human social behavior: An anthropological perspective*. North Scituate, Massachusetts: Duxbury Press, 1979.

Blau, P. M. *Exchange and power in social life*. New York: Wiley, 1964.

Chagnon, N. A. Genealogy, solidarity, and relatedness: Limits to local group size and patterns of fission in expanding populations. *Yearbook of Physical Anthropology*, 1975, *19*, 95–110.

Chagnon, N. A. Mate competition, favoring close kin, and village fissioning among the Yanomamö Indians. In N. A. Chagnon & W. G. Irons (Eds.), *Evolutionary biology and human social behavior. An anthropological perspective*. North Scituate, Massachusetts: Duxbury Press, 1979.

Darwin, C. *On the Origin of Species*. (A facsimile of the first edition with an introduction by Ernst Mayr). Boston: Harvard Univ. Press, (1859), 1967.

Hamilton, W. D. The evolution of altruistic behavior. *American Naturalist*, 1963, *98*, 354–356.

Hamilton, W. D. The genetical evolution of social behaviour. I, II. *Journal of Theoretical Biology*, 1964, *7*, 1–52.

Hamilton, W. D. The moulding of senescence by natural selection. *Journal of Theoretical Biology*, 1966, *12*, 12–45.

Hamilton, W. D. Extraordinary sex ratios. *Science*, 1967, *156*, 477–488.

Hamilton, W. D. Selfish and spiteful behavior in an evolutionary model. *Nature*, 1970, *228*, 1218–1220.

Hamilton, W. D. Geometry for the selfish herd. *Journal of Theoretical Biology*, 1971, *31*, 295–311.

Hamilton, W. D. Altruism and related phenomena, mainly in the social insects. *Annual Review of Ecology and Systematics*, 1972, *3*, 193–232.

Homans, G. C. *Social Behavior. Its Elementary Forms* (Rev. ed.) New York: Harcourt, 1974.

Lewontin, R. C. The units of selection. *Annual Review of Ecology and Systematics*, 1970, *1*, 1–18.

Sahlins, M. On the sociology of primitive exchange. In M. Banton (Ed.), *The relevance of models for social anthropology*. ASA Monograph. London: Tavistock, 1965, 139–236.

Sahlins, M. *The Use and Abuse of Biology*. Ann Arbor: Univ. of Michigan Press, 1976.

Trivers, R. L. The evolution of reciprocal altruism. *Quarterly Review of Biology*, 1971, *46*, 35–57.

Trivers, R. L. Parental investment and sexual selection. In B. Campbell (Ed.), *Selection and the Descent of Man*. Chicago: Aldine, 1972, 136–179.

Trivers, R. L. Parent–offspring conflict. *American Zoologist*, 1974, *14*, 249–264.

Walster, E., & Walster, G. W. Equity and social justice. *Journal of Social Issues*, 1975, *31*, 21–43.

West-Eberhard, M. J. The evolution of social behavior by kin selection. *Quarterly Review of Biology*, 1976, *50*, 1–33.

Wiessner, P. *A study of reciprocity among Kalahari Bushmen*. Doctoral Thesis, Univ. of Michigan, 1977.

Williams, G. C. Pleiotropy, natural selection, and the evolution of senescence. *Evolution*, 1957, *11*, 398–411.

Williams, G. C. *Adaptation and Natural Selection*. New Jersey: Princeton Univ. Press, 1966.

Williams, G. C. *Sex and Evolution*. New Jersey: Princeton Univ. Press, 1975.

8

Social Network Influence on the Dyadic Relationship

CARL A. RIDLEY
ARTHUR W. AVERY

I. Introduction

In recent years there has been an increased interest in conceptualizing and, to a more limited extent, explaining, dyadic development and functioning (Altman & Taylor, 1973; Huston, 1974; Levinger & Snoek, 1973; Lewis, 1972). Although these and other conceptualizations of relationship development appear to be useful, we are here concerned with what appears to be a conceptual blindness to the potential influence of the social environment, particularly the immediate social environment, on dyadic development.

The assumption made at the outset of this chapter is that there are variations in the way primary dyadic relationships develop and that some of these variations can be better understood than they usually are by conceptualizing this development from a social network perspective. Thus, we will argue that an understanding of dyadic development is facilitated by understanding the social networks within which the partnership is initiated, maintained, and in some cases, terminated. What follows is a brief description of the social network concept, including a discussion of the influence of social networks on dyadic relationships.

SOCIAL EXCHANGE IN DEVELOPING RELATIONSHIPS

II. Social Networks

The term *network* has been used most extensively in sociological and anthropological analyses, and in mathematical graph theory. Most of this work has focused on the concept of personal or social networks—defined as those individuals with whom a particular person interacts directly (or could potentially interact) and their interconnection (Boissevain, 1974; Katz, 1966). Extensive time will not be devoted here to reviewing the vast literature on the network concept. The reader is referred to Barnes (1969), Boissevain and Mitchell (1973), Mitchell (1969, 1974), or Whitten and Wolfe (1973) for a more comprehensive review of the concept and its development.

Since the present chapter focuses on the influence of social networks on dyadic relationships, the term *personal* or *social network* is used in reference to those persons (e.g., significant others, other dyads, social groups) with whom one or both of the dyad members is in *actual* contact (see Katz, 1966, for a definition and description of actual and possible networks). To clarify this definition, let us refer to Figure 8.1, which presents the parameters of a dyadic social network. The letters A and B indicate the dyad partners. The area within the circles surrounding each letter refers to the social network of each partner. The area of intersection between the two circles (AB) represents those persons who are network members of both partners. Although we recognize the possible differential effects of network members on the dyad, depending on whether they are members of one or both partners' social network, we will not deal with this distinction in the present chapter; rather we will view members of either or both partners' social network as members of the dyad's social network.

In an excellent discussion of network interaction, Boissevain (1974) compared interaction within networks to a communication circuit. He noted that in both instances certain individuals were in contact with each other, although the nature of their interaction was unspecified. He went on to say, however (and we agree with him), that a social network

is more than a communication network, for the messages are in fact transactions. By transaction I mean an interaction between two actors that is governed by the principle that the value gained from the interaction must be equal to or greater than

Figure 8.1   Parameters of the dyadic social network.

the cost (value lost). If the transaction is reciprocated in the sense that goods and services are returned, and thus flow in both directions, it is then useful to speak of exchange [pp. 25–26].

The basic foundation of the Boissevain (1974) explanation of network interaction appears to rest in exchange theory, in that transactions between an individual and his network, although sometimes unilateral, will over time usually develop a pattern of exchange of goods or services. From a dyadic perspective, then, the process may be viewed as an exchange of goods or services between the dyad members and other persons within the dyadic network. It should be noted, however, that some dyad network interactions may be maintained on a coercive or mutually hostile basis in which the apparent rewards to the dyad members are exceeded by the costs (Patterson & Hops, 1972). Such would be the case if (a) the rewards were less obvious to the dyad members than the costs, or (b) the costs to the dyad members were less than the costs of comparable alternatives for the dyad. In the former, a marital dyad may maintain what appears to be a costly relationship with one or both parents, with the long range goal of inheriting valued goods or services. In the latter, a marital couple having prominent parents in a small town may find having a negative relationship with their parents less costly than losing most of their other social relationships (i.e., incurring social isolation), which might result if they discontinued interaction with their parents.

As might be expected from an exchange theory perspective, the pattern of goods and services exchanged between the dyad members and persons within the dyadic network may become imbalanced over time. Person A provides more valued goods or services to Person B than B is able to (or desires to) reciprocate. In many cases this results in A's having greater influence (power) over B. Boissevain (1974) carried the effect of power differences within the network one step further, to include the total social environment:

A person's network thus forms a social environment from and through which pressure is exerted to influence his behaviour; but it is also an environment through which he can exert pressure to affect the behaviour of others. It is the reservoir of social relations from and through which he recruits support to counter his rivals and mobilizes support to attain his goals [p. 27].

If, as Boissevain (1974) proposed, the social network plays an important role in the achievement of individual or, in this case, dyadic goals, it would seem essential to understand the basic structure of networks. Are certain structures more likely to result in dyadic goal achievement than are others? What factors affect network development and maintenance? In the following section we will explore in greater detail the interactional and structural network components that have a marked effect on the development of the social network and thereby influence, directly or indirectly, the developing partnership.

III. Interactional Criteria

The relationship between the dyad members and the persons within the dyadic network may be examined in terms of (a) their role relations (diversity of linkages), (b) exchange content, (c) degree of reciprocity (directional flow), and (d) the temporal nature of the interaction. The following is a brief description of each of these interactional criteria.

A. Diversity of Linkages

One of the most important characteristics of a network involves the role relationships between the dyad members and others within the dyadic network. The term *role* is used in reference to the norms and expectations that apply to a particular position. A given dyad, for example, plays a number of different roles, including perhaps the role of parents or neighbors. In each of these roles, the dyad comes in contact with other individuals as well as other dyads and groups. If the social relations between the dyad and others are based on a single role relation it is termed *uniplex* (or *single-stranded*), whereas a relation that covers many roles (e.g., friend, neighbor) is termed *multiplex*, or *multi-stranded*, (Gluckman, 1955; Wheeldon, 1969). In discussing various role relations, Boissevain (1974) noted that over time uniplex relations tended to become multiplex relations and also that multiplex relations were likely to be stronger than uniplex relations since in the former the strands (roles) tend to reinforce one another.

B. Exchange Content

By the term *exchange content* (Kapferer, 1969), we are referring to the elements of the transaction (both material and nonmaterial) between a given dyad and others within the dyadic network. The particular elements exchanged will of course depend on the individuals involved, their goals, and the situation in which the transaction takes place In a sense, then, the nature of the elements exchanged is indicative of the dyad's and other network members' investment in the social relation.

C. Directional Flow

The term *directional flow* (or *directedness*) refers to the direction the elements move (are exchanged) in transactions (Kapferer, 1969). With respect to directionality, the elements exchanged may be equal, unequal, or complementary. In any case, the directional flow, whether symmetric or asymmetric, is a general indicator of the individuals' levels of investment in the social relation.

D. Frequency and Duration of Interaction

Both *frequency* and *duration of interaction* are potentially important variables in network interaction (Reader, 1954; Mitchell, 1969). Frequency of contact, although often an indicator of the investment of an individual or dyad in a social relation, does not always imply a high level of involvement in the relationship. Duration of contact, on the other hand, is likely to be a better indicator of involvement, since it is a measure of the amount of time (a limited resource) that individuals spend with each other (Boissevain, 1974).

IV. Structural Criteria

A. Size and Degree

Size and *degree* are two of the most important structural characteristics of a network. Network size (i.e., the number of persons included in the network) is particularly significant because it represents the factor against which most other structural components are compared. The degree of a network is simply the mean number of social relations that each person has with others in the same network—i.e., the extent to which the persons are on the average connected to the network (Niemeijer, 1973). Niemeijer (1973) presents an excellent description of the relationship between the size, the degree, and the density of a network, including an explanation of how to measure degree.

B. Density

Cubitt (1973) and others (e.g., Barnes, 1969; Noble, 1973) have pointed out that the term *density* has been defined differently by a number of researchers (e.g., what Barnes (1969) and Cubitt (1973) call density Bott (1971) calls connectedness). For our purposes, we will define density as *the extent to which members of the dyadic network have links (i.e., social relations) with other members of the network independently of the dyad members.* Density may be measured by the formula

$$200a/n \ (n-1)$$

where a refers to the actual number of links in the network excluding those with the dyad members and n to the total number of persons in the network including the dyad (adapted from Mitchell, 1969). Density, then, is a function of both the size and the degree of a network. As Niemeijer (1973) notes, the density of a network will vary directly with degree and inversely with size.

C. Intensity

The *intensity* of a network link refers to the degree to which the dyad members are willing to respond to the expectations of the network or particular network members and, therefore, are willing to forego other considerations in fulfilling the expectations associated with these ties (Mitchell, 1969).

V. Network Influences

Figure 8.2 presents a hypothetical social network for a given dyad. The larger circle in the center of the network represents the dyad members; the smaller circles surrounding the dyad members represent others in the dyadic network. The persons within the network are encircled by an "imaginary" dotted line, drawn merely to illustrate the extent of this particular network.

Thus far in the chapter we have examined the structural and interactional characteristics of the social network (Part A in Figure 8.2). Before moving on to a more detailed presentation of the way in which the social network influences the dyadic relationship, we must first identify a number of important agents that influence the development and functioning of the social network (Part B in Figure 8.2). These influences include biological, physical, and social factors that play a potentially significant role in network structure and interaction and, hence, affect the influence of the social network on the dyadic relationship. The following is a brief description of some of the major network influences identified in sociological and anthropological analyses. Other important factors of

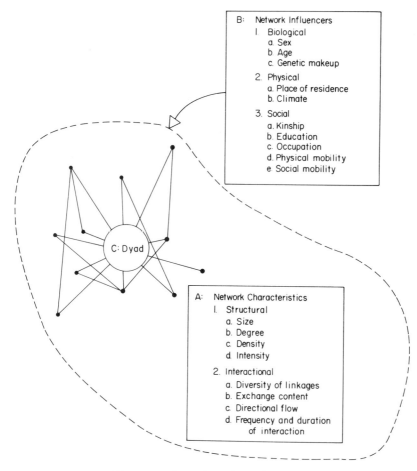

Figure 8.2 Hypothetical social network.

course could be listed, but our goal here is merely to familiarize the reader with several of the more significant biological, physical, and social influences on social networks.

A. Biological Factors

Certain biological factors, such as sex, age, and genetic makeup, have an important effect on the size and structure of an individual's personal network. An attractive female, for example, is often likely to have more relations with males than a less attractive female or one who puts less emphasis on her physical attributes. The resulting increase in the number of males in her personal network, however, may result in decreased relations with other females—many of whom may be jealous of her physical attributes.

Changes in the size and structure of a person's network over time, and the resulting effects of these changes on the individuals involved, have received little attention to date. Recently, however, more extensive research on life-cycle variations within networks, especially among older persons, has been undertaken (e.g., Shulman, 1975). There are indications that numerous structural aspects of a network change over time. When a person is young, the number of his closest relations is small, with a high degree of density and multiplexity characterizing them. As a person grows older, his network of closest relations grows larger, with an accompanying decrease in both density and multiplexity. With old age, the individual's network of closest relations again grows small, with a subsequent decrease in density and multiplexity (Boissevain, 1974). In one of the more recent studies on life-cycle variations in network patterns, Shulman (1975) investigated life-cycle variations in (a) the types of relationships that make up the network, (b) the stability of the network, (c) the content of the network relationships, and (d) the structural aspects of personal networks. He concluded that network size and structure were markedly affected by life-cycle variations:

> From the consideration of these findings we would conclude that the nature of close relationships does vary with life cycle changes and that at each stage people tend to establish and sustain networks of relationships geared to the needs and concerns of their particular stage of life [p. 820].

B. Physical Environment

Besides the biological factors previously noted, the physical environment in which a person lives has a potentially marked effect on the structural form of the resulting personal network. The person's immediate physical environment, or place of residence, is thought to play a significant role in the resulting size and structure of the personal network. Perhaps the major distinction in immediate social environments is to be made between small, isolated communities and large urban centers. Persons living in small self-contained communities are likely to have both comparatively high density and comparatively high multiplexity in their social relations, with, consequently, a comparatively rapid flow of information within the network (Barnes, 1954, 1969; Gluckman, 1955). Individuals in large urban centers, on the other hand, are likely to maintain uniplex relations, and with a comparatively large number of persons, and to have a comparatively low density within the network.

Climate is another characteristic of the physical environment that is likely to influence the nature of the personal network developed (see Sewell, 1966; Sewell, Kates, & Phillips, 1968). It is a factor, as Boissevain (1974) observes with "which most readers have had personal experience but find difficult to explain [p. 74]." Concerning the effects of climate on social relations he makes a main distinction between warmer and colder climates. His summary on the influence of climate conditions on social relations is excellent:

> All other things being equal, in a warm country, as compared [with] a cool one, the size of the first order zones will be larger, and as a result the density will be lower, as will [be] the multiplexity. Though frequency of interaction is relatively high, many of the contacts are relatively superficial: they are non-committal, for one does not have to cross thresholds to interact. On the other hand, in a cold country, social networks will tend to be smaller, with the result that the relative density will tend to be higher, as will multiplexity. Since friends must cross the threshold and enter into the personal domain of the house, it follows that persons there will maintain fewer friendships but that these are more intense than in warm climates [p. 77].

C. Social Influences

In addition to the biological and physical environmental factors that influence personal network formation and structure, several social factors, among them kinship relations, occupation, educational level, and geographic and social mobility, play an important role in social networks. The following is a brief description of each of these factors.

1. KINSHIP

Kinship relations have long been viewed as agents of support and exchange in personal networks (see Adams, 1968; Sussman, 1959, 1965). The significance of kinship ties within a person's network was illustrated clearly in a recent study by Shulman (1975). Using a structured interview format, the author found that approximately 41% of all persons in an individual's social network were kinrelated. The influence of these kinship relations on the behavior of the individual (or the dyad) will of course depend on the culture, and the quality of the social relation, as well as on a number of other factors. Boissevain (1974) suggested, however, that when the kinship part of a person's social network was centered in the person's residential area, the resulting network would likely have both high density and a high degree of multiplexity. This situation would likely result in greater network agreement regarding norms and values as well as in potentially more pressure for conformity under prescribed circumstances.

2. EDUCATION AND OCCUPATION

Like wealth or time, education is a valuable resource in exchange relations. Because it gives prestige and can be used to gain certain ends, it is clearly a form of power (Boissevain, 1974). Generally speaking, the more education an individual has, the larger will be the network and the lower its density and multiplexity. This is often the result of the fact that individuals frequently establish more social relations during the years that they are being educated than at other times. With respect to the social networks of less educated persons, they are likely to be smaller and have more multiplex links. As might be expected, the network of a less educated person, because of its structure and size, has greater potential to initiate social pressure to have the person conform to the norms and values of the network members.

3. PHYSICAL AND SOCIAL MOBILITY

In several instances, physical mobility has been shown to have a significant effect on the size, structure, and stability of social networks (see Bott, 1957; Mogey, 1956; Young & Wilmott, 1957). Once a person moves, the size and structure of his network changes—its size increases, its density decreases, and its multiplexity is likely to decrease (Boissevain, 1974). As Toffler (1970) has pointed out, we are living in a geographically mobile society in which people move a number of times during their lives. With each move, future moves become easier, and there is an increase in network size and a decrease in network density and multiplexity.

Like physical mobility, occupational status is also an influencing factor in social mobility. People move to get ahead in their careers, to increase status and social prestige. Like residential change, social mobility has a marked effect on personal networks.

VI. Social Exchange within Dyads

Let us again refer to the hypothetical social network presented in Figure 8.2. Thus far we have discussed both the structural and interactional characteristics of networks (Figure 8.2, Part A) and the primary physical, biological, and social influences of network structure and interaction (Figure 8.2, Part B). In these discussions we have seen that social networks vary tremendously depending on the differential effect of various factors influencing the networks. It might be concluded at this point, then, that social networks differ in many respects and that their impact on the developing dyad will depend on a number of important factors, including the structural and interactional characteristics previously outlined and the nature of the dyadic relationship itself. Just as networks have differing characteristics, including such things as the types of goods and services exchanged and the nature of the transaction itself, so also dyad relations vary along many dimensions. One important dimension in which dyads differ is the type of exchange patterns existing in the dyad itself. In short, one might speculate that the nature of social-network influences on the developing dyad will depend heavily on the type of exchange relations which exist between dyad partners (Figure 8.2, Part C).

Addressing this issue, we will describe five common types of dyadic exchange patterns. Our intention will be to explore the influence of the social network on each type. We will first briefly review the major assumptions of social exchange theory that are necessary for a thorough understanding of the major dyadic social exchange patterns to be presented in the next section.

VII. Social-Exchange Theory Assumptions

Complete descriptions of social-exchange principles can be found in a number of sources (such as Blau, 1964; Homans, 1974; Thibaut & Kelly, 1959). A recent review of social-exchange principles (Burns, 1973) includes a particularly clear presentation of the major assumptions of social-exchange theory:

1. Social behavior can be explained in terms of rewards, where rewards are goods or services, tangible or intangible, that satisfy a person's needs or goals.
2. Individuals attempt to maximize rewards and minimize losses or punishments.
3. Social interaction results from the fact that others control valuables or necessities and can therefore reward a person. In order to induce another to reward him, a person has to provide rewards to the other in return.
4. Social interaction is thus viewed as an exchange of mutually rewarding activities in which the receipt of a needed valuable (good or service) is contingent on the supply of a favor in return (usually immediate) [pp. 188–189].

VIII. Types of Dyadic Exchange Patterns

Individuals in a relationship are guided in their actions toward each other by their orientations (attitudes) to relationship exchange. When partners have considerable freedom to define their own exchange style, they are likely to be matched on symmetry in orientations (i.e., rarely does a person look out solely for his partner if the partner is, in fact, only concerned with himself or herself). Asymmetrical relationships do, however, appear particularly when norms exist to support them—e.g., the dominant–submissive pattern found in parent–infant relationships and in many husband–wife relationships (Carson, 1969).

Before we examine in detail the types of exchange found in relationships, it should be noted that the relationship-exchange typology to be presented does not represent the full range of exchanges found in either symmetrical or asymmetrical dyadic relationships, since actual relationships usually have a mixture of characteristics from a variety of exchange orientations. Thus, what is presented here is an exchange typology, not a relationship typology. In a later section of this paper we will give examples of how these exchange types might be linked in actual relationships.

The one asymmetrical exchange type presented here represents a typical pattern of husband–wife interaction when the relationship norms are sanctioned according to culturally expected sex-role behavior. This particular typology is introduced in the paper to serve as an analytical device assisting in the identification of the influence of social networks on a wide variety of social relationships.

Table 8.1 presents a typology of exchange patterns in relationships (the typology was adapted and expanded from Burns, 1972; Burns, 1973; Burns & Cooper, 1971; and Sahlins, 1965, 1968). Exchange types one through four are symmetrical; exchange type five is asymmetrical.

A. Type I: Mutually Exploitative

A Type I exchange pattern corresponds in many ways to classical economic market behavior, in which the focus is on short-run individual maximization of rewards. One implication of self-orientation is that each person in the relationship is largely indifferent to the partner's preferences. It is the individual's responsibility to protect his or her own interest in the exchange or face the result of poor "profit" in the interaction. When exchanges do occur, partners usually insist on immediate reciprocation.

An often observed Type I exchange pattern appears when divorcing marital partners attempt to maximize their benefits as economic goods are divided. The exploitative nature of this interaction can be concealed by successfully manipulating the partner to believe that the person has an "other-orientation" and is, therefore, acting in the other's best interest. Once each partner becomes aware of the other's orientation, however, mutual distrust develops and cooperation is diminished. Type I ex-

TABLE 8.1
Typology of Exchange Patterns[a]

Type I: Mutually exploitative		
A has pure self-orientation and believes B to have the same toward him or her	← Reciprocity →	B has a pure self-orientation and believes A to have the same toward him or her
Type II: Mutual consideration		
A has joint self–other orientation and believes B to have the same toward him or her	← Reciprocity →	B has joint self–other orientation and believes A to have the same toward him or her
Type III: Mutual benevolence		
A has a pure positive orientation toward B and believes B to have the same toward him or her	← Reciprocity →	B has pure positive orientation toward A and believes A to have the same toward him or her
Type IV: Mutually hostile		
A has pure negative orientation toward B and believes B to have the same toward him or her	← Reciprocity →	B has a pure negative orientation toward A and believes A to have the same toward him or her
Type V: Considerate–benevolent		
A has a pure positive other orientation toward B and believes B to have a self–other orientation toward him or her	← Reciprocity →	B has a self–other orientation toward A and believes A to have a positive other orientation toward him or her

a Adapted and expanded from Burns (1973).

changes are frequently short-lived, involve much haggling and conflict, and often result in withdrawal and a disruption of exchange.

B. Type II: Mutual Consideration

In Type II exchanges, partners are aware that each has a self–other orientation (i.e., there is a cooperative approach to exchange, in which at any given time either partner may give up something in order that the other partner may get a fair deal). The pair develops and implements what might be called an "exchange packet" that has outcomes that are fair to both partners. The goods and services that are part of the packet are the same or are of comparable value (i.e., they may swap kisses or exchange them for a back rub). The exchange packet is usually restricted to a limited and specific number of exchanged goods and services, and the satisfaction derived from the exchange is the major reason for maintaining the relationship. The quid-pro-quo basis of exchange is made possible by a commitment to maintain the goodwill and trust of one another, the an-

ticipation of future exchanges, and subscription to—in Gouldner's (1960).
phrase—the "norm of reciprocity."

There are several possible sources of conflict when Type II exchanges
are employed. First, there could be a lack of satisfaction with either the
exchange packet (i.e., the nature of what is being exchanged is not perceived to be equivalent) or the way in which the packet is being exchanged (e.g., although the exchange may be perceived as equivalent, one
or both individuals may give up their resource because their partner
identified the exchange as an expectation or obligation). Second, there
may be an inability or unwillingness to expand or contract the behaviors
currently included in the exchange packet. Third, the "self" and "other"
components of the self–other orientation are in such delicate balance that
certain situational factors could result in one component being weighed
more heavily than the other. Fourth, an imbalance in resources or power
could cause conflict in the relationship.

C. Type III: Mutual Benevolence

Type III behavior is based on both partners' having a positive other-
orientation in the relationship. Each partner, for example, is relatively
happy in the relationship, labels the relationship as a positive one, and, as
a result, is concerned about the wellbeing of the partner. Both dyad
members often seem more concerned with being sensitive to their partner's needs than concerned with whether particular gifts or behaviors are
reciprocated or rewarded. Obviously, exchanges do take place, but they
are interlocking exchanges in a complex matrix of relationship behaviors,
and are a result of an existing and committed social relationship. The
exchange packet may remain unspecified with regard to content, place, or
time—making it difficult to compare the relative value of the goods or
services exchanged. Evaluations of fairness are made on the basis of a
person's perception of the extent to which the partner is sensitive to the
person and the person's needs (both short-term and long-term). This type
of exchange may develop gradually from ongoing rewarding interaction
between partners. Early interaction may be characterized by the counting
of specific goods or services that are given and received. It would appear,
then, that after continued positive interactions, a desired state of feeling
based on the positive interaction (e.g., happiness) becomes the primary
basis for continuing this type of interaction. We are implying not that the
counting of exchanged behaviors necessarily stops but that the state of
feeling increases in significance and becomes a more important criterion
for evaluating the exchange. There are no doubt wide individual variations in the degree to which counting continues even when there is a
positive state of feeling. If one or both dyad members become dissatisfied
(e.g., the desired feeling decreases), they may well attend more closely to

the specific goods or services exchanged and, for all practical purposes, may return to an early stage of this exchange pattern in which they are again more cognizant of the specific goods or services exchanged. The competent performance of an extensive array of behaviors is often necessary to keep the partners from returning to the counting phase of this pattern as well as from developing the relationship problems that may result when the desired states of feeling of one or both partners decline to an unsatisfactory level. In some sense, then, both Type II and Type III exchange patterns are contingent on the partner's evaluation of the exchange packet. In Type II exchanges, this assessment is based primarily on the perceived equivalency of the resources exchanged; in Type III exchanges, it is based on the development and maintenance of a desired state of feeling, such as happiness.

D. Type IV: Mutually Hostile

Both partners in Type IV exchanges have negative exchange orientations (i.e., each tries to minimize the partner's chance of attaining goals). Both are aware of each others' orientation, and the exchange packet might be stated as follows: "You hurt me and I am going to hurt you in return." The rewarding quality of the interaction consists in being successful at inflicting dissatisfactions on the partner that exceed those doled out by the partner. Even if one partner "wins," so to speak (gets less hurt than the other), the result of this type of conflict interaction is to become suspicious of the partner's intentions for interaction and highly sensitive as to when the next bout will take place. The content of the conflict interaction could include a wide or a narrow range of behaviors dependent in part on the participants' tolerance for conflict and the degree of hurt that has been inflicted—the more severe the hurt, the more extensive the range of conflict tends to be (Rausch, Barry, Hertel, & Swain, 1974). Conflicting interaction coupled with a negative orientation results in a breakdown of open communication and exchange of information, and generally inhibits cooperation. The vicious cycles produced by conflict make the exchange pattern resistant to change. Any change in the exchange pattern is most likely to come about through conditions external to the relationship or by relationship termination (see Patterson & Hops, 1972, for an excellent description of causes, processes, and outcomes of coercion games between marital pairs).

E. Type V: Considerate–Benevolent

This particular asymmetrical relationship has been identified because it is found so often in long-enduring intimate heterosexual relationships such as marriage (Scanzoni, 1972). In Type V exchanges one partner has a positive other-orientation while the other partner has a self–other orientation. Both partners possess different but valuable goods and services, which are exchanged between them. The self–other oriented partner possesses more resources, or more valuable ones, and therefore has more power in the relationship. The other-oriented person, through what appears to be (but, as noted earlier, is not) contingency-free giving, encourages the partner to reciprocate in a like manner at least to a certain extent. Although the relationship is not equal in terms of valued behaviors exchanged, balance in relationship exchanges is maintained by adherence to the norm of reciprocity applied to the more powerful partner and the weaker partner's ability to withdraw valued resources. Mutual fairness and satisfaction is achieved with this system of exchange when partners are not equal in resources possessed and exchanged.

Type V exchanges remain satisfying and largely conflict-free so long as the distribution of resources does not change significantly. However, should the other-oriented partner increase his or her resources, or perhaps deliver goods or services in a more pleasing way, changes in the distribution of behaviors might be necessary. A refusal to redistribute behaviors on the partner's part will result in relationship dissatisfaction and conflict. Also, dissatisfaction could result in a decrease in the more powerful partner's resources (e.g., losing economic resources with retirement).

IX. Sequencing of Exchange Patterns within Dyadic Relationships

To this point we have attempted to demonstrate that there are important differences in the types of transactions within relationships and that the nature of exchange is tied to the orientation of exchange of the relationship participants. The task now becomes the placing of these types of exchange types into ongoing relationships.

Although it is possible to conceive of an ongoing relationship being characterized by only one type of exchange, there are probably several types of exchange that exist simultaneously or in sequence within most relationships. Perhaps the most typical sequence within close relationships is a movement from Type II exchange to Type III exchange. The early stage of Type II exchange has a very restricted exchange packet, and a greater emphasis on the "self" aspect of the self–other orientation. Positive early interaction expands the exchange packet and allows the "other" aspect of the self–other orientation to become more active. Type II exchange becomes Type III exchange when (a) exchanges in the relationship become extensive with a corresponding increase in the difficulty of keeping track of or in controlling the exchange packet (i.e., the goods or services exchanged) and (b) partners have developed mutual trust with respect to the fairness of the exchange. Although some of the processes that result in movement from Type II exchanges to Type III exchanges help to maintain Type III exchanges within the relationship, there seem to be cognitive and behavioral adjustments by dyad members that stabilize Type III exchange patterns that are not necessary to establish or maintain the Type II exchange pattern. Members of the dyad may or may not be fully aware of these adjustments. It appears that many dyads with elaborate exchange packets attempt to simplify the exchanges by (a) developing a saliency hierarchy of exchanged behaviors with, the more important exchanges being monitored and controlled most closely, and (b) developing rules of fairness in relationship exchanges—making it less important to evaluate the fairness of each exchange (which is a characteristic of Type II exchanges). It should be noted that saliency hierarchies and fairness rules are produced not only be the impulse to simplify complex exchange packets but also by relationships characterized by predominantly mutual positive affect. So long as the state of feeling is positive, the relationship rules are followed, and the important exchanges continue to take place, Type III exchanges remain stable. Conversely, relationships which have largely Type III exchanges may deteriorate when the positive feeling state is no longer present, the relationship rules are violated, or important goods and services are no longer exchanged. When Type III exchanges begin to break down, it is likely that the often unstable Type I (mutually exploitative) or Type IV (mutually hostile) exchanges will result, as the dominant exchange pattern. Stable close relationships with many Type III exchanges might be expected to have "episodes" of Type I and Type IV exchanges. Some of these hostile exchanges based on interpersonal conflict may signal perceived exchange violations and thus provide a possible basis for exchange corrections—perhaps by increasing the mixture of Type II and Type III exchanges.

X. Social Network Influence on Dyadic Relationships

As noted in our earlier discussion of the major assumptions of social-exchange theory, the influence of, for example, Person A on person B depends to a large extent on Person A's having resources desired by Person B. An analogous statement of the influence of the social network on the dyad can be made. In large part, the influence of the social network on the dyad will depend on the social network's having resources desired by the dyad. Unless the social network can confer rewards or punishments on the dyad, its effects might well be negligible.

If we assume that the social network has sufficient resources to have an influencing effect on the dyad, one might then want to know under what conditions the social network will exert an influence on the dyad and what the nature of the influence will be.

In the light of these preliminary remarks we will discuss in this section several of the more important factors related to the nature and strength of the social network influences on the dyad. They include (a) network characteristics, (b) network resources, (c) the nature of the network–dyad relationship, and (d) dyadic exchange patterns.

A. Network Characteristics and the Network—Dyad Relationship

The structural and interactional characteristics discussed earlier play an important role in determining the nature and strength of the social network influences on the dyad. Although we will not attempt to fully identify the influence of these characteristics here, we will discuss several examples of propositions that, we believe, should serve to highlight some of the possibilities.

In our earlier discussion on the diversity of linkages, we noted that multiplex relations were likely to be stronger than uniplex relations, since roles tend to reinforce one another. All things being equal, then, we posit the following:

PROPOSITION 1: *Persons within the network that have multiplex relations with the dyad have greater potential to influence the dyad than persons with uniplex relations with the dyad. (This assumes, among other things, that both the uniplex relations and multiplex relations have similar resources.)*

A person who is, for example, a neighbor, colleague, and tennis partner of the dyad may have the potential for greater influence on the dyad than another person who has a uniplex relationship with the dyad (e.g., a post office employee).

Density is another characteristic that potentially has a great influence on the network–dyad relationship. As Boissevain (1974) noted, persons' perceptions of their network will likely affect their behavior. The same, no doubt, would hold true for a dyad.

PROPOSITION 2: *The network will influence the behavior or expected behavior of the dyad in accordance with the dyad's perception of the density of the network.*

For example, if the dyad members are trying to make a decision whether or not to live together, the possibility that one or both sets of parents may learn about this (e.g., by way of another person in the dyadic network) may certainly affect their behavior.

B. Network Resources and the Strength of the Network–Dyad Relationship

1. VALUE OF THE NETWORK RESOURCES TO THE DYAD

Perhaps the most important variable affecting the strength of the social network influence on the dyad is the amount of resources possessed by the social network that are desired by the dyad.

PROPOSITION 3: *The greater the resources possessed by the social network that are desired by the dyad, the greater will be the influence (i.e., power) of the social network over the dyad, and the greater will be the dependence of the dyad on the network. Conversely, the fewer the resources possessed by the social network that are desired by the dyad, the less will be the influence of the social network over the dyad, and the less will be the dependence of the dyad on the network.*

The strength of the social network influence on the dyad will also be determined in part by the scarcity of those network resources desired by the dyad.

PROPOSITION 4: *The greater the scarcity of resources possessed by the network and desired by the dyad, the greater will be the social network influence on the dyad. Conversely, the less scarce the resources possessed by the network and desired by the dyad (i.e., the dyad has alternative means for obtaining the resources), the less will be the social network influence on the dyad.*

2. INTERNAL NETWORK AGREEMENT AND DYAD BEHAVIOR

Another key factor in determining the strength of the network influence on the dyad is the amount and type of agreement among network members regarding the dyad's behavior or expected behavior.

PROPOSITION 5: *The network will have greater influence on the dyad if all members of the network are in agreement on the behavior or expected behavior of the dyad.*

If there is disagreement among network members regarding the behavior or expected behavior of the dyad, the dyad is likely to receive contradictory messages from the social network regarding appropriate or desired behavior.

PROPOSITION 6: *If the social network is not in agreement regarding the behavior or expected behavior of the dyad, the dyad will be influenced most by those members of the network who (a) have the resources most desired by the dyad, and (b) are most likely to confer the resources on the dyad, and will be least influenced by those network members who (a) do not have the resources desired by the dyad or (b) are least likely to confer the resources on the dyad.*

As before, if those resources desired by the dyad can be obtained from other sources, those network members possessing the resources may have less influence on the dyad than they otherwise would.

C. Nature of the Network–Dyad Relationship

Another important factor in determining the influence of the social network on the dyad involves the degree to which the network (as a unit) and the dyad agree on the appropriate or expected behavior of the dyad.

PROPOSITION 7: *If the network and the dyad agree on the behavior or expected behavior of the dyad, the network will influence the dyad by (a) conferring rewards on the dyad, and (b) minimizing costs to the dyad.*

PROPOSITION 8: *If the network and the dyad disagree on the behavior or expected behavior of the dyad, the network will influence the dyad by (a) withholding resources from the dyad, and (b) inflicting punishments on the dyad.*

The degree to which the social network influences the dyad in the aforementioned directions will depend in part on the relationship between the behavior desired by the dyad and the norms of the network.

PROPOSITION 9: *The social network will be most supportive of the dyad when the behavior or expected behavior of the dyad supports those norms valued by the network. Conversely, the social network will be least supportive of, and in many cases opposed to, the behavior or expected behavior of the dyad when the dyad does not support (or opposes) the norms of the network. When the behavior or expected behavior of the dyad is in opposition to the network norms, the network will attempt to influence the dyad to behave in accordance with network norms. The network will attempt to influence the behavior or expected behavior of the dyad less if the behavior in question is not closely associated with the norms of the social network or it is more individualized to the dyad itself.*

D. Dyadic Exchange Patterns and the Network–Dyad Relationship

To this point we have developed propositions concerning the influence of networks on dyads based on the idea that by knowing (a) the structural and interactional characteristics of the network, (b) the resources possessed by the network, (c) the network consensus in the application of network resources, (d) the extent to which dyadic exchanges are normatively governed, and (e) the consensus between network norms and dyadic application of these norms the strength and nature of the network influence on the dyad relationship can be better understood. The propositions in this section are built on the idea that the influence of networks on dyads can be further clarified by knowing (a) the dyadic exchange patterns and (b) the network norms.

Propositions 10 and 11 specify the relationship between network norms and conflict exchange patterns.

PROPOSITION 10: *Networks generally will not support both regularized hostile and nonhostile exchanges—that is, network norms tend to support only one predominant class of exchange patterns: either conflict (Types I and IV) or non-conflict (Types II, III, and V), but not both.*

It should be noted that in actual dyads it is relatively rare for the dyad to consistently exhibit large amounts of both conflict and nonconflict exchange patterns.

PROPOSITION 11: *Most networks have norms that support nonconflict exchange patterns within close relationships (exchange Types II, III, and V). Thus, conflict exchange patterns (exchange Types I and IV) are not likely to be supported by the network.*

As was argued earlier in this chapter, it is difficult to move from Exchange Pattern II to Exchange Pattern III without conflicting interaction between partners; that is, relationship conflict signals violations in exchange packets and helps provide the impetus for movement between exchange patterns. The proposition that follows describes the network influence on the dyad during this and other exchange-pattern transitions.

PROPOSITION 12: *Networks are likely to have a strong influence on the dyadic relationship when the dyad is in transition between exchange types. If the transition is toward an exchange pattern that is normatively* prescribed, the network will be supportive (e.g., Type II to Type III). If the transition is toward a nonnormative exchange pattern, the network will be nonsupportive (e.g., Type II to Type IV) and will attempt to reinstate the prescribed exchange pattern (e.g., reinstate Exchange Pattern II).

These propositions are based on the assumptions that the collective network or network members possess sufficient resources valued by the dyad to make it rewarding for the dyad or its members to pursue interaction with the network or its members. Should this not be the case, the dyad or its members will (a) terminate interaction with their existing social network, or (b) seek out or respond to a new network that possesses valued resources.

These propositions constitute an initial attempt to formulate predictions concerning the influence of social networks on relationship interaction using exchange theory concepts. They are in no way intended to be inclusive or definitive, but are presented simply to demonstrate the types of issues that need to be addressed within an exchange theory framework.

XI. Summary and Conclusions

The purpose of this chapter has been to explore the potential influence of the social network on the dyadic relationship. The task was accomplished in several steps. First, we identified some of the major structural and interactional characteristics of social networks likely to affect dyadic interaction. Second, we discussed several predominant biological, physical, and social factors that influence network structure and interaction and thus affect, directly or indirectly, the behavior of the dyad. Third, we presented a typology of exchange patterns that typify dyadic relationships. Finally, we developed a number of exploratory propositions designed to describe the nature of the social network influence on the dyad under prescribed circumstances.

In the process we have determined that social networks are important factors in dyadic interaction. The relationship between social networks and relationship interaction is, however, a complex one and greatly in need of conceptual and empirical work. As a conceptual base, social exchange theory (with particular emphasis on the exchange of valued resources) seems useful for this type of analysis.

This chapter, we hope, has provided a framework within which to assess the value of social exchange theory as a conceptual base for explaining social network influence on the dyadic relationship. The nature of this influence will perhaps be clearer when we begin to do the following: (a) clarify and operationalize the types of exchange patterns proposed in this paper, in order that empirical work can be undertaken using them, (b) develop procedures for more effectively measuring the exchange of resources between network members and between the network and the dyad, (c) assess the effects of social networks on the developing dyad (i.e., view exchange of resources developmentally and focus on exchange at different developmental levels), (d) assess the influence of the network on the dyad at times of crisis or of conflict in the dyad, (e) assess the influence of the network on individual dyad members rather than solely on the dyad as a unit, and (f) determine the influence of the dyad on the network (e.g., the degree to which the dyad selects persons to be part of their network). Only when these and other issues are addressed will we be able to adequately understand the potential influence of the social network on the dyadic relationship.

References

Adams, B. N. Kinship in an urban setting. Chicago: Markham, 1968.

Altman, I., & Taylor, D. Social penetration processes: The development of interpersonal relationships. New York: Holt, 1973.

Barnes, J. A. Class and communities in a Norwegian island parish. Human Relations, 1954, 7, 39–58.

Barnes, J. A. Graph theory and social networks: A technical comment on connectedness and connectivity. Sociology, 1969, 3, 215–232.

Blau, P. Exchange and power in social life. New York: Wiley, 1964.

Boissevain, J. Friends of friends. Oxford: Basil Blackwell, 1974.

Boissevain, J. & Mitchell, J. C. Network analysis: Studies in human interaction. Paris: Mouton, 1973.

Bott, E. Family and social networks. London: Tavistock, 1957.

Bott, E. Family and social networks. (2nd ed.) London: Tavistock, 1971.

Burns, T. A structural theory of value, decision-making, and social interaction. Paper read at the Symposium on "New Directions in Theoretical Anthropology," Oswego, New York, May, 1972.

Burns, T. A structural theory of social exchange. Acta Sociologica, 1973, 16, 183–208.

Burns, T., & Cooper, M. Value, social power, and economic exchange. Stockholm: Samhällsvetareförlaget, 1971.

Carson, R. C. Interaction concepts of personality. Chicago: Aldine, 1969.

Cubitt, T. Network density among urban families. In J. Boissevain & J. C. Mitchell (Eds.), Network analysis: Studies in human interaction. Paris: Mouton, 1973.

Gluckman, M. The judicial process among the Barotose of Northern Rhodesia. Manchester: Manchester Univ. Press, 1955.

Gouldner, A. J. The norm of reciprocity: A preliminary statement. American Sociological Review, 1960, 25, 161–179.

Homans, G. C. Social behavior: Its elementary forms. (2nd ed.) New York: Harcourt, 1974.

Huston, T. L. (Ed.) Foundation of interpersonal attraction. New York: Academic Press, 1974.

Kapferer, B. Norms and the manipulation of relationships in work context. In J. C. Mitchell (Ed.), Social networks in urban situations. Manchester: Manchester Univ. Press, 1969. pp. 181–244.

Katz, F. E. Social participation and social structure. Social Forces, 1966, 14, 199–210.

Levinger, C., & Snoek, J. *Attraction in relationship: A new look at inter-personal attraction.* New York: General Learning Press, 1973.

Lewis, R. A. A developmental framework for the analysis of pre-marital dyadic formation. *Family Process*, 1972, *11*, 17–48.

Mitchell, J. D. (Ed.) *Social networks in urban situations.* Manchester: Manchester Univ. Press. 1969.

Mitchell, J. C. Social networks. In B. J. Siegel, A. R. Beals, & S. A. Tyler (Eds.), *Annual review of anthropology.* Palo Alto, California: Annual Reviews, 1974.

Mogey, J. M. *Family and neighborhood.* London: Oxford Univ. Press, 1956.

Niemeijer, R. Some applications of the notion of density to network analysis. In J. Boissevain & J. C. Mitchell (Eds.), *Network analysis: Studies in human interaction.* Paris: Mouton, 1973.

Noble, M. Social network: Its use as a conceptual framework in family analysis. In J. Boissevain & J. C. Mitchell (Eds), *Network analysis: Studies in human interaction.* Paris: Mouton, 1973.

Patterson, G. R., & Hops, H. Coercion, a game for two: Intervention techniques for marital conflict. In R. C. Ulrich & P. Mountjoy (Eds.), *The experimental analysis of social behavior.* New York: Appleton-Century-Crofts, 1972.

Rausch, H. L., Barry, W. A., Hertel, R. K., & Swain, M. A. *Communication conflict, and marriage.* San Francisco: Jassey-Bass, 1974.

Reader, D. H. Models in social change with special reference to southern Africa. *Journal of African Studies*, 1954, *23*, 11–33.

Sahlins, M. D. On the sociology of primitive exchange. In M. Banton (Ed.), *The relevance of models for social anthropology.* New York: Praeger, 1965.

Sahlins, M. D. *Tribesmen.* Englewood Cliffs, New Jersey: Prentice-Hall, 1968.

Scanzoni, J. *Sexual bargaining.* Englewood Cliffs, New Jersey: Prentice-Hall, 1972.

Sewell, W. R. D. (Ed.) *Human dimensions of weather modification.* Chicago: Univ. of Chicago Press, 1966.

Sewell, W. R. D., Kates, R. W., & Phillips, L. E. Human response to weather and climate. *Geographical Review*, 1968, *58*, 262–280.

Shulman, N. Life-cycle variations in patterns of close relationships. *Journal of Marriage and the Family*, 1975, *37*, 813–821.

Sussman, M. B. The isolated nuclear family: Fact or fiction? *Social Problems*, 1959, *6*, 333–340.

Sussman, M. B. Relationships of adult children with their parents in the United States. In E. Shanas & G. Streib (Eds.), *Social structure and the family: Generational relations.* Englewood Cliffs, New Jersey: Prentice-Hall, 1965.

Thibaut, J. W., & Kelley, H. H. *The social psychology of groups.* New York: Wiley, 1959.

Toffler, A. *Future shock.* New York: Random House, 1970.

Wheeldon, P. D. The operation of voluntary associations and personal networks in the political processes of an inter-ethnic community. In J. C. Mitchell (Ed.), *Social networks in urban situations.* Manchester: Manchester Univ. Press, 1969.

Whitten, N. E., Jr., & Wolfe, A. W. Network analysis. In J. J. Honigmann (Ed.), *Handbook of social and cultural anthropology.* Chicago: Rand McNally, 1973.

Young, M., & Willmott, P. *Family and kinship in East London.* London: Routledge, Paul & Kegan, 1957.

9

Personality and Exchange in Developing Relationships

ROBERT C. CARSON

I. Introduction

The idea that the personalities of individuals who are in some relationship to one another contribute importantly to what transpires in that relationship is so commonly accepted as to appear banal. Similarly commonplace is the observation that the implicated process of inter personality engagement is to a large extent governed by exchange principles; that is, that relationships develop and are sustained to the extent that reward–cost ratios are hedonically optimal, in non impersonal ways, for each participant in behavioral transactions that occur between participants, and that such transactions are normally mutually contingent. The general acceptance of these notions notwithstanding, however, they have not thus far proven very powerful at the level of precise empirical confirmation, especially if viewed from the standard of their capacity to predict relationship events. It would nevertheless seem premature to abandon this type of application of exchange theory, partly because of its enormous intuitive appeal, and partly because it has not yet received a comprehensive and fair test.

A number of rather perplexing problems will require solution before any such comprehensive testing can be accomplished, some of them—

247

such as the problem of subjective values or utilities—very general, and some of them more specifically related to whatever we mean by exchange in regard to personality processes. In part, this chapter is an attempt to identify some of the larger of these unsolved problems. More generally, I hope to lay out a foundation for thinking about personality and inter-personality in exchange terms. As the course is to a large extent un-charted, not to say hazardous and intimidating in its complexity, I shall confine myself to a fairly broad level of analysis, leaving the hard part to more patient and courageous souls.

Unlike most individuals interested in exchange theory, my own background is a clinical one. This item of biography would perhaps be irrelevant were it not for the fact that, as a young clinician, I was pro-foundly influenced by the work of another and very seminal clinician, Harry Stack Sullivan. As is well known, Sullivan conceived of personality as a largely interpersonal phenomenon, a conception that in itself suggests his pertinence to my topic. Less well known—and more specif-ically pertinent here—is that he was an early exchange theorist. I shall have more to say about the latter fact in due course. For the present, it is obligatory that I propose some working definition of personality, and there seems no better place to begin than with Sullivan.

II. The Nature of Personality

A. Sullivanian Theory

Sullivan (1953) defined personality as "the relatively enduring pat-tern of recurrent interpersonal situations which characterize a human life [p. 110]." The potentially most troublesome word here is "pattern," and Sullivan, with characteristic style, defines it as "the envelope of insig-nificant particular differences [p. 104]." Thus, personality is an enduring, recurrent, characteristic form of engagement of other persons that is discernible by virtue of the "insignificant particular differences" in which it may manifest itself from one occasion to another. The principal under-lying process determining personality, so defined, is the individual's self system or self dynamism. The latter is a highly complex schema by means of which the individual processes information about himself and others, sometimes veridically (syntaxis) and sometimes not (parataxis). De-velopmentally, this schema arises from accommodations to incoming information, much of it in form of reflected appraisal of the characteristics of the self. Later, the major operating principle becomes that of assimila-tion, such that incoming information is increasingly rendered consistent with previously existing schematic elements. It is painful, or "costly," for the individual to be confronted with discrepant information. The self system minimizes such costs through its control of awareness. It must be acknowledged that this is a condensed and modernized version of Sullivan's personality theory; I do believe it to be an essentially accurate one.

Insofar as these ideas imply a degree of transsituational consistency in the significant behavior of persons, they touch certain basic issues that currently dominate the area of personality research. It seems necessary to give a measure of attention to these issues before proceeding, because they involve the essential validity of the personality construct, and because they introduce additional complexities to the problems under consideration—complexities that have thus far not been addressed to any great extent by empirical research. I refer, of course, to the situationism–dispositionism–interactionism controversy, which has recently received a thorough airing in *Interactional Psychology and Personality*, edited by Endler and Magnusson (1976). Unless we allow for a substantial and systematic dispositional element in the behavior of persons, there would seem to be little point to the personality construct and therefore to the purported subject of this paper.

B. The Interactionist Resolution

Anyone familiar with the history of psychology will recognize that the controversy in question is by no means new (see Ekehammar, 1974). The reasons for its persistence as an issue appear to be intimately tied to the differing methodological styles of researchers in the personality field, some emphasizing correlational and some experimental approaches, along the lines of what Cronbach (1957) has described as the "two disciplines of scientific psychology." As pointed out by Bowers (1973), among others, correlational and experimental methods are selectively blind, respectively, to situational and dispositional influence on behavior, and—what is widely misunderstood—neither approach has a monopoly on the understanding of causation at the theoretical level, causation being, at bottom, a construct applied to empirical relationships of whatever source.

The outcome of the controversy is now discernible. Some would argue that it always has been. In any event, a variety of evidence reviewed by Bowers (1973) and Sarason, Smith, and Diener (1975), and presented in many of the selections of the Endler and Magnusson (1976) volume, points to the widespread existence of potent person-by-situation interaction effects in studies whose designs permit their exposure. Moreover, this conclusion appears justified in spite of the well-reasoned technical precautions voiced by Golding (1975) concerning the assessment of interaction effects in studies not involving subject preselection on "person" variables.

Person-by-situation interaction in the determination of behavior may conceivably occur on two quite distinct bases, mechanistic and organismic (Endler, 1975). According to the mechanistic interpretation, such interactions reflect merely the divergent and unique conditioning histories of individuals, such that similar behaviors across persons are evoked and maintained by differing stimulus curcumstances, and that phenotypically similar stimulus circumstances would be expected to produce, in different individuals, different conditioned responses. The simplistic view of the organization of human behavior implied in this position has been amply challenged on many fronts in recent years and requires no commentary here.

The organismic interpretation is essentially a cognitive or information-processing one: Persons respond individualistically to the situations with which they are confronted because, to at least some extent, they construe those situations in idiosyncratic ways. This is basically the conclusion to which Mischel (1973) was drawn in his recent, important reconceptualization of personality, and thus organismic variables have found their way back into a psychology of personality perversely dominated in the 1960s by views that excluded the person (Carlson, 1971).

It goes without saying that the most important situations encountered by persons in their daily living consist of other people and their behaviors, particularly those behaviors that are directed toward the subject-person. To a large extent, then, the essential things we need to understand concern the manner in which persons perceive, construe, subjectively quantify, etc., the signals coming to them from other persons in their life space. This is the issue on which I especially want to focus. There is another sense in which the person may be said to create his own situations, as was emphasized recently by Wachtel (1973); that is, by behaving in such a way as to control the real-world situations with which he is characteristically faced. I do not want to suggest by neglect that I regard such processes as unimportant. On the contrary, I have analyzed them extensively in an earlier work (Carson, 1969), and I shall return to them briefly later in this chapter. For now, however, I want to emphasize the matter of possible systematic idiosyncracies among persons in their construing of other people and their behavior. This seems an equally promising means, although in some ways a neglected one, of understanding person-by-situation—that is, largely, person-as-subject-by-person-as-object—interaction in the determination of complex social behavior. In interpersonal processes, of course, this subject–object distinction is simultaneously bidirectional, which is only one of several perplexing methodological challenges that pervade the field.

C. Personality and Construal Style

It would seem from what has been said thus far that much of what we normally regard as personality-contingent behavior is based on the differing and distinctive ways in which persons construct reality from the sensory information available to them, particularly that emanating from their relationships with other people. Such a view, made explicit in George Kelly's (1955) system, is hardly novel. As we have seen, Sullivan (1953) seems to have had much the same idea. Unfortunately, a rather vast literature in person perception provides little elucidation of the supposedly implicated processes (Schneider, 1973; Shrauger & Altrocchi, 1964), mostly because it does not really address the substantive issues implied here, or does so in an insufficiently sophisticated manner (Carson, 1975; Golding, 1977). Some more recent and promising work in this area will be reviewed later.

Personality manifests itself in behaviors that are somehow and to some extent distinctive for the person. The implication of the preceding remarks is that these distinctive behaviors are based in turn on distinctive ways of perceiving–construing the social environment. To infer as much should not be unduly surprising, inasmuch as a cogent argument can be made that *all* behavior is based on perceptual processes. Powers (1973), for example, in a rather impressive treatise, tells us that the *function* of behavior is to *control* perception, to cause perceptions to meet certain criterial specifications (cf. Bruner, 1957). These criterial specifications, or what may be termed "reference signals," constitute the outputs of an elaborately hierarchicized cybernetic control system, a control system whose operating characteristic is to reduce the mismatch or "error" between reference signal and input. Is it possible that persons differ systematically in the nature and magnitude of their higher-order reference signals—in the zero-points and scalar properties of the subjective metric by which they process incoming information? I would think so. And if they do, then they will perceive the world somewhat differently, and their behaviors in the world will reflect those distinctivenesses. Conceived in social interaction terms, the intermeshing of personalities becomes a matter of understanding the constructions (or misconstructions) persons make about what is going on between themselves and others. Presumably, such constructions are not without hedonic significance to interaction partners. These processes will be examined in the pages that follow.

III. Personality and Commodities of Exchange

Having outlined in broad terms a conception of what personality is and of the manner in which, to a large extent, it seems to function in mediating relationships between the person and the environment, we are now in a position to return to the main issue: the exchange process as related to the personalities of the individuals engaged in exchange. I shall focus on the implications of our analysis for some of the basic properties of interpersonal relationships.

A. Resources to be Exchanged

Foa and Foa (1974) have developed a useful taxonomy of resource classes based on both empirical and conceptual analysis of exchange in social relationships. These resource classes, which are obviously nonindependent at the behavioral level, are love, status, information, money, goods, and services. Conceived in exchange terms, then, social relationships consist of the giving, taking away, receipt, and loss of quantities of these types of resources as the parties to the relationship negotiate their interactions. The underlying idea is that persons have needs to receive (and perhaps to give or to take away) varying amounts of the substances of these resource dimensions in the network of social relationships in which they engage, and indeed that the basis for such engagements is the opportunity provided thereby for need fulfillment.

Personality manifests itself chiefly in those contexts that are relatively unconstrained by potent situational requirements (such as stringent social-role prescriptions), in agreement with the "naive psychology" of attribution theory. Hence it is in less structured and less formal relationships (more intimate ones) that we would expect to find the greatest effect of personality upon exchange processes. This observation has implications for the types of resources (needs) most likely to be involved in more intimate forms of exchange (Levinger, 1974). In general, from this standpoint we would expect love and status (or their opposites) to be maximally significant items of exchange, information and services less significant items, and money and goods virtually insignificant ones. There is a great deal of evidence, in fact, that social behavior in relatively unconstrained contexts is systematically ordered to a very substantial degree along principal dimensions whose poles may be designated *hate* and *love*, and *dominance* and *submission*—or *activity* versus *passivity* (Benjamin, 1974; Briar & Bieri, 1963; Brown, 1965; Carson, 1969; Foa, 1961; Leary, 1957; Mehrabian, 1972; Wish, Deutsch, & Kaplan, 1976). Given this rather impressive consensus, and given the need for some economy in presentation, I shall organize what follows mainly in terms of exchanges of these two types of resources and their combinations. It may be noted in passing that many of the alleged basic needs of persons as represented in classical personality theories, including that of Freud (where these needs are represented as libidinal and aggressive instincts in their so-called "masculine" and "feminine" forms), may be located rather comfortably within the space defined by these two dimensions, conceived to be bipolar and orthogonal to each other. Also to be noted is the fact that

information is a frequent by-product of exchanges of these other resources, as in the important case of self-information derived from reflected appraisal.

In summary, we might say that personality enters into exchange processes largely by virtue of transactions involving the resources of love and
status. Consistent with this view is the fact that informal social interaction
appears to be to a large extent organized in terms of communications
containing varying amounts of these two bipolar factors, or components.
The factors, of course, exist at a more abstract level than does the specific
content of any particular communication, and in this sense they represent a
kind of metacommunication that tends to define the nature of a given
relationship at any point in time (Walztawick, Beavin, & Jackson, 1967). For
example, as I write these words I am also necessarily taking a particular
stance or position toward my imagined audience. It is one in which I
assume a quasi-instructional—or, in a sense, dominant—position within (I
hope) an altogether friendly affectional context. It might be said, then, that
for this immediate period my proposed exchange with my audience is one
in which I shall lead and they will be, in a sense, passive, and in which we
will provide some measure of mutual affiliative regard, one to the other. I
will also offer information to my audience, and by doing so I must inevitably seem to claim a certain advantage in status, of a circumscribed sort. But,
then, this is clearly not the type of unconstrained and informal relationship
on which I particularly want to focus in the present analysis.

B. Personality as Characteristic (Preferred) Exchange

I have elsewhere (Carson, 1969), consistent with prior formulations by
Leary (1957), developed at some length the argument that persons exhibit
regularities or consistencies in the extent to which, in Foa and Foa's (1974)
terms, they give or take away love and status in their relationships with
others. To the extent that such is the case, it qualifies nicely as a Sullivanian
definition of personality. I shall not repeat that entire argument here, but
rather point out some limiting conditions in respect to the general idea.

The most important of these limiting conditions has already received
considerable attention—namely, the widespread evidence of the dependence of social behavior on interactions of dispositional and situational
factors. If persons do indeed have propensities to behave in certain ways,
then it is obvious that they do not always follow their propensities, and that
the behavioral output of any given propensity, while perhaps systematically related to it, may be substantially affected by situational constraints. When the matter is put thus, the entire controversy about dispositions and situations takes on an air of ludicrousness. One wonders how

anyone could possibly take it seriously, even granting the ecological un-representativeness of much of the available research bearing on personality.

Certainly one of the more common factors mitigating the frank behavioral expression of personal propensities in interpersonal encounters, even in those in which impersonal, formal constraints are minimal, is the behavior of the other person in the encounter, who of course has propensities of his or her own. It is for this reason, indeed, that perhaps all but the most routine and established relationships between people contain obvious elements of negotiation as the parties seek ways of maximizing their joint outcomes. In short, one's preferred mode of encounter is not always likely to be accepted by the other, a possibility necessitating a certain adaptability of one's behavioral output to the particular interpersonal context. So it is, at least for persons who are adaptable, or "adjusted." For maladjusted persons, the problems of social life can be, and usually are, rather more grim than the relatively easy and flexible negotiations in which most of us engage as a matter of course.

I think it is no accident that nearly all general theories of personality, containing as they do strong traitlike concepts, grew out of clinical practice. One of the characteristics of the typical maladjusted person—and this assertion comes close to being tautological—is that his/her behavior varies little with changing social requirements; that is, it is less situationally specific than that of the more socially competent (Bem, Martyna, & Watson, 1976; Leary, 1957; Millon, 1969; Moos, 1968; Raush, 1965; Raush et al., 1960; Snyder, 1974). The traits of the maladjusted person are therefore more salient and obvious, so much so that they tend to inspire the creation of dispositional causal theories to account for them. The traits of the typical college sophomore, should he have any (and I am sure he does), are by contrast much more subtle and elusive. Dispositional constructs, while not necessarily less relevant to the latter than to the former populations, are thus applied with greater facility in the case of maladjusted persons. For reasons of clarity, therefore, I shall orient much of the discussion that follows around persons who exhibit a degree of inflexibility, or maladjustment, in their interpersonal behavior, I think that what I shall say is not without pertinence on a larger scale, however.

To return to the more general issue, it should again be noted that, in proposing to discuss exchange processes involving affiliation and status, we will largely eschew discussion of specific behavioral acts. Our resources are broad, categorical ones. At this sort of very general level it seems likely that the behavior of persons, whether normal or maladjusted, will in fact be more consistent across situations than a more fine-grained analysis would suggest. There are, after all, many different ways to be dominant, loving, hateful, or submissive. Basically, then, we will be discussing personality in terms of the *stylistic* qualities of a person's social behavior.

Leary (1957) distinguished sixteen varieties of interpersonal style, these being the segments created by imposing eight equidistant diameters upon an imaginary circle (psychometrically, a circumplex) describing the two-dimensional space of hate–love and dominance–submission. This typology and its octant variant are unduly cumbersome for our purposes; a quadrant variant of the same scheme seems more suitable, and can be utilized with only a modest loss in precision (Carson, 1969). Accordingly, we shall be dealing in what follows with four types of interpersonal styles: affiliative dominance, affiliative submission, hostile submission, and hostile dominance. Needless to say, the range of behavioral acts within each category is very broad; for our purposes, these variations will tentatively be regarded as insignificant particular differences. Many persons, and especially those whose behavior is considered maladaptive, manifest their personalities in large part by enacting a preponderance of behavior that is codable within one or another of these categories. The "preferred-exchange" implications of this circumstance are perhaps already discernible to the reader; they will be given more explicit attention shortly.

C. A Possible Superordinate Need: Self Confirmation

I earlier made the suggestion that information was a common by-product of transactions involving other resources, specifically information about the self. Presumably, persons are not uninterested in their status or lovability in the eyes of the other, and information about these attributed qualities is deeply embedded in the behavior of the other toward oneself. As we have seen, a principal function of the Sullivanian self-system is the control of awareness, particularly awareness about one's own characteristics. The ideas of a number of other personality theorists, notably Adler (Ansbacher & Ansbacher, 1956) and Rogers (1959), contain major elements that are very similar to this one of Sullivan's.

If, in keeping with Sullivan (1953), the reasonable assumption is made that persons have a stake in controlling the informational content of others' behaviors toward them, then there would seem to be no more direct means of accomplishing this end than that of controlling the other person's behavior. A potent strategy in any such undertaking would be the manipulation of the other person's outcomes in such a way that he or she is "trained," so to speak, to provide confirmatory feedback. This conception of process has been strongly emphasized in the Sullivanian extensions proposed by both Leary (1957) and Carson (1969). Secord and Backman (1961, 1965) have advanced an essentially similar notion. The exquisite delicacy of such negotiated self-confirmation in relationships that extend over time is suggested in the social penetration theory of Altman and Taylor (1973).

Marlowe and Gergen (1969), in concluding their extensive review of personality processes in social interaction, suggest that some form of self theory is the most likely prospect for providing a much needed integration of the diverse findings in the field. I am advocating a similar type of integration here. While it may be profitable for analytical purposes to concern ourselves with separate needs, resources, etc., the overriding goal of most persons in their social relations seems to be very much a matter of maintaining their selves as going concerns.

D. Personality, Exchange, and Relationship Survival

I have referred to Sullivan as an early exchange theorist. Specifically, he saw interpersonal relationships (what he called "integrations" or "integrated situations") as developing or not developing as the particular mesh of the personalities involved dictates, a mesh that was unmistakably conceived as determined by reward–cost considerations. His thinking in this area is well summarized by what he called his "theorem of reciprocal emotion":

> Integration in an interpersonal situation is a reciprocal process in which (1) complementary needs are resolved, or aggravated; (2) reciprocal patterns of activity are developed, or disintegrated; (3) foresight of satisfaction, or rebuff, of similar needs is facilitated [Sullivan, 1953, p. 198].

This rather brief statement of Sullivan's is sufficiently rich and comprehensive in meaning to serve us well as an organizing format for moving forward in our analysis. Let us explore each of its three elements in the light of the prior discussion, adding such additional pertinent observations as seem appropriate. We begin with the matter of need complementarity.

IV. Complementary Needs and Resource Exchange

The origin of the hypothesis that interpersonal attraction is determined at least in part by the level of reciprocity obtaining in the need profiles of the individuals involved is lost in antiquity. Certainly it predates Winch's (1958) less than compelling attempt to demonstrate its importance in mate selection, as evidence by the existence of a variety of ancient—and often contradictory—proverbs and aphorisms relating to the matter. The history of empirical research in this area, dominated as it has been by global hypotheses regarding the alleged importance of similarities or differences in need structures, has been characterized by conceptual confusion and methodological opacity (Kerckhoff, 1974; Marlowe & Gergen, 1969; Rosow, 1957). Fortunately, the issue for us is a rather simple and straightforward one, and we can proceed directly without addressing the more general problem.

In limiting our discussion to the exchange of resources in the areas of status and love, we have also delimited a corresponding set of needs. Resources and needs, of course, are reciprocally related; one person's resource is, virtually by definition, another person's need. We assume, then, four basic types of expressive–receptive needs that characterize persons as personalities: to love (or be loved), to hate (or be hated), to dominate, and to submit. It remains only to specify the complementarities among them, a rather obvious matter.

The term *complementarity* is used in several different ways in the psychological literature. We use it here to refer to a condition in which there is an expressive–receptive match such that the behavioral expression of a given need of Person *A* will tend to produce satisfaction of a corresponding (complementary) need of Person *B*, the recipient. In general, then, complementarity is a matter of correspondence of needs on the hate–love axis. Needs to dominate or to submit, by contrast, are "fulfilled", so to speak, by their opposites. The distinction between expressive and receptive needs is an important one conceptually, although it is not always easy to distinguish between them at the behavioral level. For example, is loving behavior consistently expressed toward someone indicative of a need to give love, to receive it, or both? Is behavior expressive of hate, aside from its instrumental value in intimidation, almost always wholly expressive, or may it also serve as a bid or prompting for the receipt of behavior in kind from the other? In clinical situations, where, for example, the individual may harbor pronounced fears of interpersonal tenderness, the latter seems a not uncommon happening. Unfortunately, the research literature is largely silent on these matters.

If, according to Sullivan, complementary needs in an interpersonal relationship are not resolved they become aggravated, or intensified. While this frustration–intensification notion seems intuitively reasonable up to a point, it is also true that relationships do not normally survive severe frustration of the needs of one or more of the participants, as exchange theorists have pointed out. If the individual believes he or she can get a better outcome deal elsewhere, as in Thibaut and Kelley's (1959) comparison-level-for-alternatives (CL_{alt})-concept, his or her dependence on the current arrangement is thereby seriously compromised, and he or she may leave it.

One additional consideration in complementary need satisfaction, or its lack, is the limited range of substitutability of one resource for another that is more appropriate to the particular exchange situation. Foa and Foa (1974) have developed and documented to some extent the argument that perceived compensation for the provision of a given type of resource varies according to the extent to which the repayment is similar along dimensions of particularism (i.e., it matters *who* does the giving) and concreteness. Thus, money would be in most instances an unsatisfactory compensation for love. One can readily imagine, then, needs becoming aggravated in a relationship not so much because the pertinent resource is unavailable in the other person, but because it is offered at the wrong times; the problem is one of coordination (see, for example, Gottman *et al.*, 1976).

V. Reciprocal Patterns of Activity

From a certain point of view, the foregoing discussion of need complementarity is a gratuitous one. The kinds of needs we are considering are highly abstract entities whose ultimate referent is the patterned (in the sense already defined) consistency of the behavior of individuals to whom such needs are attributed. The concept of need complementarity, therefore, reduces itself finally to the question of systematic sequential dependencies of some duration and mutuality in the patterned behavior of persons as they interact with each other. Somehow, persons who enter into a relationship with each other must develop reciprocal patterns of activity that mesh in ways that allow each of them to derive a modicum of outcome profit. It is behavior that must be complementary, then, not necessarily needs. Presumably, the satisfaction of dispositional needs contributes importantly to the learning and maintenance of these reciprocal behaviors, especially, perhaps, in long-term relationships characterized by a high degree of mutual penetration (Altman & Taylor, 1973). However, in keeping with our earlier analysis, we should remain alert to possible extra personal factors that may also contribute to behavioral meshing, either directly or in interaction with personal dispositions.

The number and variety of these more impersonal regulators of interbehavioral integration are potentially very large. Many have the character of general social norms, as in the case of the reciprocity norm itself (Gouldner, 1960), or the norm of distributive fairness (Leventhal, 1976). Others are, if you will, mini-norms formulated at varying levels of explicitness within particular relationships in order to obviate problems of power and interdependency (Thibaut & Kelley, 1959; Carson, 1969). Power itself, in the sense of the possession of resources of high (positive or negative) value to the other, may obviously be utilized in the service of enforcing behavioral complementarity.

Whatever the sources, and they might be normative in part, there is a growing body of evidence indicating a type of induced behavioral reciprocity in respect of behavioral initiations that are strongly dominant, submissive, loving, or hateful. Behaviors containing salient elements of these qualities tend, statistically, to provoke complementary behaviors in the recipient (Benjamin, 1974; Celani, 1974; Heller, Myers & Kline, 1963; Kronberg, 1975; Leary, 1957; Raush, 1965; Shannon & Guerney, 1973). In terms of the quadrants of the interpersonal behavior circumplex noted earlier, the relationships may be summarized as follows:

Initiator Behavior	Probable Respondent Behavior
Affiliative dominance	Affiliative submission
Affiliative submission	Affiliative dominance
Hostile Submission	Hostile dominance
Hostile dominance	Hostile submission

It is important to note that these contingencies are not firm predictions. They are statistical probabilities above a certain base rate for the respondent behaviors in question. Many other factors, including the respondent's own proclivities, determine actual reactions; for example, it appears difficult to generate submissive responding in a contemporary college undergraduate population if the dominance of the initiator's message has a hostile quality and is of only mild amplitude (Kronberg, 1975; Shannon & Guerney, 1973). The general consistency of the available evidence, however, suggests that there are certain payoff advantages in responding in complementary fashion to an initiator's implicitly conveyed definition of the affectional quality and hierarchical status arrangement of the relationship situation of the moment; that is, that there is an increment of reward or a minimization of costs for responding in this rather than some other way, independent of other reward–cost considerations in a particular interaction sequence. A more detailed discussion of this type of exchange transaction may be found in Carson (1969). The main implication of these notions is that they provide a beginning understanding of the manner in which a person may utilize complementarity pressures in controlling the vis-à-vis behavior of an interaction partner. Celani (1974) has provided an interesting demonstration of the effective use of such a stratagem in controlling client behaviors in psychotherapy relationships.

In sum, we have identified here another, and conceivably quite potent, situational factor (the other person's behavioral style) that may interact with a person's dispositions in affecting his behavioral outputs in the complex negotiation space that any interpersonal relationship represents. The more "neurotic," or inflexible, the person, the more difficult he or she will be in any such negotiations, and the fewer will be his or her interaction partners, as many fall by the wayside in being driven below their own CL_{alts} in attempting to comply with the behavioral demands placed upon them—unless, that is, they are sufficiently fortunate to find someone with a complementary "bag." The striking interdependency of many neurotic relationships is probably not unrelated to the very low CL_{alts} of the persons involved.

VI. Foresight of Future Satisfaction, or Rebuff

A. Foresight in the Particular Relationship

The limits of Sullivan's meaning concerning the impact of rewards received and costs incurred upon the anticipation of comparable outcomes in the future is not entirely clear. Conceivably, he intended it to apply only to the immediate, particular relationship, in which case it becomes a rather routine observation. Each encounter with a particular other person is quite obviously a learning experience from which one can predict, within limits, the outcomes one might reasonably expect in subsequent encounters with that person. Presumably, most people either seek out or avoid interactions with familiar others based upon such anticipations. Much of the voluminous literature on interpersonal attraction (Huston, 1974) can be interpreted as providing general support for this idea. Edquist (1973), incidentally, working within the framework proposed here, has added an interesting and perhaps nonobvious finding to this literature: namely, that hate-disposed persons tend to prefer similar others as interaction partners (and affiliatively disposed, affiliative others). His results on the dominance–submission dimension, however, were not in line with predictions, possibly because of the limited and brief nature of the interactions involved in the experiment.

B. Foresight Generalized

The notion that the foresights, or anticipation, acquired in particular relationships—especially, perhaps, one's earlier and more significant ones—might generalize to new relationships is thoroughly consistent with Sullivan's thought (e.g., the concept of parataxic distortion), whether or not he intended this meaning in the statement previously quoted. It is a powerful idea, one related to several other enduring concepts in the psychology of personality, including that of transference. The idea is powerful because, in part, it draws attention to the possibility of self-fulfilling prophecy as an important element in the maintenance of persistent styles of interaction with the social environment.

Let me illustrate by pointing to the circular effects that we might theoretically expect to be generated in regard to the four types of interpersonal style previously identified. I begin with the component dimensions: hate–love and dominance–submission. Fortunately, self-fulfilling-prophecy effects in respect of the first of these dimensions, hate–love, have already been described in some detail by Kelley and Stahelski (1970), under the rubrics of competitiveness and cooperativeness. Subsequent research by Miller and Holmes (1975) and Kuhlman and Wimberly (1976) modifies somewhat, but does not substantially alter, the Kelley and Stahelski argument. Kelley and Stahelski note that, in playing "Prisoner's Dilemma" and other such games, randomly selected subjects tend to sort themselves into two groups, cooperators and competitors. Indeed, such differences exist prior to the actual play itself, in the form of the goals subjects will freely choose when asked to do so. Some say that they are concerned with the other person's winnings as well as their own; and others say they are concerned only about themselves and intend to play against the other player. When the game begins, then, the cooperative and competitive types deploy their divergent strategies.

Under such circumstances it does not take very long for the cooperative player in a mixed-type dyad to recognize that he is being had. Typically, he shifts his manner of play so that it becomes ever more like that of his competitive partner, and Kelley and Stahelski review an impressive array of evidence demonstrating such shifts in the initial cooperator's behavior. That is, the play of the initially cooperative person in short order begins to look like the play of his more competitive partner—indeed, from the standpoint of the latter the cooperator's defensive behavior is presumptive evidence that *he* is a competitor, too. Generalizing, we see that such a process is apt to lead to a rather homogeneous type of experience of other persons in the life of the competitor, and a rather grim one at that. He discovers, lo and behold, that other persons are uniformly aggressive and competitive. Moreover, there is a great deal of evidence, reviewed by Kelley and Stahelski, that the competitor does not appreciate his own contribution to his experience of competitiveness in others. Hence, he tends to conclude that the world is just that way; he *expects* hostility from others.

Now, contrast this with the experience of the cooperatively disposed person. Should his gaming partner have goals similar to his own, there is a fairly prompt resolution of the difficulties inherent in the game situation, and the two will usually fix a cooperative strategy that may persist through a very long series of plays. If, however, our cooperator is paired with a competitor, he shortly shifts his strategy (assimilates to the competitor), and the two become fixed in a mutually aggressive and often self-defeating series of interchanges. Moreover, and this is important, the cooperator will be aware that his now competitive style of play was forced upon him by his exploitative partner. Should the partner's strategy shift to a cooperative one, the cooperator can and does shift back to his preferred mode. The cooperator's experience with others, if we may generalize once again, is, in contrast to that of the competitor, heterogeneous in respect to cooperation–competition. Unlike the competitor, he does not automatically assume that the other will be competitive, and he can afford to wait and see what the other person is going to be like, adjusting his own reactions accordingly. It is my contention that the disposition to hate and the disposition to be agreeable as individual difference variables operate in everyday life in much the same way as do competitiveness–cooperativeness in the Kelley and Stahelski (1970) analysis. Snyder, Tanke, and Berscheid (1977), in an interesting experiment involving self-fulfilling prophecy in heterosexual relations, have recently provided additional support for this contention.

What about dominance–submission? Does it operate in any way analogously? Several considerations suggest that it might. Most obviously, in many everyday interactions things just do not happen unless someone takes the initiative. In other words, submissiveness, passivity, or nonassertiveness in any degree tends to create a leadership vacuum such that, if there is to be a relationship at all, its development must depend on the instigative (dominant) actions of the other person. Joint passivity rapidly becomes uncomfortable to parties to an encounter. Beyond that, the dominant or leading role seems to be a valued one in at least our own culture; so, given the opportunity, many individuals are likely to step in to fill a leadership vacuum, if only for the status elements it offers. The experience of someone who is dispositionally passive, then, is that the other can usually be counted on to assume a dominant position vis-à-vis him. That is to say, the world of people who comport themselves passively is one largely populated by dominant, assertive others. I suppose there might be a persistent standoff in the case of two people equally strongly committed to a passive position, but it is difficult for me to imagine, and I suspect it is fairly rare.

The experience of the dominantly disposed person is more varied. He will encounter persons prepared to contest his assumption of dominance, as well as those entirely content with it. He will therefore experience the world as heterogeneous in respect of the dispositions to dominate or to submit.

Moreover, each type—dominant and submissive—will tend to have his expectancies confirmed. One would not expect assimilation effects comparable to the situation for hate–love, but a contrast effect—if I may continue the psychophysical-judgment metaphor—might sometimes occur when a person predisposed to relative passivity is forced into a less passive stance by a more passive other. What is much more common, I suspect, is that such incipient encounters simply never develop enough to constitute a serious challenge to already formed expectancies. Unfortunately, there seems to be little empirical research to either confirm or unconfirm these conceptions in any direct way, although certain of Smelser's (1961) findings on the social perception biases of dominant and submissive subjects can be interpreted to support the general notion.

If we take our four interpersonal style types, and if we integrate this conception with the immediately preceding analysis of the probable reactions of others to behaviors varying on the dimensions of hate–love and dominance–submission, it is possible to come up with some very tentative predictions about the kinds of interpersonal experience that will be associated with each type of (relatively strongly) preferred style. Or, more specifically, it is possible to predict the kinds of interpersonal experience persons of each type will be *unlikely* to have in their relations with others. The predictions follow straightforwardly from the above analysis, and may be summarized as follows:

Preferred Style	Deficit Experience In
Hostile dominance	Affiliative dominance, affiliative submission
Hostile submission	Affiliative dominance, affiliative submission, hostile submission
Affiliative submission	Hostile submission, affiliative submission
Affiliative dominance	———

To the extent that experience in the interpersonal world influences one's expectancies about it, some important differences in (largely unrecognized) own-behavior-contingent expectancies are depicted here. For example, the rigidly hostile–dominant personality (what I refer to informally as the Watergate syndrome) lives in a world in which love is largely unknown; it is a jungle, and in that jungle there are only winners and losers. The so-called Machiavellian (Christie & Geis, 1970) is a case in point. The hostile–submissive personality—for example, the typical schizophrenic—also lives in a jungle, but one in which, besides himself, there are only winners (Carson, 1971). It is only the affiliative–dominant individual who, by this analysis, has an essentially unconstrained experience with others, an experience that should enable him or her to be relatively unbiased when assessing the behavior of others. Perhaps significantly, affiliative dominant individuals do not tend to become psychotherapy clients, except when suffering from psychosomatic disorders (Leary, 1957).

It is reasonable to assume that persons tend to enact behaviors that are congruent with the behaviors they anticipate from others. When persons enact them, the behaviors of others tend to confirm the expectancies the persons bring to the interpersonal situation. Thus, the hostile–dominant person anticipates a hostile reception and enacts behaviors in accord with that expectation; lo and behold, he finds his expectancies confirmed in the actively or passively aggressive response he receives, and his beliefs about the nature of the social environment (i.e., that it consists of winners and losers) are thereby materially strengthened so as to sustain additional hostile–dominant behavior. The question where it all begins is, of course, an important one theoretically. But, given the evident circularity, I suspect it is going to be difficult to sort out the answer.

VII. Construal Style Revisited

We have now, in a sense, come full circle. Having at the outset suggested, on the basis of the apparent outcome of the personalism–situationism controversy, that personality processes reduce in large part to individual differences in the perceptual–cognitive realm, we have come to much the same conclusion via a more complicated but more narrowly focused route in the course of the subsequent discussion. Moreover, it appears that there may be substantial and mutually supportive relationships between a person's more characteristic social behavior and the manner in which the person construes the social environment. The more rigid the person's behavior, particularly in regard to hostility and passivity, the more constricted we would expect these constructions to be. Consider, for example, Raush's (1965) summary statement, which bears on this issue, of the differences between normal and hyperaggressive children:

> Whereas earlier studies suggested that situations were not as discriminable for very disturbed children, the present data suggest additionally that behavioral events themselves are less differentiated by the very disturbed children. There was evidence that the groups of children differed rather little in their responses to unfriendly acts; rather, it was acts thought by coders to be friendly which differentiated the groups, the disturbed children more often responding *as though such acts had hostile meaning* [pp. 497–498; italics added].

Gottman *et al.* (1976) have demonstrated effects comparable to these among distressed adult couples. As was suggested earlier, there is a fair amount of evidence of individual differences in interpersonal construal style scattered throughout the literature (Duck, 1973; Jackson & Messick, 1963; Kelly, 1955; Messick & Kogan, 1966; Pederson, 1965; Sherman, 1972; Walters & Jackson, 1966), most of it peripheral to our main concerns here. A recent study by Golding (1977) is germane indeed, because it concerns the very kinds of personality variables around which this chapter has been organized. Golding provided subjects previously tested on a variety of individual difference measures with a set of systematically derived "interpersonal vignettes," and asked them to make attributional judgments about the psychological content of these samples of interpersonal behavior. Using elegant mathematical procedures, he then related individual differences of subjects to the attributional biases they displayed.

No adequate summary of Golding's very complicated results can be attempted here. In general, however, it may be said that they tend to support at least certain aspects of the interpersonal quadrant-based conceptions presented before. A sampling of the findings may suffice to illustrate the general trend. Desirable–dominant (our affiliative–dominant) subjects, in contrast to the other types identified, showed little evidence of a generalized attributional set, as would be expected. Affiliative (affiliative–submissive) subjects tended to produce low variance in their attributions concerning dominance–submission, but very high variance in those concerned with hate–love. They also tended to overattribute both friendliness and hostility in vignettes where these elements were present, and they tended to overattribute dominance in those involving hostility or hostile–dominance. "Machiavellian" (hostile–dominant) subjects showed generally low variance in their attributions, which, in contrast to those of other subject types, were determined principally by variations along the dominance–submission dimension in the stimulus materials; these subjects also tended to markedly overattribute both hostility and submissiveness. Unfortunately, Golding seems not to have discovered a clear hostile–submissive type in his subject pool given the personality measures he employed. The available findings, nevertheless, seem quite in line with the independently derived conceptions presented earlier. Interpersonal perception data obtained by Terhune (1968) in a study of personality and conflict are similarly intriguing when considered from this conceptual standpoint.

VIII. Conclusion

Have we left exchange theory far behind in all of this? I think not. We have merely shifted the focus away from the subjective value of the other's behavior in some intrinsic sense to the subjective value of perceptions or constructions of that behavior on the part of the subject–person. Some such perceptions–constructions are more rewarding, or costly, than others, depending upon the perceiving individual's psychological organization, or personality. To influence the behavior of the other, by whatever means, is an effective way to maintain one's own perceptions in an optimal hedonic range, but it is not the only way; one can also assimilate the incoming information, whatever it may be, to preferred cognitive categories—at least to some extent—should the other prove intractable. What I am suggesting, essentially, is that as far as personality is concerned, the currency of the exchange process appears in large measure to be symbolic in character. People, as personalities, need other people in order to sustain personally important cognitive structures of some historical precedence. It seems to me that such a view is quite consistent with the previously mentioned thesis developed by Powers (1973); that *all* behavior serves the function of controlling perceptions within some reference-signal range. A detailed analysis in these terms strikes me as a rather difficult task, however, and I therefore leave it for another time and place.

References

Altman, I., & Taylor, D. A. *Social penetration: The development of interpersonal relationships.* New York: Holt, 1973.

Ansbacher, H. L., & Ansbacher, R. R. (Eds.) *The individual psychology of Alfred Adler.* New York: Basic Books, 1964.

Bem, S. L., Martyna, W., & Watson, C. Sex typing and androgyny: Further explorations of the expressive domain. *Journal of Personality and Social Psychology*, 1976, *34*, 1016–1023.

Benjamin, Lorna S. Structural analysis of social behavior. *Psychological Review*, 1974, *81*, 392–425.

Bowers, K. S. Situationism in psychology: An analysis and critique. *Psychological Review*, 1973, *80*, 307–336.

Briar, S., & Bieri, J. A factor analytic and trait inference study of the Leary Interpersonal Check List. *Journal of Clinical Psychology*, 1963, *19*, 193–198.

Brown, R. *Social psychology.* New York: Free Press, 1965.

Bruner, J. S. On perceptual readiness. *Psychological Review*, 1957, *64*, 123–157.

Carlson, Rae. Where is the person in personality research? *Psychological Bulletin*, 1971, *75*, 203–219.

Carson, R. C. *Interaction concepts of personality.* Chicago: Aldine, 1969.

Carson, R. C. Disordered interpersonal behavior. In W. A. Hunt (Ed.), *Human behavior and its control.* Cambridge, Massachusetts: Schenkman, 1971.

Carson, R. C. *Phenomenological implications of interactionism in the study of interpersonal relations.* Symposium paper presented at the American Psychological Association meetings, Chicago, 1975.

Celani, D. P. *The complementarity hypothesis: An exploratory study.* Unpublished doctoral dissertation, University of Vermont, 1974.

Christie, R. & Geis, F. L. Studies in Machiavellianism. New York: Academic Press, 1970.

Cronbach, L. J. The two disciplines of scientific psychology. American Psychologist, 1957, 12, 671–684.

Duck, S. W. Personal relationships and personal constructs. London: Wiley, 1973.

Edquist, M. H. Interpersonal choice and social attraction among four interpersonal types. Unpublished doctoral dissertation, Duke University, 1973.

Ekehammar, B. Interactionism in personality from a historical perspective. Psychological Bulletin, 1974, 81, 1026–1048.

Endler, N. S. The case for person-situation interactions. Canadian Psychological Review, 1975, 16, 12–21.

Endler, N. S. & Magnusson, D. (Eds.) Interactional psychology and personality. New York: Wiley, 1976.

Foa, U. G. Convergences in the analysis of the structure of interpersonal behavior. Psychological Review, 1961, 68, 341–353.

Foa, U. G., & Foa, E. B. Societal structures of the mind. Springfield, Illinois: Thomas, 1974.

Golding, S. L. Flies in the ointment: Methodological problems in the analysis of the percentage of variance due to persons and situations. Psychological Bulletin, 1975, 82, 278–288.

Golding, S. L. Individual differences in the construal of interpersonal interactions. In D. Magnusson & N. S. Endler (Eds.), Personality at the cross-roads: Current issues in interactional psychology. Hillsdale, New Jersey: Erlbaum, 1977.

Gottman, J., Notarius, C., Markman, H., Bank, S., Yoppi, B., & Rubin, M. E. Behavior exchange theory and marital decision making. Journal of Personality and Social Psychology, 1976, 34, 14–23.

Gouldner, A. W. The norm of reciprocity: A preliminary statement. American Sociological Review, 1960, 25, 161–179.

Heller, K., Myers, R. A., & Kline, L. V. Interviewer behavior as a function of standardized client roles. Journal of Consulting Psychology, 1963, 27, 117–122.

Huston, T. L. (Ed.) Foundations of interpersonal attraction. New York: Academic Press, 1974.

Jackson, D. N., & Messick, S. Individual differences in social perception. British Journal of Social and Clinical Psychology, 1963, 2, 1–10.

Kelley, H. H., & Stahelski, A. J. Social interaction bases of cooperators' and competitors' beliefs about others. Journal of Personality and Social Psychology, 1970, 16, 66–91.

Kelly, G. A. The psychology of personal constructs (2 Vols.). New York: Norton, 1955.

Kerckhoff, A. C. The social context of interpersonal attraction. In T. L. Huston (Ed.), Foundations of interpersonal attraction. New York: Academic Press, 1974. Pp. 61–78.

Kronberg, C. L. Interpersonal style and complementary response evocation. Unpublished doctoral dissertation, Duke University, 1975.

Kuhlman, D. M., & Wimberley, D. L. Expectations of choice behavior held by cooperators, competitors, and individualists across four classes of experimental game. Journal of Personality and Social Psychology, 1976, 34, 69–81.

Leary, T. Interpersonal diagnosis of personality. New York: Ronald, 1957.

Leventhal, G. S. Fairness in social relationships. Morristown, New Jersey: General Learning Press, 1976.

Levinger, G. A three-level approach to attraction: Toward an understanding of pair relatedness. In T. Huston (Ed.), Foundations of interpersonal attraction. New York: Academic Press, 1974.

Marlowe, D., & Gergen, K. J. Personality and social interaction. In G. Lindzey & E. Aronson (Eds.), Handbook of social psychology. (Vol. 3.) Reading, Massachusetts: Addison-Wesley, 1969.

Mehrabian, A. Nonverbal communication. New York: Aldine-Atherton, 1972.

Messick, S., & Kogan, N. Personality consistencies in judgment: Dimensions of role constructs. *Multivariate Behavioral Research*, 1966, *1*, 165–175.

Miller, D. T., & Holmes, J. G. The role of situational restrictiveness on self-fulfilling prophecies: A theoretical and empirical extension of Kelley and Stahelski's triangle hypothesis. *Journal of Personality and Social Psychology*, 1975, *31*, 661–673.

Millon, T. *Modern psychopathology*. Philadelphia: Saunders, 1969.

Mischel, W. Toward a cognitive social learning reconceptualization of personality. *Psychological Review*, 1973, *80*, 252–283.

Moos, R. H. Situational analysis of a therapeutic community milieu. *Journal of Abnormal Psychology*, 1968, *73*, 49–61.

Pedersen, D. M. The measurement of individual differences in perceived personality-trait relationships and their relation to certain determinants. *Journal of Social Psychology*, 1965, *65*, 233–258.

Powers, W. T. *Behavior: The control of perception*. Chicago: Aldine, 1973.

Raush, H. L. Interaction sequences. *Journal of Personality and Social Psychology*, 1965, *2*, 487–499.

Raush, H. L., Farbman, I., & Llewellyn, L. G. Person, setting and change in social interaction: II. A normal-control study. *Human Relations*, 1960, *13*, 305–333.

Rogers, C. R. A theory of therapy, personality, and interpersonal relationships as developed in the client-centered framework. In S. Koch (Ed.), *Psychology: A study of a science*. (Vol. 3.) New York: McGraw-Hill, 1959.

Rosow, I. Issues in the concept of need-complementarity. *Sociometry*, 1957, *20*, 216–233.

Sarason, I. G., Smith, R. E., & Diener, E. Personality research: Components of variance attributable to the person and the situation. *Journal of Personality and Social Psychology*, 1975, *32*, 199–204.

Schneider, D. J. Implicit personality theory: A review. *Psychological Bulletin*, 1973, *79*, 294–309.

Secord, P. F., & Backman, C. W. Personality theory and the problem of stability and change in individual behavior: An interpersonal approach. *Psychological Review*, 1961, *68*, 21–32.

Secord, P. F., & Backman, C. W. An interpersonal approach to personality. In B. A. Maher (Ed.), *Progress in experimental personality research*. Vol. 2. New York: Academic Press, 1965.

Sherman, R. C. Individual differences in perceived trait relationships as a function of dimensional salience. *Multivariate Behavioral Research*, 1972, *7*, 109–129.

Shannon, J., & Guerney, B., Jr. Interpersonal effects of interpersonal behavior. *Journal of Personality and Social Psychology*, 1973, *26*, 142–150.

Shrauger, S., & Altrocchi, J. The personality of the perceiver as a factor in person perception. *Psychological Bulletin*, 1964, *62*, 289–308.

Smelser, W. T. Dominance as a factor in achievement and perception in cooperative problem solving interactions. *Journal of Abnormal and Social Psychology*, 1961, *62*, 535–542.

Snyder, M. Self-monitoring and expressive behavior. *Journal of Personality and Social Psychology*, 1974, *30*, 526–537.

Snyder, M., Tanke, E., & Berscheid, E. Social perception and interpersonal behavior: On the self-fulfilling nature of social stereotypes. *Journal of Personality and Social Psychology*, 1977, *35*, 656–666.

Sullivan, H. S. *The interpersonal theory of psychiatry*. New York: Norton, 1953.

Terhune, K. W. Motives, situations, and interpersonal conflict within prisoner's dilemma. *Journal of Personality and Social Psychology: Monograph Supplement*. Part 2, 1968, *8*, 1–24.

Thibaut, J. W., & Kelley, H. H. *The social psychology of groups*. New York: Wiley, 1959.

Wachtel, P. L. Psychodynamics, behavior therapy, and the implacable experimenter: An inquiry into the consistency of personality. *Journal of Abnormal Psychology,* 1973, *82,* 324–334.

Walters, H. A., & Jackson, D. Group and individual regularities in trait inference. *Multivariate Behavioral Research,* 1966, *1,* 145–163.

Watzlawick, P., Beavin, J. H., & Jackson, D. D. *Pragmatics of human communication.* New York: Norton, 1967.

Winch, R. *Mate-selection: A study of complementary needs.* New York: Harper, 1958.

Wish, M., Deutsch, M., & Kaplan, S. J. Perceived dimensions of interpersonal relations. *Journal of Personality and Social Psychology,* 1976, *33,* 409–420.

10

A Dynamic
Interactional Concept
of Individual and
Social Relationship
Development

RICHARD M. LERNER

I. Introduction

In indicating that the exchange approach to social behavior has a clear interdisciplinary flavor, Emerson (1972) also stressed that the approach has not implied an attempt to integrate various disciplines. However, in this book we have scientists from several disciplines who, however different their perspectives, have contributed to a work that might reinforce the idea that exchange notions indeed have interdisciplinary integrative utility.

My own discipline, developmental psychology, has not traditionally embraced ideas compatible with social exchange. As will be seen in more detail later, developmental psychology has often engaged, for example, in debates about molar versus molecular analyses of individual development (see Looft, 1973), and ignored the interactive components of behavior. This exclusion has often led to a failure to consider the social reciprocities that are now beginning to appear in the developmental literature (Bell, 1974; Hartup & Lempers, 1973; Lewis & Lee-Painter, 1974). As such, this exclusion has resulted in omitting an exploration of the utility of social-exchange notions in describing and understanding the association among individual development, social processes, and relationship development.

271

SOCIAL EXCHANGE IN DEVELOPING RELATIONSHIPS

If, as many social scientists assert, it is only through interaction that we can study human behavior without distortion, then it is incumbent on developmental psychologists to ascertain the relevance of all theories pertinent to such interchange.

While I hope this chapter represents one step in this integrative direction, I am aware that on the other side of the interdisciplinary coin there exist sociologists and social psychologists who do not see the relevance of developmental psychological notions to the attempt to understand social behavior. We may surmise that one basis of this lack of interest is the awareness of the history of developmental psychology's lack of concern with social interaction as a dimension of individual development, a history I have just alluded to. However, as both Homans (1969, 1974) and Emerson (1972) have pointed out, other reasons for a lack of concern exist. For instance, debates concerning issues of reductionism and emergence have often led sociologists to view a consideration of psychological principles, developmental or otherwise, as being inappropriate. Thus, people taking this position need to be convinced that notions of individual development are worth considering.

How can we convince developmentalists, on the one hand, and sociologists, on the other, that there exist conceptual resources within both disciplines that provide the basis for balanced exchanges? Although such a rewarding exchange may be initiated by members of either discipline, I will attempt to do this from my perspective as a developmental psychologist. As such, I believe that we must first briefly consider the models of human beings that have traditionally been advanced in developmental psychology, and then consider a third model which has recently begun to be elaborated (Lerner, 1976, 1978; Looft, 1973; Riegel, 1972a, b, c, 1975, 1976). This third model is labeled differently by various authors; for example, it is called "relational" by Looft (1973), "transactional" by Sameroff (1975), "dialectical" by Riegel (1975), and "dynamic interactional" by Lerner (1978). Yet, whatever it is termed, this model stresses that relations—interactions—are the necessary foci of concern in human behavior, and as such the model leads to a concept of development that stresses that reciprocal interchanges—most importantly, between an individual and the others in his or her world—are inevitable components of behavior development and functioning. Thus, in asserting that reciprocal social relations are unbiquitous and necessary components of individual behavior we will see that many issues beclouding the relevance of developmental psychology for sociologists (e.g., reductionism and emergence) may be seen as pseudoissues, and in addition, this individual–social process integration will provide a conceptual basis for an extension of principles of reciprocal individual development to principles of relationship development.

II. Mechanistic and Organismic Models of Human Development

At least since the West Virginia Life Span Development Conferences, in the late 1960s and early 1970s (cf. Baltes & Schaie, 1973; Goulet & Baltes, 1970; Nesselroade & Reese, 1973), developmental psychologists have paid increasing attention to the models of human nature that guide their theoretical and empirical endeavors. Although such concern was certainly evident much earlier, most notably in the volume *The Concept of Development*, edited by Harris (1957), conference papers by Reese and Overton (1970), Overton and Reese (1973), and Looft (1973) indicated that two alternative paradigms or world views have provided the major basis for theorizing in developmental psychology. These two positions have been termed the "mechanistic view" and the "organismic view."

Looft (1973) has argued that these two views represent divergent, but general, models of development. That is, they are epistemological and metaphysical models that determine the parameters of lower-order, more specific theoretical and empirical activities (p. 28). Moreover, Looft asserts that, because of the belief that these positions have quite different truth criteria, it has often been argued that they are irreconcilable (Overton & Reese, 1973; Reese & Overton, 1970). Because the characteristics of these models are well known in the social sciences, and because they have been reviewed extensively elsewhere (Lerner, 1976; Looft, 1973) we need only note the major ideas associated with each.

The mechanistic paradigm is a natural-science position, stressing quantitative change, continuity, and reductionism, whereas the organismic paradigm is an epigenetic position stressing qualitative change, discontinuity, and emergence (Bertalanffy, 1933; Harris, 1957; Lerner, 1976; Looft, 1973). Although it is important to recognize that the lower-order, theoretical positions derived from the respective models do not necessarily have to fit perfectly with the superordinate models, several reviewers (e.g., Lerner, 1976; Looft, 1973) have found developmental theories categorizable on the basis of these two divergent models. In other words, though members of the family of theories (Reese & Overton, 1970) derived from one model may differ among themselves in their specific details, they are in agreement on the fundamental nature of humans (Looft, 1973).

Accordingly, because of the fundamental differences between theories derived from the alternative models, other issues about human development have been raised. Skinnerian theory has been nominated (Looft, 1973; Lerner, 1976) as the exemplar of a position derived from the mechanistic model. In it humans are seen as reactive, their open-ended development controlled by external stimulus events. Alternatively, the theories of Piaget and Kohlberg are exemplars of positions derived from the organismic model. In them humans are seen as active, their closed-ended development derived from variables having an internal focus.

A. Towards a Contextual–Dialectic Model

While both models of human development have led to both theories and research advancing our knowledge, some reviewers of the implications of these models have been quite pessimistic about reconciling what may seem to be unbridgeable paradigms (cf. Reese & Overton, 1970). Other reviewers (e.g., Looft, 1973; Riegel, 1972a, 1975) however, view these two models as just a thesis and an antithesis in need of a synthesis. Looft (1973), emphasizing the prescriptive nature of models, advocates a new model, one entailing a new view of reality, and one therefore that may lead to different assumptions about human nature, and accordingly, to different theories, concepts, hypotheses, and finally, facts of development.

As indicated earlier, attempts at such a synthesis have occurred. While these attempts may be seen as being primarily derived from the organismic tradition, they are derived also from conceptual compromises between this view and the mechanistic one (see Lerner, 1976). These attempts are compatible in that they all lead to a view of human development as essentially interactive, rather than just active or reactive. Contributions to this third model have derived from many sources. Heinz Werner's (1957) notion of orthogenesis is a major contribution. This notion posits that developmental change involves both continuous and discontinuous processes: hierarchic integration, on the one hand, and differentiation, on the other. Development is thus seen as a dialectical synthesis (Lerner, 1978) among such processes, and it is held (Werner, 1957) that *all* developmental changes take an orthogenetic form. While we will have reason to reiterate this conception in our discussion of relationship development, we may here note that contributions to this third model have also come from T. C. Schneirla's (1957) notions of probabilistic epigenesis; that is to say, that the phenomena that characterize developmental change arise from a dynamic interaction between nature variables, such as maturation, and nurture variables, such as experience. The contribution of each source of development is influenced by the quality and timing of the other; the status of one determines the status and hence the effect of the other. Most recently, contributions to this third model have evolved as a consequence of Klaus Riegel's (1975, 1976) specification of a dialectical view of development, and Pepper's (1942) quite compatible discussion of the contextual world view. Rather than stressing that development is either internally or externally derived, or either a closed or an open system, or either unidirectional or even bidirectional, this alternative model conceives human development as the "confluence of many interrelated and changing systems and subsystems including the biological, social, cultural, and historical [Looft, 1973, p. 51]."

As I have indicated earlier, derivatives from this model are labeled differently: for example, "transactionalism," "dynamic interactionism," "probabilistic epigenesis," "contextualism," or simply, "dialecticalism." Yet the unifying theme among the derivatives is *interaction relations*. As such, the principles of these relations, the ideas that relate to the structure of the exchanges among elements, and not the elements themselves (Looft, 1973), are the primary concern of approaches derived from this model.

B. Dynamic Interactionism and Social Exchange

Although social-exchange theory did not derive from this third model, it does appear compatible with it. Burgess and Nielsen (1974) define social exchange "as a form of interaction whereby two or more actors provide each other with services or activities each finds rewarding [p. 44]," and they note that this "suggests a direct exchange between actors with a focus on reciprocal outcomes [p. 44]." Hence, the invariant presence of reciprocities in exchange relations and the focus on interdependent relations in theories and concepts of development derived from the dynamic interaction model we have been discussing represent a major congruity in the conceptual schemes. Accordingly, this congruity represents our point of entry into an analysis of the utility of developmental notions derived from this third model for understanding social exchange and developing relationships.

To begin this analysis, I will first offer a conception of development derived from views compatible with this third model of human nature. This conception will culminate in a theoretical specification of the necessary role of reciprocal social interactions in individual development. In turn, this dynamic interactional interpretation of individual- and social-process development will provide a basis for understanding the development of repeated social interactions among developing organisms. Accordingly, we will turn to a consideration of the empirical evidence that exists in support of our theorizing, and in so doing we will see if notions of social exchange are in fact compatible with empirically verified patterns of dyadic interaction that do appear as salient components of individual development. This latter analysis, focusing on research about the infant–caregiver dyad, will allow us to point to issues that social-exchange theory must address. For example, we will point to issues relating to broadening the definition of *reward;* that is, we will address the questions why cognitive developmental variables must be incorporated into exchange notions and how they can be. To attain these goals we must begin by offering a concept of development.

III. Components of Development

Although various conceptions of development, consistent with a contextual-dialectic model, have been devised (e.g., Bertalanffy, 1933; Kuo, 1967; Riegel, 1975; Schneirla, 1957; Werner, 1957), all positions appear amenable to a common, albeit general, definition of development. *Development* refers to *systematic changes in the organization of an organism,* an organism that is seen as a functional, adaptively oriented, relatively open system throughout its life (Lerner, 1976). Development is then a concept basically biological in emphasis (Harris, 1957), in that it considers how progressive changes in a system's properties subserve an organism's adaptive functioning. Development thus refers to how the whole system—the individual—utilizes its processes to adjust to a continually changing environment, and, in turn, how such an environment is continually and progressively modified by an individual itself undergoing alterations. Thus, the study of development is the assessment of how organismic processes are altered to coordinate with extraorganism processes, and how these latter processes are altered to coordinate with organism processes. In short, the study of development is the study of organism–environment relations.

This conception of development indicates the continuous interdependency of organism and environmental processes and, as such, indicates that the bases of the changes that characterize development lie in the parameters of this interdependency. To understand this dialectical intermeshing, the nature of such organism and extraorganism variables, and the characteristics and outcomes of their interfaces, must be evaluated. To facilitate this discussion it will be useful to consider the details of the present author's model of dynamic interactional development, illustrated in Figure 10.1. Our point of entry into this model is a consideration of intraorganism processes.

A. Maturation

Maturation refers to processes of growth—that is, progressive alterations in the physical and physiological systems of an organism by tissue accretions—and to processes of differentiation—that is, progressive

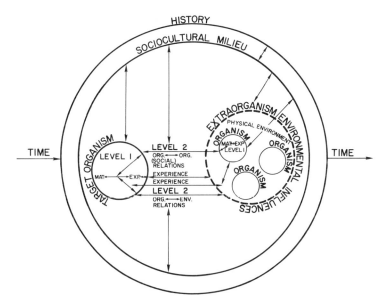

Figure 10.1 A dynamic interactional model of development.

changes in the structural interrelations of growing systems (Schneirla, 1957). Although these organism processes have often been considered as nature variables independent of experiential influence (Gesell, 1929; Hamburger, 1957), this conception of development indicates that such processes are in fact interdependent with experience. Thus, the quality of the changes labeled "maturational" is shaped by the quality and timing parameters of the experiential context in which the changes occur. Regarding them as such, let us consider the interdependent contribution of experience.

B. Experience

Experience is a broad term denoting all stimulative influences acting on the organism over the course of its life span (Schneirla, 1957). As such, experience can contribute from the moment of conception (e.g., in providing the nutritional milieu of the ovum) until death, and hence we may speak of the intrauterine and extrauterine contributions of experience. The contributions take the form of *trace effects,* a term denoting organismic changes resulting from experience and limiting the effects of future experience (Schneirla, 1957). For example, the effects resulting from the intrauterine experience of rubella will provide limits on the influences of later experience (e.g., if blindness has developed). Similarly, diseases (e.g., scarlet fever) at an earlier ontogenetic point may leave trace effects (heart defects) altering the possible outcomes of experiences (e.g., various physical education programs) at later points in ontogeny.

However, all these effects of experience are limited also by the maturational status of the organism. The same experience may lead to a different development outcome depending on the maturational level of the organism. For instance, excessive maternal stress during pregnancy may lead to either a cleft palate or a normal palate depending on whether growth and differentiation are at an early embryonic stage or at the late fetal stage. Thus, just as experience provides a basis of growth and differentiation—maturation, it may be noted, proceeds at different rates and with different outcomes depending on the nutritional–health status of the mother—we see that the effects of experience are limited by the individual's maturational level. Finally, we must note that since temporal covariation of the various parameters of these interdependent sources is not constant across all members of a species, lawful individual differences will emerge. A consideration of this individuality is important.

C. Organism Individuality and Its Role in Development

As each person's maturation–experience interactions intermesh to provide a distinct individual, this individual concomitantly interacts differently with his or her environment as a consequence of this individuality. In turn, these new interactions are a component of the individual's further experience, and thus serve to further promote his or her individuality. Endogenous maturation–experience relations provide a basis of organism individuality, and, as a consequence, differential organism–environment (exogenous) relations develop.

Although, as is illustrated in Figure 10.1, the endogenous maturation–experience interactions are not discontinuous with the exogenous organism–environment interactions, it is appropriate to differentiate between these two sets of interactions in order to indicate how they are interdependent. As is shown in the figure, a conception of interaction levels is useful here. The organism's individual developmental history of maturation–experience interactions (what I will term *Level 1 development*—a term analogous to Riegel's, 1975, *inner-biological developmental level*) provides a basis of differential organism–environment interactions; in turn, differential experiences accruing from the individual developmental history of organism–environment interactions, or *Level 2 development* (a term analogous to Riegel's, 1975, *individual-psychological developmental level*), provides a further basis of Level 1 developmental individuality.

The parameters of this process are summarized in the figure. Thus, the target organism in the figure is unique because of the quality and timing of endogenous, Level 1 maturation—experience interactions. Yet the experiences that provide a basis of Level 1 development are not discontinuous with other, extraorganism experiences influencing the target individual. The target interacts with environmental influences composed of other organisms (themselves having intraindividual, Level 1 developmental distinctiveness) and of physical effects. These Level 2 interchanges will also show interindividual differences because of Level 1, intraindividual distinctiveness. Thus, the feedback received as a consequence of these differential interactions will also be different among individuals, and will promote further Level 1 and Level 2 individuality. This process provides the basis of a circular function (Schneirla, 1957) between an individual and its environment, a function having important implications for the understanding of organism—organism relations.

D. Circular Functions and Organism—Organism (Social) Interaction

Other individuals are part of a person's experiential context, and these others will interact differentially with people. It is these interactions that constitute the feedback to the individual providing a further differential basis of development.

Such circular functions have been identified at various phyletic levels (see Lerner, 1976). On the human psychosocial level Thomas and his colleagues (Thomas, Chess, & Birch, 1970; Thomas, Chess, Birch, Hertzig, & Korn, 1963) suggest that the developmental characteristics of a child promote differential reactions in his or her socializing agents (e.g., parents), and these different reactions provide a further basis for the child's development. In a study of children's behavioral style, or temperament, Thomas *et al.* (1963, 1970) report that children whose individual pattern of temperament comprised adaptable, rhythmic behaviors of moderate intensity and positive mood evoked interactions with their parents that were different (e.g., in such dimensions as parental approach—withdrawal tendencies, and warmth—coldness) from those interactions established among parents of children whose pattern was composed of relatively unadaptable, arhythmic behaviors of high intensity and negative mood. As one index of the developmental outcome of such differential child—parent interactions, Thomas *et al.* (1970) report that of those children in their sample who developed psychological disorders, a higher proportion came from the latter, difficult-child group than from the former.

1. SOCIAL RELATION PROCESSES AS A PARAMETER OF INDIVIDUAL DEVELOPMENT

Although organism interactions with animate and non-conspecific organisms certainly exist, and at least for the latter type of interactions circular functions are also certainly involved, the conspecific organism–organism interaction—the social relation—has been used to exemplify the nature of circular functions. This was done because it is believed that development by its very nature is basically a social relation phenomenon.

As is depicted in Figure 10.1, other individuals are an obvious component of the typical experiential world of any person, and on this basis alone relations with these others are inextricable dimensions of ecologically valid developmental milieus. Yet conspecific relations are particular organism–environment relations. These Level 2 interchanges invariably involve processes of reciprocal stimulation and hence interdependent influencing; and moreover, especially at the human psychosocial level, they involve relations with stimuli on the basis of stimulus association value, or meaning, rather than merely on the basis of stimuli's immediate physiological import (see Lerner, 1976; Schneirla, 1957; Tobach & Schneirla, 1968). Hence, organism–organism interactions appear to be a special, as well as an invariant, component of human developmental processes. In fact, the results of social isolation experiments—for example, those summarized by Harlow and Harlow (1962) and by Tobach and Schneirla (1968)—indicate that individuals deprived of such apparently basic social relations develop aberrant social and nonsocial behaviors.

Moreover, until the transitions between organic and inorganic matter are better understood, it appears tenable to assume that any living cell comes into existence on the basis of a relation to another living cell (Tobach & Schneirla, 1968). Thus, the dependency for existence of one organism on another appears basic to all life matter, and suggests that organisms exist basically in relation to one another. As such, the study of the social bond—the multidimensional social relations between conspecifics—becomes not just one important, or merely one interesting, concern of developmentalists, but rather represents the study of an essential, core component of the development of all individuals. As Tobach and Schneirla (1968) have asserted, "No existing form of life is truly solitary and no organism is completely independent of others at all times in its history [p. 505]."

2. SOCIOCULTURAL–HISTORICAL PARAMETERS OF INDIVIDUAL AND SOCIAL DEVELOPMENT

Our dynamic interactional model views individual development as invariably embedded in reciprocal social relations, and leads to the view that development is basically a social as well as a biological phenomenon. In addition, our model indicates that debates about reductionism and emergence, when raised as issues relating to the continuity or discontinuity between individual and social behavior, are pseudoissues based on inappropriate dichotomies. As derived from our present model, and, also, as stressed by Lewis and Lee-Painter (1974), Hartup and Lempers (1973), and Looft (1973), all behavior is socially interactive. For example, Lewis and Lee-Painter (1974), in discussing the issue of the direction of effects in socialization research, assert that "any study—regardless of direction—that fails to consider the dyadic relationship cannot accurately describe the elements. Once we consider the dyad we must at once conclude that *both* actors actively and significantly influence each other [p. 46]."

However, in addition to stressing individual–individual reciprocities, our model has other components which should be noted. As is suggested in Figure 10.1, all organisms involved in social reciprocities are developing. Thus, not only is the effect of the target organism on others moderated by its developmental level (e.g., the effect of a toddler having a temper tantrum differs from that of an adolescent having one), but also these effects and the feedback received are influenced by the developmental levels of the other organisms in the social relation. An experienced parent will probably be differently affected by a child's tantrum from the way an inexperienced one is, and the child-rearing-related feedback the child gets from the parent will in part be determined by such a developmental difference. However, the probability of the occurrence of a particular child behavior, the concomitant evaluation of the behavior by such others as parents, and the modes (such as child rearing practices) of dealing with the behavior by these others are dependent on the sociocultural milieu of the relation. As is seen in Figure 10.1, people are always embedded in a sociocultural setting. Parents in one setting may be more or may be less permissive than parents in another. Furthermore, the sociocultural milieu also influences the physical setting of any social interaction, and it may be expected that in physical environmental situations varying in such socioculturally related variables as noise level, pollution level, housing conditions, crowding, and recreational facilities, the quality and timing of person–person exchanges will show variation and provide differential feedback to all involved individuals.

Moreover, it must be recognized that all sociocultural milieus are embedded in history—the outermost circle of Figure 10.1. A middle class sociocultural milieu of the 1930s did not include some variables, such as the pervasive influences of television, that typify this milieu in the 1970s. Hence, the profound effects of such variables (see Stein & Freidrich, 1975) on the nature of the sociocultural setting, on social relations occuring in this setting, and on individuals embedded in these relations could not have even existed in the earlier era. Of course, there exist reciprocal effects of the individual, of the dyad, and of each of the levels shown in Figure 10.1 on all of the other levels in this figure. These reciprocities have been detailed elsewhere (see Lerner, 1978; Lerner & Spanier, 1978).

Finally, time cuts through all these interfaces, and has a different meaning at each of the different levels. Days, weeks, months, or years may be the appropriate temporal divisions to use in assessing whether significant individual relational developments have occurred. However, years may be the smallest appropriate division assessing the implications of changes in the physical environment, and decades, or even centuries (Sarason, 1973), may be the only appropriate temporal divisions for assessing the implications of history on all these subordinate yet interdependent levels. In addition to such objective temporal metrics, time may have a different subjective meaning at each of the levels of Figure 10.1. For example, the meaning of having to wait a year for an event may vary in relation to the developmental level of an individual. For a young child or an aged adult such a delay may be unbearable, whereas for a young adult, planning a vacation, such a temporal delay may seem quite tolerable and appropriate.

3. CIRCULAR FUNCTIONS AND SOCIAL PROCESSES: THE ROLE OF PHYSICAL CHARACTERISTICS

In order to illustrate the utility of our circular functions notion, let us consider a specific example of social processes among individuals. As was already indicated, our model indicates that any person has an individual history of Level 1–Level 2 interactions, which are based on both organism–environment and social relations, and which bring the person into any situation with particular characteristics. These characteristics may be either physical attributes—body type, physical attractiveness level, racial type, sex type, and so on—or behavioral attributes (e.g., temperamental style, assertiveness, dominance, altruism). The target person's individuality in one or more of these dimensions will promote differential reactions in others, which will feed back on the target to affect further development.

As a consequence of the possession of different body types, children elicit different personal and social evaluations from their peers and adult supervisors. Lerner and Korn (1972) have shown that chubby 5-, 15-, and 20-year olds receive negative evaluations, whereas children of average build who are of these ages receive positive personal–social evaluations from others. Not only are the individual physical characteristics that the person brings to the interaction situation associated with differential appraisals, but also there is evidence that social interaction consistent with these appraisals occurs. In samples from within both American and Japanese cultural settings (Lerner, Iwawaki, & Chihara, 1976; Lerner, Karabenick, & Meisels, 1975; Lerner, Venning, & Knapp, 1975) kindergarten through sixth-grade children showed interpersonal approach responses to average-build male and female stimuli, and proxemic withdrawal responses to chubby male and female stimuli.

Moreover, since chubby physiques are seen as low in physical attractiveness and average builds are associated with higher physical attractiveness (Berscheid & Walster, 1974), these relations linking body build and social appraisal–interaction may be an instance of a more general relation between social variables and physical attractiveness. Evidence in support of this inference exists. Dion and Berscheid (1972) found that by the latter part of the nursery school term, boys and girls high in attractiveness were judged as more popular by their peers than were boys and girls low in attractiveness. Furthermore, the peers saw the low attractiveness children as more likely than high attractiveness children to display maladjusted behaviors, such as hitting or yelling at the teacher. In turn, the high attractiveness children were seen as more likely than the low attractiveness children to display behaviors related to better school adjustment.

Dion (1972) provides additional evidence suggesting that the attributes people bring to encounters may affect the nature of their exchanges. College-aged women evaluated identical transgressions of high and low physically attractive children to be less severe and less characteristic of a chronic personality disposition when emitted by the former type of child than by the latter. Similarly, Clifford and Walster (1973) reported that experienced sixth-grade teachers evaluated identical report cards more favorably when these records were associated with a physically attractive child. Finally, early and late maturing adolescent males, who may be divided into relatively high and relatively low physical attractiveness groups, respectively, on the basis of their body types (see McCandless, 1970), were differentially rated by peers and adults. Boys of the former group received higher personal and social ratings than boys of the latter group (Jones & Bayley, 1950).

These data indicate that physical characteristics are associated with differential reactions among other people in the person's social milieu. However, the circular function notion derived from our dynamic interactional model indicates that another, critical component of this social process should exist. These differential reactions should constitute feedback for the target people, feedback affecting further development. For example, based on differential appraisals of personality–social behavior, school adjustment, perceived popularity, and academic potential, children possessing different physical characteristics should be differentially channeled into the development of contrasting behaviors in these do-mains. In short, a self-fulfilling-prophecy process may be expected to exist such that children low in physical attractiveness will show less adjust-ment, more negative peer relations, poorer school performance, and, in general, more negative personal feelings and self concepts than will children high in physical attractiveness.

Consistent with this prediction, Lerner and Lerner (1977) found that among fourth- and sixth-grade males and females, high physically attrac-tive children had more positive and fewer negative peer relations than low physically attractive children, and were rated by teachers as higher in academic adjustment and ability. Likewise, physical attractiveness was significantly related to current grade-point average, as well as to grade-point average in each of the two preceding school years; and physical attractiveness was related to a standardized measure of actual social adjustment. Thus, physically attractive children were somewhat more socially adjusted than were their unattractive peers and actually achieved better grades. Similarly, Mussen and Jones (1957) report that the self concepts and feelings of psychological adjustment on the part of the early and late maturers studied by Jones and Bayley (1950) were consistent with the differential peer and adult appraisals accorded these groups. Late maturers showed evidence of prolonged dependency needs, negative attitudes toward parents, feelings of instrumental ineffectiveness, and a negative self concept; early maturers showed evidence of feelings of being able to play adult roles in social situations, positive attitudes toward parents, feelings of instrumental effectiveness, and a positive self concept.

Furthermore, McCandless (1970) summarizes data indicating that these developmental differences between early and late maturers, which first occur in their adolescent years, have implications for later, adult social-relationship developments. Into middle age the personality and social-interaction advantages of the early maturers are maintained: They are more likely than the late maturers, for instance, to play leadership roles and to be in a job supervising others. Similarly, Jackson and Huston (1975) find evidence of personality differences among college females consistent with the notion that physically attractive people show higher scores on positive behavioral attributes (Jackson and Huston focused on assertiveness) than do physically less attractive people.

Although data such as these are certainly not definitive, primarily because of research design issues (see Baltes, 1968; Lerner & Lerner, 1977), they do present support for the view that characteristics of organism individuality play a significant role in social exchanges. However, we have indicated that such social processes must be understood as being significantly embedded in sociocultural–historical milieus. Hence, we would expect that the implications of organism individuality may be expected to vary in relation to differences in such milieus. Although little relevant data have been collected, what findings do exist are consistent with our model. For example, Mussen and Bouterline-Young (1964) report that the implications of early and late maturing during the adolescent period vary in relation to sociocultural embeddedness. First-generation-American early-adolescent males born to immigrant Italian parents show self concepts similar to those of the early-maturing American adolescents born to American-born parents, studied by Mussen and Jones (1957). However, the Italian–American early-maturers showed negative attitudes toward parents, similar to those of the late-maturers of the Mussen and Jones (1957) study. On the other hand, early-maturing Italian adolescents born to native-Italian parents had self concepts unrelated to their physical status, but maintained attitudes toward their parents comparable to those of the early maturing adolescents studied by Mussen and Jones (1957).

Thus, while the data we have reviewed indicate that social processes based on organism individuality occur among people ranging in developmental levels from nursery school through middle age, the content and feedback implications of these processes are influenced by the sociocultural setting. Moreover, although collected for different purposes, the data of Nesselroade and Baltes (1974) indicate that the socializing impact of a sociocultural setting is further influenced by the historical era; and the data reported by Baltes and Schaie (1974) likewise indicate the significant role of historical context in intellectual development within adult and aged groups. Accordingly, although our model of organism–organism reciprocities is a general one, it can only be adequately employed when understood in the context of all the levels of interaction illustrated in Figure 10.1.

In sum then, the present dynamic interactional model stresses the necessity of conceptualizing any level of analysis—from inner-biological to historical—as inextricably related to all other levels. The model thus points to the view that knowledge about any one level is, at best, a probabilistic statement to be held as tentative until it is ultimately explicated by the higher-order interaction effect in which it is embedded. Furthermore, the model indicates that individual development cannot be completely understood independent of the social relations in which the individual is involved. Since it is always the case that such relations must involve interdependent, developing organisms, the relation of these organisms, when existing over the course of repeated interactions, must develop also. When the Level 2 organism–organism interchanges of our model involve exchanges between the same two organisms over time, a *relationship* may be said to exist. It is both appropriate and necessary to consider the nature of the developmental changes these relationships may or may not progress through.

IV. Relationship Development

As was indicated at earlier points in this chapter, when individual development is conceptualized from a dialectically derived viewpoint it may be seen as being composed of processes describable through the notion of orthogenesis (see Lerner, 1978). Moreover, it is held (see Werner, 1957) that any phenomenon that develops may be described by this principle. Accordingly, relationship development appears to also involve orthogenetically based parameters. Consideration of these parameters leads to a specification of relationship development as involving a progression from an initial, global and, unidimensional *basis* of interchange to eventual, differentiated, multidimensional, multilevel, and hierarchically organized *bases* of interchange.

A. Developmental Level and Rate of Development of Each Member of the Relationship

The dialectically based notion of orthogenesis is that processes of individual development proceed from states of relative globality to ones of relative differentiation and hierarchic integration. Thus, for any dyad one may assess the *level*, or stage, of differentiation–hierarchicization that exists for each member, and, through some sort of repeated-measures design (a sequential one, for instance), the *rate* at which each individual is developing through this level also may be assessed. This evaluation will lead to a specification of one of four types of relationships that may exist for a particular dyad at the time of relationship initiation. As can be seen in Figure 10.2, when a relationship begins the members of the dyad may be at similar or at different levels, which may or may not be progressing at similar rates; relationships may therefore exist at one of four types of symmetry—Box 1 representing a relationship of maximum symmetry;

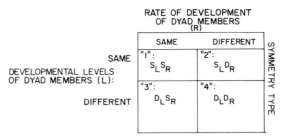

Figure 10.2   The type of symmetry at which a relationship exists is dependent on the developmental levels and rates of development of the dyad members.

Box 4, one of least symmetry; and Boxes 2 and 3, relationships of inter-mediate symmetry. Of course, as any of these relationships develops—along the lines we will presently suggest—its placement into another of these symmetry categories is possible. In fact, it may be that depending on the content area of a particular relationship (e.g., employer–employee, graduate student–mentor, mother–child) particular sequences of sym-metry occur over the course of the relationship's development.

For example, in the graduate student—mentor relationship, the rela-tionship may, typically, be initiated within symmetry type 4. The stu-dent's level of knowledge development is less than that of the mentor (in respect to the domain of graduate study); but while the student is acquiring with relative rapidity further knowledge and skills as he or she moves (asympototically) toward the level of knowledge of the mentor, the mentor is already at a given level, which is relatively more stable. How-ever, as the relationship progresses it may be locatable in other boxes in Figure 10.2, and ultimately, if the initial basis of the relationship reaches fruition, it will be locatable in the first box: both student—now former student—and mentor will exist at comparably stable levels of knowledge–skill attainment.

Relationships initiated on the basis of other content reasons may start and proceed through other sequences. Any relationships, nevertheless, at any point in its development should be categorizable in terms of the categories of Figure 10.2. Although future empirical inquiry will be necessary to indicate where relationships of particular contents begin and where they progress, in terms of their symmetry status over time and of how deviations from normative symmetry sequencing may affect relation-ship quality and stability, we may at this point specify two principal parameters of relationship development that should characterize a rela-tionship of any content and of any initial symmetry type. These parame-ters derive from a further analysis of the orthogenetic nature of develop-ment.

1. GLOBALITY TO DIFFERENTIATION–HIERARCHIC INTEGRATION

In the example of the graduate student—mentor relationship it was implied that the basis for relationship initiation was an academic enter-prise. The transaction would probably be initiated on the basis of an exchange of knowledge and skills (from the mentor) for capable work and assistance (from the graduate student). However, as the relationship prog-resses (if it does progress) other reasons for continued transactions may become relevant (Homans, 1974). The graduate student may want advice about job placement or counseling on how to strike a balance between professional and personal development goals; the mentor may come to regard the graduate student as integral to the further development of his or her work and as a personal friend. Moreover, it should be noted that both initial and new bases for relationship maintenance may exist simultaneously, but that each set of bases may exist at different developmental levels. While the initial dimension of the relationship may still exist at its initial—or, more probably, a developmentally changed—level, any new dimension will upon its emergence follow its own developmental course. One may have considerably differentiated knowledge about someone's intellectual and professional abilities, while still having very general knowledge about his or her personal-intimate characteristics. The point is that new dimensions of a relationship do not automatically and immediately reach the highest developmental level involved in the relationship.

What this example indicates then is that when a relationship is initiated there is typically a single, general basis (physical attraction between dyad members, being assigned as a graduate assistant to a professor, giving birth to a child) for interaction. Thus, relationships exist as relatively global, unidimensional structures at their initiation; as they progress, not only does this general basis become more particularized but, also, other dimensions of the relationship emerge. A relationship may begin because the dyad members are physically attracted to each other. This attraction may wax, wane, or become more particularized (e.g., "I like her eyes, but not her teeth," or "He has a nice body except for his thighs"). And it may become embedded in other, and perhaps more salient, domains of interchange (e.g., the person is reliable, or disloyal, or affectionate, or aloof).

To summarize, while relationships are initiated as relatively global, relatively unidimensional interchanges, in accordance with the orthogenetic principle they proceed to states of differentiation; for example, the single base becomes more particularized, as when the graduate student learns that the mentor is very strong theoretically (but more so in some areas then others), good in writing ability, but only average in data analytic abilities. In addition to such differentiation, other bases for relationship maintenance emerge as a consequence of repeated interchange, and thus relationships develop into multidimensional phenomena. As these other dimensions of interchange become operational, they too follow an orthogenetic course, and thus, the multiple dimensions of a developing relationship exist at multiple developmental levels. While each basis of the relationship thus has its own developmental course, all dimensions exist in a hierarchical integration, both within and between dimensions, and they all subserve the functioning of the relationship. In essence, relationships develop toward differentiated, multidimensional, hierarchically integrated levels. Such a developmental progression is illustrated in Figure 10.3.

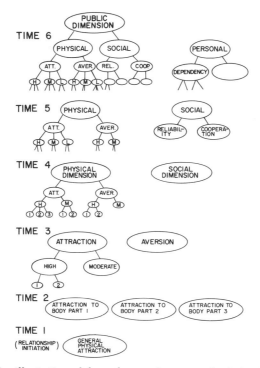

Figure 10.3   An illustration of the orthogenetic nature of relationship development.

In this figure the relationship is initiated at Time 1 on the basis of physical attraction between the individuals. At Time 2 this attraction has become more differentiated, as attraction to particular body parts is seen; these less global components may be conceptualized as bipolar dimensions, and thus a particular body part may have a negative weighting. By Time 3 this negative–positive differentiation becomes further particularized, and within-dimension hierarchicization appears; in addition, an aversion domain emerges. By Time 4, attraction is high or low to particular body parts, but this attraction domain becomes contrasted with the independent, and now differentiated and hierarchicized, aversion domain, but, too, they have been subordinated to a more general physical dimension. In addition, a social dimension of interchange has emerged, in an orthogenetically initial, global state. Development at Time 5 involves a further orthogenetic progression of the physical dimension and further differentiation of the social dimension; and Time 6 development sees not only further progression within each of these domains, but also their integration within a superordinate public dimension and the emergence of a personal dimension. Of course, an infinite number of times of relationship development could be depicted, and this means that such de-

velopment is an open, continually changing system. Moreover, the intervals between depicted times need not be equivalent, and the duration of
the relationship is unimportant to the depicted nature of structural progression; that is, both short- and long-term relationships should follow an
orthogenetic course. Finally, relationships do not have infinite durations,
and orthogenetically derived notions will allow us to speak, in a moment,
about relationship dissolution.

At this point, however, we should indicate that the present view of
relationship development is compatible with the one presented by
Levinger and Snoek (1972). However, although their model stresses progression from noninteraction (unilateral awareness) to a global, surface
contact, through (in the present terms) more differentiated minor and then
major intersections, it does not consider the multidimensional, hierarchically organized nature of relationship development emphasized in the
present model. In other words, although the progressions described by
Levinger and Snoek (1972) are part of relationship development, they are
not sufficiently complete. One must consider not only the basis of relationship initiation and changes in that domain, but also the emergence
and development of additional domains, that is, what Homans (1974) has
described as "the elaboration of relationships."

Such consideration requires analysis of the developmental levels of
the dyad members, and the type of symmetry implied by these levels.
Although a Type 4 symmetry (see Figure 10.2) may characterize numerous relationships, one may conceptualize any symmetry type itself as a
bipolar dimension and consider the import of the *degree* of a given type
$(D_L D_R$ for instance) in characterizing a particular relationship.

To understand this point we must first recognize that not only will
each dyad member's developmental level and rate of development determine the symmetry type of the relationship, but it will also determine the
nature of the orthogenetic progression illustrated in Figure 10.3. For
instance, how global each member's conceptual basis for relationship
initiation is will determine the level of globality of the initial relationship,
the rate of differentiated developmental progressions, and the timing (and
nature) of the emergence of other dimensions of the relationship. New
mothers will have a more global conception of motherhood than will
experienced mothers, and a first romantic relationship is perhaps based
on more global and more socially stereotypic conceptions of love and
erotic involvement than is a romantic relationship initiated after considerable experience in earlier ones. Either of these latter relationships (i.e.,
those involving experienced mothers or experienced lovers) will still
begin as relatively global—the particularities of the other dyad members
are not yet known, and, until they are, the person is necessarily placed in
a relatively general category (e.g., "my new baby" or "my new lover").
However, the *rate* of orthogenetic progression to more advanced levels

will be different (e.g., more rapid) for dyads involving these developmentally advanced members. Yet, since dyads having developmentally advanced or unadvanced members may be categorized in the same symmetry box when the relationship is initiated, the developmental status of each member of the dyad must be known in order to fully account for all types of variation in a relationship's development (e.g., its rate of differentiation–hierarchicization, and hence its rate of sequencing through the four symmetry categories).

2. OSCILLATION (VARIABILITY) LEVELS OF RELATIONSHIPS

A second parameter of relationship development, derivable from our orthogenetic position, may be specified. Not only do the components of relationships become multidimensional, and thus multilevel in developmental status and multirate in progression, but they also become *multidirectional*. The components of relationships cannot be both static and, at the same time, responsive to the continually changing contingencies in a continually changing environment. If a developmental phenomenon (an organism or a relationship) did not show plasticity, it would not be adaptive and viable. In fact, it may be the case that one basis of both organism demise (or severe maladaptiveness) and relationship dissolution is that the dimensions (components) of the phenomenon do not exist with degrees of plasticity sufficient to adapt to the continual changes of the environment. Thus, akin to a notion of dedifferentiation, the dimensions of a relationship may be conceptualized to exist as fluctuating phenomena, variable in the direction of either more or less globality or differentiation–integration. The level of affection exchanged in a relationship, for example, does not always remain the same, either across the range of the relationship's duration or within a particular segment of the relation. Partners may move from an exchange of love to an exchange of hositility relatively rapidly, or affection may decrease or increase in intensity over a long time span. The point is that oscillation—the variability in behavior associated with a relationship—may be considered for any content domain both within and between temporal segments.

Not only may relationship oscillation occur within a particular content dimension (as in the ups and downs of marital affection), but it also can be seen between content dimensions. In dependence on the level of globality–differentiation–integration that exists within each of the dimensions, one may expect interdimensional differences in levels of intradimensional variability. For example, it may be hypothesized that the more global the status of a particular dimension (i.e., the more stereotyped the behavior; Lerner, 1976) the less the level of oscillation, and that oscillation increases as differentiation proceeds.

One implication of this oscillation parameter is that the components of relationships, depicted in Figure 10.3, should be drawn as theoretical probability distributions rather than as circles. An empirical question becomes raised about the appropriate depictions of these distributions. It is logically clear that they need not appear normal, and, in fact, one might predict that in successful, adaptive relationships—for example, marriages having high levels of marital satisfaction (Spanier, 1976)—such distributions would be negatively skewed. For instance, in a highly valued marriage one might expect the preponderant majority of variation in the affection dimension to exist between average and high. Similar predictions could be made for other dimensions of the relationship (e.g., trust, sharing), and one could in fact validate measures of marital satisfaction through interrelation with the various intradimensional oscillation distributions that may exist. Thus, those distributions that approached normality should be associated with marriages having intermediate levels of marital satisfaction; those distributions that were positively skewed should be found with marriages having low satisfaction. Moreover, in any distribution—whatever its form—where variability is minimal, the probability of the relationship's dissolution should be high. Minimally oscillating relationships would not have a sufficient repertoire of responses to employ in the face of the continually changing demands placed on the relationship by a continually changing world (cf. Riegel, 1976). Alternatively, however, relationships involving maximal oscillation also should be associated with high probabilities of dissolution; here, continual readjustments and reappraisals would be involved, and this might mean that the relationship's repertoire of responsiveness would have no more than a random chance of matching the changing demands placed on it. Accordingly, since either minimal or maximal oscillation may lead to relationship dissolution, it may be that there exists an oscillation range that is adaptive for relationships of specific developmental characteristics and attribute domains.

A relationship might survive one or even a few minimally or maximally oscillating dimensions—especially at early levels of relationship development, when fewer dimensions exist, and when they exist as relatively more global (i.e., behaviorally stereotyped) and hence as less variable; but no relationship could be expected to survive when most, and especially key, dimensions exist as having relatively minimal or maximal variability. If this should happen the relationship would dissolve and, in a sense, return to a state analogous to its initial one. It will exist in a global state of the no-longer-existing. In a sense, all relationships develop towards this end, as when the death of a dyad member occurs. However, pre-death dissolutions (e.g., divorces) obviously occur. It is the role of future research to delineate the variables influencing the oscillation characteristics of relationships making them relatively adaptive and successful or unviable and dissolvable. Some early suggestions were made by Homans (1974) and Thibaut and Kelley (1961) when they discussed the roles that such processes as satiation and alternative sources of reward may play in determining the value of a particular relationship at a particular point in time.

In sum, not only do individuals follow developmental progressions involving dynamic interactional change, but, because such development is necessarily social and exchanges are often repeated with the same organisms over time, the basis is provided for relationship developments that also follow such a course. As is the case with individual ontogeny, relationships develop from a state of globality, initiated typically on the basis of a single, general dimension of interchange, to a state of increasing differentiation and hierarchic integration. Numerous dimensions of such open-ended relationships emerge, each following its own orthogenetic course, and these multiple bases show oscillation characteristics that not only covary with the developmental level of the dimensions within which they are embedded, but also have import for the relationship's adaptive maintenance or its dissolution.

V. Implications for Social Exchange

Support for this model of individual and social development has been provided through the presentation of data involving physical characteristics of organism individuality. In addition, support based on some behavioral data (e.g., temperament) has been indicated. While these discussions have often been cast in terms compatible with social-exchange theory, to this point in the chapter no specific evaluation of the relevance of data supporting our model to social exchange has been made. Do social-exchange notions allow us to understand these data? If so, what are the implications of these data for the further development of social exchange theory?

Information needed to address these questions may be derived from studies of the effects of infants on their caregivers (see, for example, Lewis & Rosenbaum, 1974). Considerable data on infant–caregiver interactions have been generated. Because traditional conceptual emphases in socialization research, stressing the static, unidirectional influences of caregivers of infants, have failed to account sufficiently for the variation in children's personality and social development (cf. Hartup & Lempers, 1973; Rheingold, 1969), several researchers have begun to evaluate the infant's role in the development of these processes, and the interrelationship of this contribution to that of the parent. In fact, in summarizing some of these data Rheingold (1969) describes the infant–mother dyad in

terms consistent with a notion of reciprocal exchange of mutually rewarding behavior. She says, "Although we can talk about who socializes
whom, neither the infant's contribution nor the parent's can be separated
when the dyad is studied in real life situations. The child's behavior
modifies the parent's behavior, even as his behavior is being modified by
theirs. As variables for analysis they are completely confounded . . . [p.
789]."

Thus, aside from the compelling fact that there exist considerable
data, it is apropriate that we evaluate our dynamic interactional notions
vis-à-vis exchange notions through reference to the literature on infants'
effects on caregivers. This dyad, because of its ontogenetic primacy, is
perhaps most interesting to those concerned with individual development; on the other hand, this relationship is of particular concern to those
primarily interested in socialization. Moreover, because a consideration
of the development of this relationship allows us to see implications not
only for individuals and dyads but also for somewhat larger and especially important groups—families—it seems particularly important to determine the relevance of exchange notions to these data. Finally, although
our dynamic interactional ideas, and their relevance to exchange, may
seem to apply at older age levels, and with encounters at these levels
based on physical attributes, it is important to consider whether this
applicability holds for relationships involving dyad members at perhaps
one of the most disparate degrees of Type 4 symmetry (see Figure 10.2).

A. Empirical Support for a Dynamic Interactional Model of Exchanges in Individual and Social Relationship Development

1. EFFECTS OF THE INFANT ON CAREGIVERS

Does the infant affect its caregiver, and are such affects interactional?
Bell (1974) indicates that parents respond to their infants in one of two
ways. First, they respond to the infant's presence and distress—
discomfort-related behaviors by emitting life support and protection behaviors. They respond to the infant's crying and fussing in order to avoid
undesirable immediate and long-term effects. Bell (1974) contends that
from the parents' point of view this system of interaction is an aversive
one. Hence, it is clear that decrements in infant distress behavior would
be rewarding to the parent—they would confirm to the parent his or her
success as a caregiver. In turn, these parenting behaviors are associated by
the infant with the diminution of presumably noxious stimuli. The second system of parental response that Bell identifies also involves an

exchange of rewarding behaviors, but here, since both parent and infant behave so as to maintain the other's behavior, the system is an appetitive one. For example, vocalizations by the infant are exchanged with parental vocalizations and perhaps also touching. An example of this system is found in data reported by Lewis and Lee-Painter (1974). The looking behavior of an infant elicits more maternal vocalization than its touching behavior, but maternal touching and vocalization appear to evoke equal levels of infant vocalization.

Although this information indicates that parental behaviors may indeed be contingent on infant behavior, is the nature of the relationship interactive? The data just cited seem to indicate that it is, and additional evidence reported by Lewis and Wilson (1972) supports this conclusion. Although finding no overall differences between middle class and working class mothers in the frequency of vocalization in the presence of their infants, a difference in the interactional use of vocalizations did obtain: Middle class mothers were more likely to respond to their infants' vocalizations with a vocalization than were working class mothers. The respective percentages were 78 and 43. Similarly, Lewis (1972) reports that interactional sex differences also occur: Female infants are more likely to respond with a vocalization to a maternal behavior than are male infants, although no total amount of vocalization difference exists between the sexes.

Parenthetically, I might point out that Lewis' data are an excellent example of how one's model-derived theoretical assumptions influence one's research. Earlier, I mentioned the prescriptive role of models in science, and pointed out that, eventually, different models lead to different facts of development. Lewis and Lee-Painter (1974) show that if a unidirectional model for socialization effects governed the analysis of their data, and interactional notions were ignored, one would conclude that there are neither maternal social-class differences nor infant sex differences in vocalization behavior. Thus, although the point has been made before (e.g., Werner, 1957), it bears repeating: The parameters of our methodology are never unrelated to our theoretical assumptions.

Although I will address methodological issues further in my conclusions, at this point I would like to return to an analysis of infant effects. We have seen some evidence that infant–parent behavior is interactional. But to further substantiate this view we must assess whether and how the infant can initiate reciprocal exchanges.

2. INFANT INITIATION OF EXCHANGES

If the infant is not merely reactive, he or she must be capable of initiating a flow of interactive behavior, maintaining it, and terminating it. Data indicate that infants do have such competencies. Bell (1974) indicates that in the first few weeks of life crying elicits caregiver approach behavior, and such approach increases the likelihood that visual, olfactory, and tactile stimuli provided by the infant can elicit other caregiver behaviors. As was pointed out earlier, such interactions represent an aversive system to the mother, and her behavioral role in the relation is to reduce or diminish the infant behavior. For example, in a study that illustrates how developing infant characteristics alter the exchanges in the infant–mother dyad—an important point we will return to presently—Wolff (1966) reports that by a few weeks of age infants' crying behavior comes to follow a predictable cycle. Infants move from a state of quiescence to soft whispering, then through gentle movements, rhythmic kicking, uncoordinated thrashing, and finally intense crying. As the pattern of changes emerges and, in accordance with orthogenetic differentiation, becomes predictable to the mother, a response to one of the behaviors in the sequence might avert others. Kicking, for instance, might become a discriminative stimulus for caregiving, which in turn would be maintained by termination of an aversive sequence (Bell, 1974).

Such exchanges are not automatic, however. The mother will not respond to every infant cry. While it remains for future research to discern the situational and maternal variables predictive of those instances when infant behavior does not elicit caregiving, there is some evidence that, consistent with our interactional model, suggests that noncaregiving behavior is influenced by infant behavior also. Infant crying can become so excessive that it disrupts or terminates the flow of interactions. Robson and Moss (1970) found that mothers reported decreases in their feelings of attachment toward their three-month-old infants if crying and other demands for physiological caregiving did not decrease, as they do in most infants. Moreover, data from the previously cited Thomas et al. (1970) study of temperament suggested that developmental differences between easy and difficult children might arise as a consequence of the differential levels of energy their caregivers had to expend in order to maintain a relationship with them. Difficult children, having as one of their salient characteristics low behavioral regularity (rhythmicity), might be in a relationship with their parent that is prototypic of one above the adaptive oscillation range; the apparently maximal oscillation of the child might mean that the parent's caregiving behaviors could not successfully follow any preplanned sequence. Thus, not only may the infant's difficult behavior be a primary negative reinforcer but, in the context of this relationship, it would also serve to punish parental caregiving behavior. Excessive aversive-system-initiating behavior by the infant may require that parents expend too much of the caregiving or love resources, and lead to relationship termination.

Consistent with this possibility are data reported by Bell and Ainsworth (1972). Analyzing the relation between infant crying and maternal ignoring of crying in the four quarters of the infant's first year, they report that the more an infant cried in any one quarter the more the mother ignored the cry in the subsequent quarter. These data suggest that for some infants their behavior was excessive enough to exceed their mothers' caregiving tolerance limits. After caregiving behavior failed to lead to a decrement in crying, the mother began to withdraw the more the infant cried; this led to increased crying and further maternal withdrawal (Bell, 1974).

3. BALANCING OF EXCHANGES BETWEEN INFANT AND CAREGIVER

The above data indicate that infant–mother dyadic relationships are interactional, and that the infant is capable of initiating and maintaining a relationship if initiation behavior does not exceed caregiver limits; that is, if a rewarding alteration in infant state follows caregiving behavior. In other words, although most infants cry and fuss, this aversive behavior is typically alterable by parent caregiving, and the infant–mother relationship does not usually break down. Still, when crying–caregiving exchanges do not lead to an alteration in infant state, then the infant–mother relationship does break down for a period. These alternative instances of infant–mother interactions suggest that the dyad exists in a social exchange relation involving temporal oscillation within a range of relationship adaptiveness (i.e., maintenance, in this case).

Brazelton, Koslowski, and Main (1974) report that the maternal attributes most necessary for maintaining interactions with an infant are the development of a sensitivity to the infant's capacity for attention and understanding the infant's need for either complete or partial withdrawal after a period of attention. Cycles of attention–nonattention were found in all periods of prolonged interaction, and Brazelton et al. (1974) interpreted nonattentive, looking-away behaviors as reflecting the infant's need to maintain some control over the amount of stimulation taken in during an intense interaction period.

Thus, infants' behaviors contribute to a dynamic balance of exchanges between themselves and their caregivers. Not only do parents similarly contribute to such a balance in exchanges when infants' behaviors are too intense, as we have seen, but they also do so when behaviors are not intense enough. Bell (1974) indicates that extreme lethargy in infants elicits in parents various behaviors designed to intensify the infants' activity levels. We see that, consistent with a biphasic approach–withdrawal conception (Schneirla, 1965), an actor makes approach, intensifying behaviors when exchanges become unbalanced through too little stimulation from the other, and makes withdrawal behaviors when exchanges become unbalanced through too much stimulation from the other.

The maintenance of such a dynamic exchange is predicated on each actor's behavior being capable of conditioning by the behavior of the other. For example, if the mother's behavior cannot manipulate the excessive crying state of her infant, then her caregiving behaviors are not being rewarded, and, as we have seen, she may withdraw from exchange. The relationship does not involve sufficient oscillation, and it moves toward dissolution. Thus, state alterability of infants in response to caregiving efforts is an important contributor to the maintenance and termination of stable exchanges. For instance, Escalona (1968) reports that mothers stimulate sleepy infants in order to bring them into a state appropriate for interaction, and then often must act to quiet the infant when a behavioral state too intense for interaction obtains. In turn, Brazelton (1962) reports that if an infant's state is unalterable by the mother, markedly negative effects on her may ensue. In short, an infant-behavior characteristic that provides reward for parental caregiving behavior is state alterability (Bell, 1974). This observation leads to a consideration of the nature of reward in social exchange.

VI. The Nature of Reward in Social Exchanges

As we have already noted, a social exchange involves an interaction wherein actors provide each other with rewarding behavior (Burgess & Nielsen, 1974). We have just seen that infant state alterations contingent on parental caregiving behaviors reward such parent actions. Although social exchange notions appear to fit the data of mother–infant dyadic interchanges, these notions do not necessarily tell us why the behaviors of one actor are rewarded by those of the other. What they do tell us, however, is that they do serve this function. While this observation may lead into a discussion of the tautology alleged to be involved in the operant principles on which exchange theory is based, such a digression is neither necessary nor useful. Homans (1974) has argued that a tautology may in fact have an appropriate use within a theoretical system, and Burgess and Akers (1966) have, in any event, clearly indicated that operant principles are not necessarily tautological. Yet, these same authors assert that it is both empirically and logically useful to be able to define a phenomenon independently of the propositions that apply to it, and it is this need that I now address.

Although in detailing exchange notions Emerson (1972) says that "we will not presume to know the needs and motives of men [p. 45]," it is precisely such information that may provide independent knowledge of when and why certain behaviors of one actor are rewarding to another. It is this information that may extend, therefore, the utility of exchange notions for understanding the development of the infant–parent dyad.

Having concluded that infant-state alterability is the characteristic that rewards caregiving actions, we may inquire into the nature of this reward. Why is such alterability rewarding? If, as we might suppose, some notion of a confirmation in role-appropriate or normative behavioral expectations is invoked in answer to this question, then we might further ask if such cognitive variables are moderated by the caregiver's developmental status in regard to other cognitive domains. For example, the salience of role-appropriate behavior or the importance of being normative may be expected to vary according to whether the caregiver is at a concrete or a formal operational stage of thought or whether the caregiver is at a conventional or a postconventional level of moral reasoning or whether the caregiver is at one of these stages of thought and one of these levels of moral reasoning. One's appraisal of one's role as a socializer would vary according to these cognitive levels. Thus, differences in cognitive status may be expected to lead to contrasting conceptualizations of the meaning of the infant's behavioral alterability, and hence such differences would contribute to determining when and why a given level of alterability was rewarding. Here we may recall the Brazelton et al. (1974) findings that mothers must develop sensitivity to and understanding of infants' needs for cyclical stimulation levels in order to maintain interactions with them, developments that are obviously dependent on the cognitive level of the mother. Similarly, in the already noted study by Wolff (1966) it was seen that if mothers could discriminate emerging sequentiality of infants' crying behavior they could avoid much of an aversive procession of events. Thus, consistent with our model, the developmental level of dyad members must be considered in order to understand the nature of relationship progression, e.g., its rate and sequencing of symmetry types.

Both Feffer (1970) and Sameroff (1975) have provided models specifying how cognitive development in adults provides a parameter of the nature of the social relationships they will have, and Sameroff (1975) has looked at the mother's cognitive level as a way of understanding the variability in outcomes of infant–parent relationships. He suggests that when abnormal child behavior develops it can be related to exceptional caregiving based on a mother's cognitive inability to make developmental sense of her child's behavior; he hypothesizes that a flow of negative transactions is started that creates a self-fulfilling prophecy.

Thus, what we may see at this point is the utility of considering the developmental status of the parent in attempts to understand, independent of observation of a particular interaction, why certain infant behaviors may or may not be rewarding. Similarly, developmental changes in the infant's behavior appear to contribute to the status of that behavior as a reward for caregiving. Bell (1974) describes a developmental sequence wherein infants show decreases in durations of fussing and crying and increases in durations of wakefulness and attentiveness. This relative alteration from a modal state of intense negative behaviors to one of milder, positive ones elicits approach behaviors in mothers, behaviors perhaps regulated by an approach–withdrawal system like the one we noted earlier. In any event, Jones and Moss (1971) have found that infants in the awake–active state tend to babble more when alone than when the mother is present; the emergence of this behavior in the context of infants' now modal awake–active state may represent a novel stimulus to the parent, and so may serve as a cue to the parent that the infant is developing behavior states indicative of healthy development. That is, the emergence of expected behaviors may provide a discriminative stimulus for the parent that development is proceeding along expected or desired lines. Moreover, Bell (1974, p. 9) reports that when interaction is initiated on the basis of novel babbling, the infant often discontinues the babbling and shifts into a reciprocal relation in which the mother vocalizes or touches and the infant responds by smiling and vocalizing. Watson (1966) has termed such interaction series "contingency games," and Bell (1974) has indicated that the infant's ability, emerging after about three months of age, to engage in such reciprocal games rewards the parents' approach behaviors.

Such data as these indicate that developmental characteristics of each of the actors in an exchange contribute to determining why the other's behavior is rewarding, and whether and how the relationship they are embedded in will develop. The infant's behavior moves from being dominated by fussing and crying—behaviors related to physiological need states in early infancy—to being dominated by wakefulness, attentiveness, and reciprocal social games, such as in the sequence I have just described. Thus, in accordance with our orthogenetic model of relationship development, the types of behaviors infants exchange with caregivers are different as the infant interaction system moves from a predominantly aversive one to a predominantly appetitive one. Moreover, even the nature of the stimuli that reward appetitive behavior would be altered as a consequence of developmental changes in the person. We have seen that, for the parent, the rewarding aspects of infant alterability must be understood in the context of the parent's appraisal of how well the infant's behavior matches, or the extent to which it is discrepant with, role and socialization expectations, evaluations which are moderated by the caregiver's cognitive level. Similarly, whether or not the parents' caregiving behavior rewards appetitive, social behaviors by the infant may be dependent on the infant's expectations about what should obtain in social interchanges. Thus, it has been reported that after the infant can recognize and discriminate the mother from others, and has developed some elementary notion of time, "anticipatory protests occur when behaviors are shown by the mother that have been associated in the past with separation [Bell, 1974, p. 4]." Here, then, we see that cognitive developments in the infant—relating to such things as schemas of object permanence and the emergence of representational ability—must be considered when attempting to understand why a given maternal behavior may at one time maintain an appetitive exchange and at another time disrupt it.

Lewis and Lee-Painter (1974) have made a similar point. Immediately preceding behaviors are not the only ones that may initiate an interaction. Rather, since these authors conceive of behavior as a circular flow or as reciprocal interchanges, they argue that any one of the behaviors in such a series may initiate an exchange, and that the developing cognitive abilities of the actor—retention, recall, and representational ability, for example—need to be understood in order to determine when and why past behaviors can play an initiating or a maintaining role, or both roles, in an exchange.

VII. Conclusions

In conclusion, we may return to the issue of whether useful conceptual exchanges can occur between those whose primary interest is individual development and those who are primarily concerned with social relationships. Derivations from our contextual-dialectic, dynamic interactional model suggest that developing attributes of the person need to be considered in attempting to understand the nature of exchanges in developing social relationships (see Reigel, 1975; Sameroff, 1975; Tobach & Schneirla, 1968). As Tobach and Schneirla (1968) assert: "The nature of the stimuli reciprocally exchanged between two or more animals in a social group is dependent upon the stage of development of each of the participating group members, as well as upon the group situation and factors affecting the stability of its organization [p. 505]."

The data we have reviewed are consistent with this assertion and suggest that individual developmental processes are inextricably related to social reciprocities. Developmental changes in dyadic relationships such as those between infant and caregiver not only are consistent with exchange notions but seem to provide a basis for understanding that important parameters of reward in social exchanges involve developmental attributes of the actors. Burgess and Nielsen (1974, p. 429) have noted that if there is a motivational assumption in basic social-exchange theory, if there is any statement about why particular behaviors are rewarding, it is one of hedonism. However, Emerson (1972, p. 87) has speculated that exchange theory may be strengthened if it considers concepts from theoretical systems that have to do with cognitive functioning. Our preceding suggestions about understanding aspects of social exchange through integration with interactive concepts of development—cognitive or otherwise—may thus be a step in the direction of moving exchange theory beyond a simple drive-reduction model of social behavior and, in so doing, of extending its utility to those concerned with cognitive domains of social behavior.

In turn, exchange notions seem particularly useful in aiding developmentalists understand the interactional nature of human development. The major problem with notions of interactions such as we have derived from our model is a theoretical–methodological one. Although our model stresses interactive relations as the main concern in developmental analysis, no totally satisfactory data-gathering model that will allow the researcher to focus primarily on the interaction per se rather than on its elements has been derived from current contextual-dialectic concepts (cf. Lewis & Lee-Painter, 1974; Looft, 1973). These remarks, however, suggest that exchange notions may contribute to the development of such a model. The focus in exchange theory on the exchange relation per se, and the theory's conceptual specification of the role that repeated observations will play in revealing basic structural aspects of this relation—e.g., in balance notions—hold considerable import for developmentalists. Exchange notions, used in conjunction with descriptive sequential research (cf. Baltes, 1968), with manipulative studies, and with age-simulation investigations (Baltes & Goulet, 1971), may substantially contribute to providing developmental psychology with the theoretical and methodological tools necessary for understanding interactionally based development. Through such exchanges, we may learn how the development of an individual is derived from dynamic interactions among maturation, physical experience, other individuals, the social, cultural, and historical contexts, and, ultimately, him- or herself.

Acknowledgments

The author thanks John R. Knapp, Wesley Jamison, Marsha Harshbarger, and Victor Barocas for their critical readings of and discussions about various drafts of an earlier version of this chapter. The comments of the editors of this volume were also extremely helpful in sharpening my style and honing my thinking, and their contributions are hereby acknowledged. Finally, I have profited greatly from a series of exchanges with Ted Huston concerning relationship development. Many of the ideas expressed in this chapter about this topic were stimulated by him. The shortcomings of the presentation stem, of course, totally from me.

References

Baltes, P. B. Longitudinal and cross-sectional sequences in the study of age and generation effects. *Human Development*, 1968, *11*, 145–171.

Baltes, P. B., & Goulet, L. R. Exploration of developmental variables by manipulation and simulation of age differences in behavior. *Human Development*, 1971, *14*, 149–170.

Baltes, P. B., & Schaie, K. W. *Life-span developmental psychology: Personality and socialization.* New York: Academic Press, 1973.

Bell, R. Q. Contributions of human infants to caregiving and social interaction. In M. Lewis & L. A. Rosenblum (Eds.), *The effect of the infant on its caregiver.* New York: Wiley, 1974.

Bell, S. W., & Ainsworth, M. D. Infant crying and maternal responsiveness. *Child Development*, 1972, *43*, 1171–1190.

Bertalanffy, L. *Modern theories of development.* London: Oxford Univ. Press, 1933.

Berscheid, E., & Walster, E. Physical attractiveness. In L. Berkowitz (Ed.) *Advances in experimental social psychology.* New York: Academic Press, 1974.

Brazelton, T. Observation of the neonate. *Journal of the American Academy of Child Psychiatry*, 1962, *1*, 38–58.

Brazelton, T. B., Koslowski, B., & Main, M. The origins of reciprocity: The early mother-infant interaction. In M. Lewis & L. A. Rosenblum (Eds.), *The effect of the infant on its caregiver.* New York: Wiley, 1974.

Burgess, R. L., & Akers, R. L. Are operant principles tautological? *The Psychological Record*, 1966, *16*, 305–312.

Burgess, R. L., & Nielsen, J. McC. An experimental analysis of some structural determinants of equitable and inequitable exchange relations. *American Sociological Review*, 1974, *39*, 427–443.

Clifford, M. M., & Walster, E. The effect of physical attractiveness on teacher expectation. *Sociology of Education*, 1973, *46*, 248–258.

Dion, K. K. Physical attractiveness and evaluations of children's transgressions. *Journal of Personality and Social Psychology*, 1972, *24*, 207–213.

Dion, K. K., & Berscheid, E. *Physical attractiveness and social perception of peers in preschool children.* Mimeographed research report available from the authors. 1972.

Emerson, R. M. Exchange Theory, Part 1: A psychological basis for social exchange; Exchange Theory, Part 2: Exchange relations and network structures. In J. Berger, M. Zelditch, & B. Anderson (Eds.), *Sociological theories in progress.* Volume 2. Boston: Houghton Mifflin, 1972.

Escalona, S. *The roots of individuality.* Chicago: Aldine, 1968.

Feffer, M. Developmental analysis of interpersonal behavior. *Psychological Review*, 1970, *77*, 197–214.

Gesell, A. L. Maturation and infant behavior pattern. *Psychological Review*, 1929, *36*, 307–319.

Goulet, L. R., & Baltes, P. B. (Eds.), *Life-span developmental psychology: Research and theory.* New York: Academic Press, 1970.

Hamburger, V. The concept of development in biology. In D. B. Harris (Ed.), *The concept of development.* Minneapolis: Univ. of Minnesota Press, 1957.

Harlow, H. F., & Harlow, M. K. Social deprivation in monkeys. *Scientific American*, 1962, *207*, 137–146.

Hartup, W. W., & Lempers, J. A problem in life span development: The interactional analysis of family attachments. In P. B. Baltes & K. W. Schaie (Eds.), *Life-span developmental psychology: Personality and socialization.* New York: Academic Press, 1973.

Harris, D. B. (Ed.), *The concept of development.* Minneapolis: Univ. of Minnesota Press, 1957.

Homans, G. C. Prologue: The sociological relevance of behaviorism. In R. L. Burgess & Bushell (Eds.), *Behavioral sociology.* New York: Columbia Univ. Press, 1969.

Homans, G. C. *Social behavior: Its elementary forms* (Rev. ed.) New York: Harcourt Brace Jovanovich, 1974.

Jackson, D. J., & Huston, T. L. Physical attractiveness and assertiveness. *Journal of Social Psychology,* 1975, *96,* 79–84.

Jones, M. C., & Bayley, N. Physical maturing among boys as related to behavior. *Journal of Educational Psychology,* 1950, *41,* 129–148.

Jones, S. J., & Moss, H. A. Age, state, and maternal behavior associated with infant vocalizations. *Child Development,* 1971, *42,* 1039–1051.

Kuo, Z. Y. *The dynamics of behavior development,* New York: Random House, 1967.

Lerner, R. M. *Concepts and theories of human development.* Reading, Massachusetts: Addison-Wesley, 1976.

Lerner, R. M. Nature, nurture, and dynamic interactionism. *Human Development,* 1978, *21,* 1–20.

Lerner, R. M., Iwawaki, S., & Chihara, T. Development of personal space schemata among Japanese children. *Developmental Psychology,* 1976, *12,* 466–467.

Lerner, R. M., Karabenick, S. A., & Meisels, M. Effects of age and sex on the development of personal space schemata towards body build. *Journal of Genetic Psychology,* 1975, *127,* 91–101.

Lerner, R. M., & Korn, S. J. The development of body build stereotypes in males. *Child Development,* 1972, *43,* 912–920.

Lerner, R. M., & Lerner, J. V. Effects of age, sex and physical attractiveness on child-peer relations, academic performance, and elementary school adjustment. *Developmental Psychology,* 1977, *13,* 585–590.

Lerner, R. M., & Spanier, G. B. A dynamic interactional view of child and family development. In R. M. Lerner & G. B. Spanier (Eds.), *Child influences on marital and family interaction: A life-span perspective.* New York: Academic Press, 1978.

Lerner, R. M., Venning, J., & Knapp, J. R. Age and sex effects on personal space schemata towards body build in late childhood. *Developmental Psychology,* 1975, *11,* 855–856.

Levinger, G., & Snoek, J. D. *Attraction in relationship: A new look at interpersonal attraction.* New York: General Learning Press, 1972.

Lewis, M. State as an infant–environment interaction: An analysis of mother–infant behavior as a function of sex. *Merrill-Palmer Quarterly,* 1972, *18,* 95–121.

Lewis, M., & Lee-Painter, S. An interactional approach to the mother-infant dyad. In M. Lewis & L. A. Rosenblum (Eds.), *The effect of the infant on its caregiver.* New York: Wiley, 1974.

Lewis, M., & Rosenblum, L. A. (Eds.), *The effect of the infant on its caregiver.* New York: Wiley, 1974.

Lewis, M., & Wilson, C. D. Infant development in lower class American families. *Human Development,* 1972, *15,* 112–127.

Looft, W. R. Socialization and personality throughout the life span: An examination of contemporary psychological approaches. In P. B. Baltes & K. W. Schaie (Eds.), *Life-span developmental psychology: Personality and Socialization.* New York: Academic Press, 1973.

McCandless, B. R. *Adolescents: Behavior and development.* Hinsdale, Illinois: Dryden, 1970.

Mussen, P. H., & Bouterline-Young, H. Relationships between rate of physical maturing and personality among boys of Italian descent. *Vita Humana,* 1964, *7,* 186–200.

Mussen, P. H., & Jones, M. C. Self-conceptions, motivations, and interpersonal attitudes of late- and early-maturing boys. *Child Development,* 1957, *28,* 242–256.

Nesselroade, J. R., & Reese, H. W. (Eds.), *Life-span developmental psychology: Methodological issues.* New York: Academic Press, 1973.

Nesselroade, J. R., & Baltes, P. B. Adolescent personality development and historical change: 1970–1972. *Monographs of the Society for Research in Child Development,* 1974, *39*(1).

Overton, W. F., & Reese, H. W. Models of development: Methodological implications. In J. R. Nesselroade & H. W. Reese (Eds.), *Life-span developmental psychology: Methodological issues.* New York: Academic Press, 1973.

Pepper, S. C. *World hypotheses: A study in evidence.* Berkeley: Univ. of California Press, 1942.

Reese, H. W., & Overton, W. F. Models of development and theories of development. In L. R. Goulet & P. B. Baltes (Eds.), *Life-span developmental psychology: Research and theory.* New York: Academic Press, 1970.

Riegel, K. F. The influence of economic and political ideology upon the development of developmental psychology. *Psychological Bulletin,* 1972, *78,* 129–141. (a)

Riegel, K. F. On the dialectics of cognitive changes during the life span. Paper presented at the Ninth International Congress of Gerontology, Kiev, U.S.S.R., July, 1972. (b)

Riegel, K. F. Time and change in the development of the individual and society. In H. W. Reese (Ed.), *Advances in child development and behavior. Volume 7.* New York: Academic Press, 1972. (c)

Riegel, K. F. Toward a dialectical theory of development. *Human Development,* 1975, *18,* 50–64.

Riegel, K. F. The dialectics of human development. *American Psychologist,* 1976, *31,* 689–700.

Rheingold, H. A. The social and socializing infant. In D. A. Goslin (Ed.), *Handbook of socialization theory and research.* Chicago: Rand McNally, 1969.

Robson, K. S., & Moss, H. A. Patterns and determinants of maternal attachment. *Journal of Pediatrics,* 1970, *77,* 976–985.

Sameroff, A. Transactional models in early social relations. *Human Development.* 1975, *18,* 65–79.

Sarason, S. B. Jewishness, blackishness, and the nature–nurture controversy. *American Psychologist,* 1973, *28,* 962–971.

Schneirla, T. C. The concept of development in comparative psychology. In D. B. Harris (Ed.), *The concept of development.* Minneapolis: Univ. of Minnesota Press, 1957.

Schneirla, T. C. Aspects of stimulation and organization in approach/withdrawal processes underlying vertebrate behavioral development. In D. S. Lehrman, R. Hinde, & E. Shaw (Eds.), *Advances in the study of behavior.* New York: Academic Press, 1965.

Stein, A. H., & Friedrich, L. K. Impact of television on children and youth. In E. M. Hetherington (Ed.), *Review of Child Development Research. Volume 5.* Chicago: Univ. of Chicago Press, 1975.

Spanier, G. B. Measuring dyadic adjustment: New scales for assessing the quality of marriage and similar dyads. *Journal of Marriage and the Family,* 1976, *38,* 15–28.

Thibaut, J. W., & Kelly, H. H. *The Social Psychology of Groups.* New York: Wiley, 1961.

Thomas, A., Chess, S., & Birch, H. G. The origin of personality. *Scientific American,* 1970, *223,* 102–109.

Thomas, C., Chess, S., Birch, H. G., Hertzig, M., & Korn, S. J. *Behavioral individuality in early childhood.* New York: New York Univ. Press, 1963.

Tobach, E., & Schneirla, T. C. The biopsychology of social behavior of animals. In R. E. Cooke & S. Levin (Eds.), *Biologic basis of Pediatric Practice.* New York: McGraw-Hill, 1968.

Watson, J. S. The development and generalization of "contingency awareness" in early infancy: Some hypotheses. *Merrill-Palmer Quarterly,* 1966, *12,* 123–135.

Werner, H. The concept of development from a comparative and organismic point of view. In D. B. Harris (Ed.), *The concept of development.* Minneapolis: Univ. of Minnesota Press, 1957.

Wolff, P. H. *The causes, controls, and organization of behavior in the neonate.* New York: International Universities Press, 1966.

11

Sexual Involvement and Relationship Development: A Cognitive Developmental Approach

JUDITH FRANKEL D'AUGELLI
ANTHONY R. D'AUGELLI

I. Introduction

In their book, *Is Sex Necessary?*, James Thurber and E. B. White (1929) discuss what was once termed "the battle of the sexes" in circa-1920 fashion. Yet many of their observations still ring true. Not only does sex remain necessary, its role in relationship development remains important. Thurber and White describe the following episode:

[A young man] has been sitting, we'll say, on a porch with his beloved. They have been talking of this and that, with the quiet intimacy of lovers. After a bit he takes her in his arms and kisses her—not once, but several times. It is not a new experience to him; he has had other girls, and he has had plenty of other kisses from this one. This time, however, something happens. The young man, instead of losing himself in the kiss, finds himself in it. What's more, the girl to him loses her identity—she becomes just anyone on whom he is imposing his masculinity. Instead of his soul being full of the ecstacy which is traditionally associated with love's expression, his soul is just fiddling around. The young man is thinking to himself:

"Say, this is pretty nice now!"

Well, that scares him. Up to this point in the affair he has been satisfied that his feeling was that of love. Now he doesn't know what to think. In all his life he has never come across a character in a book or a movie who, embracing his beloved, was heard to say, "This is pretty nice," unless that character was a villain. He becomes a

SOCIAL EXCHANGE IN DEVELOPING RELATIONSHIPS

mass of conflicting emotions, and is so thoroughly skeptical and worried about the
state of his heart that he will probably take to reading sociological books to find out
if it's O.K. to go ahead, or whether, as a gentleman, it's his duty to step out before he
further defames a sweet girl and soils her womanhood [pp. 75–76].

This highlights two aspects of sexual behavior (and we can define
this embrace as such) that social scientists sometimes forget: that sexual
behavior *occurs between two people,* and that it has *meanings* for both
involved. Furthermore, the consequences of sexual interaction for the
relationship between the partners differ depending upon the meanings
they attach to the interaction. An understanding of the event Thurber and
White describe could well begin with a scrutiny of distal sociocultural
norms, but the proximal interpersonal environment in which the behavior
occurs would likely be more informative. The reasons for this include the
specific relevance and richness of the proximal relationship for analyzing
how individuals and couples come to define and attribute meaning to
interpersonal issues and events, including sexual ones. While the influence of the larger cultural context on any individual's thinking and
behavior cannot be denied, it must be remembered that cultures are not
homogeneous and that individual variants on complex cultural themes
are of the greatest importance in understanding individual differences.

A comprehensive understanding of sexual involvement and relationship development must address three sets of proximal variables: person
variables, interaction variables, and relationship variables. *Person variables* include each interactant's cognitions, emotions, and behaviors. For
example, moral reasoning is a cognitive variable; sex guilt is an emotional
variable; and, prior sex experience is a behavioral variable. *Interaction
variables* are those which characterize the interpersonal transactions
which take place between partners. The key interactive factors in any
relationship can be described in terms of dominance–submission and
affection–hostility dimensions (Foa, 1961; Foa & Foa, 1974; Leary, 1957;
Schaefer, 1965). Finally, *relationship variables* involve patterns, goals,
and meanings of interactions to the couple over the life of the relationship. One example might be increasing mutuality of self-disclosure over
the course of a set of sexual interactions. Each person (A and B) brings
person variables (cognitions, affect, and behavior) to a dyadic interaction.
The nature of the interaction, described by interaction variables, results in
further contact or termination. Later interactions are a joint function of A
and B's person variables and a new factor, their interaction history. (Note
that some person variables may change as a result of interaction while
others remain constant. A clear example is an individual who has had his
or her first sexual experience. This person will enter a subsequent interaction with different behavioral skills, though other personal traits may be
unaltered.) The relationship between A and B consists of the accumulated

interactions of the past, present interactions, and any anticipated (planned or fantasized) interactions.

At present, the literature on sexual involvement concentrates on person variables often of a distal nature, such as religion and socioeconomic status. There is surprisingly little direct study of the relationship between different person variables and sexual behavior. There is even less empirical work on the vicissitudes of interaction over time or on relationship variables related to sexual behavior. This chapter has as its purpose the articulation of one approach to sexual involvement linking person, interaction, and relationship variables. The conceptualization of the relationship between the interactive context of sexual behavior and its meaning for each person and for their relationship is the critical problem: Does, as Masters and Johnson (1975) assert, the sexual relationship mirror the interpersonal relationship? This, indeed, exemplifies the more generic problem of relating social behavior to social relationships. We are in general agreement with Harré and Second (1972) who argue that a mechanistic model has severe limitations in the area of social behavior since *meanings* are crucial to understanding interpersonal phenomena. We will attempt to make the case that social behavior and social relationships can be linked heuristically using a cognitive–developmental framework that delineates qualitative individual differences in the processes by which personal and interpersonal meaning are ascribed to social behavior. Although we will start with a discussion of sexual behavior, we end by suggesting that a broader focus, on relationship development, is a profitable avenue for the future.

II. Person Variables Influencing Sexual Involvement

What propels, impels, or simply allows an individual to engage in each progressively more intimate sexual activity? What person, interaction, or relationship variables are associated with graduation from willingness to engage in necking—lip kissing and tongue kissing, as well as hugs and caresses—in premarital sexual relationships to willingness to engage in light petting: allowing the caressing of clothed and unclothed chest or breasts? Or, in marital relationships, what frees the individual and couple to use coital positions other than the "missionary position" or, if they have not yet done so, to engage in oral–genital activities? Extramarital sexual relationships are subject to similar issues: What factors govern a married person's willingness to engage in increasingly intimate sexual activities with someone other than his or her spouse? What influences the timing of progressive involvement? Do people who have at least engaged in marital coital experiences, if not premarital, more readily agree to intercourse in extramarital or postmarital relationships? Several factors—prior sexual experience, sex guilt, and level of affection—are reviewed to address these questions.

A. Prior Sex Experience

Alice Roosevelt Longworth's experience, related in Fleming and Fleming (1975), is probably exceptional: "I hadn't kissed anyone when I got married, heavens to God, no. Nor afterwards either. I always thought it was a revolting habit [p. 182]!" More common is the progression recalled by Clifford Irving (in Fleming & Fleming, 1975):

> I was taking girls out from the age of twelve onward. After a couple of times there would generally be a kiss at the door. When I was thirteen or fourteen I began kissing girls on the lips, generally closed-mouth kisses. A French kiss was a big thing. You were on your way then. And in New York City, at least, we had this shorthand which we used to describe sexual progress. If you could kiss her, that was a single. If you could feel her breasts, that was a double [p. 107].[1]

Progressive sexual experience seems to occur in a predictable sequence over an individual's sexual history. On this basis, sex researchers such as Brady and Levitt (1965), Bentler (1968a,b) and Curran, Neff, and Lippold (1973) have been able to derive and confirm empirically Guttmanized sexual experience scales. It is rare, for example, to find that a woman has engaged in caressing male genitalia without having first engaged in lip kissing, tongue kissing, having her clothed breasts caressed, having her unclothed breasts caressed, having her genitals caressed, and having her breasts orally caressed. The sequence is slightly different for men.

In addition to predictable sequentiality, prior sex experience correlates directly with subsequent sexual attitudinal and behavioral permissiveness. The more sexually experienced the individual, the more liberal are standards both for self (Reiss, 1967) and, even more, for others (D'Augelli, 1971). Increasing behavioral intimacy appears to be facilitated by prior sexual experience to a similar but lesser degree: Generally, the greater the sexual experience prior to the current relationship, the more willing the individual to engage in behaviors of high intimacy (D'Augelli, 1971, 1972; D'Augelli & Cross, 1975; Mosher & Cross, 1971; Nichols,

---

[1] This quote and the ones on pages 316, 317, and 318 are from *The First Time*. Copyright © 1975 by Karl Fleming and Anne Taylor Fleming. Reprinted by permission of Simon & Schuster, a Division of Gulf & Western Corporation.

1970). Prior sex experience, then, has a disinhibiting effect on sexual intimacy in later relationships.

Interaction between prior sex experience and relationship factors is suggested by data by Peplau, Rubin, and Hill (1977) with respect to coitus. In a 2-year study of dating couples from four colleges, they found that the prior experience of *both* partners affects sexual behavior in the current relationship. When both partners were sexually experienced— that is, had earlier engaged in intercourse—the overwhelming majority (94%) of the couples had intercourse together during the 2-year span of the study. However, when both were virgins only half of the couples (50%) had intercourse within that relationship. Most interesting were findings regarding relationships in which only one partner had previously had intercourse. When the female was experienced, all couples began to engage in intercourse at some point in their relationship over the 2 years; male virgins, in this study, apparently could not resist sexual opportunities provided by their experienced partners. However, in those couples in which the male had previously engaged in intercourse, only two-thirds of the couples began to have intercourse. Thus, while prior sex experience is related to progressive sexual involvement, a two-person focus seems necessary for meaningful prediction.

B. Sex-Guilt

Gagnon and Simon (1970) suggest that learning about sex in our society means learning about guilt; sexual development may be said to involve learning how to manage one's guilt. Sex guilt is conceptualized by Mosher (1965, 1968) to be a dispositional variable which exerts restraining effects on sexual behavior and attitudes. According to Mosher (1965), higher sex guilt may lead the individual to inhibit sexual expression. It has been demonstrated that sex guilt is negatively related to the level of intimacy of a person's premarital sexual activities (D'Augelli, 1971, 1972; Mosher & Cross, 1971; Nichols, 1970). If individuals high in sex guilt engage in behaviors beyond their personal boundary, they experience guilt feelings. Those with lower sex guilt are less likely to experience feelings of guilt over behaviors beyond their standard. Findings by other investigators who inquired about guilty feelings in relation to sexual activities support this (Bell & Blumberg, 1960; Christensen & Carpenter, 1962; Ehrmann, 1959; Kinsey, Pomeroy, & Martin, 1948; Kinsey, Pomeroy, Martin, & Gebhard, 1953; Kirkendall, 1961; Reiss, 1967). Reiss' (1967) data suggest that those most prone to guilt are least likely to engage in intimate sexual transactions, though once engaged in, few are likely to stop because of guilt feelings. Of those he studied, significantly more reported growing to accept the originally guilt-producing behavior than those who ceased such behavior. Bell and Blumberg's (1961) findings indicate similar percentages of women reporting guilt about petting but doing so despite their feelings (25%) and those reporting regret about not being more intimate (20%). In their sample, 41% felt some guilt at intercourse, but said that it was not a sufficient deterrent.

Sex guilt, a person variable, has been found to interact with relationship variables. Indications of this are seen in Ehrmann's (1959) early study of premarital sexual behavior. Inquiry about remembered guilt feelings yielded different responses depending upon the depth of the relationship in which the particular sexual activities took place. Despite not wanting greater intimacy, a majority of women (86%) accepted their partner's urging, especially with friends. Acceptance of such urging was less frequent with loved ones, and least with acquaintances. Men were less often coerced than women, but some women indeed initiated sexual advances toward greater intimacy. Reasons for submission to partner's urging included force, especially with acquaintances, and the desire to please, especially with loved ones. Ehrmann's findings are, of course, dated.

D'Augelli's (1971, 1972) findings offer more recent, though less direct, support for the influence of relationship status on willingness to engage in increasingly intimate sexual activities. Asked about specific sexual experiences with unloved and loved partners, participants in the studies reported significantly less intimate experiences with unloved partners, whereas experiences of increasing intimacy occurred with loved partners, especially in the present. Reasons for noninvolvement with unloved partners varied, but tended to cluster around "moral issues" and "no desire." Reasons for noninvolvement with loved partners included "feared loss of respect" and "fear of pregnancy" as well as "moral issues."

In studies some years ago, men seemed to experience greater guilt the more the relationship meant to them (Kirkendall, 1961), particularly if they held the double standard (Ehrmann, 1959). Concomitantly, men were found to be less willing to engage in very intimate sexual behavior within a formalized relationship, such as engagement. Of those who did so, however, fewer experienced guilt than those who had intercourse within a less formalized relationship of strong emotional attachment (Kirkendall, 1961). More recent studies suggest that this double standard is less prevalent today (D'Augelli, 1972; Komarovsky, 1976). Sex, particularly intercourse, appears increasingly frowned upon in relationships considered inauthentic. The men who participated in Komarovsky's (1976) study were more likely to experience guilt in relationships of lesser value to them than in important, emotionally intimate relationships. Moreover, forcing sex on the woman was generally disdained and guilt-producing. Indeed, the men reported that it was meritorious in their peer groups to turn down opportunities for coitus in less meaningful relationships. Said one, "One comes away with assorted shame, worries. . . . Sleeping around is, after all, a kind of lackluster mutual masturbation [Komarovsky, 1976, p. 62]."

Thus, guilt about sexual involvement is widely experienced but varies in intensity and behavioral impact depending, in particular, on prior experience, personal standards, and relationship quality. Guilt feelings about progressive intimacy are becoming less prevalent in meaningful relationships. Contributing to this is an increase in egalitarianism in sexual standards and in attitudes regarding relationships. Such a change is an example of the effect of broad cultural changes on the proximal environment of the couple.

C. Level of Affection

Meaningfulness of relationships is to some degree externally recognizable by public labels: casual dating, going steady, informal engagement, engagement, cohabitation. There once existed a rule of thumb that socially approved sexual progression was necking with a casual date, light petting with a steady, and heavy petting or even intercourse with a financé(e). Seriousness of sexual involvement assessed via such indicators is indeed correlated with extent of sexual involvement (D'Augelli, 1971). However, currently a more powerful variable may be level of affection. While the socially approved level of sexual intimacy covaries to some extent with relationship status, the public status of a relationship seems to have fewer implications for permitted depth of sexual involvement than does felt affection, emotional commitment, and partner consensus about intimacy.

Ehrmann (1959) found a clear relationship between affection and premarital sexual behavior. Degree of affection was viewed in terms of perceived relationship intimacy, defined as *relationships of no intimacy (acquaintances)*, of *moderate intimacy (friends)*, or of *high intimacy (lovers)*. The more intimate the relationship, the more permissive were the attitude and the behavior, the more willingly was the behavior engaged in, and the more pleasure was reported to have been experienced. Affection for partner was a critical factor in engaging in and enjoying sexual intimacies. Reiss's (1967) important work demonstrates the shifting standard regulating sexual behavior in the direction of increased emphasis on relationship considerations and on egalitarianism. D'Augelli (1971, 1972) reconfirmed the general association found by Ehrmann (1959) between level of affection and willingness to engage in increasingly intimate sexual behaviors.

D'Augelli (1971, 1972; D'Augelli & Cross, 1975) found that the relationship standards implicit in an individual's sexual philosophy were highly associated with personal limits on sexual intimacy (this will be discussed in detail later in the chapter). Recent data (Peplau, Rubin, & Hill, 1977) further suggest that sexual intimacy and emotional intimacy are importantly linked, especially for women. Patterns varied, however, among three groups labeled *traditional*, *moderate*, and *liberal*, in terms of their premarital sexual permissiveness. Traditionals permitted limited sexual intimacy in the context of evolving emotional intimacy; intercourse was not sanctioned except within the bounds of a permanent commitment. For moderates, sexual intimacy paralleled emotional intimacy. Sexual exploration and pleasure became possible as the relationship deepened. Sexual intimacy did not require emotional intimacy for liberals. Partners could enjoy sexual intimacy without necessarily feeling affection, although they indeed may. The investigators found that first intercourse for moderates occurred an average of six months after they defined themselves as "going together." Liberals, on the other hand, reported having first intercourse in a particular relationship an average of one month prior to defining themselves as "going together." For those with liberal premarital sexual standards, then, sexual intimacy may facilitate the development of emotional intimacy and emotional commitment. It may be that the actual level of emotional intimacy is similar for liberals and moderates at the time of first intercourse, but that the need for expressed emotional commitment differs. This interpretation is supported by the data of D'Augelli (1971, 1972) in samples roughly comparable to those of Peplau, Rubin, and Hill. In any case, one generalization from these data is that moderates and liberals are less concerned with prohibitions of sexual actions in their formulation of sexual standards than are traditionals. For those with traditional standards, the avoidance of premarital intercourse is of central concern regardless of the meaning of the relationship.

As Kirkendall and Libby (1966) note, a shift is in process from act-centered moral concerns to person- and relationship-centered moral concerns. The data of Reiss (1960, 1966, 1967) and others (D'Augelli, 1971, 1972; D'Augelli & Cross, 1975; Hunt, 1974; Kirkendall, 1961; Kirkendall & Libby, 1966) suggest that the crux of the "sexual revolution," as it is termed, is the emphasis on the interpersonal relationship between partners rather than on sexual acts. Reiss' data in particular demonstrate a movement away from the traditional double standard to a more egalitarian standard, with degree of affection or partner agreement as the central issue in sexual decision-making within relationships.

In summary, it is clear that person variables such as sex guilt, prior sex experience, and level of affection do influence sexual conduct. Yet, it is also evident that these variables are becoming less important in regulating progressive sexual involvement while relationship issues are becoming increasingly important. That is, relationship issues are coming into focus as significant factors in understanding sexual conduct, achieving prominence in reported personal standards as well as in scientific investigation. It is necessary to analyze the roles of person variables in conjunction with relationship (and interaction) variables in regulating sexual involvement rather than simply to assess any one set of variables in isolation.

The critical factor in sexual intimacy seems to be the individual's present context, particularly the present relationship, whether it be premarital (D'Augelli & Cross, 1975; Komarovsky, 1976; Spanier, 1976), marital (Edwards & Booth, 1976; Hunt, 1974) or postmarital (Hunt, 1974). Indeed, the presence of an emotionally committed partner-in-relationship is an important factor in engaging in and enjoying sex in old age (Pfeiffer & Davis, 1972). Hunt characterizes the currently predominant cluster of sexual ethics as "liberal-romantic" rather than "radical-recreational." That is, relationship issues are the crucial issues for progressive sexual involvement—affection, emotional commitment, social and personal identity as a couple, and other relationship-relevant variables. Sex is primarily a social behavior, and progressive sexual involvement is to a large extent contingent upon relationship development. Sexual exchange in social relationships is one way of conceptualizing the relationship development process.

III. Relationship Variables: Sex and Social Exchange

There is surprisingly little discussion of sex in the literature on social exchange. The index to Homans's revised edition of his classic on social exchange (1974) contains no reference to sexual behavior. Yet sexual behaviors are social behaviors indeed, and they may be viewed in exchange terms. As Scanzoni notes in Chapter 3 of this volume, sex is an interpersonal resource that most people can supply and most desire to receive.

Sexual social behaviors are deceptively simple in character. Although particular sexual behaviors may be fairly easily observed and described, the social and interpersonal contexts in which they occur serve to complicate and define in idiosyncratic ways the meanings of those behaviors. For example, Altman and Taylor (1973), using a social-exchange framework, argue that three broad factors are involved in relationship development: the personal characteristics of participants (person variables), the outcomes of exchange, and the situational context. The same sexual act can be given different meanings by these factors. Individuals differing in affectional needs will interpret intercourse in different ways (personal characteristics); those who feel valued by their sexual partner are likely to maintain the relationship (outcomes of exchange); and partners who freely engage in sexual activity will evaluate it differently from those who are forced to participate (situational context). In its simplest form, social exchange theory would view any sexual behavior in respect to its costs and profits. One woman clearly conveyed this notion to Masters and Johnson (1975): "I feel used, but I also feel that I'm doing my duty. He supports me and the children, and if this is what he wants, that's what I do [p. 45]." Enduring indifferent, if not poor, sexual intercourse was her acknowledged cost for the gain of being supported. Given the relationship context of sexual behavior, another way of defining the situational context, an analysis of the outcomes of exchange would necessarily have to deal with the different reward value (profit) of sexual behavior at different phases of relationship development.

One source of difficulty in empirically examining this issue has been the lack of a framework for viewing relationship development. Levinger (Levinger, 1974; Levinger & Snoek, 1972) and, more recently, Scanzoni (in Chapter 3 of this volume) have been among the few to hypothesize about differing sexual involvements within the framework of relationship development. The models are similar.

A. Levels of Relatedness

Levinger and Snoek (1972) identify three levels of relatedness through which relationships evolve: unilateral awareness, surface contact, and mutuality. Scanzoni also identifies three levels, or stages, in relationship development: exploration, consolidation, and commitment. Sexual attraction may occur at any level of relatedness.

In the Levinger and Snoek model, at the first or the unilateral awareness level the other is known only in terms of external characteristics: Impressions and inferences form the basis for predicting possible rewards that might accrue from further interaction. Inferred reward potential is critical. In terms of sexuality, Levinger and Snoek suggest that self-centered fantasies would predominate. To illustrate, consider this recollection (in Fleming & Fleming, 1975):

> I was walking down the steps at school one day and this beautiful blond boy . . . stepped out into the courtyard and the sun came out at that moment on his head, and I remember stumbling down the steps and saying, "Who is that?" He didn't know it, but he got laid right then and there. I just felt there was Adonis. That was the one, whether he wanted to go along with it or not. I was ready [p. 213].

At the surface contact level, interactions proceed largely by role performances in which relatively little unique personal information is exchanged. When sexual attraction exists and if sexual activities are engaged in at this level, the individual's personal profit-seeking would dominate the interchange. Again, consider the example above. The girl set about pursuing her Adonis that very day, discovering information about his family, his school life, his girls, and so on. She used the information in two ways: first to attract him by changing her image—her hair style, clothes, and even social affiliations—and, second, to plan a "chance" meeting. It took him a week to ask her out, to a football game that she detested going to: "On the way home we necked—no touching, no French kissing. But when he kissed me I knew the initial lustful look I had gotten was right on [p. 214]." Five months later, after slowly working through the series of progressively intimate sexual exchanges, they finally had intercourse: "I remember his saying, 'Are you sure?' I said, 'For godsake, I'm sure.'" She asserts that she had caught him offguard and was able to propel him and herself toward intercourse as she had planned from the first.

Finally, relationships at the mutuality level are characterized by shared knowledge and awareness. The partners assume mutual responsibility for the quality of the relationship and for the quality of the other's experience in the relationship. At this level, communication about and alertness to the partner's desired outcomes occur. Sexual involvement in relationships at the mutuality level is characterized by a we-centered viewpoint. Levinger and Snoek (1972) suggest that the more mutual and committed the relationship, the greater the partner's awareness of the mutual significance of the other's feelings. The woman's relationship with Adonis continued for some time, apparently becoming somewhat more mutual with improvement in their sexual transactions. Indeed, they decided to get married. They were not truly sexually compatible, however, for she required more frequent and intensive sexuality than did he; he felt she made extreme demands on his sexual energy. Furthermore, he wanted her to quit acting in order to support him through school. Given these conflicts, she ultimately decided that the relationship would not work out.

B. Relationship Stages

Scanzoni (see Chapter 3 of this volume) considers three stages necessary to understanding relationship involvement and solidarity: exploration, consolidation, and commitment. The exploration stage of relationship development is, like the awareness and surface-contact levels, said to be individualistic. Scanzoni suggests that utilitarian bargaining for personal rewards marks this stage. No sense of dyadic interest has yet been developed. Scanzoni notes that it is possible that sex *may* be the only interest sphere shared by partners in an exploratory relationship. The experiences of the woman mentioned above provide another illustration, a very concrete one indeed. The same woman recalls having a crush on a boy at age 8 and peering down at him in the boy's partition of the bathroom. He later followed her to the bathroom and told her he would like to see her with her dress off: "I've seen other girls in their slips and nothing will happen and if you let me see you we'll go steady [Fleming & Fleming, 1975, p. 209]." The exchange in this very early exploratory relationship is clear; indeed, they did go steady for several months. Sexual progression in this relationship, however, went no further than kissing.

Scanzoni doubts, however, that such purely sex-based exploratory relationships are generally established. Rather, he asserts that sex (especially sexual intercourse) is more likely to be exchanged in the consolidation stage of relationships. Expansion and linkage of shared interest spheres are the keynotes of this stage. Decision-making about the relationship itself is implied, and decision-making processes become more complex. Attraction, mutual reciprocity, rectitude regarding relationship norms and generalizable "deals" from one interest sphere to another mark this stage. Sex may be one of the new common-interest spheres, usually preceded by additional ones. One man's experiences as a teenager demonstrate the sharing of several interest spheres, including sexual activity:

> I was a virgin until I was eighteen. . . . I had one important steady girlfriend between the ages of eleven and eighteen—all through high school. The kind of relationship we had consisted of going to the movies, hours and hours on the telephone and going for long walks. Occasionally we would walk from Brighton Beach, hand in hand, to her house in Crown's Point. Every now and then we would stop and neck. I was a very romantic kid. . . . She was the first important girl in my life [Fleming & Fleming, 1975, p. 68].

The commitment stage is characterized by an essential solidarity in the relationship, accompanied by behavioral and emotional interdependence. Furthermore, a consistency of relational inputs over time is observed and expected. A critical element in developing commitment is what Scanzoni terms the "maximum-joint-profit process." This process involves negotiation to promote common interests rather than individual advantage. It carries with it reciprocation as felt obligation, which accrues the more one observes the partner engaging in mutuality. Last, trust is involved, trust that the partner will provide desired inputs to the relationship and will not harm the relationship or the individual partner. Both these processes—maximum joint process and trust—consolidate commitment in a relationship, according to Scanzoni (similar analyses are offered by Huesmann & Levinger, 1976 and by Huston & Cate, 1977.)

Sex as exchange in such relationships is characterized by mutuality and agreement on terms. One 48-year-old paintshop foreman implicitly expressed these aspects of a committed relationship and sexual exchanges within a committed relationship:

> I wasn't planning ever to marry again, but then I met a girl I liked, and *more* than liked. After a while I realized she was someone I hadn't thought existed anywhere. I didn't feel the least fear of getting totally wrapped up in her, *and she felt the same about me.* Our sex was just fine—about as good as any I'd been having—but it was *only part of the whole magoo*—and we both knew after a few months that we just had to be married to each other. It's still a big thing in our lives, and yet *not* a big thing, in a way—I mean, it's not what we're thinking about, or planning or working on all the time, it's just there, part of us, like breathing and sleeping [Hunt, 1974, p. 253; italics added].

Sexual exploitation of one partner is unlikely, since it would decrease maximum joint profit, particularly because the exchange rules at the commitment stage generally preclude advantages to one partner at the cost of the other.

C. From Egocentrism to Reciprocity

Thus, transitional development in relationships, including sexuality, is thought to move from egocentric fantasies of self-gratification to reciprocal exchanges and concern with rewards not only satisfying to the individual but also supportive of the relationship. Indeed, the ultimate relationship reward may eventually become a satisfying relationship, "a common property to be enjoyed, protected, and enhanced [Levinger & Snoek, 1972, p. 14]." We conceptually integrate the relationship progression models of Levinger and Snoek (1972) and Scanzoni (see Chapter 3 of this volume). Thus, we view relationship development as logically evolving in the following fashion: from no contact to awareness to surface contact to exploration to consolidation to commitment to mutality.

Levinger and Snoek and Scanzoni argue that the exchange of intimate sexual activity is least likely early in relationships. However, when sexual behavior occurs early, it is, they assert, oriented to self-reward. Engaging in sex becomes more probable at some middle phase of progressive involvement, with bargaining still based on individual satisfaction but perhaps more related to relationship-role expectancies. Sexual exchanges in highly developed relationships are most likely characterized by reciprocity and concerns for the sexual satisfaction of the partner as well as those of the self. Sexual exchanges earlier in relationship involvement are more likely to entail some personal cost for each partner because of the predominantly individualistic attitudes and behaviors. Potential long-term gain is great *if* the relationship indeed progresses to commitment or mutuality.

Scanzoni notes that sex has the unique capability of generating high degrees of extensive interdependence quite suddenly and apart from other decision-making processes that contribute to solidarity and commitment. As a type of social behavior, sexual behavior is distinguished by its intense physical intimacy. This physical intimacy may promote feelings of emotional intimacy. According to Scanzoni, the resulting interdependence may initially be intimate but shallow. Hopes and expectations may be raised for consolidation or for further, extensive commitment that may or may not evolve. However, the advancement of the relationship to further stages may be spurred by the emotional intimacy associated with sexual intimacy. On the other hand, sexual involvement may be the result of relationship decision-making processes. For example, one woman explained her decision to have intercourse as follows:

> The relationship was very close but kind of unsteady. I wasn't sure I wanted to have intercourse. Then I realized that having intercourse was the most logical step for our relationship to go any place. If this basic idea is understood by both parties—the fit of sex in the relationship—then they can find other things in the relationship. Having intercourse has strengthened our relationship [quoted in D'Augelli, 1972].

The exchange process implicit in sexual involvement can be viewed on many levels, but perhaps the most significant is the exchange of overt and covert communications about the past, present, and future of the interpersonal relationship in which the sexual behavior is occurring. Progressive sexual involvement and progressive relationship involvement generally proceed simultaneously. Most often, this encompasses moral decision-making about allowable sexual intimacies given the nature of the relationship and personal sexual standards. It is our thesis that personal decision-making about sexual involvement within relationships is much influenced by the individual's moral reasoning and sexual philosophy as well as by sexual standards and guilt. Further, each person's moral orientation to relationships is involved, as reflected in personal relationship reasoning, a concept to be discussed later in the chapter. Lastly, the relationship reasoning of the partners together suggests limits for their decisions regarding sex in their relationships.

IV. Sexual Decision Making and Moral Reasoning

The study of the moral meaning of sexual involvement provides a clear example of the importance of personal and dyadic evaluation construals for interpersonal life. Sexual decision making entails an evaluation of a certain act against internalized moral standards. One method of examining the way individuals and couples reason and give meaning to sexual behavior is through a cognitive–development approach. Kohlberg's model of moral development (1958, 1963, 1969, 1971) provided a framework for three important studies in this area.

The Kohlberg model suggests that researchers focus less upon the content of sexual attitudes than upon the structure or process of reasoning underlying sexual morality. Kohlberg defines moral reasoning as a cognitive developmental variable characterized by emerging structural changes in the person's logic–value system. These changes occur as a function of the developing individual's interaction with the social environment. Kohlberg postulates three levels of moral reasoning—preconventional, conventional, and postconventional—and two stages within each level. Each stage is characterized by a type of thought distinguished by a qualitatively unique consistency of logic and values in judging moral dilemmas. On the basis of cross-cultural and longitudinal evidence, Kohlberg (1971) asserts that the stages represent an invariant universal development sequence. The developmental progression is from reasoning based on meeting egoistic needs with little role-taking and concrete reciprocity, through reasoning based on fulfillment of roles and others' expectations, toward reasoning based on the application of abstract principles to moral conflicts. Relativity of moral standards and reciprocity of social behavior are based on complex role taking and reflect values of trust and mutuality in social contracts. The stages are defined in Table 11.1. The way individuals reason about moral dilemmas typically is evaluated through structured interviews. An example of a dilemma concerning specifically sexual issues is the following:

> A high school girl's parents are away for the weekend and she's alone in the house. On Friday evening, her boyfriend unexpectedly comes over. They spend the evening together in the house and after a while they start necking and petting. (a) Is this right or wrong? Why? Are there any circumstances that would make it right? (Wrong?) (b) What if they had sexual intercourse? Is that right or wrong? Why? (c) Does the way they feel about each other make a difference in the rightness or wrongness of having sexual intercourse? Why? What if they are in love? What does love mean and what is its relation to sex?

Moral reasoning about sexual behavior—that is, judging what is right or good in sexual behavior—can be based on a variety of value sets: fulfilling personal wants, attaining approval for well-intentioned role-bound behavior, acting consistently with perceived social rules, or achieving consensual agreement between partners. Moral reasoning about sexual relationships usually involves the predominance of one of these sets.

The crucial point is that a moral or "right" decision for one individual or couple may be an immoral decision for another, depending on how they reason about it. Deciding to have premarital sex, for example,

TABLE 11.1
Moral-Reasoning Orientations[a]

Level I: Preconventional: Moral value resides in external, quasi-physical happenings, in bad acts, or in quasi-physical needs rather than in persons and standards.

  Stage 1: Obedience and Punishment: Egocentric deference to superior power or prestige, or a trouble-avoiding set. Objective responsibility.

  Stage 2: Instrumental Relativism: Right action is that which instrumentally satisfies the self's needs and occasionally others'. Awareness of relativism of value to each actor's needs and perspective. Naive egalitarianism and orientation to exchange and reciprocity.

Level II: Conventional: Moral value resides in performing good or right roles, and in maintaining the conventional order and the expectations of others.

  Stage 3: Personal Concordance: Good-boy, good-girl orientation. Orientation to approval and to pleasing and helping others. Conformity to stereotypical images of majority or natural role behavior, and judgment by intentions.

  Stage 4: Law and Order: Orientation to "doing duty" and to showing respect for authority and maintaining the given social order for its own sake. Regard for earned expectations of others.

Level III: Postconventional: Moral value resides in conformity of the self to shared or shareable standards, rights, or duties.

  Stage 5: Social Contract: Recognition of an arbitrary element or starting point in rules or expectations for the sake of agreement. Duty defined in terms of contract, general avoidance of violation of the will or rights of others, and majority will and welfare.

  Stage 5B (formerly 6): Universal Ethical Principles: Orientation not only to actually ordained social rules but to principles of choice involving appeal to logical universality and consistency. Orientation to conscience as a directing agent and to mutual respect and trust.

---

[a] Adapted from Kohlberg (1971, pp. 164–165). Reprinted with permission.

may be viewed as morally right to an individual reasoning at the instrumental-relativist stage (Stage 2) if he or she will get pleasure from it; whether the partner will get pleasure from it or not is not an issue, except insofar as the partner's displeasure may affect the individual's own experience. To an individual reasoning at the social-contract stage (Stage 5), having premarital sex may be viewed as morally wrong, even though pleasurable, if both partners do not agree that it should be an aspect of their sexual relationship. Greater maturity of moral judgment is reflected in the latter because the individual is basing the decision on the application of personal principles concerning contractual relationships.

Three studies have directly examined the role of moral reasoning in premarital sexual behavior: those of Jurich and Jurich (1974), D'Augelli (1971), and D'Augelli (1972).

A. Moral Reasoning and Sexual Standards

Jurich and Jurich (1974) investigated the association between moral reasoning and premarital standards in a sample of 180 unmarried undergraduates. In a personal interview, each individual was asked to describe his or her personal standard about premarital intercourse and to respond to four of Kohlberg's moral dilemmas, two general and two sexual. Personal sexual standards were classified into five categories: abstinence prior to marriage, double standard, permissiveness with affection, permissiveness without affection, and nonexploitive permissiveness without affection. The first four are Reiss's (1960), the last was coined by the Jurichs. In nonexploitive permissiveness without affection, the morally correct decision is based on the *couple's* agreement to pursue particular sexual behaviors without necessarily affirming love for each other. This is contrasted with permissiveness without affection by which standard sex is considered legitimate any time, under any circumstances—the issue of taking advantage or exploiting the partner is irrelevant or not considered. The Jurichs found moral maturity to be strongly associated with choice of sexual standard. They found the standards to be ordered, in terms of *decreasing* moral maturity, as follows: (a) nonexploitive permissiveness without affection, (b) permissiveness with affection, (c) double standard, (d) abstinence, and (e) permissiveness without affection. There were significant differences in cognitive moral development between those endorsing nonexploitive permissiveness and those endorsing permissiveness without affection. The former standard was related with the highest moral-maturity scores; the latter was related consistently with the lowest. Moral-maturity scores for permissiveness with affection were significantly higher than those for permissiveness without affection and significantly lower than those for nonexploitive permissiveness. The scores associated with abstinence and the double standard were not significantly higher than those associated with permissiveness without affection, but were significantly lower than those associated with nonexploitive permissiveness.

The Jurichs conclude that premarital standards differ in degree of logic and cognitive differentiation. Some standards are absolutistic, whereas others allow relativity of application. Those standards of greater relativism of perspective inherently demand greater role-taking and decision-making and in this study were associated with higher moral maturity.

B. Moral Reasoning and Individual Sexual Behavior

Judith Frankel D'Augelli (1971) studied the relationship between premarital sexual behavior and moral reasoning in college women. In addition to completing a measure of sex-guilt, an inventory of sexual behavior, and a moral-judgment interview, the women were categorized in terms of their "sexual philosophy," a variable that emerged from interviews. Sexual philosphy is a composite variable that taps an individual's articulated concept of his or her premarital sexuality based on sexual standards, expectations for relationships, and attitudes toward past and future sexual experiences. Six distinct sexual philosophies were identified. They are presented in Table 11.2.

The concept of sexual philosphy, though considered a personal rather than an interpersonal variable, involves a definite relationship orientation. As is evident in the descriptions of the six categories in Table 11.2, a critical aspect of sexual philosophy is the type of relationship within which the individual decides to engage in specific sexual behaviors manifesting his or her personal standard. Further, the concept includes reference to the preferred locus of sexual decision-making within the relationship, whether it be the couple, the partner, or the individual himself or herself.

The results of the study were as follows: Women who oriented at law-and-order reasoning (Stage 4) were significantly higher in sex guilt than those at other stages. Furthermore, these women were also significantly more likely to be virgins than those orienting at other stages. Law-and-order reasoning was thus associated with greater sex guilt and with virginity. It is reasonable to assume that women who judge moral-dilemma situations with regard to upholding perceived social rules used such reasoning as a foundation for their decision to refrain from intercourse. Their moral assessment of the issues is emotionally bolstered by their disposition to high sex guilt.

Adamant virgins most often oriented at the law-and-order stage. They also manifested high sex guilt. According to the interview data, they decided that they must obey the social sanction against premarital coitus. From interview material, it appears that their reasoning was based on the judgment that sexual intercourse was counter to prevailing social or religious rules. As their sexual philosophy suggests, relationship parameters were less important to them in decisions regarding sexual actions than the legal status of the relationship was. Sexual activities other than intercourse could be safely engaged in within the context of premarital relationships, but decisions regarding the extent of sexual involvement tended to revolve around social standards and religious values. As one woman said:

> Society's views on premarital sex are more liberal than they used to be but not drastically. I would place my own views within society's. I agree that intercourse should be saved for marriage as an expression of the vows, but I feel that petting should be allowed before marriage. I have been heavy petting with my boyfriend, but it's not conceivable to me that I would have intercourse before marriage.

TABLE 11.2
Sexual Philosophy Categories

1. *Inexperienced Virgins:* These usually have little dating experience until college. Their dating relationships have not been serious or involved. They have not thought much about sex, the kind of relationship they desire, or about themselves. They may be moralistic about sex, although not necessarily. They have a close relationship with their parents and do not want to hurt them. Their sexual experience has usually been kissing, necking, or light petting.

2. *Adamant Virgins:* These are set in their idea that intercourse should be saved for marriage: "Virginity is a gift for the spouse" is a predominant theme. However, they may say that premarital intercourse is permissible for others—it is up to the individual. They say that they do not feel guilty about light or heavy petting but that they would feel guilty about going further. They often attribute control to the partner and presently pet with someone special. They do not usually confine themselves to one partner. There is a sense that the marriage license is important in assuring that the partner is the "right" one. Their family or religion is often mentioned as directly influencing their sexual views.

3. *Potential Nonvirgins:* These often say that given the right situation they would have intercourse. They say that they have not yet been in the right situation or have not yet met the right person. They feel that premarital intercourse is morally acceptable, but they have a high fear of pregnancy. They seem to want more security than they have in their present relationships, at least at the point of development in the relationship, and the ideas of commitment and love are important to them. They seem frustrated by their cautiousness or inconsistency.

4. *Engaged Nonvirgins:* These have had intercourse with, usually, one person only, although not necessarily. This person is usually considered someone very much loved and may be the fiancé(e). Often, marriage or some future commitment is mentioned, but the important thing in justifying the sexual behavior is the partners' love and commitment to the relationship. The relationship is described as very close and very important, and the development of that relationship is of high value to them. They usually have discussed sex with their partner. Morality is considered an individual's personal concern.

5. *Liberated Nonvirgins:* These engage in sex in a freer way than do others. They have a freer, looser life style and are not interested in the security of the relationship as much as in the relationship itself. Sex within the context of the meaning of the relationship is important, and what is stressed is the agreed-upon meaning for the two partners. The physical act is valued for its pleasure. Reciprocal pleasure-giving as well as other reciprocities are important.

6. *Confused Nonvirgins:* These engage in sex without real understanding of their motivation, the place of sex in their lives, or its effects on them. There is usually some ambivalence about having had intercourse under these circumstances, especially if there have been many partners. The relationships between them and their partners gradually terminate. They seem generally confused about themselves and may be characterized as having a diffuse identity. Sex is seen as a pleasure and a need; it also seems to be the means to an end, an attempt to establish relationships.

Inexperienced virgins did not use one stage of moral reasoning predominantly more than others. In their interviews, however, they tended to focus on love as an important facet of a relationship in which they might become sexually involved:

> *I lightly petted with one guy because we're a little more than friends and we have fun when we go out together. I'd never get more involved with someone I didn't care about. For me, I must know I care, that I'm in love.*

Reflection on their relationships yielded recollections of uncertainty and concerns about getting hurt. Another woman whose most sexually intimate experience at age 19 had been light petting explained:

> *I liked him as a person, but we knew neither of us was ready to settle down. Maybe we're both in love—I'm unsure of what love is. I have standards but they kind of get messed up if I think I'm in love. They're rigid. I kind of hold myself aloof to avoid being hurt. I hold back from a relationship.*

No predominant stage orientation was found for *potential nonvirgins.* In discussing their sexual decision-making, they all allowed for the possibility of premarital intercourse under certain conditions. These included experiencing mutually deep love, becoming engaged, and deciding jointly with a partner to have intercourse. One subject, when asked how she went about making her decisions concerning her sexual standards, shared these thoughts:

> *The present more for my age group is that intercourse is morally okay in a meaningful relationship if there is mutual agreement. It is not okay if it will hurt either person. The older segment is not geared to delve into the psychological implications, the relationship. They're conditioned to the view that marriage comes first. My own views: I don't morally condemn intercourse before marriage. I think now it would be an upsetting experience for me, but it would be okay if I did it rationally, if I thought about it first. An affair wouldn't be wrong for me if I loved him and vice versa, and we didn't hurt each other . . . if we agreed.*

A small number of *engaged nonvirgins* oriented at law and order, stressing the formalistic aspects of their relationships, such as engagement, as considerations for their behavior:

> *We were almost engaged then. Intercourse before marriage is okay if you love each other and are going to be married. I think I'm moral. I try to do what's right.*

Most engaged nonvirgins, though, oriented at the social-contract or the personal-concordance stages of moral reasoning. Those who used social-contact reasoning stressed the application of principles of consensus in their relationships. For instance:

> We approached having intercourse mutually. We are very open with each other, as I believe you have to be, and we communicate well sexually. Earlier, I was preoccupied with the question of virginity, and where the rule to maintain it derived from. I concluded that it was a function of society and particularly the male double standard. No basis for it really, if the two people agree and they are in love. That is, for me personally. I wouldn't condemn others who sleep with guys they don't care for. I wouldn't, I don't think.

An emphasis on affection was seen in the discussions of engaged nonvirgins who used personal-concordance reasoning. Mutuality was defined in terms of the special role of lovers, with its attendant expectations and assumed reciprocities. One woman expressed it as follows:

> With my present boyfriend, I had intercourse because I decided it was okay if I was in love and he loved me. I came to a different decision than before because he is a special case. We both have respect for each other.

Liberated nonvirgins tended to use social-contract reasoning. Their emphasis was on reciprocal communication, trust, and mutual agreements, and expression of the importance to them of the quality of the relationship. Sex could be engaged in for physical pleasure or for its meaning for the relationship as long as the partners agreed on the nature of the relationship and on the role of sex within the relationship. For example:

> When I was old enough to understand, I decided not to remain a virgin. I decided to experience sex fulfillment and happiness without marriage. It was important to find someone who could satisfy me emotionally and I waited for a long time. We had a good emotional relationship, though our relationship was very physical too. We discussed having intercourse. I wanted to find out his thoughts about my decision and how he felt. We were complementary. And we were fulfilling what we both wanted. In my other relationships since, it's been important to me for the decision to be mutual as well. Discussing it openly is the only way.

Confused nonvirgins using predominately instrumental-relativist reasoning. Their explanations of their sexual relationships manifested a superficial sense of reciprocity based on what might be gained from the partner if they allowed intercourse. They appear to have been motivated to seek affection through sexual encounters, which their low sex guilt facilitated. Unfortunately, they rarely found warmth in their relationships and they tended to express resentment.

> *I've had intercourse with eight men. I'm feeling fairly stupid now—I have a bad reputation and I didn't even get what I was looking for. The relationships were not satisfying at all.*

Thus moral issues are quite important in decision making about sexual involvement. The ways in which individuals thought about such issues as affectional roles, social rules, personal fulfillment, and dyadic consensus differed depending on their moral-reasoning orientation and sexual philosophy.

C. Moral Reasoning and Couples' Sexual Behavior

The third study (D'Augelli, 1972) was an attempt to examine similar issues for *couples*. Focus on the couple as a unit *and* as individuals led to complex findings, and we will only highlight the results. For example, partners' sex guilt was found to be significantly correlated ($r = .39$, $p <$ .01), and male sex guilt found to be the most important variable predicting the couple's sexual experience. Male sex guilt was the best predictor of the couple's current sexual experience. Female sex guilt was the third most critical factor. The following interaction illustrates the meaning of this. In a conjoint interview, a couple stated:

> M: *We decided to pet—light petting I guess—because that's the usual pattern I follow and I enjoy sex. She doesn't, so I try not to do what she doesn't like. Though she didn't like light petting at first, she didn't mind it after we started. She's not afraid of everything as she used to be.*
> F: *I would like him to leave me alone more (sexually), but we do stop when I want to. I don't usually engage in sex except necking. Why we decided to pet I can't figure out! I don't mind now.*

The male partner, low in sex guilt, though concerned about the woman's feelings, was clearly responsible for shifts in their sexual intimacy. The woman, however, does seem to have had some effect on his attitudes toward their sexual intimacy and there is some sense of perceived agreement.

Another interesting finding was that the male's orientation to law-and-order reasoning was the second most critical variable predicting the couple's sexual experience. When both partners or just the male partner oriented at law and order, it was unlikely for the couple to have had intercourse. When the woman oriented at law and order, it was possible that she had had intercourse provided her partner oriented at other stages.

Sexual philosophy was found to relate to modal moral reasoning in ways generally consistent with the results of the earlier D'Augelli (1971) study. Quotes from the men will be cited in this section to illustrate these points. In this study, as earlier, women liberated nonvirgins were likely to be at the social-contract stage. Adamant virgins were more likely than those of other sexual philosophies to orient at law and order, as in the prior study, but in this study they oriented to the personal-concordance stage. The few female confused nonvirgins were oriented to Instrumental Relativism, as previously.

For males, as for females, results indicated that it was especially likely for adamant virgins to orient at law and order. One adamant virgin expressed his view as follows:

> Premarital intercourse is simply wrong. It should be saved for marriage—marriage is more than a piece of paper. Sex belongs in marriage, according to society.

Potential nonvirgin men generally oriented at the personal-concordance stage. For them, love in a mutual relationship tended to be emphasized. Reports of not having met the so-called "right person" were common.

> Sexual intercourse is not wrong. You need sexual outlets, expressions. It's natural. The important thing is that you are sincere and are emotionally tied to the person. If not, then it is wrong.

For some potential nonvirgins, their partner's wishes were the inhibitor:

> I was into heavy petting with her. She loved me and I was infatuated. I didn't go further because she didn't want to.

Liberated nonvirgins and engaged nonvirgins were more likely to orient at social contract. Liberated nonvirgins viewed sexual involvement as contributory to relationship involvement. Like the women in the earlier study, they stressed open discussion as vital to sexual decision making. One man said:

> Having sex can be part of building a relationship. The way people feel about each other makes a difference to me—they

*must be open and frank. If they both agree, then sex is right. I feel
that what I'm doing now is acceptable to my partner and me and
that's what counts.*

For engaged nonvirgins, the relationship was also primary. In the words
of one man:

*I now consider premarital intercourse to be right, at least for me.
I have decided to allow myself to be influenced by my own
experiences rather than conventional social mores. I feel that it
depends on the relationship. The relationship should be a good
one, a meaningful one, but not necessarily having anything to do
with marriage. The relationship is important in itself.*

While some confused nonvirgin men oriented at law and order, more
were found to use instrumental-relativism thinking. The emphasis for
them was on sexual prowess and numbers. Relationships were treated
casually, with little indication of genuine involvement, in contrast to
liberated nonvirgins and engaged nonvirgins.

*I've had intercourse with 20 to 25 girls. Most were casual rela-
tionships. Maybe 3 or 4 were close. The first time I was scared. I
felt that premarital sex was wrong. But that experience did contribute to a change in my standards. I was curious about sex and
felt good that I could tell the guys I wasn't a virgin. I used to feel
guilty. Now I feel that if I take precautions so there is no pregnancy, then it's okay. That's what's important for society.*

In general, then, findings for men parallel the results of the earlier study of women alone. Furthermore, partners of similar sexual
philosophies were significantly likely to be similar in moral-reasoning
orientation. However, the results of this study suggest that women may
participate in sexual behaviors beyond their personal preferences or may
inhibit their preferences (as social-contract women with law-and-order
partners did) to maintain a given relationship. One male was unusually
explicit about his "rules of the game," suggesting that his partner may
have held a different standard but acted to maintain the relationship:

*I had intercourse with my girlfriend when we both thought we
were in love. My standards determined our behavior. I keep my
standards and have yet to find a girl who won't incorporate
them.*

In contrast, for couples similar in moral reasoning and sexual philosophy,
it is likely that their decision making about sexual involvement will
parallel their shared orientation, mediated by their respective disposi-

tions to sex guilt. In a conjoint interview, one partner explained the couples' decision to have intercourse this way:

> Our relationship was a good long one. We got along well together and had great fun. Both of us felt that intercourse before marriage was fine. At least in special relationships. We had intercourse because it was the ultimate thing to do.

From the three studies described, it is clear that the variety of sexual moralities that exist have differing implications for sexual behavior and for relationships. The relationship as a moral issue has become an important factor in choosing one's sexual standard, as the Jurichs (1974) have shown. Whether the focus is on affection in the relationship, on mutual agreement in the relationship, or on both, the Jurichs's results demonstrated that greater moral maturity was associated with standards reflecting relationship concerns than with the traditional or double standards in which the sexual act is emphasized. D'Augelli's research offers further support and demonstrates that sexual behavior as well as standards are related to moral reasoning. Furthermore, the interpersonal context of sexual involvement—in other words, the interpersonal relationship—is a critical factor in sexual decision making.

The implication of the research is that the study of sexual behavior must be placed in a relationship-development context. Each sexual encounter has the potential to encourage relationship development since each interactant enters the encounter with a personal concept of the implications of sexual behavior for the relationship with this partner. That is, the personal meaning of sexual behavior vis-à-vis relationship development is implicitly present. For instance, Hunt (1974) relates this reflection shared by a 23-year-old female who reexamined the meaning of sexual behavior for her own relationship development:

> Actually, I did take somewhat of a chance the second time around, not waiting for it to be love but sleeping with him as soon as I felt he was genuinely interested in me and would deal with me honestly. And it was only after we started sleeping together that the relationship developed real depth—much more than my first affair—and the sex, as a result, has become more satisfying than ever before [p. 170].

Although in earlier relationships, sex was permissible in the context of a love relationship, in this particular relationship sex had a distinctly different meaning. In this second relationship, sex was not equated with love nor did it necessarily foreshadow relationship permanency. It did, however, imply a development of the relationship. On the basis of different personal meanings of sexual behavior for relationships, engaging in intercourse or other sexual behavior may be viewed by different individuals as acceptable in any impersonal relationship, in a close but not necessarily intimate relationship, in an intimate relationship, or in an intimate and long lasting relationship only. Thereupon, the sexual act itself implies for them the type of involvement. It is also worth noting that meanings change in the course of an individual's life-span, as the preceding example shows.

Given a relationship orientation, examining the interpersonal decision-making process is critical to understanding sexual involvement. This is the crux of our thesis. The implications of the sexual behavior for the relationship and for the individual must be considered. One partner may inhibit sexual involvement unless a future commitment is expected and likely; the other may consider intimate sexual behavior as acceptable in any caring friendship regardless of future commitment. Relationship reasoning underlies interpersonal decision making. Viewing the overt behavior without considering the individual reasoning processes of each partner and of the dyad as a unit leads to a view of two bodies coupling instead of two people with unique pasts, presents, and futures engaging in personally and interpersonally meaningful, goal-related behavior. A couple involved in deciding, spontaneously or cautiously, about sexual involvement of whatever form is implicitly engaged in relationship development. Relationship reasoning is proposed as a means of tapping individual and dyadic perspectives on this process.

V. Relationship Reasoning

A. Introduction

Relationship reasoning is viewed as a cognitive dispositional variable similar to moral reasoning. It is the individual's way of reasoning about interpersonal relationships, and it is the basis for deliberate decision making regarding the current and future nature of one's interpersonal life. Most critically, relationship reasoning is involved at decision-making points in which the individual or dyad is confronted with a choice as to the future course of a particular relationship. These decision points concern change within the relationship, whether involving issues moving towards relationship initiation, enhancement, or dissolution. Clearly, decisions about sexual behavior are related to the process of relationship development. However, the development of interpersonal relationships involves the exchange of other classes of resources as well (see Turner, Foa, & Foa, 1971). Because of this, a broader conception of relationship development than one emphasizing sexual involvement seems needed.

The relationship reasoning process underlies the ascription of meaning to one's own behavior and to the behavior of others with whom one is involved. It should be noted that this involvement may be actual or fantasized. Therefore, from a given individual's perspective, the same behavior observed by self and an uninvolved onlooker will have different meanings, depending upon the relationship(s) involved. For example, a smile observed by a partner-in-relationship and an onlooker will be interpreted differently and is perceived to hold distinctly different implications for the recipient's subsequent action toward the smile-giver. The smile, to the partner, is interpreted in the context of a very specific relational context; the onlookers, however, unless fantasizing or anticipating a relationship with the smile-giver, may disregard the act or may interpret it as connoting an existing relationship between the other two. Future plans for the relationship in response to observed, interpreted behavior, especially complex plans (e.g., becoming engaged), are decided upon using the relationship reasoning process.

B. Levels of Relationship Reasoning

Three levels of relationship reasoning are proposed: egoistic reasoning, dyadic reasoning, and interactive reasoning. Six stages of reasoning development are conceptualized. Each individual is presumed to operate at a maximal stage as far as individual development is concerned. The maximal level, as discussed earlier, may differ from the modal level. The general assumptions of a social cognitive development model are taken. The implicit continuum, paralleling Kohlberg's moral development continuum, emphasizes transition from reasoning and relationships based on an individualistic, cost–benefit orientation to a dyadic role-bound orientation to a dynamic, consensually interactive orientation. The levels and stages are described as follows.

LEVEL 1: EGOISTIC REASONING

Relationship reasoning is based essentially on a simple cost–reward analysis, with the individual's cost–benefit ratio as the primary factor. The individual does not view costs and rewards as emergent from the relationship per se, but from the partner. What the individual will give is dependent on the likely returns from the partner. Interpersonal interactions are seen as opportunities to give or to receive in concretely reciprocal ways, and there is little concept of long-term interpersonal reward. The conceptualization of the relationships' normative structure is unilaterally decided, in that each partner acts on his or her own view of the relationship's norms with little direct reference to the partner's views. Relationship change is viewed as a matter of personal rewards and costs,

and the locus for change is perceived to lie with the individual. The·
optimal relationship is one that provides the most immediate benefits for
the individual.

Stage 1: Interpersonal Punishment Avoidance Decisions are reasoned on the basis of minimizing personal loss and avoiding physically,
psychologically, or socially punitive repercussions as a function of the
relationship. Consideration of unpopular, nonpreferred relationship
choices at decision points are based upon the probabilities of avoiding
punishment or the assessment of the likelihood of being negatively
evaluated. Little value is placed upon the other's feedback, needs, or
concerns except insofar as they relate to assessing probabilities of
punishment. The optimal relationship is barely considered; indeed, the
conception of relationship is superficial and poorly articulated.

Stage 2: Interpersonal Instrumentalism Decisions are reasoned on
the basis of increasing personal gain with as little loss as possible. Rewards (physical, psychological, and social) in the context of the relationship are of utmost importance. Interpersonal interactions are viewed as
opportunities to receive from the partner. Giving of self or from self is
dependent upon what and how much will be received, thus demonstrating a superficial reciprocity. Decisions are based on what the partner will
do or will be influenced to do for the individual, and the individual will
seldom give any more than the maximum likely to be attained. There is,
however, little conception of long-term reward. The optimal relationship
is one that provides the most essentially immediate benefits for the individual.

LEVEL 2: DYADIC REASONING

Relationship decisions are based on the perceived expectations of the
partner, as consistent with role stereotypes or standards. The other's view
of the relationship is of central importance to the individual's relationship
decision making. Reciprocity is based on role responsibilities, as is relationship change. Choices at decision points support the couple's socially
defined conception of their relationship, sometimes to the detriment of
personal rewards. Emergent relationship qualities are more a function of
the expectation of a certain kind of mutual relationship consistent with
social definitions than a function of idiosyncratic dyadic definitions. That
is, the dyad makes idiosyncratic decisions regarding the relationship
within the bounds of perceived social expectations and requirements
because of perceived obligations to uphold them. Locus of control for
change within the relationship is perceived to lie largely with the partner
whose role responsibilities are perceived or are socially defined as includ-

ing dominance and control. The optimal relationship is one that provides the most conducive conditions for fulfilling the partner's expectations and enacting one's role(s) within the relationship.

Stage 3: Interpersonal Concordance Decisions are reasoned on the basis of the perceived but not necessarily explored expectations of the partner and significant others in the relationship environment. Perceptions based largely upon well-meant role stereotyping of the partner's view of the relationship are of central importance to decision making within the relationship. Unpopular or nonpreferred choices at decision points are justified as well-intentioned and "for the best," in terms of the relationship. Reciprocity as well as relationship change are based on role responsibilities and intentions to fulfill perceived needs or desires. The optimal relationship is viewed as one that provides the greatest fulfillment of stereotypical role demands as couched in the partner's perceived expectancies.

Stage 4: Social Convention Orientation Decisions are reasoned on the basis of the broadly social definition of the relationship, with societal givens and normative expectations providing the standards. The partner's expectations are important insofar as they reflect or are consistent with socially established rules and conventions. Unpopular or nonpreferred choices at decision points are justified on the basis of perceived standards of external authorities and institutionalized role norms. Reciprocity and relationship change are based on institutionalized role demands and conventions. The impetus is toward maintaining the status quo and the given order of the larger society despite possible divergence form idiosyncratic dyadic or personal preferences and definitions.

LEVEL 3: INTERACTIVE REASONING

Relationship decisions are based upon the couple's consensually developing conception of their relationship. The couple's conception of their relationship is dynamic and fluid, open to change based upon agreed-upon responsibilities and norms that are subject to changing needs and values. Choices at relationship decision points are made through shared effort and discussion, with the *explicit* expectation that both partners contribute to the decision-making process. Their own conception of interaction is more critical to their behaviors than stereotypical or role-derived concepts. The locus of control is felt to lie with the dyad; change results from a process of sharing in which each partner accurately takes the other's point of view and examines the consequences of potential change for self, partner, and dyad. Reciprocity is a function of both individual decisions and relationship norms. The optimal relationship is one which allows for the creation of dyad-specific norms.

Stage 5: Socially Based Contracting   Decisions are reasoned on the basis of the couple's developing perspective of socially agreed upon norms and roles and their fit with personal preferences. Social givens, viewed as consensually arrived at agreements, are important to them, and are explored for their relevance to the emerging relationship. Reciprocity and relationship change are functions of individual decisions based on social-relationship norms. Mutuality and compromise are valued. The optimal relationship is viewed as one in which both partners derive mutually satisfying norms founded on social givens.

Stage 6: Interpersonally Based Contracting   Decisions are reasoned on the basis of the couple's emerging conception of their idiosyncratic relationship roles and norms. Their own concept of interaction is most important to their relationship decision, with a reciprocal process of decision making as central. Socially based and role-derived concepts are relevant only as consistent with the couple's mutually agreed upon roles. Some individual autonomy is provided in decision making because it is considered essential to ideal personal development. Reciprocity and relationship change are functions of individual decision and relationship norms that have been interpersonally explored and agreed on. The optimal relationship is one which allows for the creation of dyad-specific norms that may or may not overlap with social norms or relationship definitions.

Relationship reasoning, like moral reasoning, is an indirect mediator of overt behavior. The translation of thoughts into action is controlled by many factors, ranging from situational contingencies to personal skillfulness. Generally, it is hypothesized that relationship reasoning would most directly affect behavior when relationship issues are salient to the interactants and when conscious decision making occurs. Strains in the present relationship will also heighten the role of relationship reasoning in behavior, whether such strains are internally produced (e.g., as when one partner announces a wish for a different type of relationship) or externally produced (e.g., as when an outside event, such as the birth of a child, alters the situation). It must be remembered that behavioral predictions in this area are bound to be imperfect: the complexities of the interaction of both partners make a simple unidirectional causal model of dubious value. Rather, studying what dyads consider to be important decisions and the processes whereby these decisions are made is more likely to generate useful explanations of interpersonal behavior (see Peterson, 1975).

These three relationship-reasoning levels are hypothesized to form an invariant relationship development sequence as do Kohlberg's moral reasoning levels. However, it is assumed that at any point in time, an individual will be involved in relationships differing in depth of involvement. Because of this, a person maximally capable of interactive reasoning in an intimate or long-lasting relationship will likely be involved in other relationships that she or he "manages" using egoistic and dyadic reasoning. For example, a married man contemplating an extramarital affair could use interactive reasoning in discussing this with his lover, but use dyadic reasoning with his subordinates at work and egoistic reasoning with a stranger on a bus. Because in most people's lifespan there are quantitatively fewer intimate relationships than those of lesser closeness, the modal reasoning would likely be lower than the maximal. Whether an individual achieves the highest type of relationship reasoning depends partially on the achievement of formal operational thought, though this is best considered a necessary but not sufficient condition.

1. Meaningfulness. The foundation of this social–cognitive developmental view ultimately rests on the individual's cognitive capacities and abilities. Thoughts about behaviors and behaviors-in-relationship are of primary concern. Contextual influences resulting in specific interpersonal acts are of secondary interest. Indeed, the acts themselves (for example, sexual behaviors) are important only to the degree of perceived consistency or inconsistency with the individual's reasoning. Essentially what is being proposed is that cognitive processes act as interpreters of behaviors and that, as far as the individual is concerned, there are important and trivial interpersonal behaviors. What is viewed as important or trivial by a partner-in-relationship may be interpreted differently by outsiders to the relationship. Even the partners themselves may not interpret the same interpersonal acts as important from their individual reasoning perspectives. The point is that the ascription of meaning to interpersonal behaviors stems from the personal salience of those behaviors based upon one's relationship reasoning. Salience may be associated with one's ideals for relationships or with one's goals for a specific relationship. Ascription of importance is also influenced by historical factors in one's relationship history, particularly prior interpretations and related consequences.

In relating his experiences in essentially surface-contact relationships in which exchange of sex was the purpose of affiliation, one man (in Fleming & Fleming, 1975) demonstrates differential ascription of meaning to intercourse:

> She spent the night at my place and the morning came. She got out of bed and was getting dressed and I lazily got up and said . . . "When will I see you again?" We'd had a good night, nothing wild and exciting. We liked each other, nothing more, no

> promises. . . . And she said, "Like man, I'll be around." Wow, I was crushed. . . .
> Then I realized that . . . I would never get over the feeling that there is a commit-
> ment involved, that I am taking something from a woman, and that sex, even after
> all the experiences, is something very special [p. 118].

In this example, it is clear that the interactants in this relationship placed
different meanings on their sexual transaction and had different expectations for the relationship. The interpretations of partners-in-relationship
are likely to become more similar as their relationship progresses. In
Masters and Johnson's view (1975), accommodation and negotiation are
the key processes in conveying, understanding, and satisfying one's own
and one's partner's personal meaning in sexuality. Accommodation and
negotiation were necessary for Lois and Don White (in Masters & Johnson,
1975), for whom touching became a relationship issue. Lois liked to
express affection by touching and was comfortable doing so in public. To
Don, touching was a cue for sex, and he became embarrassed and frustrated in public:

> I'd say "Hey—we're starting to make out in public, and we can't do anything about
> it. So cut it out till we get home." We'd talk like that, and she'd say, "Well, I'm not
> making out, I just wanted to touch you." And there was the conflict because I would
> feel: when you touch me it means we *have* to make out. Recently we've had a lot of
> discussions about that and I think we both understand each other a lot better [p.
> 217].

The social contract implied here is in the process of modification to better
fit both partners' sexual values and their views of the relationship. We
suggest that relationship reasoning underlies the process of accommodation and negotiation. Lois and Don are reviewing the meaning and fit of
public affection in their relationship as a function of their commitment to
each other. Their discussions are oriented toward understanding how
each one interprets the same behaviors and what the meaning is for their
relationship. This can be viewed as the process of renegotiating an un-
clear contractual clause based on interactive reasoning. For a couple in
which one or both partners are oriented to dyadic reasoning, the renegotiation process might be based on the socially approved interpretation of
such behaviors rather than on the idiosyncratic needs of the partners.
Indeed, the renegotiation process might be hampered because of the
limitations of the partners' reasoning capabilities.

   2. Cognitive development.   Developmental differences in cognitive
reasoning processes are important to assessing individual variation. A
fundamental tenet of the social–cognitive developmental perspective is
that thought processes and interpersonal abilities dependent upon
these cognitive abilities develop in a qualitatively advancing manner.
Relationship-reasoning processes are seen as a subset of cognitive-

reasoning processes influenced by and influencing the social environment. Therefore, while the cognitions involved concern with self vis-à-vis others, one's conceptualization becomes increasingly complex with development over the life span as a result of social interaction experiences as well as physical maturity.

Cognitive limits on individual relationship reasoning are implied. Due to differences in basic cognitive capacities and in social environments, individuals vary in their abilities to articulate and conceptualize their interpersonal lives. This view suggests, despite the oblique association of reasoning to behavior, that there may be cognitive reasons underlying the inability of certain individuals to engage in intimate, sharing relationships. For example, a fairly accurate conception of the partner may be a prerequisite for an intimate relationship since it underlies and allows prediction of the partner's feelings, thoughts, and attitudes that in turn facilitates mutually satisfying interactions. One woman involved in a second marriage put it this way:

> I had a very unhappy first marriage, which seemed fine to a lot of people but was really unrewarding. We just didn't talk to each other. I came into this second marriage thinking "I'll be damned if I want to fail again." You think about the other person more; your perceptions are sharper. Instead of being hung up with all sorts of angers and other concealed feelings, you're busy trying to figure out what's really bugging him. And I think [he] does the same for me [In Masters & Johnson, 1975, p. 207].

3. Intraindividual variability. Complementing interindividual differences in relationship reasoning is intraindividual variability in such reasoning. Although individuals are theoretically capable of reasoning about relationships at a particular level, it does not follow that all relationships are subject to the qualitative processing of that particular level. Like moral reasoning, an individual's relationship reasoning may be viewed in modal, maximal, or range terms. The modal level is that which most often characterizes the individual's reasoning. The maximal level is the highest level manifested by the individual. The range of reasoning is the span of levels that the individual uses among all his or her reasoning about all his or her relationships. An analysis of the individual's relationships will reveal a variety of relationship types: some conducted using fairly primitive, egoistic notions of immediate costs and benefits, while others demonstrate mediation by symbolic reinforcements and formal or informal contractual agreements. Modal, maximal, and range-of-relationship reasoning are all worthy of attention as far as developmental advance and intervention are concerned. Factors regulating the individual's application of reasoning type must be delineated.

4. Reasoning as interaction. Thus far, the discussion of relationship reasoning has focused on reasoning as an individual ability. However, implicit in the discussion has been the extension of relationship reasoning to the actual transactional relationship process. Relationship reasoning is viewed as characterizing thoughts about interactions with others and as providing themes for the patterns of ongoing interactions by partners-in-relationship. In this view, a relationship is defined both by the reasoning processes of each of the two partners and by the interaction of the partners' conceptualizations.

The reasoning capabilities of partners may be similar or dissimilar in respect to their current levels of reasoning within that relationship. Indeed, the degree of congruence in relationship reasoning may be a useful dimension to examine in seeking an explanation for change within a relationship. A degree of dissimilarity introduces a dynamic quality to relationship development and may produce a tension that leads to enhancement or to termination of a relationship. Each partner's conception of the present relationship—its rules, roles, responsibilities, limits, and boundaries, in other words, its meaning structure—serves as a framework by which to implicitly and explicitly plan behaviors and evaluate their outcomes. Stambul and Kelley (Chapter 5 of this volume) provide evidence which suggests substantiation of the importance of relationship-reasoning content to relationship development and transactions: Norms and role-definitional processes were found to be primary in relationship development, rather than power per se. Presumably, partners differ in their conceptions of, and methods of arriving at, the relationship's meaning structure, as a Laingian analysis would suggest (Laing, Phillipson & Lee, 1972), and interdyad differences would certainly exist as well. While homogeneity of reasoning patterns—the processes by which a relationship's meaning structure is articulated—need not exist for relationship development, recognition and articulation of differences would seem a preliminary step towards relationship intimacy.

C. Process of Relationships

This model has implications for the process of relationships. A dyad can be homogeneous or heterogeneous as far as the partners' reasoning orientations are concerned. The partners may differ in their reasoning capacities per se; they may also differ in their tendency to apply a particular reasoning orientation to the particular relationship, particularly depending on the stage of the relationship. Prior to long-term commitment in a relationship, partners may screen on the basis of differences regarding conceptions of relationships through verbalized idealizations and manifested relationship decision-making behavior. However, this screening may not result in similarity as much as the avoidance of obvious incompatabilities. Such dimensions especially remain unexplored in depth until decisions are imminent.

Facilitation or inhibition of relationship development is largely dependent upon how recognition of differences is handled. For example, if the female partner is operating at the socially based contracting stage of interactive reasoning, while her male partner operates at the social-convention orientation of dyadic reasoning, differences in meanings attributed to interpersonal behaviors and divergent plans for the relationship may arise. In this case, the woman's reasoning about the relationship may itself serve to advance her partner's reasoning. In an adamantly sexist relationship, however, the reluctance to listen to, much less adapt, the woman's views might cause conflict and impede the partner's own growth as an interactant.

On a different level, we hypothesize that couples similar in relationship reasoning but operating at egoistic or dyadic levels might individually or dyadically develop beyond their current stage or even advance a level with the continuance of the relationship. In a sense, this is the process of social interaction mitigating egocentrism, but in a relationship context. However, it is most reasonable to assume stability of the couple's homogeneity unless other influences are operative such as advances in reasoning facilitated by one or both partners' experiences in heterogeneous relationships outside the current one.

Further, it should be stated that a relationship adjustment satisfying to the partners can occur at any level of relationship reasoning, especially for dyads with homogeneous reasoning. In addition, adaptation to imbalances can occur if the relationship provides additional rewards and if few alternatives exist. Indeed, before the relaxation of divorce laws, partners were strongly committed to a certain type of relationship and adapted to it because few alternatives existed. The current increase in divorce rates may signal, among other things, the release of heterogeneous couples from previously unnegotiable contracts. In sum, dyads homogeneous with respect to relationship reasoning might verbally report greater dyadic satisfaction. Nonhomogeneous couples might report less satisfaction but may also have the potential for greater intimacy and mutuality, having to work harder and longer with negotiation and accommodation processes.

VI. A Model for Sexual Involvement in Relationships

Relationship reasoning has the potential to provide substance in examining relationship interaction and partners' conceptualizations of relationships. As far as sexual behavior is concerned, it is suggested that the study of relationship reasoning in conjunction with other variables such as moral reasoning, sex guilt, and sexual philosophy represents a viable direction to pursue in the theoretical conceptualization of interpersonal sexual behavior.

Our view is that sexual decision-making is structured by the relationship reasoning of the partners and is given content by their sexual philosophy and sexual moral reasoning. Both sexual philosophy and sexual moral reasoning interact with sex guilt, which tends to inhibit sexual expression. Relationship reasoning would seem to be the pivotal factor in determining the process of decisions—their locus in the relationship— and the ongoing development of the relationship, whereas sex guilt, sexual philosophy, and sexual-moral-reasoning orientation influence partners' sexual expression within the relationship. Given heterogeneity of orientations within a relationship, the dominant partner, traditionally the male, will tend to initiate sexual decision making. Peplau, Rubin, and Hill (1977) suggest that the female partner still tends to limit intimacy, consistent with traditional role ascriptions. However, when both partners in such relationships reason interactively about relationships, role dominance ought to be irrelevant to the outcome of their decision making. Rather, the outcome may be influenced by the standards of the partner with the greatest sex guilt.

Stage-of-relationship development, defined in terms of shared knowledge, level of affection and trust, and commitment, may influence sexual decision-making in conjunction with relationship reasoning. Recall the integrated model of relationship development described earlier in the chapter. Relationship reasoning may be conceptualized as evolving similarly. As suggested earlier, the relationship reasoning of one individual may vary among his or her relationships. In addition, each new relationship may exert a pull for first reasoning at egoistic levels, progressing to dyadic levels, and perhaps reaching interactive levels as the relationship progresses. That is, one factor regulating the initial application of a particular reasoning orientation may be the stage of relationship development. Limits on relationship-reasoning capability, however, would delimit the range of reasoning, no matter what the stage of relationship. It should be noted that the stage of reasoning, in turn, would limit the level of the relationship as well, as Lickona (1974) has argued.

The nature of an initial relationship may influence here-and-now reasoning of an egoistic nature regardless of the modal or maximal reasoning stage of the person. Assuming unilateral awareness as the first stage of a relationship, for instance, it would not be surprising to find each individual reasoning at Stage 1, Interpersonal Punishment Avoidance. The main concern is avoiding rejection. Exchange concepts are perhaps most relevant in this stage and in Stage 2. Questions regarding potential gain versus serious losses of esteem, pride, and confidence in extending one-self to a new partner would be seriously considered. Potential gain might well include sexual gain, in the broader sense of a possible sexual partner in a meaningful relationship or in the narrower sense of more immediate sexual exchanges. Recent data (Peplau, Rubin & Hill, 1977) suggest that sex is an important goal in seeking dating partners, more so for men.

In a surface-contact relationship, the decision having been made to engage in initial interaction, interpersonal-instrumentalist reasoning—still egoistic—may be functional. "What might I get out of continuing this relationship?" is an important concern, especially given comparison level for alternatives. In D'Augelli's studies (1971, 1972; D'Augelli & Cross, 1975), confused nonvirgins often placed greatest emphasis on sex as an immediate reward. Their hopes were that sexual exchanges would lead to relationship intimacy; their relationship reasoning was especially in-strumental. However, it is also conceivable that liberated nonvirgins might at times note that sex was the critical reason for entering a specific relationship, but they would differ from confused nonvirgins by not viewing sex as instrumental to relationship development. Sexual attrac-tion might be the initial motivating factor in entering such relationships, but their relationship reasoning would stress interactive processes in sexual decision making rather than egoistic ones. For them, partner hon-esty and consensus are crucial relationship factors no matter what the exchange.

In an exploratory relationship, it is likely that relationship reasoning would be dominated by interpersonal concordance. As discussed earlier, the formulations of Levinger and Snoek (1972) and Scanzoni (Chapter 3 of this volume) suggest role expectancies would predominate in decision making at this stage. The less the shared knowledge of the other, the more influence social roles and expectations of significant others have. Explor-atory relationships probably include sexual transactions of some sort. Sex guilt is likely to play a larger role at this stage than at later ones for inexperienced virgins, adamant virgins, potential nonvirgins, and en-gaged nonvirgins. Confused and liberated nonvirgins would probably be willing to engage in sexual intercourse; whether they would be im-mediately willing to engage in variations in intercourse is less likely. As Hunt (1974) and Masters and Johnson (1975) suggest, evolving trust between partners is a key factor in willingness to experiment sexually. Such trust would be minimal in an early exploratory relationships.

At the consolidation stage, social-convention reasoning might functionally predominate for those couples who are able to reason at this level. However, for those able to reason interactively, such reasoning would no doubt be evident. Consolidation implies greater shared knowl-edge, overlapping interest spheres, and emerging trust and joint-profit processes (Scanzoni, Chapter 3 of this volume). The relationship begins to have meaning to the partners beyond the here and now. Sexual transactions may become less limited. Inexperienced virgins may never have experienced this relationship depth as yet. If they do, they may be willing to engage in necking or light petting, but would go no further. To be more intimate implies more depth than they can grasp or indeed can feel safe with. Moreover, their high sex guilt limits their exploration. Adamant virgins may be willing to light pet or heavy pet, particularly clothed (D'Augelli, 1971, 1972). If consolidation involves formal engagement, adamant virgins may engage in oral–genital activities and will probably pet to orgasm. At least the male partner will experience orgasm; the female may or may not. Engaged nonvirgins may heavy pet, probably without oral–genital involvement, at this stage. However, petting to orgasm may occur.

The commitment stage of a relationship will draw interactive reasoning from those capable of it. Socially based contracting will first be observed and may be followed by interpersonally based contracting. The relationship itself is critical here. The meaningfulness in terms of depth, quality, and maximum joint profit becomes the pivot. The partners make contracts with each other regarding norms and roles. Their commitment is recognized. For engaged nonvirgins, commitment may be defined in terms of love or in terms of the explicit agreements about the relationship as well as degree of affection. They would be willing to engage in intercourse once commitment is defined. Adamant virgins may find commitment in a marital contract; once married, intercourse is morally permissible. The extent of sexual intimacies at this stage of the relationship is bounded by sex guilt, trust, and present interactions—how good the partners feel about each other, the degree of disclosure and sharing, and so on. The greater the trust, the more intimate the sexual exploration will be allowed to be.

Finally, mutuality in relationship is best understood as a dynamic stage in relationship development. The more mutual the relationship the greater the trust and self-confidence within the relationship and the more the willingness to explore (Masters & Johnson, 1975). Joint profit processes and a concomitant concern for satisfying the other's perceived and heard needs, as they arise, would be likely to encourage greater intimacy and experimentation. Sex guilt and personal preferences or dislikes would limit the extent of this outer boundary in sexual transactions.

The transition from one level of relatedness to another can occur rapidly or very gradually. Various factors interact to speed up or delay transitions or, for that matter, decisions to terminate. Among these factors is relationship reasoning. Those who are capable of higher-order reasoning are likely to overcome the relationship-stage pull toward lesser reasoning. They may apply the more salient higher order concepts and processes to both assessing the state and progress of the relationship and to acting in the relationship. Application of higher-level processes—for example, partner consensus on idiosyncratic role behaviors—is likely to promote within-relationship progression toward consolidation, commitment, and mutuality. If partners differ in their relationship reasoning and cannot find consensus in defining their relationship, the decision to terminate may be made. Otherwise, their further sharing of increasingly intimate experiences—sexual and otherwise—will tend to broaden the range of overlapping interest spheres and resources for exchange. In turn, greater relatedness is likely to result.

Movement toward progressive sexual intimacy parallels the development of intimacy in other spheres, or, in some instances, anticipates such intimacy. For sexually conservative people, publicly defined relationship development provides key reference points for permissible sexual intimacies within the bounds of personal sex guilt. For sexually moderate people, personally defined relationship development provides the reference points. Sex guilt is less prominent a factor in decision making. For sexually liberal people, relationship development is less salient a factor than others. Sexual liberals involve two groups of people who differ greatly in their understanding of expectations for relationships. Liberated nonvirgins focus on interactive processes early in relationships and engage in sexual intimacies earlier than others. Their sexual exchanges are based on relationship factors other than expected commitment; low sex-guilt facilitates. Confused nonvirgins, on the other hand, focus on instrumental processes using sex as exchange for hoped for relationship commitment. Low sex guilt probably enables them to engage in sexual intimacies early in relationship affiliation, but their very involvement is intertwined in desired relationship commitment.

VI. Summary

The critical elements of interpersonal relating involve the psychological situation of the relationship itself, the meaning of interpersonal behavior as perceived by the partners-in-relationship, and decision-making processes about relationship development. The following are propositional statements of the model:

1. Interpersonal relationships are conducted by and develop via decision-making processes.
2. Relationship reasoning, the underlying interpersonal decision-making process, is a social–cognitive developmental process that evolves and changes over the life span as a result of maturation and experience.

3. There are individual differences in the development of relationships.
4. Individuals differ in the qualitative differentiation of their reasoning about relationships.
5. Although individuals can operate at a maximal level of reasoning about relationships in general, their actual relationships vary in respect to the operative reasoning processes such that modal reasoning may differ from possible maximal reasoning.
6. Interpersonal relationships develop as a complex function of the relationship reasoning of both interactants, their behavioral acts (verbal and nonverbal), and their shared implicit and explicit definitions of and plan for their relationship.
7. Development within a relationship consists of changes in each partner's unique conceptions of the desired relationship, and modifications in the dyad's explicit understanding of each partner's conception.
8. Movement toward intimacy (sexual or nonsexual) in a relationship occurs with relationship development evolving from an essentially socially defined to an essentially couple-defined conception of the relationship.
9. More highly developed relationships are generally characterized by a shared understanding of the idiosyncratic, couple-specific nature of the relationship.

Progressive sexual involvement, it is suggested, parallels relationship development to the extent that sex guilt allows. Sexual philosophy, specifying behavioral intimacies permissible within the bounds of particular levels of relatedness, is a key to the extent of intimate involvement likely for each individual. Relationship reasoning is the key to the definition and progression of the relationship, in respect to the individual and in respect to the couple's conception of their relatedness and their future. A fitting example of the process by which a couple arrives at a consensus about sexual activity and relationship development is provided by e. e. cummings (1954, pp. 288–289):

> *may i feel said he*
> *(i'll squeal said she*
> *just once said he)*
> *it's fun said she*
> *(may i touch said he*
> *how much said she*
> *a lot said he)*
> *why not said she*
> *(let's go said he*
> *not too far said she*
> *what's too far said he*
> *where you are said she)*

may i stay said he
(which way said she
like this said he
if you kiss said she
may i move said he
is it love said she)
if you're willing said he
(but you're killing said she
but it's life said he
but your wife said she
now said he)
ow said she
(tiptop said he
don't stop said she
oh no said he)
go slow said she
(cccome? said he
ummm said she)
you're divine! said he
(you are Mine said she)

References

Altman, I., & Taylor, D. A. *Social penetration: The development of interpersonal relationships.* New York: Holt, 1973.

Bell, R. R., & Blumberg, L. Courtship stages and intimacy attitudes. *Family Life Coordinator,* 1960, *8,* 60–63.

Bentler, P. M. Heterosexual behavior assessment—Males. *Behavior Research and Therapy,* 1968, *6,* 21–25. (a)

Bentler, P. M. Heterosexual behavior assessment—II Females. *Behavior Research and Therapy,* 1968, *6,* 27–30. (b)

Brady, J. P., & Levitt, E. E. The scalability of sexual experiences. *Psychological Record,* 1965, *15,* 275–279.

Christensen, H. R., & Carpenter, G. R. Value-behavior discrepancies regarding premarital coitus in three Western cultures. *American Sociological Review,* 1962, *27,* 66–74.

Cummings, E. E. *Poems 1923–1954.* New York: Harcourt, 1954.

Curran, J. P., Neff, S., & Lippold, S. Correlates of sexual experience among university students. *Journal of Sex Research,* 1973, *9,* 124–131.

D'Augelli, J. F. *Moral reasoning, sex-guilt, sexual attitudes, and parental behaviors as related to women's premarital sexual behavior.* Unpublished master's thesis, University of Connecticut, 1971.

D'Augelli, J. F. *The relationship of moral reasoning, sex-guilt, and interpersonal interaction to couples' premarital sexual experience.* Unpublished doctoral dissertation, University of Connecticut, 1972.

D'Augelli, J. F., & Cross, H. J. Relationship of sex-guilt and moral reasoning to premarital sex in college women and in couples. *Journal of Consulting and Clinical Psychology,* 1975, *43,* 40–47.

Edwards, J. N., & Booth, A. Sexual behavior in and out of marriage: An assessment of correlates. *Journal of Marriage and the Family,* 1976, *38,* 73–81.

Ehrmann, W. *Premarital dating behavior.* New York: Holt, 1959.

Fleming, K., & Fleming, A. T. *The first time.* New York: Simon and Schuster, 1975.

Foa, U. G. Convergences in the analysis of the structure of interpersonal behavior. *Psychological Review,* 1961, *68,* 341–353.

Foa, U. G., & Foa, E. B. *Societal structures of the mind.* Springfield, Illinois: Thomas, 1974.

Gagnon, J. H., & Simon, W. *The sexual scene.* New York: Aldine, 1970.

Harré, R., & Secord, P. F. *The explanation of social behavior.* Totowa, New Jersey: Rowman and Littlefield, 1972.

Homans, G. C. *Social behavior: Its elementary forms.* New York: Harcourt, 1974.

Huesmann, L. R., & Levinger, G. Incremental exchange theory: A formal model for the progression of dyadic social interaction. In L. Berkowitz and E. Walster (Eds.), *Advances in experimental social psychology* (Vol. 9). New York: Academic, 1976.

Hunt, M. *Sexual behavior in the 1970's.* Chicago: Playboy Press, 1974.

Huston, T. L., & Cate, R. *Social exchange in intimate relationships.* Paper presented at Conference on Love and Attraction, Swansea, Wales, 1977.

Jurich, A. P. & Jurich, J. A. The effect of cognitive moral development upon the selection of premarital sexual standards. *Journal of Marriage and the Family,* 1974, *36,* 736–741.

Komarovsky, M. *Dilemmas of masculinity: A study of college youth.* New York: Norton, 1976.

Kinsey, A. C., Pomeroy, W., & Martin, C. *Sexual behavior in the human male.* Philadelphia: Saunders, 1948.

Kinsey, A. C., Pomeroy, W., Martin, C., & Gebhard, P. *Sexual behavior in the human female.* Philadelphia: Saunders, 1953.

Kirkendall, L. *Premarital intercourse and interpersonal relationships.* New York: Julian Press, 1961.

Kirkendall, L., & Libby, R. W. Interpersonal relationships—crux of the sexual renaissance. *Journal of Social Issues,* 1966, *22,* 45–59.

Kohlberg, L. *The development of modes or moral thinking and choice in the years 10 to 16.* Unpublished doctoral dissertation, University of Chicago, 1958.

Kohlberg, L. The development of children's orientation toward a moral order. *Vita Humana,* 1963, *6,* 11–33.

Kohlberg, L. Stage and sequence: The cognitive-developmental approach to socialization. In D. Goslin (Ed.), *Handbook of socialization theory and research.* Chicago: Rand McNally, 1969.

Kohlberg, L. From is to ought: How to commit the naturalistic fallacy and get away with it in the study of moral development. In T. Mischel (Ed.), *Cognitive development and epistemology.* New York: Academic Press, 1971.

Laing, R. D., Phillipson, H., & Lee, A. R. *Interpersonal perception: A theory and a method of research.* New York: Springer, 1966.

Leary, T. *Interpersonal diagnosis of personality.* New York: Ronald Press, 1957.

Levinger, G. A three-level approach to attraction: Toward an understanding of pair relatedness. In T. L. Huston (Ed.), *Foundations of interpersonal attraction.* New York: Academic Press, 1974.

Levinger, G., & Snoek, J. D. *Attraction in relationship: A new look at interpersonal attraction.* Morristown, New Jersey: General Learning Press, 1972.

Lickona, T. A cognitive–developmental approach to interpersonal attraction. In T. L. Huston (Ed.), *Foundations of interpersonal attraction.* New York: Academic Press, 1974.

Masters, W. H. & Johnson, V. E. *The pleasure bond.* Boston: Little, Brown, 1975.

Mosher, D. L. Interaction of fear and guilt in inhibiting unacceptable behavior. *Journal of Consulting Psychology,* 1965, *29,* 161–167.

Mosher, D. L. Measurement of guilt in females by self-report inventories. *Journal of Consulting and Clinical Psychology,* 1968, *32,* 690–695.

Mosher, D. L., & Cross, H. J. Sex guilt and premarital sexual experiences of college students. *Journal of Consulting and Clinical Psychology,* 1971, *36,* 27–32.

Nichols, M. F. *The relation of parental child rearing attitudes to the sexual behavior and attitude of women.* Unpublished master's thesis, University of Connecticut, 1970.

Peplau, L. A., Rubin, Z., & Hill, C. T. Sexual intimacy in dating relationships. *Journal of Social Issues,* 1977, *33,* 86–109.

Peterson, D. R. *A plan for studying interpersonal relationships.* Paper presented at the Conference on Interactional Psychology, University of Stockholm, Sweden, 1975.

Pfeiffer, E. & Davis, G. C. Determinants of sexual behavior in middle and old age. *Journal of the American Geriatrics Society,* 1972, *20,* 151–158.

Reiss, I. L. *Premarital sexual standards in America.* New York: Free Press, 1960.

Reiss, I. L. (Ed.), The sexual renaissance in America. *Journal of Social Issues,* 1966, *27.*

Reiss, I. L. *The social context of premarital sexual permissiveness.* New York: Holt, 1967.

Schaefer, E. S. A configurational analysis of children's reports of parent behavior. *Journal of Consulting Psychology,* 1965, *29,* 552–557.

Spanier, G. B. Perceived sex knowledge, exposure to eroticism, and premarital sexual behavior: The impact of dating. *Sociological Quarterly,* 1976, *17,* 247–261.

Thurber, J. & White, E. B. *Is sex necessary?* New York: Harper, 1929.

Turner, J. L., Foa, E. B., & Foa, U. G. Interpersonal reinforcers: Classification, interrelationship, and some differential properties. *Journal of Personality and Social Psychology,* 1971, *19,* 168–180.

12

Relationship Initiation and Development: A Life-Span Developmental Approach

DOUGLAS C. KIMMEL

I. Introduction

Social relationships are located in the unfolding time perspective of the individual participants. All persons bring their own unique developmental history to each new relationship they initiate. And those relationships that endure have a time framework and a developmental history of their own. Thus, transient encounters represent the intersection of the participants' developmental histories. And enduring relationships represent the convergence of the individual's development with the relationship's development. In either case, developmental vectors are relevant to the interaction.

However, these developmental vectors have seldom been considered in the study of social relationships. For example, most studies of relationship initiation and development have been conducted with college students as subjects. Since college students tend to have a set of developmental characteristics that are different from the developmental characteristics of persons of different ages, it is likely that these developmental factors may affect the nature of the relationships being studied. Thus one might question whether these studies provide information that can be generalized to persons with different developmental histories—such as young children, middle-aged adults, or elderly persons.

351

SOCIAL EXCHANGE IN DEVELOPING RELATIONSHIPS

In addition, many studies of social relationships tend to focus on transient encounters that may be significantly different from those enduring relationships that have a developmental vector of their own. For example, Huston (1974) noted that over 80% of research findings about interpersonal attraction are based on studies of strangers with only a single measurement in time. While it is obvious that the vast majority of an individual's social encounters are transient relationships (with bank tellers, bus drivers, and others, including strangers) and that all relationships begin as initial encounters, the majority of a person's meaningful relationships do have a significant developmental vector. From a life-span developmental perspective, these enduring relationships would seem to deserve much more research attention than has been given to them in the past.

Thus, the focus of this chapter will be on enduring relationships that have a developmental vector over time. It will be argued that the age of the participants in a relationship is a significant variable for understanding the nature and meaning of the relationship. Chronological age is, of course, only a rough index of development through the life-span, but the developmental perspective implies that the nature and meaning of relationships may be different at age 5 from what they are at age 25 or 50 or 75.

There are three goals of this chapter: (a) a critique of the social-exchange framework from a developmental perspective and recasting of the framework into a perspective that may be more useful from a life-span view of relationships; (b) a review of developmental issues and processes that are relevant to relationship initiation and development; and (c) an integration of the major themes of life-span social interaction to suggest new directions for research on social relationships throughout the life-span.

II. Critique and Recasting of Social Exchange Theory

Social-exchange theory as developed by Homans (1961), Thibaut and Kelley (1959), and others has had a profound influence on many aspects of sociological and social–psychological research and thinking. It has also been subjected to a variety of critiques. For example, Gergen (1976) noted:

> First there is the mechanistic form of the theory that often segments the human into discrete units and treats him as a passive automaton. Many find such views repugnant and would be more inclined to join humanistic psychologists who contend that we must embrace the individual as an autonomous, organismic whole. The

very manner of objectifying the other is viewed by many as an alienating activity—setting people against each other—highly undesirable if one wishes to establish a cooperative society. The economic metaphor is also a source of displeasure to many. This marketplace mentality, it is said, distorts normal social activity and mocks "relations of the spirit." In the same vein, to assume persons are bent primarily on increasing their own social profit is viewed by some as both jaundiced and inaccurate. Still others view the entire theory as a derivative from capitalistic ideology, which invites people to treat each other as commodities to be bought and sold [pp. 71–72].

Despite these and other critiques, the theory appears to be well supported by a variety of empirical data from a range of fields. Even Thibaut and Kelley's (1959) startling assertion—"We assume that the amount of reward provided . . . can be measured [at least in theory] and that the reward value of different [self-defined] modalities of gratification are [theoretically] reducible to a single psychological scale [p. 12]"—can be accepted by the present writer with only minor additions that are not inconsistent with the original formulation of the theory.

However, from a developmental perspective, the social exchange theory appears to have three major drawbacks. First, the implicit model of the human person in the theory appears to contrast with the developmental model of the person. On the one hand, developmentalists are inclined to view the person as a biosocial being that consciously draws upon its past and holds expectations about the future and that manifests both change and continuity over time. On the other hand, the social-exchange model implies a static conception of the person and seems to imply that the person in the theory is a kind of general man—one who seems to this writer to be distinctly masculine, middle class (white), American, and between 20 and 45 years old. Perhaps exchange theorists would have little difficulty applying the theory to any group they might choose to study; but the economic computer at the core of the general man, continually computing the cost, reward, and CL_{alt} may not be as salient for describing the social behavior of children at play, mothers or fathers caring for their children, grandparents babysitting, residents in a nursing home, or a person aiding another through a bereavement period as it would be for describing achievement-oriented, competitive social behavior. This general man may also be uniquely American. For example, Kandel and Lesser (1972) report on the considerable differences between American and Danish adolescents:

Americans emphasize achievement more than Danes; Americans emphasize getting somewhere, establishing oneself, and, in this way, gaining the respect or recognition of the community. Central here is a concern for the respect of others, and the belief that it is won by achievement. For example, a much larger percentage of American than Danish parents and adolescents emphasize being a leader in activities, earning money, having a good reputation. Furthermore, the majority of American parents and adolescents believe that the best way to get ahead in life is to work hard, a belief maintained only by a very small minority of Danes, who, in contrast, emphasize getting along with others as the best way to get ahead in life. Comparing the two, we might say that Americans believe that achievement gains the testimony of others to one's worth, which then permits self-acceptance. Danes, in contrast, want to get along with others, to be accepted as someone dependable, in personal rather than achievement terms. The distinction is between winning the regard of others through achievement (characteristic of the American outlook) and simply gaining acceptance as a person (characteristic of the Danish outlook) [pp. 169–170].

Certainly rewards and costs in the social-exchange framework could be interpreted broadly to apply to social interactions in both cultures. But the model seems more consonant with "winning the regard of others" (or just winning) than with "gaining acceptance as a dependable person."

The second major drawback to social exchange from a developmental perspective is the implicit assumption of *justice* in the model. Lickona (1974) has noted that lovers are likely to use a Marxist conception of justice in their relationship (from each according to ability; to each according to need) rather than the equity notion of justice implicit in the social-exchange model. However, a life-span developmentalist is likely to question the relevance of any assumption of justice in social relationships, especially for older adults. One important lesson the study of aging teaches is that the belief in justice is a myth. People do not necessarily get what they deserve. Good people get cancer or are paralyzed by strokes. Important relationships are ended and grief is an increasingly common experience with aging. Coping with impossible situations, living with ambiguity at the mercy of uncontrollable forces and still surviving is not an uncommon set of experiences for aging persons (of any chronological age). The concept of justice in relationships, or any notion of turning a profit in relationships becomes irrelevant; instead, the task is one of finding a few rewards despite the costs. Rubin and Peplau (1975) found that:

Believers in a just world have been found to be more likely than nonbelievers to admire fortunate people and to derogate victims, thus permitting the believers to maintain the perception that people in fact get what they deserve. . . . Believers in a just world have been found to be more religious, more authoritarian, and more oriented toward the internal control of reinforcements than nonbelievers. They are also more likely to admire political leaders and existing social institutions, and to have negative attitudes toward underprivileged groups [p. 65].

They also note that "everyone may have a version of the just-world belief in early childhood (Piaget's "immanent justice"), but some people outgrow the belief quickly and some apparently never do [p. 65]."

The third major drawback to social-exchange theory is that the context of the relationship, especially the developmental context of the participants, is not explicitly considered. One succinct example may highlight this point: "The desire to play cowboys and Indians greatly declines between childhood and adulthood, so that by age 20 this desire is not likely to serve as a basis for forming attachments, no matter how important it may have been at age 5 [McCall, 1974, p. 227]." Certainly an exchange theorist would recognize this obvious fact and would implicitly include such developmental factors in any research study. However, it is possible that not only the reinforcement values but also the process of attending to and comparing reinforcement values may change with age. It would be very interesting, for example, to add developmental variables to such exchange-theory research designs as computer-dating methodologies for studying attraction. Would prepubescent children, college sophomores, middle-aged adults, and elderly persons respond in similar ways (differing perhaps only in reward values given to various partners)? Or would major characteristics of attraction be found to differ across the life span? Some studies have been carried out with children from the exchange framework (see Lott & Lott, 1968), but by and large, developmental factors have seldom been explicitly considered by exchange theorists. Some of the relevant developmental factors that may be important for understanding relationship initiation and development will be discussed below; and some of the specific research possibilities will be suggested in the conclusion of this paper.

III. Social Interactions and the Personality System

Because of these drawbacks in the social-exchange framework, this chapter will attempt to recast the discussion of social interaction into a framework more useful for a life-span developmental analysis. The first step will be a discussion of the function of social relationships in human life and the interrelation of social interactions with the self and the personality system. The next step will be a description of a symbolic–interactionist model of enduring social relationships.

George Herbert Mead (1934) argued that biological evolution provided humans with the ability to become objects to themselves in a social group—a characteristic that differentiates humans from other animals (some of whom also have social interactions in well-developed social groups). This ability to be an object to oneself is the foundation of Mead's (1934) concept of the development of the self. "The self, as that which can be an object to itself, is essentially a social structure, and it arises in social experience. . . . It is impossible to conceive of a self arising outside of social experience [p. 204]." Thus, one of the basic biosocial functions of social interaction is the creation and development of the self, which is the hallmark of our humanness, in this view.

It is conceivable that human evolution depended upon and enhanced the capacity for social interaction. Perhaps the long postreproductive period (for women) in the human life cycle is an indication of the biosocial importance of social interaction between a few old persons who are not parents and younger members of the group. As Margaret Mead (1972) suggested, survival of the species may have depended on some old persons remembering where to go for water during a drought, or on how to survive other historically rare occurrences. If it were not for reasons such as this, it is difficult to understand why humans have a long postreproductive life. There is likely some survival advantage—perhaps greater stability, perhaps a way to store social history and traditions—that depended on social interaction during our long evolutionary process.

Thus, it may be assumed that the capacity, necessity, and inclination for social relationships is "wired in," so to speak, to the human organism. Other biosocial predispositions such as territoriality, dominance hierarchies, and sexual drives may also incline human beings to engage in social interactions.

G. H. Mead's emphasis on the importance of social interactions for the development of the self is well known. The child gradually develops a self by taking the attitude of the other toward itself. As the child grows older (and cognitive development increases), the attitude of several others are taken at once (as in the example of the baseball game where the child must be aware of the positions and expectations of all the players on the field). Later, the child becomes able to take the attitude of the generalized other, which evolves to an abstract generalized other (with the advent of formal operations, in Piaget's scheme). In adulthood, the person has the ability to take the attitude of other individuals toward the abstract characteristics of the social order (such as religion, morality, or politics). That is, the complex cooperative processes of adult human society are possible only in so far as every individual is able to take the attitude of all other individuals who are involved in those social processes and is able to direct his or her own behavior accordingly.

In adulthood, then, the complex network of an individual's social interactions are interwoven into the fabric of the person's self, which is at the heart of the personality system, through the process of taking the attitude of the other toward oneself. This process begins as early as the child begins to differentiate itself from others and begins to understand itself as an object separate from those persons with whom it interacts. Certainly, this process involves various aspects of social learning, but the growing perception of oneself as a person reflects the diversity and pattern of social interactions (especially with significant others). In adolescence and young adulthood when the social interactions are increasingly selected by the person, they reflect, support, and extend the person's sense of personhood and identity—which includes but is not limited to the prevailing standards of social norms and conventional social reinforcements. During this period there may be a kind of centrifugal movement in the personality system from the organism out toward the social environment. In later life there may be a relative deemphasis of social interaction and an "increasing interiority" of the personality (Neugarten, 1968).

The interrelation of social interactions with the other components of the personality system is diagrammed in Figure 12.1. The various parts of the personality system are described in detail elsewhere (Kimmel, 1974). The model was developed to describe the simultaneous processes of change and consistency in the personality during adulthood. It represents

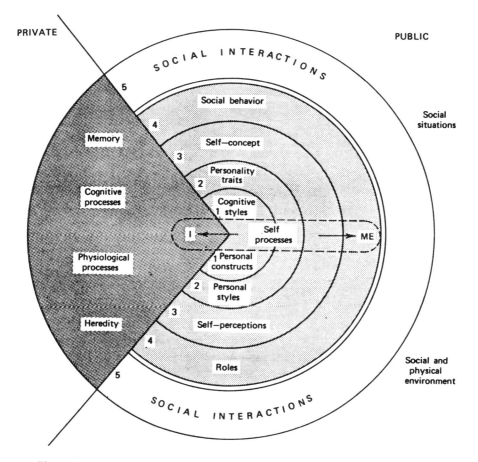

Figure 12.1 Interacting aspects of the personality system. [From D. C. Kimmel, *Adulthood and Aging*. New York: Wiley, 1974.]

the interaction of private aspects (such as memory and physiological processes) with public aspects (such as personality characteristics, social roles, and social interactions) in a dynamic system in which change in any part of the system will bring change in the other parts of it. The boundary of the person is represented by the shaded areas; but the model clearly implies that the personality system includes social interactions and the social environment as well as more traditional components of personality.

Social interactions are conceived quite broadly in this model; they include transient, enduring, and repetitive (but trivial) relationships. For example, an enduring relationship would be interwoven with many layers of the personality system (Altman & Taylor, 1973). In contrast, a transient relationship would typically have no important impact on the personality (except, of course, for those rare fleeting experiences that do remain with us and affect us, despite their short duration). Meaningless repetitive relationships (with bus drivers, bank tellers, and so on) tend to enhance the consistency of the personality system because the interaction is clearly prescribed by social norms; in a sense, such interactions are as much a part of the social environment as they are social interactions.

Just as social interactions may affect the other components in the personality system, so also the different components in the system may affect social interactions. Physiological factors, personal styles, memory, and cognitive styles may each (or all) affect the pattern, meaning, and satisfaction of various social interactions at any point in time. McCall (1974) provides a good example of this interaction:

> Had Jill met Jane on a morning when she was feeling fresh and energetic, she might have asked whether Jane played tennis. Meeting Jane this afternoon when she is tired and depressed, Jill does not even think to inquire. Desire for a given type of reward—such as the intrinsic gratifications of playing tennis—is not an individual constant. Satiation, fatigue, deprivation, and changes in situation can sharply affect level of desire [p. 227].

Thus, social interactions, in this view, are completely interwoven into the human personality system. They have probably played a crucial role in human biological and social evolution. And they clearly play a major role in the development of the human self and the human personality. Conversely, the other major components of the human personality affect social interactions on a moment-by-moment basis. From the perspective of G. H. Mead (1934), social interactions are experienced by the *I* aspect of the self on a moment-by-moment basis; the *I* aspect also allows the continual possibility of novelty and change. (In social-exchange terms, this means that the reward–cost expectancies may change at any point in time; and since they exist only in the *I* they are unobservable and unmeasurable except at second-hand, as it were, as the *I* becomes a *me*.)

If this is true, then social interactions cannot be studied apart from the other components in the participant's personality system. At a common-sense level, this implies that an understanding of an aged man's social interactions requires consideration of *memory* (of his developmental history, of past interactions, and of past interactions with this person), *cognitive development* (and possibly some degree of memory loss), *physiological factors* (such as present health), and even *hereditary predispositions* in addition to *cognitive styles, personality characteristics, social roles*, and his perception of his *social and physical environment* (as well as the other components shown in Figure 12.1). At the same time, it would be recognized that the meaning of the interaction exists in the interaction itself (Mead, 1934), so that the individual's experiencing of that interaction is likely to be closer to its actual meaning than an outside observer's experiencing of the interaction.

IV. Symbolic–Interactionist Approach to Social Relationships

Clearly, the perspective and assumptions in the preceding discussion are those of the symbolic–interaction framework. McCall (1974) has extended that framework somewhat and used it to analyze one aspect of social relationships—attraction. His perspective is quite consonant with this present analysis. He emphasizes the interaction of social relationships and the participant's *role identity, situational factors*, the role of *alter* in the interaction, and the processes of *presentation of the self* (Goffman, 1959) and *altercasting* ("Not only does ego's performance express an image of who *he* is, but it also simultaneously expresses an image of whom he takes *alter* to be [McCall, 1974, p. 223]"). In this framework the process of social interaction is somewhat different from the description given by social-exchange theory, according to McCall (1974):

> Ego must, first of all, somehow reconcile the role he improvises for himself (in response to the role imputed to alter) with the demands of his own salience hierarchy [of role identities]. Second, he must also reconcile his improvised role toward alter with the demands of *alter's* salience hierarchy. The content of one or more of alter's salient role identities may dictate that ego act toward him in an altogether different fashion than indicated by ego's own improvised and expressed role.
> Although the moves of each party are thus motivated by the reward–cost considerations underlying their salience hierarchies, these moves take the form of

insinuations about identities. The negotiation is fundamentally a process of bargaining over the terms of exchange of social rewards, yet it does not assume the outward appearance of a crude naming of prices. Rather, the negotiation takes the form of a subtle (often tacit) debate over who each person is. Each move is expressed through a change (or a refusal to change) in the presentation of self or in altercasting [p. 224].

Thus, the process deals with defining and agreeing upon the role identities of the participants in that situation. It may be that if ego successfully convinces alter of ego's role identity, this is rewarding to ego; or if ego's role identity is relatively congruent with ego's ideal self, this will be rewarding to ego. Or, if alter successfully understands ego's role identity and accepts it, this may be rewarding to ego. These rewards are different from the customary rewards or costs in social interaction, since they do not necessarily depend on whether alter provides customary social profits to ego. In fact, ego may choose not to relate to alter (despite the reward value of alter), because ego cannot convince alter of ego's role identity in that situation. Conversely, ego and alter may continue an enduring relationship because ego and alter accept each other's role identities (which are relatively high in each person's salience hierarchy of role identities) despite the fluctuating costs and rewards of that social relationship.

McCall (1974) also lists five characteristics that lead one person to engage in an enduring relationship with another person:

1. *ascription,* the linkage among persons owing simply to their occupancy of social positions that happen to be interrelated;
2. *commitment,* the fact of having privately and publicly pledged oneself to honoring an exchange agreement with alter;
3. *investment,* the fact of having expended scarce personal resources, such as money, time, and life chances, in the enterprise of establishing interaction with alter;
4. *reward dependability,* the personal knowledge that alter is a dependable source of various social rewards; and
5. *attachment,* the incorporation of alter—and especially alter's actions and reactions—into the contents of one's various conceptions of self [pp. 218–219].

As was noted earlier, the life-span developmental perspective in this chapter focuses our interest primarily on enduring relationships. Such relationships may arise from any of these five interpersonal bonds. It may be noted that these interpersonal bonds clearly recognize the developmental vector in relationships. Also, they diminish the importance of a continuing economic computation of costs and rewards. An enduring relationship (such as a marriage) may be maintained for any or all of these five reasons despite relatively high costs and relatively low rewards in comparison with alternate relationships. In some situations enduring relationships will be maintained even with very high costs and essentially no rewards (as in a relationship with a terminally ill person).[1]

In summary, the symbolic–interactionist approach to relationships seems to provide a framework for understanding social relationships, especially enduring relationships, that is consonant with the life-span developmental perspective. It allows developmental changes over the life-span to be included in the analysis of relationships—as shifts and reordering of the salience hierarchy of role identities with increasing age—and it allows the developmental vector in enduring relationships to be considered in the theoretical analysis. This perspective also avoids the other major shortcomings of social exchange theory—the implicit assumption of the general man, functioning as an economic computer, and the assumption of justice in social relationships. In addition, the perspective developed by McCall elaborates on the dynamic interaction between the person and the social relationships in the personality system. That is, the personality system describes the individual participant in the relationship; the symbolic–interactionist framework describes the process of that interaction at any point in time.

V. Developmental Themes and Relationships

The life-span developmental perspective on social relationships assumes that the nature and meaning of relationships is affected by the participant's age, where age is an index of the multiple factors that make up the vector of human development from conception to death. This section of the chapter will discuss some of the relevant factors in that developmental vector that seem to be particularly important for understanding social relationships. It should be noted that relatively little research has been done on relationships from a developmental perspective, and most of this existing research concerns children or elderly persons (in addition to the great mass of research that has been done on college sophomores that might be taken as research on the developmental period of late adolescence among relatively elite samples). Thus, although some research data will be presented, this chapter has not attempted to represent a review of research findings. Instead, six general factors that affect the developmental vector will be discussed in relatively brief terms. The intent is to point out issues and to raise research questions for the

[1] A significant difficulty in the social-exchange framework is that rewards may be viewed so broadly as to lose all meaning. It might be argued that the reduction of guilt in a relationship with a terminally ill person would be a reward, or that self-sacrificing behavior is rewarding. This would be an example of explaining everything and therefore nothing.

further study of social relationships from a life-span developmental framework.

A. Cognitive Development

In the diagram of the personality system presented in Figure 12.1, cognitive processes are included as one of the four major private components of the personality system. It may be clear that the way one thinks about and conceptualizes one's environment and social relationships (as well as oneself) will be a major factor in determining the nature and meaning of social relationships. As Piaget has demonstrated, cognitive processes change and develop in an orderly sequence through childhood and (at least) early adolescence (see Piaget & Inhelder, 1969). His work is too well known to review here, but a brief sketch of the major themes of cognitive development will suggest the importance of it for an understanding of social relationships.

The sensorimotor period begins with the new-born infant unable to differentiate itself from other persons. Thus it is unable to perceive that it is engaging in social relationships. However, Freedman's (1975) work on smiling in blind infants suggests that the infant may have a "wired-in" mechanism to promote care and concern in social relationships even at this early period. Gradually, the child begins to perceive the separate existence of others and to discriminate one person from another in its social environment. At this point, rudimentary social relationships become possible for the infant. With the advent of language, the nature of social relationships takes a quantum jump, since the ability to communicate in what Mead (1934) calls significant symbols provides the basic means for taking the attitude of others toward oneself. This development of language and the cognitive realization of object permanence, by which the child recognizes that physical objects and other people continue to exist even when out of the child's sight marks the end of the sensorimotor period. At this developmental point the child would be capable of actual social relationships for the first time; however, these relationships would be expected to be infused with illogical and magical thinking characteristic of the preoperational period of development.

This next period, preoperational, is a transition from sensorimotor to logical operations. The lack of logic in this period is manifested by the child's egocentricism. In relationships this would be manifested as a "lack of differentiation between the child's own viewpoint and those of other persons [Looft, 1972]." During this period, Piaget has observed what he calls "private speech," which is not designed for communication, and a general inability to separate the perceptions of the world from what later come to be recognized as logical conceptions of the world. Thus, social relationships with imaginary playmates may be at least as significant as relationships with real persons during this period; and relationships with real persons are likely to be egocentric in the sense of being distorted by the child's nonlogical perceptions.

Logical thought begins with the stage of concrete operations, when the child is freed of the confines of its own perceptions and can understand concrete relations between objects that are physically present. According to Looft (1972), the child's egocentricism at this stage is an "inability to differentiate between mental products (resulting from his newly acquired operations) and perceptual givens [p. 77]." That is, the child believes it can analyze problems accurately, but cannot shift from one perspective to another in a logical manner, as some problems require. In Mead's framework, the child is now able to take the attitude of significant others toward itself, but is not able to take the perspectives of all of the others simultaneously (as in the game of baseball) and confuses the generalized other with significant others. In terms of relationships, the child at this stage of development would be expected to be able to form realistic relationships with other persons who are physically present—for example, in dyadic chumships (Sullivan, 1953)—but would have less ability to integrate differing patterns of relationships in social groups and would be likely to form unrealistic (imaginary or romantic) relationships with persons who are not physically present.

Formal operations bring the next quantum jump in the child's cognitive development (although some persons may reach this level only in adulthood, if at all). This developmental stage allows the adolescent to think in abstractions and to systematically shift perspectives in solving problems. According to Looft (1972), egocentricism is manifested in this stage also: "The adolescent fails to differentiate between the events to which his own thought is directed and those about which others are concerned [e.g., in political activism or adherence to an ideology]. . . . The adolescent takes the other person's point of view to an extreme degree [p. 79]." For Mead, one would now be able to take the attitude of the generalized other (an abstraction), as well as to take the attitude of abstract (fictional or historical) other persons toward oneself. This stage of cognitive development may be thought to allow complex, reciprocal relationships to exist in which the person would be able to understand and appreciate the differing perceptions of several others at once. However, the egocentricism of adolescence might interfere with full acceptance of other's views, especially if they are seen as illogical, irrational, or ideologically incorrect.

The importance of these different stages of cognitive development for understanding the meaning and nature of social relationships may be seen in studies such as those of moral development (Kohlberg & Gilligan, 1971) and the development of gender identity (Kohlberg, 1966). In moral development, the child's evolving sense of ethics progresses from a hedonistic orientation in early childhood through an ethic of social conformity in middle childhood, perhaps reaching as high a level as the one implied in the phrase "the greatest good for the greatest number" during adolescence. Such ethics would appear to affect the nature of social relationships—and especially the person's conceptions of rewards and costs of social relationships—and would differ at various periods of development. Similarly, the research on gender identity indicates that the salience of the gender of others evolves from unknown to concrete (based on physical appearance only) to a highly significant aspect of social interaction (and possibly may continue to evolve toward androgyny for some).

While it is not clear whether there is an additional stage beyond formal operations that may be reached by some persons during adulthood, it would seem that the egocentricism of adolescence is gradually tempered by early adult development—at least for most persons. However, it may be that some persons do not reach formal operations at all (Kohlberg & Gilligan, 1971); this phenomenon is not well understood at present. In addition, some of Kohlberg's data on moral development suggest that adolescents may reach levels corresponding to formal operations, but actually operate on lower levels because the level of cognitive style in the culture does not support the formal thinking style. Perhaps a parallel in our society would be persons who think on a formal-operations level on some tasks but who operate on a concrete or even preoperational level when their car does not start or a light switch does not work. It may be that this same phenomenon occurs in social relationships when magical (preoperational) thinking is employed instead of a logical analysis—as in some relationship problems that lead a person to seek psychotherapy (see Raimy, 1975).

Some data have indicated that in late life a regression in cognitive development may take place (Papalia, 1972). Since these data are not longitudinal and the concept of regression is usually not appropriate for aging persons (the changes are usually more complex than this term suggests), these findings should be treated with caution. In general, however, it would seem that the situations in which the aged person is functioning (i.e., in new situations, long-term relationships, or in institutional settings) would require different levels of cognitive functioning, so that formal operational thinking might be used less frequently by older persons particularly if their social situations tend to be familiar and nondemanding. Physiological factors as well as other aspects of the personality system would also be involved in the level of cognitive functioning in older adults (as in persons of all ages); this is reflected in the model proposed earlier in which all of the components of the personality system are in continual and mutual interaction. Thus, social interactions at different points in the life span would be expected to be affected by a variety of factors that change over time. Cognitive development is one of these factors that has received considerable research attention and would appear to be significantly relevant to the life-span evolution of social relationships.

B. Other Childhood Factors

The childhood years provide a tremendous expansion of the child's ability to form, understand, and engage in social relationships. Both the nature and the meaning of these relationships expand by quantum jumps as cognitive processes develop and as the child's social world expands to include a diversity of significant others. At the same time, the child's ability to perform social roles and to engage in more and more complex social relationships advances dramatically. Loevinger's (1976) summary of research and theory on ego development provides one model of significant developmental change that would be relevant to social relationships. For example, each of the stages of ego development she describes is associated with a different interpersonal style. Related interpersonal effects of psychosocial development can also be inferred from the work of Erikson (1968). And Newman (1976), in her review article, focused specifically on the development of social interaction in childhood.

Returning briefly to the personality model presented in Figure 12.1, it may be noted that the relatively enduring aspects of the personality system would be formed during the childhood years. That is, those components of the system closest to the center of the diagram (Levels 1, 2, and 3) have been found to be highly consistent over time (Mischel, 1968) and it is likely that the stability of these factors results from the interaction between hereditary–physiological processes and the child's early experiences in social relationships. For example, personal constructs are those basic ways in which persons perceive and organize their world. Perhaps some infants are born with a predisposition to conceptualize in (for instance) "large" or "small" categories. However, such categories are constructed through the learning of language and the process of cognitive development; and they represent an individual's blend of parental and social constructs. As was suggested earlier, the reward–cost model for evaluating social relationships may be a peculiarly American way of viewing relationships. In the present context, it may also be a particular personal construct that is used as a framework for viewing one's social world. As such, it was probably learned from parents and significant others during childhood. In contrast, a more prevalent construct among Danish adolescents may be dependable–undependable, based on the Kandel and Lesser (1972) findings.

To take one more example, personality characteristics are another component of the personality system that undoubtedly owe much of their stability to childhood social interactions—and perhaps also to hereditary factors (Thompson, 1968). Put simply, some enduring childhood relationships (especially with parents) tend to have extremely long-lasting effects on the person's later perception of other persons and interpretation of social relationships. In addition, some characteristic styles of responding in social relationships can be attributed to the person's personality characteristics that clearly reflect earlier developmental events and relationships.

Taken together, these various developmental influences would be likely to affect the meaning and pattern of social relationships. The evolving developmental vector of cognitive development or ego development would suggest a progressive change in the meaning and pattern of relationships. And the relative continuity of personal constructs and personality characteristics would suggest enduring predispositions to respond in ways that were learned in childhood. This would imply that there may be cultural differences, idiosyncratic differences, and developmental differences in the child's initiation and development of social relationships. For example, persons at varying points in Loevinger's (1976) sequence of ego development may view the nature and meaning of relationships in significantly different ways. Similar research questions could be posed about the interaction of cultural factors, cognitive and ego development, and sex differences in relationship formation and development. Studies such as these would add to our knowledge of child development and might also further refine social exchange theory or determine the limits of its applicability to social relationships across the life span.

C. Preadolescent Social Relationships: Chumships

Harry Stack Sullivan (1953) described the developmental epochs of childhood and adolescence, emphasizing the interpersonal experiences and changes that are crucial for the development of the person. He noted that:

> Just as the juvenile era was marked by a significant change—the development of the need for compeers, for playmates rather like oneself—the beginning of preadolescence is equally spectacularly marked, in my scheme of development, by the appearance of a new type of interest in another person. These changes are the result of maturation and development, or experience. This new interest in the preadolescent era is not as general as the use of language toward others was in childhood, or the need of similar people as playmates was in the juvenile era. Instead, it is a

specific new type of interest in a *particular* member of the same sex who becomes a chum or a close friend. This change represents the beginning of something very like full-blown, psychiatrically defined *love*. In other words, the other fellow takes on a perfectly novel relationship with the person concerned; he becomes of practically equal importance in all fields of value. Nothing remotely like that has ever appeared before. . . . [The] child begins to develop a real sensitivity to what matters to another person. And this is not in the sense of "what should I do to get what I want," but instead "what should I do to contribute to the happiness or to support the prestige and feeling of worth-whileness of my chum" [p. 245].

These chumships provide the preadolescent with his first experience of intimacy. (Sullivan is explicitly discussing males, although it is reasonable that many of his concepts may apply to females as well.) This intimacy experience is not necessarily related to genital contact, since it is "that type of situation involving two people which permits validation of all components of personal worth [p. 246]." It provides an opportunity to see oneself through another's eyes, to learn to value oneself by valuing another person who is similar to oneself and who values one, and to correct various misperceptions about oneself.

Thus, these chum relationships represent another quantum jump in the nature and meaning of social relationships. They set the stage for sexual intimacy—when the adolescent seeks to involve a person (usually of the opposite sex) in a relationship that is as intimate as his relationship with his chums, but one that also includes what has been called the "lust dynamism"—and for the adolescent issues of identity. These relationships also play an important role in validating oneself as a worthwhile and acceptable person. Insofar as this is a salient characteristic of some preadolescent relationships, it would seem that such chumships would be maintained because of the importance of the mutual acceptance of each other's role identities. Moreover, reward dependability and attachment (McCall, 1974) may further strengthen these chum relationships, so that they are not maintained by relative social status and prestige. It might therefore be hypothesized that the reward–cost model would have less ability to predict which chumships would be maintained than it would to predict which dating partners, for example, might be selected during early adolescence (when rating and dating are often consciously synonymous).

D. Adolescence: Identity and Transitional Relationships

Erik Erikson has described the identity issues that reach their apex in adolescence so widely that his central points do not need to be repeated here (see Erikson, 1968). It is apparent in his discussions that identity is an interpersonal issue and that one's identity is always formed in the context of social relationships (with a probable contribution from formal operational thinking skills). One of the clearest examples of the importance of relationships in resolving the identity issues is represented in those transitional relationships characteristic of adolescence described by Goethals and Klos (1970).

An important aspect of the process of identity formation involves trying out new relationships and new aspects of oneself in relationships. In preadolescence, this often occurs in a chumship; in adolescence the relationship may involve romance and even sexual intimacy, but the goal of the relationship may be more to learn about oneself than to learn about the other person. Often this process involves a kind of bouncing one's self and identity off another person to gain feedback about oneself. Indeed, the actual character of the person one is relating with may be irrelevant if he or she provides some social rewards, thereby increasing one's self-esteem.

It is plausible that these relationships may typify the kind of social interactions that the social-exchange framework describes. Since much of the social-exchange research has used the prototypic college sophomore subjects, perhaps the theory has its clearest utility for this developmental group.

However, these relationships are described by Goethals and Klos as transitional because they are serving as a bridge from the identity issues of adolescence to the intimacy issues of young adulthood. They are often important relationships, for they may provide significant input into the identity formation process, so that when the participants emerge from the relationship, they may have a much firmer sense of identity. Thus, in this developmental view, these transitional relationships serve primarily to clarify the person's sense of identity (although, of course, some persons may continue this process well into adulthood).

Intimacy, in Erikson's view, is possible only when both participants have a firm sense of identity so that intimacy represents a "fusing and counterpointing of identities (Erikson, 1968)." In the symbolic–interaction framework, intimate relationships would be maintained because of investment, commitment, and attachment. Though the social-exchange model may be quite useful for understanding initial attraction in eventually intimate relationships, it is less clear whether it is as useful for understanding enduring relationships in which rewards, costs, and alternative relationships may be superseded by perceived investment, attachment, and commitment to the relationship, as McCall (1974) has proposed. An additional research area would focus on the developmental vector of the intimate relationship: In what ways do the rewards, costs, and power of attachment, commitment, and investment vary as the relationship evolves over time? Does the proverbial seven-year itch or the recently discovered midlife crisis have an effect on these dimensions of intimate relationships? These questions have already set the stage for the next developmental topic: adulthood.

E. Adulthood: Intimate and Intergenerational Relationships

Social relationships in adulthood are as complex as human adults in a heterogeneous society can imagine. Neugarten (1968) once asked:

> What terms shall we use to describe the strategies with which such a person [a business executive, age 50, who makes a thousand decisions in the course of a day] manages his time, buffers himself from certain stimuli, makes elaborate plans and schedules, sheds some of his "load" by delegating some tasks to other people over whom he has certain forms of control, accepts other tasks as being singularly appropriate to his own competencies and responsibilities, and, in the same 24-hour period, succeeds in satisfying his emotional and sexual and aesthetic needs? [p. 140].

Salient relationships during young, middle and late adulthood are almost always those relationships that endure over a period of time—such as intimate relationships, intergenerational relationships and confidant relationships. In an important sense these enduring relationships are the hallmark of adulthood. In McCall's (1974) terms, *ascription* (as in relationships with neighbors and co-workers) *commitment, investment, reward dependability* and *attachment* (as in intimate and kin relationships) would be particularly salient factors in understanding these enduring relationships.

With the passage of time, the length of these enduring relationships increases until death begins ending the relationships—clearly a more frequent occurrence as one grows older and some persons may actually outlive most of their significant long-term relationships. As was noted earlier, these enduring relationships have a developmental vector, so that they accumulate a history, a reliability, and a firm place in one's sense of "identity," "intimacy," "generativity," and "integrity" (to use Erikson's terms). Moreover, as persons grow older their interaction experience increases (Kimmel, 1974), and they gain greater experience and skill in forming, managing, and ending long-term relationships. There may also be a greater selectivity and concentration on significant (rather than peripheral) relationships beginning in young adulthood and continuing on as commitments are formed and evolved (White, 1966).

It would seem that the context of the relationship would be especially significant for understanding adult social relationships. Some enduring relationships with friends, co-workers and spouse(s) have a distinct quality of intimacy—yet they differ in their context. Other relationships serve other needs (such as affiliation or achievement) and other important functions in one's life-space. And still other relationships are intergenerational: with one's parents or with one's children and grandchildren. Each context would be expected to affect the nature of the relationship as well as its development and its meaning. For example, Neugarten and Weinstein (1964) examined the differeing styles of grandparenting, noting the marked differences between the parent and grandparent roles.

Although relatively few studies of these complex adult relationships have been reported, one recent study by Shulman (1975) concluded that "The nature of close relationships does vary with life-cycle changes and that at each stage people tend to establish and sustain networks of relationships geared to the needs and concerns of their particular stage of life [p. 820]." He also noted that a majority of the relationships in the network "had been in existence for at least 11 years." Most of the respondents said that they maintained these relationships because they were "enjoyable"; other prominent reasons were "obligation" and "need" (especially for kin ties).

The importance of the context and the developmental vector in adult relationships is also suggested by data from studies of marital satisfaction through the family cycle. Rollins and Feldman (1970), for example, found that the percentage of wives who were very satisfied with their marriage declined from about 75% at establishment and new-parent stages to less than 10% at the "launching-center" stage, when the adolescents were leaving home. Satisfaction rebounded strikingly, however, with over 80% of the wives reporting they were very satisfied in the aging-family stage. These cross-sectional findings obviously include only those couples whose marriage remained intact (possibly inflating the extent of the increase in satisfaction after the children left and the parents retired), but they do make clear the importance of the developmental questions: At what point in the life cycle are the data relevant? In what developmental context? In which kind of relationship?

The relatively sparse data and the importance of social relationships of various kinds during adulthood clearly suggest the need for many more studies of the developmental course in relationships and in networks of relationships during the adult years. One continuing study of friendship as reported by persons at four different periods of the life-span (Lowenthal et al., 1975) suggests some of the possibilities for future studies of adult social relationships:

> That the sex of the individual rather than his or her stage in life accounts for most of the variation within our sample is well documented. . . . Within each gender, the qualities attributed to close and to ideal friends is surprisingly constant across the four life stages, men tending to emphasize shared interests and activities, women commonly more concerned with affect and reciprocity. The men apparently wished that their friends were different, or that their own capacity for friendship

were different, since they did often emphasize affect and reciprocity in discussing ideal friends. Women at all stages also tended to provide more complex descriptions of friends than men did. At the preretirement stage, however, both sexes were more likely than the younger cohorts to provide elaborate and subtle descriptions of their friends—suggesting that, with pressures of job and family easing off, these men and women had more time to develop awareness and appreciation of the unique individuality of others. The relatively simplistic descriptions of friends offered by the middle-aged women (in marked contrast to the oldest women) was yet another indication that these women facing the postparental phase of life may have been preoccupied with intrapsychic problems [p. 227].

One additional example of important social relationships in adulthood is confidant relationships. Lowenthal and Haven (1968) noted that those aged persons who had a confidant (a close and trusted friend) maintained relatively high levels of morale despite the various social losses inherent in aging, such as widowhood and retirement. In fact, widowed persons with a confidant were found to have higher morale than married persons who did not have a confidant; and retired persons with a confidant were as high in morale as working persons without a confidant. Thus, their data indicate that a confidant relationship serves to buffer the individual against the impact of the loss of other important relationships.

While the Lowenthal and Haven data apply only to older persons, it would seem that confidant relationships would be important for young and middle-aged adults as well. Perhaps the need for a close, trusted friend, such as a chum, in Sullivan's description of preadolescence does not end in adolescence (although its importance may vary with developmental factors); it may continue to be an important source of confirmation of one's more salient role identities and may be particularly significant during periods of crisis, resocialization, or role loss. This suggests several hypotheses for research on the importance of a confidant relationship throughout the life cycle (or from preadolescent chumships to old age intimate friendships). For example, would such relationships be strengthened during periods of crisis? Would the presence of a confidant relationship protect the morale of the person (regardless of age) from the full effect of the crisis? And would such relationships be especially important in crises involving role loss or resocialization since the person's new role identity needs to be formed and affirmed?

F. Death and Relationships

All enduring relationships eventually come to an end. Perhaps no characteristic of relationships calls attention to the developmental vector as clearly as this fact.

The termination of a relationship that once was important to a person may bear some similarity to the process of bereavement and dying that Kübler-Ross (1969) described. There may be some initial (and recurring) need to deny that the relationship is ending; there may be some anger that the relationship is ending and some grieving about it; there may also be some bargaining, some depression over the importance of what is being lost, and eventually some kind of acceptance of what has to be. However, when a relationship is terminated and both persons go on living (as in a divorce), one does not lose the person—only the relationship. When death brings an end to a relationship, there is a finality to the ending that precludes the possibility that one day one might be able to reestablish that relationship again. Thus the process involves grieving for the relationship and for the person. Both were unique and neither can ever be duplicated again.

The process of saying goodbye to someone who is dying can be so important in a relationship that the last few weeks or months can expand in time perspective to equal years of ordinary relations. Research in relationships that are known to be ending because of terminal illness may find that the social-exchange framework is especially inadequate for understanding these relationships. That is, it may be that in such relationships the costs would be disregarded and the profit concept would be meaningless for the persons involved.

This consideration of death and relationships raises the question of whether the social-exchange framework may be most relevant in relationships in which the participants implicitly assume that the relationship is immortal. Most persons probably tend to live as if they—and their relationships—were going to continue forever. But this is obviously a delusion, despite the prevalence of the denial of death in our society.

In this philosophical sense, the life-span developmental perspective clearly calls our attention to the fact that the developmental vector has an end point. If this perspective is taken seriously, it implies that our important relationships have a special significance because they evolve over time, and because they are finite. Just as the awareness of one's own mortality can affect the style and meaning of living, so also the awareness of the finiteness of one's important relationships may affect the quality and importance of the relationship. For example, one might be less willing to procrastinate in correspondence or to leave various kinds of unfinished business in one's relationships if the finiteness of the relationship were more fully acknowledged in one's consciousness—it just might happen that this goodbye will be the final goodbye. Possibly this realization of the finiteness of relationships would also imply that the social profit in relationships has little to do with reward or cost, but instead has something to do with our attempts to find meaning and humanness during our limited life-span as mortal human beings.

There is another aspect to this connection between relationships and dying that was briefly noted earlier. This is that the termination of relationships through the death of the other person may increase one's awareness of the finiteness of one's own life. As one's parents die, as one's friends die (some of whom may be younger than oneself), one comes to realize more and more clearly that one's own death lies ahead. There are other cues too, of course, that begin to shift the time perspective to time-left-to-live sometime during the middle years (Neugarten, 1968); but many of a person's contacts with death come through relationships. And it is through relationships that one comes to learn about the different styles and types of dying. These experiences become more frequent with age; and it is not uncommon for old persons to read obituaries regularly to see which relationships have ended recently (just as younger people may read their alumni newspaper to see what accomplishments their college friends may have reported). Thus, the study of the beginning, evolution, and ending of relationships may hold important lessons about who we are and where we are going in our own developmental progression.

VI. Social Factors and Relationships

The life-span developmental approach to an understanding of relationships calls attention to sex differences, sociocultural differences, and life-style differences as they interact with age differences in relationship initiation and development. If the examination of these factors separately is not unique to the developmental perspective, the concern with the interaction of these factors with age is a central focus of developmentalists.

To take only one example, what has been called *ageism* in the United States (Butler, 1969), we note its effect on the availability of heterosexual relationships for elderly women, the avoidance of close relationships with elderly persons, and the inaccurate stereotypes about the loss of sexual desire and capacity in old age. This social stigmatizing of the euphemistic "senior citizen" may affect the older person's desire and ability to form the same kinds of meaningful relationships that younger people form as a matter of course. We tend to segregate old people as if all old people were only interested in relating to other old people; we tend to assume that all old people do not want young children around (but that young adults do); and we hold to many other stereotypes that imply that old people do not have the same kinds of human needs, desires, and interests that are in fact an essential aspect of every person's humanness.

If anything, old people are more varied in their personalities, interests, and attitudes than younger people. They have had a lifetime of experience and a wider variety of relationships to produce this individuality than young people; and the personality shift toward "increased interiority" (Neugarten, 1968) further manifests this individuality. And yet we tend to assume that stereotypes about all old people are more accurate than stereotypes about young people; in reality, the reverse may be more correct, although every stereotype or generalization has important exceptions.

In terms of relationships, it is possible that ageism results in part from a fear of establishing a close relationship with an old person. This fear might reflect the irrational belief that one might contract aging (as if it were a disease) from too close contact, or the denial of our own mortality in that aged persons may remind us of our own eventual aging and death. Perhaps the reluctance to form relationships with old people also reflects our discomfort with the finiteness of relationships: After all, why initiate a relationship with an old person, who (we assume) is going to die in a few years?

One recent study of sex differences in intimate friendships in old age (Powers & Bultena, 1976) dealt with some of the relevant social factors in relationships as they interact with age for a group of Midwestern persons between 70 and 95 years old. They found (contrary to stereotypes about sex differences) that men interacted with more individuals and had more frequent contacts with other persons than the women (especially with friends, neighbors, spouses, children, and their children's families); women had more frequent contacts with what were termed "intimate friends" (even more contact than with spouses) and with "other relatives" than men did, however.

Kin relationships were important, as one-third of the intimate friends were relatives (for both men and women). Both men and women averaged weekly contact with their intimate friends, although some did not see their friends as often as once or twice a year. One-third of these close friends were younger than 60 (average age of the respondents was 77), but most were relatively close to the respondent's age; few of the intimate friends were much older than the respondents—only one had an intimate friend over 10 years older.

Most of the close friends were of the same sex as the respondent, although one-third of the men's friends were women (and the data suggest that close friends of either sex tend to be substitutes for a spouse among men, since men without intimate friends tended to be married). Nearly one-third of the women had never had a close friend except the spouse, but those who had established an intimate friendship nearly always established another friendship when they lost the previous one.

These data suggest that social relationships remain important throughout the life-span, but that the social factors associated with aging affect the composition of the person's friendship network. Riley and Foner (1968) also note the continued importance of relatives, neighbors, and friends for aged persons, but point out the lack of data on the evolution of friendship patterns through the adult years. The existence of intimate friends whom one does not see even once or twice a year may be difficult to explain from the social-exchange framework, but is not very puzzling from a developmental perspective. However, we need to begin studying the developmental vectors of the variety of friendship patterns as they interact with the other developmental factors in the life cycle to gain a full understanding of the nature and meaning of human relationships as they interact with the developmental vector of the human life-span.

VII. Research Possibilities in Life-Span Social Interaction

The life-span developmental perspective raises a number of questions about the nature of the evolution of social relationships at different points in the life cycle. Four of these issues are central to a more complete understanding of human relationships, and each suggests questions that can be answered only by developmental research.

First, it is clear that relevant dimensions of social relationships change with age. Increased skill in forming relationships and in relating with persons may be expected to result from growing older, but is this an accurate assumption? What are the similarities and differences in intimate friendships at different points in the life cycle? What effect does greater experience with relationship termination have on relationship formation in later life? And what are the relevant dimensions of relationships that change (or that remain consistent) throughout the life-span?

Second, each of the five types of enduring relationships noted by McCall evolve with age (ascription, commitment, investment, reward dependability, and attachment). But what are the similarities and differences in the evolution of these types of enduring relationships? Some would be expected to be more easily replaced than others when the previous relationship is terminated; yet each type of relationship may be expected to continue in some form into old age. How do these types of relationships differ at various developmental points in the life cycle?

Third, it is apparent that the goals, context, expectations, and meaning of relationships change at different points in the life course. For example, these aspects of relationships would clearly be different for a school-age child, an adolescent, a young parent, and an old person. Would it be possible to examine relationships within a life-span perspective such as Erikson's (1968) to explore the differences in the nature and meaning of enduring relationships in respect to autonomy or identity or integrity (for instance)?

Fourth, the complex of factors that interact to produce the developmental vector of an individual's life cycle would be expected to influence the establishment and evolution of the individual's social relationships. Age–sex norms, physiological changes, disease, experience, and cognitive development are some of these interacting factors that need to be explored for their effects on patterns of interpersonal relationships throughout the life-span.

Since social relationships make up much of the fabric of human development, it would seem to be important to explore the complex interactions between human development through the life-span and the patterns of social relationships. However, it seems clear that the social-exchange framework may not be an adequate perspective for this task, particularly because the developmental perspective emphasizes enduring relationships that evolve over time and are, by definition, finite relationships that inevitably have an end point. Different perspectives, perhaps drawing from symbolic–interaction theory and a model of the personality system such as the one presented in this paper may be more useful approaches. However, the task will be a very complex one and much more data needs to be gathered on the evolution of relationships throughout the entire life-span.

References

Altman, I., & Taylor, D. A. *Social penetration: The development of interpersonal relationships.* New York: Holt, 1973.

Butler, R. N. Age-Ism. Another form of bigotry. *Gerontologist,* 1969, 9(4, Part 1), 243–246.

Erikson, E. H. *Identity: Youth and crisis.* New York: Norton, 1968.

Freedman, D. G. *Human infancy.* New York: Halsted Press, 1975.

Gergen, K. J. Social exchange theory in a world of transient fact. In R. L. Hamblin & J. H. Kunkel (Eds.), *Behavioral theory in sociology.* New Brunswick, New Jersey: Transaction Books, 1976.

Goethals, G. W., & Klos, D. S. *Experiencing youth: First-person accounts.* Boston: Little, Brown, 1970.

Goffman, E. *The presentation of self in everyday life.* Garden City, New York: Doubleday, 1959.

Homans, G. C. *Social behavior: Its elementary forms.* New York: Harcourt, 1961.

Huston, T. L. *Foundations of interpersonal attraction.* New York: Academic Press, 1974.

Kandel, D. B., & Lesser, G. S. *Youth in two worlds.* San Francisco: Jossey-Bass, 1972.

Kimmel, D. C. *Adulthood and aging: An interdisciplinary, developmental view.* New York: Wiley, 1974.

Kohlberg, L. A cognitive-developmental analysis of children's sex-role concepts and attitudes. In E. E. Maccoby (Ed.), *The development of sex differences.* Stanford, California: Stanford Univ. Press, 1966.

Kohlberg, L., & Gilligan, C. The adolescent as a philosopher: The discovery of the self in a postconventional word. *Daedalus,* 1971, *100,* 1051–1086.

Kübler-Ross, E. *On death and dying.* New York: Macmillan, 1969.

Lickona, T. A cognitive-developmental approach to interpersonal attraction. In T. L. Huston (Ed.), *Foundations of interpersonal attraction.* New York: Academic Press, 1974.

Loevinger, J. *Ego development: Conceptions and theories.* San Francisco: Jossey-Bass, 1976.

Looft, W. R. Egocentricism and social interaction across the life-span. *Psychological Bulletin,* 1972, *78,* 73–92.

Lott, A., & Lott, B. A learning theory approach to interpersonal attitudes. In A. G. Greenwald, T. C. Brock, & T. M. Ostron (Eds.), *Psychological foundations of attitudes.* New York: Academic Press, 1968.

Lowenthal, M. F., & Haven, C. Interaction and adaptation: Intimacy as a critical variable. *American Sociological Review,* 1968, *33,* 20–30.

Lowenthal, M. F., Thurnher, M., Chiriboga, D., & Associates. *Four stages of life.* San Francisco: Jossey-Bass, 1975.

McCall, G. J. A symbolic interactionist approach to attraction. In T. L. Huston (Ed.), *Foundations of interpersonal attraction.* New York: Academic Press, 1974.

Mead, G. H. Mind, self, and society. In A. Strauss (Ed.), *George Herbert Mead: On social psychology.* Chicago: Univ. of Chicago Press, 1964. [Originally published: *Mind, Self, and Society.* C. W. Morris (Ed.), 1934.].

Mead, M. Long living in cross-cultural perspective. Paper presented at the meeting of the Gerontological Society, San Juan, Puerto Rico, December, 1972.

Mischel, W. *Personality and assessment.* New York: Wiley, 1968.

Neugarten, B. L. Adult personality: Toward a psychology of the life cycle. In B. L. Neugarten (Ed.), *Middle age and aging.* Chicago: Univ. of Chicago Press, 1968.

Neugarten, B. L., & Weinstein, K. K. The changing American grandparent. *Journal of Marriage and the Family,* 1964, *26,* 199–204.

Newman, B. M. The development of social interaction from infancy through adolescence. *Small Group Behavior,* 1976 (February).

Papalia, D. E. The status of several conservation abilities across the life-span. *Human Development,* 1972, *15,* 229–243.

Piaget, J., & Inhelder, B. *The psychology of the child.* New York: Basic Books, 1969.

Powers, E. A., & Bultena, G. L. Sex differences in intimate friendships of old age. *Journal of Marriage and the Family,* 1976, *38,* 739–747.

Raimy, V. *Misunderstandings of the self: Cognitive psychotherapy and the misconception hypothesis.* San Francisco: Jossey-Bass, 1975.

Riley, M. W., & Foner, A. *Aging and society.* (Vol. 1). New York: Russell Sage Foundation, 1968.

Rollins, B. C., & Feldman, H. Marital satisfaction over the family life cycle. *Journal of Marriage and the Family,* 1970, *32,* 20–28.

Rubin, Z., & Peplau, L. A. Who believes in a just world? *Journal of Social Issues,* 1975, *31,* 65–89.

Shulman, N. Life-cycle variations in patterns of close relationships. *Journal of Marriage and the Family,* 1975, *37,* 813–821.

Sullivan, H. S. *The interpersonal theory of psychiatry.* New York: Norton, 1953.

Thibaut, J. W., & Kelley, H. H. *The social psychology of groups.* New York: Wiley, 1959.

Thompson, W. R. Genetics and personality. In E. Norbeck, D. Price-Williams, & W. M. McCord (Eds.), *The study of personality: An interdisciplinary appraisal.* New York: Holt, 1968.

White R. W. *Lives in progress.* (2nd Ed.). New York: Holt, 1966.

PART IV

Epilogue

13

Dynamic Theories of Social Relationships and Resulting Research Strategies

JAMES A. WIGGINS

I. A Theoretical Introduction

This chapter will examine research strategies for analyzing dynamic theories of social relationships. Because the appropriateness of a research strategy is dependent on the particular features of a theory (at least an *explicit* theory), the parameters of the various dynamic theories must be identified. However, as my commission is to prepare a methodological treatment, the theoretical review will be brief, thereby risking the chance of omitting portions of someone's favorite theory—possibly even those included in this volume. (See Huston & Levinger, 1978, for a thorough review of the literature focusing on informal social relationships.)

The first issue concerns the way theories differ in their conceptualization of a social relationship. First, some theories focus on a single variable, be the variable an observed behavior or an inferred attitude. The behavior could be (a) differential contact with or without periodic sampling of alternatives; (b) positive behavior, such as altruism, helping, smiling, entering into contracts of commitment; (c) positive information, such as a promise of positive behavior, approval, self-disclosure or eye contact. The emphasis could be on either the amount or the variety (i.e., breadth) of such behavior or information. The attitude variable may include (a) social perception, such as viewing the participants in the relationships as one; (b) interpersonal attraction, such as liking or loving; (c) beliefs (or positive attributions) about another person or the relationship, such as trust or "heaven-made"; or (d) behavioral disposition, such as wanting to be near someone. On the other hand, conceptualizations of anti-social relationships focus on avoidance, aggression, threats, alienation, hate, and negative impressions. Theories differ in their treatment of the association between social and anti-social relationships, with some conceptualizing them as opposite ends of a single variable (i.e., the nature of a relationship) and others viewing them as two distinct variables that can sometimes be orthogonally or even positively related (i.e., the intensity or intimacy of a relationship).

An alternative view sees social relationships somewhat more abstractly, as a cluster of related variables (factor or dimension). Exchanges of eye contact, gifts, and kisses may all be viewed as components of a social relationship; but a theory might specify that the frequency of kissing is more important in conceptualizing the relationship than either eye contact or gift giving. Yet other theories conceive of social relationships as involving multiple factors, where specific variables are seen as being highly interrelated within a factor but only moderately related between factors. For example, social relationships may be viewed as having three relatively orthogonal dimensions: (a) reward–punishment, (b) power–dependence, and (c) intimacy–formality. Any relationship can be viewed as lying somewhere in the three-dimensional space. (Most of the conceptualizations found in this volume include little variation in the last dimension, since they have been formulated with romantic relationships in mind and thus ignore other primary relationships of equal length, such as parent–child bonds or friendships; secondary relationships, such as between business associates or students and teachers; or more complex role relationships, where the role players are replaced periodically with new participants.)

Research strategies are also influenced by the theorist's approach to the explanation of social relationships. Many theories of the dynamics of social relationships are primarily descriptive, in that they detail the various paths or stages characterizing the typical development of a social relationship. Of course, this is the antecedent step to efforts to explain variation in the development of relationships. The perspectives of several disciplines have been addressed to explanation. Psychology has contributed both cognitive and behavioral models. At least three kinds of cognitive models are represented: (a) cognitive consistency or attitude-change models, whose major mechanism is the minimization of tensions; (b) rational-choice models, whose major mechanism is expected utility; and (c) developmental models, which rely on age-related mechanisms involving information processing skills on which it is assumed some of the other cognitive variables depend. The developmentally based models usually have more complex conceptualizations of a social relationship. Behavioral models also have interesting variations: (*a*) reinforcement models, which emphasize the effect of unilateral or reciprocal contingencies involving rewards and punishments; (*b*) social-network models, which focus on the import of the participants' being involved in several overlapping relationships; and (*c*) ecological models, which focus on the system of interdependent relations among multiple behavioral and environmental variables. Anthropology and sociology focus on variables that are relatively common to those individuals within a society or group (culture and norms) but dissimilar to those individuals representing different societies or groups. The resulting models attempt to (*a*) explain variation in social relationships in terms of intersocietal or intergroup (for example, social class, race, religion) differences, (*b*) explain these associations in terms of the cognitive and environmental variables developed in psychology (such models usually assume that differences in cultural or social *groups* are equivalent to the differences in cultural and social *conditions*), or (*c*) emphasize how the effects of the cognitive and environmental variables are modified by the intersocietal or intergroup variables.

Finally, the choice of a research strategy depends on the conceptualization of the dynamic features of social relationships. Social relationship dynamics involve the study of change rates or the association of the state of the relationship and time. The current language used to describe changes in social relationships is very limited. Continuous descriptions involve relationships which (*a*) remain constant (steady rate), (*b*) become progressively more stable or less stable (increasing or decreasing rate), or (*c*) possess repeated periods of becoming progressively stable interrupted by periods of progressive instability (cyclical rates). Momentary fluctuations are viewed as variations around an equilibrium. At the present time I know of no attempt to describe change rates involving *structural* changes in multivariate conceptualizations of social relationships, unless one is simply interested in counting the number of factors or dimensions characterizing a social relationship over time; for example, integration–differentiation. Descriptions of discontinuous change rates normally involve a small number of variations in rate such as can be classified verbally. Such categories are sometimes referred to as "stages" or "epochs." Stage models view social relationships as going through successive periods of very low change rates separated by periods of relatively high change rates.

Most of the discussion of change in social relationships can also be applied to the description of the explanatory variables used to account for the variations in social relationships. The only major distinction among the various models involves those descriptions of discontinuous changes in explanatory variables (i.e., variables operationalized by a single experimental intervention or a natural event such as a birth of a child) and those descriptions of relatively continuous rate changes (e.g., the availability of alternatives or the support of one's parents). A change in the social relationship may result from multiple rate changes in an explanatory variable. The influence of a current environmental condition may be modified by earlier conditions. An example would be the contrast effect in the interpersonal attraction literature. Resulting changes in social relationships may be permanent or temporary (i.e., revert to a prior change rate). Models seldom specify the time lags between the change in explanatory variables and each change in a social relationship. A permanent or temporary change in a social relationship might follow an environmental change immediately or be delayed for a period of time. The "momentary reversal" sometimes mentioned in reinforcement models is an example of an immediate but temporary change. Finally, dynamic models of social relationships emphasize the possibility of reciprocal causality (i.e., nonrecursive models), whereas most of the current static models of social relationships suggest recursive models, by distinguishing between independent and dependent variables. Dynamic models view any variable as potentially performing both functions. I will elaborate each of these points in my subsequent discussion.

II. A Methodological Introduction

The discussion of research methods for analyzing the dynamics of social relationships will be organized around factors affecting social scientists' confidence in the validity of statements pertaining to such relationships. Such discussion usually reflects the strong influence of Donald Campbell and his associates (for example, see Cook and Campbell, 1975), and this chapter is no exception.

The first kind of statement whose validity may be of concern involves the relationship between concepts and measurements; that is, *concept validity*. How valid is a statement which makes the claim that a concept is accurately measured or a measurement accurately conceptualized? Approaches to evaluating the conceptual validity of static variables focus on the internal consistency or predictive consistency of multiple cross-sectional measures. Methods of inferring the conceptual validity of dynamic variables also focus on the stability of measurement trends. The second kind of statement whose validity may be of concern involves the relationship between two or more concepts; that is, *propositional validity*. How well can the changes in one concept be predicted from changes in other concepts? Whether concerned with the propositional validity of static or dynamic variables, much of propositional validation concerns itself with the argument that the proposed association is uncontaminated by the effects of unspecified variables (i.e., extraneous, confounded, or spurious variables). Propositions involving dynamic variables also suggest the temporal sequence and time lags among the changing values of the concepts. The third kind of statement whose validity may be addressed concerns the correspondence between the available samples of indicators, persons, times, and setting conditions, and the assumed populations of these units to which one wants a concept or proposition to apply; that is, *generalization validity*. Normally, most concepts and propositions are phrased in the most general terms, suggesting little about the researcher's intent as to the specific conditions under which they apply or do not apply. However, it is usually safe to assume that any particular conceptualization or proposition is intended to apply beyond the specific conditions under which it is empirically examined. In some instances, the researcher may have little ultimate interest in the validity of a statement under the precise conditions in which it is tested. So it is of some concern to be as explicit as possible about the population conditions, the sampled conditions, and the correspondence between the two. Whereas persons or places have represented the generalization concerns of cross-sectionality-based theories of social relationships, time (or occasions) has been a major focus of dynamic theories.

The verification of conceptual, propositional, and generalization statements of dynamic processes requires a methodology that is itself in the process of being developed. New methods are being created, old methods extended, and some simply borrowed from other areas of inquiry. Although each of the validity concerns may be addressed separately, it may be best to envisage them together, in a complex model. In any single piece of empirical research, some validity concerns may have to be tentatively assumed while others are examined. It may always be too impractical to gather enough data to evaluate simultaneously all validity concerns. Only cumulative research projects whose only differences are systematic can hope to provide estimates of all aspects of the model.

III. Concept Validity

Concept validity is concerned with the accuracy with which a concept is measured or, conversely, a measurement conceptualized. To some degree, this is an inferential process, since the concept which causes or is caused by the measurement is assumed to be unmeasurable without some error. Thus, any measurement may reflect (a) the designated concept, (b) other undesignated concepts, or (c) some combination of both. The problem is to decide which. If it can be determined that what is reflected is the designated concept, then the measurement is said to be a valid measure of that concept.

A. Cross-sectional Constructs

The ability to decide what a measurement reflects is dependent on three things: (a) the number of indicators, (b) whether the multiple indicators are acquired on a single or on multiple occasions, and (c) the degree to which some of the indicators reflect the undesignated concepts or allow for the elimination of their effects. Let me begin by focusing on indicators obtained on a single occasion, with the assumption that multiple indicators provide more accurate measurement than a single indicator. Two types of errors are to be considered: random and nonrandom (i.e., systematic) measurement errors. If one is addressing random measurement error alone, each indicator will be viewed as reflecting both (a) something the indicators have in common (assumed to be the designated concept) and (b) something unique to that particular indicator (random, undesignated concepts). If the several cross-sectional indicators possess more commonality than uniqueness, then they should meet two empirical criteria. First, the relationships between the measures of the designated concept and other variables should remain relatively consistent across the several indicators (assuming that it is the same variation being predicted in each case). Such predictive consistency could be explained in terms of the similarity in the epistemic relationships between the designated concept and the various indicators (Costner & Schoenberg, 1973). Although practical when dealing with two or three indicators, this criterion becomes cumbersome when dealing with many indicators. The alternative is to demonstrate a strong relationship among all indicators. Internal consistency or unidimensionality could be explained the same way as predictive consistency. Both predictive and internal consistency methods test the validity of statements for the absence of random measurement error.

The choice of a particular validation technique rests on the types of indicators to which the methods are applied. First, a choice must be made between qualitative and quantitative methods. By "qualitative" I am not referring to the fact that many theories include multivariable or multifactorial conceptions of social relationships. Appropriate methods would be used to verify the qualitative distinctiveness of each concept. By "qualitative" I am referring, rather, to the level of measurement of a particular concept. Most qualitative measures assume only binary values; for example, mate selection. On the other hand, many measurements (and corresponding conceptualizations) are quantitative. For example, reinforcement theories use frequency of contact, and cognitive consistency theories use liking intensity. Second, the validation methods must be applied to indicators intended to reflect the entire concept. I shall call such indicators *full indicators*. Many indicators are only *part indicators*, in that as individual indicators they are intended to reflect only a portion of a concept. Several part indicators are needed to capture the entire complexity or quantitative range of a concept. Such part indicators would have to be combined into a full indicator before methods of concept validation could be applied; for example, if one were to conceptualize relationship development as involving both positive and negative behaviors but that intimate couples vary in their resulting behavior ratios (i.e., some are high on positive behaviors and low on negative behaviors, whereas other relationships *of equal development* are high on negative behaviors and low on positive behaviors). Some method of combining corresponding positive and negative indicators (e.g., gazes and glares) would have to be accomplished before applying traditional validations procedures.

But nonrandom measurement error remains a problem. It is only reasonable to assume that each indicator will reflect more than a single source of commonality; that is, the designated concept as well as undesignated concepts (nonrandom measurement error). The only way to distinguish among the alternative sources is to designate conceptually as many of the sources of measurement error as possible and to use methods that will isolate their effects on the measurements. For example, if *liking* is the designated concept, one should be sensitive to the possibility that the indicators may reflect *loving*. Distinctive indicators of *loving* should be included, and, empirically, they should be unique with respect to the indicators of *liking* (using predictive and internal consistency). Similarly, one might suspect that a questionnaire measurement of *liking* may reflect a reaction bias to the method of measurement. Different kinds of instruments, as well as direct measures of reactivity, should be included in the research design. Another possible source of nonrandom measurement error may be the calibration of the instrument. A metric conceptualization of romantic involvement might be measured using four categories: dating, going steady, engaged, and married. However, the actual variations in romantic involvement might be greater within the last category than between the other three. Empirically distinguishable sets of categories might suggest that one of the sets (dating, going steady, engaged, married 1, married 2, . . . married k) should be conceptualized as *romantic involvement* while the prior indicator would more reasonably be conceptualized as *normative involvement*. In addition, many measures provide biased estimates of actual variations at levels of high intensity or deviation. The methods volume of *The Handbook of Social Psychology*

(Lindzey & Aronson, 1968) contains useful discussions of methods-related, nonrandom error common to various measurement procedures; for example, observation, the questionnaire, the interview, content analysis.

B. Dynamic Constructs

For those interested in the dynamics of social relationships, a major concern must be with the validity of a concept-measurement association across repeated occasions. As several indicators at one point in time may reflect designated or undesignated concepts, or both, measurements at successive points in time may also reflect either or both factors. Again both random and nonrandom measurement errors are to be considered. The indicator on each occasion may reflect (a) something the repeated measurements have in common and that was correctly assumed to be the designated concept (reliable, valid, and sometimes stable indicators), (b) something the repeated indicators have in common and that was incorrectly assumed to be the designated concept (reliable but invalid indicators), or (c) some undesignated concept(s) unique to the measurement at that particular time (unreliable indicators).

Instead of focusing on the internal consistency of cross-sectional indicators, attention is drawn to the empirical identification and interpretation of the trends in dynamic indicators. Once a trend is designated, are the deviations from the proposed trend best conceptualized as random or nonrandom (i.e., autocorrelated)? The sources of nonrandom error could include methodological effects due to repeated testing, repeated treatment, and measurement regression as well as the systematic changes in external variables. An illustration may be of some assistance. Figure 13.1 shows hypothetical marital satisfaction data gathered on the first of each month for a 12-year period. First of all, it would be a mistake to describe the data in terms of a simple average-marital-satisfaction score, because

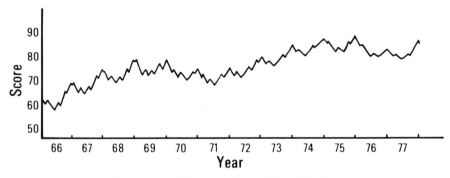

Figure 13.1 Hypothetical marital satisfaction scores.

such a description would suggest that the deviations from the average score were random. Subjecting the data to eyeball scrutiny or statistical tests of randomness (e.g., serial correlation or the Von Neumann ratio) should invalidate such a statement. Second, although the data look irregular over the 12-year period, they could be described in terms of a general, stable increase in marital satisfaction. However, again the deviations—this time from the trend—are not random. There are at least two cycles in the data. The first cycle appears to last 5–6 years. The second cycle (nonrandom deviations from the first cycle) is shorter, appearing to be almost annual, reaching a high about the end or the beginning of each year and falling to a low about midyear. Beyond this point it is hard to distinguish between random and nonrandom deviation. But if the data were gathered using repeated testing, separated by intervals of only 1 month, of the same individuals and using the same instrument, it would probably be reasonable to assume that part of the remaining variation was not random due to test–retest effects. Thus, any set of longitudinal data may contain several sources of systematic variation. The data set must be decomposed, in order that theoretical statements will describe as much of the systematic variance as possible with the assumption that the residuals are random.

The first identification attempted might be that of a single long-term trend—if for no other reason than a zest for parsimony. In order to do this, one must be able to screen out the possible systematic cycles and random variations. In some instances it may be possible to "eyeball" such a trend. Given the nonspecific trend conceptualizations that have dominated the scanty dynamics literature, this is a real possibility. Although the newer mathematical models (usually associated with simulation efforts, such as those of Huesmann and Levinger, 1976) offer a great deal more flexibility in such conceptualizations, limited verbal descriptions will probably continue to dominate the field for some time. However, it may be useful to at least note the corresponding mathematical functions in anticipation of the increasing specification that should develop in the future. (See Table 13.1.)

Short of actual mathematical functions, a moving average may be constructed to describe a general trend. By replacing each value at a point in time by the average of values at preceding and succeeding points, variations are of course removed. How much is removed is determined by the number of successive values included in each average. In the marital-satisfaction illustration, averages based on twelve successive values should remove the annual cycle; 60–70 values would have to be used to eliminate the longer cycles.

In determining the validity of statements describing the dynamics of a variable in terms of a general trend (whether determined by least squares or by moving average), some evidence must be provided that the devia-

TABLE 13.1
Change Functions

Each of the following functions belongs to a family of simple polynominals whose general expression is

$$y_t = a + bx + cx^2 + dx^3 + \cdots.$$

where
  a = the y intercept
  b = the slope, or the rate change in Y, at the origin
  c = the rate of change of the slope at the origin—the degree to which the curve is bent
  d = the rate of change in the degree to which the curve is bent

Verbal	*Visual*	*Mathematical*
Stable		$y = a + bx$ (linear)
Accelerating		$\log y = a + bx$ (logarithmic)
Decelerating		$y = a + bc^x$ (modified exponential)
Decelerating		$y = 1/a + bc^x$ (logistic)
Cycle		$y = a + bx + cx^2$ (second-degree parabola)
Cycle		$y = a + bx + cx^2 + dx^3$ (third-degree parabola)

tions from the trend are random. The general trend can be removed from the data through subtraction or division procedures to disclose the deviations of interest. A moving average could be constructed from the adjusted data to assist in the identification of cycles of nonrandom variations. Care must be taken to assure that the variations removed by the moving average do not include both random and nonrandom errors. Long-term cycles may include short-term cycles. To guard against this possibility, the constructed moving average representing the cycle should be removed from the adjusted data, and the readjusted data examined for shorter-term cycles.

  The method of removing average is less effective in completely removing variations as the duration and amplitude of the variations become less consistent across the time series. Changing cycles can be examined by dividing the data into blocks of time and plotting each block independently, as one would look for interaction effects in a block-design experiment. The slopes would indicate cycles; the levels would indicate trends (i.e., changes in cycles).

  In addition to nonrandom deviations due to cycles imposed on a general trend, autocorrelation may result from short-term repeated-testing effects. Those effects may be examined by intercorrelating the measurements for several n-lagged time periods so as to produce a function showing changes in the magnitude and direction of the correlation as the time interval increases. The specification of the length of the autocorrelation effect provides a basis for deciding the number of values to include in each average of a moving average.

Some might feel more comfortable with the position that data such as the hypothetical marital-satisfaction data could be accurately described by statements referring to an average, a trend, or either of two cycles. All statements would be valid. For example, Heise (1977) has proposed a theory of affect control in which attitudes operate at two levels, a fundamental (or moving-average trend) and a transient (short-term cycles). If one takes this position, one should be clear as to specifying that the validity of the particular statement is based on the assumption that deviations are *not* random but rather capable of autocorrelation. Doing so will have the consequence of restricting one's use of normal estimates of standard error and, therefore, tests of significance.

Jöreskog and Sörbom (1976) have developed a path analytic method (and a corresponding computer program, LISREL) of statistically estimating and testing alternative models involving longitudinal data. It includes estimates of possible autocorrelation due to repeated testing. Models that do not specify this particular autocorrelation error can be compared to those that do (what is called a "test-specific factor") to see which provides the best fit to the data.

As an alternative to estimating autocorrelation, attempts may be made to eliminate it. For example, if one suspects that answering questions about business or personal relationships will affect answers to the same questions if repeated a short time later, different but equivalent questions should be used for each administration. The equivalency of indicators would be determined during pretesting using the same predictive and internal consistency for testing construct validity. Similarly, subjects being exposed to a repeated-treatments design may respond differently to the initial exposure from the way they respond to subsequent exposures. If this is a possibility, reexposure should be delayed until the effect of the previous exposure has been eliminated and the baseline recovered. Finally, experimentalists should be sensitive to the possibility of turning random error into nonrandom error by assigning subjects to experimental groups on the basis of extreme (high and low) pretest scores or correlates of pretest scores. Given random-measurement error, regression may occur on subsequent measures so that high scores will decrease and low scores will increase.

The analysis of the dynamics of multivariate conceptualizations of social relationships is pretty much limited to a consideration of changes in factor structures and factor loadings and, as a result, to data meeting the related assumptions (Bentler, 1973). Although not particularly useful for the analysis of gradually changing trends or cycles, factor-analytic methods can be used to verify statements involving major changes by extracting information concerning the number of definable factors relating to a time dimension. The previously mentioned Jöreskog method is one example. Great care should be taken in providing a theoretical basis for the particular rotation solution applied to the data. An as yet incompletely explored possibility (which has gotten mixed reviews) would be the removal of the time dimension from the factorial matrix by applying factor-analytic techniques, not to the values at successive occasions but directly to values representing certain change functions (Nesselroade and Bartsch, 1976).

Some theoretical trend statements involve qualitative as opposed to quantitative changes. Such statements usually refer to (a) invariant sequential patterns of different responses, as opposed to systematic changes in the value or magnitude of the same response, and (b) the amount of time to advance from one level to another, as opposed to the rate of change of a single response. Figure 13.2 shows sequential patterns containing sets of responses where (a) each behavior displaces the preceding one (i.e., disjunctive responses) or (b) each lower-level response is retained as the higher-level responses develop (i.e., cumulative responses). Disjunctive responses are illustrated by the many formal forms of address and initiators of conversation that mark the beginning of a relationship and that give way to informal forms (usually abbreviated) marking an advanced stage. Cumulative responses are illustrated by the introduction of a lover to one's friends before and during the introductions to one's relatives. A less restrictive model might allow the termination of responses to produce a different sequential pattern than that of the acquisition of the same responses. Following an exact specification of the proposed sequential pattern, its validity can be examined using the same scalogram-analysis techniques that are used in evaluating the internal consistency of a set of responses (Bentler, 1971; Guttman, 1944; Leik & Matthews, 1968; Loevinger, 1948).

Raush's use of Markov process analysis provides an interesting

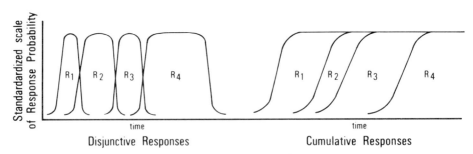

Figure 13.2 Qualitative change.

method of identifying a quantitative trend involving the development of two persons' reactions to each other (Raush, 1972). Once a set of circumstances establishes the initial probabilities of each person's reactions to the other, and, assuming the causal effects extend only a single measurement (i.e., Lag 1) and external circumstances do not change, the direction and the slope (speed) of the trend representing the development of the relationship can be predicted. Particular probabilities might predict a rapid transition from initial positive impressions to stable romantic love. Other probabilities might result in the projection of a cyclical relationship varying between periods of harmony and conflict. Departures from the predicted trends would provide an indication of a change in variables external to the simple structural relationship.

All of the longitudinal methods suffer two disadvantages: time and possible autocorrelation. The researcher's reaction is usually that of taking another look at cross-sectional methods. This is particularly tempting when the researcher feels confident he can argue that all persons pass sequentially through a series of points or stages; for example, ages, grades in school, positions in an organization, stages in romantic involvement. Other responses are then the target of interest. How do these responses change as individuals progress through the sequence? Instead of identifying a trend in a variable as each person or dyad passes through the successive points, a trend across points may be located using different persons at each point. Data-collection time would be shorter and autocorrelation problems would be avoided—but in exchange for what? Although it may be possible to argue that the points specified the same for all persons, these points were, in all probability, not experienced under the same historical conditions. Thus, a host of extraneous variables must be added to a theoretical model. Moreover, there is no way to investigate the various change functions for the unit of analysis of greatest interest, that of the individual person or social group. In other words, analyses based on measures of change per se are precluded. The theoretical statements of interest usually require such measures. One compromise between cross-sectional and longitudinal designs would be to obtain shorter longitudinal data on a set of cross-sectional samples such that the units of analysis in the longitudinal series are partially overlapping. This is a particularly useful method if units can be matched on the basis of their change functions during the overlapping periods.

IV. Propositional (Internal) Validity

Many of the theoretical statements concerning the dynamics of social relationships involve proposed associations between *different* concepts. If truly concerned with dynamics, such propositional statements should make explicit reference to the *directionality* of the variables involved. At least three aspects of the temporal sequences of the changing values may be specified. First, the statement may propose an order of change among two or more variables. A recursive association would suggest that changes in A will precede but not follow changes in B, or vice versa. A nonrecursive association would suggest that the changes are reciprocal; that is, changes in one or both variables both precede and follow changes in the other. A correlational association suggests there is no time lag separating the changes in A and B, but that instead, the changes occur simultaneously. (Of course, one should be reminded that the term *correlation* is frequently used when a propositional statement fails to specify directionality.) Second, the statement may propose a specific time lag separating the various changes. Here caution must be exercised in specifying the total change in a single variable; that is, the overall trend. If a change in one variable precedes a *temporary* change in a second variable, the latter could be conceptualized as two changes with two corresponding time lags (i.e., the time to establish steady-state and the time it is maintained before returning to baseline). Third, if the statement proposes a nonrecursive association with related time lags, it could propose a specific pattern to the system. The effect of the reciprocal changes among the variables could be monotonic trends (i.e., amplification) or cycles (i.e., control). The trends or cycles could remain constant over time, or they could exhibit changes of increasing magnitude (i.e., unstable) or decreasing magnitude (i.e., stable). Finally, if the statement explicitly proposes a correlational association with time lags involving repeated simultaneous changes, I simply refer you back to the previous discussion of the trend analysis of multivariate conceptualization. The only distinction between the analysis of the dynamics of multivariate conceptualization and correlational association is conceptual. The only empirical basis of differentiation would be the higher correlations expected in the former case. A discussion of the verification procedures would be very repetitive.

Again, let me note that the major problem with assessing the validity of propositional statements involving directionality is the same as that for assessing the trends of single concepts. Data must be accumulated at enough points in time to be sure that the complete effects have been indicated, and must be spaced closely together in order to be sensitive to the exact time lag(s). *Nothing can replace or be substituted for such data.*

Let me illustrate these alternatives—again using hypothetical data for a proposed recursive association. In Figure 13.3, the dependent variable is the daily record of the number of occasions on which either member of a work pair gave the other some assistance at his job. The independent variable is the presence or absence of an individual or group quota

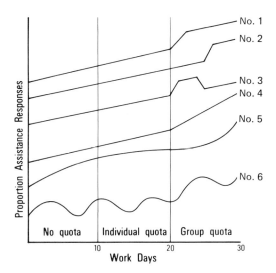

Figure 13.3 Hypothetical work assistance data.

system. (The dependent variable has already been averaged to provide smooth trends.)

Although all work groups show an increase in assistance rates at the introduction of the individual quota system, none show a change in the trend that was established prior to the introduction. In other words, the assistance rates at any point in time (before or after the change) can be explained in terms of the assistance rates at prior points in time without taking the change in the quota system into account. Whatever the circumstances were that produced the trends when there was no quota system simply maintained the same trend during the existence of the individual quota system.

On the other hand, all of the trends show some alteration when the group quota system is introduced. The first three groups show an increase in the level of the trend (a in the polynominal), the first being an immediate, permanent change, the second being a delayed change (time lag about 7 working days), and the third being an immediate, temporary change (time lags of 0 and 6 working days). The fourth group shows an increase (immediate and permanent) in the slope of the trend (b in the polynominal). Group 5 demonstrates a change in the curvature of the slope (c in the polynominal). Group 6 appears to have cycles of job assistance the level of which is simply increased during the introduction of the group quota system. Thus, although the data would support a general statement that a change from an individual quota to a group quota system will produce a change (in the positive direction) in the job assistance rate whereas a change from the absence of an individual or a group quota system to an individual quota does not produce a change, they do not account for the specific trend changes. Neither do the data afford the opportunity to validate any statement referring to the effect of other kinds of qualitative changes. For example, what would be the effect of changing directly from the absence of any quota system to a group quota system?

In this particular hypothetical situation, the independent variable was a qualitative change. An elaboration of a general model involving the effects of changes in quota systems could include quantitative changes in the two quota systems; for example, changes in the amount of work output for the same amount of pay. The quantitative changes could be conceptualized in terms of trends, resulting in the possibility of proposing and investigating the effects of changes in the various components of the trend; for example, level and slope.

As real data will, typically, not be as "neat" as this hypothetical set, one will usually turn to a statistical analysis to aid in making a decision as to the validity of a propositional statement. One has two choices, although the choice may be dictated more by the quantity of data available than by the model one is attempting to assess. Both involve fitting regression lines before and after the change in the independent variable and then examining them for significant differences in level or slope. A safe assumption either of no autocorrelation or of fewer than fifty data points will point to (or limit one's choice to) the ordinary least-square methods. (See Bock, 1975, for a discussion of various repeated-measures designs based on ordinary least squares.) Given more than 50 data points, the autocorrelation assumption does not have to be made and generating-function procedures may be employed. (See Box & Jenkins, 1970; Box & Tiao, 1975; & Glass, Willson, & Gottman, 1972, for a discussion of the procedure.) It should be noted that by increasing the space between data points one may increase one's confidence in the absence of autocorrelation due to some sources (e.g., repeated testing) and, thus, increase the appropriateness of the more practical ordinary least-squares methods. However, one does so at the risk of decreasing one's confidence that the data points are sensitive to short-term changes.

[I have ignored discussion of situations in which group comparisons are made on the basis of a single measurement before and after a change in an independent variable. Previous discussions (Bock, 1975) have focused on the inappropriateness of (a) gain scores given measurement error and regression effects and (b) covariance analysis as a substitute for randomization in initially equating groups.]

The above discussion has been predicated on the assumption that the association is recursive. Changes in the quota system could affect changes in job assistance but not vice versa. What is the empirical basis for this assumption? It would not be unreasonable to propose that quota systems are introduced as a result of low job assistance or low productivity, a possible correlate. Once a high level of job assistance or productivity is reached, the quota system could be withdrawn (possibly because quota systems are expensive to maintain). However, in the present hypothetical data, it would appear that the two quota system changes were made under similar conditions in the job assistance trend and in both cases under steady-state conditions (i.e., no indications of a change in trend prior to the interventions). Similarly, the postintroduction trends are identified while the quota systems are in stable-state.

In many data sets, it is more reasonable to stipulate nonrecursive than recursive associations. Parent–child interaction could be a case in point. The data set in Figure 13.4, again hypothetical, involves the semidaily observations of (a) father's abuse of his oldest child and (b) that child's aggressiveness toward the father. (Conceptually, it may be cleaner to think in terms of their mutual abuse.) The relationship between the two variables is clearly reciprocal, with changes in each following changes in the other. However, the time lags for the two components are different, but constant. A change in the frequency of the father's abuse is followed approximately two days later by a change in the frequency of the child's aggression. (This has to be approximate, for some precision has been lost as a result of semidaily observations.) In turn, a change in the latter is followed 6–8 days later by a change in the former.

The positive effect of each variable on the other results in the monotonic amplification of both variables. Abuse increases aggression, which drives up subsequent abuse; subsequent abuse increases aggression even more—and so on. However, the rate of change is dampened over time and eventually reaches a steady state (or equilibrium) of very high

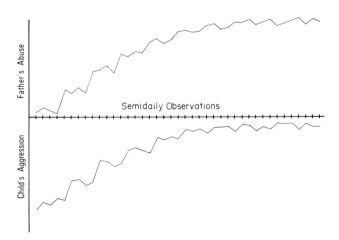

Figure 13.4 Hypothetical parent–child interaction data.

rates of abuse and aggression. The trends of both variables could be described using an exponential curve. Unfortunately real data might indicate constant rate changes in both variables (linear trends) or even increasing rate changes (logarithmic trends), either of which could "explode" the social interaction when the upper limit of the variables is eventually reached.

Of course, the effects of this particular reciprocal relationship could be altered by the presence of another set of relationships. Suppose that the child's aggression triggers the abuse of the mother (2-day time lag), which, in turn, results in a decrease in the child's aggression (4-day time lag), followed by a decrease in abuse, and that when the mother's abuse is withdrawn, it results in another round of the child's aggression and the mother's abuse. In this reciprocal association, the changes in each variable counters the changes in the other, the result being that both variables oscillate between periodic increases and decreases in their respective rates to form a cyclical trend. In addition, the amounts of rate change remain constant over time. (The magnitude of each oscillation could have increased or decreased. In the latter case, the mother's abuse and the child's aggression would reach a stable state.) The net effect of the mother–child interaction on the behavior of the father and the child would be a decrease in the amplification of the child's aggression and the father's abuse. The latter will occur as a result of the fact that the father is frequently responding to a degree of child aggression that has been suppressed by the mother's abuse. On the other hand, the mother's abuse will periodically increase (the upper limit of the oscillation), because she is responding to increasing degrees of child aggression by the father–child interaction. The analysis would become more complex by postulating a direct association between father's abuse and mother's abuse in addition to the indirect association resulting from their common nonrecursive associations with the child's aggression. For example, if the association were negative with a 2-day time lag (i.e., an increase in father's abuse is followed 2 days later by a decrease in mother's abuse), a change in the father's behavior would produce two changes in the mother's behavior— the first occurring two days later (the direct effect) and the second some four days later (the indirect effect of father on child and, in turn, child on mother).

An additional complexity to the analysis of dynamic social relationships is that each of the above descriptions was simplified by basing it on the deterministic assumption that the probability of social behavior is either 0 or 1. Although this may be a practical first approximation, one will ultimately want to relax this assumption in favor of a probabilistic model. Raush's analysis of the interaction process among family members uses transitional probabilities in a Markov chain (Raush, 1972).

Nonrecursive associations also lend themselves to another conceptual complexity that is popular among ecologically oriented social scientists. Whereas one may begin an analysis by viewing the separate parts of the social relationship in cause and effect terms, one might alternately conceive of the relationship as a single system reacting to (or interacting with) external forces. The changes in the social relationship would be viewed as being initiated by an external force (i.e., environment, social networks, biological or evolutionary factors) but with all subsequent changes simply reflecting the system's reaction in terms of a gradual transition from one stage, epoch, or stable state to another. Thus change due to external forces would again be reflected in changes in trends.

If the verbal descriptions of this kind of process are complex, their statistical analysis is horrendous. Most of the readers of this volume are familiar with the analysis of microsequences of qualitatively conceived and measured behaviors. The data for such an analysis is usually obtained from an unbroken sequence of observations that provide a scenario of designated persons engaging in designated behaviors (categories, but the intensity sometimes also observed) at designated points in time. Behavior is probably the only phenomenon to be examined in such a continuous manner, given our conceptualization of the more permanent nature of cognitive phenomena such as attitudes. The frequencies of recursive and nonrecursive sequences as well as correlational patterns are, then, (a) subjected to chi-square analysis to see if particular sequences or patterns occur more frequently than would be expected by chance or (b) compared for different groups of persons in terms of their having different personal characteristics or of their having been exposed to different environments. The complexity of the analysis increases rapidly as the length of the behavioral sequence increases.

Most of the other familiar techniques for the analysis of quantitative variables were devised for use with panel data collected at a small number of time points. Thus the techniques were not intended to shed much light on questions involving time lag or the specific patterns resulting from a nonrecursive association. Instead their purpose was restricted to the evaluation of the strength of the nonrecursive association.

The cross-lagged panel correlation technique was devised to determine whether one variable (A) was a stronger cause of a second variable (B) than the reverse. Although the initial proposals involved the comparison of the magnitudes of two cross-lagged correlations ($r_{A_1 B_2}$ and $r_{B_1 A_2}$, subsequent revisions of the technique have rightly proposed the comparison of the partial correlations ($r_{A_1 B_2 \cdot B_1}$ and $r_{B_1 A_2 \cdot A_1}$) (Pelz & Andrews, 1964). Two equally strong partials, especially in comparison with the simultaneous correlations ($r_{A_1 B_1}$), would suggest a nonrecursive association, whereas significantly different partials might suggest a recursive association. Heise (1970) proposed the structural equation approach as an alternative using path coefficients as estimates of the lagged effects of each variable on the other. Wohlwill, Fusaro, and Devoe (1969) have developed a procedure that extends the cross-lagged method to the examination of qualitative change. As noted, the procedures are of little use in evaluating time lags. Instead, the success of each of these procedures is predicated on the assumption that the time lag of any possible causal association has been properly identified and measurements made at the appropriate intervals. Each further assumes that the association is not correlational and that the time lags for all parts of the association are about the same.

Data gathered at several points in time allow an examination of alternative time lags or, assuming only brief lags, allow enough replications of the analysis to examine the stability of the causal process. If no changes are indicated, the replications could be pooled to provide more precise estimates of the underlying dynamics.

Although many researchers, especially experimentalists, have frowned upon the use of structural equation techniques for the causal analysis of social dynamics, it is probably safe to assume that their applications will actually increase in frequency in the years to come. Until recently, analyses have been primarily restricted to the application of the ordinary least-squares method (OLS) to cross-sectional data in order to examine what was assumed to be the stable state of a recursive association. Of course, it was legitimately noted that estimates obtained by OLS were biased and inconsistent if the measures of the independent variables were unreliable. In addition, OLS could not transform cross-sectional data into longitudinal data in order to verify the directionality of an association. Estimates of measurement error had to be obtained before incorporating OLS. For example, Jöreskog's technique (LISREL) combines a factor-analytic technique for estimating measurement error with OLS for estimating recursive associations. The directionality had to be verified via some other methods or, as was more often the case, simply assumed. In the event that there was some reason to believe (or assume) the association was nonrecursive, the two-stage least-squares method was used to obtain estimates although this necessitated the risky task of identifying "instruments"—that is, variables which were *assumed* to have no involvement in the nonrecursive association but to have effects on some but not all of the variables in the association. Given the availability of longitudinal data, lagged values of variables become the obvious candidates for instruments. This is the logic behind the cross-lagged procedures just mentioned. Thus, longitudinal data increase the apparent utility of structural equation techniques. But nonrandom (correlated) error remains a problem. As the earlier discussion of autocorrelation noted, the best way to deal with the problem is to have a direct measure of the residual cause creating the disturbance, or a theory specifying its effects and enough data to obtain proper estimates. The test-specific factor in the Jöreskog procedure serves this function. Otherwise, the generalized least-squares method provides truer estimates of associations given the presence of autocorrelation.

However, if autocorrelation exists as a function of a nonrandom residual cause linking repeated measures, the same residual cause could link independent and dependent variables via the lagged values of the dependent variable. Thus lagged values would represent inappropriate instruments for the assessment of nonrecursive associations. (See the Smith discussion, 1978, of the research by Tesser & Paulhus, 1976.) The solutions to this specific problem are the same as those applied to the general problem of the control of any nonrandom residual cause (i.e., extraneous variables, confounding variables, alternative explanations, spurious associations, threats to internal validity). Can one verify that the residual causes in which one is not immediately interested are unrelated to those of immediate interest, at least for the data at hand? It depends on two conditions, (a) the specification and measurement of the residual causes and (b) the appropriateness of and opportunity to employ experimental designs with randomization of relatively unspecified residual causes.

In most instances, the verification of control depends on the identification of the residual cause. Such residual causes may be only residual in respect to a specific research proposition derived from a theoretical model that includes the causes as part of the model. More probably, what is one researcher's designated cause is another's residual cause. Therefore, every effort must be made to work within a complete theoretical model to aid in the identification of potential residual causes. Given corresponding measures, structural equation techniques will provide estimates of the direct effects of the designated cause independent of the indirect effects produced by the *specified* correlated residual cause. If the model is relatively simple and the association between causes less than strong (either naturally or by experimental manipulation), the independent effects of the designated cause may be examined using cross-classification techniques. The latter have the advantage of exploring the possibility of interactions before the various estimates are averaged. On yet other occasions, residual causes are only inferred by assuming they are correlated with a specified surrogate variable. For example, both time and persons are assumed to represent many variables. The same person is assumed to represent relatively unchanging values of cognitive variables, at least within a brief time-span. Different persons drawn from different backgrounds probably represent different variations. However, different persons at the same point in time may represent the same historical events. As time passes, both personal characteristics and environmental events are assumed to change. Experimentalists make frequent use of surrogate residual causes when they assume that the real residuals are being held constant when they expose each subject to multiple treatments or when they compare experimental and control groups at approximately the same point in time. They also assume that real residuals are being randomized when subjects are randomly assigned to treatments. Even though randomization may represent the only hope of controlling unspecified residual causes, it too is not without its limitations (even if one assumes it achieved its intent). Nonrobust associations may be masked by the effects of the residual cause(s). The opportunity to explore the possibility of interactions involving the residual cause is not possible. And, what is possibly most important for the investigation of dynamic phenomena, there is no guarantee that the randomization will remain in effect over a period of time. Given nonrecursive associations, the effected dependent variable will feed back on the values of the independent variables altering the orthogonal association between them.

V. Generalization (External) Validity

A third kind of research concern is the correspondence between the available samples of indicators, persons, settings, and time and the assumed populations to which generalization is desired; that is, generalization validity. (I have departed from tradition by including a discussion of indicator generalization, or content validity, as a case of generalization validity instead of including it as part of concept validity.) The most powerful validation of generalization is drawn from a research situation in which the desired population can be clearly designated and a representative sample can be drawn from this designated population. A less powerful alternative to the latter is to use a sample of modal units of concern such that one's findings might apply to the largest segment of the designated population. A less powerful alternative to the clearly designated population is to use a wide range of the units of concern without being able to specify the exact population that they represent. One would be generalizing *across* units (having demonstrated the absence of statistical interaction) as opposed to generalizing *to* a population. To date, most researchers have found it easier to designate a population of persons than populations of indicators, settings, and time. Thus, most of the *practical* concerns of generalization validity have been placed on using a range of indicators (multimethods), persons (different sexes, ages, occupations), settings (laboratory and natural), and time (dynamic theories). I will illustrate the problems of practical generalization validation by referring to three areas familiar to those interested in investigations of social relationships: experimental methodology, crosscultural research, and time sampling.

As many of our ideas about social relationships are based on experiments, it is probably worthwhile to quickly review the traditional criticisms. First, it is certainly true that most experimentalists fail to specify any kinds of populations to which they propose their empirical findings apply (and we continue to use tests of significance as though this were not the case). Convenience sampling is the norm. Second, the range of units employed is frequently limited, often with the intent of strengthening propositional validity. The behaviors and attitudes examined are usually of low complexity and intensity. As a result, most of the theoretical statements may be applicable only to the initial development of social relationships. The exceptions are usually those experiments conducted in a therapeutic situation where the participants are willing to subject themselves to extensive measurement and provocative manipulations. Although the participants are typically undergraduates and the setting is a room on or near a college campus, some experimentalists are concerned enough about generalization to examine their propositions across sexes or races as well as across one or more situational variables. Similarly, although the number of occasions sampled is usually very small, a few experimentalists will obtain data (using simple measurement) at 50–200 points in time. Even then, however, the findings may be more applicable to informal than formal interaction. A related criticism is that only molecular units are examined and that little attention is given to molar units. For example, most propositions investigated apply to individual persons or small groups. Whether these propositions (or some variants) apply to aggregates of persons, or groups, remains relatively uninvestigated. One exception is the interest of experimentalists in the effects of both contingent (individual occasions) and correlational (aggregated occasions) reinforcement. Such interest will probably increase in the future as a result of the increasing participation of experimentalists in policy analysis where many programs are implemented at the aggregate rather than the individual level. Finally, experimentalists must contend with the criticism that the conditions of their investigations are unique and share little variance with the conditions in the real world. One of the principal conditions is the presence of the experimenter with his measurements and manipulations. As a result, experimentalists have spent a great deal of time attempting to identify experimenter effects or disguising their experiments as part of natural events. A more controversial issue centers on experimental control procedures that establish orthogonal associations among independent variables. Ecologically oriented theorists suggest that such orthogonal associations seldom occur outside experimental situations. Instead, interdependence is the normal rule. If this is true, the concern with independent effects is irrelevant, unless one is interested in "what-if" propositions.

Of almost equivalent concern has been our focus on middle-class

Americans. Recently, Triandis encouraged APA members to "explore universals of social behavior. By universal is meant a psychological process or relationship which occurs in all cultures [Triandis, 1978]." In order to attain this generality, one has to use concepts that are at a high level of abstraction. Such abstractions are readily available in our disciplines. The problem comes in the development of measurements whose contents reflect the broad parameters of the abstract concepts. Consider a measurement of the concept of romantic love which would be applicable to the various cultures of the world. Most researchers do very little to suggest their population of indicators, because only a few will be relevant to the specific research situation at hand. This is readily seen in situations where the same concept is operationalized in different ways by different researchers, particularly those doing research in different cultures. Thus, we may have different validated propositions involving romantic love among middle-class Americans, Italians, Eskimos, Samoans, and Chinese. Although of equal propositional validity, these propositions may differ in the degree to which they can be used to explain romantic love in other cultures. It may be that our conceptual scheme could be so interdependent that several culture-specific concepts could be definitionally subsumed under a more culture-free concept, allowing one a basis for moving from the more abstract to the less abstract in a way that would allow the high-level abstractions a greater impact on one's choice of measurements. Lonner (1978) has recently reviewed the cross-cultural literature in an effort to identify concepts of greater cultural generality. Several of the concepts are relevant to investigations of social relationships. Rather than discuss the problems associated with such efforts, let me simply refer you to discussions by Werner and Campbell (1975) and Echenburger (1973) focusing on the establishment of equivalence of different indicators in different cultural environments. (As noted earlier, many sociological and anthropological investigations of social relationships focus on cultural variations in social relationships, as opposed to concentrating on cultural universals.)

Finally, the sampling of time or occasions is of critical importance to the development of dynamic theories of social relationships. The importance of time samples in the identification of trends was previously noted. Too few occasions may not result in the identification of short-term oscillations or delayed changes. Equally important is the possibility that different propositions are applicable at different points in a relationship. What applies during the initiation of a relationship might not apply as the relationship continues. For example, Kerckhoff and Davis' (1962) "filtering theory" proposed that initial contact of heterosexual persons may best be explained by background similarity. However, subsequent contact may be better explained by attitude similarity, and even later contact probably results from satisfied complementary needs. Reinforcement-oriented theories have suggested that there are distinctive propositions explaining the initial acquisition, the maintenance, the extinction, and the reacquisition of behavior. For example, Molm and Wiggins (1978) have shown that under some conditions social exchange can be maintained by noncontingent reinforcement although the initial establishment of the exchange required contingent reinforcement. In such instances it is more useful theoretically to consider time as a surrogate for variables related to the history of the development of the social relationship. Increased understanding of a particular kind of social relationship will increase our capacity to specify the time sampling appropriate for empirical investigations of such relationships, and vice versa.

VI. A Final Note

The methodological literature concerning the empirical investigation of the dynamics of social relationships is very spotty and disorganized, owing to its relatively undeveloped status. Instead of attempting to touch all the methodological bases, using a general schema familiar to social psychologists, I have concentrated on organizing the issues of concern to those interested in dynamics. Although my discussion of any given method could not do justice to its particular development, I hope that enough has been said concerning its applicability to the analysis of social relationships to encourage your further in-depth study. If you have not as yet immersed yourself in the dynamics methodology, now is the time to do so (a course in econometrics is a good beginning), because the area will develop more in the next 5 years than in all the years till now combined—and the current developments are already sufficiently complex.

My underlying thesis (and I hope it wasn't lost in the detail) was that theory and methods are usually correlated. The conceptualization of a parameter of a social relationship influences the choice of data collection techniques, the number of indicators, the number and spacing of successive repetitions of the indicators, and the concept-validation procedures. (And in view of experience with particular methods, the relationship is nonrecursive.) It has often been asserted that a theory that generalizes across several methods is better than one restricted to a particular method. There is a valid point to be made here. In some instances, validity can be increased using multiple methods. On the other hand, some methods were developed in order to address specific kinds of theoretical statements. Thus, the more explicit a theoretical statement (including its assumptions), the more obvious the methods required to evaluate its validity. I am always amazed at the number of graduate students who after taking several methods and statistics courses do not associate various theoretical statements with the appropriate research design and analysis procedures. As I suggested at the beginning, our verbal (theoretical) statements involving social relationship dynamics are both limited and somewhat disorganized. We are only beginning to speak what might be termed a "dynamics language." Though simply perplexing to some, to others such developments represent a welcome revitalization of old interests—a new frontier.

References

Bentler, P. M. Monotonicity analysis: An alternative to linear factor and test analysis. In D. R. Green, M. P. Ford, & G. B. Flamer (Eds.), *Measurement and Piaget*. New York: McGraw-Hill, 1971.

Bentler, P. M. Assessment and developmental factor change at the individual and group level. In J. R. Nesselroade & H. W. Reese (Eds.), *Life-span developmental psychology: Methodological issues*. New York: Academic Press, 1973.

Bock, R. D. *Multivariate statistical methods in behavioral research*. New York: McGraw-Hill, 1975.

Box, G. E. P., & Jenkins, G. M. *Time series analysis: Forecasting and control*. San Francisco: Holden-Day, 1970.

Box, G. E. P., & Tiao, G. C. Intervention analysis with applications to economic and environmental problems. *Journal of the American Statistical Association*, 1975, *70*, 70–79.

Cook, T. D., & Campbell, D. T. The design and conduct of quasi-experiments and true experiments in field settings. In M. D. Dunnette & J. P. Campbell (Eds.), *Handbook of industrial and organizational research*. New York: Rand McNally, 1975.

Costner, H., & Schoenberg, R. Diagnosing indicator ills in multiple indicator models. In A. S. Goldberger & O. D. Duncan (Eds.), *Structural equation models in the social sciences*. New York: Seminar Press, 1973.

Echenburger, L. H. Methodological issues of cross-cultural research in developmental psychology. In J. R. Nesselroade & H. W. Reese (Eds.), *Life-span developmental psychology: Methodological issues*. New York: Academic Press, 1973.

Glass, G. V., Wilson, V. L., & Gottman, J. M. *Design and analysis of time-series experiments*. Boulder, Colorado: Colorado Associated Univ. Press, 1972.

Guttman, L. A basis for scaling qualitative data. *American Sociological Review*, 1944, , 139–150.

Heise, D. R. Causal inference for panel data. In E. Borgatta, & G. Bohrnstedt (Eds.), *Sociological methodology*. San Francisco: Jossey-Bass, 1970.

Heise, D. R. Social action as the control of affect. *Behavioral Science*, 1977, *22*, 163–177.

Huesmann, L. R., & Levinger, G. Incremental exchange theory: A formal model for progression in dyadic social interaction. In L. Berkowitz & E. Walster (Eds.), *Advances in experimental social psychology*, (Vol. 9.) New York: Academic Press, 1976.

Huston, T. L., & Levinger, G. Interpersonal attraction and relationships. *Annual Review of Psychology*, 1978, *29*, 115–156.

Jöreskog, K. G., & Sörbom, D. Statistical models and methods for analysis of longitudinal data. In D. J. Aigner & A. S. Goldberger (Eds.), *Latent variables in socioeconomic models*. Amsterdam: North-Holland, 1976.

Kerckhoff, A. C., & Davis, K. E. Value consensus and need complementarity in mate selection. *American Sociological Review*, 1962, *27*, 295–303.

Leik, R. K., & Matthews, M. A scale developmental process. *American Sociological Review*, 1968, **33**, 62–75.

Lindzey, G., & Aronson, E. (Eds.), *The handbook of social psychology*, (Vol. 2). Reading: Addison-Wesley, 1968.

Loevinger, J. The technique of homogeneous tests compared with some aspects of scale analysis and factor analysis. *Psychological Bulletin*, 1948, *45*, 507–529.

Lonner, W. The search for psychological universals. In H. C. Triandis & W. W. Lambert (Eds.), *The handbook of cross-cultural psychology*. Boston: Allyn and Bacon, 1978.

Molm, L. D., & Wiggins, J. A. A behavioral analysis of the dynamics of social exchange in the dyad. *Social Forces* 1979, *57*, 1157–1179.

Nesselroade, J. R., & Bartsch, T. W. Multivariate experimental perspectives on construct validity of the trait-state distinction. In R. B. Cattell & R. M. Dreger (Eds.), *Handbook of modern personality theory*. New York: Halstead, 1976.

Pelz, D. C., & Andrews, F. M. Causal priorities in panel study data. *American Sociological Review*, 1964, *29*, 836–848.

Raush, H. L. pProcess and change—A Markov model for interaction. *Family Process*, 1972, *11*, 275–298.

Smith, E. R. Specification and estimation of causal models in social psychology: Comment on Tesser and Paulhus. *Journal of Personality and Social Psychology*, 1978, **36**, 34–38.

Tesser, A., & Paulhus, D. L. Toward a causal model of love. *Journal of Personality and Social Psychology*, 1976, **34**, 1095–1105.

Triandis, H. C. Some universals of social behavior. *Personality and Social Psychology Bulletin*, 1978, **4**, 1–16.

Werner, O., & Campbell, D. T. Translating, working through interpreters, and the problems of decentering. In R. Naroll & R. Cohen (Eds.), *A handbook of methods in cultural anthropology*. New York: Columbia University, 1973.

Wohlwill, J. F., Fusaro, L., & Devoe, S. *Measurement, seriation, and conservation: A longitudinal examination of their interrelationship*. Paper presented at the meeting of the Society for Research in Child Development. Santa Monica, California, March, 1969.

Author Index

Numbers in italics refer to the pages on which the complete references are listed.

A

Abrahams, D., 51, *60*, 126, *133*
Adams, B.N., 231, *245*
Adams, J.S., 99, 103, 125, *131*
Adler, A., 255
Aigner, D.J., *406*
Ainsworth, M.D., 296, *303*
Akers, R.L., 298, *303*
Alexander, R.D., 5, 198, 200, 201, 204, 210, 211, 212, 213, 214, 215, 217, 218, *220*
Altman, I., 8, 10, 15, 16, *25*, 107, *131*, 144, 158, 159, 160, 166, *167*, 174, *176*, *191*, 223, *245*, 256, 258, *266*, 315, *347*, 358, *376*
Altrocci, J., 251, *268*
Anderson, B., *303*
Anderson, V.E., 127, *132*
Andrews, F.M., 399, *407*
Ansbacher, H.L., 255, *266*
Ansbacher, R.R., 255, *266*
Arber, S., 70, *98*
Arnold, W.J., *131*
Aronson, E., 56, *58*, 108, 109, *131*, *267*, 388, *407*
Aronson, V., 51, *60*, 126, *133*
Avery, A.W., 5, 13, 19, 22, 23, 184, *193*
Austin, W.G., 103, 116, 117, *131*

B

Backman, C.W., 125, *131*, 256, *268*
Bakke, E.W., 120, *131*
Baltes, P.B., 273, 284, 285, 302, *303*, *304*, *305*
Bank, S., 258, 264, *267*
Banton, M., 221, *246*
Baral, R., 14, *26*
Barclay, A., 104, *131*
Barnes, J.A., 224, 227, 228, 230, *245*
Barry, W.A., 237, *246*
Bartsch, T.W., *407*
Bayer, A.E., 70, *96*
Bayley, N., 283, *304*
Beals, A.R., *246*
Beavin, J.H., 253, *269*
Bell, R.Q., 271, 294, 295, 296, 297, 298, 300, 301, *303*
Bell, R.R., 311, 312, *347*
Bell, S.W., 296, 300, *303*
Bem, S.L., *266*
Benjamin, L.S., 252, 259, *266*
Bentham, J., 4
Bentler, P.M., 310, *347*, 392, *406*
Berger, J., *303*
Bergler, E., 126, *131*
Berkowitz, J., 59

409

Berkowitz, L., 131, 303, 348, 406
Berlyne, D., 35, 36, 38, 54, 58, 59
Bernard, J., 7, 25, 106, 125, 131
Berscheid, E., 13, 14, 15, 17, 25, 43, 48, 49,
  50, 51, 52, 55, 59, 60, 73, 75, 77, 98, 99,
  100, 101, 104, 106, 115, 116, 117, 125, 126,
  127, 131, 133, 176, 183, 191, 268, 283, 303
Bertalanffy, L., 273, 276, 303
Bieri, J.A., 252, 266
Birch, H.G., 279, 296, 305
Birchler, G.R., 25, 28, 164, 165, 167
Blake, J., 68, 96
Blau, P., 12, 25, 41, 59, 65, 66, 68, 76, 77, 80,
  87, 90, 91, 94, 96, 97, 106, 110, 111, 115,
  125, 131, 203, 207, 221, 233, 245
Blood, R.O., Jr., 112, 185, 191
Blumberg, L., 311, 312, 347
Bock, R.D., 396, 406
Bohannan, P., 126, 131
Bohrnstedt, G., 115, 127, 131
Boissevain, J.P., 21, 22, 25, 223, 224, 226,
  230, 231, 232, 240, 245, 246
Bolles, R.C., 34, 59
Bolton, C.D., 159, 161, 167
Booth, 315, 347
Borgatta, E. F., 139, 167, 406
Borgia, G., 217, 220
Bott, E., 22, 25, 228, 232, 245
Bottomore, T., 87, 96
Boulding, E., 110, 131, 191
Bouterline-Young, H., 285, 304
Bowerman, C.E., 139, 167
Bowers, K.S., 249, 266
Box, G.E.P., 396, 406
Boye, D., 43, 59
Bradburn, N.M., 156, 164, 165, 168
Brady, J.P., 310, 347
Braiker-Stambul, H.B., 9, 17, 139, 141, 144,
  160, 164, 165, 167, 340
Brazelton, T.B., 297, 298, 299, 303
Brehm, J.W., 23, 25, 124, 131, 184, 191
Briar, S., 252, 266
Brickman, P., 69, 70, 71, 96
Brim, O.G., Jr., 139, 167
Brock, T.C., 377
Brothren, T., 55, 58
Brown, J.S., 161, 167
Brown, P., 186, 191
Brown, R., 252, 266
Bruner, J.S., 251, 266
Buber, M., 191
Buckley, W., 76, 89, 96
Bultena, G.L., 374, 377

Burgess, E.W., 7, 25, 112, 127, 131, 167
Burgess, R.L., 7, 12, 25, 74, 96, 164, 189, 275,
  298, 301, 303, 304
Burns, T.A., 233, 234, 235, 245
Burr, W.R., 9, 25, 98
Bushell, D., 12, 25, 304
Buss, A., 131
Butler, R.N., 373, 376
Byrne, D., 41, 59

C

Campbell, A., 185, 186, 191
Campbell, B., 221
Campbell, D.T., 384, 404, 406, 407
Campbell, J.P., 406
Caplow, T., 163, 168
Carlson, R., 250, 266
Carpenter, G.R., 311, 347
Carroll, J., 27
Carson, R.C., 5, 138, 168, 234, 245, 250, 251,
  252, 253, 255, 256, 259, 263, 266
Carterette, E., 58
Cate, R., 318, 348
Cattell, R.B., 407
Celani, D.P., 259, 266
Cerreto, M., 105, 123, 127, 132
Chadwick-Jones, J.K., 12, 25, 86, 87, 97
Chagnon, N.A., 209, 214, 220, 221
Chapman, J., 51, 59
Chapman, L., 51, 59
Cheever, J., 14, 25
Chein, I., 43, 59
Cherlin, A., 185, 186, 191
Chess, S., 279, 296, 305
Chihara, T., 283, 304
Chiriboga, D., 370, 377
Christensen, H., 98, 131, 311, 347
Christie, R., 263, 267
Clark, K., 19, 26
Clifford, M.M., 283, 303
Clore, G., 14, 26
Cohen, A.R., 124, 131, 184, 191
Cohen, R., 407
Cole, C.L., 9, 28
Coleman, J.S., 64, 95, 97
Collins, R., 71, 82, 85, 97
Colson, E., 68, 97
Converse, P.E., 185, 186, 191
Cook, T.D., 384, 406
Cooke, R.E., 305
Cooper, M., 234, 245
Coser, L.A., 72, 90, 91, 93, 97
Costner, H., 386, 406

Cottrell, L.S., Jr., 142, *167*
Cromwell, R.E., 73, *97*, *98*
Cronbach, L.J., 249, *267*
Cross, H.J., 310, 311, 313, 314, 315, 343, *347*, *348*
Cuber, J., 7, *26*, 186, *191*
Cubitt, T., 227, 228, *245*
Cummings, E.E., *347*
Cunningham, J., 137, 139, 141, 164, *168*
Curran, J.P., 310, *347*
Cutright, P., 185, *192*
Czajka, J., 70, *98*

D

Dahl, R.A., 73, *97*
Dahrendorf, R., 62, 91, *97*
Darley, J., 43, *59*
Darwin, C., 202, 203, *221*
D'Augelli, A. D., 5
D'Augelli, J.F., 5, 310, 312, 313, 314, 315, 320, 322, 323, 328, 329, 331, 343, 344, *347*
Davis, G.C., 315, *349*
Davis, K., 68, *96*
Davis, K.E., 9, 13, 17, 19, *26*, 46, *59*, 183, 184, *192*, 404, *407*
Davis, M.S., 87, *97*
Day, H.I., *59*
DeBurger, J.E., 139, *167*
Dermer, M., 43, 48, 49, *59*
Deutsch, M., 6, 7, 10, 11, *26*, 28, 71, 77, 78, *97*, 190, *192*, 252, *269*
Devoe, S., *407*
Diener, E., 249, *268*
Dion, K. K., 17, *26*
Dion, K.L., 14, 17, *25*, *26*, 183, *191*, 283, *303*
Donnenwerth, G.V., 109, *132*
Douvan, E., 105, *132*
Dreger, R.M., *407*
Driscoll, J.M., *59*
Driscoll, R., 13, 17, 19, *26*, 184, *192*
Duchnowski, A., 41, *60*
Duck, S.W., 9, 14, *26*, 265, *267*
Duncan, O.D., *406*
Dunnett, M.D., *406*
Durkheim, E., 21, *26*

E

Echenburger, L.H., 404, *406*
Eckland, B.K., 182, *192*
Edquist, M.H., 260, *267*
Edwards, J.N., 315, *347*
Ehrmann, W., 311, 312, 313, *348*

Ekeh, P.P., 12, *26*, 63, 66, 68, 69, 70, 72, 76, 77, 80, 86, 89, *97*, 190, 191, *192*
Ekehammer, B., 249, *267*
Elder, G.H., Jr., 127, *132*
Ellis, D.P., 61, 63, 64, 66, 68, 69, 77, 80, 86, 87, 89, *97*
Emerson, R.M., 5, *26*, 73, 74, *97*, 271, 272, 298, 301, *303*
Endler, N.S., 249, *267*
Engels, F., 82, *97*
Erikson, E.H., 365, 367, 368, 375, *376*
Erikson, K.T., 23, 24, *26*
Escalona, S., 298, *303*
Exline, R., 54, *59*

F

Fairchild, R.W., 139, *167*
Farbman, I., 254, *268*
Farber, B., 86, *98*, *132*, 161, 167
Faris, R.E.L., *96*
Faucheux, C., 125, *133*
Faw, T., 54, *59*
Fazio, R., 51, *60*
Feffer, M., 299, *303*
Fei, J., 17, *25*
Feld, S., 164, 165, *167*
Feldman, H., 362, 370, *377*
Festinger, L., 124, *132*
Figley, C., 54, *59*
Firestone, S., 82, *97*
Fischer, C.S., 23, *26*
Flamer, G.B., *406*
Flaubert, G., 20, *26*
Flavell, J., *59*
Fleming, A.T., 310, 316, 318, 337, *348*
Fleming, K., 310, 316, 318, 337, *348*
Fogarty, M.P., 80, *97*
Foa, E.B., 22, *26*, 109, *133*, 174, 175, *192*, 252, 253, 258, *267*, 308, 332, *348*, *349*
Foa, U.G., 22, *26*, 109, *132*, *133*, 174, 175, *192*, 252, 253, 258, *267*, 308, 332, *348*, *349*
Foner, A., 374, *377*
Foote, N.N., 159, *167*
Ford, M.P., *406*
Fouraker, L., 77, *98*
Fox, A., 69, 70, 78, *97*
Freedman, D.G., *376*
Freedman, S., 99, 125, *131*
Freud, S., 82
Friedman, M., 49, *58*
Friedrich, L.K., 281, *305*
Fromm, E., 13, *26*, 105, *132*

Furstenberg, F.F., 83, 84, 97, 185, 192
Fusaro, L., 407

G
Gadlin, H., 21, 26
Gagnon, J.J., 311, 348
Garrison, R.L., 127, 132
Gary, A.L., 107, 133
Gebhard, P., 311, 348
Geis, F.L., 263, 267
Gelles, R.J., 93, 97
Gerard, H., 50, 51, 52, 59, 60
Gergen, K.J., 25, 26, 27, 168, 192, 256, 257, 267, 353, 376
Gesell, A.L., 277, 303
Gibson, J.J., 33, 59
Gilligan, C., 363, 364, 377
Glass, G.V., 396, 406
Glick, P.C., 7, 19, 27
Gluckman, M., 226, 230, 245
Goethals, G.W., 368, 376
Goffman, E., 359, 376
Goldberger, A.S., 406
Goode, W.J., 93, 97, 112, 139, 167, 186, 192
Goslin, D.A., 305, 348
Gottesman, I. I., 127, 132
Gottman, J., 188, 192, 258, 264, 267, 396, 406
Goulden, C.E., 220
Goulding, S.L., 249, 251, 265, 267
Gouldner, A.W., 62, 63, 64, 76, 80, 82, 97, 236, 245, 258, 267
Goulet, L.R., 273, 302, 303, 305
Graziano, W., 15, 43, 48, 49, 55, 59
Green, D.R., 406
Greenberg, M.S., 27, 168, 192
Guerney, B.G., Jr., 188, 192, 259, 268
Gurin, G., 164, 165, 167
Gurvitch, G., 87
Guttman, L.A., 392, 406

H
Hage, J., 6, 7, 27
Hamblin, R.L., 98, 376
Hamilton, W.D., 198, 203, 217, 221
Hamburger, V., 277, 303
Hammerlynch, L.A., 193
Handy, L.C., 193
Harlow, H.F., 280, 303
Harlow, M.K., 280, 303
Harre, R., 33, 59, 309, 348
Harris, D.B., 273, 276, 303, 305
Harrison, A.A., 182, 192
Harroff, P.B., 7, 26, 186, 191

Hartup, W.W., 271, 281, 293, 303
Hatch, C.D., 127, 132
Hatfield, E., 8, 11, 12, 112, 113, 116, 205, 207
Haven, C., 371, 377
Heath, A., 64, 73, 74, 80, 88, 89, 97
Heider, F., 39, 59
Heise, D.R., 391, 399, 406
Heiss, J.S., 158, 167
Heller, K., 259, 267
Henzi, 112
Hertel, R.K., 237, 246
Hertzig, M., 279, 305
Hetherington, E.M., 305
Hill, C.T., 20, 26, 159, 183, 184, 186, 192, 311, 314, 342, 343, 349
Hill, R., 98, 158, 168, 177
Himmelfarb, S., 44, 59
Hinde, R.A., 8, 26, 305
Hobbes, T., 3
Holmes, J.G., 261, 268
Holmes, S.J., 127, 132
Holter, H., 68, 71, 97
Homans, G.C., 12, 24, 26, 36, 59, 63, 66, 68, 73, 80, 92, 93, 97, 179, 192, 205, 207, 208, 219, 221, 233, 245, 272, 287, 290, 293, 298, 304, 315, 348, 352, 376
Honigmann, J.J., 246
Hoogland, J.L., 198, 220
Hops, H., 112, 132, 141, 168, 188, 189, 193, 229, 237, 246
Howard, R.D., 198, 220
Hubbard, M., 51, 60
Hudson, 112
Huesmann, L.R., 10, 13, 15, 16, 17, 26, 27, 107, 108, 132, 139, 168, 170, 171, 175, 176, 192, 318, 348, 389, 406
Hunt, M.M., 186, 192, 314, 315, 319, 331, 343, 347
Hunts, D.E., 59
Huston, T., 5, 12, 14, 26, 28, 54, 59, 67, 97, 126, 131, 132, 181, 183, 192, 223, 245, 260, 267, 284, 304, 318, 348, 352, 376, 377, 381, 406

I
Ingersoll, H.L., 159, 167
Inhelder, B., 362, 377
Inkeles, A., 97
Insko, C.A., 14, 28, 126, 133
Irons, W.G., 198, 220, 221
Irving, C., 310
Iwawaki, S., 283, 304

J

Jackson, D.D., 105, *132*, 253, *269*
Jackson, D.J., 284, *304*
Jackson, D.N., 265, *267*
Jacobson, P.H., 186, *192*
Jaffe, D.T., 187, *192*
Jenkins, G.M., 396, *406*
Johnson, V.E., 309, 316, 338, 339, 343, 344, *348*
Jones, A., 120, 127, *132*
Jones, E., 39, 46, 50, *59*
Jones, M.C., 283, 284, 285, *304*
Jones, S.J., 300, *304*
Joreskog, K.G., 391, *406*
Jorgensen, B.W., 9, *27*, 108, *132*, 183, 184, *193*
Jourard, S.M., 107, *132*
Jurich, A.P., 322, 323, 331, *348*
Jurich, J.A., 322, 323, 331, *348*

K

Kafka, J.S., 144, 145, *168*
Kahn, G.M., 107, *133*
Kandel, D.B., 353, 365, *376*
Kanouse, D., 39, *59*
Kapferer, B., 226, 227, *245*
Kaplan, S.J., 6, 7, *28*, 252, *269*
Karabenick, S.A., 283, *304*
Kates, R.W., 231, *246*
Katz, F.E., 224, *245*
Kelly, G.A., 251, 265, *267*
Kelley, H.H., 9, 10, 12, 13, 17, 18, *28*, 36, 39, 40, *59*, *60*, 75, 77, 88, 95, *97*, *98*, 137, 138, 139, 141, 142, 159, 164, *168*, 170, 171, 172, 173, 179, 182, 223, *246*, 257, 259, 261, 262, *267*, *268*, 293, *305*, 340, 353, *377*
Kerckhoff, A.C., 9, *26*, 67, *97*, 183, *192*, 256, *267*, 404, *407*
Kiesler, S., 14, *26*
Kimmel D., 5, 357, 369, *376*
Kimmel, M.J., 18, *27*
Kinsey, A.C., 311, *348*
Kirkendall, L., 311, 312, 314, *348*
Kirpatrick, C., 163, *168*
Kiser, C.V., 127, *132*
Kline, L.V., 259, *267*
Klos, D.S., 368, *376*
Knapp, J.R., 283, *304*
Koch, S., *268*
Kogan, N., 267, *268*
Kohlberg, L., 274, 321, 322, 323, 333, 337, *348*, 363, 364, *376*, *377*

Komarovsky, M., 112, 120, *132*, 312, 313, 315, *348*
Korn, S.J., 279, 282, *304*, *305*
Koslowski, B., 297, *303*
Kronberg, C.L., 259, *267*
Kubler-Ross, E., 372, *377*
Kuhlman, D.M., 261, *267*
Kuhn, A., 74, *97*, 100
Kunkel, J.H., *98*, 376
Kuo, Z.Y., 276, *304*

L

Laing, R.D., 343, *348*
Lambert, W.W., *407*
Langer, E.J., 189, 190, *193*
Lanzetta, J.T., 38, 40, *59*
Lawrence, D.H., 18, *27*
Layton, B.D., 14, *28*, 126, *133*
Leary, T., 252, 253, 254, 255, 256, 259, 264, *267*, 308, *348*
Lederer, W.J., 105, *132*
Lee, A.R., 343, *348*
Lee-Painter, S., 271, 281, 295, 301, 302, *304*
Lehrman, D.S., *305*
Leik, R.K., 10, 19, *27*, 65, 66, 71, 74, 78, 86, 87, *98*, 392, *407*
Leik, S.A., 10, 19, *27*, 65, 66, 71, 74, 78, 86, 87, *98*
Lempers, J., 271, 281, 293, *303*
Lepper, M., 51, *60*
Lerner, M.J., 10, *27*
Lerner, J.V., 284, *304*
Lerner, R.M., 5, 65, 67, 272, 274, 276, 279, 280, 282, 283, 284, 286, 291, *304*
Lesser, G.S., 353, 365, *376*
Leventhal, G.S., 258, *267*
Levin, S., *305*
Levine, D., *131*
Levine, R., 43, *59*
Levinger, G., 5, 6, 8, 9, 10, 12, 13, 14, 15, 16, 17, 20, 23, *26*, *27*, 33, 35, *60*, 107, 108, 112, *132*, 139, 140, 144, 145, *168*, 170, 171, 173, 174, 175, 176, 179, 180, 181, 182, 183, 186, 187, 189, *192*, *193*, 223, *246*, 252, *267*, 290, *304*, 316, 317, 318, 319, 343, *348*, 381, 389, *406*
Levi-Strauss, C., 63, 68
Levitt, E.E., 310, *347*
Lewin, K., 161, *168*, 179, *193*
Lewis, M., 271, 281, 293, 295, 302, *303*, *304*
Lewis, R.A., 9, *28*, 223, *246*
Lewontin, R.C., 198, *221*
Libby, R.W., 314, *348*

Lickona, T., 342, 348, 354, 377
Lindzey, G., 267, 388, 407
Lipetz, M.E., 13, 17, 19, 26, 184, 192
Lippold, S., 310, 347
Lipset, S.M., 68, 97
Llewellyn, L.G., 254, 268
Locke, H.J., 112, 116, 139, 164, 165, 166, 168
Locke, J., 3
Loevinger, J., 365, 366, 377, 392, 407
Longfellow, C., 187, 193
Longworth, A.R., 31, 310
Lonner, W., 404, 407
Looft, W.R., 272, 274, 275, 281, 302, 304, 362, 363, 377
Lott, A.J., 67, 98, 355, 377
Lott, R.E., 67, 98, 355, 377
Lowenthal, M.S., 370, 371, 377
Luker, K., 70, 84, 98

M

Maccoby, E., 376
MacDonald, M.G., 105, 123, 127, 132
Madsen, K.B., 34, 60
Magnusson, D., 249, 267
Maher, B.A., 268
Main, M., 297, 303
Markman, H., 188, 192, 258, 264, 267
Marlowe, D., 256, 257, 267
Martin, C., 311, 348
Martyna, W., 254, 266
Marwell, G., 6, 7, 27
Marx, K., 4, 83
Mash, E.J., 193
Maslow, A.H., 41, 60
Mason, K.O., 70, 98
Masters, W.H., 309, 316, 338, 339, 343, 344, 348
Matthews, M.A., 392, 407
Mathews, V.D., 139, 165, 168
May, R., 105, 132
McArthur, L.Z., 51, 60
McCall, G.J., 137, 159, 168, 355, 359, 360, 361, 367, 368, 369, 375, 377
McCall, M.M., 70, 86, 87, 98, 106, 125, 132
McCandless, B.R., 283, 284, 304
McClintock, C.G., 97, 142, 168
McCord, W.M., 377
Mead, G.H., 159, 168, 355, 356, 358, 359, 363, 377
Mead, M., 356, 377
Mehrabian, A., 55, 60, 252, 267
Meisels, M., 283, 304

Messet, B., 104, 133
Messick, S., 265, 267, 268
Michael, J., 27
Mihanovich, C.S., 139, 165, 168
Miller, D.T., 261, 268
Millon, T., 254, 268
Mills, J., 105, 132
Mill, J.S., 4
Mischel, T., 348
Mischel, W., 250, 268, 365, 377
Mitchell, J.C., 82, 98, 224, 228, 245, 246
Mogey, J.M., 232, 246
Moles, O.C., 193
Molm, L.D., 405, 407
Monson, T., 43, 48, 49, 59
Moos, R.H., 254, 268
Morris, C.W., 377
Moscovici, S., 99, 132
Mosher, D.L., 310, 311, 348
Moss, H.A., 296, 300, 304, 305
Mountjoy, P., 168, 246
Murphy, G., 43, 59
Murstein, B.I., 33, 37, 60, 105, 112, 123, 126, 127, 132
Mussen, P.H., 284, 285, 304
Myers, R.A., 259, 267

N

Nagy, G., 14, 15, 27
Naroll, R., 407
Nassiakou, M., 6, 7, 28
Neff, S., 310, 347
Nehls, E., 18, 27
Nesselroade, J.R., 273, 285, 304, 305, 406, 407
Neuringer, C., 27
Neugarten, B.L., 369, 370, 373, 374, 377
Newcomb, T., 9, 27
Newman, B.M., 365, 377
Newman, H.M., 189, 190, 193
Nichols, M. F., 310, 311, 349
Nielsen, J. M., 12, 25, 74, 96, 275, 298, 301, 303
Niemeijer, R., 227, 246
Nisbett, R., 39, 59
Noble, M., 227, 246
Noonan, K. M., 198, 215, 220
Norbeck, E., 377
Norton, A. J., 7, 19, 27
Notarius, C., 188, 192, 258, 264, 267
Nunnally, J., 41, 54, 59, 60
Nye, F. I., 98, 187, 193

O

Olson, D.H., 73, *97*, *98*, 112, 144, 145, *168*
Orden, S. R., 156, 164, 165, *168*
Ort, R.S., 164, 166, *168*
Ostrom, T.M., *377*
Overton, W.R., 273, 274, *305*

P

Palmer, M., 120, *132*
Papalia, D.E., 364, *377*
Parelius, A.P., 70, *98*
Parker, R., 41, *60*
Patterson, G. R., 7, 16, 17, *27*, 105, 112, *132*, 141, *168*, 188, 189, *193*, 225, 237, *246*
Paulhus, D.L., 401, *407*
Payne, J., *27*
Pedersen, D.M., 265, *268*
Pelz, D.C., 399, *407*
Pepitone, A., 43, *60*
Peplau, L.A., 20, *26*, 177, 183, 186, *192*, 311, 314, 342, 343, *349*, 354, *377*
Pepper, S.C., 274, *305*
Person, L.G., *268*
Peterson, D.R., 336, *349*
Pfeiffer, E., 315, *349*
Phillips, L. E., 231, *246*
Phillipson, H., 343, *348*
Piaget, J., 274, 354, 356, 362, *377*
Pitts, J. R., 62, *98*
Pomeroy, W., 311, *348*
Porter, L., *27*, *192*
Powers, E.A., 374, *377*
Powers, W.T., 251, 266, *268*
Price-Williams, D., *377*
Pruitt, D.G., 18, *27*

R

Raimy, V., 364, *377*
Rands, M., 6, *27*, 173, 174, *192*
Rapoport, R., 80, *97*, 177, 193
Rapoport, R.N., 80, *97*, 177, *193*
Raush, H.L., *27*, *132*, 237, *246*, 254, 259, 264, *268*, 393, 398, *407*
Ravagli, F.L., 18
Reader, D.H., 227, *246*
Reed, E.W., 127, *133*
Reed, S.C., 127, *133*
Reese, H.W., 273, 274, *304*, *305*, *406*
Regan, D., 51, *60*
Reid, J.B., 7, 16, 17, *27*
Reik, T., 41, *60*
Reiss, I.L., 82, *98*, 310, 311, 314, 323, *349*

Rheingold, H.A., 293, *305*
Ridley, C.A., 5, 13, 19, 22, 23, 184, *193*
Riegel, K.F., 272, 274, 276, 278, 292, 301, *305*
Riley, M.W., 374, *377*
Robson, K.S. 296, *305*
Rodgers, W.L., 185, 186, *191*
Rogers, C.R., 255, *268*
Rollins, B.C., 89, *98*, 370, *377*
Rosenberg, M., 100, *133*
Rosenblatt, P.C., 23, *27*
Rosenblum, L.A., 293, *303*, *304*
Rosenhan, D.L., 51, *60*
Rosenzweig, M.R., *27*, *191*
Rosow, I., 257, *268*
Ross, H.L., 51, *60*, 185, 186, *193*
Rottman, L., 126, *133*
Rousseau, J.J., 3
Rubin, M.E., 258, 264, *267*
Rubin, Z., 10, 11, 17, 20, *26*, *27*, 55, *60*, 105, 112, 123, 126, *133*, 177, 183, 184, 186, *192*, *193*, 311, 314, 342, 343, *349*, 354, *377*
Ryder, R., 144, 145, *168*

S

Saeed, L., 182, *192*
Sameroff, A., 272, 299, 301, *305*
Sarason, I.G., 249, *268*
Sarason, S.B., 282, *305*
Sahlins, M., 205, 211, 212, 213, 214, *221*, 234, *246*
Sampson, E.E., 10, 11, 12, *27*, 190, *193*
Sawhill, I.V., 185, 186, *193*
Scanzoni, J., 8, 12, 13, 16, 67, 69, 70, 71, 73, 83, 84, 85, 90, 93, 94, *98*, 106, 110, *113*, 125, 164, 165, *168*, 178, *193*, 238, *246*, 315, 316, 317, 318, 319, 320, 343
Schaefer, E.S., 308, *349*
Schaie, K. W., 273, 285, *303*, *304*
Schenitzki, D.F., 77, *97*
Schoenberg, R., 386, *406*
Schultz, D.A., 94, *98*
Schneider, D.J., 251, *268*
Schneirla, T.C., 274, 276, 277, 279, 280, 297, 301, *305*
Scott, J.F., 68, *98*
Secord, P., 33, *59*, 125, *131*, 256, *268*, 309, *348*
Secord, R.F., *131*
Senn, D.J., 9, *27*, 108, *132*, 183, *193*
Sewell, W.R., 231, *246*
Shanas, E., *246*

Shannon, J., 259, 268
Shanteau, J., 14, 15, 27
Shaver, K.G., 42, 60
Shaw, E., 305
Sherif, M., 167
Sherman, P.W., 198, 220
Sherman, R.C., 265, 268
Shrauger, S., 251, 268
Shulman, N., 24, 27, 230, 231, 246, 370, 377
Shurkus, J.P., 180, 193
Siegel, B.J., 246
Siegel, S., 77, 98
Sills, D.L., 97
Silverman, I., 126, 133
Simon, W., 311, 348
Skinner, B.F., 273
Slater, P.E., 23, 28
Smelser, N., 97
Smelser, W.T., 263, 268
Smith, A., 3, 4, 28
Smith, E.R., 401, 407
Smith, R.E., 249, 268
Snoek, J.D., 5, 8, 10, 27, 33, 35, 60, 108, 132,
    144, 145, 168, 176, 182, 193, 223, 246, 290,
    304, 316, 317, 319, 343, 348
Snyder, M., 44, 51, 52, 60, 254, 262, 268
Sörbom, D., 391, 406
Spanier, G.B., 9, 28, 282, 292, 304, 305, 315,
    349
Sprey, J., 91, 98
Spuhler, J.N., 127, 133
Stahelski, A.J., 261, 262, 267
Stein, A.H., 281, 305
Steinmetz, S., 93, 98
Stephan, W., 43, 60
Stewart, P., 106
Storer, N.W., 106, 133
Straus, M., 91, 93, 98
Strauss, A., 377
Strauss, E., 51, 60
Streib, G., 246
Stroebe, W., 14, 28, 126, 133
Sullivan, H.S., 248, 251, 253, 255, 256, 257,
    261, 268, 363, 366, 367, 371, 377
Sussman, M.B., 112, 231, 246
Swain, M.A., 237, 246

T
Talaber, R., 6, 27, 173, 174, 192
Tanke, E., 52, 60, 262, 268
Taylor, D.A., 8, 10, 15, 16, 25, 107, 131, 144,
    158, 159, 160, 166, 167, 223, 256, 258, 266,
    315, 347, 358, 376

Tedeschi, J.T., 16, 28
Teichman, M., 109, 133
Terhune, K.W., 265, 268
Terman, L.M., 139, 164, 166, 168
Tesser, A., 401, 407
Thibaut, J.W., 12, 13, 18, 28, 36, 40, 60, 75,
    88, 95, 98, 125, 133, 137, 138, 142, 159,
    168, 170, 171, 172, 173, 179, 182, 193, 233,
    246, 257, 259, 268, 293, 305, 352, 353, 377
Thiessen, V., 177, 193
Thomas, A., 305
Thomas, C., 279, 296, 305
Thomas, D.L., 89, 98
Thomas, E.J., 188, 189, 193
Thompson, V.D., 14, 28, 126, 133
Thompson, W.R., 366, 377
Thurber, J., 307, 349
Thurnher, M., 370, 377
Tiao, G.C., 396, 406
Titchener, E.B., 35, 60
Tobach, E., 280, 301, 305
Toffler, A., 107, 133, 232, 246
Triandis, H.C., 6, 7, 28, 407
Traupmann, J., 8, 11, 12, 112, 113, 115, 116,
    127, 128, 129, 130, 133, 205, 207
Trivers, R.L., 198, 208, 210, 213, 221
Turner, J.L., 109, 133, 322, 349
Tyler, S.A., 246

U
Udry, J.R., 126, 133
Utne, M.K., 8, 11, 12, 112, 116, 128, 133,
    205, 207

V
Valins, S., 39, 51, 59, 60
Vandenberg, S.G., 132
Vassiliou, V., 6, 7, 28
Venning, J., 283, 304
Veroff, J., 164, 165, 167
Vincent, J.P., 7, 25, 28, 164, 165, 167

W
Wachtel, P.L., 250, 269
Waller, W., 112, 115, 133, 158, 159, 168
Walster, E., 13, 14, 25, 43, 50, 51, 59, 60, 73,
    75, 77, 98, 99, 100, 101, 104, 106, 107, 115,
    116, 117, 125, 126, 127, 128, 129, 130, 133,
    183, 191, 219, 221, 283, 303, 348, 406
Walster, G.W., 14, 25, 73, 75, 77, 98, 99, 100,
    101, 103, 106, 107, 115, 116, 117, 125, 127,
    128, 129, 130, 131, 133, 176, 191, 219, 221
Walters, H.A., 265, 269

Watson, C., 254, *266*
Watson, J.S., 300, *305*
Watzlawick, P., 253, *269*
Wallin, P.W., 7, *25*, 112, 127, *131*, 164, *167*
Wallis, K.M., 116
Walshok, M.L., 83, *98*
Weber, M., 76
Weick, K.E., 104, *133*
Weiner, B., 39, *59*
Weinstein, K.K., 370, *377*
Weiss, R.L., 7, *25*, *28*, 112, *132*, 164, 165, *167*, 188, 189, *193*,
Werner, H., 274, 276, 286, 295, *305*
Werner, O., 404, *407*
West-Eberhard, M.J., 198, 209, *221*
Wheeldon, P.D., 226, *246*
White, E.B., 307, *349*
White, R.W., 369, *377*
Whitten, N.E., 224, *246*
Wiessner, P.A., 209, 214, *221*
Wiggins, J.A., 405, *407*
Williams, G.C., 198, *221*
Willis, R.H., *27*, *168*, *192*
Willmott, P., 232, *246*

Wills, T.A., 112, *132*
Wilson, C.D., 295, *304*
Wilson, M.O., *167*
Wilson, V.L., 396, *406*
Wimberley, D.L., 261, *267*
Winch, R., 257, *269*
Wish, M., 6, 7, *28*, 252, *269*
Wohlwill, J., 9, *28*, *407*
Wolfe, A.W., 224, *246*
Wolfe, D.M., 112, 185, *191*
Wolff, P.H., 296, 299, *305*
Worthy, M., 107, *133*

Y

Yoppi, B. 258, 264, *267*
Young, M., 232, *246*
Young, P.T., 34, *60*
Yussen, S., 41, *60*

Z

Zadney, J., 51, 52, *60*
Zand, D.E., 78
Zelditch, M., *303*
Zelnik, M., 84, *97*

Subject Index

A

Affection, 17, 21, 24, 120, 313–315

Age, and relationships, 351, 353, 356–357, 361, 375

Altruism, 3, 4, 10, 18, 62–64, 77–82, 100–101, 205, 219, 234, *see also*, Exchange; Reciprocity

nepotism, 202–220

Approval, 13–15, 17, 56–57, 183, 260

Attachment, parent–child, 296–297, 360, 367

Attention, 35–48, 54–57

Attraction, 14–15, 17, 41, 54–55, 66–67, 173, 178–181, 184–188, 352

Attribution

processes, 41–47, 51, 189–190, 265

theory, 38–39

B

Bargaining, 71–76, 336

Bereavement, 372

C

Close relationships

behavioral manifestations of, 8

conflict in, 157–164

and exchange, 10–12, 18, 104–106, 112–130, 174–175

nature of, 6–8, 106–111, 171, 174–176

Cognitive development, and relationships, 362–366

Cohabitation, 84–85

Commitment, 10, 19–21, 23, 24, 84, 86–94, 180, 184, 318–319, 344, *see also* Interdependence; Levels of involvement

Comparison level, 18–19, 88–90, 92–94, 171–173, 178–179, 182–183, 185, 225

Comparison level for alternatives, 16, 18, 48, 69, 74–76, 87–90, 92–94, 125, 171–173, 178–179, 182–183, 185, 186, 225, 257–258, 260, 343, 353, 361

Complementarity, 256–260, *see also* Similarity

Conflict, 7, 64, 90–94, 147, 150–155, 186, 188–189, 237, *see also* Hostility; Violence

escalation of, 141–142

levels of, 137–142, 234–235

resolution of, 91–92

Conflict of interest, 3–4

Costs, 36, 83, 140, 142, 225, 233, 242, 247–248, 334, *see also* Rewards

Costs, (*cont*)
  and evolutionary theory, 205–207
  and power, 73–74
  and relationship initiation, 12–21, 49–50
  and rewards, 39–41
  of terminating marriage, 187–188
Courtship, 10, 136, 142–157, 183, 218, *see*
  also Premarital relationship
  conflict in, 149–157, 164
  parental influence, 19, 184
  stages of, 145–146, 150–151
  transitions in, 148–155

D

Dating, 14–15, 43–47, 115–116, 123, 125,
  127–128, 145–146, 148, 155, 183, *see*
  also, Courtship
Dependence, 20, 40–49, 94, 173, *see also*, Interdependence
  selective attention, 41–47
Development,
  and exchange theory, 353
  individual, 276–285
  individual differences in, 282–285, 355–
  359, 361
  models of, 273–276, 382
  ontogenetic versus phylogentic, 198–202,
  274
  research approaches, 9–10
Dissolution, *see* Divorce; Relationships
Divorce, 19, 126, 184–188, *see also*, Relationships
Dominance, *see* Interpersonal style; Power

E

Equality, *see* Equity
Equity, 10–12, 235–237, *see also* Inequity;
  Justice
  definitonal formula, 101
  and love, 104–106
  measurement of, 112–113
  perceptions of, 102, 108, 120–121
  restoration of, 103–104, 114, 119–122
  theoretical formulation of, 100–104
Evolutionary theory, 198–202
  natural selection, 198–202
Exchange
  collectivistic approach, 63, 66, 68–70, 72,
  188, 190
  individualistic approach, 12, 63, 72, 188,
  190
  motivation for, 3–4, 10–13, 18, 34, 62–64,
  66–67, 77–82, 86–87, 100–101, 175,
  182, 208–211, 234–238, 287–288,

  319–320, 333–340, 353–354
  social context, 12
Exchange theory
  assumptions of, 233, 275
  critique of, 352–355, 368
Explanation, 298, 383–384, 393–402
  levels of analysis, 4–5, 198–208, 272,
  278–282, 382–383
Extramarital relationships, 129–130, 186–
  187

F

Filter theory, *see* Levels of involvement
Friendship, 70, 94, 366–367, 370–371,
  374–375

H

Hostility, 7, 92–94, 163–164, 225, 237, 239,
  263, 397–398, *see also*, Conflict; Violence

I

Identity, and relationships, 367–368
Inequity, *see also*, Equity
  and distress, 102–103, 113–119
  reactions to, 115–119, 127–130
Inputs, *see* Investments
Interdependence, 6, 9, 13, 110, 155–156,
  175, 319–320
  and ambivalence of dependency, 17–18
  and conflict, 73, 137–142, 157–164
  and investments, 72
  co-residence, 85–86
  economic, 84–85, 89, 185–186
  expansion of, 15–19, 79–86
  levels of, 138–142, 148–150, 171
  maximum joint profit and trust, 76–78
  measurement of, 8, 13, 110
  norms regulating, 62
  properties of, 137–142
Interpersonal style, 255, 259, 262–265
Intimacy, *see* Close relationships, Identity
Investments, 8, 11–12, 16, 72, 80, 87–88,
  101–102, 177–178, 183, *see also*, Equity
  and natural selection, 210–211

J

Justice, 73–76, 82–84, 91–92, 113, 354, *see*
  also Equity, Power

K

Kinship, 7, 21, 24, 202–220, 231, 374

L

Levels of involvement, 5–6, 65–94, 157–

160, 183, 287–291, 316–320, 342–343, 360
  awareness, 5, 33, 35–37, 316
  commitment, 86–94, 318–319, 344
  expansion, 79–86, 318, 343
  exploration, 65–79, 318, 343
  mutuality, 5, 13, 317, 344
  premarital relationships, 145–146
  and sex, 316–320
  surface contact, 5, 13, 316–317, 337–338
Love, 20, 55, 120, 183, 186, 205, 218, 257–260, 325–326, 331
  exchange theory, 10–12, 104–105
  interdependence, 8, 17–18, 107
  and premarital relationships, 147–148, 150–155
  as a resource, 109, 174

M

Markov process, 392–393, 398
Marriage
  attractions and barriers, 180–181, 184–188
  commitment in, 86, 88
  conflict in, 7, 150–155, 164–167
  dissolution of, 184–188
  equity in, 105, 116–130
  law of marital infidelity, 55–56
  research, 9, 164–167
  satisfaction, 115–119, 164–167, 178, 185–186, 188–189, 292, 370, 388–391
  social control of, 19, 23
  violence in, 94
Mate selection, *see* Courtship
Measurement of relationships
  cycles, 388–393
  measurement error, 387–388
  rate of change, 383–384, 388–389
  sequential analyses, 388–401
  structural change, 383, 391–392
  time sampling, 404
  validity, 384–405
Moral reasoning, 320–332
  and relationship reasoning, 333–340
  and sexual behavior, 323–332
  and sexual standards, 322–323
  stages of, 320–322
Motivation, 34, 39, *see also* Exchange
  and conflict, 160–164

N

Natural selection, *see* Evolutionary theory
Needs, 40–41, 172, 257–258
Network, *see* Social network

Norms, 62, 68–69, 138, 141–142, 158–159, 234, 243–244, 258, 299, 335

O

Obligations, *see* Reciprocity
Outcomes, *see* Rewards; Costs

P

Parent–child relationships, 19, 65, 88–89, 94, 187, 202–211, 279, 281, 293–298, 397–398
Perception, 33–34, 41, *see also* Social perception
  expectations, 52
  importance of stimuli, 38–40
  novelty of stimuli, 39, 55
Personality theory, 248–250
Physical attractiveness, 14–15, 50–54, 120, 122, 126, 182–183, 229, 282–284, 289
Physical characteristics and social relations, 282–285, 289
Power, 40–41, 48, 64, 73–76, 89–90, 125, 236, 240–244, 255, 259
Premarital relationships, *see also* Courtship
  development of, 9–10, 17
  parental response to, 19
  and sex, 310–314, 322–332
  termination of, 20
Profit, *see* Rewards; Costs
Propinquity, 13–14, 21–24, 37, 182, 230

R

Reciprocity, 10–12, 62–64, 66, 174, 301, 335, 397–398
  complementarity, 256–257
  contrasted to nepotism, 208–211
  and equity, 124–126
  and evolutionary theory, 203–205, 211–212
  expectations of, 14–15, 176, 189
  and love, 104–106
  mother–infant, 294–298
  obligations, 62–64, 66–67, 72, 75, 77, 80, 142, 318
  patterns of, 234–238
Reinforcement, *see* Rewards; Costs
Rejection, *see* Approval
Relationship dimensions
  change in, 291–293, 296–297, 383
Relationships, 6–7, *see also* Close relationships; Levels of involvement
  adolescent, 367–369
  adult, 369–371

Relationships (*cont.*)
  barriers, 20, 178–181, 185
  cross-generational, 370
  cross-sectional approaches, 386–388, 393
  and death, 371–373
  deterioration, 19–21, 25, 188–189, 236–239
  dimensions of, 6–7, 381–382
  dissolution, 181–188, 237, 292
  duration, 48–49, 107, 121, 123, 176, 188–190, 227
  initiation, 13–15, 24
  kinds of, 6–7, 173, 208–220, 233–239
  life-span changes in, 351, 353, 370–371, 375–376
  longitudinal approaches, 9–10, 389–393
  preadolescent, 366–367
  reasoning about, 333–340
  research approaches, 9–10, 32–34, 111, 198–200
  social context of, 21–24
Reproductive success, 202–203, 211
Resources, 13–16, 40
  economic, 84–85, 89, 185–186
  and equity, 125–130
  and evolutionary theory, 204, 210
  and needs, 257
  of networks, 241
  and sexual behavior, 70, 72–74, 82–84
  types, 108–110, 174, 252–253
  violence, 93
Retirement, 122
Rewards, 4, 6, 11–20, 140, 142, 173–176, 225, 233, 242, 247–248, 259, 298–299, 333–337, 355, 360–361, 367, 383, 405, *see also* Costs
  attention and attraction, 54, 56–57, 188–189
  and confidence, 78–80
  and costs, 39–41
  expectations for, 18–19, 50–54, 56–57, 74–75, 178, 183, 260
  and evolutionary history, 205–207, 217–219
  and restoration of equity, 11–12, 103–104
  sexual interaction, 315–316
  value of, 108–109

S

Self-concept
  and social interaction, 355–359
  validation of, 359–361, 367

Self-disclosure, 8, 107, 150–155
Self-fulfilling prophecy, 51–54, 261–264, 284
Self-interest, *see* Exchange, motivation for
Sex, 82, 84, 120, 177, 186, 202–203
  and affection, 313–315
  experience, 310–311
  exploitation, 319
  extramarital, 129–130, 186–187
  guilt, 311–313, 323–325, 328
  and moral reasoning, 320–332
  and social exchange, 315–316
Sex differences, 115–119, 136, 177, 182, 216, 311, 328–330, 374
Sex-roles, 70–73, 80, 82–84, 234
Sibling relationships, 215
Similarity, 48, 50, 67, 177, 183, 260, *see also* Complementarity; Equity
  behavioral, 16–17, 80–82, 172, 260
  in status, 14–15, 50, 125–127
Social context, 37, 187, 190–191, 230, 281–282, 404
Social control, 21–24, 40, 100, 104, 184, 230–231, 240–244
Social exchange, *see* Exchange
Social networks, 5–6, 19, 21–24, 126, 184, 187, 190–191, 211–215, 383
  across the life-span, 230
  and community size, 21–24, 230–231
  characteristics of, 21–24, 226–228
  definition of, 224–225
  influence on dyad, 240–244
  kinship, 231
  withdrawal from, 5–6, 23
Social perception, 33–34, 39–40, 42–47, 124
Status, 14–15, 50, 109, 125–127
Stereotypes, 49–50, 373–374
Submission, *see* Interpersonal style; Power
Symbolic interaction, 359–361

T

Trust, 8, 17, 77–79, 81–82, 318

V

Validity
  external, 385, 402–405
  propositional, 384–385, 393–402
  concept, 384–393
Violence, 7, 92–94, 397–398, *see also* Hostility